John McGahern was born in Dublin in 19
Ireland. A graduate of University College Dublin, he worked a..
school teacher and held various academic posts at universities in Britain,
Ireland and America. He was the author of six highly acclaimed novels and
four collections of short stories, and the recipient of numerous awards and
honours, including a Society of Authors Travelling Scholarship, the American-
Irish Award, the Prix Etrangère Ecureuil and the Chevalier de l'Ordre des
Arts et des Lettres. *Amongst Women*, which won both the GPA and the *Irish
Times* Award, was shortlisted for the Booker Prize and made into a four-part
BBC television series. McGahern died in 2006.

Frank Shovlin is Professor of Irish Literature in English at the Institute of
Irish Studies, University of Liverpool. He was educated at University College
Galway where he took his BA and MA degrees before moving on to St John's
College, Oxford, where he completed his DPhil. He was a British Academy/
Leverhulme Senior Research Fellow for 2018–19.

Further praise for *The Letters of John McGahern*:

'Magnificent . . . All credit to Shovlin for bringing the artist, neighbour, friend
and lover to such brilliant, refracted light.' *Irish Times* (Book of the Day)

'Remarkable . . . A treasure trove . . . Both the man and the writer come
vibrantly alive . . . Such is Shovlin's remarkable scholarship throughout this
800-page collection of McGahern's letters that it is worth reading for its an-
notations alone.' *Irish Independent*

'Shovlin has clearly done Trojan work . . . There is much to savour . . .
Throughout his life [McGahern] never lost the epistolary habit, writing hundreds of letters filled with warmth, wit and empathy.' *The Times*

'The publication of McGahern's letters was always going to be an event in
Irish culture . . . The present volume, meticulously annotated and edited by
Shovlin, does not disappoint . . . If the settled view of McGahern is not exactly upended, the letters nevertheless offer a more complex, less soft in some
respects, image of the writer . . . Poignant . . . McGahern does not always
appear in these letters as quite the saint . . . The letters of McGahern's mature
years are punctuated by many striking asides . . . He offers a few snippets
of his personal philosophy that will resonate with fans of the fiction . . .

McGahern is caustic about the Irish literary scene over his own lifetime – usually amusingly so.' *Times Literary Supplement*

'[McGahern's] letters have been immaculately collected and edited by Shovlin in this welcome volume . . . Fascinating . . . They provide a unique inside view of the making of a writer who from the outset was a steely, single-minded and fiercely ambitious lyric novelist . . . There are also sporadic appearances of the luminous prose writer . . . Most are pithy and refreshingly cosmopolitan exchanges . . . One of the greatest pleasures of reading the letters is the chance to savour the peppery one-liners . . . [They] confirm his sense of style and the almost religious importance of writing [and] show how extraordinarily constant his sense of literary vision – or mission – was.' *Literary Review*

by John McGahern

fiction
THE BARRACKS
THE DARK
NIGHTLINES
THE LEAVETAKING
GETTING THROUGH
THE PORNOGRAPHER
HIGH GROUND
AMONGST WOMEN
THE COLLECTED STORIES
THAT THEY MAY FACE THE RISING SUN
CREATURES OF THE EARTH: NEW AND SELECTED STORIES

non-fiction
MEMOIR
LOVE OF THE WORLD: ESSAYS
(edited by Stanley van der Ziel)

plays
THE POWER OF DARKNESS
THE ROCKINGHAM SHOOT AND OTHER DRAMATIC WRITINGS
(edited by Stanley van der Ziel)

The Letters of
John McGahern

edited by

FRANK SHOVLIN

faber

First published in 2021
by Faber & Faber Ltd
The Bindery, 51 Hatton Garden
London EC1N 8HN

First published in the USA in 2021

This paperback edition first published in 2023

Typeset by Donald Sommerville
Printed in the UK by CPI Group (UK) Ltd, Croydon CR0 4YY

A CIP record for this book is available from the British Library

ISBN 978-0-571-38741-0

MIX
Paper | Supporting
responsible forestry
FSC
www.fsc.org   FSC® C171272

Printed and bound in the UK on FSC® certified paper in line with our continuing
commitment to ethical business practices, sustainability and the environment.
For further information see faber.co.uk/environmental-policy

2 4 6 8 10 9 7 5 3 1

For Madeline McGahern

I think that the difficulty of dealing with letters is that they are never quite honest. Often out of sympathy or diffidence or kindness or affection or self interest we quite rightly hide our true feelings.

JOHN McGAHERN
Letter to Sophia Hillan
19 January 1991

CONTENTS

JOHN McGAHERN'S WORKS

All published by Faber in London.

The Barracks (1963)
The Dark (1965)
Nightlines (1970)
The Leavetaking (1974)
Getting Through (1978)
The Pornographer (1979)
High Ground (1985)
Amongst Women (1990)
The Power of Darkness (1991)
The Collected Stories (1992)
That They May Face the Rising Sun (2002)
Memoir (2005)
Creatures of the Earth: New and Selected Stories (2006)
Love of the World: Essays, ed. Stanley van der Ziel, int. Declan Kiberd
   (2009). Abbreviated in footnotes as LOTW.
The Rockingham Shoot and Other Dramatic Writings, ed. and int. Stanley
   van der Ziel (2018)

INTRODUCTION

'I am no good at letters': so writes a twenty-nine-year-old John McGahern to Mary Keelan, an American graduate student whom he had met in Dublin in the summer of 1963 and with whom he had entered a lively epistolary friendship. After confessing this perceived weakness, he explains more about his relationship with the letter as a form: 'I have written more to you than to anyone ever, there's something unreal about them, they're neither life nor anything, but it's nice for them to come.'[1]

And yet, despite this avowed discomfort in the face of letter writing, McGahern would write a host of revealing, forthright and intriguing missives to a variety of people over the course of his life, from close friends to professional contacts, fellow writers and family. That said, it was clear from the outset of this editorial task that I was not dealing with a writer like W. B. Yeats or T. S. Eliot, where multiple volumes would be needed to chronicle the various communications sent out to the world by the author over the years. 'I don't like writing letters,' McGahern tells one correspondent in 1960. 'So I seldom do – which physics nothing.'[2] He was not a voluminous letter writer, though there is no year – and not many months in any year – for which I could not find a letter or an email between the first adult communication contained in this volume, penned to his good friend Tony Swift in December 1957, and March 2006 when, in the midst of his final illness, he dictated emails and letters to his wife Madeline. Published here are about three-quarters of the letters I have managed to track down. Left out were those instances that were repetitive of points made better elsewhere or that were so brief and unrevealing that they added little to our sense of the man and his work. I know that there must be correspondence out there that I have failed to locate and I am also aware of some elusive runs of letters that people feel sure they possess but have been unable to find for me. In some cases recipients preferred to keep correspondence private. Doubtless more letters will emerge after the publication of this volume that will help future biographers and scholars of the work to come to a still fuller picture of McGahern and his life.

1 Letter to Mary Keelan (1 June 1964).
2 Letter to Paddy Swift (5 September 1960).

That said, I am aware of no long run of correspondence to which I have not had access and I am confident that the letters reproduced and annotated here give an accurate sense of the writer's epistolary life.

McGahern's confession to Keelan about the difficulties of writing a true letter and yet his happiness in receiving same is not surprising, for he liked to read other people's letters. Among his favourite books were W. B. Yeats's *Letters on Poetry to Dorothy Wellesley*; Franz Kafka's *Letters to Milena*; and Rainer Maria Rilke's *Letters to a Young Poet*. The first of these he gifted to Mary Keelan during that intense friendship of 1963–64, the last to another friend of Dublin's early 1960s, Nuala O'Faolain. So fond was McGahern of John Butler Yeats's letters that he undertook to bring forth a new edition in 1999 for both a French and an English audience. 'The letters', he writes in his lively introduction, 'have given me pleasure for many years. They can be gossipy, profound, irascible, charming, prejudiced, humorous, intelligent, naive, contradictory, passionate. They are always immediate.'[3] In that introduction McGahern provides a potted history of the letters as they came to publication over the years and is amused by how much Yeats enjoyed seeing his own epistolary handiwork in print, quoting the old man on the subject: 'I have a copy which I constantly read and find very illuminating. Swift confesses to something of the sort with his own composition.'[4]

We can say with near certainty that McGahern did not feel about his own letters as Yeats or Dean Swift did about theirs. One never gets the sense when one reads a McGahern letter that it was composed with permanence or posterity in mind. His letters, while often spasmodically beautiful, are not self-conscious works of art. But one might argue that the correspondence, because he is not writing self-consciously, is all the more truthful and revealing. There is a noticeable change in handwriting from the late 1950s cursive, careful script still under the sway of schooldays and teacher training, to the later small, jagged block letters that populate the great majority of his correspondence. As early as 1961, McGahern's penchant for handwriting over typing was irritating his fellow Irish writer John Montague as the two of them exchanged letters on the subject of a proposed anthology of new Irish writing: 'Your handwriting is so bad that it brings me comfort since mine (which people have always found terrible) couldn't come within an ass's roar of yours for incomprehensibility. You also write on both sides of light

3 John McGahern, 'Introduction', in John Butler Yeats, *Letters to His Son W. B. Yeats and Others 1869–1922*, ed. Joseph Hone, abridged and with an introduction by John McGahern (London: Faber, 1999), 24.
4 Quoted in McGahern, 'Introduction', 23.

paper, thus ensuring that the script on one side is blotted out by the other. You should buy a typewriter.'[5] Only a small number of McGahern's letters are, in fact, typed, and those that are tend to be of a businesslike nature in communication with publishers and agents about contracts or royalties. Very occasionally, in transcribing the work, a word has proved illegible and is marked so by me in square brackets; when McGahern makes an obvious error in leaving out a word, I have inserted that word in square brackets, unless its absence reflects his personal style of speech and prose. I have let oddities of spelling and punctuation stand unremarked. McGahern never felt confident enough to type his own handwritten manuscripts. Prior to the later 1960s and meeting Madeline, he paid for professional transcription of his work. Much of the £100 he won in 1962 as the AE Memorial Award for sections of the still incomplete debut novel that was to become *The Barracks* in 1963, for instance, was absorbed in paying for half a dozen copies of the work to be typed.

McGahern, contrary to certain received views of him as an isolated gentleman farmer, or what he calls in one note composed towards the end of his life 'the myth of Farmer John', travelled a good deal and lived at many addresses in Ireland, England, the United States and France.[6] This facet is especially true up to the mid-1970s when he and Madeline moved to a modest cottage in Foxfield, Co. Leitrim. 'Madeline, as well as I,' he writes to an editor at the American publisher Alfred A. Knopf in October 1975, 'is tired of climbing other people's stairs. It's eleven years of having no place now.'[7] For most letters McGahern supplies an address, for some I have had to rely on postmarks, and for others I have made educated guesses based on dates and contexts. Where the address is not provided, I have used square brackets around what seems the likeliest place of origin. The use of such brackets has also been my practice when estimating dates of composition, although there are a few occasions where the guess has to be as vague – as in the case, for instance, for many of John's letters to his sister Dympna from the late 1950s to early 1960s – as just supplying a year rather than a day or a date.

In terms of my footnoting practice, a short biography of each correspondent is supplied for the first letter or email. Where possible, these biographies include year of birth and, where applicable, year of death. When a question arises in a letter that appears not to be addressed in the footnote, the reader

5 John Montague to John McGahern (22 October 1961). John Montague Papers, University of Victoria, British Columbia.
6 Email to Stanley van der Ziel (14 February 2006).
7 Letter to Jonathan Coleman (14 October 1975).

can assume that it was not possible to supply an answer despite my best efforts. The only alternative to this method would have been to footnote 'unknown' whenever I had failed to track down fully the source of the piece of information or the answer to some question that arose within the letter. Very occasionally I have chosen to do this if I thought it helpful to the reader. I have kept editorial comment – especially as it relates to the interplay between the life and the work – to a minimum. So, for instance, I have not found it necessary to comment on the ways in which McGahern's December 1957 letter to Tony Swift breaks into second person singular narrative to describe first person action, just as occurs at length in *The Dark*. Usually I have thought it best for readers to come to those sorts of conclusions themselves. But there are occasions where I felt it better to give some guidance and provide links between biography and fiction, such as in one letter to Dympna of December 1964 when he describes enthusiastically a particular chair he has seen in St Petersburg – a chair that reappears in an early draft of 'My Love, My Umbrella'.

What would McGahern have thought about an edition of his letters being made public? Given his general suspicion of literary biographies, I think we can surmise that he would have disliked the idea. He was resistant to permitting the reader access to the private workings of the author's mind and sensibility. 'Sometimes I am uneasy when I remember all the letters hanging about your flat,' he writes to Patrick Gregory, his first American editor.[8] Gregory reassures him that there is no cause for concern, though it has been much to the benefit of this project that Gregory, in fact, carefully kept much of this correspondence and donated it to the National University of Ireland Galway after McGahern's death and where it can be consulted today.

One 1976 letter to Madeline about his efforts to complete the collection of short stories that would appear two years later as *Getting Through* sees McGahern commenting ruefully on the tension between the private world of the artist and the public world of the audience: 'Even to me the book of stories are finished, once I counterpoint Along the Edges with the story of the day. So another private act is becoming public, another nail visible in the wood'.[9] The publication of *The Letters of John McGahern* means that a large new number of such nails become visible to the reading public for the first time. I do not regret that this should be the case: McGahern's books retain their majesty today as surely as on the dates of first publication. It is a measure of the work's peculiar power that no amount of archival delving can

8 Letter to Patrick Gregory (18 November 1966).
9 Letter to Madeline McGahern (June 1976).

diminish what stands as one of the most consistently superb fictional oeuvres of the twentieth century. These letters will reinforce the already deep respect for McGahern's work among his readers and hopefully open him to a new and fortunate audience.

LOCATION OF THE LETTERS

The name at the top right of each letter denotes the current holder or location. 'TS' stands for typescript. The following is a list of the full details of the location of those letters that are held in institutional archives and libraries (a shortened form is used in the text):

Alan Ross Papers, Brotherton Library, University of Leeds
Alfred A. Knopf, Inc. Records, Harry Ransom Center, University of Texas
   at Austin
BBC Written Archives Centre, Reading
Brian Friel Papers, National Library of Ireland
Charles Monteith Papers, Stuart A. Rose Manuscript, Archives, and Rare
   Book Library, Emory University
DeWitt Henry, *Ploughshares* Papers, Emerson College Archives
Eoghan Ó Tuairisc Papers, National University of Ireland Galway
Frances Kiernan Papers, Manuscripts and Archives Division, The New York
   Public Library, Astor, Lenox, and Tilden Foundations
Frances McCullough Papers, Special Collections and University Archives,
   University of Maryland Libraries
Irish Academy of Letters, National Library of Ireland
John McGahern Papers, National University of Ireland Galway
John Montague Papers, University of Victoria, British Columbia
London Magazine Papers, Harry Ransom Center, University of Texas
   at Austin
Lyric Theatre/O'Malley Archive, National University of Ireland Galway
Macmillan Archive, University of Reading
Mary Lavin Papers, University College Dublin
Michael Hamburger Papers, Brotherton Library, University of Leeds
Michael McLaverty Archive, Linen Hall Library, Belfast
Niall Walsh Papers, National University of Ireland Galway
Patrick Gregory Papers, National University of Ireland Galway
Paul Durcan Papers, National Library of Ireland
Paul Muldoon Papers, Stuart A. Rose Manuscript, Archives, and Rare Book
   Library, Emory University

Peter Fallon Papers, Stuart A. Rose Manuscript, Archives, and Rare Book
   Library, Emory University
The Review Correspondence, Brotherton Library, University of Leeds
Robin Robertson Papers, Brotherton Library, University of Leeds
Russell and Volkening Papers, Manuscripts and Archives Division,
   The New York Public Library, Astor, Lenox, and Tilden Foundations
Seamus Heaney Papers, Stuart A. Rose Manuscript, Archives, and Rare
   Book Library, Emory University
Seán Brehony letters, National University of Ireland Galway
Thomas Kilroy Papers, National University of Ireland Galway
Tom Paulin Papers, Stuart A. Rose Manuscript, Archives, and Rare Book
   Library, Emory University
X Papers, Lilly Library Manuscripts, Indiana University

THE LETTERS

1943

Memoir

[*Corrmahon, Aughawillan*]

[*April 1943*][1]

Dear Daddy,[2]

Thanks very much for the pictures. I had great fun reading them.[3] I hope you are well. Come to see us soon. We got two goats. Uncle Pat does not like them. Will you bring over my bicycle please and games. We are all well. I was gugering for Uncle Pat Thursday.[4]

Goodbye from Sean to Daddy

1 For this letter in its full context, see *Memoir* (2005), 76. At the time McGahern was living with his mother and siblings near her place of work, Aughawillan National School, Co. Leitrim. His father was living in the garda barracks at Cootehall, Co. Roscommon where he held the rank of Sergeant.

2 McGahern's father was Francis McGahern (1901–77), commonly known as Frank or, to non-family members in later years, 'the Sergeant'.

3 McGahern's father had, the previous Christmas, gifted his then eight-year-old son a book of the *Irish Independent* comic strip 'Count Curly Wee and Gussy Goose' along with a small bicycle.

4 Pat McManus (1904–88), a brother of McGahern's mother Susan who would, in later life, go on to become one of McGahern's closest friends and is in part the model for the fictional character of 'The Shah' in *That They May Face the Rising Sun* (2002).

Gugering is the act of dropping seed potatoes into holes in the ground, usually work for an adult and child. The adult would dibble or make a hole in the ground with a '*stibhín*' or home-made wooden tool; it was usually the child's job to drop the seed potato into the hole before the adult covered it over with soil. The word, particular to Co. Leitrim and parts of neighbouring counties Longford, Cavan and Roscommon, likely derives from the Irish word '*gogaide*' meaning 'haunches' or 'hunkers'.

1957

Tony Swift
[*Madeline McGahern*]

57 Howth Road
Clontarf
[*hereafter 57 Howth Road*][1]

14 December 1957

Dear Tony,[2]

Many thanks for your letter. I was discharged yesterday but must attend daily for treatment. I am weak, a little sore but the worst is over.[3] I hope to go home about Wednesday.[4]

Sunday was a cold night and rain spitting across the Liffey. I walked out to try and rid away the nervousness. You were right about many things: they knew it was cold but they might have been talking about Siberia. They took my clothes away and the doctor examined me and I wrote till morning. When I would hear the nurse coming I used to stuff the paper sheets under the clothes and pretend to be reading; she was very serious about me not sleeping and offered to give me tablets.

And in the morning they dressed me up like the fatted lamb. Then the pain – a big pain in my head and my pulse sledging the time out up top and the scald of blood caking. You could only think of lines of poems or that Monica was coming in at half-seven or that the colour of the ceiling was a

---

1 McGahern lived at this address throughout most of his time as a teacher at *Scoil Naomh Eoin Baiste*, colloquially known as Belgrove Boys' National School, Seafield Road, Clontarf, Dublin from December 1956 to July 1964. He had a room in this large, three-storey house owned by the Lightfoot family.
2 Tony Swift (1935–2022), Dublin friend of McGahern's whom he first met in a city centre dancehall. The Swift brothers – particularly Tony's older brother Jimmy – quickly became vital parts of McGahern's social and aesthetic life.
3 McGahern had spent a period in Dr Steevens' Hospital, Kilmainham, Dublin for an operation on a deviated septum.
4 Home, at this point, was still the garda barracks in Cootehall, Co. Roscommon.

sickly green.[5] Not really thoughts at all. Then you'd examine every square foot of the ceiling to see if it was flaking and count up to a hundred several times. Paw for your watch, and Jesus, only five minutes gone. You'd want to call out but something kept shouting: must keep quiet; lie down; and keep your dirty mouth shut.

Then you'd say: offer this up for your sins or for Christ on the Cross and you'd grin might-as-well and give a horrible smothered chuckle. Something funny about that, like a man paying his income tax from patriotic motives.

Matron comes round with a nurse and murmurs poor boy. You begin to feel very sorry for yourself and want to cry. But something shouts up: Can it; dry up; get to hell you mooning crosseyed manspawn.

And you are going gallant when two visitors come. You smile and try to talk and long for the Seven Furies to stuff them down the jacks and pull the chain. And they go with self-pity and repugnance mixed up all over their comforter-of-the-sick mugs. The nurse didn't see them coming in and put them out when she found them. May she have a strong man and a cartload of bawling sons!

And the night-nurse gives you tablets and an injection and the pain dies down. But the sweat keeps breaking out and you long for a cool, clean knife. Later in the night she calls the doctor; they talk for a while; and you get another injection.

In the morning they took out the plugs – it was like coming back to life again. Everything about you are lovely, wonderful things and the smallest things that happened – like a nurse's giggle or a rattle of plates – seemed never to have happened exactly like that before. You smiled at everyone and your smile seemed infectious. Only for soreness you could shout out or dance or rig up an altar and say mass.

And the days went by in a blue dream. You hated to see visitors come because they changed it and, then, hated to see them leave because they changed it again. The young nurses would come and tell you where they came from; that the Head Sister was drinking gin in the doctor's rooms last night (naughty Brasser); and ask you if you knew people they knew. When someone would come they'd rattle the trolley like mad and make off with a tray. And then, by jingo, they kick you out.

This pen must have limped along for nearly an hour now and I'm afraid I was writing for my own benefit for quite a part of it. I am writing on a big,

5 Monica McGahern b. 1939, John's sister. Monica was then living in Dublin and was working in Accounts at the Department of Industry and Commerce, Kildare Street.

brown box beside the fire – all my precious poems and notebooks are in it. I sit here all evening after coming from the hospital, dream mad short stories and lecherous poems aloud to the bloody heart of Jesus on the mantelpiece. Then I write letters that should have been written six months ago; I'm in great form for letter-writing. I saw a half-baked poem sticking out of a book to-day and, by the loose women of Ireland, did I put it out of sight, quick.

The sky was dark yesterday, so dark that I thought it might snow. I wanted to be at home for it. That hour before the snowstorm – that's peace for you: the birds winging like hell for the woods; all the cold melting out of the air; the hare hopping along the thick hedge, and the trees waiting, still as a held gasp. I love the snow. It makes the white gull turn grey as she swings over the Red Barrel and the black cattle stand like sin in the converted fields.

I liked Kavanagh's little verse though it's tinged with sentiment.[6] I thought Auden good too, but I dearly wanted to knock him down from his impeccable, pious horse. That's a sign, I suppose, that he is really good. I have a poor opinion of the English Poets of this century.[7] Even Eliot is more satirist than poet.[8] Thomas, Graves, Raine and maybe Barker I'd pick – and they are minor poets.[9] I nearly forgot some of Lawrence, though, he is too unequal.[10] I suppose it all boils down to the [illegible] of that, Sean Sufferin Duck Mac Eachran is the undiscovered country.[11]

But, no! I am not really the literary man you half-don't-know-whether-I-am-or-not. Life for me is a physical thing like a woman. I love the bitch and try and tell all sorts of things because I must. I tell her the things she has been told before and she wipes her arse with them. I dream of shaking the whore out of her standing some day. Come a day, gone a day! God send Sunday. But recognition:

6 McGahern was a lifetime admirer of the poetry of Patrick Kavanagh.

7 This poor opinion of contemporary British poetry soon changed, with Auden, Philip Larkin and W. S. Graham, in particular, becoming important touchstones for McGahern.

8 As McGahern grew older and read more he lost this suspicion of Eliot and was particularly fond of Four Quartets.

9 Dylan Thomas (1914–53), Robert Graves (1895–1985), Kathleen Raine (1908–2003), George Barker (1913–91).

10 D. H. Lawrence (1885–1930), whose novel Sons and Lovers (London: Duckworth, 1913) was a particular favourite of McGahern's.

11 McGahern was always known at home as Seán rather than John, and as a teacher he tended to use his full Irish-language name of Seán MacEachran, a common practice among Irish primary school teachers of this era.

Pillicock sat on Pillicock Hill.[12] I could ravel and rave out my befuddled mind like this for hours.

But enough. Listen, Tony, I know I should rewrite this into some readable form but I just haven't the goddamn energy. I know you will not be critical. I can almost hear the ghost-voice of my mother:

'Anything worth doing, is worth doing well'.

Ay! and the big men and the little men and the men that are neither big nor little; the men that rule the earth and the men that the earth rules and the careless men that pass indifferently and swiftly over the earth, neither holding, or being held by it; they are all clay and a clay with a great fire in it, that will blaze into an eternal day.

I can only wish you a happy Christmas
Sean McEachran

---

12 Spoken by the Fool in Act 3, Scene 4 of Shakespeare's *King Lear*, a play that would in later years become an important influence on McGahern's 1990 novel *Amongst Women*.

1958

Tony Whelan
[*Madeline McGahern*]
57 Howth Road

16 July 1958[1]

Dear Tony,[2]

I was delighted and very grateful to get your letter. You have much to be thankful for – a fairly satisfying job and the opportunity of meeting interesting people.

But it hardly matters where you are! Suffering cannot be better developed in one part of the world than another. 'A man that doesn't make an eejit out of himself makes nothing' is a Roscommon truism. London may be the meeting place of the world; it seems to me that the meetings are no different in London than in Cootehall. Maybe I am wrong? But I do not find life easy here: it is very lonely. No one seems to even know about literature anymore; to realise death. So many things, opinions have been said about Ireland that it is laughable to say more. But Ireland must be the pagan country in the sun: religion is mere ritual; Jesus a sugar-daddy equivalent of the English the-thing-you-know-old-boy; heaven a holiday resort that everyone who contributes to the monthly fund is guaranteed to reach – hardship free. I shouldn't have begun this. I am just bitter and must sound like one of those opening-of-the-mission things.

1 This date is an error on McGahern's part. The letter was posted to Whelan's London address from Dublin on 14 June 1958 and forwarded on to his Kilkeel, Co. Down address. Such dating errors are not uncommon in McGahern's correspondence.
2 The late Tony Whelan, from Kilkeel, Co. Down. McGahern first met Whelan in a London hostel in the summer of 1954 when he was seeking work during a vacation from St Patrick's teacher training college, Drumcondra. For an account of their friendship, see Tony Whelan, 'Working at the mill', *The John McGahern Yearbook*, vol. 2 (Galway: National University of Ireland, 2009), 28–41.

I still teach in Dublin. I often fear I shall grow old among the Primers and children who care as little about learning as I do about teaching.[3] I finished my degree this week; it may be useful.[4]

As long as you believe in yourself nothing can happen you. Your proper books must be your life, to shape experience, to be able to leave life with some grace.

I picked these poems for you from nine or ten that I attempted since Christmas. I have no opinion on them. I wouldn't send them anywhere – I would hate getting them back, you see! I would like to believe that they are not without merit. But it is possible that they have not.

I have been saving money. I hope to go to London and spend a few weeks going through France and Italy. I had intended to stop at St Ann's but would prefer to avoid it if I knew of a place, not too dear.[5] Do you know of any? Or would you think it better to stop in the hostel? I would be going there early in July.

I can only thank you for writing and hope to hear from you again. Perhaps you might be able to spend some evening with me in London?

Very sincerely yours,

Sean

'Poem'

The leaves wither on the trees
The wind whirls them free
And the rain batters them
Into the earth again

3 In a letter of 29 September 2005, Tony Whelan writes to congratulate McGahern on *Memoir* and reminds him of this letter written nearly fifty years before: 'Incidentally you might be interested to know that I have come across a letter you wrote to me in July 1958 in which you say "I often fear I shall grow old among the primers and children who care as little about learning as I do about teaching." I'm sure I must have kept this letter because I thought that this would not be your fate.' Madeline McGahern Papers.

4 McGahern had studied for an evening BA degree in English, Irish and Economics at University College Dublin (UCD), 1955–8.

5 St Anne's was a Catholic hostel on the Underwood Road in London's East End. It is the address used on McGahern's National Insurance card issued for December 1953–December 1954. See McGahern Papers, National University of Ireland Galway (NUIG), P71/1253.

My love was young and soft as the growing leaves
You blighted it and time swept slowly away –
I offer you my peace that is of the world's peace
A triumph [?] sodden as torn earth under the rain.

The leaves of love are shed
And scattered with the dead
The tree is bare and stark
And waiting for the dark.

Our love is gone and we are naked as the tree
Helpless and terribly alone on this bare hill
Waiting for this dark frustration to be crushed
By the deadening clasp of our simple clay

The leaves and tree are gone
They are dead, dead and gone
Beaten into earth again
Again, again and again

When passing generations make frenzied sound about us
When our rotten flesh a richer earth has made
Suckle a casual worm on your clayey breasts
And send him wriggling in search of my heart.

The tree shall rise again
To the wind and driving rain
It shall clothe and shed
And mix with us, the dead

When he curdles into me and makes us one
You and I shall madly shake our companion clay
And startle the ancient grubs and growing grasses
With our ridiculous comical laughter

'Song Over A Child'

O turn your face to the wall, my child, and weep
Away the dream unquiet sleep that ages keep
For innocence; in sleeping still believe
That sleep is all we need to take from life to leave . . .

And all the weeds of your unknowing know,
The gardens growing, waters flowing deep and slow,
For holy wheat will clothe your soul with grace
And word [*illegible*] each squandered passion on your
     wasted face.

O turn, turn over your face, old face, asleep
In innocence, and bathe in deeper sleep.

'The Cross'

I

The shudder through our flesh forgets
To ripple to its sob
And we are sure the shadow met
In the night is ours at last
And that a cross on the road is turned
To the rectangular beast.

II

Arm on arm, crossed, our lips
Feel on the throat, the hair,
Their certainty of what we are –
We stuff our mouths with flesh
To choke the locust yell of the cross
Within a skin-tight mesh.

III

A beating of seed in the bloodshot dark
Wears naked the sated bone
And failure of love leaves us undone
In the passion contracted shadow
Of the ríb, as we móve, crúcifórm,
Through the níght's uneásy flow.

[untitled and partially damaged poem]

[*illegible line*]
[*illegible*] of dancing heels
Farther than the [*illegible*] mad tattoo
On the empty booming drum

Once you were soft and warm arm
And men discussing that took it
And left hard pride and a coldness in you
              And the longing

[*illegible*] you I pity and hate
[*illegible*] that gave pride
And left taking more than they gave.
Come! I will dance thee as well as they.

I shall [*illegible*] thy cold breasts
Warm the dull twylight between them
With a pity gentler than love
And hate fiercer than passion

That the fear [?] loses its hardness
And the coldness of spurned pride
[*illegible line*]
[*illegible line*]

You! You there! Standing in the hall
Spurning the twisted paper with nervous flick,

Rests at my feet, while the drumsticks
Clatter yonder, with a bump and a frump.

You like the paper at my feet
Alone and sulked with no man to dance
Rage in the heart that lurks not
In the brazen face, but the twisted paper at my foot

Mad that no man takes your hand
And fiercely presses your cold breast
And lays his burning cheek to yours
And rocks you to the [illegible] beat.

Which should I hate the baulked
Bitter in you or pity the [illegible] in you
That could so [illegible] itself to wait
For the vulgar food of a man

The Spoiled Poet Takes his Ordination Vows

(temptation)

No faith or love ordains me:
I take the living death with hands
That feel no flesh or blood in cups
Worn frail from centuries of use,
Too much religion have my people
From rearing priests on stingy acres
Till they have come too priestly now
To root the bitter soil and breed.

No want of serving man of God
Bids me relinquish common ways
The comfortable closeness of flesh,
Of thigh and mouth for sodden dreams.
None but the terror of blindfold lust
Has put this chalice to my lips
That I may drain its anguish part,
The confusion of eternity.

The room is swept; the crucifix
and candles near the tidied bed.
I fix belief on every sense
That fondled hopeless guilt in life.
What matter what is chosen now?
It all was chosen minds ago –
I only change the changeless time
And make the waiting years go slow.

(I would not have sent you these only you asked; I picked them because
they seem different from one another; transcribing them and comparing them
with their passion they seem very slight.)[6]

6 These are the only known surviving poems written by McGahern, and all exhibit
the heavy hand of, particularly, Patrick Kavanagh and Gerard Manley Hopkins,
writers McGahern would continue to admire for the rest of his life.

1959

Michael McLaverty Archive

57 Howth Road

13 January 1959[1]

Dear Mr McLaverty,[2]

I have wanted to write to you for some time, but I have found it difficult to address you. I have never written to an author before. I am a native of North Roscommon, and work in a National School in Dublin.

I came across Truth in the Night when I was in the Training College; I read it several times that month.[3] Since then I read and enjoyed most of your work. School for Hope is the novel I think greatest: Truth in the Night gave me most enjoyment – to read it was like coming into a new country. For many chapters I thought The Choice was to be your best novel, but it reminded me too much of Balzac's Le Medicin de Campagne – a book I never liked.

More than a year ago, I read The Circus Pony in the Dublin Magazine.[4] I hope you don't think me stupid when I say it is better than any of your work. I thought it captured the same strange wonder of K Mansfield's The

---

1 McGahern's first letter to Michael McLaverty. This particularly rich run of correspondence which resides in the Linen Hall Library, Belfast has previously been edited by John Killen as *Dear Mr McLaverty: The Literary Correspondence of John McGahern and Michael McLaverty 1959–1980* (Belfast: The Linen Hall Library, 2006). For the purposes of my edition I am using the original documents. My conclusions about the exact contents of the letters are at slight variance to Killen, with occasional changes in guessed dates and difficult-to-read words. I am also replacing Killen's italics with the original underlining of words.

2 Michael McLaverty (1904–92). Ulster novelist and short story writer who, when McGahern began writing to him, was headmaster at St Thomas's Secondary School, on the Whiterock Road, Belfast.

3 McGahern attended St Patrick's College, Drumcondra, Dublin, where he studied to be a primary school teacher, October 1953–June 1955.

4 Michael McLaverty, 'The Circus Pony', *Dublin Magazine*, XXXII, 4 (1957), 23–35.

Young Girl, or Vision by Corkery.[5] It so excited me at the time that I read it to the class I teach; but they were too young. I have a younger brother and sister at home, and at Christmas I took the story with me; I shall never forget the way it affected them. I couldn't draw their impressions of the story from them, but I found the little girl reading the story secretly a few days later.[6]

I shall leave this letter as it is; were I to rewrite it, I wouldn't have the courage to post it – you see, I tried it once before.

But I do not want to make a display of my personality. I believe that it is a great achievement for any man to state, even once, a measure of his experience truthfully. Your books have given me a better appreciation of life as well as their own pleasure.

I want to thank you and wish you the health to write many more,

I am
Very Sincerely
John McGahern

Michael McLaverty Archive

57 Howth Road

22 August 1959

Dear Mr McLaverty,
It is possible, perhaps, that you remember me writing to you – last Christmas. I want to thank you for your kindliness, and the stories you told me about. Only for I am aware that you are a busy man I would have written sooner.

I had read all the stories you mentioned except Ivan Ilyich; it is the greatest of them all.[7] Some years ago I read Resurrection and an Oxford Press

---

5 In a return letter of 23 January 1959, McLaverty agrees with McGahern about the power of Corkery's overlooked story 'Vision', which appeared in *Earth out of Earth* (Dublin: Talbot Press, 1939). He suggests that McGahern should write to Corkery and provides an address. There is no correspondence from McGahern among Corkery's extensive papers at University College Cork. For McLaverty's reply, see Killen (ed.), *Dear Mr McLaverty*, 17.

6 The two children at home in Grevisk at this point were Dympna b. 1942 and Frankie b. 1943.

7 In a letter of 23 January 1959, McLaverty had suggested to McGahern that he read for his 'own private enjoyment' Tolstoy's 'The Death of Ivan Ilyich'; Mary Lavin's 'The Small Bequest'; and Frank O'Connor's 'Uprooted'. He also suggests some reading for the classroom. See Killen (ed.), *Dear Mr McLaverty*, 17.

selection of his tales.[8] I was probably too young to like them. While I rushed over and over again through all Dostoyevsky wrote I neglected Tolstoy. I was working at the time I read Ivan; it so excited me that I had to put it away until I was finished. Now I am reading through his novels. I thought Ivan a far greater story than Joyce's The Dead, though not unlike it. Also, I thought – especially in My Husband and I – I saw the seeds of Proust's great novel: the quarrel about the changing of love in time, and, indeed the French [*illegible*] at the end of Ivan Ilyich. War and Peace is probably greater than The Magic Mountain. These comparisons are idle things.

I was sorry to see Patrick Kavanagh make a fool of himself about your writing; though, I don't expect you minded your name being linked with Hardy's. Kavanagh is an irresponsible critic and a careless poet. It is a pity he doesn't take more care with his poems because he is richly gifted. Do you know:

> 'But satire is unfruitful prayer,
> Only wild shoots of pity there,
> And you must go inland
> And be lost in compassion's ecstasy . . .
>
> Bring in the particular trees
> That caught you in mysteries . . .
> Ignore power's schismatic sect,
> Lovers alone, lovers protect.'[9]

I am only linking lines at random out of my memory.

I saw your Wild Duck included in a pocket anthology of Irish stories. It is a poor selection and I don't think that particular story does you justice. It is a

---

8 Tolstoy's last novel, *Resurrection* (1899), is the one paperback present in Fr Gerald's bookcase in *The Dark* (1965).

9 Quotes from Patrick Kavanagh, 'Prelude', first published as 'From a Prelude' in the *Irish Times* (12 February 1955). Collected in the British literary periodical *Nimbus* later that year and in *Come Dance with Kitty Stobling* (London: Longmans, Green and Co., 1960). McGahern recalls his first encounter with the poem thus: 'I wish I could open a magazine now with the same excitement with which I once opened *Nimbus*'. See McGahern, 'The Solitary Reader', *LOTW*, 92. In the instruction to 'go inland/And be lost in compassion's ecstasy', the poem is an important influence on *The Leavetaking* (1974). In 1964 McLaverty gifted McGahern his copy of Kavanagh's rare first collection, *Ploughman and Other Poems* (London: Macmillan, 1936).

pity you have no following in this country, but I doubt very much if anybody has. As for my own part, I would look forward to your next book.

My own first novel has gone to the publishers. It is a trying time waiting for some word back. If it was either accepted or rejected I could settle back to work again, and some peace. Perhaps, if it is published, you might do me the honour of reading it.[10]

I come from the country between Boyle and the Arigna mountains, near the Leitrim and Sligo borders, about twenty miles from Castlerea.[11] Lough Key is there, the scene of the love story of Una Bhán and Tomas Láidir; it has an island for every county in Ireland with broken-down castles and churches. It is very lovely in the ring of the mountains. Castlerea has the fat land – lazy men and cattle. A Kerry schoolmaster used to say that from walking behind their bullocks the Roscommon men and women have become like them. It might be wiser not to pass on this information to your friend. This is [an] untidy letter, but if I were to write it again I mightn't post it. I wish you well and thank you again for your kindness.

Sincerely
John McGahern

Dympna McGahern
[Madeline McGahern] (TS)

57 Howth Road

[*Early 1960s*]

Dear Dymphna,[12]
I was so glad to get your letter, but you were hardly right in thinking that I was trying to evoke Grevisk for you.[13] It was no more than an attempt,

---

10 In fact, McGahern's first novel, *The Barracks*, was not published until 1963. It is likely that he is referring here to 'The End or the Beginning of Love', which was never published but seems to have been read by London publishing companies Barrie and Rockliff, MacGibbon & Kee, Hamish Hamilton and Hutchinson.

11 McGahern mentions Castlerea because McLaverty told him in a letter of 23 January that his best friend's wife was 'Fallon from Castlerea'. See Killen (ed.), *Dear Mr McLaverty*, 17.

12 Dympna McGahern b. 1942, John's youngest sister. He spells the name with an 'h' throughout the correspondence. These letters to Dympna form part of the Madeline McGahern Papers.

13 Dympna was still living at home then in Grevisk, Boyle, Co. Roscommon with her father, stepmother and brother Frankie.

schoolmasterish enough perhaps, to tell you that you can't describe something through an emotional fog, that you must imagine it clearly and then select its most essential images. Like the petrol can . . .[14]

You should try to come to terms with the people about you and with your work: if you can't endure them find devices to avoid them or to see as little of them as possible or to get clear of them altogether; if you dislike your work set about getting another kind of work. To do any of these things you'll have to discipline yourself and work. There is no such thing in life as freedom, only the freedom to choose and that not always. And our choices impose their own tyrannies on us, but only a person who fails, who gives everything up as hopeless can become wooden. Lamb didn't let the wood get into his soul – how could one piece of wood say that an office makes people into other pieces of wood?[15] Only a thinking person could recognise such a thing. I, at least, have no wish to be a lily of the field. I would not want to be a lesser thing than I am. I can, by discipline and honesty and work, be greater. TO GIVE UP is to go in the direction of the lily or the piece of wood or the pig. To lose our consciousness or our souls. It is only because your mind has some idea of beauty that a lily is more so than a pig.

I was glad to know that you are reading. Read many books. Not until you have read many books – bad ones and good ones – will you know what you want. And always read what you enjoy. But now that you are young read several and many books because even now the time is slipping away from you that leaves a lasting impression on your life. Until you have read many books do not have too many opinions about them: because it is only by comparison that books no more than most things are good and bad. But ask yourselves some time if this or that has anything to do with your own life. Is it your idea of truth or of beauty?

Do not trouble much about others. They have to shape their own lives, and finally it is their own responsibility. Seldom does it do any good, hardly ever, mostly harm. If they need help it is usually in some simple concrete way – a word, or some money for food or shelter. And the world is so full of squalor that it is usually only possible to help our friends. Frankie's trouble is laziness and he'll have to pay a little price which, whatever about whether it will do

14 Dympna and John exchanged work with each other for critical comment.
15 A reference to Charles Lamb, 'The Superannuated Man' (1833), an essay that reflects on the drudgery of office work: 'I had grown to my desk, as it were; and the wood had entered into my soul.' McGahern was interested in the figure of the working drone and how one might fight such servitude, as evident in a later fascination with Herman Melville's 'Bartleby, the Scrivener'.

good or harm, will certainly have more EFFECT than any coaxing. And even he might yet find HIMSELF.[16]

Write and if there is anything you think I could help you with I would try as hard as I know how.

Love,
Sean

Dympna McGahern
[*Madeline McGahern*] (TS)

57 Howth Road
Dublin

[*Late 1950s–early 1960s*]

Dear Dymphna,

Thank you very much for your letter. I have holidays now and I'll work a little and then go home perhaps. I'm not leaving the country. It's dull heavy weather and you fall asleep over work. Still it goes constantly and well enough.

I always found I.R.A. narratives boring in the extreme.[17] But then I never [*found*] these external dramas exciting. What Curiosity I have is what impact they made on the individual concerned. I've found they've made none, or only accentuated some stupid hatreds. The real drama of life doesn't go on in war, the drama of all our lives under God, but how our consciences weigh the triumphs and disasters of each day. It does not matter what way our lives pass, somebody could make a walk through the woods as passionately vivid as an ambush, provided he loved it, that is all that matters. Only what is felt with passionate intelligence is really exciting. And only life understood in its death is vital. It is strange how people who have lived face to face with it in war hardly ever understand it outside some glorification or other, dying for faith and fatherland etc., it saves them thinking for themselves. All great saints and artists turned their backs on Mass excitements and lived in the

---

16 Frankie disliked school, quarrelled with his father and eventually left for London as an adolescent, helped by his siblings and escorted aboard the night crossing to Holyhead by John.

17 Ernie O'Malley's account of his part in the Anglo-Irish War of 1919–21, *On Another Man's Wound* (London: Rich & Cowan, 1936), later becomes an exception to this critical preference.

War of their own selves, to find a peace outside the fickleness of days and crowds.

I send you this little book of poems and hope you like them. Read the poem on page 61 first, it is on a painting of Brueghel's, which shows the fall of Icarus, by a single white leg disappearing into the water while every thing goes about its daily business and pays no attention.[18]

Margaret comes sometimes. Monica I saw a fortnight ago. What's Fr. at now?[19]

Write soon and with all my love,
Sean

18 The poem to which McGahern is referring is W. H. Auden's 'Musée des Beaux Arts', written in December 1938 and first published under the title 'Palais des beaux arts' in the Spring 1939 issue of *New Writing*. It was first collected in *Another Time* (London: Faber, 1940). The poem's title derives from the Musées royaux des Beaux-Arts de Belgique in Brussels, which Auden had visited and where he had seen *Landscape with the Fall of Icarus*, normally attributed to Pieter Bruegel the Elder (c. 1525–69). Given the pagination, the Auden volume that McGahern must be sending to Dympna is a paperback that forms part of the Penguin Poets series, selected by the author and published in 1958.

19 Margaret and Monica McGahern, both sisters then living in Dublin. 'Fr.' presumably refers to McGahern's younger brother Frankie, then living in Grevisk with Dympna.

1960

Lyric Theatre/
O'Malley Archive (TS)

36 Victoria Street
South Circular Road
Dublin[1]

17 January [1960][2]

Dear Editor,[3]

I was born in Dublin in 1934, but was brought up in the West of Ireland, for the most time in North Roscommon.

I have not appeared in print. My first novel was finished a few months back and was recommended by another writer to his publishers, Hamish Hamilton. They are still considering it.[4]

I mention these in case you find my story suitable for publication and because of the bibliography at the back of your quarterly.[5]

Although I am in an unfair position, I would like to say how much I enjoyed Yeats in the Dagg Hall last year.[6] Such evenings happen rarely in Dublin.

Sincerely,
John McGahern

---

1 McGahern's sisters Monica and Margaret then lived at this address. Monica was in the Civil Service and Margaret in the Eastern Health Board. McGahern occasionally used it as his postal address.

2 This letter is misdated 17 January 1959 by McGahern.

3 To Mary O'Malley, editor of *Threshold* magazine.

4 Referring to the ultimately unpublished 'The End or the Beginning of Love'. The MS resides among the McGahern Papers at NUIG.

5 McGahern had a section from *The Barracks* published in *Threshold* in 1962 under the title 'Waiting'.

6 In September 1959 the Lyric Theatre of Belfast put on a four-day run of Yeats's *Oedipus at Colonus* and *The Death of Cuchulain* in the Dagg Hall, Westland Row, Dublin.

15 February 1960

Dear Michael McLaverty,

I want to accept your invitation, for which I am deeply grateful.

I have taken the liberty of sending you nearly ¼ of the mss. I would rather you saw my work first because I would feel easier meeting you. I tried to put in as little as possible but I cannot see less giving you any idea of what it is about. If this is an impertinence I beg to shelter under the famous awkwardness of the young.

I brought very little away of the work as I conceived it. It grows very little in my eyes in the past few months. So you need have no fear of being even painfully just.

I had not hoped for your interest when I wrote to you in September. I wrote because I owe much to your own work, of living Irish prose writers I admire your works most. You cannot know how your card delighted me.

Sincerely,

John McGahern

9 March 1960

Dear Michael McLaverty,

Your kindness in sending a card with the New Yorker made me very happy and I would have thanked you sooner only I know that you can have little time on your hands.

The story is indeed as bad as you said it was – not really a story at all. Something strung hurriedly together for that fat fee the New Yorker pays and he has probably an easy wicket. His new novel is coming out shortly. It is unlikely to be, on the N. Y. evidence, much of an event.[7]

---

7 McLaverty had sent McGahern the New Yorker issue of 30 January 1960 that published 'The Wild Boy', a story by the Irish writer Benedict Kiely (1919–2007). Kiely's novel The Captain with the Whiskers was published in 1960 by Methuen.

I managed to borrow a copy of Bird Alone and, although you spoke well of it, I couldn't like it.[8] I found it difficult to distinguish anything through the fog of rhetoric. Characters, emotions, even simple situations blurred in his exceedingly skilful manipulations of words – and this quickly became for me the drone of a bore. He said one very good thing about friendship and even this was spoiled for me by appearing too neatly parcelled – all wrapped in shiny blue ribbon. I wished that somebody would nail a 'grocer's calendar' on the wall and say something ordinary, instead of all these beautiful turned phrases melting into one another like clouds. Have you ever felt that more skill can be as worthless as the total lack of it?

But it is only fair to say that I may be biased against O Faoláin. I have had no contact with him except through his work and it has always seemed phoney to me – the man in the work. Somewhere in his journals Da Vinci says, an unskilful man who is honest is far more likely to achieve something than a great craftsman who has no honesty. This sounds all very solemn and Hemingway said a solemn writer is always 'an owl, a bloody owl.'[9] And as far as O Faoláin is concerned, I may be blind as one.

I rang Mrs Walshe and she received me with great kindness.[10] I think she is the most charming and interesting woman I ever met. She said many good things but she has the unusual gift of seeming to say everything as if she was saying it specially for whoever she is speaking with. I also found that our vision of life and writing had much in common and that – deplore it how we may – is the most exciting discovery of all. As she invited me again I can only hope that it wasn't all from kindness and I must be careful not to wear out my welcome. I hope this doesn't sound too drunken.

Although most of the children in the school where I teach come from comfortable homes there is a small slum in the middle of Clontarf. This year I happen to have ten from there – eight to nine years old – and what I learn shakes me. Any scar will nearly always fester. I notice how they huddle apart from the other children in the playground. It is strange that while their shoes are leaking that they can always muster money for drill costumes or a shining

8 Seán O'Faoláin's second novel, published in 1936 by Jonathan Cape. By the time of this letter's composition O'Faoláin (1900–91) was one of the grand old men of Irish letters and had an international reputation as a writer of short stories.

9 The quote is from *Death in the Afternoon* (New York: Scribner, 1932): 'A serious writer is not to be confounded with a solemn writer. A serious writer may be a hawk or a buzzard or even a popinjay, but a solemn writer is always a bloody owl.'

10 American-born, Irish novelist and short story writer Mary Lavin (1912–96). She married William Walsh in 1943. Her work was admired by McLaverty and he encouraged McGahern to meet her.

new red tie and blue suit for First Communion – any outward show. Why I probably tell you these things is that only to day I discovered that the sweaty smell of decay, nauseatingly strong from some of them, comes from them sleeping in their clothes. It is difficult to reconcile the desire to do nothing but write ('I intend to give up this scribbling', Byron said in one of his letters), even a cushioned civil service life, with all the human suffering about us.

But there's not much danger of me doing much these days. With the eternal scraping of the tubular steel chairs and a great roarer with his class at the other end of the ballroom – it is really that – there's not much left when you try to work. Slow-quick, quick-slow. Sometimes it seems funny – and that saves the day.

I want to thank you for the wonderful evening you gave me in the Ivanhoe.[11] One of the things that overjoyed me was not to feel that there was much difference between the man and his work. I think not many writers would have as much patience with a young person.

Although I have gone on for too long, one thing more: if you happen to read Thomas Mann's Felix Krull* I would like to hear what you think.[12] He is a writer that I love; and it is my favourite among his work.

I must not forget to wish you luck with the novel you are working on.

> V. sincerely
> John McGahern

*Penguin

---

11 Hotel and bar located in the Carryduff area of suburban Belfast.
12 Mann's final, unfinished, novel. First published in 1954.

James Swift
[*Madeline McGahern*]

Grevisk
Boyle
Co. Roscommon
[*hereafter Grevisk*]

Easter Sunday[13] [*1960*]

Dear Jimmy,[14]

I am sending you one of Dymphna's poems – I wrote it out as she has only one copy of the magazine – and <u>she</u> hopes you will like it. I would like to think she will be a poet one day, and, yet, I would spare her its devil's-dance – the eating into the heart.

I can never write from here, not even letters – which are the easiest passer away of time. It is constantly tense, egotism both greedy and afraid, once savage, wasting away as a kill-joy, gnawing at its own loneliness and despair. Because all men must suffer and die in our own image, they should be worthy of all our compassion which is beautiful in the ideal – The Tempest – but impossible in life because of our own, each of us, need of love. We rarely find the perfect union of male and female, positive and negative.

And yet it is more lonely than a golden dream today; the sun on the fields around the house, bunches of wild daffodils between the tall, churchyard evergreens, and here and there patches of forget-me-nots – they grow profusely in small wild patches in our land – making blue the coming green of grass. The shell of a blackbird's egg, so palely blue, fallen under the trees. This morning I found my first cowslip: it has the modest scent of any flower.

13 Sergeant Frank McGahern retired from *An Garda Síochána* in autumn 1958 and moved from the garda barracks in Cootehall to a fine stone house, once part of the Rockingham estate, in nearby Grevisk with his second wife Agnes McShera and two youngest children, Dympna and Frankie.

14 James 'Jimmy' Swift (1919–2004), the eldest of a large Dublin family whom John first met through Jimmy's brother Tony (see letter to Tony Swift of 14 December 1957). Jimmy Swift quickly became one of McGahern's closest friends and his most important intellectual influence, introducing him to Proust, among other writers. He is fictionalised as 'Lightfoot' in *The Leavetaking*, a name McGahern borrowed from his landlord at 57 Howth Road. The closeness of the friendship is reflected in McGahern's decision to dedicate his first novel, *The Barracks*, to Swift. The letters to Swift form part of the Madeline McGahern Papers.

And do you know – 'Where the bee suck, there suck I/In the cowslip's bell I lie.'[15]

I was at the crossroads today as well. A girl from England took our photographs. Watching the carloads of girls pass in their summer frocks and the band wagons for the Easter dancing with the big instruments on top. In spite of the usual buffoonery it was a failure. Nothing but lonliness and a craving for an excitement that will not come. They were glad to break up to cycle to a funeral. I remember the war Sundays of my childhood and soldiers dancing with the people I knew. I am sad for my own sake: it is a society breaking up into loneliness, the last loneliness is death.

I have no news of my brother but it is easy to be dramatic for its own sake. Only for the poem I wouldn't write. Most of the letters of this kind that I have ever got seemed phoney. 'The sun slanting through mists and the blooming [*illegible*] and flowers in every hole and corner.' (But) Even as I write this there is a thrush singing on the Drooping Ash that's just before our house. For me the tree of quiet sorrow. I would bring all the people I love to hear that song in this evening. Which could not be done, because even if they could come, it would be a still greater miracle if they were not busy with their own beauty, deaf to my evening. It is impossible to gather even one or two, except with, maybe, the miracle of art. 'We live as we dream – alone.'[16] If there is much foolishness remember I scribbled, not separating the wheat if any.

John

James Swift
[Madeline McGahern]
[No address]

[*No date*][17]

Dear Jimmy,
A complete disregard for language and preoccupation with the wringing of diverse matter into a kind of wholeness are, in my own opinion, only too

---

15 Sung by Ariel for Prospero, Act 5, Scene 1 of Shakespeare's *The Tempest*.
16 Quoting here from the character Marlow in Joseph Conrad, *Heart of Darkness* (Edinburgh: Blackwood, 1902). 'No, it is impossible; it is impossible to convey the life-sensation of any given epoch of one's existence… We live, as we dream – alone.'
17 Very fine, cursive handwriting and lacerating self-criticism suggest an early date of late 1950s or early 1960s.

pathetically obvious on these pages. In a work of art clarity of language and clarity of vision are inseparable: a vision of life cannot be conveyed, even to satisfy your own ear, without the power over social intercourse; language for its own sake becomes merely ridiculous. This is obvious on all levels of life – from gossip to high art.[18]

Indeed I would be grateful for any adverse criticism. The scenes are not smoothed one into the other: the descriptive narrative is slipshod. I have taken more care with the dialogue and it should be obvious. The couple who read it gave it too much praise: my sister is the only one who has faulted it constantly, and of these, later chapters, I have [*illegible*] her criticism.[19] She read the love scenes and said that they were no more than popular writing – an awkward Steinbeck – and she considers the hayfield scene with Mahoney crass sentimentality.[20] She is, of course, entitled to her opinion which I believe honest but, at the same time, it is necessary for myself to keep writing. That is why I want you to be honest rather than kind.

John

18 Not known what McGahern is referring to here, but it seems to be an especially harsh reading of his own work – not uncharacteristic in his dealings with Swift at this early point in his career.

19 Dympna is almost certainly the sister in question. Couple unknown.

20 While the mention of Mahoney might suggest that this letter refers to drafts of what becomes *The Dark*, it more likely refers to sections of 'The End or the Beginning of Love', McGahern's unpublished novel on which he was working through the late 1950s and early 1960s, in which the name Mahoney is also used for a central character.

James Swift
[*Madeline McGahern*]

6 King Edward Road
Leyton
London E. 10
[*hereafter 6 King Edward Road*][21]

[*August 1960*]

Dear Jimmy,

I shall be going home soon, and I shall see you then, if Providence is still watching us – for I suppose that is more exact, since it must be more miraculous to be alive than to be dead.

I still live alone with my brother. And it is too much – for me, and for him.[22] We have nothing in common, except memories, and these have become so distorted by our opposite visions that only in irrelevances are they alike. He is young, I know. But he is so like my father. And despotism and intolerance are the most detestable things in humanity. They have fathered every filthy plague.[23]

Why should I trouble you, except that the rain outside goes with complain, and I only meant to tell that I intend to go home soon.

I have met most of those about Paddy, but I'll leave it till we meet. He is coming down the East here one of these evenings. I like him very much.[24]

21 McGahern's sister Rosaleen began her married life with Jimmy Craig at this address before moving on to a large house at 23 Forest Drive West, Leytonstone in 1964, a house she shared for many years with her sister Breege and family and in which McGahern frequently stayed. The sisters worked as nurses in the nearby Whipps Cross Hospital.

22 McGahern regularly spent summers in London through the later 1950s and early 1960s.

23 McGahern's younger brother Frankie left home for England with his father's permission on 2 April 1960 on the understanding that Rosaleen would take him in. John was likely sharing a room with Frankie in Rosaleen's at King Edward Road during his summer holidays from teaching duties at Belgrove. There was a gap of nine years between Frankie and John. On Frankie's move to England, McGahern's worries and his brother's ultimate success in the world, see *Memoir*, 236–9.

24 Paddy is Patrick Swift (1927–83), Irish artist and younger brother of James 'Jimmy' Swift.

The MSS came from Tony. I must thank him. I am afraid he hadn't much of a holiday here.[25]

I used to work here during the day – for myself, of course, for, if you have a little money, I have long come to realize that Time is by far the most valuable currency, but a friend of mine has died suddenly and the sense of futility, as it often does with me, sucks away all energy; there is no will to work.[26]

I saw a very beautiful scarf on a young girl at Mass last Sunday, softly black like a pall, hung with cloth bells, exactly like fuchsia bells, only they were green and yellow as well as that lovely velvety red of fuchsia. I was wondering if she made it herself. It was very lovely.

I am looking forward to seeing you very much, and I hope all of you are well,

John

Dympna McGahern
[*Madeline McGahern*] (TS)

57 Howth Road

[*1960*]

Dear Dymphna,
Thank you for the letter and I hope you like the book, they're all quite good, except the rubbishy Paddiad.[27]

It's a fearful price for a room, but you could pay almost as much here.[28] I think it's good to be on your own, you need that even as much as you need people, if you will ever get grip and vision on your life's passion.

I work mostly. It is real suffering but I get more and more power and control and increasing need for it in the difficulty of the work. I can never bear to write much about it: it has its own life.

In what hall did you meet Adrian? What does he work at now? I saw Noel Garvey from a bus passing through O'Connell Street: it was Thursday

25 Tony Swift.
26 Donncha Ó Céileachair (1918–60), a teaching colleague of McGahern's in Belgrove. He was a scholar of the Irish language and had worked on Tomás de Bhaldraithe's Irish-English Dictionary. He died on 21 July 1960 after a very short illness having contracted polio.
27 'The Paddiad' was the closing poem of Patrick Kavanagh's *Come Dance with Kitty Stobling*.
28 Dympna moved to London in 1960.

and Corpus Christi; and I thought probably a cheap excursion day. It made me wonder about many things. I heard the processional singing last Sunday coming from the distance of a calm day: 'Holy God we praise Thy name': it made me feel so sick and desperate that I had to turn away from my working, such a homesickness for lost days, and the little veiled girls with their white crepe and silk ribbons on cardboard boxes full of rose petals, and the gold canopy and candles and red surplices, the line of women and straggling shamefaced men in front, and our father in all his uniform at the bridge, and kneeling in the shade of evergreens at Regans, or the people, hankies down, and the ringing of the small altar bell in all the vastness of the day.

> Be sure and write in a little time.
> With all my love,
> Sean

X Papers (TS)

57 Howth Road

5 September [*1960*]

Dear Paddy,[29]

I would have written before now but I wasn't sure of your address. I send you these things too. They're of poor interest, but since they're so like Hamilton's, you may as well see them – and that'll save me the embarrassment of trying to explain. I was writing for the MS back, so I don't care, and I'll work it out so much better. It'll be a real, real work then: and they can say what they want to about it.[30]

The insistence that to string a few lunatic situations into a plot is more valuable and difficult than to give passion and pattern to the lives of people being eroded out of their existence in the banality and repetitiveness of themselves and their society is the real maddening thing. I better leave it so! But the autobiography stunt! Very few of the situations in the book ever

---

29 Paddy Swift was, at the time of this letter's composition, co-editing *X: A Quarterly Review* with David Wright (1920–94), a South African-born writer and man of letters. *X* was a top-quality quarterly that ran for seven issues and was as much interested in the visual arts as in literature.

30 The MS referred to is almost certainly the unpublished novel 'The End or the Beginning of Love', extracts of which appeared in *X* as McGahern's first publication. It had been considered (and presumably rejected) by Hamish Hamilton. See letter to Mary O'Malley of 17 January 1960.

happened in my life – in that sense, it is no more mine than the Man in the Moon's autobiography; THE WHOLE BOOK owes everything to my experience, the way I suffered and was made to laugh, the people I have lived among, the landscape and the books I liked, – in that way it is as auto as I was capable of making it. But it is seldom possible to be ourselves in real life: because of the need FOR MONEY, for friends, for a beloved, or even, I suspect, because of the need to have enemies. And if you feel you must be a responsible individual in some manner, and can't or do not wish, or feel that it's not enough to be a saint, then you have little choice but to try some artifice. The common notion that you can make an art out of your life, refinements of pleasure etc, is pure moonshine as far as I see it. There must be some morality. You might as well call the philanderer a lover. While there's the need to be a responsible individual, and you don't turn to saint, it seems to me that the need to be an artist must remain, a whole lifelong.[31] And that's a hell of a long way from writing AUTOBIOGRAPHY. You may not like what I say. Do not mind. I hate this laying down of the law. And I am always eventually sorry. But this thing has annoyed me.

Forgive me too if this isn't very coherent. I don't like writing letters. So I seldom do – which physics nothing. It is so easy to be anything except honest here: surely the art for the saint or the madman, or so I have often thought.

Your mother was so excited with the Drawing. I never saw any one so delighted I think, when Tony brought nothing, that she thought you might pass her by. People dislike strangers speaking intimately about the ones they love. Even though I felt strange there, I was very glad for her.

I saw no mushrooms while I was at home, even though I used to go down the long sheep paddocks of the Demesne nearly every morning to the spring river – for drinking water. We used to get canfuls there. It must be that the land is cold after the weeks of rain.

There was loads of apples and plums, lovely long wine-coloured Victorias, and the pears are marvellous. A pair of old pear trees shelter under the stone belfry at the house. It was for calling the workmen: where we live was the nursery farm for the House once and Milady Rockinghams used walk there.[32] I never saw it in its heyday but they still talk about it round. A few things like the belfry, several evergreens and a few walnut trees, stray apple become crab-trees, the stone roads under the grass, wild mint or rose and thousands of narcissi in the pastures in Spring are all that tell now. Kathy and Julie

31 'a whole lifelong' is inserted in pen.
32 This passage refers to the land around McGahern's father's house in Grevisk, Co. Roscommon, once part of the Rockingham estate.

should have been there, for the house is full of windfalls.[33] A pity I cannot bring you there. You could live there cheap as the dead.

I could easily have put Una's name with yours on the letter.[34] Even though I haven't she will still know that she's not far from my mind. It is no more than a distaste of the form of address. But I'm sure she won't mind. Jimmy was delighted with her regard.

You might remember me to the Wrights and Cronins, George Barker.[35]

I've started tricking with the novel, and I'll soon be working. There'll be two this time. Then I'll be able to get on out of it for good.[36] The work is the only frightening thing. But it's more than enough.

You might find time to drop me a line. Be certain to. I enjoyed so much being there with you. I'll never forget it.

John

Tony Whelan
[*Madeline McGahern*]

57 Howth Road

Wednesday evening [*postmarked 8 September 1960*]

Dear Tony,
Your card came this morning. And thank you very much for the kind invitation.[37] I am so sorry that I cannot go.

You see: last week I came back from home; the week before that, from London. I am desperately trying to build up the shambles, trying to get some order into my working life, after it all. I feel if I go down I'll only be side-stepping. It's so easy to go on and on at that, bogging deep and deeper, little by little; and it's such an impossible mountain of work it frightens me, that I'll not have sufficient will, and take some carrion comfort. I would love to

---

33 Paddy Swift's daughters.

34 Oonagh Ryan (1929–2012) was Paddy Swift's wife, sister of John Ryan who had edited *Envoy* magazine in Dublin, 1949–51.

35 'George Barker' is inserted in pen. David Wright, Anthony Cronin and George Barker were all closely associated with – and contributors to – *X*.

36 To get out of teaching, which McGahern always found difficult despite his talents in the classroom.

37 The letter is addressed to Whelan's home in Kilkeel, Co. Down and presumably is in response to an invitation to visit him there.

go down. I ask you to forgive me, but I am sure you will understand me, working yourself at the same mill.

I hope you will thank your mother for me. I would have loved to meet her again. But I hope I shall yet: though we do not often get time, to have the power taken away when we at last have the time.

I hope you will write to me very soon. I wish you well with your life and your work, now as always.

It is so degrading to be back at school again. I was very close to the dead person.[38] You see a door opening, and you imagine him where you have often seen him. He was younger looking than his years. You cannot see him again, that is the terrible thing, he no longer exists, as we ourselves will find the day when we can neither see or be seen. And the fulsome obituaries makes one embarrassed that are coming out in the gaelic magazines. No wonder Yeats, an Irishman, said that the sentimentalist deceives himself, the rhetorician his neighbours.[39]

With every good wish,
Sean

Michael McLaverty Archive

57 Howth Road

[*21 September 1960*][40]

Dear Michael McLaverty,
Thank you for your letter and kind enquiries. I felt a need to tell you what O Cealleachair intended had he lived.

I will be published in <u>X</u>, a London Quarterly edited by David Wright and Patrick Swift, next January. They invited me to London to meet them last summer. And there they introduced me to other writers.

I saw Mary Lavin a few weeks ago. She is a very charming person. She is sadly very busy, and always crowds of people about her.

---

38 Donncha Ó Céileachair, McGahern's colleague at Belgrove National School.
39 From W. B. Yeats, 'Ego Dominus Tuus': 'The rhetorician would deceive his neighbours,/The sentimentalist himself'. This poem was much admired by McGahern and remained an important inspiration throughout his artistic life, becoming a key touchstone in the composition of his final novel, *That They May Face the Rising Sun*.
40 Date marked in pencil, possibly by McLaverty or archivist.

I was delighted to learn you are working away at your novel. But I understand only too well what it is, the impossibility, of serving two masters. I shall look forward eagerly to it.

I hope you are well, and your family.

And with every good wish,
John McGahern

X Papers

57 Howth Road

[*Autumn–winter 1960*]

Dear Paddy,

I am sending you the episodes. I cannot leave them alone here – so many new cracks appear every day. And they have become an excuse for not really beginning again.

III and IV are continuous, but I think they are better split. IV is cut down very much, and they are all I'm afraid much changed. Are they all right? Or can you pick out much idiocy? If you can, you will tell me.

I would like to call it all when finished, The Grindstone, but 'episodes' are probably simpler and better now, – whatever you think.[41] There are a few words less than five thousand.

It was sharp and cold with frost until this evening, but a miserable, heavy rain without wind is coming down outside. If I had money I would always escape these wretched city winters.

Are you both well? I was to send Oonagh a lovely story by Thomas Mann: in a small red and black cover, thick creamy paper and wide margins, and a strange watercolour inset of a young girl asleep beside her bugle and rocking horse, such as you never see now. I have searched high and low, and yet it must be in the house. When I can lay my hands on it, I'll send it.

All the newspapers are on strike here. I hope they do not settle it too quickly.

I am seeing Jimmy tomorrow. You'll hardly come home for long now.

I send you my love and hope that both of you are well.

John

41 The piece was published as John McGahern, 'The End or the Beginning of Love: Episodes from a Novel' in *X: A Quarterly Review* (March 1961).

Dympna McGahern
[*Madeline McGahern*]

57 Howth Road

[*1960*]

Dear Dymphna,
Your letter came this morning. There's never need to worry about your letters to me. I'll always like them. Write what you feel, for if you get the idea that you must write well they will all become artificial. Write as you would talk to me. But you need never fear my reception of them. They please, delight me so much.

I waited down by the Bus Station to see you but they told me of all your annoyance. It was unfortunate but I'm sure you don't care very much – about the job.

Auntie is here in the Cancer Hospital. It's all so dreary and depressing. She is herself, which is a great deal less than her situation. But it's so depressing that I'll not go into it. I have to trudge out every so often to see her.[42]

I saw on The Herald how Mick Farry drownded on his way home from Henry's as far as I could make in the drain the Cootehall side of Murphy's Hill.

I have been busy lately, such a frightening amount of work to do yet. And it wears your heart out of the drudgery at school. But I am not complaining. You cannot have your loaf and the eating. It is a choice – a free choice.

Joseph Conrad, you may have read some of his novels of the sea, I think said: 'We live as we dream, alone.'[43] Nothing else is possible, to live in the light of our longings and conscience. I used to rare [*rear*] against the petty, repetitive lives of people. It is only a waste of time, Dymphna. We have only one brief life to live; we can live no other here. So why trouble too much with how the others live? You must live your own: and what it is will come to you if you have patience: and you will need much courage and discipline. As we are we are almost nothing: but I believe we can almost make ourselves into anything. By Discipline and Work. It is a difficult, bitter way, but there is

---

42 McGahern's aunt Maggie from Ballinamore, a particular favourite of his. Visitations by the narrator to a sick aunt in a Dublin cancer hospital form an important subplot in *The Pornographer* (1979).

43 A favourite quotation of McGahern's. See letter to Jimmy Swift of Easter Sunday [1960].

No Other. You must follow whatever your aspirations are. It will not matter whether you succeed or fail. What is success? What failure? Who knows?

Some writing of mine is coming out in London at the end of January. Maybe the girls told you. If you are writing home, do not mention.

Write to me often. I will answer you. If you are distracted do not be too long in writing again even if I don't answer for a time.

The longer the time passes, against what most people think, the less there's to tell. Letters cause more letters, talk more talk, and even silence blossoms in silence.

> I hope you are very well
> And with all my love
> Sean

Dympna McGahern
[*Madeline McGahern*]

Grevisk

[*Late December 1960*]

Dear Dymphna,

Thank you very much for your card and letter. Spent all Christmas here. Miserable with snow and rain. I didn't get past the house. Daddy is in bed with the cold and I'm foddering the cattle these last days. Everything looks cold and hungry, patches of snow still on the fields, and the withered thistles blowing black.

Margaret was at home but she went back on Wednesday. I tomorrow.

Congratulations on the C. Service. I thought you got a very high place.[44]

Pat came up Christmas Day with the usual sweets and bottle of squash.[45] It's strange how these little gifts, so marvellous once, go with the years, lose their excitement and meaning, and are carelessly left there all night, and only look sad like broken dolls.

The cards were damp and we had to spread them over the Rayburn. Many of the same little sayings you remember well.

---

44 Dympna did the Civil Service clerical exam in 1960 after her Leaving Certificate examination as did hundreds of others. She excelled by achieving eleventh place in the country but was not called to a vacancy for two years due to a pause in recruitment. She went to London but returned to take the job, which supported her through an evening degree course in Commerce in UCD.

45 McGahern's uncle, Pat McManus of Ballinamore.

The comic-opera of Margaret and Pat holidaying in Germany was discussed. 'The man said,' Pat said 'that it'd be all ready by Easter – at the latest – definitely I aksed him.'

So it is gone. I do not think I'll write for some weeks. I have a fearful amount of work in Dublin. And you'll be coming to Dublin soon.

With much love,

Sean

1961

Michael McLaverty Archive (TS)

57 Howth Road

[23 *January 1961*]

Dear Michael McLaverty,
You may remember that I asked you the one evening we met about the translating of your work into Gaelic. Donncha O Ceilleachair wanted to know if you would wish it. He died last summer, suddenly in a few days.

He was a friend of mine and it is hardly for me to praise him; but it was generally believed that he was the only Gaelic writer of distinction or promise among those who were still young. Corkery knew him from when he was a boy. And O Ceilleachair's first book is dedicated to him.[1]

I don't believe that translation into Gaelic was important for you, and now that O Ceilleachair is dead the whole Gaelic business looks even more quixotic to me than it was before. But I was glad that he should want to translate it. I first put your work in his way and it was a real sign of his love. He looked upon you as the first writer of prose since Joyce and maybe Corkery.

It is a small thing, sentimental may be, but he had probably intended to tell you what I have said, and I feel easier that you should know.

Intelligence is so often a flatterer and Honesty a fool that real praise is rare.

I hope that you are well and that you enjoyed your holidays.

With Good Wishes

John

1 In a letter of 30 January 1961, McLaverty replies that Corkery had mentioned Ó Céileachair. He also congratulates McGahern on the (rare) typed letter: 'I take it that the typewriter is a good sign of work to come.'

[*Early 1961*]

Dear Paddy,

If you wish you can keep the old title.

My dislike is that it has novelettish overtones – something soft or vague.

The Grindstone

Episodes from a Novel

would to my mind be truer.[2]

But if it would embarrass after having announced it, or if it would cost you extra money, or if you think the old title looks better, leave it.

Would The Grindstone seem hard and repellent, too much so? My fear was that the clumsiness and vagueness of The End – would offend real taste and not be true? But I do not know. What does David think?[3] Which do you like?

But do whatever suits the best, whichever you like more, for I could never get a satisfying title.

If it's not set up would you make these small changes? The last sentence at the end of the long par. on page 7 in the MS change to:

They felt closer to each other, the pain of their essential loneliness easy, until the next hurt or failure or sin.[4]

And change the first sent. in same paragraph to:

Ideally confession is made to God, which means nothing to the senses, it is no more than a (substitute to there).[5]

Changes underlined. Forgive me for causing you so much trouble.

Could you drop me a note to tell what you decide on?

2 An undated letter from Patrick Swift on X notepaper reveals some debate about what the extract should be titled: 'The End or etc by far best title. I shd. have said The Grindstone more novelettish.' Madeline McGahern Papers.

3 David Wright, Swift's co-editor at X.

4 The sentence appears in X as follows: 'They felt closer to each other, the pain of their essential loneliness at rest until the next sin, the next hurt, the next failure.'

5 The sentence appears in X as follows: 'Ideally confession is made to God, which means nothing to the senses, it is no more than a sophistical balm for pride; the real need is to confess sensually to another man, a need as old as original sin, as emotionally intimate as the act of hatred or of love.'

But I leave the deciding to you, whichever you like the best.

Love

John

Faber

57 Howth Road

16 March 1961

Dear Mr Monteith,[6]
Thank you for your letter of the 14th March concerning the extracts that appeared in X.[7]

It is a first novel that was actually accepted for publication, but by then, I could not in conscience publish it without serious revision. The pieces in X are part of the revision.

In the revising another novel evolved which owed nothing to the first. I felt I must leave the revision aside for a time and finish and try to publish this new work. The publishers do not seem to like this delaying and I am not happy with the position.

6 Charles Monteith (1921–95), editor, publisher and Fellow of All Souls College, Oxford. A native of Lisburn, Co. Antrim, Monteith was educated at the Royal Belfast Academical Institution and Magdalen College, Oxford. His time at Oxford was interrupted from 1940 to 1945 by war service in the Royal Inniskilling Fusiliers, which took him to India and Burma. Rising to the rank of Major, he was seriously wounded in the legs; all his life he would suffer from impaired mobility. Before his army service he obtained a first class degree in English; after the war, he obtained a further first class degree in Law, was MA in 1948 when he won a prize scholarship to All Souls. He completed a BCL in 1949 and was called to the Bar at Gray's Inn. His colleague at All Souls was Geoffrey Faber, of the publishing house Faber & Faber; Monteith joined that firm in 1953, becoming a director the following year, vice-chairman in 1974 and chairman from 1977 to 1980. His first great success at Faber was in spotting the worth of an already much-rejected manuscript from William Golding that became the multi-million-selling *Lord of the Flies* (1954). Golding went on to win the Nobel Prize for Literature in 1983. McGahern grew quickly to like and trust Monteith, whom he fictionalises in *That They May Face the Rising Sun* as the gentlemanly Robert Booth.
7 This is McGahern's first letter to Charles Monteith. Monteith had written to him c/o X on 14 March: 'I was very interested in the extracts from your novel which are published in the current number of "X". If by any chance you haven't yet made arrangements for its publication I would be absolutely delighted if you would give us an opportunity to consider it.' This quote and all subsequent quotes from Monteith to McGahern come from documents held in the Faber archives unless otherwise stated.

I sent the first part of this new work to the editors of X who have just written to say that they consider it a real advance and exciting.[8] Whether this opening (13,000 words or so) would be too slight for you to make me an offer or not I do not know. If you consider it possible, I could let you see a copy.[9]

I hope this does not seem all confusion. I am not bound by any contract or agreement. Naturally the idea of you publishing me is enormously attractive.[10]

Yours sincerely
John McGahern

Faber

57 Howth Road

22 March 1961

Dear Mr Monteith,

Thank you for your letter of the 20th March and I enclose the first part of the new novel. I'm sorry that there should be a few smudges, it is my own copy, the original wasn't returned from X. I am now working at the chapters that end the novel, and it is all coming clear.

The other novel is quite safe, and it can be finished with a few months work, and I'll be glad to offer it to you when it's done.

I retained the name Mahoney and the grouping of the children – they only serve as a kind of chorus in this work – simply because it evolved out of the other work, and they'll probably be changed in the last writing.

I go to London at Easter. I feel sure that I'll have to accept or turn down the contract that was offered to me then.[11] While I know and appreciate that you

8 In an undated letter on X notepaper, Patrick Swift had written to McGahern about the work on the new novel, soon to become The Barracks: 'It's a real advance. Very exciting. I still think the first book worth preserving but this is clearly a finer job, sharper and keener.' Madeline McGahern Papers.

9 Monteith replied on 20 March that he would like to see the 13,000 words and – when revised to McGahern's satisfaction – the first novel.

10 It is not surprising that any young writer should want to publish with Faber, but McGahern had developed a particular love and admiration for the work of T. S. Eliot, then still a director at the firm. He stayed with Faber throughout his career despite strong interest from other publishing houses.

11 The firm of Barrie and Rockliff, which was responsible for publishing X, was keen on offering McGahern a contract for 'The End or the Beginning of Love'.

must be a busy and public man, I'd be grateful if you give me some intimation where I stand with you before then.[12] An unknown writer, as I am, cannot risk easily the bird in the hand.[13]

Though this has nothing to do with business, Faber and Faber published more their share of the writers I at one time or still love, and I was flattered and deeply grateful that my work attracted your attention.

Yours sincerely

John McGahern

Faber

57 Howth Road

[*Late March 1961*]

Dear Mr Monteith,

I'm sorry for troubling you again. What has happened is that I've been asked to meet the directors Easter Week for to come to some agreement.[14] As I'll be in London all that week I wondered if I managed to put off the meeting till the end of the week would it be possible for me to see you or phone you on Tuesday or Wednesday. If it would be, could you leave some instructions waiting for me at 6, King Edward Road, Leyton E. 10 and I'd be grateful.

It must sound all pressing and vulgar. But I'd rather be published by F. and F. than anybody else. And yet, in the end, I'll <u>need</u> some publisher.[15]

And please forgive me for trying your time and patience so much.

Sincerely

John McGahern

12 Easter Sunday 1961 fell on 2 April.

13 Monteith writes to McGahern on 24 March assuring him that he will read the extract as quickly as possible, though possibly not before Easter: 'If I'm not able to manage it by then I really would be grateful to you if you would keep things open with the other firm for a week or two afterwards.'

14 The directors of Barrie and Rockliff.

15 Monteith prioritised the reading of the extract and wrote again to McGahern on 29 March: 'The portion of A BARRACK EVENING which you sent me has been read here by several people – including myself of course – and I am delighted to let you know that we have all been extremely impressed by it. So much so in fact that we would certainly be willing to make an agreement with you now for the publication of the novel when it's finished.'

James Swift
[*Madeline McGahern*]

6 King Edward Road

[*April 1961*]

Dear Jimmy,
Just a note. Not met many people yet. Wrights, Paddy and Higgins. Barker in Rome. Cronin in Dublin – his father is sick which suits.

Fabers delighted with the new stuff and want to offer agreement. Very conflicted with Bunting – who'll have a fit they say.[16] So giving the whole business to a lit agent.[17] MacGibbon and Kee worried and Buchanan Brown going round the pubs saying Paddy diddled him out of the MS.[18]

16 John Bunting was an editorial assistant at Barrie and Rockliff. Bunting telegrammed McGahern on 31 January 1961 as follows: 'Paddy Swift gave me manuscript your novel stop tremendously impressed and want to publish but must first consult co-director stop probably too good to sell stop congratulations and admiration stop'. Madeline McGahern Papers. Barrie and Rockliff became Barrie and Jenkins in 1964 after a merger with Herbert Jenkins, notable as publishers to P. G. Wodehouse and Irish writer Patrick MacGill among others.

17 A. D. Peters was the agency McGahern used in this period. His work was dealt with by Michael Sissons (1935–2018).

18 In an undated letter, Patrick Swift apologises to McGahern for his slowness in getting the MS to Martin Green at MacGibbon & Kee, but assures him that they are considering it: 'Buchanan Brown has the mss. No question, by the way, of hawking since we only bother with the people we know. Martin Green wrote the most flattering report I've ever seen or heard of. B-B has this too. If you cd. do this it wd. help: write a note to B-B to say the mss must be regarded as a draft or whatnot & that you are doing something else with the material – in this case he might be able to get you an advance cash if the U.S. take.' In another, later, undated letter Swift tells McGahern that Barrie and Rockliff wish to publish the MS, and clearly at this point there is another MSS (*The Barracks*) in play: 'Yr. original MSS is very good & if they brought that out you could also do the other – but if you want the new one that's what you must get.' It is evident from a further undated letter that Buchanan-Brown was unsuccessful in finding an American publisher for the MS: 'I happened to have occasion to see Buchanan Brown the other day and asked about your bk. I could see through his façade of polite enthusiasm that Abelard Shitmans was not for you.' Swift's curt dismissal of publishing house Abelard-Schuman is typical of the informal tone he takes with McGahern in their dealings. Madeline McGahern Papers.

There's some hostility amongst crowd I think to Faber. Apparently the last thing they did was to reject Kavanagh with D. Wright's recommendation.[19]

Hope to see you soon. The wedding this morning. Some of the warming up hilarious.

Love
John

Tony Whelan
[*Madeline McGahern*]

6 King Edward Road

[*Spring 1961*][20]

Dear Tony,

There's a job going in the Subsidiary Rights Department of Cassells, an assistant to John Sundell.

Start £700-800 going to £1200.

Use Michael Sissons name from A. D. Peters as your reference, it'll be useful.

A little experience is necessary, but not much, or perhaps none.

I tried to ring today. No reply.

Good luck,
Sean

---

19 The Irish poet Patrick Kavanagh had an ambivalent relationship with X and its two editors. Though published in the magazine, he was difficult to deal with, as Patrick Swift outlines in an undated letter to McGahern on X notepaper: 'I had a very funny encounter with P.K. arising from Jimmy telling me of your story re the old man's gossip about you in the Dub. pubs. Meself & DW confronted him – without specifically telling him of the detail – with the accusation that he had said we were taken in etc. [. . .] I'm so bored with his monstrous disloyalty & betrayal of all kinds of friendships & regard that I dropped his new things which were set up for this issue & I think we'll have no more of him. Meanwhile he tries to get David to take some poems which David won't do etc.' Madeline McGahern Papers.

20 This dating must remain an educated guess.

Macmillan Archive

57 Howth Road

25 April 1961

Dear Teresa Stacco,

Thank you for your kind and extremely courteous letter in which you
mentioned that Mary Lavin had told you about my work.[21]

After publication in <u>X</u> I received a number of offers and my agent decided
to accept a contract which Fabers offered for the publication of this, a second
novel, when it's finished. My first novel was accepted some months ago but I
decided to withdraw it.

So I am not at present free to offer you work. But if my present relationship
changed I would be glad to go to you first. And I was grateful and flattered
by the attention of such a famous house as yours.

Yours sincerely
John McGahern

Faber (TS)

57 Howth Road

25 April 1961

Dear Mr Monteith,

Thank you for your very kind letter. I had been disturbed and unable to work
for the last weeks, as the others did not let me change easily, and your letter
gave me new faith.

I would be delighted to meet you and will certainly let you know when
next I go to London.[22]

If you have no further need of the opening chapters you could possibly
send them; but if they are any advantage I can easily get them off A. D. Peters

21 Mary Lavin was then with Macmillan both in the US and the UK. In 1959 the firm
had published her *Selected Stories* and in 1961 *The Great Wave and Other Stories*. In
1964 Macmillan published *The Barracks* in the US.
22 On 21 April Monteith had written to McGahern apologising for not having been
in a position to meet him when he called at Faber after Easter. Peter du Sautoy, then
general manager of the company, met with McGahern on that visit.

as I believe Barrie & Rockliff are returning them there. I shall not be needing them for some time.

I am beginning to take up my work again and I am sure I'll fulfil your trust in me. I consider it an honour indeed to be able to appear on the list of Faber & Faber.

Yours sincerely

John McGahern

Dympna McGahern

[*Madeline McGahern*] (TS)

57 Howth Road

29 April 1961

Dear Dymphna,

Thank you so much for writing to me. Have you decided to change anywhere yet? Or will you just stay on where you are for a time? Do you read much now? You must be careful, what you read and do now will shape the whole richness of your lifetime. Do try and be alive to things all day, not bored or superior to others or critical or clever or full of notions and opinions. Remember that life is eternally passing – for others as for yourself and they too have to endure it in the lonely cell of themselves.

The long disturbing mess about the publishing is at an end at last, thank God. Faber and Faber will publish when it is finished. I am trying to work this week, and what I have to do frightens me very much, what I have set myself, it [*is*] almost impossible, and all sorts of failure and the long hours and the precious days of summer going on outside. Somehow, I know I will do it, for I believe in life itself, and then life itself is given to that faith.

No news from home. I wrote Rose a long letter looking for information, and I hope it doesn't cause her too much trouble.

I was at a lovely play by Tennessee Williams one evening last week and that is all exciting. Did you ever read Checkov's tales? You should if you can, and those libraries near you are marvellous, nothing at all like them here.[23]

---

23 Dympna was then living in London.

Did you ever read any poems of Andrew Marvell? They are really exciting.[24]
                    Rather in haste. Will write you soon
                    With all my love
                    Sean

Michael McLaverty Archive

57 Howth Road

19 June 1961

Dear Michael,[25]
Thank you for your letter and kind invitation. I am deeply grateful. Though what I had intended was to go down and back to see you the same day. Sometimes I cannot sleep in strange houses. So if I do not stay more than one day you will understand. And I am looking forward very much to seeing you.

I was sorry to see you so caught in school and I hope you'll be able to work soon again. My own work goes slow but well.

Send Maeve Brennan, but if it causes much trouble, don't bother. I'd be glad.[26]

I could not keep a diary of things or work, it would seem too self-conscious, a kind of dramatization of the role of the artist. Though many such are marvellous to read, ones like Stendhal's, but they were obviously written out of private need. I have no such. There would be no excuse and I know I could never use them. I often think the realest reason I write is, having lost my formal faith, I am self compelled to pray or praise. If I did not need to do it I would stop tomorrow, but there seems little else.

I hope you are well and wish you every good thing.
                    John

24 Marvell remained one of McGahern's favourite poets. He gifted a Marvell collection to Madeline Green, his future wife, on her birthday in October 1967, in the early weeks of their courtship.
25 This letter does not appear in Killen (ed.), *Dear Mr McLaverty*.
26 Probably a reference to the Maeve Brennan (1917–73) story 'The Beginning of a Long Story' that appeared in the *New Yorker* of 4 February 1961. McLaverty was a subscriber to the magazine, in which Brennan regularly appeared.

[Late June 1961][27]

Dear Michael,

Thank you for your letter and The New Yorker. I won't have holidays till the 7th July and I wonder would the following Thursday, the 13th, or any other day, be suitable to you if I went down.

I found the story a coarse exposition of human longing, vulgar, and the writing leaden with statement.[28] The people for me had no reality or dignity, they were not seen with any vision, or in the pity of their passing lives. As often in the pages of The New Yorker I found she was superior or at least indifferent to these people, something a human being I think cannot be, and definitely no artist, for are we not all accursed together in our nature? I think your own work is the very antithesis of this story; but who am I, for often I have differed with the judgement of people I respect, and they with me. Taste is an incalculable and personal thing. There is no such [*thing*] as good taste, only purity, faithfulness to your own personality and that is too close to Aquinas for comfort. I am sorry, for I was really prepared to like the story. The unknown Stendhal said a very funny thing in his journals, marvellous I think: 'I must stop myself reading all modern fiction, for it makes me monstrously vain.'

> With every good wish
> John

[Early July 1961]

Dear Michael,

Thank you for your card. The train is actually supposed to arrive at 10.56, it's sometimes a little late with the customs. It is a weekly excursion and unlikely to be in the usual timetable. It leaves here at 8.30.

27 This letter is not included in Killen (ed.), *Dear Mr McLaverty*.
28 See letter of 19 June. Clearly McLaverty has sent McGahern the Maeve Brennan story as it appeared in the *New Yorker* and the two men differ strongly on its merits.

If the date has a meaning for you, the town has for me, for I spent one of the most dreadful weeks of my life there at seventeen, desperately in love and with only my paltry seventeen years to offer. I've even a kind of a dread going, though I always laugh when I think of Belfast. From habit and convention and cleverness we often smother our real selves afterwards for the sake of vanity or security.

I am looking forward very much to meeting you there.

John

Faber (TS)

57 Howth Road

5 July 1961

Dear Mr Monteith,

Thank you very much for your letter and enclosure. I would have no hesitation in entering for the prize but I imagine it might be pretty futile.[29] The literary Ireland is much a single house, without a figure of any real authority, and I've no connection with it. They are practically all either friends or enemies, I fear such confinement doesn't breed tolerance, and it'd be unlikely to be given to anybody outside. It'd be more likely to be decided on literary politics than on quality. But there's little to lose by entering, and if you feel this may not be true, I'd enter. I'd rather, if you don't mind, leave the decision with you and be grateful.

I've about half of the first writing finished – 40,000 or so – and I believe I've more power than ever before. I hope it'll please you when it's finished.

The Barrack Evening will not be its title, it was only a provisional title for the opening, but I'm sure you are aware of this and that it was only in the agreement to fill a legality.

Yours sincerely
John McGahern

29 In a letter of 4 July, Monteith had suggested that McGahern enter for the AE Memorial Award. On 7 July he wrote: 'It would certainly help, I'm sure, if you were to say, when you submit it, that you already have a firm contract with us for its publication when complete.'

John Montague Papers

57 Howth Road

[December 1961]

Dear John,[30]
I'm sorry I can't type this, the machine is broken, because I know my hand is terrible.[31]

I hate burdening you with more reading but I venture this in the hope it may solve both our problems. I mark the part I think makes sense in itself and I'd be glad if you could put in the first 3 pages as well, though they can be done without. It's only ½ the length of Chapter II, less than 7,000, and I think it can stand by itself better than any other parts of the opening chapters. The <u>fucking</u> can hardly cause trouble, it has no sexual significance, it only lights the breakdown of civility.[32] I'd be pleased if you like it enough to use and would be grateful if you could let me know how you feel about this suggestion as soon as you can manage.

30 John Montague (1929–2016), born in New York City before moving back to Ireland as a child, was one of Ireland's leading poets of the mid-to-late twentieth century. In addition to many volumes of poetry, he published two collections of short stories and two volumes of memoir. In 1998 he became the first occupant of the Ireland Chair of Poetry and in 2010 was made a Chevalier de la Légion d'honneur, France's highest civil award. At the time of the composition of this letter, Montague was living in Paris, was editing *The Dolmen Miscellany of Irish Writing* in association with Liam Miller of the Dolmen Press in Dublin, and was arranging for sections of what would become *The Barracks* to be published there.
31 Montague found McGahern's handwriting all but indecipherable as he complains in a letter of 22 October 1961: 'Your handwriting is so bad that it brings me comfort since mine (which people have always found terrible) couldn't come within an ass's roar of yours for incomprehensibility. You also write on both sides of light paper, thus ensuring that the script on one side is blotted out by the other. You should buy a typewriter.' John Montague Papers, University of Victoria. McGahern did not take the advice and rarely typed anything, either letters or fiction.
32 McGahern's use of this word would later be the subject of a series of letters between himself and Charles Monteith at Faber, and with his American editor Patrick Gregory at Knopf. The extract finally used by Montague for *The Dolmen Miscellany* consists of what would eventually form the opening eleven pages of *The Barracks* and does not contain the word 'fucking'.

Thank you for the letter, and congratulations on Encounter.[33] I was glad and somehow reminded of a beautiful thing of Yeats in the Autobiographies. 'I am growing jealous of other poets and we will all grow jealous if we don't know each other and so share in each other's triumph.'

I've been plagued with an old illness and my work has been going slow, though I'm finishing the last part of Ch. IV.

You felt the structure of the work fairly truly. There are the 3 opening chapters; a long IV in 4 distinct parts, the early time pattern gets completely broken up; and then 3 chapters in the manner of the first 3 leading away. I'm grateful for what you said about the first chapters. It'll all have to be revised again.

The husband and the police come vitally into Chapter IV and for the first time independently of the woman's vision. She dies in the second last chapter and the work ends in a triumph in violence for the less conscious vision, the social vision, before the children, who have only the function of a chorus, draw the blinds, as the novel began, on the mystery of another evening.

I think what you say of the need for structure true, but I think it must be unique or organic, growing out of the struggle with the material, and not a superimposed structure as in Joyce and Eliot. No matter how great that achievement, it ends in academic sterility, and I think our generation must move in the opposite direction – to survive and grow.

I was only brooding over the uneasiness of Dublin. Thinking it my failure more than yours. When do you expect to have your book of stories ready?[34] Does Peters help you with any of them? What do you think would be a good book of Faulkner's to begin with?

With this illness I've not been out and haven't seen John Jordan or anybody since I last wrote.[35]

If I get any money I hope to leave this school and go abroad when I've this work finished.

33 Montague's poem 'The Country Fiddler' was published in Encounter, vol. XVIII, no. 5 (May 1962). Later that year 'Reconstruction' appeared in vol. XIX, no. 1 (July 1962); and 'Cathedral Town' in vol. XIX, no. 6 (December 1962).
34 Montague was working towards his first short story collection, eventually published as Death of a Chieftain (London: MacGibbon & Kee, 1964).
35 John Jordan (1930–88), a star undergraduate contemporary of Montague's at UCD, followed by graduate study at Oxford. He joined the English faculty at UCD in 1959. A regular reviewer in the Irish Times, he edited Poetry Ireland from 1962 to 1968. His essay reviewing the work of Thomas Kinsella, Desmond O'Grady and John Montague, 'Off the Barricade: A Note on Three Irish Poets', was published in The Dolmen Miscellany of Irish Writing (Dublin: The Dolmen Press, 1962), 107–16.

I'm sorry this letter's so long and had to send this new thing to read but I'm full of hope it'll settle things. I'd be glad if you could let me know soon. And I wish you a happy Christmas.

John

1962

Faber

57 Howth Road

24 January 1962

Dear Mr Monteith,
I have been approached to publish part of the novel I have almost completed. By a Dolmen Press Miscellany of the younger Irish writers – Aidan Higgins, Brian Moore, Thomas Kinsella etc – edited by John Montague. And by a special edition of <u>Threshold</u> (Belfast) edited by Dr Roger McHugh with work from the established names down. Would you have any objections or what is a publisher's attitude to such prepublications?[1]

I entered the first 35,000 or more for the AE and got back a letter last week wanting to see more chapters and/or a synopsis of the work as a whole – whatever that may mean! I shall be greatly astonished if I am given it and naturally grateful to you should it happen.[2]

Yours sincerely
John McGahern

1 Monteith consulted with Peter du Sautoy on this subject and the latter agreed in a memo of 30 January that 'any advance publicity that will get his name more widely known is likely to be helpful both to him, to us'. Monteith wrote to McGahern on the same date to say that Faber had no objection to the extracts appearing 'provided that the extracts they use are not more than 5,000 words each'. *The Dolmen Miscellany* was published in Dublin in September 1962 with John Montague as editor and Thomas Kinsella as poetry editor. Declaring in a short preface that the main link between the writers collected therein was an 'obvious desire to avoid the forms of "Irishism" (whether leprechaun or garrulous rebel) which have been so profitably exploited in the past', the *Miscellany* was the first Irish publication to bring McGahern to print. A passage from the middle of Chapter 3 of *The Barracks* in which Elizabeth Reegan visits the doctor, titled 'Waiting', appeared in *Threshold*, 17 (1962), 10–16.
2 Modelled on the Guggenheim Fellowship, the AE Memorial Fund Award was established through the auspices of the Irish Academy of Letters to promote literary excellence in Ireland and support a projected work to be finished. Candidates had to be born in Ireland and aged under thirty-five. The first recipient of the award was

Faber

57 Howth Road

10 February 1962

Dear Mr Monteith,

I have been awarded the AE Prize for <u>some chapters of an unfinished novel</u>. It is the first time the award has been made to a work of fiction.[3]

Please accept my deep gratitude, for were it not for your insistence I wouldn't have dreamed of entering.

Yours sincerely
John McGahern[4]

X Papers

57 Howth Road

15 February 1962[5]

Dear Paddy,

Please excuse this letter, it's with some fear I write this, because I do not know.

They've given me the AE here, for what reason I don't know, and it was only after publisher pressure that I entered. It has no real meaning for you or me or anybody who even knows what the activity is, but I thought to tell you, and Jimmy said you wouldn't mind, because if you and David hadn't

---

Patrick Kavanagh, beating a young Brian O'Nolan (Flann O'Brien) to the prize of £100. Bank of Ireland was the trustee of this award, which was funded via an original endowment of £900 with the prize to be awarded once interest developed sufficient capital. When McGahern entered in 1962, the awarding committee was made up of Professor J. J. Hogan (UCD); Professor P. W. Edwards (Trinity College Dublin); James F. Meenan (Royal Irish Academy); Constantine P. Curran (Royal Dublin Society); and Arland Ussher (Irish Academy of Letters).

3 Monteith writes about the award of the prize in an internal memo dated 13 February: 'This should lead to some useful publicity in Ireland, since this Award has much the same sort of standing there as the Somerset Maugham award here.'

4 In pencil on this letter, Monteith has written: 'Mr. du Sautoy, this is excellent news I think.' And du Sautoy has replied in pencil: 'Mr. Monteith, congratulations to you too! I'm very glad.'

5 Mistakenly dated 1961 by McGahern.

printed me in X̲ I'd still be unprinted. And please do not think I'd write this for any vulgar reason.

I still remember that publisher's Easter with pain, disgust and self-disgust, and, more than anything, pain.

I hope you are well and Oonagh and that your work goes well. And I'd be grateful if you'd remember me to David and (if you don't mind this letter) that I asked you to tell him I got the thing.

Love
John

John Montague Papers

57 Howth Road

21 February 1962

Dear John,
Thank you for your letter. I've given the MSS to Liam Miller, it is barer and more perfect now, and shorter.[6]

I went 3 sentences beyond your mark – to Casey being told come in. I do not think you can have objections, if I stopped before announcing Casey it might seem a short story and it can't be judged in that context; by going 3 sentences on the sense of the evening's flow is kept, the sense of time, not the flare of a moment of the short story.

Would you be satisfied to print this?[7]

John McGahern was born in Dublin in 1935 and is at present living there. He was brought up in different parts of the country and in London.

I leave it to you to say where the only time I was published was in X. I think the less the better. Write and tell me what you think.[8]

---

6 Liam Miller (1924–87), Irish publisher. A graduate in architecture of UCD, Miller married Josephine Browne in 1947, and together they founded the Dolmen Press in 1951. The press operated in Dublin from 1951 until Miller's death on 18 May 1987.
7 The extract did indeed end with Casey being summoned to 'Come in' by Sergeant Reegan.
8 This short biographical note is both intriguingly vague and remarkably inaccurate. McGahern was born in 1934, was brought up only in Leitrim and Roscommon and not at all in London. The final note as published in *The Dolmen Miscellany* reads as follows: 'John McGahern was born in Dublin (1935) but brought up in various parts of the country. Some of his work has appeared in X magazine, and he was awarded

I'd have written sooner but I have this ghastly illness back again. Does your work go well?

With good wishes
John

Michael McLaverty Archive
57 Howth Road

23 February 1962

Dear Michael,
I was delighted with your letter and to know that you are well.

For a little while, the morning it came, I was excited as a schoolboy with the Award, and then afterwards there was the blank inscrutable face of my work that knows nothing of awards or rewards, but only faith and passion and suffering and the long availability, which we call work, will move. The most gladness my success, if so little can be called that, has brought, apart from my friend's sake, is to affirm in my bones that all success and failure are private. What happens outside that are either lucky or unlucky accidents. For all art approaches prayer.

I hope you'll be able to work well soon. The hustling world is always full of those rumours and they rarely come to anything in the case of the established firms, though the finding of another publisher will have no difficulties for you, it will simply be a choice.

I hope your wife and family are well and with every good wish

John

John Montague Papers
57 Howth Road

[*Spring 1962*]

Dear John,
I'm sorry to trouble you but Sissons in A. D. Peters is kicking up about not being told of the publication agreement and I'd be grateful if you write and

---

the A.E. Memorial Award recently for sections from a novel in progress, one of which appears here.' See *The Dolmen Miscellany*, 118.

tell him the price (I think it's £15) and the no of words (a little less than 4,000).[9]

It's all my fault. I did something else without consulting him and he's annoyed with me.[10]

I hope you are well and that you'll write soon. Please forgive this.

With good wishes

John

Faber

57 Howth Road

10 April 1962

Dear Mr Monteith,

I've been approached to submit work by <u>The Transatlantic Review</u>. I have 4,000 to the <u>Dolmen Press Miscellany</u>, and 2,000 to <u>Threshold</u> of the novel. What would your attitude be to giving <u>The Trans Atlantic</u> some of the novel or to giving away more of it?[11]

I am sorry to trouble you with these small things but I thought it better to make sure.

With good wishes

Yours sincerely

John McGahern

9 Michael Sissons of the A. D. Peters Literary Agency, London acted for McGahern for a number of years in the 1960s and 1970s. He had written to Montague as early as 11 September 1961 to broker the agreement between McGahern and *The Dolmen Miscellany*.

10 Montague has pencilled in the margin here: 'Sold chapter to Threshold for ⅓ what I was offering!'

11 Monteith replied on 12 April that he had no objection, but that he felt the word count ought to be limited to 2,500. A passage from the closing pages of Chapter 1 of *The Barracks* appeared in the *Transatlantic Review*, 12 (Spring 1963), 5–15.

57 Howth Road

12 April 1962

Dear John,

I've been ill and have to give up writing this time and I am going home today. Yesterday I gave the proofs back to Millar. He showed me the new cover, which I think is for the best.

So I just want to wish you success with your miscellany; and to say that I am sorry for my part in the fact that we could not come to easier agreement.[12]

With good wishes
John

Faber

57 Howth Road

15 June 1962

Dear Mr Monteith,

I forward a copy of the completed novel with this letter and I am hoping very much you will like it. I call it <u>The Barracks</u>, almost in despair of finding a true title. Is it any use, do you think? Or does any other come into your mind?

I keep the original, because unfortunately it was typed on very thick paper, and is extremely bulky; but if you would prefer the original typescript I can send it to you immediately. If I make some precision changes in the copy I keep, is it possible to substitute it for your copy when it goes to the printers?

12 Montague again comments in pencil on this letter about his annoyance that he believes McGahern gave an excerpt to Roger McHugh at *Threshold* for a third of the price he was paid for the extract published in *The Dolmen Miscellany*. In a letter of 3 August 1962 Michael Sissons writes to Montague: 'Thank you for your letter of August 1st and the cheque for £20. Despite what you say, I'm afraid that I have still split it up £15 to McGahern and £5 to Plunkett. I know how tight your budget was for this, but honestly I don't think you have been hard done by. In effect, you have had first bite at 1st serial rights in a novel which has aroused a great deal of interest: if the offer had come from anyone else, I would probably have turned it down, at least until we had time to explore serial rights here. The Plunkett story is not a new one, and I think this is a fair distribution.'

Some of the words in the dialogue are doubtful, but I am hoping they may be publishable, because in no place has it sexual significance – it indicates a kind of social breakdown. The AE Award people passed it, they were given to page 140 (4 chapters).

I shall be in London in July or August and if you want me for anything I'd be delighted to make myself available.

And I want to thank you for the confidence you gave me while I was still at work, and for your courtesy every time I wrote to you.

Yours sincerely
John McGahern

Michael McLaverty Archive
57 Howth Road

19 June [*1962*]

Dear Michael,
Thank you for <u>The Guardian</u>, I recognised your hand, and it was very kind of you to think.

I withdrew the first novel, Fabers will publish what I'm working at when it's finished. It goes slow and back-breaking.

I often wonder how your own book is and wish it so well.

It's rather difficult with Mary Lavin. I couldn't enjoy her recent book, some of it I actively disliked. And she is always asking about her work and I don't know how on earth I can go to see her.[13]

I thought to go down to Belfast some day this summer and I hope it may be possible to see you.

With every good wish,
John

13 Most likely refers to *The Great Wave and Other Stories* (London: Macmillan, 1961).

Lyric Theatre/O'Malley Archive

57 Howth Road

24 June 1962

Dear Mrs O'Malley,[14]

Please forgive me for approaching you like this.

I gave Dr McHugh an extract from a novel for the next issue of <u>Threshold</u> on very short notice.[15] It was on the understanding that he'd allow me to make some alterations in the proofs, if I needed. As I believe he is in America I wondered if you could allow me to see the proofs before I leave here in a fortnight's time. I'd be very grateful.

Yours sincerely,
John McGahern

James Swift
[*Madeline McGahern*]

6 King Edward Road

[*July 1962*]

Dear Jimmy,

I enclose Stanislaus's Notebook, it's not published yet, keep it for me, it is fascinating.[16]

14 Mary O'Malley (1918–2006), founding editor of *Threshold*. Born Mary Hickey, Mallow, Co. Cork, she was an Irish theatre director, the founder of Belfast's Lyric Players Theatre.
15 Roger McHugh (1908–87), Irish academic, author, playwright and politician. He was educated at UCD where he went on to spend his academic career, teaching McGahern when he pursued his degree there in the late 1950s. In 1966 he was appointed the university's first Professor of Anglo-Irish Literature and Drama. He was guest editor of the issue of *Threshold* in which McGahern's extract from *The Barracks* appeared and remained a loyal admirer of McGahern's work for the rest of his life.
16 A reference to *The Dublin Diary of Stanislaus Joyce*, published by Faber in 1962, and available in certain quarters earlier in that year as an uncorrected proof copy. Jimmy Swift replies that 'It is wonderful and can undoubtedly take its place with the finest Journals, even perhaps with the great ones, Swift, Stendhal, Kiekegaard.'

Also a story. You saw it years ago but it bears no resemblance to that now. I thought it good but when the typescript came back it did not come violently to life for me. Could you scribble a note when you read it and tell me if I should send it away? These days are so crazed with suffering now that I have no calm to see anything.[17]

It'll soon be over, I say again and again all day like a prayer. I have no real hope, only it drags on and on, and I know I am coming to the end of my strength, I cannot endure much more.

Tell me truly about the story, since my own judgement's gone. What you say will neither delight or shatter me, since I don't care about the work. It was written in a crazy fit and I suspect it deeply.[18] And forgive me.

Love,
John

Faber

6 King Edward Road

17 July 1962

Dear Mr Monteith,
Thank you for your congratulations and warm and generous praise, it delighted me, and I am really grateful. I came to London today and I am staying some weeks. I look forward very much to meeting you, whenever you find it most convenient for you.

(i) Page 75. You are quite right about the names of the regiments and in substituting Ulster Rifles.[19]

McGahern was a great admirer of Stanislaus Joyce's account of his life with James, *My Brother's Keeper* (London: Faber, 1958).

17 Refers to a broken love affair.

18 The story in question was 'Coming into his Kingdom', first published by the *Kilkenny Magazine*, 10 (Autumn–Winter 1963) and in the short story anthology *Voices*, ed. Robert Rubens (London: Michael Joseph, 1963). It was McGahern's first story to appear in print and was eventually collected as the third story in *Nightlines* (1970) and in *The Collected Stories* (1992). But McGahern's doubts about it clearly persisted till the end with his choosing not to include it in *Creatures of the Earth* (2006).

19 In a letter of 6 July 1962 Monteith suggested a handful of changes to the MS of *The Barracks*. The first such reads: 'I ventured to make two corrections here to the names of the British regiments you mention. Inniskilling Fusiliers should be spelt like that; and since the Connaught Rangers (which were spelt like that) were disbanded

(ii) Dun Laoghaire is the correct spelling, though in the modern thing it'd probably be Laoire; but it would be Laoghaire in Elizabeth's time.[20]

(iii) Page 232, end of 2nd Paragraph. I changed to: the expenses of her last illness and burial eating up most of the profit he had calculated as well as all her savings, the savings that had meant so much to her now only a pathetic little sum against the flood of bills –. It should, I think, take care of Elizabeth's money.[21]

I have gone through the 'fuckings'. I could eliminate all Reegan's, indeed every one except three or four in chapter 3, the doctor's dialogue, used to shock Elizabeth's awareness into a harsh, despairing world of a particular consciousness. I don't know how I can really leave out these without harming the work. I am indeed anxious not to harm the sales, and I would be pleased to try to find a satisfying compromise, if it is possible. Could we leave it till we meet?[22]

---

when the Irish Free State was founded I have substituted the Ulster Rifles – which are still going strong. I do hope that is all right.' The extract of *The Barracks*, titled 'Waiting', that appeared in *Threshold* saw McGahern refer to '*The Connacht Rangers and Enniskillen Fusiliers*'. See *Threshold*, 17 (1962), 11.

20 The second of Monteith's corrections reads: 'Is Dunlaoire the correct spelling? I have got an impression that there's a "gh" somewhere in it.'

21 The third correction reads: 'You mention the fact that Elizabeth's illness and hospital fees had eaten up most of the money which Reegan had made from his turf contracting; but you don't mention Elizabeth's own money which Reegan would presumably have inherited after her death. I think this should be taken care of somehow since these accumulated savings of Elizabeth's feature quite largely in the story.'

22 Again, in Monteith's letter of 6 July he had addressed the issue of the potentially offensive word: 'We have no objection in principle to printing the word "fucking" which is used occasionally in the dialogue and I don't think that nowadays there would be any legal risk in doing so in this country. I think I ought to point out to you, though, that if we do print this word it is likely to have two results which would to some extent impair the sales of the book. Some libraries and bookshops, particularly in the Provinces, do still have fairly strong objections to buying books which contain such words and expressions; and moreover, – and this is probably more important than usual in the case of THE BARRACKS – the retention of this word would of course almost certainly lead to your novel being banned in the Irish Republic. I am quite happy to leave the final decision about this to you and if you really do insist on the word going in it will go in.' In the published novel the word is used only by Halliday, Elizabeth's one-time London lover. It occurs on four occasions over five pages in Chapter 3, always for emphasis rather than bearing any sexual connotation.

Thank you again for your praise and I look forward very much to meeting you, whenever it's convenient for you.

Yours sincerely

John McGahern

P.S. Do you find the title satisfactory?

James Swift

[*Madeline McGahern*]

6 King Edward Road

[*Summer 1962*]

Dear Jimmy,

Thank you for writing, for more than that with so much work on your hands. What you say about the end is I think true, only if I succeed it'll have to be in the same manner that I failed in. What's predictable and organic is really boring more and more, and I dream of letting in sudden destructive light to see if we can endure its terror in the ecstasy of deeper being. Out of boredom, out of fear, I've read dozens of books here and except for one or two they were all the same book: as if they'd come out of some contented collective consciousness, with sloth the presiding portrait on the wall. Or so it seems, though nothing seems the same for long these days, and it'll be pretentious rubbish before it reaches you. Then you want to swear, and that never changes.

Tomorrow I go to Paris.[23] Barker was here and is gone. I see Elizabeth, Carmi, Rosie, Dom from time to time.[24]

I was delighted you liked the Diaries, they'll last out a lot of louder shouting.[25]

---

23 Where McGahern visited John Montague.

24 Barker is the poet George Barker; Elizabeth is Elizabeth Smart (1913–86), the Canadian poet and novelist. Her book *By Grand Central Station I Sat Down and Wept* (London: Editions Poetry London, 1945) detailed her romance with George Barker. Carmi is T. Carmi (1925–94), the literary pseudonym of Carmi Charney, an American-born Israeli poet and editor of *The Penguin Book of Hebrew Verse* (Harmondsworth: Penguin, 1981). Dom is probably Carmi's close friend Dom Moraes (1938–2004), the Indian poet and winner of the Hawthornden Prize while still an undergraduate at Jesus College, Oxford for his collection *A Beginning* (London: Parton Press, 1957). I have been unable to identify 'Rosie'.

25 Stanislaus Joyce's diaries.

Thank you more than anything for what you said, it was very beautiful from day to day, I need it more than ever in my life to keep before my mind. And I try to pray that I'll be given enough ridiculous courage to see it through.[26]

John

James Swift
[*Madeline McGahern*]

6 King Edward Road

24 July 1962

Dear Jimmy,

Thank you for your letter, it was very kind of you not to keep me watching, and what you say I think will happen – The Barracks. The publishers are satisfied. And I think, in the real sense, that a title is better blank, without much life of its own, and then to take its meaning from the work, to split itself off from associations of its own and to become simply the book. At any rate I find this notion attractive to my own way, unless we happen on a miracle, I am deeply grateful for you giving the thing your thought.

I am not meeting Faber till next week. Peters took me to lunch, they say that they are excited about the book, and will give it priority treatment, whether or not they mean what they say has meaning at all. I meet Elizabeth, Carmi, who had pneumonia but who's recovered and gone to France, Dom, Higgins and David and Pip once, etc. They remember you affectionately.

I went out of curiosity and old gratitude to see Lawrence Little, who is rather good and nice, and in a frightful state of confusion.[27]

---

26 Jimmy Swift writes in an undated letter from this period in which *The Barracks* was at an advanced stage of gestation: 'London is a wonderful & stimulating place but it can also be very tiring, when dealing with difficult matters. I have been thinking about the title of the novel since then. As I said before, what I'd like is a title that would convey something of the depth & significance of the book, but such a title has to be just right or it sounds phoney. [. . .] What about Yeats' "Love's Bitter Mystery"? I was also thinking of something to indicate the essential loneliness, the revelation of a private world, "In that Solitude" or "Gathered in Silence": However none of these, nor any others I thought of, are good enough or near so. [. . .] I'm inclined to think it may be as well to keep The Barracks.' Madeline McGahern Papers.

27 Little was author of a sensationalist novel about a reform home for delinquents, *The Dear Boys* (London: The Harborough Publishing Company, 1960).

My brother went to hospital out of a slum room today: I do not believe in success or comfort, except as allowing space for all manner of human graciousness that comes from the vision of our situation, and that seems vanity and rubbish in the light of that room in Whitechapel and my brother and the letter to the Casualty Dept of the London Hospital in his fingers stained with cigarette smoke and so many memories.

This girl didn't write. I suffer much, especially the times before the different posts come, but it's despair now and regret, not much of the sickness and desperation of before. I go to Mass often. It's the only place these days I can find the calm to see the Mystery. It's strange, at seventeen I believed I'd rise one day to true prayer by great effort, and now I smile to see myself reduced to it. We are played strange tricks.[28]

I know you dislike writing, but we'll meet soon,
John

Something that'll amuse you. After P. and D. W. wrote to Auden, [*illegible*] told me, he went over to Auden afterwards.[29]
'Those people that were here from X said you were their friend and I'm afraid I can't congratulate you on your choice.'
'Why? What happened?'
'Well they sat here and talked and drank all my gin and the deaf one asked for another bottle.'[30]

Faber

57 Howth Road

[*8 September 1962*]

Dear Charles,[31]
I can't thank you sufficiently for your kindness and understanding in London. I was afraid going and with you I enjoyed myself very much. I am deeply grateful.

---

28 McGahern was emerging from a broken love affair with a young woman he had met in Dublin whom he referred to in later years as 'the dark haired girl'. The deep pain he felt in the wake of the breakup partly inspired plotlines in *The Leavetaking* and in several of his stories.
29 P. and D. W. are Paddy Swift and David Wright.
30 David Wright was deaf.
31 McGahern's first letter to Monteith to address him so familiarly.

I'm sorry the copy of the first novel should be so ragged. I don't think it's fair for me to say anything about it now except that I began it when I was 22. There is no hurry with it back, and you can read it when you find the time.[32]

I hope you enjoy your holiday very much and that we'll be able to see each other before too long.

With every good wish

John McG

Faber

57 Howth Road

[*11 September 1962*]

Dear Charles,

Thank you for both your letters, and of course take as long as you wish over the reading of the novel – what I marvel at is that you should want to read it at all, with all the compulsory reading you have to do.[33]

I thought Gore Grimes letter silly and irresponsible when it arrived, he went to no trouble to find the facts, but mostly advised you and me on the use of language, his letter is all vague – 'it may be but I think' – except for the Lady Chatterly which everyone knows about.[34] Since then I've been seeking advice, Dr Roger McHugh also gave his opinion and sounded others, from reputable people in the Universities as well as on Boards, he was guest editor of <u>Threshold</u> and would have printed the objectionable passage then, he wanted to, but I did not want so long a piece published.

The opinion is that the book would not be banned: and that, if it was, the ban would be almost certainly lifted on an appeal. It has filtered out that the

32 Refers to 'The End or the Beginning of Love', which remains unpublished.

33 Monteith had written to McGahern on both 6 and 10 September.

34 With Monteith's letter of 6 September, he included a letter from C. J. Gore-Grimes, a Dublin solicitor from whom Faber had sought advice on the possible issues arising from use of the word 'fucking' in *The Barracks*. Writing on 31 August, Gore-Grimes commented that the Censorship Board 'is much more intelligent and liberal than the former ones', but then went on to list his concerns: 'I have not seen, except as I say in a legal report, the word "fucking" published in full in any novel in Ireland. Usually it is printed as f— or in some other form [. . .] I would say that it would be wiser not to publish the word in full.' Monteith makes clear in his accompanying letter that he will back McGahern if he wishes to retain the word in full.

book was given the AE Award on an unanimous vote and one of the judges, Professor Hogan, is actually a member of the Appeal Board.[35]

Gore Grimes says – 'Iris Murdoch is an established and serious writer and it may be that An U. Rose contains the word but is unbanned' – and makes no reference to the AE Award which I notice you suggested to his attention, it is the National Literary Award, given usually to poetry, for the first time to a work of fiction, by judges representing these institutions: University College Dublin; Trinity College; Irish Academy of Letters; Royal Dublin Society; Bank of Ireland.[36] If that's not the Establishment I don't know what is. Dr McHugh and the body of opinion he drew on cannot see them risking even a first ban, the thing would be so comic that it'd be certain to attract wide publicity to the Censorship and the Book both here and in England.

Also I see in the Dolmen, which you probably have by this since you've advertised there, that Aidan Higgins has printed more than once FUKKEN which is even coarser than fucking.[37]

I do also think that f..... would harm the book, it'd put an artificial look on the Doctor's dialogue.

It may be possible actually to sound the Censorship Board through the AE Judges, and I'll try to do so immediately if you think the course is necessary or advisable.

Have you any idea of the actual month of publication?[38]

I regret to cause you all this nuisance and wish you a lovely holiday. I envy you very much, and wish I could be with you.[39]

John

35 Professor J. J. Hogan of UCD.
36 Iris Murdoch's *An Unofficial Rose* was published by Chatto & Windus in 1962.
37 Aidan Higgins, 'Helen Langrishe Goes Home' appeared on pp. 12–26 of *The Dolmen Miscellany*. As the eponymous Miss Langrishe returns by bus to her Kildare home, she hears once again the flat Kildare accent: 'They were natives of Kildare, for she recognised the grudging inflections and flattened vowels. I fukken well this, I fukken well that, I fukken well never . . .'
38 Monteith replies on 13 September that it is too early to predict a publication date and reasserts his backing for McGahern in his use of language: 'you can be assured that I'm completely on your side since you feel so strongly about it'.
39 Monteith was about to leave for a holiday in Morocco.

[20 *September 1962*]

Dear Michael,
Thank you very much for writing to me in London: I looked in Foyles and a few other shops on the Charing Cross Road but I had no luck in finding the books.

Are you well? And you will let me know if you come to Dublin?? When and where are your stories coming out?[40]

I write little, except a story of the break-down of innocence in a child.[41] I came to almost the end of my world after finishing the book. I fell in love with some one: there is little end of pain in sight; and I am too troubled most of time to get any of the calm to work. I walk and walk, and some people I can talk to have shown me real charity.

I came across lines of Edwin Muir I thought you'd like:
. . . A man and woman building their changing house on patient mutability.[42]

I hope you are well and happy and that we'll see each other soon.

With every good wish
John

Faber

57 Howth Road

[22 *September 1962*]

Dear Charles,
Thank you very much for writing. I'm afraid your tolerance and kindness make me feel a troublesome person, and it's not true. I did not think Gore-

---

40 McLaverty had been discussing the possibility of publishing an anthology of his stories with his US editor Cecil Scott at Macmillan. These plans fell apart at the death of Scott and no anthology appeared until the 1970s.
41 'Coming into his Kingdom'.
42 McLaverty sent McGahern a copy of Muir's *Autobiography* with a letter dated 25 November 1962.

Grimes's opinion a really considered one but I'd go as far as ever possible to help and save you trouble.[43]

John

Michael McLaverty Archive

57 Howth Road

30 September 1962

Dear Michael,

Thank you for your criticism and very warm praise. All my masters wrote with care: and you were one. I'd have sent you the Dolmen, only I thought you'd have your hands too full, and I am sending you the book in spring. I must read the proofs very carefully at the places you drew attention to, it was kind of you to tell me, and I am grateful.[44]

I am disappointed that you could not come, but as long as we meet before long. Or if I can get free from this worry soon I'll go down to see you.

I am almost as delighted as you that you have a prospect of leisure, and you must do your real work.[45] It is easier to be a headmaster than to write, with your gifts, and you cannot squander your uniqueness even to do another kind of good.

Is your wife any better?

I am trying to take up threads of my work again, but painfully.

43 Monteith had written on 20 September: 'I am delighted to say that this is to let you know that everybody agreed at our editorial committee yesterday that we would take our courage in both hands and print the word "fucking" in full. Like you, I don't really think there will be any trouble; and certainly it strikes me as a much more rational and honest thing to do than to go on printing f-.'

44 In a letter of 27 September 1962 McLaverty had praised McGahern for his piece in *The Dolmen Miscellany* and pointed out a few turns of phrase he thought less well judged: 'There were one or two places where my Northern eye or ear stumbled, found the rhythm upset, or the object blurred. I tripped on "blinded windows" and would have preferred "that beat on the slates and on the windows". And in the dialogue found that the addition of "on us" knocked off balance the line "rich Americans didn't run off with a girl like you." And a point that seemed to me to lack general truth was Regan's use of "bejasus" in front of his children.' For a full transcript of the letter, see Killen (ed.), *Dear Mr McLaverty*, 27–8.

45 McLaverty, as headmaster of St Thomas's Secondary School, Belfast, had been supplied with a secretary, which left him with more time to write.

We must meet very soon, somehow; and with every good wish until then.

John

Faber

57 Howth Road

[*Mid-October 1962*]

Dear Rosemary,[46]

I hope the enclosed may be of use to you.[47] It's the best I can think of in the time. And I am hoping it's not too disgraceful. If you think it can be improved you are free to change any part you think might be improved.

I enjoyed very much meeting you in the summer and hope you are still well.

With good wishes

John McGahern

Faber

57 Howth Road

22 October 1962

Dear Rosemary,

Thank you very much for your letter. I found the blurb excellent, except for two things, which I ventured to change for the dustjacket.

There are no 'intrigues' in the book, so I changed to the 'stagnated life etc.' and substituted 'to love and live' for 'to love her husband and children.'[48] I hope very much they do not lessen its impact, and that you approve. Do you think them all right?

46 Rosemary Goad worked at Faber from 1954 until her retirement in 1989, frequently alongside Charles Monteith. In the late 1970s, she became the first woman working within the company to join the Board of Directors.

47 Goad had written to McGahern on 6 October asking him to attempt a 200-word draft blurb for *The Barracks*. His typed effort is enclosed and is in turn amended in pen by a Faber employee, probably Goad.

48 Goad had made a suggestion that the blurb ought to say that Reegan rages 'against the intrigues of the policemen & their wives'.

Do you think would it be good to put AE Memorial Award Novel in small print with the title on the front jacket? Why I mention it is I see prizes announced this way as well as in the blurb. Do you intend to print a photo?[49]

Hope you are keeping well and with every good wish

John

Faber

57 Howth Road

[*Early November 1962*]

Dear Rosemary,

Many thanks for your kind letter and help. Would the enclosed be any good? I'd like it to be as short as possible. Or would it be possible to add it to the blurb, and put both under the photo on the front inside slip of the dust jacket. If so the first two sentences of the enclosed might do. That's the way I'd like it best. What do you feel?

If any more publicity was needed, it should be easy to give it at publication time, but I feel too much does not look very good on the book itself. I'd go for adding to the blurb John McGahern was born in Dublin in 1935 and brought up in various parts of the West of Ireland. His prose has already attracted attention on its appearance in various literary magazines. And put all under the photo.[50]

Please tell me what you feel?

With every good wish

John

49 McGahern did not entirely get his way with the changed wording. While 'intrigues' is removed, the relevant text on the dustjacket reads: 'Against the background of the changing countryside, the rituals of the Church, the stagnating lives of the policemen and their wives, she fights for strength to love and live.' That the book won the AE Memorial Award is mentioned in the final sentence of the blurb.

50 The wording that ultimately appeared under McGahern's photograph on the dustjacket was as follows: 'John McGahern was born in Dublin in 1935, and brought up in various parts of the West of Ireland. He attended St Patrick's and University College, Dublin, and has worked in many places, including London. He is now living in Dublin.'

14 November 1962

Dear Charles,

I've had a letter from Peter Lennon, he's Paris Correspondent for the Manchester Guardian, and his editor suggested that he publish a collection of his interviews with writers, his articles etc.[51] He favours Fabers, if he's acceptable, and wrote to me for an address. I gave him yours, and I hope this is all right.

He's been published in the New Yorker and Atlantic Monthly and he's half-way through a novel Little Brown commissioned on some early chapters.[52] I found him an intelligent person of great integrity and charm, and though he did not ask me to write to any one, only for an address, I thought it better to tell you. And I hope it was all right to give him yours.

I hope you are well after the holidays. I wondered during the Cuban crisis what it was like in Fabers.[53] Will you ever get to Dublin? It's almost Christmas now.

With every good wish, and affection
John

---

51 Peter Lennon (1930–2011), a native of Dublin who spent many years in Paris with *The Guardian*, becoming a friend of Samuel Beckett. He is best known for his 1968 film *The Rocky Road to Dublin*. In August–September 1964 he introduced McGahern to the woman who would become his first wife two months later, the Finnish radio and theatre producer Annikki Laaksi.
52 The novel never materialised.
53 A thirteeen-day (16–28 October 1962) standoff between the US and the USSR concerning Soviet ballistic missile deployment in Cuba, usually seen as the closest the two countries came to open conflict during the Cold War. The crisis forms a background to McGahern's short story 'Sierra Leone'.

Faber

57 Howth Road

24 November 1962

Dear Rosemary,
I think you've managed everything marvellously, and as there's only this one thing more, will you please forgive me?

I don't want to say <u>educated</u> about those institutions: they're awful priestly places, they give me the creeps to even think about yet. I'd like to say just

<u>He attended St. Patrick's and University College, Dublin</u> if you would accept that.

I think they'll be just facts, names to the English reader: and I really want to lump both together. St. Patrick's will appear to them, if they think about it, as a school before University.

I think also it'd be as well to print the usual thing denying any association of the character with living people.

I want to say that you've been extremely patient and good with me, in everything, the blurb and photo and note.

I really feel guilty over all my niggling with words.
Are you well? I have started another novel, and am very excited.

                    John

Faber

57 Howth Road

28 November 1962

Dear Charles,
The first part of the proofs came today and I was disturbed to see fucking printed f___. Is it that they were printed before the Board's decision, or some mistake?[54]

---

[54] Monteith replied on 30 November to assure McGahern that this was a printer's error.

I hate to trouble you at this busy time, and I do hope you are happy and well.

With all good wishes
John

Michael McLaverty Archive

57 Howth Road

7 December 1962[55]

Dear Michael,

Thank you very much for your letter and the Muir, your kindness moved me, and I can only try and accept as generously.[56] The reason I delayed writing was in the hope that I could read some of the book first, but then the huge proofs of the novel came, and I went almost crazy reading through them. It seems very marvellous from the first glances, and it deserves a more quiet time, over Christmas I'll read it, and then write.

I told Elizabeth your criticism and praises: she was grateful and delighted. I think she's a very beautiful person.[57]

I disagree with you over Bartleby: it seems to me a beautiful and shocking vision of all-is-vanity, and the last passage a pure poem.[58]

---

55 Mistakenly dated 1963 by McGahern.

56 Edwin Muir, *An Autobiography* (London: Hogarth Press, 1954).

57 Elizabeth Cullinan, Irish-American writer (1933–2020). Worked in the 1950s as a secretary at the *New Yorker* and had work published there. Spent a period in Ireland in the early 1960s where she grew friendly with McGahern. Of Cullinan, McLaverty had written to McGahern in a letter of 25 November 1962: 'Her stories are good. They are cool and calm and precise.' See Killen (ed.), *Dear Mr McLaverty*, 28–9. Cullinan first brought McGahern's work to the attention of William Maxwell at the *New Yorker*. Maxwell wrote to her after the magazine decided to accept 'Strandhill, the Sea': 'you must now revise your belief that you don't know how to tell a good manuscript from a bad one. You have changed. You have learned. And if you see any more of this calibre floating around Dublin, start them on their way to me.' McGahern Papers, NUIG, P71/1171. The story was published as 'Summer at Strandhill' in the *New Yorker* (21 September 1963).

58 McGahern had loaned McLaverty a selection of Herman Melville's work. In his letter of 25 November, McLaverty had commented: 'I read two of the stories, Bartley and Billy Budd, the latter, I feel, the better and would repay re-reading. Bartley is fascinating on a first reading, but I doubt, since it leans too much on the element of curiosity, that I would enjoy it as much on a second reading.' 'Bartleby, the Scrivener'

I am sorry that I could not get to Belfast, but I will go in spring. My life will be less a mess then, and we can laugh.

Are you well? And your work? I am looking forward for the story for Christmas.

Everything is settled about the book now: Faber are lovely people to be with.

Please give my kindest regards to your wife and daughter, and with many thanks

John

————

(1853) was one of the pieces of literature most admired by McGahern – in November 1967 he gave a compelling lecture in Belfast with the story at its root. See Richard Murphy, *The Kick: A Life Among Writers* (London and New York: Granta Books, 2003), 261–2.

1963

Michael McLaverty Archive

Grevisk

[January 1963]

Dear Michael,

Thank you for sending me the story at Christmas.[1] I enjoyed and admired it very much, reminding me in some ways of The Dead, it read true and cruelly sad. The one word that grated on me was – the whistle <u>flared</u>, associated with flame or light, not sound, though I can see the effect.

The only other thing that troubled me, and this may be totally personal, was the unconsciousness of both man and woman: how little troubled either of them seemed by fear or doubt here at the end of their life; both seemed equally monstrous, his indulgence in what the saccharine protests of conventional righteousness made sentimental almost worse than her bored unconcern, and neither seemed to have <u>learned</u> or <u>seen</u> anything.

All this may be personal objection to the people, not valid to the story as you see it, and I would be very interested if you had time to tell me how you see them. The writing was all so accurate and beautiful that I will not dwell more.

I enjoyed Muir, it is often moving and beautiful, though to me lacking in integrity and consequently intensity too, what is uniqueness.[2] What Yeats said about Wordsworth came back and back to me as I read: his poetry lacks excitement and grows old before him because of a clinging to an alien morality, a morality of life or society, not the morality that is created in the vision of the work. You can have perfection of the life or work, but not of both.[3] Purity of heart is to will one thing. And it seemed to me that Muir's

---

1 'After Forty Years', which was not published until 1968. See Michael McLaverty, *Collected Short Stories* (Dublin: Poolbeg Press, 1978), 92–101.

2 Referring to Muir's *Autobiography*, gifted to McGahern by McLaverty in November 1962.

3 A position best laid out by W. B. Yeats in his late poem 'The Choice', as McGahern well knew.

social life, his life in society and his dream of it alone, was more vital for its translation into Art. What confirmed me in this was his statement about suffering on the bottom of the second last page – he says he learned many truths from suffering, yet he'd have been better without it. He had dream of an earthly paradise for himself. An artist accepts for me everything utterly, and loves it, once he first accepts the first sin in its absurdity as completely as the saint accepts life as a VIA. To regret one thing is to regret everything. Goodness and Virtue are the best disguises for egotism, they cloak it most perfectly from the person himself.

Though often it is very beautiful, miles above the run-of-the-mill, but I am always disturbed in work where there doesn't seem utter and total involvement, I think you need a certain contempt for life to attain it in work.

I hope you've had a happy Christmas, there was beautiful weather here, white frost, raw mornings, and the sun calm and golden on the open trunks of the trees in the evenings after three. Relatives call, the old clichés of kindness: dances, going off in cars, to the Roseland and Cloudland and Dreamland, to do the Twist and the Madison.[4] Conformity spreads.

Thank you for the story and the Muir. I hope you are well, and I wish you luck in the New Year, and please give my regard to your wife and daughter.

John

Faber

57 Howth Road

3 January 1963

Dear Rosemary,

Thank you very much for writing. I contacted Mr Fitzgerald with the publication date, he is the producer of Spectrum, and he is putting me on, he says, on March, the first days, about 2 weeks after the 22nd of February.[5] He will be in London for the February one, producing Stephen D. in St Martin's,

---

4 These three ballrooms, opened between 1959 and 1961, were the creation of impresarios Jim and Albert Reynolds, brothers from Rooskey on the Leitrim–Roscommon border. The Roseland was situated in Moate, Co. Westmeath; The Cloudland in Rooskey; and The Dreamland in Athy, Co. Kildare. Albert Reynolds (1932–2014) went on to a successful career in politics, serving as Taoiseach from 1992 to 1994.
5 Jim FitzGerald (1929–2003) was a Dublin-born actor, theatre director and television producer. In the early 1960s Telifís Éireann appointed him head of drama.

and he wants to produce <u>The Barracks</u> himself.[6] He says that he imagines the programme will do the sales more good once the book is in the shops, than 2 weeks before.

The book, based on having won the AE a year ago, was in the gossip columns of The Irish Times, with a photo, and an announcement of publication at the end of February.[7] The woman who owns the Eblana bookshop in Grafton Street said she was writing to Mr Brennan after this publicity in <u>The I. Times</u> and hopes that you'll be able to give her a photo or pictorial material to stage a central display in the window.[8]

With every good wish for the New Year
John

Faber

57 Howth Road

8 February 1963

Dear Charles,
Thank you for returning the typescript and for your lovely letter, which delighted me, though I do think that your praise of my first novel is too generous.[9] But I had hoped with all my heart that you might like it, the reason

---

6 FitzGerald won acclaim in 1962 with his production of Hugh Leonard's *Stephen D.* The production, an outstanding success in Dublin, transferred to London where it played to packed houses.

7 The popular 'Irishman's Diary' column in the *Irish Times* of 2 January 1963 pointed to the February publication of *The Barracks*, describing McGahern as 'a diffident and self-contained young writer who prefers to let his work speak for itself'. The piece was accompanied by a photo of McGahern.

8 The earliest entry for this shop in *Thom's Dublin Street Directory* is 1954 where it is listed as 'Eblana Book Shop Ltd., library contractors, booksellers and stationers, 46 Grafton Street'. The business seems to have been there until 1979 when it moved to 50 Middle Abbey Street. Mr Brennan is Ben Brennan, the owner.

9 On 28 January 1963 Monteith had written to McGahern about his impressions of the first novel, 'The End or the Beginning of Love': 'Now that I have read it I have been kicking myself for not having done so long before now. It really is a quite extraordinarily sincere, impressive and moving book – and, I thought, absolutely beautifully written. I know your feelings about not publishing it – and indeed I can quite see that to publish it would probably be impossible since so much of the material in it has in fact been used over again – in a rather different context and from a slightly different angle – in THE BARRACKS. And I am right in thinking, am I not,

I was reluctant to let you read it was that I cannot understand how you are not sick and sated with so much compulsory reading, and though I admire utterly such a passion, coming as it must from extraordinary generosity, yet I almost believe it would be an act of real affection to keep you from one more.

I have recovered my strength from a disastrous affair, which I fear made me poor company for you in London in the summer, and I am writing well, at least I am more excited than ever before, and, I know, better.

Are you well and very busy? Had you a nice time at Christmas? Will you, do you ever think, venture to Dublin?

The most thing I'll fear for on the 22nd – after all the encouragement, and extreme kindness you showed me – is that the book will, before the strange public, justify your trust.[10]

With all good wishes, and much gratitude.

John

P.S. Could you just possibly hand this list to the Dispatch Department, I'd post it to them but I am not sure, to place to my account one of the copies I give rather reluctantly, but since I have nothing more to do with the person bitterness is too stupid, it's too stupid anyhow.

I'll be terribly grateful if you do this.

J.

Faber

57 Howth Road

[February 1963]

Dear Charles,

It was so kind and considerate of you to telegram, and I am really grateful.

I got the books by going to the Customs in a rage with your telegram. They gave me the parcel immediately, saying that all parcels were delayed by the weather, which I am inclined to doubt. The 1-2-1963 was the postmark. They have no authority to hold such a parcel. I wondered if I should make an official complaint.[11]

---

that the "vocation" theme which is handled so beautifully in THE END OR THE BEGINNING OF LOVE is going to be the central thread of your next book?'

10 *The Barracks* would be published on 22 February 1963.

11 Monteith attaches a brief memo to this letter, dated 12 February 1963, which reads: 'The McGahern mystery solved. Irish inefficiency, not Irish pruriency.'

I do hope you manage to keep free of the illnesses of this time of year, it kills me. Written in haste.

Yours always
John (McGahern)

Faber

57 Howth Road

22 February 1963

Dear Charles,
Thank you very much for your letter. In the same post, a letter came from Mr. Michael Sissons, which disturbed me very much. I mentioned in a reply to a letter that I wrote to Rosemary about the Eblana and wondered why nothing happened and he took it on himself to ring. I am terribly sorry that it should have happened. She has been always very kind and helpful to me. And I would be really grateful if you could tell her how I feel. It would be such relief to know that she is not annoyed. My God, what an awful stupid business I made of a petty affair.[12] There's worse here. My father says that the book's an immoral disgrace and has called here from the country with that priest of my adolescence. I am afraid I am just living on my nerves. I would wish the next days out of my life.

But please explain to Rosemary and I'll never forget it. Oh, it was so stupid, so petty a thing to even mention.

As always
John

12 Presumably Sissons had made a fuss with Goad of the fact that the Eblana bookshop had not featured *The Barracks* in its window in the way McGahern had hoped for.

57 Howth Road

26 February 1963

Dear Mr Rigney,[13]

Thank you very much for your letter – it was extremely kind.

I used always wait for your classes in Drumcondra with excitement. There you introduced me to many things that were to enrich my life, Yeats above all, and the joy of rhythmic speech. People could grow in those classes; there was never any stultifying pressure of examination; and there was excitement I will always be grateful.

I hope you are well, and Mrs Rigney and your children.

Yours sincerely,
John McGahern

Faber

57 Howth Road

20 March 1963

Dear Mr du Sautoy,[14]

I want to thank you very much for the telegram you were so kind to send me on publication day. The only reason that this is so belated is that for me it was rather ghastly and I was upset and did hardly anything. Because I treasured it very much.

With good wishes
John McGahern

---

13 This uncatalogued letter at NUIG can be located among the Patrick Gregory Papers. It was donated to the library by Mary Rigney, daughter of the recipient, James Rigney, a faculty member and English lecturer at St Patrick's College, Drumcondra. Rigney had presumably written to McGahern to congratulate him on the publication of *The Barracks*.

14 Peter du Sautoy (1912–95). Director at Faber 1946–60, vice-chairman 1960–71, chairman 1971–7; OBE 1964, CBE 1971.

[*21 March 1963*]

Dear Michael,
Thank you for your very kind letter. It was honest and true, and I am sincerely grateful.

That I do not agree with it is perhaps simply the difference of our visions, our personalities: I have reasons too; but I think it better, what you said most beautifully in regard to Chekov once, to just bow. It is all any of us can do, we have accused ourselves of what we are already.

I often wonder how your own work goes, it must be almost finished now, and I look forward with excitement.

I do very little work, though I have finished three stories, and I'll send them to you when they're published.

The experience of coming out in a book was ghastly; I think it'll be a long time before I can go home. Mary Lavin is gone to Paris, will be soon to America. I often see Miss Cullinan, she is a very beautiful person. I will miss her very much when she goes home.

I hope Mrs McLaverty is well, and you too, and not too overworked in the school.

                With gratitude and all my good wishes
                John

                                            Faber

                              57 Howth Road

10 April 1963

Dear Rosemary,
Thank you so much for your letter, it delighted me. There was no need in the world to feel sorry, I always marvel how you and Charles have time to write to me at all, with so many people, so much business. I am so glad the flowers pleased you. When they'd gone I began to worry if I sent them too impulsively, that they might embarrass you arriving so at the Office, and now I am so glad.

It was a rather awful experience, the first few days of the book. It is utterly gone now. I want to thank you so much for the effort you so obviously put behind the book, the way it appeared in the shops, and the advertising you gave it. All your work made me feel guilty and inadequate. To a certain extent I have forgotten The Barracks; the reviews, except the awful sensation of the first weekend, don't affect me, except that I wished they were so much better so that they might justify your work and faith and Charles's. I hope it doesn't lose money. They say in Dublin that it's been the bestselling novel here for years, but of course Dublin is only a small place. And it got a rave notice on the radio tonight. Some very nice letters came, and Hamish Hamilton admired it very much and said he was quite jealous. All I care much is that you won't find your marvellous effort misplaced.

I am afraid my family are not reconciled and won't. I am not wanted at home this Easter. It's strange how one learns to be alone. It was such a nightmare house to grow up in too.

I am writing better than ever before, but slowly. I was emotionally ill most of the year, and hadn't strength for the new novel until lately, but I wrote some stories and they are coming out later in the year. If you'd like I'd be glad to send them but I know you can have very little time for reading, you must have so much to do.

When you get this you'll be back from France. I hope you've had a wonderful holiday. I'd be delighted that you've done so much for The Barracks if it didn't make me feel so guilty.

So I hope you are happy and keep very well and with every good wish
John

Joe Kennedy
57 Howth Road

22 April 1963

Dear Mr Kennedy,[15]
Thank you for your letter, and it was very kind of you to write to me.

15 Joe Kennedy b. 1935, a Dublin journalist who had first met McGahern in a Drogheda café and boarding house in 1956 when McGahern taught in the town. Kennedy was then a junior reporter on local newspaper *The Argus* and had digs in the boarding house. Kennedy joined the *Irish Independent* as a junior sub-editor shortly afterwards, remained for about a year, and then went to London where he freelanced with a news agency and a weekly paper before becoming production editor

I haven't been very well lately and hardly at all in town or around, and I'd rather wait until I am really out of this mess before ringing. I'll be glad to ring you then if it will please you.

No, at least I cannot place that meeting, but then when I see you the places and times I am sure will come.[16]

> I hope you are well and with good wishes
> John McGahern

Faber

57 Howth Road

3 May 1963

Dear Charles,

I was so delighted to get your letter, though I would have loved more if you could have managed Dublin. I would have liked to have taken you out one evening here.[17]

------

of an industrial magazine for the bakery industry. Kennedy returned to Dublin in 1960 to work with the *Evening Herald* where he stayed until 1973 working variously as a production sub-editor/feature writer; features editor; and deputy editor, writing features on entertainment and the arts. When *The Barracks* appeared Kennedy wrote to McGahern at Faber seeking an interview. In 1973 he joined the *Sunday World* as editor, staying for five years before leaving to freelance. He worked with the *Evening Press* on the 'Dubliners Diary' column for two years, 1983–5, freelanced again and returned to Independent Newspapers aged fifty where he remained as a news sub-editor, occasional writer and book reviewer, until retirement at sixty-five. He continues to contribute a nature column to the *Sunday Independent* to the present. This is the earliest surviving letter to Kennedy, and the formal salutation suggests it is the first. The two men went on to correspond sporadically for the rest of McGahern's life. Kennedy is in part the model for the character of Maloney in *The Pornographer*.
16 Kennedy had presumably reminded McGahern of their meeting in Drogheda eight years previously.
17 Monteith had written to McGahern on 23 April: 'THE BARRACKS really has, I think, established you as somebody to be reckoned with. Almost without exception, reviewers took the book seriously – as it deserved to be taken – and were quite clearly impressed by the talent it showed. Our sales people tell us that it goes on selling very steadily – if not spectacularly – and certainly we are altogether satisfied and happy about it. In the Irish Republic of course sales have been particularly good; and apart from one or two thick headed people – like the reviewer in the Cork Examiner – most Irish critics have really gone to town about you.' Thinking of the *Lady Chatterley's Lover* case that had been through the English courts in 1960, the reviewer in the

I fear I got an anxiety neurosis or it was never far away over The Barracks: that it had disappointed you, got meagre reviews, was selling poorly etc., and all the trust and kindness you gave.

There was frightful shindy at home. I think I mentioned how I was visited here. Then my abused sisters were summoned from the East and West for conference – my brother who is in London again and has a pretty wild career behind him is considered for years in worse light than me, so was not brought into the presence for fear of sacrilege – and I was formally expelled from my home and poor inheritance. I got a note, 'The blinds are drawn, the lamp lit, and an ex Sergt of police prefers to ponder in the dark until the lamp shows light or at least flickers, and the rest is silence.' It was then I realized that the old blackguard was enjoying himself as never before in his life. He made speeches. 'If he can write, why can't he write about South America or some of those exotic places, and he'd make more money. They ran Brinsley McNamara's father, you know, out of Delvin,' and the collar of the coat is pulled up to the ears even in sunshine, and the face assumes the proper aspect for [a] journey to Calvary, but no cross was ever carried with such capers of interior delight.[18] The local bumpkins say they'll 'dip' me if I ever show my face again in Cootehall. The priests in Ballinamore removed the book from the Co. Leitrim library where my aunt lives as unfit for parochial consumption. It's such an absurd country, but from a safe distance I am as well to enjoy it quietly too. I was looking at North West Tyrone on the map, it's not very far away, but I didn't know the name of your homeplace.[19] It was good, though, that Mr Gore Grimes's advice proved wrong.

I had a nice card from Richard Murphy before Christmas saying you said to look me up and I wrote saying I'd be glad of course to meet him and to congratulate him on his Sailing to an Island. I admired it very much, its

---

Cork Examiner of 23 March 1963 wrote that 'Mr. McGahern sullies his book with expressions which a London jury in a famous trial found acceptable but which a great number of others most certainly do not.'

18 The case of Brinsley MacNamara's The Valley of the Squinting Windows (Dublin: Maunsel & Co, 1918) represents the most infamous instance of unofficial censorship in twentieth-century Ireland. The novel portrayed Irish rural life as stultifying, censorious and backward, and its appearance led to an outcry among the people of Delvin, Co. Westmeath of which MacNamara (born John Weldon) was a native. Local people, outraged by the book, burnt it publicly and withdrew their children from Weldon's father's school in protest.

19 Monteith occasionally mentioned his Tyrone connections to McGahern in letters. When he went back to Ireland in the years McGahern knew him, it was to Castlederg, near the Donegal border, where his brother lived.

formal exactness above all, but it is not the personal poetry that excites me most.[20]

I'll be glad to send you the stories when they come out but I have no idea what it must be like to work in publishing and I won't mind how long you take to read them. Macmillan are to publish The Barracks in America.[21]

If I can get enough work done I'll go to London in summer if I can. I would look forward very much to seeing you then.

And I'd like to thank you more than I can say for all you did for The Barracks, it made me feel just unworthy.

I hope you are very well.

Yours always

John (McGahern)

It must have been very exciting publishing The Dyer's Hand.[22]

20 Richard Murphy (1927–2018), Irish poet. *Sailing to an Island*, his first collection of poetry, was published by Faber in 1963 and he went on to have a fruitful relationship with the firm. Murphy became a good friend of McGahern's through the 1960s and into the early 1970s and was responsible for suggesting to McGahern that he apply for a post at Colgate University, Hamilton, New York, thus beginning an association that began in 1969 and continued intermittently right up to 2001. Having engineered a first meeting between Murphy and McGahern in mid-May 1963, Monteith follows up with a letter of 27 May: 'I'm absolutely delighted that you and Richard Murphy got on so well together. I rather thought that you would – and I've already heard from Richard how very much he'd enjoyed meeting you. It would be wonderful, wouldn't it, if we could all manage a weekend together on Inish Boffin sometime this summer?' The hoped-for meeting in the west of Ireland that summer did not transpire. Murphy lived for several years in Cleggan, Co. Galway and arranged accommodation for McGahern and Madeline Green there in 1970–1.

21 Monteith replies in a letter of 6 May regarding the Macmillan publication in the US: 'I really am absolutely delighted. [. . .] I've got an idea that it might do very well in the United States – where there is, of course, a very large Irish public.' Monteith's optimism was misplaced. Knopf – which would go on to publish *The Dark* in the US – had passed over the opportunity to publish *The Barracks*.

22 W. H. Auden's book of essays was published by Faber in 1963. It became a favourite book of McGahern's.

24 May 1963

Dear Michael,
I thought today that you must have your novel finished or almost now.[23] So I'd like very much to wish it very well, and I have little doubt about its quality.

The school excursion goes to Belfast on the 19th of June, Wednesday three weeks. The boys I teach are too small to go, but I'd travel if I thought I might be able to see you, at the school, or if you mightn't be too busy.[24]

We are to have the same publisher in America, which pleases me very much.[25] I do not get much work done. My life is in a bit of a mess. And I may go away from here soon.

I hope you are well and able to work. I'd be very pleased if you gave my regard to your wife and daughters.

> With all good wishes
> Yours always
> John

Joe Kennedy

57 Howth Road

31 May 1963

Dear Joe,[26]
I am sorry you were disappointed.

I have been down with terrible flu since last Saturday, and not yet at work, only struggling on my feet now.

---

23 *The Brightening Day* (London: Macmillan, 1965).
24 McLaverty responds on 26 May to say that McGahern would be a welcome visitor and that he would like to introduce McGahern to a young member of staff who 'is endowed with taste and discernment and has read and reread passages in your book with unstaled admiration for its style and quiet power'. This staff member was Seamus Heaney. See Killen (ed.), *Dear Mr McLaverty*, 31.
25 Macmillan, McLaverty's American publisher, also published *The Barracks*.
26 Full letter written in pencil, as though in haste.

I'm afraid that you met me at the most chaotic time of my life.

This person will be on my hands till the end or almost the end of June. Then she goes.[27]

I wouldn't get too worried about what you say. We all fail. No one real succeeds. We fail ourselves and we fail one another. So I don't think anything matters very much. Certainly writing solves nothing. I often curse the day I began.[28]

But I'll ring you, and I am looking forward to a long evening when things are easy. Isn't it better wait for that when our minds won't be elsewhere? Than to have a broken hour or two.

John

Joe Kennedy
57 Howth Road

23 June 1963

Dear Joe,

Thank you for letting me see your story. It was rather beautiful and evocative but it didn't, for me, come to life till the last paragraph. I do not trust very much my own judgement. Writers are not often critics. So I gave it to someone I admire and I am afraid his opinion was the same as mine.[29]

I hope you are well. I'll ring soon and we'll have a good evening.

John

27 Refers to a love affair with the Dublin journalist Joan Kelly. For a more detailed discussion of this, see letter to Jimmy Swift of 28 January 1979.
28 Kennedy had shown McGahern some of his own attempts at writing fiction.
29 Kennedy had sent McGahern a four-page typescript of a story he had written called 'Honeymooners', set in Paris.

Mary Keelan

57 Howth Road

17 October 1963

Dear Mary,[30]

Thank you so much for writing to me. Always write to me so, differently so only if it's nearer Mary Keelan, and I don't know how you could imagine me bored, or anything of such kind, with you. I thought you very beautiful. I was more sorry than you could know that last evening. That we had no time to go out to lots and long evenings together. There's hardly more to say?[31]

And for the twilight time to America and the movie that sounds so beautiful you saw with Rosanne. Is her real life, her dream, maimed too?[32]

There was a lovely September, blues in the changing branches of the Howth Road you could look for hours at. And now the rain has started. Easier for me, it seems always when the rain is outside that you miss no real marvel by working, the world is dead or sleeping or something.

Write me and tell me many things about yourself, about everything if you can, even your love or loves. Do you ever intend or wish to leave the University?

It doesn't matter much about what I've written, they're dead and finished now.

Only once have I been in Grafton Street since, but I remember you in so many places.[33] So write to me soon.

Love
John

30 Mary Keelan, an American graduate student whom McGahern met in Dublin, summer 1963. Keelan was in her third year of graduate study in English literature at the University of Chicago, specialising in Medieval and Renaissance Studies, with a thesis on the idea of mirth in early Tudor drama. She and McGahern were introduced by Richard Murphy whom Keelan had met at his home in Cleggan, Co. Galway via Liam Miller of the Dolmen Press and the Dublin poet Thomas Kinsella to whom she was introduced at a Chicago poetry reading earlier in the year. This is the first extant letter of several sent by McGahern to Keelan over the course of a year.

31 Keelan had made plans to visit Irish relatives on that last evening in the country and could not change them.

32 Roseanne was a disabled first-year graduate student at Chicago whom Keelan was asked to help orient to the English Department.

33 Keelan and McGahern got on very well from the moment they met and spent time browsing the bookstores along the Liffey quays. In total they spent no more than two days together.

Michael McLaverty Archive

57 Howth Road

3 November 1963

Dear Michael,

Thank you so much for your kind letter, and your kindness to the story, though it is very slight, and spoiled. If it interests you the original (my) opening read:

'The tennis ball went hop-catch-hop under his hand on the street in front of Park's Guest House, grains of sand from the street coming on the grey fur of the ball, its hopping slowing to the rhythm of the conversation that droned from the benches before the flower-bed; red bells of the fuchias vivid behind and some roses and gillyflowers, the earth around the roots of everything speckled with sea-shells, overhead the weathered roughcast of the walls of the house.'[34]

I am struggling with a novel, nearly half crazy, most of it down without shape or make, ages of work before me yet. I get a lot of sickness too, which doesn't make things easy.

But what I want most to say is how delighted I am you are working. I am looking forward (for long) to it very much. I don't know why you don't throw up the job, absolutely. I wish I were in your boots. You can't do 2 things like that.

I have to go to Belfast when I get the first awful draft of the novel down, and to see you, if you don't come south before then.

Please keep well, and work, and remember me to Mrs McLaverty.

With every good wish,

John

34 An alternative opening to 'Strandhill, the Sea'. This story as McLaverty would have read it was first published under the title 'Summer at Strandhill' in the *New Yorker* (21 September 1963). It was republished with amendments as 'Strandhill, The Sea' in the *Irish Press* (27 April 1968) and first collected in *Nightlines*.

Mary Keelan

57 Howth Road

[*Postmarked 7 November 1963*]

Dear Mary,
Thank you for your letter, such a long and lovely letter, and I was very glad
that you are well and happy.

It was taking to the rain when I was writing last time, and it has kept to the
rain. I've been away from work with a throat, after I was better there were
a few real heavens of days, looking from the bed out at the greyness over
by the railway line, and the fire, no desires in the world, then days sitting in
the cane armchair.[35] But the first day I worked the nightmare and terror was
back, and restlessness, wanting to leave the four walls, hunger for movement
and any distraction. The struggles with images in reality, awareness of the
human predicament with the whole nervous system, its transmutation into
images and rhythm, they do something terrible to life, and no turning back.

You are very lucky to have so many friends, and they are more than
lucky to have you. Strange what you say about a woman loved, I do not
think it is ever so for a man. To be loved is almost to lose his identity, but
I have often noticed this difference. I hope she is lucky. It's a world of such
inherent calamity. And the thing that only a love affair exists in its tragedy,
erotic love of any passion, the lunacy of the subjective dream. Marriage is a
very different thing of course, a social thing, but I often dream that it gives
strength, allowing the miracle of two real people finding each other in their
ripeness. I would wish this for you more than anything.

I wouldn't worry too much about your brother, remember there must be
something in him that choose that girl, or allowed himself to be chosen so, it's
more him than anyone can hope to understand. Now about Roseanne, very

35 McGahern struggled much with illness in the late autumn of 1963 as he tried to
forge ahead with what would become *The Dark*. In a letter of 15 November 1963,
Charles Monteith writes to him: 'Richard Murphy got to London last night. I was
most terribly distressed to hear from him that you had been so ill; but it's a very great
relief to know that you are better now. Don't – please don't – overstrain yourself
by pushing on with the new book too fast. It won't, honestly, pay in the long run.'
The description is of McGahern's room at 57 Howth Road from which the main
railway line running north out of Dublin is visible. Keelan first met McGahern in the
downstairs parlour room there in beautiful summer weather.

few women have a deep religious sense, only social religion, establishment. You'd do no good to tell.

I went out to Skerries Sunday last where my sister has a lovely house by the sea and we went walking over the strands with the children, it was fine for once.[36]

I met my father too at a railway station, a terrible fiasco it was too, by accident.

A letter came from a man in Victoria, British Columbia which I thought you might know. The story I gave you came out in the Anthology, it had some American writers too.[37]

I go back to the school tomorrow, not that it disturbs me much by now.

I hope you write to me soon. That you keep well and very happy. I want you to know very much that you are one of the most beautiful women I have ever met. I wish I was in Chicago just to take you out.

With much love
John

Faber

57 Howth Road

[*16 November 1963*]

Dear Charles,
Thank you so much for remembering me in Greece, I was delighted.

I am sending you two slight stories under different covers, as I promised, and please do not read them until you feel you have time. The N. Yorker story is much spoiled by editors, but it was only written to keep a private fear away.[38] The <u>Voices</u> is being published under different covers but I think a book is nicer and I would like you to have it.[39]

---

36 McGahern's sister Monica, who married Paddy Gilligan, lived in the North Dublin seaside village of Skerries from 1963 to 1967. McGahern was a regular visitor.
37 Presumably refers to the appearance of 'Coming into his Kingdom' in the Robert Rubens-edited anthology *Voices*. Other writers included in the selection are Doris Lessing, Jean Rhys and Patrick White.
38 A reference to 'Summer at Strandhill' in the *New Yorker* (21 September 1963).
39 'Coming into his Kingdom' was first published in the *Kilkenny Magazine* (Autumn–Winter 1963). It was later published in the anthology *Voices*. Monteith writes to McGahern in a letter of 28 November 1963: 'This morning's book page of The Times solved the mystery about your second short story. There's a review of

I finished the first draft of the novel, and it almost finished me. Awful physical squalor. There's so much work yet, struggle for form mostly, but it's so much far better than anything I've ever done.

I hope you have a happy time with Richard and please remember me most affectionately to Rosemary.

Yours
John

Faber

57 Howth Road

[*21 November 1963*]

Dear Charles,

Thank you so much for your extremely kind letter. No – it wasn't overwork was the trouble. Images of old horror started to come at me without warning and with horrible violence, atmospheres of evil. For weeks I lived in a state of pure panic. They'd always come suddenly. And the only time I was free of them was strangely when I was working with them.

You need have no fear in the world that I'd force this book. All I've ever written seems now but just one preparation for it.

Don't be in any hurry to read the stories, only when it's pleasant and easy. They don't matter much. The N. Yorker particularly is pretty much of a doodle.

I hope you enjoy Richard with you. I wish I could be in London too.

Love
John

VOICES in which it's picked out for special mention. Very many congratulations. I am ordering a copy of VOICES for myself and I'm looking forward enormously to reading the story.'

Faber

57 Howth Road

1 December 1963

Dear Charles,

Thank you for your kind letter. <u>Voices</u> was mailed to you. Though it's not much I meant it as a small present. Would it ever have got mixed with the MSS post to Faber?

I had a letter from Peter Suschitsky and I am going to meet him this afternoon.[40]

I am hoping to be able to work again soon. I don't know if I'll go anywhere for Christmas. Though it's self-deception – no one has really any home to go to – it's disturbing not to be able to go as in the habit of all the Christmases before.[41]

I have to speak in the University this week. I wouldn't have agreed, but it doesn't matter since I'm stopped working. It's strange to go back a sort of honoured fool to the same place I went eager and wide-eyed to once, a far better person than now.[42]

I often think of you, and how you must be half crazed with the Christmas trade.

With love
John

40 In a letter of 20 November, Monteith had passed on a request from Rosemary Goad to McGahern: 'She has asked me, by the way, to give you a message about a photographer called Peter Suschitsky whom she knows and is, apparently, very good. Suschitsky will be visiting Ireland very shortly; and Rosemary has given him your address and asked him to get in touch with you. She hopes you will agree to sit for him for another few photographs since she would like a really good one for future publicity.' Suschitsky's portrait of McGahern appeared on the dustjacket of the American (Knopf) first edition of *The Dark*. Suschitsky b. 1941 went on to a distinguished career as a cinematographer. Among his best-known works as director of photography are *The Rocky Horror Picture Show* (1975), *The Empire Strikes Back* (1980) and the later films of David Cronenberg.

41 McGahern's father had temporarily broken with him over the publication of *The Barracks* and the usual Christmas in Grevisk was not possible.

42 Presumably a visit to UCD arranged by Professor Roger McHugh.

Mary Keelan

57 Howth Road

[*December 1963*]

Dear Mary,

Thank you for your letter, and the photos I shall treasure so, you look so lovely against the branches, with the long hair, and the face that never seemed so Asiatic before, almost a girl in some strange way.

There was real grief here for Kennedy, realer than I ever saw it for anything or anybody, it took some days for even sentimentality to get to the surface. It didn't move me much, public catastrophies are too big for me or something, only the ceremonies did.[43]

I finished the first draft of the book, it's safe now, but for me it's only the certain beginning of toil and toil, and I am not allowed work now, attacks of panic and other nuisance, and they tell me I've got much older looking, so I'll send you no photos. It's strange to have no house or home too but leave it so.

I don't know, if 'it can ever be other between us', you know as much about it as I do, there are two people, the makings of a lot of things, some of them frightening, and against them the constant dream.

I'll be as honest as I can, I don't know why except I know you or trust you, I've never spoken as closely to anyone as you, and certainly never written to anyone so, not even when I was most in love.

When you came I was actually working. I didn't tell you so but it was only to make things easy that I made excuse. There was something I immediately recognised in you that I never met before. And I do not think I ever regretted anything, quietly, as much as your going, that we could not have gone out to evenings and evenings, into whatever we were or were not.

All my days till a year or so, more, were a turmoil. I was in love without wanting it, only admitting it to myself when driven to the wall of desperation, a writer without wanting, alive without wanting. Love was a way into all kinds of destruction, mostly the will to destroy my art.[44]

I am certain now. I failed, I have its authority and calm, but I do not accept it. If I love again it will be with enough humility to try to build a passing house. That is all. You must have the strength to be honest. All it will be is

43 President John F. Kennedy had been assassinated in Dallas on 22 November 1963.
44 McGahern had come through an intense love affair in 1962, leaving him deeply wounded. See letter to Jimmy Swift [July 1962].

a beginning but it will be real. And you must not be literary or annalitical or even reasonable, you must want too. And if you don't there won't be any suffering now, perhaps regret, and that is clear too.

Some ordinary things. The Barracks is to be published in America in the early year, you must just be there for me when it is. I don't think it'll do well and I don't care. What I will soon begin to make pure cannot go unnoticed.

I spoke in the University on Wednesday, it was strange to go back to the rooms I had gone years before. It was awful, but a few minutes after I began to speak I forgot. Even a priest who questioned me about what I'd said about art and religion agreed with me, as I with him. It was strange, I'll tell you some time, how absolute human authority grew about me in moments. I could not err because I had admitted it.

Write soon, very soon. I've never written for so long before, to anyone.

Do be careful with that 'Poet'.[45] A beginning, the turmoil of talent, is nothing, it's strewn with it, youth. Be tolerant and distant, as you already seem to know, to oppose him you'd have to love him or hate him, and too many people live their occupations thus. He'll meet his match, it'll probably show or care nothing about his talent, and why should it? – and very, very few come purely through this. They are the few that matter.

I'll leave you now. Sunday I have to go to Jury's to have pictures taken for Faber on Sunday. Next week I'll be working again.

Often I will have to think of you.

With much love,
John

Mary Keelan
57 Howth Road

[*December 1963*]

Dear Mary,

Thank you for your letter, more than any other letter you ever wrote, I write only hurriedly in the hope that I may find you before Christmas, Christmas Evening above all.

I won't be at home for the first time in my life but I shall think of you all that day I love and hate so much. May you be very happy, with those with you.

---

45 Richard Murphy.

I hope it goes well with the doctors and the Professor, but please do not worry too much, you'll bring peace anyhow.[46]

No, I wasn't teasing you. Monica and I had one sense in common, we could tell our father's footsteps on the cement from the hall, what mood he was in, how to react. We had to. It hasn't died either.

I too wish you were here. The distance is a real curse but you will come or I will go, before too long.

And don't believe in those schools of writing. The God cannot come out of the Machine.

I am a Romantic, who could not be in this age of conformity and mediocrity and mass squalor, but I have hardness now and authority that I never had, even if it's only authority of failure.

So write to me, please, and we may be lucky enough to love together, now that the <u>chance</u> is given both ways.

John

Tony Whelan
57 Howth Road

18 December 1963

Dear Tony,

I was glad that you are well and happy and that you enjoyed that last evening, I had thought you were depressed or bored or something at the end of it. So I am glad I imagined wrong.

I finished a first rough draft of the novel, but got ill, and I'm not supposed to work for some time, but I'm sick of here, I want to go, but the work is far too important to me to risk it in change, but I wish it was done.

It must be nice to be in Kilkeel for Christmas, I hope you are happy. I'll send a card there to your mother.

I'll stay in Dublin, maybe go out to friends for the day, but I hope to work mostly.

I met Kate O'Brien, an evening in the Hibernian, not worth describing, so many silly evenings.[47] I find literary people bore me to almost the point

---

46 Refers to the serious illness of a member of the Keelan family.
47 Kate O'Brien (1897–1974), Irish novelist whose work was admired by McGahern. The Hibernian is a private club at 9 St Stephen's Green, Dublin, in operation since 1840.

of violence. You can find less and less reality in life as you grow older. But I suppose it doesn't matter a curse.

So I wish you happy Christmas and I hope you write whenever the wish comes

Love
John

Mary Keelan

57 Howth Road

28 December 1963

Dear Mary,

Thank you so much for your letter, for the plain card I liked, and more than anything for your love.

Christmas, it's gone, I never hated it so much; a time for festival or celebration should be a secret time in a man or a woman's days, not this loud and drunken time of year. And all life at all times seems to be moving into this mass horror more and more.

But how are you, my love? Are you well? And don't be confused over the convent. The Catholic Church is the one church I know, and it is beautiful. All society and organization is full of squalor, nothing can escape it, but I know it's not that that matters, it's the word, and the word made flesh in introspection and public ceremony. And you can't escape life in a convent, or anywhere.[48] We all would if we could. It's not really a choice. It's a compulsion. Perhaps we have all our own ways.

I wish so much you could be here, or I in America, we would be so much clearer. What will happen to the sea? Do you ever think about it? What can happen, and there cannot be great time, can there?

You ask me about the book, I have started on the last read of it, and you will know why I cannot discuss it much.[49]

It deals with private conflict. Conflict between the ideal (fixed days in the order and dedication of the priesthood moving out into certainty) and between woman (the world or dream of sensual happiness in confusion). Between father and son, between talent and circumstance, in a world of

---

48 Keelan had friends who entered the religious life – she and McGahern had probably been communicating about one such friend.
49 Here McGahern describes his work on what becomes *The Dark*.

mouths moving to close on mouth or dream. Cruelty, frustration, dreaming, loneliness, image that should be hard and clear as the people and the days. I know it doesn't tell you much, but it's more than to anyone, and in the end only the writing matters.

Did I tell you that I lectured in the University, a brief statement, and am now almost as much a Professor as your sweet self?[50]

Write and tell me about you, won't you. We must be clear, and practical. Once I am finished this book I feel I shall be free? It may not take so long now. And you?

I hope things went well with the Silverston laird, and the whole days, and tell me.[51]

With much love,
John

---

50 McGahern had spoken at UCD.
51 A reference to Professor Theodore Silverstein, a University of Chicago medievalist, who was Keelan's thesis advisor at the time. Silverstein (1904–2001), born in Liverpool and raised in Boston, Massachusetts, was among the most distinguished literary medievalists of the twentieth century.

1964

Faber

57 Howth Road

[January 1964][1]

Dear Rosemary,

Thank you very much for your kind wishes and the photos. They seem more than good to me, and interesting, but it's an awkward subject for the actual animal to indulge in.

I've done little but work since Christmas, and I'm half-way through this writing, it'll be the second last, and it's taken real form at last, it's been finished twice before without any shape, but I've broken it completely at last. I may be finished in the summer if I don't get another attack.

It's fantastically more exciting than The Barracks. The only thing that its eroticism is sure to cause trouble here but I'm hoping to be gone.

How are you? I hope very well and not too driven crazy with work. I often think of you.

With my love
John

Mary Keelan

57 Howth Road

[Postmarked 14 January 1964]

Dear Mary,

Thank you so much for your letter; and the copies of the Review.[2] I'll write you a long answer but I am not well again. It's marvellous that you are

---

1 Marked 'filed Jan 64' in Faber archives.
2 Keelan was then literary editor of the *Chicago Review*, a magazine founded in 1946 and published quarterly in the Humanities Division at the University of Chicago.

coming. My only hope is that I'm not a scarecrow for you then. Only I've completely broken through the novel, it's taking real shape now, and I can't leave off. It's very strange, after 6 years struggling, suddenly it breaks.

No, it wasn't strange, I thought you marvellous even then, but prejudice is far stronger in most cases than instinct, and there wasn't enough time, you'd probably imagine that I was that way with the whole world if I tried. But you are wiser and more patient. Let us wait and see.

I read the play: and disliked it, it was too cloying or sweet, a kind of chocolate box tragedy or suffering, and I don't know what. I don't trust my judgement much. I haven't general taste.[3]

One short story I read, and thought fantastic, sheer precision, sheer savage everything, was Kafka's METAMORPHOSIS, just around Christmas.

Why won't you tell me about your trouble? Are you in trouble or who? You must if you are.[4]

Don't get yourself down with the teaching, you can't. Write to me. When I'm out of this cursed attack I'll be better.

And with all my love,
John

Mary Keelan
57 Howth Road

[*Postmarked 22 January 1964*]

Dear Mary,
Thank you for your letter, it was marvellous to get.

I was looking through work for you but they're not good except a nouvelle The Going and I want to write it again. So I'll not send it. But one day I'll write it again. I'll send you this instead, taken just after Christmas. You may notice changes, especially my hair going.

The attacks were attacks of panic without warning, and blind. The specialist said they precipitate natural weaknesses, apparently hair in my case and bones, centuries of pain.

I'm alright though for the time. I only tell you since you asked. It's not pleasant, anyone's sickness.

---

3 Unidentified play most likely read by McGahern in the *Chicago Review*.
4 Keelan was facing a stressful time with a family illness.

I don't go out much, except for walks, it's summer weather almost, I never saw such a mild and lovely January. The book goes easy at last, and very quickly but that may change.

I saw Richard Murphy off to Africa before Christmas. He met the editor of The Sunday Times who commissioned a long poem and paid for it with a return air ticket.[5] The commission was sent to me for criticism. It's so hard to say anything about competent rubbish, except that some parts are more competent or less than others. What was disturbing he acted on my advice and changed it, but they know nothing, these people, except about the world.

So he stood me lunch on his way. He was in great glee. Some lovelorn millionairess gave him a cake in London with £10,000 in it, it's supposed by the way to be a secret, but he's probably told everyone it by this as a secret. He gave me an expansive lecture on the importance of public relations, publicity etc., for the writer. The poetry end is rather coming. But the money is marvellous. But I like him, he's such a great manager, except he loves it so much that he's obvious.

Do you ever have contact with Kinsella?[6]

There's a John Montague going to America from here and he may read in Chicago. He's a gossip, he may amuse you with it, but be careful as far as trusting him with anything goes. Don't.

I don't think it matters about the Review. If it's fun or you can get something concrete out of it, do it. If it's not, then it doesn't matter?

When exactly would you be likely to come? How long will you be able to stay?

If I am still teaching then I don't get holidays till July the 4th or 5th.

Please don't worry too much and with so much of my love, it'll be so much easier in the summer, we'll know one way or the other then.

> With all my love
> John

5 Murphy had by chance met Leonard Russell – then chief literary editor of the *Sunday Times* – on the pier in Cleggan in May 1963. By the end of June Russell had commissioned Murphy's long African-themed poem 'The God Who Eats Corn'. See Murphy, *The Kick*, 234–6.

6 Thomas Kinsella (1928–2021), Dublin poet and civil servant who appeared in *The Dolmen Miscellany* alongside McGahern and whom Keelan had first met in Chicago in the spring of 1963.

57 Howth Road

[*22 January 1964*]

Dear Michael,
Thank you for your card, and I was truly delighted about the stories. Congratulations, many. Struggle between work and illness is the only reason they're so late.

I am back at school, two schools now, shocking exhibition of squalor in the promotion rat race. I am in the serious school now, which I dislike very much, and I may go once I finish this book.[7]

Elizabeth Cullinan went home to America for probably good.

If you do come to Dublin I hope you will tell me.

I don't unfortunately read much but I did come on a fantastic story by Kafka in a Penguin METAMORPHOSIS, so shocking accurate. I wonder would it interest you.

Please remember me to Mrs McLaverty and Maura. I hope everything is well for you too.

                              Love
                              John

                                                        Faber

                                            57 Howth Road

[*31 January 1964*]

Dear Charles,
I won the £1000 Macaulay today, so I want to let you know before it's released to the press.[8]

---

7 Belgrove School, having grown rapidly over the years, was now divided into Senior and Junior Boys. McGahern went with the Seniors, and was finding life as a teacher more and more painful. At the time of writing this letter he was at the beginning of what would be his final months as a schoolteacher in Ireland. On 21 September 1964 he formally left Belgrove on one year's unpaid leave of absence, funded by his winning of the £1,000 Macaulay Fellowship.
8 The 1964 Macaulay Fellowship in Prose Fiction was awarded to McGahern by the Arts Council of Ireland. He was informed by a letter of 30 January. The fellowship

I've broken the novel and I don't intend to make any moves or changes till it's finished, then I can go.

I hope you are very well and with much affection.

John

Mary Keelan

57 Howth Road

3 February 1964

Dear Mary,

This happened about the time of your letter, and there's been no peace since, there must have been shortage of news over the weekend and it got main item coverage on radio and tv, so there's been a plague of people and things, but the money is marvellous and it's probably the sort of thing that'll please my father too.[9]

No, Mary, I didn't want you not to see Montague, he can be very nice and amusing, but he's uncertain and talks, and all I wanted was for you to be just not too trusting, and that's all, if he calls.

I hope the analogical argument business isn't too awful, and I loved your delight in the rain, though god knows what Lawrence might make it out to be.[10]

James Swift is my dearest friend, and a very strange, quiet marvellous man; he is in his early forties, and will never marry.

I used Horace in part of the novel this week, it is very beautiful.[11]

---

had to be used in furtherance of the successful candidate's liberal education, with the only condition being that the Secretary of the Arts Council (then the novelist Mervyn Wall) should be satisfied that the money be utilised in accordance with the wishes of the donor, William J. B. Macaulay, a prominent Irish diplomat who had served in Washington DC and at The Holy See.

9 McGahern's winning of the Macaulay Fellowship. He encloses a newspaper clipping announcing the news alongside his photograph.

10 That winter quarter the required Rhetoric course Keelan was teaching was devoted to 'analogical argument', which she found very challenging but interesting.

11 The lines McGahern quotes from Horace here are used to open Chapter 11 of *The Dark*, which sees young Mahoney on a bus in Co. Cavan en route to the priest's house where he is to make his decision about a possible religious vocation. He reads Horace in preparation for his Leaving Certificate exam, which is to take place the following June.

Cur non sub alta vel platano vel hac
penu iacentes sic temere et rosa
canos odorati capillos
dum licet?

I use it in a bus. So I too was reading Latin again.[12]

I was in Howth yesterday, from Sutton by the Summit round by the Cliff Walk, pure sunshine, seagulls away out, five miles of walking, red sand under the shoes by the Cliff, one launch and a man in a black rubber suit skiing in the bay and lovers in parked cars and walking coming down into the village, the Cock Tavern in a hurry with absolute hunger. So Howth is well my love.[13]

Not for a few days will I get back to work by now, and it was going marvellous till Friday.

Write to me, and I'll have more peace next time.

All my love,
John

Mary Keelan

57 Howth Road

21 February 1964

Dear Mary,

The only reason I delayed this is that you said you'd be writing when you got back from New York, and I waited this week not to have the letters crossing, but none came, and are you well or is something else wrong?

Such cold, cold wind here now after the mildest winter I remember, premature buds and flowers getting a horrible withering.

I don't see anyone now again and I have got really down to work. The worst ordeal was getting interviewed on the tv a fortnight ago. Murphy came here from Africa, in a bad state, some poor woman who fell in love with him gave him £10,000 but while he was away lost her sanity and he had to give most of the money back. The loss of the money was a great grief.

---

12 Keelan was part of a seminar group under Professor Jerry Taylor which involved translating medieval liturgical drama.
13 Keelan and McGahern had spent much of a day together that summer of 1963 in Howth.

I saw Kinsella and Miller, a night. Miller, strangely, happened to mention you.[14] Kinsella was full of talk of America. He's a bit unexciting.

I don't agree with you very much about public acclaim, though you are as much right as I am, it's the reaction primarily of different kinds of personalities, but I side with Malte Laurids Brigge.[15]

I could have gone to you too early this summer. Harvard wanted to pay my expenses out and back to some stupid seminar there.

Write to me soon and please be happy
                    And with my love
                    John

                                    Mary Keelan
                                    57 Howth Road

1 March 1964

Dear Mary,
The reason I didn't go to Harvard is that going to Harvard for the sake of going to Harvard doesn't interest me much. You said a long time ago that it'd be better for you to come here. If I had to know I'd have gone and it would be the simplest in the world, they arrange and pay for everything, but it's too late now.

We'll have to wait, though it's hard to wait, to know anything; there is no other way. My will is the same as yours, I want you very much, but I know too much of love not to be wary, it can be a hell around you quick enough. What I most fear is that you may find the reality – me – a long way from your dream. So is that fair answer? It's honest.

---

14 Liam Miller of the Dolmen Press, an important early champion of Kinsella's work. McGahern probably did not know that Keelan had met Miller on her Irish visit.
15 *The Notebooks of Malte Laurids Brigge* was Rainer Maria Rilke's only novel and one of the most formative books on the development of McGahern's imaginative sensibility. Published first in German in 1910, the book is semi-autobiographical and fragmentary. The novel's narrator warns against the dangers of fame, describing it as 'that public destruction of one in process of becoming'. McGahern introduced Keelan to Rilke's work and she recalls the importance of *Malte Laurids Brigge* to his thinking at this time. A heavily marked-up copy of the Norton 1964 edition of the book forms part of McGahern's library. See Rilke, *The Notebooks of Malte Laurids Brigge* (New York: W. W. Norton & Company, 1964), 74.

It looks as if the book will be finished or so much so that it won't matter before your coming.

The story I gave you is coming out in America in Avon Books or something like that, an anthology of the last 20 years of British writing. Did you happen to see the Macmillan spring list or do they have those in America?

What do you do with the priest? It's a shocking situation.[16]

A girl came out today, a painter, she's a dwarf almost, she wanted me to come down with her to Wicklow it was such a fine day, but I couldn't because of work. I brought her for tea for an hour and a walk in the Park down the road. My God, children are so cruel, how they laughed at her, and shouted. I could hardly keep my own violence in control.

Over tea she asked about the Crucifixion, she's doing a Stations of the Cross. I told her that I didn't think the gesture as it happened was valid anymore, but out there in the Park, the way that Stupidity happened to you the first time, that's where and how the Crucifixion happened, that's what I wanted to say, but couldn't.[17]

I wasn't able to work for long after she drove away, but I did, that's the horrid thing. Oh my God, Mary, do you ever shiver, and wish it all over as violently as possible.

I didn't go into school this week, but did a lot of work, but I go in tomorrow, there's a Confirmation, I have to do sponsor or some other fraud.

Are you well – I wish I could call you – my Mary? I am completely, even under this work. But I'm afraid my hair comes tumbling out, as the damned specialist said it might, once it was set in motion by that attack in October. It's a curse but strange how quickly you learn not to care so much.

It is late, and I love you, but I cannot tell you that I love you utterly, it is what I want to do. But I cannot – and it is for the first time in my life – say that love needs less care than words, less discipline. My love was or has been mad and blind, my work was once, it is the direction into reality, if it wasn't there nothing would be either in me or in my work or in you. But there is what is Style. And I will tell you what I mean, what I know for the first time in my life, it would take far too long, and you probably have its intuition. And I know that is there and with it that I should sleep with you for as long

16 Likely refers to a priest in Keelan's Medieval Latin drama class who failed his doctoral qualifying exams.

17 Refers to the artist Lesley MacWeeney, b. 1936 in Dublin to a professional family and taught by a series of governesses. She had polio as a child and as a young woman enrolled in the National College of Art and also represented Ireland at the Paris Biennale in 1959 and 1961. She designed the Stations of the Cross in 1963 for Knockanure Church in Co. Kerry.

as we are able and walk together but it's for both of us and I cannot fully trust you at this distance. Does this satisfy what you ask, Mary? If it does please write as soon as you can ever. And will you tell me what you mean by 'it is not where so many think or what they think'.

Love, I suppose, is?

Will you write to me soon as you can
John

Tony Whelan

57 Howth Road

14 March 1964

Dear Tony,

I was delighted to get your letter, and thank you for your congratulations, it was a piece of real luck.

I'll go away, but I'm finishing this novel first, and I haven't thought about it in any real way. It's nearly finished but it almost killed me.

I didn't care very much for the few Devlins I read, formal and academic, but if you'd like I could get and send you a copy of the Review.[18]

I was very glad you like Chelsea. I wouldn't mind living there. You're lucky to have parties and people. London on its own can be pretty terrifying.

I read a few marvellous savage stories by Gogol, and Metamorphoses by Kafka, which I thought extraordinarily accurate, but not much else.

I hope you have a nice Easter in Manchester. I'd be grateful if you remembered me to your mother very much. I wouldn't mind going home for a few days, just to look at the woods and river and that, but there's no use growling about not.

I'd be very grateful to hear from you any time you wish to write or to see you, if you come here or I to London.

with all wishes,
Sean

18 Probably the Irish poet Denis Devlin (1908–59).

[*Postmarked 11 March 1964*]

Dear Mary,
I do not blame the priest, with you and the red coat and brass lustrous and hair high, how could I. Nor do I judge, you judge nothing as you grow, it grows a mere way of seeing, and what is shocking is only the human lunacy and tragedy, my own life there.

I wish I could tell you I walk where there is marvel but it is only in tiredness, school a nightmare of clockwatching and timewasting. Around four I wake to work. It is strange how the mind learns the habits of a dog too. But the work goes and goes to its end, but this intolerable weariness.

The only gay night was a dinner dance, carnival hats and brandy, I even fell down in the twist, but it was two days before I could work after.

What I fear most in this work is the destruction of the will to merely survive. Consciousness turned in on language destroys. I know I am less able to earn a living now than before, it is frightening in a way, but leave it.

When do you hope to come? Does your thesis go well or will it take you long to finish? Does Roseanne stay with you still or with her lover? You must have Easter holidays soon.

Will you write to me soon?
The work is narrow and savage, not like The Barracks, much of all kinds of violence, and horrible cruelty. It won't be fully as long at the B. Some of it is written in the 2nd person, I don't know how much yet.

When it's not in my head you are.
                    With all my love
                    John

16 March 1964

My Dear Mary,
No, nothing changes, except you sounded tired in the letter, but I hope Wednesday goes well.

Cold, with wind, lying on the radiators over by the windows in school all day, the class heads bent whispering, some strange sensation of endlessness from the empty corridors, and I think of you at such a weird distance, but soon it'll be different.

I move into the very last section of the book, in Galway, at the University, and I may have to go there, to get its concrete reality, the destruction of the dream.[19]

With your letter there came one from New York, a friend of mine, a photographer, Alen McWeeney, Apt 1F, 74 East 7th Street wherever that is?[20] He is nice but he has a long way to go to discover himself.

St. Patrick's Day tomorrow, drunks, industrial hordes, speeches, hurling and football matches, much alcohol.[21] Did you ever read a letter of Rilke where he said there should be no public holidays, only festivals of the spirit, a time of flowering?[22] But tomorrow all this human and understandable and brutish clutching after another identity.

I love the forsythia too, its blaze of sheer yellow, but it is too early for it to flower here yet.

So keep well, my love, and happy if you can, but it doesn't matter so much, not near so much as to keep true.

With my love
John

19 *The Dark* closes with young Mahoney's decision to quit university at Galway despite his intense effort to get there and away from his brutish father and his home.
20 Alen MacWeeney b. 1939, Dublin-born, New York-based photographer who became friendly with McGahern after taking publicity shots for Macmillan's American publication of *The Barracks* (1964). The dustjacket of that first US edition bears a black and white photograph of a rather gaunt young McGahern by MacWeeney. His sister was Lesley MacWeeney with whom McGahern was also on friendly terms. See letter to Mary Keelan of 1 March 1964.
21 The Gaelic Athletic Association Interprovincial finals – better known as the Railway Cup – were in this period played annually in hurling and football at Croke Park on St Patrick's Day before huge crowds. McGahern regularly attended matches in Croke Park, particularly gaelic football matches.
22 McGahern may be thinking of a letter Rilke wrote to his wife Clara on 19 December 1906: 'Do you remember . . . our two restrained Christmas Eves? [. . .] how much we felt even then that we must mingle our work so deeply with ourselves that its workdays would lead out of themselves to holidays, to our true holidays. Everything else is indeed only a schedule such as we had in school'. *Letters of Rainer Maria Rilke 1892–1910*, trans. Jane Bannard Greene and M. D. Herter Norton (New York: W. W. Norton & Company, 1945), 248. McGahern made a gift of this volume to Madeline Green in 1968.

Mary Keelan

57 Howth Road

6 April 1964

Dear Mary,

All your letters came, two when I was away, one Saturday. I am sorry, my hand has got shocking careless, but I'll print you this.

The book's almost finished, a week or so at most, and the last read through to try for sheer precision. I feel as if I'll never write again. Drained of every strength; and just despair, and crushing weariness, but I complain far too much.

No. I told no one. I mentioned you to McWeeney when he was going to America but only passingly, I showed him the photos, they came around that time.[23] I'm afraid I do not trust very much, this city is a village, and I'm more known than ever now. And God knows what may happen, so it's better to be free of eyes and minds not our own.

Today I was back at school. I wonder more and more what the hell anyone is doing there, but it's one way of mere survival for a time for everyone.

The train passes. The dog is at the door, he wants me to throw the ball for him in the garden, I have to go to the hospital to see my aunt, she's dying, she's incredibly stupid and frightened, the rosary beads a prayer wheel on the eiderdown. I'll tell her in the summer she and I will drink pints in Terry Dolan's, we'll come down High Street singing and amaze the town, and she will laugh and say 'Aye. If I can get out of this god-forgive-me place.'[24]

I am many times in the day with you. Write to me, send the photo, and tell me about yourself.

> With my love,
> John

---

23 McGahern and Keelan were both of a mind that they did not want any chatter about their seeing each other. Keelan never mentioned John to any other literary friends or acquaintances. Keelan had sent on some snapshots of herself taken on her back porch in Chicago. McGahern had also sent Keelan a photograph of himself taken by Alen MacWeeney, posing before a coffee cup.

24 The main subplot of *The Pornographer* sees the central character visiting his dying aunt in a Dublin cancer hospital, and giving her the sorts of reassurances imagined by McGahern here for his aunt Maggie. Maggie died on 26 June 1964.

Mary Keelan
57 Howth Road

[Postmarked 16 April 1964]

Dear Mary,
Thank you so much for your letter, and for the book, it seems very funny.

I finished the book and went through it again and it needed not much change. I'll leave it for a few days and go through it for the last time and have it retyped etc.

There was business with the New York Times, they tracked me out to the school, an absurd rush of photos out, the people not knowing what they were rushing for except on orders from some man Brown, the literary editor. They were very impressed with the orders to rush staff on aeroplanes, cables etc. which was amusing.

What does auditing a class mean, is it counting the heads? Bellow is too extrovert a writer for me, I think that legitimately belongs to the Cowboys anymore.[25]

I think you fog things, Mary. I think that woman and earth are the opposite not the same as work, which is murderous and destructive, a road that leads to the wall.

What is Notes from Underground?[26]
Did I tell you I saw Murphy one evening in Galway, and he's going to America touring in autumn, the tour'll probably be a business wow.

I get holidays on 3rd July. Come any time after, depending on planes, I could meet you in London or Paris. You could come earlier if you want to see people in London, and I'd join you there or we can decide in the next few letters, for definite.

The photo is marvellous. You're either a very modest or a very vain young woman or worse both.

Won't you write soon and I'll not be as bad as these days.

With my love
John

25 Saul Bellow (1915–2005) was in residence at the University of Chicago as part of the Committee on Social Thought while Keelan was a student there.
26 Keelan was then reading lots of Dostoevsky and recommending it to McGahern.

Faber

57 Howth Road

28 April 1964

Dear Charles,
I am very excited that you are definitely coming – Richard said it was likely – but I'd hoped before and I am absolutely delighted now, the Dolphin will be very easy for me.[27]

I finished the novel, and I am getting it typed out, it finally got cut down shorter than The Barracks but it has thirty chapters. I feel pretty lousy, I had almost to fight for my life in it.

Do you know if any other novel has gone by the name of The Pit?[28]

I hope you are well, I felt envious of both of you in Oxford, but I am looking forward very much to see you here.[29]

Please remember me most affectionately to Rosemary.
                              Yours always
                              John

                                        Mary Keelan

                                    [57 Howth Road]

[29 April 1964]

Dear Mary,
Your letter came this morning, last night I posted a note, I was worried you were so long.

27 On 24 April, Monteith had written to arrange a meeting with McGahern in the Dolphin Hotel and Restaurant, then a popular meeting place on Essex Street East, Dublin on 21 May.

28 This was still at this stage of composition the working title for what became *The Dark*. In a letter of 29 April, Monteith replies: 'My immediate feeling is that The Pit is an excellent title – but I'll check to make sure that nobody else has used it.' A later memo in the Faber archive turns up one other title by that name, a book of 1956 by F. Norris.

29 In his letter of 24 April, Monteith had referred to a weekend with Richard Murphy in Oxford that had been 'terrific fun'.

28th is Sunday.[30] I'll be free Saturday after. I can meet you that Saturday, Sunday, Monday.

I think either Paris or London is best. I'll have to use in London some of the time over the book and on business. Paris is the nicest, it's criminally expensive though for long.

If you want to see people – either here or in England, I don't know who they are, if there are – some [*illegible*] or anyplace you want to go on your own. If it was in London it'd be possible to stay with friends of mine if you wished, but that's your time, you might wish to be on your own completely.

It'd depend what you had in mind whether here or London or Paris then, a city would be far better first, and then we could go where we want. Think about it, there's no hurry to decide.

I don't want to reason or search, I think we'll have to meet and just risk it, writing won't get us nearer than we have come, and I feel pretty run over now, I find myself turning in hatred on the book, so I want to get it away, and turn it into something unreal, a publisher's project or something. It nearly killed me, I walk all day in pure weariness, but it'll be different soon.

Write to me soon.
All my love
John

Mary Keelan

57 Howth Road

[*Postmarked 6 May 1964*]

Dear Mary,

I won't have any peace until after this week, all a sweat and cursing of typescript and corrections, but it'll be over in a few days and gone away.

I know this impersonality is hard for you or for any woman, but I need you to be patient, if you press too hard or force, and it seems to be particularly American, you kill. We must have some detachment, some style, or there's only the nothingness of our flesh.

In letters we have gone almost as far as it is possible, and we'll have the patience to wait and meet, and you must understand that, or we'll make no more than egotism and disillusionment.

30 28 June 1964 was a Sunday.

No, I was never in the Italian army, but it was so charming of you to tell me, and I don't think it is foolish you.[31]

I don't know if you should hate lies so much, it's better than blind egotism, the apparent truth in righteousness' name, lies give people time to breathe, to get energy, but it seems almost the clash of two civilizations between us in that.

But write to me and I am free now, and tell people you are coming if you want, especially if you'd like to see them, and I am longing so much to see you, and come then, on that plane.

I almost hate the sight of a plane by this but I will write longer soon and in eight weeks or less we will have each other.

And for me and for yourself keep well and with my love

        John

                               Mary Keelan

                              57 Howth Road

[*Postmarked 9 May 1964*]

Dear Mary,

I am writing to you without waiting which seems self indulgence, but I felt I was too hard.

I am longing for you to come, all writing up to that is rubbish anyhow, the one regret is that I didn't go to you.

It doesn't matter where we meet, we'll go to Paris, we can be utterly alone there, in marvel, its, and ours if we are sufficient.

Tomorrow the novel goes out, into other people's problems, it is hard and beautiful, and savages all I've ever done till now.

Please keep well and beautiful for we will have to meet in our lives, it will never solve anything, you know that, and we can meet, and go together or our own ways in grace.

        With all my love

        John

---

31 Likely refers to a comment Keelan had made about a foreign-language film she had seen in Chicago.

Faber

57 Howth Road

[*9 May 1964*]

Dear Charles,
I post the novel with this, and I hope very much it wins your favour.

I don't want to say anything, it should stand or fall on its own, but there's one technical thing that's better to mention – the use of a confessional 'you' for the heightened passages after the opening, relaxing back to a third person in rest places.

I wonder, if you find it (the novel) acceptable, could you give me as soon as possible a publishing date – approximately. Since I won the Macaulay a colour supplement of the Sunday newspaper here has been chasing a feature, I'll have to say yes or no, as they work some months ahead.

Peter Lennon says the novel should make a very interesting test case with the censorship here, they're growing very selfconscious about it and might let it through, the Macaulay is a government award, donated by our ex-Ambassador to the Vatican, dedicated to the memory of ex-President Sean T. O'Kelly. And if they did ban it would attract outside attention. Lennon says it would delight him to be able to feature it in The Guardian.

Needless to say it would be much nicer not to be banned, but there's a risk probably, though there's absolutely no pornography in the book.

I look forward all the time to your coming. Please give my love to Rosemary and I send mine to you too.

John

Mary Keelan

57 Howth Road

15 May 1964

Dear Mary,
The book, it's called The Pit, is typed and gone away. It's real, and rubbishes The Barracks, but it'll be hard for many to take.

And I am perfectly alright.

The first touch of summer's here, and I walk from school, and play football with the barmen down in the Park, and drink pints of ale in the late evening.

I read two books slow and easy, The Thief's Journal by Jean Genet and a book of criticism, it deserves a better name, by Jacques Riviere.[32]

Paris is the loveliest city I know, a real style, and elegance; and we can go there, and stay in a cheap hotel and go and eat in the small restaurants. I love it more than anywhere, and I was deliriously happy and unhappy there in dead days.[33]

This day week the publisher comes from London and I am to lunch with him in the Dolphin.[34]

Now that your coming is so close it seems unreal writing except to send you my love.

John

Mary Keelan

57 Howth Road

1 June 1964

Dear Mary,

There was no reason to worry, I was only writing to find out about the book before writing, I am more than well, some lovely days of sunshine, and I was swimming, in my very poor fashion, I learned a few years ago, because we had always a boat growing up, a marvellous tarred boat with tar that melted in the heat, dead leaves on the ribs from the sally above its moorings and fish scales bedded on the tar, and it was always the passion to go fishing, on wet days and after Mass on Sundays, because always besides we had to work.

Monteith was here, and gone, he thinks the book is marvellous, and it'll be published next spring. He is firming up the contract with the agent. The agent found it 'very powerful but frightening, and hard to know at this stage how this affect sales'? It's strange what has to be lived by mostly – money.

Would you like to think if there's anything you'd like to do especially, or if you'd prefer to leave it till London, for there's plenty of time to dither, but get a visa for Spain, it'll leave us free to go there if we want to.

---

32 Jean Genet's The Thief's Journal was first published in English by Grove Press, New York in 1964. Jacques Rivière (1886–1925), French intellectual, edited La Nouvelle Revue Française from 1919 until his death. He was influential in promoting Proust to a wider reading public.
33 McGahern had visited Paris with 'the dark haired girl' in 1962.
34 Charles Monteith.

Ted Kennedy was here this week, mad scenes and foolery, but one crowd I liked started to sing <u>Happy Birthday</u> and then to laugh outrageously, it was morbid and comical and disrespectful, and I'm afraid very Irish.[35]

I was at a party and met Kinsella and his wife, it was embarrassing because I promised a few times to ring up, and never did.

Austin Clarke has a big reputation here, but mostly academic people, I have never found much poetry in his verse, competent always and obsessed with silly social hatreds, and not big enough to walk on them savagely as Swift, only a sort of academic nibbling and quibbling, a sentimentalist gone sour.[36]

The respectable literary world would bore the britches off a saint anyhow.

I read one extraordinary book last week IF THIS IS A MAN by a Primo Levi, an Italian Jew, who was in Auswich.[37]

I am no good at letters, I have written more to you than to anyone ever, there's something unreal about them, they're neither life nor anything, but it's nice for them to come.

And you mustn't worry about anything, a neurosis can start like that and grow murderous, and write to me, and with my love

John

Faber

57 Howth Road

11 June 1964

Dear Charles,

I wrote yesterday but your letter came today. I had actually started to change the passage you mentioned, to equate it with the vagueness of the priest

35 Edward 'Ted' Kennedy (1932–2009), the youngest brother of President John Fitzgerald Kennedy, was a US senator from Massachusetts from 1962 to 2009, making him one of the longest-serving senators in American history. On his 1964 Irish visit, he was greeted by large, enthusiastic crowds wherever he went. On 30 May in Limerick, his final stop of the tour, the streets were lined with 100,000 people.

36 Austin Clarke (1896–1974) was, by 1964, the grand old man of Irish poetry having been part of the Revival generation, and subsequently became a critic of the new Irish state. The Swift whom McGahern refers to here is Jonathan Swift (1667–1745).

37 Primo Levi (1919–87), a survivor of Auschwitz. *If This is a Man* was first published in 1947 by Francesco De Silva in Italian as *Se questo è un uomo*, and in English in 1959 by Orion Press. McGahern remained an admirer of this book, choosing to teach it in later years at UCD. See Stanley van der Ziel, 'Editor's Preface', *LOTW*, xxxi.

scene, but if you wish send the copy with your underlining, – I've kept a copy to substitute at the time of printing –, or I'll send you the changed copy. It simply leaves the motive of the caressing simply vague.

I was very disturbed by the possibility of the legal business, it'd be for me the last horror, I'd rather not publish. It'd never occurred to me and I think it extremely unlikely; the life of the Pit bears no resemblance physically to my upbringing. He was a policeman, I have a letter where he states he was Reegan in the Barracks, which is as cuckoo as if he was Mahoney, he is not.[38]

But what I will do is quietly investigate the position, in my own family first, and a literary opinion, and I will write you then the situation, because it has nothing to do with my feelings.[39]

I was sorry after writing to you that I was too harsh on Ben, because it was a marvellous book, but what you crave to inflict on people is not praise or happiness but greatness though we'd want to keep it from ourselves.

I'll write as soon as I can see these people.

John

38 In a letter of 10 June, Monteith had written to McGahern of legal concerns over a particular passage in *The Pit*: 'there is, as I've said, one passage which does worry me slightly; and I wonder if I could discuss it with you? It's the description on pp. 9–11 of the father in bed with the boy where the father uses the boy to excite himself sexually and eventually has an orgasm. There doesn't seem to be any doubt that what you're describing here is an actual criminal offence – I suppose that technically it would be called "indecent assault on another male" or something like that; and that makes it particularly worrying for two reasons. In the first place, I'm afraid that if we were to leave this passage in exactly as it stands the probability of an Irish banning would turn into a near-certainty. And, in the second place, (I do hope you'll forgive me for raising this) I'm a little worried by the possibility that it might give rise to libel trouble. I remember you telling me how violently your father reacted to the publication of THE BARRACKS; and I wonder if there's any possibility that he might identify himself – or be identified by his friends – with Mahoney in THE PIT? [. . .] I don't suggest, of course, that the passage should be deleted. Indeed it would be quite wrong to do so for it's a central one in the book. I do think, though, that a little toning down – even a little deliberate imprecision – might be very helpful. If you'd like me to, I'd be very willing indeed to run through it lightly with a pencil and then send it over to you so that you could see my suggested cuts and changes.'
39 Monteith replies on 15 June: 'I'm sure it would be an excellent idea – as you suggest – if you were to make some quiet personal investigations in your own family about your father's likely reactions. When you've done that do write to me again. As you'll appreciate, it's impossible for me – or anyone here – to form any sort of view about what your father's feelings are likely to be. I'm very relieved to know, though, that there aren't many factual resemblances between your own early life and upbringing in the narrative of THE PIT.'

Mary Keelan

57 Howth Road

[Postmarked 16 June 1964]

Dear Mary,

Thank you for your letter. There's not much more to write.

Please yourself about seeing Alen, it's of no consequence one way or another, and he is going out of New York for the summer I think. It doesn't matter.

We can decide best in London. I'll have some sociabilities to fulfill, and then we can get out as quick as possible, they may take the best part of a week, I'll go the 3rd or 4th of July there. You can send a note during the Oxford [*visit*], and we can arrange.[40] It is a pity I cannot meet your plane.

I saw the Kinsellas, and I went down last weekend to Murphy, who is away to America in October, I wondered did he write to you. It rained and it rained while I was there and it's raining here now.

I was at a wedding yesterday, an old friend who runs a cinema, there's something gruesome about a wedding reception.[41]

I found out about a visa, there's none needed, and nothing else I can think of. You can write to me soon and with my love

John

Faber

57 Howth Road

22 June 1964

Dear Charles,

I have made the enquiries. My sisters have read the MSS – two of them – and they felt practically certain that there would be no trouble.

They said there is only a spiritual resemblance between the man and the character, that his is closer than Reegan in the Barracks, but factually far less

40 Professor Silverstein, Keelan's doctoral advisor, was then on sabbatical in Oxford and she went to meet with him.
41 Kevin Lehane's wedding. Lehane (1921–2002) worked as a manager of various Dublin cinemas and was one of John's three closest friends in Dublin of the late 1950s and early 1960s along with Tom Jordan, a teaching colleague, and Jimmy Swift.

identifiable, and we spent our life either with our mother, a schoolteacher, or with him in the police barracks, and the name of the school can be changed.[42]

The other parts that came up were.

1. Very few of the incidents are true factually, but two are, the swinging by the chair and the stripping: these can be proved, and the house was a great deal worse than the house of the book. One of my sisters was temporarily paralized by a beating, and there is a great deal besides: this is the main reason we feel certain that there can be no trouble, my father would never dare risk this becoming public, his whole present life is a running away from it, and there are several witnesses. That is even if he could be identified with Mahoney. But the main agreement was that it is unimaginable that he'd risk the publicity.

This doesn't matter, but I have a letter where he identifies himself with Reegan, he can't be every one. Even then there was no mention of any court action, it's a private feud, private recrimination. I am quite honest, and my sisters were too, but I'd much rather talk about it to you if you feel there's need then write, if you feel there's necessity for more, because there's a horrid vulgarity in putting it down like this, and no facts are ever really true. Though I do understand that it is necessary.

I have changed the scene, but I want to revise the MSS, and possibly fill out the early part of the book, so I thought if I could bring it with me to Spain and work it over finally there, as it'd be unlikely to go to the printers till at least September, but perhaps you could tell me about this.

I intend to travel to London on the 3rd of July, and stay a few days before going down to Spain. I would look forward very much to seeing you then.

Love
John

---

42 Included with this letter in the Faber archives is an internal memo from Monteith that states: 'This is quite reassuring, I think.' In a letter of 1 July, Monteith seeks further reassurance: 'You say in your letter that "the name of the school can be changed". Does this mean that the name you use at the moment is the real one? If so, I'm sure it would be a good idea to change it anyway.'

Mary Keelan

57 Howth Road

[*Late June 1964*]

Dear Mary,
Don't worry about the change, it doesn't matter.

If you want to stay an extra day or two in Dublin to see people you liked last year do so but tell me exactly as you can what day you'll go to London. And what day then will you have to meet the Professor in Oxford?

I'll go to London on the 3rd and do what I have to do mostly alone anyhow, see the publishers etc.

You'll have plenty of time to write before I go, and I'll leave instructions and ways of contact in the American Express or where to meet me in London.

I hope you have a lovely journey and that you keep well.

It's horrible here with constant rain.

There's hardly any more, except to tell me those as near as you can, and we'll meet in London.

A safe London address or message after July 3
                                        is Mindlin
                                        11 Westerham Ave. N. 9
                                        Tele EDM 1915[43]

               Love
               John

Mary Keelan

[*Dublin*]

[*Early July 1964*]

Dear Mary,
I think the best is to meet me at The Shelley Bar in Albemarle Street at 7.30 p.m. on the 8th (Wednesday).

---

43 Murray Mindlin, anti-censorship campaigner, translator of James Joyce's *Ulysses* into Hebrew, and London-based friend. *Censorship*, the magazine edited by Mindlin, published Owen Sheehy Skeffington's article on the Irish banning of *The Dark*, 'The McGahern Affair', in its Spring 1966 number.

I'd meet the plane but I have to get photographed by some German for the Zurich publisher that afternoon and airports are wretched places to meet at anyhow.

We can eat at the Shelley. It is 3 or 4 minutes from Piccadilly Circus, ask at the Circus, or get a taxi.

Should anything go wrong I'll wait at Foyle's Bookshop the next evening at 6 p.m.—it's only an insurance.[44]

Love

John

Faber

[San Sebastián postcard]

[Postmarked 26 July 1964]

[To Charles Monteith]
It is very beautiful here, and monstrous in some way, the churches especially, and the celebrations of the anniversary of the revolution or civil war.

It is impossible to get enough withdrawnness to work and I may have to go back to Dublin to finish what I have to do. Please remember me to Rosemary.

Love

John

Joe Kennedy

Paris

[Postmarked 28 July 1964]

[To Joe Kennedy]
Probably come home soon, impossible in Spain.

John

44 McGahern and Keelan did meet in London, one evening dining with some of McGahern's extended London family. After London they went to Paris where they met up with Peter Lennon, his wife and friends. Sometime after Bastille Day they went on to San Sebastián. After a few days there Keelan went on to Madrid and McGahern returned to Paris. They again met in Dublin in August after which Keelan went back to the US and the epistolary exchange came to an end except for one autumn letter from McGahern in Helsinki and some contact many years later in 1998.

Mary Keelan

57 Howth Road

3 September 1964

Dear Mary,

I meant to write, I tried, but it was impossible, too hopeless, so let it be so.

I have resigned from where I teach and will not be here after the end of this month.[45]

I hope you got back in less of a nightmare than the coming, and that you feel well.

If you want to write here do so before the end of this month.

I do not know anything else to say or I am not able.

John

Faber

57 Howth Road

[*7 September 1964*]

Dear Charles,

I enclose the final novel and I hope it pleases you.

The main changes are:

1. The insertion of a chapter (2) p. 5 to break the horror of the beating & the sleeping.

2. The rewriting of the sleeping p. 11.

3. Corpus Christi procession p. 53 & 53A.

4. A sad-comic insertion to break the intensity of the study, bringing potatoes to Benedict for Christmas 119A.

5. A page added to end of University, I think it satisfies your valid objection to the failing. It is an affirmation, though outside the academic lunacy.

6. The use of the first person in the first p. 22 & last p. 140 (the chief) masturbation passages, to make it less mechanical in appearance.

---

45 McGahern did not resign, but took a one-year leave of absence to travel, courtesy of the Macaulay Fellowship. On attempting to return in October 1965 he was dismissed.

I cannot find a satisfactory title. I've been trying with The Stake, The Direction, Mahoney.[46]

I'll wait a while, hoping for inspiration, and if anything strikes you I'd be grateful to learn.

I am tired. I've worked like a slave. There's only one thing I'd like the numbers of chapters to be in Times Roman.[47]

Love

John

James Swift

[*Madeline McGahern*][48]

[*Berlin postcard*]

[*Late September 1964*]

At city of Berlin lunch today, strange to see Auden at reception and next table, such energy and total eye for the main chance in pleasure, torrid Portugese woman next to me Sophia de Mello Brayner something or other and told her that there was at least one good person in Carvoiero.[49] She never heard of it.

Give my love to Katherine Swift[50]

John

---

46 The typescript as sent by McGahern arrived at Faber offices just as Monteith was leaving to holiday in Greece. It was read by Peter du Sautoy and Rosemary Goad, the latter in particular having concerns about some of the sexually shocking material. Goad replies to McGahern on 28 September: 'since the revisions are a little more complicated than we'd expected (in particular, we wonder if it doesn't make for rather awkward reading using a different person for the first and last masturbation passages) we do feel that the ts. should wait for Charles and not be sent to the Production Department until after his return.'

47 Meaning in Roman numerals.

48 Undated postcard to Jimmy Swift from Berlin where McGahern was attending the Berlin Writers' Conference. McGahern was on his way to Finland to marry Annikki Laaksi whom he had met in Paris for the first time a couple of months previously via Peter Lennon and his Finnish wife Eeva Karikoski. Among the other attendees at the conference were W. H. Auden, Jorge Luis Borges, James Meredith and Derek Walcott.

49 Sophia de Mello Breyner Andresen (1919–2004), an acclaimed Portuguese poet of aristocratic background. Carvoiero was the Algarve village that Patrick Swift made his home after leaving London in the 1960s.

50 Patrick Swift's daughter.

c/o Parko
Tammitie 13
Helsinki
[*hereafter Helsinki*]

[*6 October 1964*]

Dear Charles,

I hope your holiday was marvellous, I wanted to wish you well before you went, but for some reason thought you weren't going until October the 5th.

The blurb is masterly, I think; it makes it almost impossible to ban, and it seems true to the book as well.[51]

The one change I'd make is the <u>Arts Council of Ireland</u> instead of the <u>Arts Council of the Irish Republic</u>.

Mahoney is a good title but I think it must immediately summon up the novels of Beckett – Watt, Murphy, Malone Dies – or a certain Irishness. It's a curse but if no one in Fabers can think of a concrete name I'll go through it and find some name in a few days. <u>The Stake</u> or <u>The Dark</u> seem now second best if nothing comes.[52]

I would like to dedicate the novel

To

Annikki Laaksi

I was at the Berlin Festival, which was a bore of African rubbish, but Auden spoke beautifully twice, but the city was strange, I liked it very much, marvellous wide streets, and trees, the museum I most enjoyed was ever

51 The inside cover of the dustjacket describes the book in terms keen to avoid controversy: 'His second novel [. . .] has been awaited with more than usual interest and eagerness; and it will confirm and enhance the reputation he gained with the first. Once again Mr. McGahern sets his scene in rural Ireland and his theme is adolescence, impelled forward by ambition and sexuality – guilty and uncontrollable; contorted and twisted by a puritanical and passionate religion and, above all, by a strange, powerful, ambiguous relationship between son and widower father. Against a background evoked with quiet, undemonstrative mastery, Mr. McGahern explores with precision and tenderness a human situation, superficially very ordinary, but inwardly an agony of longing and despair.'

52 Monteith replies on 9 October: 'I've been thinking about the title again – and discussing it with people here – and the one we've now decided we'd like is the second of your two suggestions, i.e. THE DARK. This does seem to me – the more I think about it – very powerful and resonant; so may we simply settle for that?'

at Dahlem, two Vermeers you could look at all day.[53] East Berlin was an intensification of the difference between France and Spain and the people were afraid.

I came up here from Berlin yesterday to see some friends, I think I'll stay here for some time, but if I decide to leave I'll write immediately.

Please remember me affectionately to Rosemary.

As always
John

Faber

Helsinki

14 October 1964

Dear Rosemary,
Thank you for your very kind letter – I am really grateful – and it doesn't matter about Macmillan, the only publishers I ever felt I had was Faber, and it is no different now.[54]

Except there'll probably be some similar reactions, and Helsinki might be an easier place for a time than Dublin.

I think The Dark is probably the best title.

Did you get holidays yet?

I went down last week-end to a town in the middle of the country, it was very strange, extraordinary forest and lake and timber rivers, the train crowded, life at all the stations, it seemed nineteenth century Russia.

I hope you are very well, and not overcome with the autumn list and work, and with my love

John

53 The Gemäldegalerie is an art museum in Berlin where the main selection of paintings belonging to the Berlin State Museums is displayed. It holds one of the world's leading collections of European paintings from the thirteenth to the eighteenth centuries. The two Vermeers are *Woman with a Pearl Necklace* and *The Glass of Wine*.
54 Goad, du Sautoy and Monteith at Faber were angry about what they felt was Macmillan's highhandedness in rejecting McGahern's new novel for publication in the US. Goad writes to Cecil Scott at Macmillan, New York on 28 September 1964: 'I feel it is rather a pity that you sent a copy of your letter direct to John McGahern, as he is extremely sensitive and may be greatly discouraged and upset.' For more, see letter to Jimmy Swift of 16 October 1964.

James Swift
[*Madeline McGahern*] (TS)
Helsinki

16 October 1964

Dear Jimmy,
I wanted to write before now but couldn't. It's rather fine looking, marvellous parks with pine and rowan, birches that are pure silver, inlets of the sea everywhere, tents of the morning market along the harbour against old buildings of Russia, but the sense of joylessness is shocking, a real dour materialism, not even light in the faces, there's no poverty at all, the cost of living more than twice that of Dublin, there are no pubs, the only place for drinking out are expensive restaurants or hotels – Quo Vadis, Jammes, Russell – and the prices are prohibitive.[55] So the whole city seems to get methodically drunk every weekend in private, and without gaiety, some of the dispair flowing into the streets and parks, I saw one stand dead as a rock with arms outstretched in the shape of a cross for longer than I could look in a freezing dusk. And the streets appear one frantic round of an eternal stations of the cross.

The book, it's to be definitely THE DARK, is gone to the printers, but it was rejected by Macmillan in terms of outrage. They even wrote to Faber. 'I was dismayed and shocked by the contents of the manuscript . . . and my first impression on a second reading was only confirmed . . . it is a most unpleasant with details that make the skin creep . . .'[56] It's not worth cursing but it doesn't make me any easier about the reception in Ireland and danger of being trapped between the devil and the North or the Arctic Circle.

55 The three places mentioned were expensive Dublin restaurants. McGahern's 'Jammes' ought to read 'Jammet's'.
56 The letter, dated 24 September 1964, condemning *The Pit* was written by Cecil Scott, editor-in-chief at Macmillan, New York to Peter H. Matson at the Harold Matson Company, New York and copied to Peter du Sautoy at Faber and to McGahern himself: 'I think it would be (and I say this in all sincerity) a great mistake to have the present manuscript published either in this country or in England for the sake of the young man's reputation. It is a most unpleasant book with details that make the skin creep, and I cannot believe from a purely commercial point of view that it has any possibilities of sales. This, of course, is secondary; we published THE BARRACKS because of its literary distinction and the promise that it held knowing that it probably would not sell. THE PIT has far less of these two qualities. John is young and no great harm would be done, if he did put this manuscript away, forgot it completely, and went on to his next book.'

Perhaps you'll write if you can find some hour. And I hope you are well. I was fooling through Ulysses and it's strange the subjective force of the hatred always on Buck Mulligan.

With my love
John

Mary Keelan
Helsinki

[*October 1964*]

Dear Mary,

I am sorry to have to answer your letter and the check from here, it is no insult, it could never be, and I too have got my own share of suffering and dispair, but I could not let it go without thanking you, so I do for both, and for the letter more.[57] It's pretty awful here.

Macmillan's rejected the book, it's to be called THE DARK, the man was 'dismayed and shocked – a thoroughly unpleasant book – without any literary distinction as THE BARRACKS – and details that made my flesh creep – without any possibility of sales.'

And he might be right but I don't give a curse and I am able to work.

I hope you are well and all your things.

I often think of the summer mess, and I cannot understand, except that everything I turn my hand to seems doomed to one kind of failure or another, I cannot understand and the more I write the more confused this becomes, and I do not know anything.

John

---

57 A note with this letter indicates that a cheque for $100 was enclosed.

[*October 1964*]

Dear Patrick,[58]
I hadn't Matson's address, it's one of the curses of having nothing here, but I cabled Peters of London.[59] I said it's urgent that you get the mss. I hate truck with them, it's as if they foul in some way the roots of the imagination, it's alright if you write for money, but I don't. I haven't the talent. Faber has the new version of the mss. All the prose has been made clearer, some added, some cut away. A river outing breaks the beating and the incest chapter. The incest is rewritten, the realistic detail taken away, but it's more rhythmic and imaginatively more vicious, an echo of the priest chapters. The masturbation is heavily rewritten, and in the first person. A Corpus Christi procession creates the attraction of the ideal versus the flesh, it was only stated before. The intense study chapters are broken by a comic chapter where Mahoney brings potatoes to the monastery as Christmas present. The university opening is totally rewritten, as well as the tone of the direction away, it becomes celebration instead of defeat.

If the mss is accepted at Knopf I'll be very happy. I'll feel I have a publisher in America for the first time, but if it doesn't, it doesn't make profound difference. If my work's any use, it'll live, and if it's not the publisher or publishers couldn't keep it alive, but I'll be delighted if it's with you.

John

58 This is the first extant letter to Patrick Gregory who was then working with Knopf in New York. Gregory was the son of literary parents: his father, Horace Gregory (1898–1982), was a poet, critic and translator. His Ukrainian-born mother, Marya Zaturenska (1902–82), won the Pulitzer Prize for Poetry in 1938. The Gregorys were neighbours of Niels Gron – father of Madeline Green who would marry McGahern in 1973 – in Snedens Landing near New York City, a wealthy enclave favoured by artists. Patrick Gregory and Madeline met as children and Gregory was responsible for introducing McGahern to Madeline in New York in February 1966. As a young man Gregory went to live in Paris, returning to work in New York as an editor. From Knopf, McGahern followed Gregory to Atlantic Monthly Press. McGahern's letters to Gregory are gathered variously in the Knopf holdings at the Harry Ransom Center (HRC), University of Texas at Austin; the James Hardiman Library, NUIG; and with Madeline McGahern.
59 Harold Matson (1898–1988) was then McGahern's American agent.

16 October 1964

Dear Patrick,

It was very kind to write so quickly and there's no trouble with Faber, they are utterly behind the book though they are prepared for censorship trouble in Ireland. For some reason Scott decided to write to Faber, they were indignant, describing it as 'hysterically prudish (the letter) and an ineffably silly decision'.

The book, it's to be finally called THE DARK, is at the printers now. I enclose the blurb Monteith has written.

Matson has the copy, perhaps it's not worth changing from him: but the only trouble is that Fabers have the revised book, and it's a good deal better. What do you think?

I haven't any reviews, they're stored up in Ireland, but I could ask Fabers to send copies of the English reviews. Is it the American or English you want?

1961 spring. Extracts from a first novel THE END OR BEGINNING OF LOVE appeared in the London Quarterly X, it first attracted the attention of publishers, I didn't want to publish it by then, but Faber gave me a contract for the Barracks.

1962. AE Memorial Award and appearance of extracts in smaller magazines

1963. Faber publication of the BARRACKS (spring). COMING INTO HIS KINGDOM (story) published in small magazines and when anthologised VOICES (Michael Joseph, picked by THE SPECTATOR as the best story of the year's anthologies). Strandhill, the Sea published by THE NEW YORKER.

1964. The Macaulay by Arts Council. American publication of BARRACKS

I am working on something modest – a love affair by an earlier death, in a dancehall.

What I want to write is a long work that I've been planning long. The world of order, the staff of a large school in their society, power and fear counterpointed against classless nightworld of dancehalls and bars and parties: between the vision in loneliness under accidental roofs and a love affair joining both worlds, a savage struggle of egos in changing balance of power, – but this description seems nonsense, – I hope an appalling comedy.[60]

---

60 What McGahern describes here is a mix of what becomes *The Leavetaking* in 1974 and *The Pornographer* in 1979.

And I'll have to wait until I am sure I have enough strength.

Remember it doesn't matter at all if Knopf don't take, it's a public matter, and has nothing whatever to do with evenings we spent or may spend together.

I must say THE BARD OF CLEGGAN gave much amusement. I'd be grateful for any account of the royal progress.[61]

And I hope you are well. I'll write about this cursed place later but it's easy to work, there's nothing else to do, except walk or go crazy.

John

Do you ever have news of Cronin?

Faber (TS)

Helsinki

24 October 1964

Dear Charles,

I am terribly happy that the changes pleased you, and thank you for both your letters, and especially the card from Greece, it seems beautiful. I met Lorna Reynolds twice. She seemed very nice. I think she has a difficult time at the University because of the Fascist/Catholic rulers there.[62] Can you tell me what ONGOS are some time, it's stayed for some reason in my mind, and I have no way of discovering here.[63] How did the hours studying Greek last winter serve you, was it difficult to follow the way the people speak?

I've applied for a visa to enter Russia and if I can get it I'll go there for some days at least. St Petersburg is only a day's journey from here. I hope to be back in London about Christmas or early January. So if the proofs are ready before Christmas it's best to send them here and I'll bring them back with me. It's rather beautiful here, everywhere inlets of the sea and a great harbour

---

61 A reference to Richard Murphy, frequently a figure of gossip, interest and amusement between McGahern, Gregory and Monteith.

62 On 9 October after his return from holiday in Greece, Monteith wrote to McGahern: 'Incidentally, I met a great admirer of yours there – Lorna Reynolds of UCD.' Reynolds (1911–2003) was then on the English faculty at UCD where she would have come into contact with McGahern when he took his night degree there in the 1950s. She was a social activist and strongly anti-censorship. She was appointed Professor of Modern English at University College Galway (UCG) in 1966.

63 Monteith had mentioned in his letter of the 9th that he had been drinking 'ouzo' with Lorna Reynolds.

and parks, full of pine and silver birch and redberried rowan and areas of stripped rock: but the place is horribly expensive, at least twice as expensive as London, there's no poverty at all, there's a real sense of materialistic dullness and puritanism in most of the faces, and then the nation seems to get methodically sozzled as a religious duty every weekend, some of it spilling into the streets in an ugly despairing way, but sometimes comic, one against a tree on a height in the park with arms outstretched in the shape of a cross, not even a muscle moving, with fumes of spirits strong at 15 yards away, and the dusk settling into a blue freeze. Other things too.

Will you want me in London or Dublin for the publication? Is it possible for you to find out a place that'd be good to go – which of the countries Greece Spain Portugal etc – that'd be cheap to live for a time, with sun, and possibly interesting.[64] Please don't go to any trouble. But if you can happen on the information easily I'd be grateful for any suggestions.

It must be a real drag to have to do jury service at this time. There seems to be one of the worst slums in Ireland in Cork city, they come to Dublin often to follow soccer, and I worked with a gang of them as a casual labourer – you don't need cards and get paid at the end of each day – on the canal a little distance to the left as you come out of Westbourne Station. I was the only one without a jail sentence![65]

John

Kopf are extremely interested in the novel: and I wonder is there any way you could loan them the rewritten copy, to a Patrick Gregory, they'd return it immediately, but if not, if it causes trouble, it doesn't matter so much.[66]

64 Monteith replies on 2 November recommending Morocco. He calculates that one can 'get from London to Marrakesh and back for less than £40'.
65 Monteith had written in his letter of 21 October approving *The Dark* to go into production that he had been landed with jury service: 'a seventeen year old from Cork who was accused of breaking and entering. We found him guilty, I fear!'
66 This PS is written by hand. On 12 November Monteith writes to Bill Koshland at Knopf praising *The Dark* and encouraging the company to publish it in the US.

25 October 1964

Dear Patrick,

I'd be grateful for any account of the Laird, he's rather marvellous, and he's totally outside any humiliation, he gave me a long account of O'Grady's visit to Cleggan, – 'I came three thousand miles to see you Mr Murphy' – and he was rather obsessed by the fact that you were continuing to address him as Murphy.[67] I explained that it was probably some unfortunate usage from France. Cronin was feeding for a long time on your account of Cleggan. In a real passion of belittlement. Ask Murphy about his first meeting with Kavanagh and keep a straight face of moral indignation if you can.

The McDaid world is such a jungle that it's impossible.[68] There's a few images. When Cronin's Riley failed here I heard Kavanagh go round McDaid's: 'Phoor Cronin. Phoor Cronin. Aah, sad, sad. His ambition was to rrite a bestseller before he was forty. Med too many enemies. Phoor Cronin. Sad. And the whife 'll cause trouble. Dissapointment. Were led to believe, ow there was big advances on the job. And he'll never ger another publisher. Because he wont sell 800 copies. It wont pay for the fucking printing even foo fum.'[69] We talked once about the solicitor side of Cronin.[70] And Cronin is hated inside as well as outside the ring. A few times Cronin got editorial power and he didn't print his friends – actually he printed the mostly dull steady respectable contributors – and he'll never be forgiven for that.[71] Only Kavanagh could do that and get away. He did. And then Cronin saying, 'But he was different. He could be generous once – at least he was to me.' I can't

---

67 O'Grady refers most likely to the Irish poet Desmond O'Grady (1935–2014) who spent much of his adult life in Paris and Rome.

68 McDaid's of Harry Street was then the liveliest literary pub in Dublin; McGahern disliked and avoided it. A thinly veiled description of Patrick Kavanagh being barred from the pub occurs in McGahern's short story 'Bank Holiday'.

69 Anthony Cronin's comic novel *The Life of Riley* (London: Secker & Warburg, 1964) was a fictionalised account of bohemian life in mid-twentieth-century Dublin. In an undated letter to McGahern of 1960–1, Patrick Swift writes: 'Poor old P.K. he's rather out of things here since Cronin won't have him'. Madeline McGahern Papers.

70 Cronin was a qualified barrister.

71 Cronin was involved in editing *The Bell* (1940–54) in its last years as its editor Peadar O'Donnell increasingly lost interest. In the later 1950s he became literary editor of *Time and Tide* (1920–79) in London.

tolerate Kavanagh but he's a real poet and that's rare, even when he's as bad as you say there's something distinctive about it. And after Beckett he's probably the only one of that whole generation though that's hardly praise. One could circle about the shindy forever but it's tiresome and it belongs more to conversation.[72]

It's rather beautiful here, perhaps I said, a harbour with a market along the cobbles, against the houses of Russian merchants and a huge white church. The sea everywhere, islands as parks, long slender silver birches everywhere, and pine and rowan with berries, areas of bare rock, it's Finland granite. There's no poverty at all. It's frighteningly expensive. More than twice as expensive as Dublin. The sense of the people is crushingly Provincialism and materialism and comfort. A sense of puritanism even in sex though the laws are among the more liberal in the world: drinking out is prohibitively expensive as Jammet's are the only places allowed and then the whole nation seem to get methodically sozzled every weekend in private, administered as some shock to the nervous system before plodding out into another dull week, and some of it spills into the streets and parks in an ugly despairing way, though it has its amusements, one against a birch tree in a freezing dusk with arms outstretched to make a crucifixion and fumes of whiskey or some spirits deadly from him at 15 yards distance.[73] Another drunk as a lord with an easel in the park with a brush in one hand and a bottle in the other painting what seemed a tree, and abusing everyone that passed in Russian. I've applied for a visa and I hope to go to St Petersburg which is only a day away on the bus when it comes. I don't like it here. I'll go back at Christmas. Write something about the election.[74] And I hope you keep well.

John

72 Gregory wrote in reply to McGahern's tales of Cronin and Kavanagh on 27 October 1964: 'Your last letter cheered me greatly. Aye, that's Kavanagh's very voice: I see him navigating among the slop-washed tables of McDaids, precariously, belligerently – like a slightly disabled man-of-war. Talent aside, he's certainly no match for Cronin, who has none of K's toughness and is riddled by pin-pricks by "bourgeois" ambition which both alarm and tickle him. K. has desires; C. has only yearnings.' Knopf, HRC.

73 Jammet's was a stylish and expensive French restaurant that traded at 45 Nassau Street, Dublin from 1901 to 1967.

74 In the US presidential election of 3 November 1964, the Democrat incumbent Lyndon B. Johnson inflicted a crushing defeat on his Republican challenger, Barry Goldwater.

Alfred A. Knopf, Inc. Records
Isokaari 5A–18
Helsinki
[*hereafter Helsinki*]

19 November 1964

Dear Patrick,

I changed my address to what's above, and I'll be here until the 5th of December. Charles Monteith wrote, the MSS is with the printers, and he said he wrote about the novel to Knopf which I certainly didn't ask him to do.[75]

I was glad about Murphy's success, and the Croke Parkers at the back were marvellous. Murphy has no sense of anything except black and white and perhaps a puzzling grey that has to be got to the root of now and again, it's his attractiveness in some way too. Will he stay in America for long? Will he base a lot of his future life there as I think he has in his mind.

I read much – Euripides was a shock and delight – I can't understand that I never came across him before – and go to the pictures. A Danish picture Day of Wrath disturbed me very much, about witch burning, made in 1943, obviously a disguised nazi picture. It gave real crushing atmosphere of evil.[76]

It begins to get cold, one day a wind so hard it was difficult to breathe.

Did you ever hear of sauna, it's a weekly ritual here, a room with three stairs of latticed wood where you sit or lie, hot air coming from heated stones, almost unbearable air, sweat pours, you beat your body from the extremities moving in with birches, and then cold shower or roll in the snow.

I hope you can write soon, it's marvellous especially here to get your letter. I am not worried about the book, it's being published. I'll be delighted if you can but if it's not possible it'll make no difference.

John

75 McGahern had changed his address from c/o Parko to Isokaari 5A–18, both in Helsinki.
76 *Day of Wrath* (Danish: *Vredens dag*) is a 1943 film directed by Carl Theodor Dreyer. The film tells the story of a young woman who is forced into a marriage with an elderly pastor after her late mother is accused of witchcraft. She falls in love with the pastor's son and also comes under suspicion of witchcraft.

20 November 1964

Dear Charles,
Thank you for all the information, it was very kind, and I look at maps and think about it, and it's a great help, but I'll probably not definitely decide till I get to London. Unfortunately the relative cheapness'll have to play a big part.

It's freak mild weather here, but a few times there was a taste of real style, air difficult to breathe it was so cold.

There's a weekly ritual here, sauna, did you ever hear? A room with latticed stairs, boiling air from hot stones, the sweat pours, you beat yourself with birches from the hands and feet into the body, and then go for a cold shower or roll in the snow. For some reason I thought of D. H. Lawrence and with the nakedness and seriousness or ordinariness I couldn't keep from laughing through the whole performance. But it was marvellous to drink frozen beer afterwards in the tiredness and listen and try to apologise. It was imagining Lawrence in the sauna caused it all.

Will you be able to send the proofs here? Have you any idea when they'll be ready? At the beginning of December I go to St. Petersburg for probably two weeks. I hope you are very well and please don't forget me to Rosemary.

Love
John

30 November 1964

Dear Joe,
Please forgive this typewriting but compared to my hand it is marvellous.

I meant to write but there was too much confusion travelling from Berlin – Auden incidentally was the only one there with the authority of a style – and I'll be here till after Christmas. I have applied for a visa to Russia, Lenningrad is only a day away on a cheap bus – and if it comes I'll go before then.

I hope to go down through Germany slowly to Rome but it seems as if I may have to go back to London after Christmas for a little time – I'd dance to go to a pub this evening – there's no such here – a puritan country if there ever was one – the only way you can buy drink is in the state monopoly ALKO shops or in prohibitively expensive restaurants where you pay to have your coat compulsorily removed.

There's nothing else to say, only it's so cold now, the sea smoking like the deballsed geography lesson – and I cannot write letters but I was wondering if I was in London after Christmas would you be able to make London on some professional excuse for a civilized drink or more.

[*In handwritten pencil:*]

As I read through the machine is even worse than the hand.

But I'll be here until after Christmas if you wish to write, and I'd be grateful. If I am in London do you think you could get across.

John

Patrick Gregory Papers

Helsinki

[*Marked '1 December 1964' by Gregory*]

Dear Patrick,

I am sorry that I gave you misleading impression, I'll be here at least until after Christmas. On the <u>5th of December</u> I go to Leningrad for a week or so and then come back here again. I think it'll be a year or more before I go back to Dublin.

Provincialism is I think only a state of mind and heart, O'Connor is as provincial as O'Brien, equal rubbish.[77] I never could like even Swim 2 Birds, it's impossible to see it without Joyce, and there's some meanness, it only cleverness, and it takes passion or savagery to make cleverness comic, when style passes beyond the conceit of vision into true humanness. Style is all that matters but I do not trust myself much, let it be. Provincialism like every other ism is primarily cowardice in the face of reality, its bravado is the easiest to see.

A Kenyon review came with serious review of the Barracks, and an extremely interesting article on Babel by his daughter.[78]

---

77 Irish writers Frank O'Connor (1903–66) and Flann O'Brien (1911–66).

78 The review of *The Barracks* was written by David Madden and appeared in the *Kenyon Review*, vol. 26, no. 3 (Summer 1964), 580–1. Madden's description of the character of Elizabeth Reegan, with its nod to Albert Camus, would have pleased McGahern: 'Carrying her own executioner within her, she becomes a kind of female

It's so cold I had to buy a cap with earflaps.

John

Seán Brehony Letters

Helsinki

[*Early December 1964*]

Dear Sean,[79]

I meant to write before now, but I cannot write letters easily, and I've lost the number of the house, so I'll have to hope this gets you through the offices.[80]

The worst of here is the expense of everything—or the unfavourable rate of exchange – twice as expensive as Dublin, and often more. There are no pubs. The only places are hotels and expensive restaurants, you've even to pay for your coat, and a meal, and the prices are prohibitive almost. Drink is sold in the Alkos, state monopoly shops, and if you want spirits you have to flash a card saying you're not an alcoholic. There's a history of prohibition, extraordinary public drunkenness – several Jesuses in imaginary states of crucifixion against the birch trees with the temperature below zero any time, almost in the park in a fume of spirits, but I'll leave it.

There was a freak, mild autumn until two months, but now it's colder than I've ever known, painful to breathe, and the sea smoking.

There's no poverty, much wealth, all the houses tall and central heated, blocks of flats, with caretakers.

A strange weekly ritual, a sauna, where you melt slowly in air over boiling temperatures from heated stones and beat yourself with bundles of birch twigs, and then drink frozen beer in a frightful thirst.

Meursault who interrogates social reality.' Nathalie Babel contributed '"No Time to Finish": Notes on Isaac Babel', 514–32.

79 McGahern's earliest surviving letter to Seán Brehony (1930–81), a native of Keash, Co. Sligo and employee of the Irish revenue service whom McGahern had first met at a wedding in 1963 and with whom he remained friendly until Brehony's death.

80 At the time Brehony lived at Calderwood Avenue, Drumcondra, an address that later features in the plot of *The Pornographer* as an absurd place of courtship between the unnamed narrator and the hapless Josephine. Nearby is the Goose, a pub which also features in the novel's plot. McGahern was a regular visitor to the Brehony home and to the Goose, 1963–4.

Anu was busy, but not now, the first night was two weeks ago, and we were married afterwards, and managed to keep it out or away from the newspapers.

It's only a day away on the bus from Leningrad, and we're going there Friday, and I'm looking forward very much. Except I hope I'm not frozen into a snowman.

We may go to London after Christmas. I have to go and Anu may as well come then as later, and go where there's sun, but there is trouble over her contract, they do not want to release her.

I hope you are well and Rita and the children. Please remember me to Rita with affection. And Joe Beirne too.[81]

If you find the will to write to me I'll be delighted and grateful.

John

Dympna McGahern
[*Madeline McGahern*] (TS)

Helsinki

[*December 1964*]

Dear Dymphna,
Thank you for the letter, I was delighted, it was in the hall when I came from St Petersburg.

I do not want to tell much, it'd be pretentious and too complicated, except the Winter Palace. Windows on the frozen Neva, the black centre running cold between shores of ice, so wide with the grace of the bridges, and sleeping eagles where the hands rest on the gold armchair.[82] Functional army lorries of

81 McGahern first met Seán and Rita Brehony in 1963 at the wedding of Joe Broin (mistakenly spelled Beirne here), a mutual friend from the west of Ireland.
82 This chair clearly made a strong impression on McGahern, and one early handwritten draft of 'My Love, My Umbrella' sees him thinking about it: 'We watched a poet in the centre of a group of overcoated admirers at the bar. He'd an overcoat too and a hat, pushed back to show thin grey strands across the crown. He was declaiming that only the quality of love mattered, not what we love, but often he regretted he'd not a richer upbringing so that the things he'd love were different. He said he'd read about a rocking chair in the Winter Palace in St Petersburg. It was Catherine's and it was also a sleigh, dogs pushed it through the streets, and on the headrest were carved sleeping leopards'. See McGahern Papers, NUIG, P71/385.

extraordinary ugliness taking heaps of muddy snow off the square where the soldiers of the Tsar marched.

And it was very easy: for Anu has fluent Russian. And in a wine shop one evening we got tipsy on a large glass of vodka and champagne. The Russians drank it like medicine and rushed immediately back into easy snow.

We leave here at the end of this month: I may leave a few days before Anu, spend time in Stockholm. Both of us go on to Copenhagen to spend a few days. And then the rest of the way to London.

I'll probably go down the centre of Finland on my own next week until Christmas.

I was very glad things are so happy at the University and that you got the fees but give them back as soon as you can because of the neurosis he is about money.[83]

I won't write again from Finland. If you will I'll be found here until the end of the month. And it goes if anything does without saying that I'll be delighted. And I hope that you will have a lovely and happy Christmas.

Love
Sean

Faber

Helsinki

13 December 1964

Dear Charles,

It was strange in St. Petersburg, and the Neva with the Winter Palace beautiful and the almost trafficless streets, and I am certain you would love the style of the hotels, the Astoria especially, and the theatre, the people endlessly drinking in the foyers in the interval, round and round as in a parade ring, but I do not want to write much now.

I leave here a few days after Christmas, for London; spending a day or two in Stockholm, and possibly the most part of a week in Copenhagen.

So I think unless the proofs come to land almost immediately it'd be better to send them to:

23 Forest Drive West, Leytonstone E. 11.

I wonder, if you would consider it, is it wise to have the proofs in the Dublin shops much in advance of publication, it's a small city, they'll go

---

83 Referring to their father, Frank McGahern.

the rounds, there could be lobbying of the censor, but it is no more than a suggestion, and you know what is best far surer than I.[84]

And I wish you a happy and marvellous Christmas, and Rosemary, and with much love.

John

---

84 An internal Faber memo of 17 December from Monteith to Rosemary Goad reads: 'I'm sure it would be wise, wouldn't it, not to distribute review copies of THE DARK too widely or too far in advance to some of the Irish papers – particularly papers like the Independent which are very closely in touch with the Government Censorship Board. We want to avoid a ban if possible – which is, I fear, probably inevitable.'

1965

James Swift
[*Madeline McGahern*]

Hotell Reisen
Skeppsbron 12-14
Stockholm Den

2 January 1965[1]

Dear Jimmy,

I am on my way to London, I'll stay here some days, and in Copenhagen, there's heavy ships from there.

Anu has work to finish, and she'll come later, before I left we were married, in a civil office along by the harbour, with the two porters of the place as witnesses.[2]

I think the proofs will be waiting in London by the time I get there, it's very old and beautiful in this part of the city, but no lightness as there was in Leningrad, it's horribly expensive too as in Helsinki, but we never saw such richness.

I am not able to write much, when I get to London I'll write, I am not sure where I'll go from there, but I'll be there several weeks, and I might go over to Ireland.

23 Forest Dr, West Leytonstone E. 11 is the best address.

I hope you are well and with love,

John

---

1 Written on headed hotel notepaper.
2 McGahern and Annikki Laaksi were married on 24 November 1964.

James Swift
[*Madeline McGahern*]

23 Forest Drive West
Leytonstone
London E. 11[3]
[*hereafter 23 Forest Drive West*]

2 February 1965[4]

Dear Jimmy,
Please forgive me for not answering before now, and thanking you, it's not easy to write.

Paddy spent one day in London. He stayed with Martin Green and saw nobody.[5] Elizabeth told me.[6] She is marvellous and has a cottage in the country but she has to leave Westbourne Terrace at the end of this week. She wanted very much to know how you are. Apparently she covered the theatre business in September, and spent a nightmare in Grafton Street, the same as Jail, even the children came with her to the theatre, and Cronin's wife roaring through the performance – a general steeplechase across to the nearest pub in the intervals.[7]

The proofs came, wide margins, it seems more attractive than the Barracks. I'll go on Thursday to the memorial lecture for Eliot.[8]

3 McGahern lived at this address with his twin sisters Breege and Rosaleen and their families for a period. The area round this part of London is brought vividly to life in Elizabeth Reegan's memories of London nursing in *The Barracks*, with Leytonstone Road given as the location of Elizabeth's lover Michael Halliday's fatal car crash.

4 McGahern has mistakenly written 1964.

5 Martin Green (1932–2015), English writer and publisher. An important figure among Irish writers in bohemian Soho of the 1950s and 1960s, he co-founded the literary magazine *Nimbus* that helped relaunch the career of Patrick Kavanagh and went on to have a leading role in the publishing houses MacGibbon & Kee and Martin Brian & O'Keefe. He co-wrote with McGahern's friend Tony White *A Guide to London Pubs* (London: Heinemann, 1965), later *The Evening Standard Guide to London Pubs* (London: Pan Books, 1973).

6 Elizabeth Smart.

7 Refers to the Dublin Theatre Festival of September–October 1964.

8 T. S. Eliot died on 4 January 1965. On Thursday 4 February McGahern attended Eliot's memorial service in Westminster Abbey. A copy of the order of service forms part of McGahern's library.

I don't know where we'll go yet. It's strange I find that not having to go to work, and most of the day alone in the streets, that's it's a sense of space and not time that comes.

What's marvellous here is the cheapness of everything after Ireland. One striking price, on my sister's table, a pot of marmalade for 1s 6d. I'd seen the same brand for about 11s 6d in Ireland.

I'll go to Dublin before I go, I'd enjoy to see you very much.

Please remember me with love to your mother and with all good wishes.

John

Faber (TS)

23 Forest Drive West

[*Late February 1965*]

Dear Charles,

Thank you for so many things, the day in Oxford that I loved so much and for your kindness in taking us on the marvellous walk of the colleges; for writing to Greece for us; and for the book that I am reading and that I'll safely return.[9] What strikes me reading it is that all the good travel books that I've read – books with information – are almost always unreadable, the way they are written.

And Anu asks me to thank you terribly much too. And to be remembered to you.

With much love
John

9 Monteith, a Fellow of All Souls College, had taken McGahern and Annikki on a tour of Oxford colleges on Sunday 14 February 1965. Monteith was advising the couple about a possible move to Greece, and had written to a connection in Thassos about setting up accommodation. McGahern thanked Monteith by gifting him a pair of amber cufflinks.

11 March 1965

Dear Michael,

Thank you for your very kind letter, it delighted me, and of course I look forward very much to The Stranger, and wish it and you well.[10]

I was disturbed a long time ago when you said you had to resign over some ugly incident, and I've often wondered since what it was.[11]

Before I left Finland I was married. Annikki – my wife – had to finish contracts – she was a producer in the Kansantheatre – City Theatre – there – and I came here and across Northern Europe alone – but she has come now. And I have to take her to meet my father tomorrow in Ireland.[12] We'll be there two weeks

    Grevisk

    Boyle

–   Co. Roscommon.

Then we'll come back to this address before going on to Spain where we've been offered a house.

Faber publish The Dark here in May. The opening of the novel comes out in the Queen magazine on the 24th of this month.[13] It'll be published later in the year in America by Knopf. I am hoping that it won't be banned in Ireland

10 *The Brightening Day* (1965) originally had a working title of *The Stranger*.

11 Fearing that his work as a school principal at St Thomas's was ruining his health and preventing him from writing, McLaverty took early retirement. See Sophia Hillan King, *The Silken Twine: A Study of the Works of Michael McLaverty* (Dublin: Poolbeg Press, 1992), 223–5.

12 Laaksi recalled this meeting in a 2006 newspaper interview: 'The moment I entered the McGahern family house in Leitrim I sensed the horror and the violence. It was stifling, I could hardly breathe and I refused to stay a second night in the place.' See Isobel Conway, '"A calculating, control freak," claims the first wife of late author John McGahern', *Sunday Independent* (28 May 2006).

13 Founded in 1861 and originally titled *The Queen*, in 1958 the magazine was sold to Jocelyn Stevens who dropped the prefix 'The' and used it as his vehicle to represent the younger side of the British Establishment. Stevens sold *Queen* in 1968. From 1970 the new publication became known as *Harper's & Queen* after a merger of two publications: *Queen* and *Harper's Bazaar UK*, until the name *Queen* was dropped altogether from the masthead. It is now known as *Harper's Bazaar*. The extract from *The Dark* appeared on 24 March 1965.

– it'd make it almost impossible to go back to teach if I want or need to – but it's not a writer's business what happens to any work once it's left his hand.

I hope you are well and that you can write soon.

And please remember me to Mrs McLaverty as I hope too that she is well

John

Alfred A. Knopf, Inc. Records

23 Forest Drive West

12 March 1965

Dear Patrick,

I am not able to tell you how happy I am, and grateful to you, and I feel I've for the first time a publisher in the way Charles Monteith is.[14] I cannot. And there's no use to try.

We go to Ireland today. My father insists he has to meet Anu. And it's easier.[15]

We come back before the 25th March. We've been offered a house in Spain and it's almost certain that we'll go, on the sea, near a Moorish village, Almeria.

Could you take a week from your holidays to come? Break your journey and come and it'd cost hardly anything and then Ireland.

Can you tell me if there's any hope when you write next?

I'll write from Ireland.

Grevisk, Boyle, Co. Roscommon if you need to write urgently.

John

---

14 Gregory had written to McGahern on 9 March 1965 to tell him that *The Dark* had been accepted for publication by Knopf. His reader's report of 19 February 1965 is instructive: 'There are few young novelists of his seriousness, talent and achievement around at the moment – we could back him with confidence.' Knopf, HRC.

15 Whatever awkwardness McGahern had felt kept him away from the family home the previous Christmas had, presumably, passed.

Joe Kennedy

23 Forest Drive West

11 April 1965

Dear Joe,
Thank you for your long letter and I was sorry too that it was the wrong day but the whole going home was too disturbing and I didn't want to stay.

We leave in two weeks. Garrucha/Almeria Spain is where we hope to stay.

6th May is the publication date. Macmillan rejected the book in America, in strangely hysterical language, 'Shocked and dismayed, a thoroughly unpleasant book full of sordid details that make the flesh creep.' Knopf will publish it there now and I am far happier with them.

Faber didn't want to send it to any of the Irish papers except the Times, I am not sure what the situation is now, but it's definitely not going to the Independent for fear of banning movement before publication. What do you think of this? It's Faber business – not mine.

I persuaded them to send you a copy on the excuse that you'd give it advance publicity just before publication but it's really only to get a free copy for you. It should come with your name to the Herald. So will you tell me if it does come. I told them that you had the photos, but do whatever you want to do yourself. Except don't give the copy to anybody and tell nobody.

It'd be ironic if the Independent announced it.[16]
I think there's a good chance that it may not be banned but Faber are much more pessimistic.

Write if you get the copy. The opening of it appeared Queen March 24th and the Sun attacked it on the grounds that it was no reading for the ladies of England.[17] So, so, so –

Will you give my love to Margaret and wish her well from me in July that both she and the child will be well and happy.[18]

16 *The Independent* was McGahern's father's newspaper of choice and generally seen as conservative, leaning politically towards support of the Fine Gael party.
17 *The Dark* was certainly an unusual choice for a high end, glossy magazine such as *Queen*. It came about as a result of John's friendship with the magazine's then literary editor, Elizabeth Smart.
18 Joe Kennedy married Margaret Johnston (1938–2002) in London in 1957. As with Kennedy's first meeting with McGahern, Joe and Margaret had met in Drogheda in the mid-1950s when Kennedy worked for *The Argus* and Margaret for the *Drogheda*

It's a pity that you cannot come over but write about what you think of the business and I'll write more leisurely before I leave. I'll be glad to be out of London soon.

I don't know where I'll live afterwards. The Finnish radio, tv want to make Anu their English representative, so she wants I think to live in London, and she didn't like Dublin.

I'm not sure what'll happen. If the book is banned there may not be much choice.

With all good wishes

John

Patrick Gregory Papers

23 Forest Drive West

[*April 1965*]

Dear Patrick,

If you think it may be too much strain to come, either on money or nervously, I do not want you to: but I'd lunch with Monteith, and he thought that four or five days in Spain would be more relaxation after Dublin/London and before New York than any strain, but I'll leave it so, and hope that you can come. And if there's reasonable prospect I think that you should book the seats, or get me to book them before I leave – about the 28th – and cancel them after if it proves to be impossible.

It's not easy to say about America but I'll try to make clear the situation.

1. I am on leave of absence from the school I used teach in until late September.

2. If the book is banned I'll probably be given permanent leave of absence since the Archbishop is my employer. May the 6th is the publication date. It'll be easier to say after that.

3. I'd like to live for sometime more in Dublin – so if there was no trouble I'd go back to teach – but Anu wants to live here after Spain until we see how possible it remains for us to live together. She disliked Ireland.[19] In

---

Independent, both local newspapers. At the time of this letter's composition, Margaret was pregnant with one of her, ultimately, five children.

19 McGahern liked living in Dublin and was keen to return there. In a letter of 4 June 1965, his great Dublin friend Kevin Lehane writes: 'I am glad to hear that you propose to return but maybe you could let me know your housing requirements. Do you propose to buy or rent or are you interested in flats at the right price.' Madeline McGahern Papers.

London she represents Finnish radio/tv and they want her to be permanent. She translates and adapts now but she may want to go back to the theatre this time next year and I must go on with my own work.

So nothing is clear, except it seems unlikely that I'll go or be able to go, but it'll be easier after May the 6th.

I meant to ask you long before but I didn't like, though I am unsure whether you prefer to be called Patrick or Pat?

It's a lovely Easter, this house is full of building workers, a huge Victorian house of 14 rooms and a long garden with white pear tree and the forsythia and apple bloom in the hedges, and they are all on holiday, and I spend all my time drinking beer with them down in the Three Blackbirds, a dark old coaching inn the same for over 200 years beside the Midland railway, and it is all light and happy, even the drunkenness is frivolous bellylaughing and hearty shouts that bear neither relation to before or after, and middling happy there I often wonder why there's always some ugliness in some way about all literary gatherings and drinkings?[20] And not here for some other reason.

> Love,
> John

Patrick Gregory Papers

23 Forest Drive West

[*April 1965*]

Dear Patrick,

I'll be sorry if you cannot come. Will you think about Barcelona? It's halfway. 90 dollars return London. 2 hours or not much more. I'll book you a pension. And take as much private time to wander alone in the streets or sit at any café you need.

Though if it's too much for your strength do not come.

---

20 In *Amongst Women*, Mark, Maggie Moran's navvy boyfriend, on his first visit to Great Meadow, fantasises about this now-defunct Leytonstone pub during the nightly saying of the Rosary: 'Mark found that as long as he made a show of mouthing the responses he did not have to pay much attention, that he could imagine who was in the Three Blackbirds at this particular moment and what they were drinking' (137). McGahern salvaged a stained-glass window featuring three blackbirds from the pub during a refurbishment and kept it in his Leitrim home.

It rained every day in Ireland. Dublin gave Anu the sense of a city drained of its best talent for whatever that's worth – but sea air sours the Guinness Joyce heard them say.

Murphy came to Roscommon. We spent three days in Cleggan. He was kind and generous but he's finally too barren for more than one evening if he's no business in the air.

I met Kavanagh by chance in a London heatwave.

'Why haven't you your shoes laced or are you tryin to imitate me?'

'They're just cooler that way.'

'I can never lace me shoes. It's the extraordinary wide feet I have. That or wear sandals.'

And much to old tunes. My friends: them bores: myself, and meself, and meself; but he has some style.

The opening of the novel came out in Queen here and I got some money.

I spoke to Charles Monteith about getting rid of the agent and he – for the first time – thought it might be no harm but to wait until after the publication – which is sensible. What do you think?

I'll write in a little time about America, it's hard to know.[21]

Write as soon as you can about the halfway Barcelona. I know cheap places there.

Love,
John

Patrick Gregory Papers

23 Forest Drive West

[*10 April 1965*]

Dear Patrick,

Change the fuck so. It is spelled. And I think what you say is right. There's only one danger I see – of making the same violence in the opposite direction and creating fuzziness; and perhaps the comma is too weak. 'Eff-u-c-kay' What do you think? Will you write and tell me! I'm very grateful; it does enforce the terror more in the real.[22]

21 Gregory was encouraging McGahern to visit the US on a promotional tour, a tour he eventually undertook in February 1966.

22 As at Faber with *The Barracks*, there were worries at Knopf over the use of the word 'fuck' in *The Dark*, where it appears on the opening page. The relevant sentence in the first US edition of *The Dark* reads: 'Eff-u-see-kay is what you said isn't it?' as

I enclose these from the agents. Barcelona as you'll see at night costs less than 80 dollars. 2.45 hours. Valencia less than 90 dollars. 2.10 hours. I can book you a pension for 2 dollars a night.

Whichever attracts you more. I'll be in both of them on my way down. If you can come, I can book you before I leave London, on the flight that is.

I leave in about 3 weeks, not more than that. I hope to be there May to September.

I'll almost certainly leave the agent after the book comes out but I'll let it lie till then.

They're a breed I cannot feel comfortable or easy with.
Write soon if you can,
John
I'll be glad to find out anything else too in London for you.

James Swift
[Madeline McGahern]
[23 Forest Drive West]

[*April 1965*]

Dear Jimmy,
I sent the money by registered letter – if by chance it failed to come tell me before I go so that we can claim – and I was very grateful.

Anu wants to send you this before we go.
There's many marvellous things, especially the beginning, but it's strange how it shows clear that nobody has more than one thing to say.[23]

Garrucha, Almeria, Spain is the address and we'll leave in about two weeks.
6th of May is the publication date.

------

compared to the British first edition (and all subsequent editions): 'F-U-C-K is what you said, isn't it?'
23 Anu had sent on some Kierkegaard, and in a letter of thanks dated 23 April 1965, Jimmy Swift writes: 'It's really too generous of her, but I'm delighted to receive it and am going to enjoy it very much. I have always found him a fascinating & attractive man, much passion & energy, he is immediately stimulating & exciting. As you say he had one thing. A disgust & bitterness drove him on to analyse the situation and his suffering in it, as of course it has so many beautiful men.' Madeline McGahern Papers.

I ran into Jordan, more and more some sort of parish priest, full of imaginary intrigues, and too drunken to be clear:[24] and Kavanagh the same last day:

'Are you takin to imitatin me or what that you're goin around without your laces tied'.

'It's that the day is so hot I'm afraid.'

'I have extraordinary wide feet.'

He started to tell about a man on the crossroads of Mucker displaying his penis for K's inspection and Jordan:

'That was in the Green Fool. And you say it's all lies. I'm catching you out every day.'

'It's Anecdote. And Anecdote is lies. It's not transformed into ART like Tarry Flynn. It's not all lies. And you'd catch me out is it? Catch me out . . . I'd like to see the day when you'd catch me out. Catch me out. Catch me fucking out is it you –'.

There was peace then in order to drive a young painter deeper and deeper into the public embarrassment of his egoism. In the name of the mother.

Write if you can and please remember Anu and me to your mother and thank her for the lovely evening and meal.

John

Seán Brehony Letters

23 Forest Drive West

[Late April 1965]

Dear Sean,

In about a week we leave here and after May the 4th we'll be in Spain.

GARRUCHA, ALMERIA, SPAIN

The book comes out May the 6th and you should have your copy before then and I'll be grateful if you refuse to loan it to anybody.

Perhaps you can scribble a note before we leave.

You are very welcome to come and Rita and I'll be delighted. If you haven't changed your mind about coming I'll write from Garrucha giving Barcelona information when I get there.

24 John Jordan, part of the Dublin literary set, then teaching in UCD. See letter to John Montague [December 1961].

Night flight London to Barcelona is £28 return and taxi from Garrucha–Barcelona is £2 - 5 - 0 single (×4 for both of you to and from).[25]

What I spoke about was EMKO that's used in Scandinavia, and after much trouble I've found out it's available here – Consumers' Association tested it and recommended it and they gave the information – Boots don't stock it in their shops and obviously don't want to sell it but they must order it for you if you ask, within 36 hours.[26]

There's nothing else and with my love to Rita and the children and to you.

John

Joe Kennedy

23 Forest Drive West

27 April 1965

Dear Joe,

Thank you for your kind letter, it's only a note, this, as we leave here tomorrow.

I'm delighted it pleases you, the book.

Perhaps you might be able to get a free or cheap trip out of the Spanish tourist office and come – it's not difficult for a newspaper person if they promise to do some stuff on it – ?

I'll write from there. There's no need to give anything to the Times because they can get the print from Fabers if they want. You should go and have a drink with Tony Lennon, he's librarian there, some evening, he is a nice person and I am sure he would like to meet you.[27]

With good wishes

John

25 The Brehonys did not travel to Spain.
26 Emko is a contraceptive.
27 Tony Lennon was the resident librarian at the *Irish Times* and brother of Peter Lennon who had introduced McGahern and Annikki Laaksi in Paris.

[*May 1965*]

[*Postcard to Patrick Gregory*]
On our way. Anu asks can a second copy be sent of Meri to London (23 Forest Drive West, Leytonstone E 11) as there's only too high a chance it may go astray in Spain, the other copy.[28] Got your letter as we left and news that Panther have bought Barracks and Dark.[29] So left in gladness.

John

James Swift
[*Madeline McGahern*]

Garrucha
Almeria
Spain
[*hereafter Garrucha*]

[*May 1965*]

Dear Jimmy,
We came a long tiresome journey in a shared taxi from Barcelona.

It is very good here: the sea in front, and the barest mountains behind, no grass, grey or red bark, a few parched olive trees, and people going by against the sea sidesaddle on mules.

Yesterday Monteith wrote that the book has been banned, it's disturbing but there's nothing to do, it's unreal there is such distance here. Anu wants to be remembered very much to you and to your mother as I do to her too.

I'll write later

John

---

28 McGahern is referring to his work on *The Manila Rope*, a farcical novel of the Russo-Finnish war by the Finnish writer Veijo Meri (1928–2015). First published in Finnish in 1957 as *Manillaköysi*, the book was published in English, translated by John McGahern and Annikki Laaksi (New York: Alfred A. Knopf, 1967).
29 Panther was then a major British publisher of paperback fiction.

[*May 1965*]

Dear Jimmy,
I was delighted when you wrote, and thank you. Publication is an ugly experience, and I was grateful to be able to be out of England. It's already got more reviews than Barracks, I was glad of the protection they gave because of the trouble, and the most unfavourable out of 40–50 was Cronin in the T.L.S., a week later.[30]
  Also a strange shower of letters, mostly stupid, by way of Faber.
I enclose two letters that came within days of each other, from Higgins, that might interest you: either destroy them or return them.[31] If it's possible to follow the why they'd be interesting.
  Do you think you'll go on any holiday this year? I began to write, a nonsense study, but this violent light here and the stream of reviews and letters from people I don't know make it even more difficult.
  Can you remember me to Tony? And with much love and respect to your mother.

    John

30 Anthony Cronin's anonymous review of *The Dark*, titled 'Swotting out of the Farm', was published in the *Times Literary Supplement* on Thursday 13 May 1965. Among the charges laid at the novel's door were the following: 'writing perhaps a little less considered than one has a right to expect from so serious an artist'; 'the novel is slightly too repetitive about everything'; 'a failure to infuse any real individual character into the hero'.
31 Jimmy Swift replies on 15 June regarding the Brian Higgins letters: 'He seems determined at being very friendly with you although his tone in regards to your work is still rather patronising. His elaborate directions and recommendations for Malaga are amusing seeing that you are not there.' Madeline McGahern Papers.

19 May 1965

Dear Charles,

Thank you for your terribly kind letter, and the newspapers, I was more disturbed than I could have known by the seizing. It was fortunate that the reviews were favourable, or I'd have no protection, I don't know what'll happen as it is if I go back.[32] Can you send a copy to Anu on my account, and I'll be grateful.

It's a lovely house, by the sea, with a burnt mountain at the back, a few stunted olives and bread trees and small goats on the eroding rock. All kinds of meat and milk or butter are expensive; but there are marvellous fish and artichokes and wines and small peaches for almost nothing. It's a pity that you cannot come. Always there's the sun, and a walled balcony with geraniums and deckchairs on the roof.

I have to thank you again too for the kindness and consideration you showed me ever since I first sent you The Dark, and how much I value it within my own quiet that's impossible to communicate.

> With much love
>
> John

I thought the Observer was a rather puerile piece of vulgarity but I suppose what does it matter.[33]

---

32 On 10 May Monteith had written to McGahern in Spain: 'THE DARK has been launched with quite a bang – as you'll see from the enclosed clippings. Excellent reviews so far – I do congratulate you on them – but also, I fear, trouble on the far side of the Irish Sea. It's very unusual, I gather, for the Irish customs actually to seize a book before it has been put on sale at all but this is what has happened to THE DARK – and we may have to wait a bit (perhaps a month or two) before the censorship board give their decision about it. But the whole thing is becoming quite a cause celebre. Quite apart from this Observer cutting there have been stories in the Daily Telegraph and, I believe, one or two other papers which I haven't so far seen; and I imagine that there will be quite a bit in the Irish papers. Your friend Murray Mindlin is of course very interested and I imagine Censorship will be taking the case up in a big way. By a happy coincidence, too, Olivia Manning – who wrote that very good review in the Spectator – is in Dublin at the moment and she is determined to do all she can.'
33 John Coleman reviewed *The Dark* for *The Observer* on 9 May 1965. It is difficult to see what so irked McGahern in this piece other than its brevity as the reviewer is

Anu sends her love to you.

[*unsigned*]

Patrick Gregory Papers (TS)

Garrucha

20 May 1965

Dear Patrick,

Thank you for writing, it came today, and I feel I cannot face America, but I'd prefer to speak with you first if it's not too late when you come, and then say finally. If it's too late I feel it'd be honester to say now that I will not come.

Yesterday, Friday, Charles Monteith wrote enclosing some extraordinary reviews, and the news of the seizure in Ireland, I was not taken unawares, but it was strange how sickening the certain knowledge was, and the sense of disgrace, my uncle at his petrol pumps and other sentimentalities and lunacies filling my brain.

Whether it'll be possible to go back to live in Dublin or not is the worst.

The sea washes to the door, and a burned mountain with a few olive trees and bread trees in the rock and scraggy strong lavender between those few trees behind, and you can stay here, it's a rather lovely house, and it'll be our delight to see you here, but can you write about the exact flight as soon as you know.

It's probably easier to keep the top address for a time, it's the nearer village. Though a dangerous roundabout on the side of the mountain, the post circling in around five side-saddle on a great mule. Charles said you were lunching with him on the 21st of June.

I hope you can write soon about the coming as I'll worry and if you think Valencia and the taxi suit you, they do not seem expensive, and they save time above all; and the road along the sea and through the orange and lemon fields from Valencia to here more than worth looking at and forgive the bad typing.

John

---

enthusiastic from the start: 'The Dark, John McGahern's second novel, fully lives up to the enthusiasm generated by "The Barracks".'

[*31 May 1965*]

Dear Michael,

Thank you for your very kind letter, I am more glad than I can say that the Dark pleased you.[34] I was in a nervous condition before I left, and afraid to send you a copy. Cecil Scott's reaction was so violent that I was afraid, so if you'd consent I'd like to give you [*a*] copy of the Knopf edition when it comes. Can you tell me when your book, The Stranger, will be published? I am looking forward to it so very much.

We live in a white house by the sea, a burnt range of mountains behind; Mojacar a Moorish village in the mountains and Garrucha, a little port 5 miles away, our two villages, it is very cheap to live, beautiful in a stark Sahara way, always the sunshine.

I write little, battering to little effect at a story but I find it always impossible to work for a long time after a book.

I read a good book by Primo Levi, The Truce, an Italian Jew, who possibly wrote a great book If This is a Man: and a very powerful novel by Henri de Montherlant Chaos and Night.[35]

I wonder if I'll be allowed back to the school because of the censorship trouble.

Are you well? And Mrs McLaverty? Did you ever contemplate coming to Spain on holiday?

The worst review of the Dark was by a Dublin public house oracle, Anthony Cronin, in the TLS.

---

34 In a letter dated 23 May, McLaverty had praised *The Dark* for its 'painful sincerity and its pared-to-the-bone style' but admitted that he had 'recoiled from one or two pages (a priest's thoughts) and wished they hadn't been there'. See Killen (ed.), *Dear Mr McLaverty*, 39.

35 McGahern's admiration for both Levi and de Montherlant persisted. *Chaos and Night* (*Le Chaos et la nuit*) was first published in English in 1964 by Weidenfeld & Nicolson. The novel's central character, Celestino Marcilla, is a disgruntled anarchist veteran of the Spanish Civil War living in exile in Paris. In his frustrated relationship with his daughter and with the world he bears a strong resemblance to McGahern's Moran of *Amongst Women*, and is described at one point as 'a pathetic King Lear'. See Henri de Montherlant, *Chaos and Night*, trans. Terence Kilmartin, int. Peter Quennell (London: Penguin, 1966), 125.

Thank you so much for your kindness to write and my good wishes as always to you and to Mrs McLaverty

John

Faber

Garrucha

31 May 1965

Dear Charles,

Thank you so much for writing to me, and for the cuttings.[36]

I imagine the censors think not too well of the customs by this, their zeal: for they're in an awkward position – whether to ban or unban.

The attack in the T.L.S. was written by a McDaid's – Dublin – writer called Cronin.

Sometime, can you tell me generally how the <u>Dark</u> has gone compared to the <u>Barracks</u>.[37]

I know a writer who lives in Paris, he's a Cambridge graduate, he's been completing the Olympia Press translation of De Sade, and he's written a novel that's been accepted by an American paperback for publication, but so far it's failed to find a British publisher. The novel was outside my sympathies, but it was clever, seemed heavily influenced by Beckett, and I wondered if it'd interest you to read for publication or, if you saw promise in it, an offer to read his next work (he is 25).[38]

I think Patrick Gregory is coming here on the 24th of June.

Anu sends her warmest regards and with much love

John

36 On 26 May Monteith had written to McGahern: 'the brouhaha in Ireland goes on; and as you'll see from the enclosed bundle of clippings, the Irish Times, at any rate, is taking a very pro-McGahern stand! That editorial, incidentally, was written by Terence de Vere White – as was the Irish Times review.'

37 Monteith replied to this question on 10 June: 'If the ban is lifted sales in Ireland should certainly be very good indeed; but in the meantime we seem to have sold over here about 18 or 19 hundred copies; and it's still going on fairly steadily. As I think I've already mentioned, we've ordered a reprint – the best of proof, I think, that we anticipate a continuing sale!'

38 Possibly Pieralessandro Casavini (Austryn Wainhouse) (1927–2014) who translated de Sade for the Olympia Press.

[*June 1965*]

Dear Joe,
Thank you for your letter, and the cuttings, though most of them had come, every day a load of them comes, the only realization is that they don't exist as maybe we ourselves don't.

I am troubled that you should be disturbed by the Observer business etc. I told Faber that I'd rather go away but if they needed me I'd stay. They said go away.

Observer rang Faber for personal information. They refused. They rang Peter Lennon in Paris. He gave it and he wrote that he was disturbed by the vulgar way they used it. As far as I can see the personal information in Irish Press [*illegible*] was based on the Observer. It also is inaccurate. We are 250 miles from Malaga.[39]

We'll come back in September if it's possible. I may read in Queens in November.[40]

I don't know who initiated the E. Press business but if you wish I'll be only too happy to steal a march on them when I come in September. That I'll answer any kind of question you want to ask honestly.

Delahunty wrote a very kind letter by way of Faber and I wrote to thank him.[41]

There's a film actress, a friend of Anu coming in a few weeks, and we both are looking forward very much to going down by way of Granada to meet her in Malaga, and bring her here. Please forgive pencil. Ink and biros have run out and I hate the typewriter.

John

39 *The Observer* and the *Irish Press* both referred to McGahern being resident in Spain.
40 McGahern did not read at Queen's University Belfast until November 1967 as part of the Belfast Festival.
41 Presumably James Delehanty (1911–94), editor of the *Kilkenny Magazine* (1960–70).

Faber

Garrucha

10 June 1965

Dear Rosemary,

I wanted to wait before writing since you know it here. The house is five miles south of Garrucha: nearly two miles on from where you turn into the mountains to Garrucha, and we find it as beautiful as you did.

I walk sometimes across the mountains into Garrucha, and Anu came once, and got fever. She's not been lucky: a scorpion bit her, lying under shoes. I'd to pour the coffee water over another one sitting in the sink. Now we've scorched all around the house with a powerful d.d.t. called S.E.X.

Roads tarred, except the one to Carboneras, and the scooter has done wonderfully, but the climb into Garrucha is a bit of a wall of death.

We get lovely cheap fish from the boats in Garrucha, and today a huge melon for 20 pasetas in the market. I go to the fountain in Garrucha, it is very beautiful, garlanded with violet leaves, I think Bougainville.

Sunday we go to Almeria for a few days and then Patrick Gregory comes. I am looking forward to his coming very much.

It was a real rumpus in Ireland and it doesn't seem very possible that I'll be going back to Dublin in September.

Do you keep well and I hope you can write something.

Anu wants to be remembered very much to you
Love
John

Patrick Gregory Papers

Garrucha

16 June 1965

Dear Patrick,

Do you have any objection to riding on a scooter? That's our means of transport between the villages, there are buses then.

1. No matter what happens I'll meet you at the airport.

2. We can bus to Murcia (265k), change and bus to Vera (103k) and scooter here (16k).

3. Scooter from Murcia after bus there from Valencia.

4. Scooter all the way.

5. The taxi.

6. Meet you at the airport and stay in that city with you, which I proposed in the beginning, the only reason that it'd take two heavy days travel off your back, though it's much nicer if you can come here, but do you enjoy travelling? In that case Barcelona is a more attractive city than Valencia.

Write soon but I'll meet you at the airport, whatever you decide, and I hope you can come here.[42]

John

Brian Friel Papers

Garrucha

3 July 1965[43]

Dear Mr Friel,[44]

Thank you for your kind and very generous letter and I was delighted that The Dark pleases you.

I am ashamed that I've never read your real work and I can only hope I am able to find A Saucer of Larks when I get to London.[45]

Until the end of August we'll stay here and where then I do not know. I was to go back to the school in Dublin in September but I am not sure if that's now possible.

I was very glad to hear that Faber are to do your play, and I hope you'll be as happy with them as I am: when I was in Helsinki last November–October

42 Gregory visited from 24 to 29 June.

43 This is the first letter from McGahern in the Brian Friel Papers, National Library of Ireland, MS 37,259.

44 Brian Friel (1929–2015) was an Irish playwright, born in Omagh, Co. Tyrone before moving with his family to Derry, aged ten. He attended St Columb's College, Derry before studying to be a Catholic priest at Maynooth. He stopped short of ordination and worked as a teacher before establishing himself as a writer of both short stories and plays in the 1960s. He went on to become one of Ireland's most distinguished playwrights, best known for works such as *Translations* and *Dancing at Lughnasa*, the former play being the first staged by the Field Day Theatre Company, co-established by Friel in 1980.

45 *The Saucer of Larks* was a collection of short stories by Friel published in the UK in 1962 by Victor Gollancz and in the USA by Doubleday.

it appeared in the newspapers there as the only interesting play of the Dublin Festival.[46]

I may be in Belfast in November or if I am in Dublin before then I'd be very glad if you called.

Very sincerely,
John McGahern

The Review Correspondence[47]

Garrucha

14 July 1965

Dear Mr Hamilton,[48]

Thank you for your kind letter, and I'd be very glad to go to Cheltenham.[49] The one thing is that while I am fairly certain I can attend I cannot be absolutely so until the end of this month. Is this too late for me?

I am sorry I have no photograph here but Faber will gladly give one and the autobiographical lines if the end of the month's not too late.

Yours Sincerely
John McGahern

46 *Philadelphia, Here I Come!* was Friel's breakthrough play, having been first performed to great acclaim at the Dublin Theatre Festival in September 1964. It was published by Faber in 1965, the beginning of a long relationship between playwright and publisher.

47 *The Review* was a literary magazine with Ian Hamilton as its driving force. It ran from 1962 to 1972 and was replaced in 1974 by the glossier *New Review*.

48 Ian Hamilton (1938–2001) was a Norfolk-born poet, critic, editor and literary scholar; he was poetry and fiction editor at the *Times Literary Supplement* from 1965 to 1973. Hamilton published McGahern's short stories in both *The Review* (1962–72) and the *New Review* (1974–9) and was one of McGahern's earliest and most important British champions. Hamilton's passion for Tottenham Hotspur FC was increasingly shared by McGahern and they regularly attended games together.

49 Established in 1949, and run over several days each autumn, the Cheltenham Literature Festival is one of the oldest continuous literary festivals in the world. In the period when this letter was written Hamilton was working as its director.

20 July 1965

Dear Sean,

I am sorry that you cannot come but I know that it could not have been easy.

Recovering from crash: jar came loose on the back of the Vespa: swung it down on the rocks from a kind of rutted dirt track: both of us badly shaken: Anu had to get six stitches around the eye: fucking machine fell on top of me: black, white and blue.[50]

Publisher here and gone. We both liked him very much, quiet and hardly American. They want me to go to America in February but I do not know what the School will do. No notice of sacking came yet.

One thing worries me. The accountant I have – Quin Westland Row – has done nothing and bills come from the income tax. He says to send them to him and then he does nothing. I wish he'd make something out so I could get rid of him.

The notion of Butlin's horrifies me a bit though with children escape from work is holiday.

If you are in Skerries would you like to call to see my sister? I am sure she'd be glad. Monica Gilligan. Hoar Rock. She is very intelligent and charming.

Do you have any word of transfer? I hope you'll be gone before October.[51]

I'll be very glad if you can write. Do you have news of Joe Beirne? Is his cousin better now?

> With love to Rita and the children.
> John

---

50 A fictionalised version of this crash features large in McGahern's short story 'Peaches'.
51 Brehony shortly got transferred from Dublin to Galway where he spent the rest of his life.

27 July 1965

Dear Charles,

I am delighted that you're well, and had such a happy rest in Ireland, because I was disturbed when Patrick Gregory told me you'd to enter hospital.

The appeal failure is bad, the whole business, but it doesn't surprise me, it got very much publicity, and, with the Irish system, from the Customs up, once any move becomes public, to revoke something amounts to one part of the machinery betraying another part of it <u>in public</u> and that's never done. I am grateful for all your care, and sorry that you'd so much trouble. I hope too that the reprinting doesn't lose you money over the appeal rejection.[52]

I am terribly glad you liked Patrick. What kind of place is the Kildare Street Club?[53] My sister wrote me a very cruel account of Richard's recent visit to my father.

Worse and worse news. The Vespa crashed. A wine jar came loose on the back, swung it down on rocks, when it swung the small wheels would [*not*] grip in the sand. The curse is that Anu'd have completely escaped except the mirror smashed on her eye, several stitches, such a curse, my own bones groaning all over after 3 weeks. I cannot think about it yet. We'd have been killed only for going slow.

> With much love
> John

I had just a letter from Dr Roger McHugh, who holds the Chair of English in U.C.D, offering to give evidence in favour of the Dark but that's too late now.

---

52 Monteith had written to McGahern on 20 July: 'We've just had the very sad news – via Easons of Dublin – that the Appeals Board has rejected our plea for THE DARK; and I don't think – though I haven't been into the position yet – that there's anything else we can do at the moment. It may well be, though – indeed I shall be very surprised if this doesn't happen – that in a year or two, or later, this decision may be reversed. In the meantime, though, we shan't be able to sell THE DARK in the Irish Republic.'
53 On 17 July 1965 Monteith dined in the elite Kildare Street Club with Patrick Gregory and Terence de Vere White, literary editor of the *Irish Times*.

30 July 1965

Dear Mr Friel,
Thank you for your letter and terribly kind offer.[54] I am very moved. What I plan to do is to go back to my place in early October in Dublin. I am on leave of absence. The Appeal Board have now rejected the Faber plea to revoke the ban. So I may get sacked. I intend to return as if nothing had happened and I have no other plans. I am anxious to live in Dublin for some more years if I can. If that's not possible I think I'll go to London.

I often heard my father say that your part of Donegal is very beautiful.[55]

I may go to Belfast to read in November.

When does your play go on in London? I'll be there through some of September. Nearly all my family are married in London.

I hope you are very happy in Donegal and with kindest regards to your wife and children.

John McGahern

1 August 1965

Dear Patrick,
Thank you very much for your letter, and Anu sends her thanks too. You cannot know how much pleasure your coming gave us.

My sister wrote a very cruel account of Murphy's antics in the house, she said you were quiet throughout.[56]

54 It would seem that Friel offered McGahern the use of a Donegal cottage to lie low in the wake of the controversy created by the banning of *The Dark*.
55 This letter was redirected from 13 Marlborough Street, Derry to Ballymanus, Kincasslagh, Co. Donegal. Frank McGahern served as a garda sergeant in Co. Donegal from 1927 to 1932 with periods in Buncrana, Burtonport, Ardara and Bundoran.
56 Gregory wrote to McGahern on 26 July 1965: 'on our trip to pick up Charles, Murphy took me to see the ruins of that great estate outside Boyle. We drove by your father's house. He was in the garden and Murphy stopped the car. I didn't particularly

I was terribly glad you liked Charles Monteith.[57] Even more so Kevin Lehane, he is my oldest friend.[58]

Fierce hot now, same as a sauna bath about noon. We'll leave at the end of August.

Did you see anything of the Daids? What has happened about the Meri? If I am able I'd be glad to do it, if it's to pay back a little of what I owe to translations.

Can you tell me when you need a decision about the American earnings?

---

want to meet with him without you – especially when I noticed how nervous Murphy was (he started out the car, then returned to put on a necktie!), but the stop had been made and there was no turning back. Your stepmother invited us in to tea and a painful silence ensued. No mention was made of the book (I was introduced by Murphy as "a Gregory" (or was it "the Gregory"?) "from Coole", and that was all. Your beautiful red-haired sister was there, and her presence was a great consolation in my troubled state. When we left, she walked with me to the gate. I had the distinct impression that she wanted to ask after you (she knew that I had visited you both in Spain), but she remained silent.' Knopf, HRC.

57 Gregory's letter to McGahern of 26 July 1965 continued: 'I won't narrate my travels and discoveries. Let me just tell you that Murphy and I picked up Charles Monteith at his home across the border and carried him back to Cleggan with us. He's a good man, and I am pleased to know him. I saw him again in Dublin the night before my return to the States. Charles and myself were invited to dine at the Kildare Club as the guests of de Vere White, and we had a fine evening together drinking brandy and talking about your book (among other cheerful and edifying topics). I would like to think of the three of us as the founding fathers of the John McGahern Fan Club.'

58 Kevin Lehane (1921–2002) worked at various Dublin cinemas and was one of McGahern's three closest friends in Dublin of the late 1950s and early 1960s along with Tom Jordan and Jimmy Swift. Gregory writes to John of his encounter with Lehane and his membership of the John McGahern Fan Club: 'An associate member of that august body is certainly Kevin Lehane. He was splendid. I called at the theater at 10 in the morning two days before my departure. Although he was on duty all that day, and free only from 7 to 9 at night, we agreed to meet for a pint before his night duty commenced. We had a pint, then another, and Tony Lennen (of the Irish Times) joined us. Kevin, realizing that the jig was up, phoned the theater and told them that he wouldn't be there that evening. We drank on until closing time – changing pubs from time to time, in lieu of the "sightseeing" tour that Kevin felt he should be offering me. He phoned me up the next morning, and in spite of his delicate condition (he has ulcers or something and really shouldn't drink at all) bravely invited me to lunch. When I return to Dublin I shall try to take better advantage of his knowledge of the city.' Knopf, HRC. McGahern reviewed Lehane's book on Dublin street life – written under the pseudonym Tom Corkery – in the Sunday Independent (4 January 1981). See LOTW, 302–4.

Shuck – still, but better, Anu too, this time I'll write no more. Anu sends her love. Does your life go any well?

John

Michael McLaverty Archive

c/o J. Vinas Campi
Consejo De Ciento 183
Barcelona

8 August 1965

Dear Michael,
Your letter came today, I'd sent a card that obviously crossed, we leave tomorrow, we'd a Vespa accident. So I am happy for my own sake that you cannot come.

We'll go in easy stages, Almeria Granada Madrid Zaragoza Barcelona Paris the vague route.

If you'd like to airmail the <u>Brightening Day</u> to the above address, it'd be something to look forward to for me in Barcelona. I'll be there for some days in about two weeks. I'd be terribly grateful and happy.[59]

I am going at the end of September to Cheltenham Festival of Literature – they pay my way from here there and on to Dublin, and they say I have nothing to do but be present in Cheltenham that week, it sounds almost too good to believe.

I'll leave Anu with my sister in London and go back to the National School in October. The Appeal Board have rejected the plea for <u>The Dark</u>. I may be asked to leave. I don't see any other alternative than to go to London then. What disturbs me very much is that the book's a religious work if it's anything at all.

The rejection by the Appeal Board means that the case is closed in Ireland.

Fishing is one of my oldest loves, I miss it here, but my sister is fanatical, she writes me long letters, and apparently it's been the best season she remembers.[60] What do you catch at Strangford?

59 McLaverty's novel was published by Macmillan, New York in 1965. McGahern thought it very poor fare, an opinion he could not hide from McLaverty. See letter to Sophia Hillan of 19 January 1991.
60 McGahern's sister Margaret (1937–2019) loved to fish and frequently took a boat out on the river at home in Cootehall with John.

Do you know Fiacc???[61] He wrote me a strange letter.
I hope I'll see you soon.
Kindest regards to you and Mrs McLaverty

John

Please forgive this terrible hand but I find it hard to write because of stiffness.

Patrick Gregory Papers

23 Forest Drive West

9 September 1965

Dear Patrick,

We reached here on the 5th, after a few miserable days in Paris in endless rain. One amusing business: the Spanish EXPRESS was an hour late for its connection to Paris at the frontier: the passport people couldn't be found: so we spent a day in the middle of the Pyrenees, waiting for the next train – rain, rich aftergrass there, blocked and overgrown streams and drains, very much as Ireland.

The Meri came. Anu is translating a chapter. I've seen some pages. And I think it'll be very amusing to translate.

I'll send you the translated chapter in a week or two. So you'll decide whether we'll finish it or not.

Anu has read it. She still likes it. She says that the main thing wrong with it is that there are too many digressions for such a short book (apparently in all his work there are endless tales) and because of this looseness it hasn't the power a clearer shape would give it.

Monteith is on holiday in Greece. A letter from Murphy with a poem about Casement.[62] He can't get the site for his house, so he's choosing [*illegible*] with green stone, overlooking the sea etc.[63] He was full of his American plans too.

I'll stay here until the 4th of October, then go to Dublin by way of Cheltenham. Anu will follow later if it's possible or easy to live in Dublin.

---

61 Padraic Fiacc (1924–2019), Belfast-born poet. Originally Patrick Joseph O'Connor.

62 Part 4 of what became Murphy's epic of Irish history, *The Battle of Aughrim* (London: Faber, 1968), focused on Roger Casement.

63 Murphy was making plans for the construction of a house in Cleggan, Co. Galway.

I wrote to the agent to ask him to write to Matson that I no longer needed him. He's refused to do so until he sees me. In about a week. I don't know what he'll try to use. Apparently Matson & Peters have formed themselves into a third combine to press translations. I suppose I can only wait and see. What do you think?

Are you well? Will you write to me soon? I'll be waiting for it very much. Anu sends you her love as I do.

John

Patrick Gregory Papers

23 Forest Drive West

2 October 1965

Dear Patrick,

I enclose a second chapter. I am sorry it's not typed – Anu is in Paris – I am in Cheltenham 4th–9th – then Dublin – and an agency would waste a week. Anu has left translation of a middle chapter. I'll do that in Cheltenham, or most of it, and send it. I've tried to make it as legible as possible.

1. I have to insist that this is a rough (as the first chapter). I've not the time to check several terms (military etc.)

2. I have no objection to the editing out of the Irishism, especially if we can improve the translation.[64]

3. If it's published I'd depend on you to check any offences so that they'd not get through. I have no experience in the world of translation.

4. Anu tells me to tell you that the dialogue is not normal speech, it's countryside and awkward and a little exotic [I know this is no use in a translation which should appear natural in its own language and world].

5. If it has to be vetted by Heinemann it must go as a draft version, a rough.

I am supposed to go to teach in Dublin on the 11th. Much rumbles of dismissal, on [*illegible*] far no notice. It won't be easy on the nerves going back.

Anu stays in Paris until things are clear, she has Platonov to translate for her old theatre.[65]

---

64 The translation is replete with Hiberno-English words and expressions such as 'arseways', 'banjaxed' and 'looderamawn'.

65 English title given to Anton Chekhov's first play (1878). The play was, in the mid-1960s, enjoying something of a revival with Faber publishing a version in 1964 translated by David Magarshack.

What is Kinsella doing in America? I liked him very much the twice I met him.[66]

I'd a card from Murphy today. No time. Address is America. No time maybe to write me. Sister engaged to somebody waiting for somebody to die to become a peer.

There's a rather lovely end to that second chapter.

Why don't you write me something about yourself?

Can you send me any of your father's translations?[67]

John

Maybe it might read better if it was typed. Write. This is best address.

Patrick Gregory Papers

23 Forest Drive West

17 October 1965[68]

Dear Patrick,

It's a long and mostly boring story, I'll try to shorten it.

The 8th May telegrammed to phone them, it was to tell me not to come. I didn't telephone and presented myself for work. They were very afraid, the teachers. The headmaster read me a note that I was suspended until the priest interviewed me, this would have to be after the 6th of November, end of his holidays. I then saw the Union: they were willing to fight sacking on the grounds of DARK; but not on a civil marriage.

I do not think I could go through the farce of a ceremony, cage Anu here, bow my head, work humbly for them; and live with myself, and work with myself.

Anu doesn't want to go through with it either, and she doesn't want to live in Dublin, which I want, but it seems impossible, it seems it must be the woman's land of London.

---

66 Thomas Kinsella spent long periods teaching in American universities, most notably at Southern Illinois University, Carbondale from 1965 to 1970 and subsequently at Temple University in Philadelphia.

67 Patrick Gregory's father was Horace Gregory, a poet, critic and translator. He was a professor of English at Sarah Lawrence College from 1934 to 1960. His best-known translation is of Ovid's *Metamorphoses* (New York: Viking Press, 1958). He became a firm admirer of McGahern's work.

68 This letter was posted in Dublin.

So I meet Anu in London tomorrow. We'll decide over the days what to do. I'll then go to see the priest after November the 6th and probably get sacked.

Nothing now can affect my work, it grows only more clear, this journey into my changing self, in search of style. But physically and financially it cannot be as easy in London as it was, but that only lies down beside the first.

23 Forest Drive West, Leytonstone, London E. 11 will be the safest address for the next few days.

I hope the translations (2 envelopes) reached you safely.

It looks almost certain now that I can go to New York next Spring if you want me to.

Lehane in the Capitol spoke very warmly about you here.[69] He finds Lennon though a nuisance, which I would too if I saw him.[70]

With all good wishes,

John

Patrick Gregory Papers

Leytonstone
London E. 11

25 October 1965

Dear Patrick,

Anu has come back here too. I'll go to see the priest in about two weeks. We are wondering what to do, searching how easy it'd be to survive here.

What the priest may present us with is the choice of getting married in the church or getting sacked. I doubt if I am able to go through with it. Also whether it'd be as possible in the school as before the Dark (a protest is already organized and waiting). Anu couldn't ever hope for any work beyond translations in Dublin. She didn't like it either. On the other side the Dublin I love, the scarcity of sufficient money for very few hours. We mull and mull but it seems it must be London.

As well there may be no choice. Anu says to thank you, that you are her dearest friend, she'd wash as well as cook: but she'll hardly come because of the airfare, and in the summer she wants to go to Finland.

I can get no work done, battering for months now at a single few pages.

69 Kevin Lehane moved between various Dublin cinemas in his work, the Capitol being one of those.
70 Probably Peter Lennon.

Write as soon as you can.
  What do you think of the business?
                John

P.S.
1. What you say about America I agree with.
2. In Cheltenham I met a poet, Michael Hamburger, some of his poems real ones, and he showed me a book of criticism just published in England that was good and sane; he said some woman scout was interested in it, on behalf of Knopf, in England; do you know anything about it?[71]
3. Saw an extraordinary film Nazarin by Bunuel.[72]

Patrick Gregory Papers

23 Forest Drive West

1 November 1965

Dear Patrick,
Thank you for writing about this business. I am in total agreement with what you say. The one trouble is that it seems to me that I'll lose no matter what happens: and also that I'll gain. And I'm almost fatalistic, that it hardly matters what way the priest or myself hop.

The question doesn't even depend on my ability to teach. It's the civil marriage. And the thing finishes on this: that I do not think I am able to go through with a religious ceremony. Even if I did, it would not be the same to teach there again, because of the DARK, and Anu – that was clear when I went back. I'll miss Dublin, a few friends.

71 Michael Hamburger (1924–2007) was a German-born British translator, poet, critic and scholar. The book of criticism may be *From Prophecy to Exorcism: The Premises of Modern German Literature* (London: Longmans, 1965). McGahern became friendly with Hamburger and wrote a number of postcards and letters to him, beginning August 1966.
72 *Nazarín* is a 1959 Mexican film directed by Luis Buñuel that follows the travails of Fr Padre Nazario as he tries to help the impoverished and downtrodden he encounters.

BBC television are doing a documentary about Barracks and Dark in January that will give some money.[73] I imagine it'd be best to go very early in February – 3rd or 4th.

I've been making some enquiries. Teaching here is a fairly terrible prospect. I have a good chance of getting an easy job on television, either in research, or assistant to a producer. We desperately need to get some rooms of our own.

I thought Hamburger's criticism sane, academic and not exciting, but I'm afraid I find ordinary sanity in criticism. I see almost exciting, positively so compared to some of the fashionable rubbish.

Write soon if you can. Anu sends you her best and kindest wishes.

As always,
John

Patrick Gregory Papers
[Dublin]

12 November 1965

Dear Patrick,

I saw the priest last night. 'That was an awful shemozzle that book made, put your foot right into it. I couldn't take you back, there'd be uproar, teaching, what are you going to do for yourself now?'

It turned out later that the command came from Archbishop.

I see the Union today. It's only a formality. I'll go to Roscommon. Then back to London. I am free to go to New York in February if it's possible to get the readings.[74]

Lehane remembers you with warmth.
I'll write from London
John

---

73 'The Dead Days', a half-hour film that was aired on BBC2 on 12 May 1966, was produced by Melvyn Bragg b. 1939 and directed by Tristram Powell b. 1940, son of the novelist Anthony Powell (1905–2000). The film was described in the *Radio Times* as follows: 'One writes about the dead days, the days that were your life, and fill you with emptiness, the places that you have known and loved, and where your imagination is in some way or other. A film about a young Irish novelist John McGahern who has just arrived in London, and whose latest book, *The Dark*, has recently been published in America and banned in Ireland.' See *Radio Times*, Issue 2217 (5 May 1966), 49. McGahern was paid 150 guineas for his involvement, plus expenses.

74 McGahern visited the United States for the first time from 7 to 28 February 1966 to coincide with the publication of *The Dark* by Knopf on 14 February. Patrick Gregory

22 November 1965

Dear Michael,

I am sorry not to have written and this is only to explain that I've been unsettled, in Ireland twice to end my affairs, and in Roscommon to see my father this last time.

I found myself suspended, without any notice, when I returned, informed by the Principal, the Manager on his holidays, and I'd to come back to be interviewed and dismissed when the good man's holiday was at an end. It came out the decision was John Charles's.[75]

As you know the Union is a paper tiger, the Church has all the power, and they'd have given me a little money to go quietly, but I refused, so the case is in their hands now, I've promised not to give the case to the press till the Union goes over the ground.

The whole business reminds me of the more savage pieces of Carleton.[76] But let it be.

We're to find some flat here, and this time of year it's a depressing prospect.

I'll probably take some temporary business till Christmas: then I go back to Ireland in January, in an advisory capacity, on a BBC short film about the world of my work, it's imagery, but they give me some money for pointing out a few trees I love etc. It might be possible to keep it simple, in the beginning was the image.

---

wrote to William Jay Smith, Department of English, Hollins College, Virginia on 7 February 1966, trying to secure a reading engagement for McGahern and pointing out that he already had two confirmed such events, at the Rockefeller Institute, New York on the 8th and at Boston University on the 17th. He describes McGahern as 'no roaring-boy of the Behan, professional-Irish clan, but a serious, dedicated, and quite original artist'. Knopf, HRC.

75 John Charles McQuaid (1895–1973), the Catholic Archbishop of Dublin and Primate of Ireland between December 1940 and January 1972. He was known for his strict conservatism.

76 William Carleton (1794–1869), a Tyrone-born writer best known for his *Traits and Stories of the Irish Peasantry* (Dublin: Curry, 1830). Born Catholic, he converted to Anglicanism and was critical of the Church of his birth. McGahern may be thinking here of a story like 'The Lough Derg Pilgrim' (1828) in which the Catholic Church is portrayed as primitive and grasping.

Knopf want me to go to America in February for the <u>Dark</u>, I'm not certain yet. American Universities want my manuscripts: and I may be able to get a life annuity from one in return for all my mss. Which'd save me going back to teach or some other rubbish.

Are you well? And Mrs McLaverty? Are you able to work?

I hope you'll forgive me such long silence.

Love

John

Patrick Gregory Papers

23 Forest Drive West

29 November 1965

Dear Patrick,

You can practically take it for certain that I will be free to come in February.

I'll ask the Boston, but it may be better to wait to see what response he makes to my letter. I enclose his letter.

No lodgings, getting desperate. Christmas so near makes it worse. Apparently the best way is get £1,000, get a loan then, and buy a house. It works that you've a house then for the price of a flat. I've made a tentative approach to Faber: that they might advance me the initial on the understanding that they get all my earnings until it was cleared off.

Impossible to work here, last Saturday a gentleman imagined the wardrobe was the toilet, got in, closed the door, pissed on the clothes, went to sleep, woke the whole house close to morning imagining he'd woken up in the grave or hell or somewhere, stark naked too when he was rescued.

I've finished the story you saw and put on the right road in Spain, <u>Why We're Here</u>, it's hard and good, I don't want to publish, I'll send you a copy.[77] That's all I've written.

I'm sorry to trouble you with all these letters and take your time away answering.

John

[77] 'Why We're Here' was first published in Ian Hamilton's *The Review* (April 1968), and was collected in *Nightlines*.

29 November 1965

Dear Charles,
Thank you and Rosemary and Eliza for the lovely lunch and day.

I was disturbed afterwards about the business of the money.

What I meant was that if I had the opportunity of some place would Faber consider advancing me more than a usual sum on the understanding that they'd recover it as quickly as possible – by the whole of my literary earnings going to them; and if that proved insufficient that I'd repay it out of a salary or by going for a year to America.

It may happen that I'll never need them to.

And if they considered it dangerous, either because of too high a risk or the setting of a precedent, it would make no difference to my relationship with the firm. I'd simply accept it.

Please forgive me for bringing it up at all yesterday, it was only out of desperation of not being able to get some quiet place ever to go on with my work.[78]

> Love
> John

[*December 1965*][79]

Dear Patrick,
Thank you for the American edition, I like it very much, it leaves the Faber – except for the offset which hardly ever looks well – streets behind.

Horsing away at the Meri over the Christmas. It could be turned into a very funny film, (1) in the way of Renoir, (2) or of Buster Keaton.

---

78 In a letter of 9 December, Monteith turned the request for money down, fearing it would mark a precedent. He suggested that he would contact the Society of Authors on McGahern's behalf, but this approach proved fruitless.

79 Gregory, in a letter of 16 December 1965, sent on the American edition of *The Dark*. Knopf, HRC.

I wrote to Boston and asked them if they could offer anything and to get in touch with you if they could.

There's no Russian entry in the passports, they stamp a visa instead, the same in East Berlin.

The position with the agent is that I have tried to get free of him twice, and the last time I was persuaded by Sissons to shelve the business until I went to America, and saw.

When will you have anything definite?

I taught a few days in a school here before Christmas and will afterwards, paid by the day.

You mentioned some writer – was it Harte – who was close to Meri, in one of your letters of some months ago, I cannot find it.[80]

I hope you have had a nice Christmas and are well.

John

80 Gregory suggested that Günter Grass might be prevailed upon to provide a blurb for *The Manila Rope* (16 December 1965). Knopf, HRC.

1966

James Swift
[*Madeline McGahern*]

23 Forest Drive West

Dear Jimmy,

I often wonder how you are. I've not written, there seemed always so little interesting or amusing to tell.

I go to New York on the 7th of February for three weeks. I don't look forward to it very much.

Seems the school business'll blow up fairly soon. The Union spent 2 months pressing the priest for an answer, he produced a jewel though, well worth the long wait,

Mr McGahern is quite well aware of the valid reason which would render his resumption of duties here inadvisable.

I've nearly the Finnish nouvelle translated, it's a good work in a minor way, very like the best of the recent films.

Did you see the Auden poem on MacNeice in one of the Sunday glossies, the end rather beautiful, when he wished he could offer him more than this egocentric rambling.[1]

Remorseless fog, blue where it can't be penetrated, utterly depressing. In Dublin there's always an expectation of some change or there'll be some crack in the sky, to little virtue certainly, but not here.

---

1 The poem in question is 'The Cave of Making', dated July 1964 in the *Collected Poems*, ed. Edward Mendelson (London: Faber, 2007), and part of a longer sequence titled 'Thanksgiving for a Habitat' which was first collected in *About the House* (London: Faber, 1966). 'The Cave of Making' was first published in *The Listener* (1 October 1964), and remembers MacNeice fondly as 'loved of women and Donegal'. MacNeice died on 3 September 1963. The poem ends: 'for your elegy/ I should have been able to manage/something more like you than this egocentric monologue,/but accept it for friendship's sake.'

I always want to laugh when I see a sun or moon over London, it seems always they've come to the wrong place.

After that recommendation, this is a poor hope, but do you think there's any possibility you may come over for some days?

We'll get some place after America, it must be immediately after, it's fairly desperate here.

I hope you can write sometime and with affection.

Please remember me to your mother

John

Seán Brehony Letters

23 Forest Drive West

17 January 1966

Dear Sean,

Thank you for writing to me for Christmas, and I was delighted that you and Rita and the children were so well, and happy in Galway.

Teaching as a temporary these last few days. Very easy. The children very dull. Bored. Treated like kings. It's real relief not to have to hammer that criminal obscenity – Irish – here though.[2]

Going to Galway has been shelved. The BBC were to make a documentary on the world of the Barracks and Dark; but if they appoint me and I accept they obviously then can't make the film. I saw a man called Weldon.[3] The appointment has been passed, but the board who controls expenditure may throw it out, as it involves office and secretary etc. I almost hope they do. And I'll see you in Galway then.[4]

Going to America in mid-February though not even that is 100% certain. With everything in the air we haven't got a place to live.

Anu goes to Finland in May.

2 McGahern taught at Whitehall Primary School, Chingford for periods between 1966 and 1968.
3 Huw Weldon (1916–86), born Prestatyn, Wales. Awarded a Military Cross for his service with the Royal Ulster Rifles on D-Day and an OBE in 1952 for his work on the Festival of Britain. At the time McGahern wrote this letter, Weldon was head of documentaries, and later controller of BBC1. He served as managing director of BBC Television from 1968 to 1975.
4 McGahern did not get a job with the BBC and did not, in fact, visit Galway until late 1970.

Can you give me advice. I paid no literary earnings tax, the Westland Row accountants never did anything, a small sum was clamped on me – £30 – while away, nothing was ever settled though it could the [*missing word*] very much. I'll have to fill tax claims here, and I wonder if you could give me any advice what to do?

How does Rita like Galway compared to Dublin? And you?

When you're writing I'd be grateful for any news.

What pubs do you go to there?[5]

You should, if you go out to Cleggan in the better weather, call on Murphy there.

> I hope you can write.
> John

> Patrick Gregory Papers
> [*23 Forest Drive West*]

[*Late January 1966*]

Dear Patrick,

I sent a letter a few hours ago, and please forgive my carelessness, I am going back on the morning [9 *a.m.*] of Monday the 28th of February.

I try very much to write a lecture and have managed 300 words or so, but there's so much sense of futility in the activity of writing, that when it comes to the secondary business – as I find too in translation – that it's an unconfident damnation of the temporary gestures, at least in work it's rooted – the temporary gesture – in the heart being watched over by the despairing head.[6]

It's as solid as the temporary tree but in 186 autumns.

The other business is a kind of impertinence but I'll leave it so

> John

---

5 When, in later years, McGahern visited Brehony in Galway, they tended to drink in P. J. Flaherty's of Lower Salthill.

6 The writing of this 'lecture' sees the birth of McGahern's intriguing artistic manifesto 'The Image', which he delivered at the Rockefeller Institute, New York City on 8 February 1966, the day after his arrival in the US. A pencil-written copy of the lecture on Knopf letterhead resides among the McGahern Papers in NUIG.

James Swift
[*Madeline McGahern*]

c/o White[7]
Powis Court
Powis Square
London W. 11
[*hereafter 7 Powis Court*]

[*March 1966*]

Dear Jimmy,

I was glad to find your letter after coming back. America was fairly murderous.

We got some place at last, it's top of the Portobello market, about a mile past where Paddy used to live in Westbourne Terrace. I hope you can sometime come.

It's almost certain I'll be in Dublin in two weeks, it's the film for the BBC.

Lennon sprang the business of the school without any consultation and I'd to give that thing to the Irish Times because of all the contradictions and [*illegible*].

I was sorry about Brian Higgins, I never knew him or had conversation with him outside crowds, but I can easily believe what you say.[8] Once I saw him leave a place, and stop some yards off to count the money in his pocket.

---

7 Tony White (1930–76) was a Londoner of half-French parentage. He was seen as the outstanding actor of his generation when an undergraduate at Cambridge – where his close friends included Karl Miller and Thom Gunn who would both go on to have stellar literary careers – but on failing to land a major film role as Romeo in Shakespeare's play he abandoned the stage and worked as a translator and in various forms of manual labour including as a gas lighter and small-time builder. He met McGahern through their mutual friend Richard Murphy with whom they shared a love for the west of Ireland, and in particular with Connemara where White lived in a primitive cottage near Cleggan, working on a lobster farm for many years. His long sojourns in Ireland allowed him to be generous with his London flat, and in this case McGahern was the beneficiary.

8 Brian Higgins (1930–65) was a Yorkshire-born poet published by X. Higgins had visited the Swift family home in Dublin at Christmas 1964 and stayed with Anthony Cronin. In a letter to McGahern of 13 January 1965, Jimmy Swift describes him as 'quite charming & very amusing'. Part of the bohemian Soho scene in the early 1960s, the biographical note in his first collection of poetry, *The Only Need* (London: Abelard-Schuman, 1960), declares that he 'was educated in 1960 at the "York Minster", Soho'.

There was something moving that I could know in the way he counted it, in total abstraction, coin over coin. And another time Kavanagh particularly brutal to him, intent on courting an English Professor, and Higgins skipping along on the outside of the lamp posts.

This is only a note, mostly to let you have the address. I hope I can see you soon, and sometime you may feel like sending a note.

John

Seán Brehony Letters

7 Powis Court

2 March 1966

Dear Sean,

This is no more than a note to let you know that I've got back from America, that we've found a flat for 6–12 months at last – it's rather lovely, a modern block, at the top of Portobello market. And to ask two things:

1. Can you give me any advice about the tax. The accountant never troubled to fix it up. I must owe not more than £100 but all expenses would have to be gone into. Which would be the worse. I've filled no form here yet.

2. Do you remember the funny police report you took Photostat of – I've lost my copy. And I wonder if you could send me a spare one, if you still have it.[9]

Two days back. Hardly able to wag. It was fairly terrible. It'd not take much more to cause an undying hatred of the human grimace and handshake, my own included. The book, it's too soon to say, started well, with the exception of a lead attack in the N.Y. Times.[10]

It is almost certain I'll be in Ireland for two weeks in a week or so for a film for B.B.C. What they plan is not fully settled.

9 McGahern may have been working on what became 'My Love, My Umbrella', which features a vignette about two city gents attacking each other with umbrellas.
10 *The Dark* was reviewed in the *New York Times* of 6 March 1966 by the Irish academic Vivian Mercier, then working as a professor in the English Department at the University of Colorado. Titled 'Growing up in Ireland', the review is a puzzling mix of opening hostility and closing praise in which Mercier ends by comparing the novel favourably with James Joyce's *A Portrait of the Artist as a Young Man* (New York: B. W. Huebsch, 1916). On the other hand it begins on a decidedly downbeat note: 'Oh Lord, here we go again – yet another novel of Irish adolescence.'

Write how you are in Galway and with love to Rita and the children.
John

Patrick Gregory Papers

7 Powis Court

6 March 1966

Dear Patrick,
We've installed ourselves in the flat, it's small but adequate, 20 yards from
the Portobello Road, the end of it, the fruit and vegetable part, the antiques
at the Notting Hill Gate end. Westbourne Park is behind. The lower part of
Kensington Gdns, the Round Pond, is 10 minutes or 15 walk away, Queens-
way; another 10 the fountains at Lancaster Gate, the Pan, the Serpentine, the
great plane trees, and at the direct end the Victoria and Albert.
I'll write you more when I know it better.
We walked there today, a lovely day of quiet sunshine, no cold in wind,
we meant to hire a boat and go rowing, but there were many boats and
boisterous, so we said we'd wait until they were at work.
What was strange was the Pan, the marvellous rats and startled rabbits
winding into the beautiful girls towards the boy: around it 5 circular bursts
of crocuses, yellow, violet and blinding virgin white, and farther back the
daffodils against the ragged bushes, the green still tight around the yellow
waiting for the starter's pistol.[11] On the water the boisterous boys and girls
in the boats, not so much people as giggling cunts and penises tottering on
the edges of their fulfilment, drunk with the imagined glimpses of their joy.
We had two pints of Watney's best bitter in the Archeries.[12] We put the world
in false order there. We were very happy. We wished you could be with us.
I've had 3 days in the school, but on Thursday I've to go to Ireland for 10
or 11 days to do the tv film on the books. The director is a Tristram Powell,
son of Anthony, what he'll make of the business is hard to imagine. I'll have

11 The Peter Pan statue is a bronze sculpture of J. M. Barrie's celebrated character in
Kensington Gardens, London. The sculpture stands about fourteen feet high and has
a tall conical form, topped by a young boy, approximately life-size for an eight-year-
old, wearing a nightshirt and blowing a thin musical instrument like a trumpet or a
flute, sometimes interpreted as pan pipes. The sides of the stump are decorated with
small figures of squirrels, rabbits, mice and fairies.
12 Watney's Red Barrel was a very popular London-brewed bitter of the 1960s and
1970s. The Archery Tavern is located at Lancaster Gate, London.

to tell them in the school that my poor father had a heart attack or something but it's a long journey from here anyhow now.

If you do not send the Jones information before Wednesday, and they still want it, can you send it c/o Lehane[13]

    Ambassador Cinema

    O'Connell Street

    Dublin.

White was reluctant to impose himself on you in spite of Richard's assurances. He asked me. (He is staying two or three days in New York.) I said you'd mentioned it and I think he may write to you. He's going by boat, in three weeks or so.[14]

I wrote to Sissons yesterday, saying that I'd not seen Matson in New York, since I'd decided I didn't need an agent there, and didn't want to complicate the business by personal feelings, so I asked him to let Matson know my feelings and to thank him for having acted for me for so long.

Could you remember me to your father and mother, and tell me how your father is, I hope he can get better soon for the selfish reason that we might have chance to talk at ease. Also I'd be grateful if you could tell the Shedlovskys how grateful I was for their kindness and good company in the Rockefeller.[15]

Though it goes without saying, if anything in the world does, I cannot end without thanking you for every pleasure or delight of the three weeks.

    John

13 Refers to New York friends of Gregory's who were planning a trip to Dublin. Judith Jones was an editor at Knopf.

14 Tony White.

15 Professor Theodore 'Teddy' Shedlovsky (1898–1976) and his wife Beatrice (1902–86). Teddy was a physical chemist, focusing his work on applying the techniques of physical chemistry to the study of biological processes. Born on 29 October 1898 in St Petersburg, Russia, he came to the United States in 1908, receiving his BSc (1918) and PhD (1925) in physical chemistry from the Massachusetts Institute of Technology. In later years he was most associated with the Rockefeller Institute in New York City. Shedlovsky was involved in numerous non-scientific activities connected to the campus community. A great lover of music, he founded the Rockefeller University Concerts in 1958 and was responsible for McGahern's first public unveiling of his most important artistic manifesto, 'The Image', at a lecture in the Rockefeller Institute on 8 February 1966. The Shedlovskys were close friends and neighbours of Patrick Gregory's parents.

Patrick Gregory Papers

Buswells Hotel
25 Molesworth St, Dublin 2

20 March [1966]

Dear Patrick,
I enclose this for the Jones. It is across the street from the Russell, practically
on the Green, and it seems an honest place. The Dolphin is closed and up
for auction. It . . . wasn't easy to find a place for them: 4 and 5th of August
is horse show week: so if it's alright they should confirm it as soon as they
can.[16]

I gave the information to McHugh, he is studying it, and will advise.
Bragg comes tomorrow. We go down to Mulligans, a castle, ancestral seat –
Pakenhams – of Powell's maternal side for filming. The crew are in the Royal
Hotel in Boyle.[17] Natives picking up handy cash for rowing boats etc. Back
in London Wednesday.

Kevin sends his cordial regards.[18]

With all good wishes,
John

Patrick Gregory Papers
[*Madeline McGahern*]

[*7 Powis Court*]

29 March 1966

[*To Patrick Gregory*]
I hope you got the Jones arrangements, and that it proves suitable, I'll let
them know if McHugh comes up with any guidance on the biography, he
took possession of the sheet Dick Jones sent.

16 Early August is always horse show week in Dublin, one of the busiest periods of
the social calendar, and therefore difficult to book hotel accommodation.
17 This hotel, now closed, features frequently in McGahern's fiction, most notably
in *The Dark*, where young Mahoney's father treats him to a fine meal to celebrate his
Leaving Certificate examination results.
18 Presumably their mutual friend Kevin Lehane.

A mixed thanks for the reviews: it's strange, in a less sophisticated way, how close to Cronin the Boston attack sounded.

I see Charles tomorrow night. BARRACKS has sold out: they are reprinting 2,000: which seems a bit ambitious to me, since the paperback of it comes out in September–October.

You said about your nephew in New York. BAY 0128 is the telephone number, if he'd like to come some evening or for lunch, or when he'd like.

A telephone message came yesterday out of the blue from O'Keefe of McGibbon and Kee, with whom I have no contact: it was a message from Conor Cruise, to know if I'd consider a writer in residenceship in New York U.[19] I have little stomach for it: the only temptation is if they'll offer very much money, O'Keefe said they would. I'll make up my own mind, but I'd be glad to learn what you think.

Bragg said if you write to him he'd hurry any request through the foreign rights department. The crew comes back this week: they'll start to cut the 'rushes' (not in the country sense): the whole may well be terrible.

You know you are now free of Matson. I was hoping Sissons would join him in protest, but no luck.

John

Michael McLaverty Archive

7 Powis Court

Easter Saturday [9 *April 1966*]

Dear Michael,
Thank you for your letter, kind as always: and I am very glad that the stories are coming out in a proper edition at last.[20]

---

19 Timothy O'Keeffe (1926–94) was an Irish-born editor and publisher who served as editorial director of the London publishing house MacGibbon & Kee and later formed his own publishing house, Martin Brian & O'Keeffe. He was instrumental in the 1960s revival of Flann O'Brien's work. Conor Cruise O'Brien (1917–2008) was an Irish politician, journalist and man of letters who at the time of this letter's composition was Albert Schweitzer Chair in the Humanities at New York University (NYU). Prior to working at NYU, Cruise O'Brien served with the Irish Civil Service from 1942 to 1962 and then as head of the United Nations operations in the Katanga Province of the Congo.
20 McLaverty had been planning with his American publisher, Cecil Scott at Macmillan, to bring out an anthology of his stories. The plans fell apart with Scott's death. See letter of 20 September 1962.

I was in Ireland for a BBC film on the books, five days; and I was glad to see the few old friends I have in Dublin.

Still Primary teaching here in London. It's a real killer, uneven classes, the poorer ⅚ almost illiterate, more a willpower struggle – who'll dominate – than teaching. I doubt if I can stand it much more. I may go into the BBC in September.

Will you tell me what happened in the school? You keep referring to it in your letters and I do not know. Apart from the fact there's a certain ease in speech I've long, for worse I suppose, gone past the point where I find anything, either good or bad, more than a matter of reflection in the awareness of my own stupidity and nothingness.

On the last lap of a Finnish translation with Anu, Heinemann and Knopf; she wanted to do it to learn English. Praise the lords when it's finished.

I met Seamus Heaney. I was too tired to wish him well with his book of verse, it'd be ungracious, and I meant to, except I was crazy tired after school, and I am uneasy with new people.[21] I'd be terribly grateful if you'd tell him so.

I hope you have a pleasant holiday and with good wishes

John

Patrick Gregory
[*Madeline McGahern*]

[7 *Powis Court*]

[*13 April 1966*]

Dear Patrick,

It's good that you come. Certainly there's place for you here, and it'll be our pleasure. I'll hardly come to Paris. One thing I notice about the dates is that if you came one week earlier I'd have a week's holidays, as I am likely to be teaching, but it isn't of much difference or consequence against what suits you.

I asked Charles about the OK offer. He said to write but careful. I wrote that I got the message. That I was grateful. That OK said I should write. That OB asked OK to ask me. And I wanted to know what salary and if my expenses were involved in return for what obligations on my part. That was all.[22]

21 *Death of a Naturalist*, Heaney's first full collection with Faber, published in 1966.
22 Refers to Timothy O'Keeffe's suggestion to McGahern that there might be an opportunity for lucrative work at NYU with Conor Cruise O'Brien. See letter of 29 March 1966.

Read or tried an article of O'Brien in this week's New Statesman. The unattractiveness and unreadableness of the prose amounts to almost an achievement, arseways.

I trust few things or people and it worsens with the years but O'Keefe absolutely. I also never know what to make of him. He is part of a pub, in it to his ears and yet outside: The Plough, in Museum Street, snowballing distance from the B. M. London version of McDaid's, outpost of Kavanagh etc., a smaller arena. The more cold and worse you treat him the more pleasant he becomes or seems, and vice versa. What he's up to I don't know: and the horribleness of this reflecting is that it's nearly always certain that an edification like OK may not know either.

He rejected, very rightly, the first book I wrote.[23] Some of it later found its way into Barracks and Dark. So this makes two letters for the burning.

I hope you send the Meri, I want to get it out of the way, I feel I should be available to another useless beginning. Read an attractive New York book with little power but valid in some small way, Tenants of Moonbloom by WALLANT.[24] Gollancz the publisher here.

John

Patrick Gregory Papers

7 Powis Court

28 April 1966

Dear Patrick,

I was disturbed when you wrote about your father, for my own sake as well as yours, I can only hope we'll meet in London. Will you tell him, if he is able.

Finished Meri. Checking it against the French. Get into despair over the fumbling incompetency of my own prose, rewriting it again. Can't read House of Green or anything else with the cursed business sweating on as it is.

---

23 McGahern offered 'The End or the Beginning of Love' to MacGibbon & Kee and had it rejected.

24 *The Tenants of Moonbloom* is a novel by the American writer Edward Lewis Wallant (1926–62). Wallant died of an aneurysm aged thirty-six with only two books published, *The Human Season* (New York: Harcourt Brace Jovanovich, 1960) and *The Pawnbroker* (New York: Harcourt, Brace & World, 1961). *The Tenants of Moonbloom* and *The Children at the Gate* were both published posthumously in 1963 and 1964 respectively by Harcourt in New York.

TV thing comes 12th of May. Kenyon offered position for next year.[25] DARK may go into a 3rd printing. We've got unexpected money for its German sale, a few days ago, publishing in Zurich.[26]

5 weeks from today Anu and I made up until you come today. It's better than several drinks to us.

Forgive the scribbling and the shortness.

Love

John

Patrick Gregory Papers

[7 *Powis Court*]

[3 *May 1966*]

Dear Patrick,
Tell Mrs Boyle that I'm the Pope; that they do use 'He-Je' in Ireland, that they go very much to the pictures.

You come on the 8th, go the 29th: When in Ireland? When in Greece? Do you wish me to make any arrangements for you before you come? That'd easy things for you.

Supposed to see Charles the 23rd of this month. Lording it in Ireland apparently last few weeks. Wheels of the novel grinding again, destruction of a spinster at the sea.

Read Confidence Man, delighted with the second half, but it reads more a sketch of a work than fleshed out.[27]

Would like to find a good dry definition of EVIL. Licking drooling whiskers over the book of Job.

Can you bring paperback Pirandello when you come?

John

25 Private liberal arts college in Gambier, Ohio. Kenyon's English Department gained national recognition with the arrival of the poet and critic John Crowe Ransom in 1937 as Professor of Poetry and first editor of the *Kenyon Review*. In a letter of 16 May Gregory agrees that McGahern was right to turn the offer down: 'nine lectures a week can hardly be considered a sinecure [. . .] It's a flattering offer to turn down, and I can't help but feel that you are right in doing so.' Knopf, HRC.
26 *The Dark* was published as *Das Dunkle* in German, translated by Elisabeth Schnack who went on to translate several more McGahern texts over the years.
27 *Confessions of Felix Krull, Confidence Man: The Early Years* is an unfinished 1954 novel by the German author Thomas Mann.

James Swift
[*Madeline McGahern*]

7 Powis Court

12 May 1966

Dear Jimmy,

Will you be able to come to London this summer? There's a whole room.

The best time for you might be July: I'll be in school all day: Anu in Finland: and you'd have the whole place to yourself all day, to go or come.

But anytime you come will delight me, and Anu if she's here. The only days I'll be away are the first days of June.

Will you write and tell me?

The BBC business came out last night, it was the usual whimsy.

I'd to fabricate an interview at Easter to stop P. Lennon whining from Dublin.

It's not worth telling.[28]

A strange image out of Proust. We go to our death as a man walking backwards down a stairs, continually looking from where he has come, the top of the stairs.[29]

Please remember me with love to your mother. I am sure she has happy Sundays in Wicklow.

Write before too long if you can.

John

28 McGahern felt that Peter Lennon's stridently anti-censorship position on the banning of *The Dark* compromised him because he did not want to be part of a polarised debate, be it of the liberal press or well-meaning others. One comment by Samuel Beckett relayed back to McGahern was the most appreciated: 'Did John *want* a protest?' He did not.

29 Swift had been responsible for introducing McGahern to Proust's work.

25 May 1966

Dear Patrick,

I'll meet you if I can get information enough about your arrival, I imagine the terminal is Victoria. If anything goes wrong the flat is modern with rectangular balconies, the Talbot Road side of Powis Square and 100 yards the city side of Portobello Road.

I was so delighted about your father, I've been enjoying very much these last weeks his Ovid, on the underground mostly.[30] Would you remember me to your mother and him before you leave, I want you to very much.

Meri is finished. With the typist. It was a mistake to attempt. I am not sorry I tried. And I'm not blaming you in any way, if you tried to take any you'd disturb me, and be plain foolish into the bargain.

Without trying to do it would not have been possible to discover the way it is.

The most any translation, not based on knowledge of the original language, can have is talent or felicity. It's much the same as somebody with talent, and possessed of no vision, trying to write.

The translation is, in every sentence, an attempt, an accumulation of attempts of imitation, without any authority, and consequently without law. The one consolation is that I'm doubtful if there's very much law to the original. There is charm.

You'll be able to inspect the messing soon. I hope you'll be able to add a few improving touches of your own, or erase some silliness.

We are still counting the days.

John

30 See Ovid, *Metamorphoses*, trans. Horace Gregory (New York: Viking Press, 1958).

Brian Friel Papers

7 Powis Court

9 June 1966

Dear Brian,

Thank you for your kind letter. I wasn't able to write for long after the <u>Dark</u>, I'm only struggling into a beginning, and what's done is too raw still to offer it.

There is one thing, and it might be more use to you than a contribution, it's a translation my wife did with me of a Finnish nouvelle (30,000) by a man called Meri; we took it on to help her English, but it was a real disaster.

He has a high reputation particularly in France, this will be his first appearance in English; it's serious work, and sometimes very funny; moral in its feel; an extract, if you liked it, might help to relieve the Irishness of an issue.[31]

It's now being typed. Heinemann and Knopf own the rights. If it'd interest you they might give permission. They bring it out next year.

If you are in London for any reason and have spare time and would like, I'd be very glad if you came here.

I'll be here all summer, most of it on my own, as Anu is going back to her old theatre work for a few months from July.

We were very grateful always for your offer of the cottage at that time, and happy for you when we saw your play become the success it now is.[32]

With kindest regard

John

---

31 Friel was guest editor of the Belfast-based literary magazine *Threshold* for its twentieth number in Winter 1966–7. Nothing of McGahern's appeared in that issue despite some indications that a story was solicited.
32 *Philadelphia, Here I Come!*

10 July 1966

Dear Patrick,

Thank you for your letter and the typescript, and more than anything for all the <u>trouble</u> with the typescript, they nearly all are improvements, and they gave me some chance.

I've gone through it three times: ½ of it is with the typist: I've spent the last 5 days on it: and I'll give the rest soon.

Nothing seems to be able to leaven the first chapters: but it's improved generally: but often I get sick that I'm not able to see or hear it anymore, as if it's outside my grip and senses.

Anu is in Finland, I sent her your love.

It was such delight for me that you came, and now that you are gone am sorry that I could not have made it nicer, that the place is so small, and it'd never be as good if you'd stayed in the hotel.

Dutch translation [contact/Amsterdam] seems certain, of the <u>Dark</u>.[33]

I enclose this curious letter, can you give me any idea how to answer it, or what to make of it?

Bea wrote a letter that they no longer need the hotel I got. What am I to do about it?[34]

Tell me how your father is? Give your mother and him my love.

I'll write a longer letter when I get the Meri away.

John

Michael McLaverty Archive

7 Powis Court

11 July 1966

Dear Michael,

Thank you for your nice postcard.

33 *The Dark* was translated into Dutch as *Het Donker* by Clara Eggink (Amsterdam: Contact, 1969).
34 Bea Shedlovsky. The Shedlovskys were planning a European trip.

Annikki has gone to Finland: she's gone as a guest director to the radio, and a production of Platonov at her old theatre; and she'll not be back until September. So she unfortunately won't be in Ireland this year, it'd be pleasant for her to meet you.

I am not sure of my own movements. I am beginning to try to work again, and I shouldn't move from the grindstone; but I may go in early August to do a tv film, they offered much, and there doesn't seem much work or embarrassment; and if I go it'd be nice if we could meet.

Do you think you may come to London?

Trudging in and out of school, it's fairly murderous, the travelling is the worst.[35] American universities have offered positions but I disliked America. I often wondered if it'd be ever possible to get a job like yours in Belfast and if it'd leave you much energy for work afterwards?

Dark going into 3rd printing: The Barracks into a 2nd: but I suppose the paperback will kill the hardback sales. The Knopf Dark is almost out of first printing.

It's still nothing to live on.

I hope you have a lovely holiday and that we'll meet soon one way or another and with sincere regard for Mrs McLaverty. I hope she is well.

As always
John

Patrick Gregory Papers

7 Powis Court

19 July 1966

Dear Patrick,

Thank you for your marvellous letter. Will you tell me what you think of the translation: I get afraid I have but the one voice: if you see any necessary need for change, make it. It's all with the typist: the fee will be 28 dollars.

Can you answer this post haste? Leo Aylen, he's the one or two most famous TV producers here (the last thing he directed here was Eh, Joe with Beckett) wants to make a film of the DARK, his first film. He believes he can get the backing and the actors. He is ready to buy a 12 month option on the book. I saw him. I tried to pour cold water but I came away with the

---

35 The daily journey from Powis Court to Chingford would have taken at least an hour and a half whether by bus, tube, bicycle or on foot.

impression that he might be able to do it, I didn't at first believe it possible. A low budget 180,000 dollars. He thinks because of his position he can give TV parts, and the part of the father and priest he'll get good actors that'll take a % cut. It may all come to nothing. But the option is a firm offer. Write me without delay what you think!

It'll be alright with Bea and Ted, I like Ted very much, and for that matter Bea.

Hamilton says the award is fairly certain.[36] Also Jebb came with the news that Lord David Cecil was caught reading DARK, it turned out for the James Tait Black award, it's in the last three.[37] I'd rather not have heard: I won't get it.

Ackerly was with Murphy, I haven't seen him since, when I write I'll ask about the book, it's unlikely, an obscene autobiography that he won't publish is what he's at. Murphy rang: he was very careful about the visit, apparently Ack fell in love with the dog: gave it powders for worms etc.[38]

Delighted your father is so well, I hope the walking business doesn't wear you out.

36 Ian Hamilton.
37 Julian Jebb (1934–84), the Cambridge-educated grandson of Hilaire Belloc, was a literary critic and BBC TV producer to whom McGahern dedicated his 1984 collection of short stories, *High Ground*. In one of his first reviews Jebb had been enthusiastic about *The Dark* in the *Sunday Times*: 'it seems to me a perfectly written tour de force. Like Robert Musil's "Young Törless" it creates a small world indelibly and without recourse to deliberate heightening effects of prose. John McGahern's gifts as a novelist are already mature with this, his second book. There are few writers in their twenties whose future work can be anticipated with such confidence and excitement.' See Julian Jebb, 'Heart of the Matter', in Tristram and Georgia Powell, *A Dedicated Fan: Julian Jebb 1934–1984* (London: Peralta Press, 1993), 165. Jebb committed suicide in 1984. Lord David Cecil (1902–86) was an Eton- and Oxford-educated critic, biographer and variously Fellow of Wadham College and New College, Oxford. Devoutly Christian, Cecil was one of the leading British cultural commentators of the day. It was not the James Tait Black prize for which *The Dark* was being considered but the Hawthornden, which was not awarded in 1966. McGahern's fellow Irishman Aidan Higgins was joint winner of the James Tait Black prize for fiction in 1966 for *Langrishe, Go Down* (London: Calder and Boyars, 1966). His co-winner was Christine Brooke-Rose for *Such* (London: Michael Joseph, 1966).
38 J. R. Ackerley (1896–1967), English author and editor, and another of McGahern's close London friends. Openly homosexual at a time when that created significant difficulties, he drank heavily towards the end of his life and died within a year of this letter's composition.

I am sorry I wasn't better when you were here, the school drains most of my joy, it'd be more charitable to blame the school.

Love,
John

Michael McLaverty Archive

7 Powis Court

22 July 1966

Dear Michael,
Do you think you could get your hands on a copy of Brian Westby for me?[39]
I'll send a copy of the American Dark in a few days.

John

Patrick Gregory Papers

7 Powis Court

31 July 1966

Dear Patrick,
Ted and Bea here and gone. I liked Ted even more than before, it's strange to see that other solitariness in total emotionalism, and when the need for defences came his changing to another person that he knew much better once and is now impatient with. Each city is his passion, that he's only able to look on with a dog's face, as he moves in increasing physical external comfort to the thirteenth station. They'd a drawing of Avignon, that they liked, that I disliked, though I didn't say so: it seemed to be true and technically extraordinary on every level except that of silence.

I won't be able to see the Jones in Dublin but they said they were to come to London. Do they know the telephone BAY 0128.

---

39 A novel by Forrest Reid published by Faber in 1934, much admired by McGahern and a likely inspiration for his story 'Strandhill, the Sea'. He may well have been turned towards this novel by Michael McLaverty who was also an admirer, as a letter of 1959 to a correspondent makes clear. See *In Quiet Places: The Uncollected Stories, Letters and Critical Prose of Michael McLaverty*, ed. and int. Sophia Hillan King (Dublin: Poolbeg Press, 1989), 198.

Writing these days. Nothing most days to show. A page today: best in terms of words so far. Like deliberately putting one's head under the yoke and then hoping to get the rest of one's person miraculously through in some way.

Is your father well? Ted said he's not seen him look better for more than twenty years.

Did you get the Meri yet? It looked fairly silly to me on the last reading.[40] Thank you for the Beerbohm, I liked it, I enjoyed it. What I found disturbing about it was its <u>total</u> reliance on the code (a reflection of reality certainly) as a substitute for reality. But then Lawrence and Hardy are the only ones in the immediate days that have proved greater than it here.[41]

I've been loaned (going to be) a copy of Brian Westby, is there any way to photostat it?

I eventually read and liked, except it has no style, the New York novel Hamilton gave me, Mario Puzo – The Fortunate Pilgrim – Heinemann here.[42] Strange, no matter how beautiful, intelligent etc. only the passion of obsession has the possibility of style.

[unsigned]

Patrick Gregory Papers

[7 Powis Court]

[Late August–early September 1966]

Dear Patrick,

Thanks for your letters and the cheque. I'll be glad to meet your nephew: has he the telephone number – BAY 0128?

I've been on the go for the most of three weeks.

Cruise O'Brien wrote, asked me to see him in Ireland. I went – Dunquin, they were kind and hospitable, the job he had in mind was for 1967–68 in NYU, to lecture to extra mural students on the 'fringe area between literature and

40 Gregory writes on 4 August 1966: 'No one, no one at all, should read the Meri as carefully, as often, as we have done. The little book obviously can't stand the strain of close, concentrated inspection.' Knopf, HRC.

41 D. H. Lawrence and Thomas Hardy remained firm favourites of McGahern's throughout his writing life.

42 Mario Puzo, The Fortunate Pilgrim (London: Heinemann, 1965). Puzo considered this his best novel and it won favourable reviews without being a commercial success. He went on to worldwide fame in 1969 with The Godfather.

politics', the salary 12,000 dollars. I wasn't able. I never knew until then of the existence of such an area.[43]

Then I went to Finland. Anu always complained I never would meet her friends. In the last ten days I met droves. A hangover a permanent fixture after the first four days. The sky blue, the girls blonde and beautiful, not forgetting Anu, the prices exorbitant, Anu busy in the radio and looking for a card to send you, trees and houses growing out of red granite against the sea, and autumn happening in one single day last week.

Anu comes home the 28th of Sept. Would you write to her about the information? C/O Parko, TEHTAANKATLL 3406/ Helsinki 15. I would try to publicize the merits of the translation too much in the blurb, because it can easily cause antagonism.

I finished two stories. I am slowly (and painfully) trying to put down the more vivid parts of the death/sex to see its possible shape.

I'll write longer very soon. Thanks for the check.

As always
John

How is your father now? And mother?

Patrick Gregory Papers
7 Powis Court

[Early September 1966][44]

Dear Patrick,
Your nephew came. He asked to stay. The people he was to stay with had gone. I found him terrible but I was as nice to him as my nerves could manage. I got him a key and told him he had to go by a certain day when I should have told him to go at once. The only poetic thing he managed was to break the alarm clock while timing his eggs. After I'd bade him goodbye, he left a note, which afforded me some amusement.

43 Gregory replies on 7 September 1966: 'In a way, I am very disappointed that the O'Brien deal didn't work out; I would have enjoyed having you in New York for a year.' Knopf, HRC.
44 Gregory writes to McGahern on 24 August 1966 to say that his nephew is travelling to England on 26 August and would like to meet McGahern.

Anu comes back the 28th. We'll have to look for a new place by the end of October. Teaching 14 mentally deficients. Have done some work. Persecuted with people, the telephone a menace.

Met Rosenthal in Ian Hamilton's for 20 minutes, on my way from school, by chance, no end depressing.[45] After the business I felt in need of immersion before I could believe that some day I might write a good sentence.

Dutch translation of the Dark was sold, and Director came from France, he was rather marvellous, serious in red trousers, a Citroen and wife and crippled mother at home 100 miles north of Toulouse, knew Proust upside-down, which endeared him.

> Sorry for such a scratchy letter
> John

Rosenthal said you were an optimist.[46]

Faber

7 Powis Court

14 September 1966

Dear Charles,
I promised you to send the Finnish publisher's name.
   It is Mr Helliman of Tammi publishers.
I saw Liam Miller for an hour last night, he was charming as ever, had enjoyed seeing you, and was flying in more than one sense.
   A very nice person was here by the name of Peter Prestcott who is an editor at Dutton.[47]

> I hope you are well
> and with love
> John

---

45 Thomas Gabriel Rosenthal (1935–2014), publisher and writer, was associated through the 1960s with Thames & Hudson, and after 1970 with Secker & Warburg.
46 Gregory responds on 16 September 1966: 'I suspect that his categorizing of me was not wholly complimentary.'
47 Peter Sherwin Prescott (1935–2004), a native of New York and graduate of Harvard, began his literary career by working for nine years as an editor at E. P. Dutton. For twenty years he reviewed books for *Newsweek*. His father, Orville Prescott, was the principal daily book critic of the *New York Times* for twenty-four years, from 1942 to 1966. Peter was, along with Julian Jebb, perhaps McGahern's

[*September 1966*]

Dear Patrick,

Thank you for writing, I was sorry I abused to you your nephew, we'll leave it so.

Rosenthal wrote, saying he hadn't time because of illness and scripts to see me, as he'd hoped, but he gave me his address, and he wanted very much for me to send him everything I write. Is he sound in the head?

I was inquisitive about your father, that's how the word 'optimistic' came up with Rosenthal, I think you may know I never discuss the few friends I have, I either say nothing or praise them, and people don't cross me usually without thinking.

Shedlovsky called on Kevin in Dublin. 'A mad scientist whose name ended in Ski called from the Rockefeller and I think I entertained him for the hour or two.'

I teach every day. I get home at five. I don't generally answer the telephone now. I leave at 7.40 in the morning.

I used leave at 8.30 in Dublin and get home at 2.30. It makes much difference. Now if I have a marvellous run I get a half a page in reasonable first competence for the day. I am not complaining. The one thing certain is that it'll be written now and that it'll be a long slow grind.

The actual work is much easier than Dublin: 15 special morons.
I got 500 Dutch Florins, it's a beautiful sound, and means £50. I was offered more to appear both here and Dublin for 30 minutes – 10 here – in moronic tv shows in the last 2 weeks.

What I find disturbing about Rosenthal, your nephew too, is the ferocious silence of the work they're fiddling about with without knowing.

Forgive a tired letter

John

---

favourite reviewer and reviewed *Nightlines*, *The Leavetaking* and *The Pornographer* for *Newsweek*.

21 September 1966

Dear Joe,
Thank you for your kind letter.

I was in Ireland for five days, came through Dublin, less than a day there, rang the office, you weren't in. I went to Finland then.

I'm able to write again after very long but it's slow and slow and horrible.

Asked to go on some show a few days ago in Dublin in October. 'The Person in Question' on tv. The money is the only temptation.

A persecution of people in London, that's the worst.

Annikki comes from Helsinki the end of this month, she's been doing her own productions there since the end of June.

Do you keep well? Is Margaret well? And the children? How do you find Dublin?

It's right that the world generally is a balls of a place.

   I hope you can visit soon
      John

Alfred A. Knopf, Inc. Records

[*7 Powis Court*]

[*Early October 1966*]

Dear Patrick,
I send you <u>Brian Westby</u>. Tell me when it comes.

 When you've finished send it to
  Michael McLaverty
  30 Derramore Drive
  Belfast 9
Register it, he's neurotic about it.

 Also send him a copy of the DARK, put it on my account.

 I was disappointed, there are a few terrible chapters, but it's still fantastically more interesting than the usual rubbish. The descriptions or evocations of the sea?

I wasn't complaining or whining about the conditions. That's how they are. One has to work in [*any way*] one has to, that is all.

Read some very interesting prose things by Leopardi, atrociously dull verse translation by Heath Stubbs.[48]

Did you know the state of Montana has taken Cronin to its arms?[49]

Anu has come back. She is well.

Can you let me see the blurb for the Meri?

Wish you could come to London for Christmas.

John

Alfred A. Knopf, Inc. Records

7 Powis Court

[*Early October 1966*]

* The description of the Irish flavour of the translation, it disturbs me, with Irish novelist already there is it not SPELLING it out?

Dear Patrick,

The one thing wrong with the blurb is that <u>Laaksi</u> is spelled wrongly. Also I doubt if I can qualify for young* anymore. What I was more interested in seeing were the biographical notes (proposed): I'll be better pleased, though, if they have been ruled out altogether. If they're not I'd like to see them.

Cronin must already be in saddle in Montana. Another McDaid's Fellow, John Jordan, is gone to the University of Newfoundland!

I paid AIRMAIL for B. Westby. It was P.O. closing time. I've a feeling the man didn't put the airmail ticket on.

The trouble I have with the work, it's snail slow, is that it must be all the time as disciplined and as explosively accurate as verse, or it's nothing: one has to live in a continual thread-the-needle hell.

---

48 Giacomo Leopardi (1798–1837), Italian poet, essayist and philosopher. John Heath-Stubbs (1918–2006), English poet and translator. His portrait was painted by Patrick Swift c. 1960.
49 Anthony Cronin was visiting lecturer at the University of Montana from 1966 to 1968.

I'll send you two very short stories, one of them you've seen, you can decide whether they're worth publishing yet or not.[50]

John

Patrick Gregory Papers

7 Powis Court

19 October 1966

Dear Patrick,

I'd a request from a Buffalo professor for 'an inscribed photo' for an exhibition in Buff. S. U. What does it mean? Would it be amusing to send him the one you took out at your parents?

Also, through Knopf, a request, from a Portugese gentleman, for signed copies of my books, he said he'd send the money. What is usual in that sort of business?

The good Leopardi prose was by Iris Origo, Oxford, in the same volume as Stubbs' dishwater verse, Selected Prose & Verse.[51]

Do Knopf have any of Knut Hamsun's books, their translations, still in print? I've a curiosity to see what they're like.[52]

---

50 In a letter of 19 November 1966 Gregory wrote admiringly of the stories – 'Why We're Here' and 'Christmas' – and told McGahern that 'Judith Jones, who is a friend of William Maxwell of The New Yorker, reminds me that Maxwell expressed his most sincere and ardent interest in your work and told her that he was eager for you to appear again in the pages of his magazine.' He goes on to ask: 'Do you want me to put his enthusiasm to the test by sending him one of the tales?' Knopf, HRC. 'Why We're Here' was eventually published in The Review, and 'Christmas' in the Irish Press (27 April 1968).

51 Dame Iris Margaret Origo, Marchesa of Val d'Orcia (1902–88), née Cutting, was an English-born biographer and writer. Her biography of Giacomo Leopardi was originally published in 1935 by Oxford University Press and subsequently much revised for republication as Leopardi: A Study in Solitude (London: Hamish Hamilton, 1953). Leopardi's Selected Prose and Poetry was edited, translated and introduced by Origo and John Heath-Stubbs and published by Oxford University Press in 1966.

52 Gregory writes in a letter of 24 October 1966 that the only Hamsun in stock is Growth of the Soil. In a letter of 5 December 1966, Gregory assures McGahern that 'The Hamsun was ordered to be sent from our warehouse on October 24th. It should be well on its way to you by now.' Knopf, HRC.

I work and have mostly nothing to show, which doesn't worry me, it's real work, an impossible beginning again.

Any news of your nephew? Or the Shedlovskys?

Kevin Lehane comes the end of the month, looking forward. For three days to the races.

The Hawthornden was, I believe, won by a William Trevor.[53] Auden reading on the tv here: terrible stuff. We're all in the club featherbed together.

Is your father improving?

How was Charles?

John

Michael McLaverty Archive

7 Powis Court

[*Autumn 1966*]

Dear Michael,

Thank you for sending Brian Westby, and your kind letter. I read it: some of it stood up; some didn't; I thought it was better; but it's a star compared to the ordinary 99.999% rubbish. I have sent it to Gregory at Knopf, (registered); he'll return it, (registered). In that way I hope to put pressure on Faber. They are conservative and worse. It doesn't surprise me, the Faber rejection. Monteith is a very nice man: it'd be nicer still if he'd be more energetic about his list.

Teaching on in the same establishment, the trouble is I see no point teaching, it's just an obvious waste of my life, the same goes for all other jobs, one place is as good as another, to keep stupid flesh for a time on the stupid bone.

Able to write but slowly.

Anu came back, with a fur coat white as the snow, she is not very happy here.

Do you come to London? For that lecture?

Forgive this scattered note and with love.

John

PS. I reminded Knopf again about The Dark: the last I heard it was close to 3,000; and selling slowly there.

---

53 Trevor won the Hawthornden Prize for Literature for *The Old Boys* (London: Bodley Head, 1964) in 1965. It was not awarded in 1966.

[*October 1966*]

Dear Patrick,
Thank you for the trouble with the F. R.[54]

Trouble is I agree; it was a shock to read it after so many years, I didn't want to prejudice you, I'd hoped you'd find for the book.[55]

I can see, though, why I liked it so much then: its rhythm, its attempt at style, above all probably its lack of 'Irishness'; and its evocation of a seaside place in my own life.[56]

I also found it was a shock too, that the passages I remembered had become completely altered in my own mind. It was strange. The Imagination and time do a fair fandango with the lady.

Do I have to pay the Dark, or can it be taken, as with Faber, from my Royalties?

Have the sales completely stopped now?
Work going badly, a scene I can't do, clearing out of the house while the woman's dying, hammering asunder of iron beds etc.[57]

Read a work Hamilton likes, The Bell Jar by S. Plath, thought it honest, but poor-poor, all the adjectives.[58]

Enclose this, it might interest. I find it pathetic.
Heard Friel earns 15,000 dollars a month.[59]

54 F. R. stands for Forrest Reid, the author of *Brian Westby*, the novel discussed here.
55 McGahern wanted to see *Brian Westby* back in print and clearly prompted Gregory in that direction. It is interesting to see him, over the course of this letter, admit to second thoughts in light of Gregory's negative response of 20 October: 'embarrassingly evasive, generally false, and ultimately muddled'. Knopf, HRC.
56 The 'seaside place' will be Strandhill, Co. Sligo. McGahern's second story to be published, 'Strandhill, the Sea', in its evocation of a young boy's tedious holiday among adults in Strandhill, bears striking resemblances to *Brian Westby*.
57 This scene, in which McGahern recalls his mother's final days, would eventually appear in *The Leavetaking* and again in *Memoir*.
58 Plath's *The Bell Jar* was first published by Heinemann under the pseudonym Victoria Lucas in 1963, but was not published under her own name in the UK until 1966. Gregory also disliked the book and rejected it in his role as second reader at Knopf.
59 In a letter of 17 October 1966 Gregory had written to McGahern about his attendance at a Broadway performance of Friel's *Philadelphia, Here I Come!* in the

Things going rapidly from bad to worse here.[60]
My young sister comes later in the week, did her evening degree, couldn't stand Civil Service anymore, going to look for work here.[61]

John

Patrick Gregory Papers

7 Powis Court

[*October 1966*]

Dear Patrick,
No place yet. My head is full of streets, loans, advances, mortgages, flats, houses, ground rents, survey fees, deposits, shady looking agents.

Not able to do any work. Crackers, crackers, crackers.

– No sign of Mr. Hamsun.[62]

See extraordinary boring letter in Irish T. from Kiely; from time to time.[63] Do you meet Farrell or any others of the brigade?[64]

Can you send me statement that I earned (not Anu & I) Meri translation money?

If you are finding difficulty with WHY WE'RE HERE I'll give it to Hamilton, who asked to publish it, he saw it when his wife typed them.[65]

Please forgive this horrible letter.

Write soon if you can.

Anu sends her love.

John

---

company of Charles Monteith, followed by a post-play party in a nearby bar: 'Friel and his wife were very pleasant and unpretentious (They asked after you and seemed to be genuinely respectful of your work.)'. Knopf, HRC.

60 A reference, almost certainly, to increasingly strained relations between McGahern and Annikki as their marriage was falling apart.

61 Dympna McGahern.

62 Gregory has written in the margin: 'it's out of stock & we're not going back to press with it yet'.

63 Benedict Kiely, whom McGahern would have seen as the personification of Irish literary chumminess.

64 Michael Farrell (1940–2000), Co. Meath-born, Ampleforth- and St Martin's College-educated Irish painter; Soho and Paris boulevardier.

65 Ian Hamilton published it in *The Review* (April 1968). Hamilton's wife at the time was Gisela Dietzel.

31 October 1966

Dear Patrick,
Sending you these, reading though not sure whether they're useless or good, I'm not able to see them anymore.

   Thank you for the Hesse. It has a few good things, the degradation esp., but generally pretty awful. It's hard to keep the expected straight face at most of the goings on. I can see the Hesse/Reade [*illegible*].[66]

   Steppenwolf is the best I read, I can't manage Magister Ludi at all.[67]

                          No other news.
                          John

31 October 1966

Dear Patrick,
It's alright about the MSS.[68]

   Any word of the Shedlovskys?
Looking forward to the Damien.[69]

---

66 Gregory may have drawn comparisons between Hesse's *Demian* (1919) and Forrest Reid's *Brian Westby*; both novels examine issues around the painful coming to consciousness of a young man.

67 *Magister Ludi* is better known as *The Glass Bead Game* (1943), Hesse's last published novel. Like *Demian*, it was a Bildungsroman.

68 Gregory had offered to return to McGahern a carbon typescript of *The Pit* in a letter of 28 October 1966, saying that he would like to keep it himself if McGahern did not need it. Knopf, HRC.

69 Gregory, in a letter of 20 October in which he writes very harshly of Forrest Reid's *Brian Westby*, had offered to send McGahern a copy of a book 'that shares some of WESTBY'S weaknesses, but which I consider much more satisfactory – Hesse's DAMIEN'. *Demian* was first published in 1919; Hesse added a prologue in 1960, thus repopularising the book. See McGahern's letter to Gregory of 10 November 1966.

Kevin came last night, in great form, consequent hangover.[70]
We'll inspect Soho, go to the Newbury races, and the Wembley international.[71]
Such cursed bad company in this dump by comparison.
Anu goes to English classes these days, they're cold, the days.

John

Is your father well?

Patrick Gregory Papers

7 Powis Court

15 November 1966

Dear Patrick,
Thank you for the kind letter. I suppose it's alright to insert father, it doesn't seem to matter much, I got into unholy despair reading through them again, they seemed so THIN.

The typing is poor, I foolishly allowed somebody who asked.

(1) Do you think it's worth having them retyped?

(2) Would it be better, it was originally intended to have the dialogue as single line (Christmas story)?

(3) Are they too slight for the bigmonied (trans Atlantic) magazines, would it be better to hold fire?[72]

Do what you think fit, you have a completely free hand. I am only sorry to inflict them on you, I'll be as well pleased if you put them in a drawer.

I met Farrell only three times, I liked him, there seemed sincerity, own but he's certainly naive, but then I don't know him in anything but superficial.[73] I gave him Ted's address. My own humble opinion of abstract art is that it can be no more than a form of interior decoration. Farrell has some good stories of Ian Stuart, and the Soho menagerie.

I write every day now, it's the only way for me.

---

70 Kevin Lehane.
71 England, who had won the World Cup three months earlier, played two November internationals at Wembley Stadium. On 2 November they played a scoreless draw with Czechoslovakia, and on 16 November they beat Wales 5–1.
72 McGahern is sending Gregory two stories, 'Why We're Here' and 'Christmas'. See Gregory to McGahern (10 November 1966), Knopf, HRC.
73 Michael Farrell, Irish painter.

What I feel for the short piece is that there's something wrong with it, it has the tension of the formal order or pattern of verse to serve as a springboard towards poetry, in the longer prose work the different parts in order/vision create the tension that forces the quality of the utterance beyond itself.

I am only thinking, I don't know.

The West business was a pathetic caper, the poetical burst down the home strait was something, Vive Moi.[74]

Sometimes I am uneasy when I remember all the letters hanging about your flat? Have you any tentative plans for next year?

John

Patrick Gregory
[*Madeline McGahern*]

7 Powis Court

25 November 1966

Dear Patrick,

The Christmas story was sent to the New Yorker 4/5 years ago: the same plot, twice or so as long, hardly any of the original language remains, and it was rejected then as too sentimental.

I meant it when I said, send them wherever you think is best, I won't worry. My own feelings are that they're so short it might be better to publish them together. It may prove not easy to get a publisher. They can be published here if it matters.

I wonder are you right about Mrs F.[75] What struck me is that she's almost anaemic, his energy too much for her, that she longed to hide in some obscure security, which isn't possible with him, that she was almost afraid of life, and afraid that he may leave her, and not able for the wear and tear of staying. Anyhow the reflection is the whole game.

I only meant when I was there in NY in your flat that there were letters about which made me uneasy since they were mine. Forgive the fear.

Able to write for 2 hours every day, it's a long run this time.

---

74 Gregory, in a letter dated 4 November 1966, had sent McGahern Anthony C. West's review of *The Dark* that appeared in *The Nation* on 7 November 1966, describing it as 'a tortured piece of prose, full of table-thumping indecision'. Knopf, HRC.

75 Most likely refers to the wife of Michael Farrell.

Reading Boswell's Johnston, feeling of Kavanagh on larger scale, many good things, but I find the continual meglamania more than a bit oppressive.

There's a note of Kafka somewhere, drunks on the way home from wedding, who seize you, and compel you into merriment, about the most oppressive merriment in the world.

As always

John

Joe Kennedy

7 Powis Court

[*14 December 1966*]

Dear Joe,

Thank you for the letter.

I hope the record business works out well for you.[76]

I didn't go on tv and won't. ITV were on again last week. I think the whole business must be pretty boring for any sensitive person in Ireland by this. I'd be glad to be left out.

Is Dublin changed, is there much life in the pubs, have many of the houses round the Cornmarket come down?

I hope you've a happy Christmas. And wish it to Margaret for me.

John

Ring up if you're in London.

The cutting is terrible, shit.

---

76 Kennedy's wife, Margaret Johnston, was from a musical family. Her siblings Adrienne, Lucy and Michael formed a very successful folk group called 'The Johnstons' in the early 1960s in their home village of Slane, Co. Meath. They signed to Pye Records in 1965, later adding Mick Moloney, then becoming a major figure in the Irish music scene, and Paul Brady, while Michael Johnston departed. Signing to Transatlantic Records in London, they released an album called *The Johnstons* in 1968.

Patrick Gregory
[*Madeline McGahern*]

7 Powis Court

[*December 1966*]

Dear Patrick,
I read through the Meri, enclosed things noticed, leave it to yourself to decide.
It's a poor work, with odd niceties.
   I'll be glad to get Mrs Odle sherry.[77]
I'll get it in the cutprice, she'll get better sherry & almost twice the quantity
that way.
   I'll borrow a postman's cap for the occasion of delivery.
Going mad, waiting for loans, not able to work.
                         Happy Christmas
                         John (over)

[*new page*]
AnuFinnish Spelling

p. 46 Jaakko Salminen
   (Jaako is wrong) 2 Ks

p. 116 Josseppi is wrong
   Must be Jooseppi
Mistake is repeated 3 times.

p. 127 Kivenappa is wrong.
Must be Kivennapa

p. 136 Alina is wrong
Must be Aliina
repeated 2 times on that page.

77 Gregory, in a letter of 16 December 1966, asked McGahern to have a bottle of
sherry sent to a family friend of the Gregorys in London. Rose Odle was the literary
executor for Dorothy Richardson. Knopf, HRC.

<u>Important</u>

1. p. 18 Is a note necessary that the Finnish for prisoner is VANKI? (as in the French edition)

2. p. 26 It should be <u>crowding</u> to the well instead of <u>crowing</u>.

3. p. 33 (question) STANDUNDER is deliberate.

4. Words left out end of p. 42, begin p. 43.

5. p. 24 Do you want him to catch his death. Ann says this is misunderstanding. Do you want to syringe his arse out? is literal, and Meri:

6. p. 73 (3 from bottom) Left out 'clever and mad'.

<u>Questions</u>. Mine. <u>Not important</u>.

p. 14 Is the 'how he managed <u>to be heard</u> better than to penetrate?

p. 46 Is <u>impasse</u> better than <u>dead-end</u>?

p. 80 '<u>Preen himself on</u>' against '<u>swagger about</u>'.

p. 90 '<u>Coffee surrogate</u>' against <u>ersatz coffee</u>.

1967

[January 1967]

Dear Patrick,
We're moving Saturday next, 28th January.
    39 Church Hill Road
   London E. 17.
It's cheap, 16 dollars p.w., and near a long market, near this school (between it and Whitechapel), and I hope I can get to my work again.[1]

It means there'll be no hurting urgency anymore, a different place can be bought if Anu can find one, and there's enough money left. I'm finished with that business.[2]

                Kindest wishes
                John

[Late January 1967]

Dear Charles,
We are leaving Powis Court Saturday. Tony White wanted it middle of February: and Richard is moving in Sunday/Monday for his visit.

We've got a place between Liverpool Street and this school, for the time being. It is as good as is possible for the area, and very cheap. I am sorry I had

---

1 The new address is in Walthamstow, very near Whipps Cross Hospital where McGahern's sisters Breege and Rosaleen worked as nurses. Now McGahern was just a 25-minute bus ride from school.
2 McGahern had been trying to purchase a leasehold interest at 30 Portland Road, W11, ultimately without success.

to give your name. The agents were extraordinarily respectable and the only way I could get it was by appearing to be more respectable than anybody else. It's 39 Church Hill Road, E. 17.

> With love as always
> John

Patrick Gregory Papers

[*39 Church Hill Road, Walthamstow*]
[*hereafter 39 Church Hill Road*]

[*23 February 1967*]

Dear Patrick,

The <u>Hamish Hamilton</u> business I can't understand, is it a mistake for Heinemann? I know Charles'd like to publish it. Will the translators get any copies.[3]

We almost bought a house with three decaying tenants, two flunkies on the ground floor, two floors free, in Portland Road, Simone Weil lived there once; it was opposite the Victorian pub T. White brought you to once, where you can walk from one street to the next only through the pub, but we couldn't get enough money from the Council, because of its condition, they'd only loan ½ the price, the price was £6,000.

Can you stay here when you come? It looks we'll be still here then. It's not like Powis Sq., but it's twice as big, and 100 times easier for somebody to stay. Or if you have business, then maybe you'd stay when you're free?

Murphy came, to my mind changed in some way, full still of notebooks and addresses and telephone numbers, but also a strong dosage of autumn or disappointment that I never noticed before, <u>almost</u> the <u>reflection</u> that the carrot wasn't worth the humiliation, but still – onwards.

Farrell wrote a note that Ted wasn't well: would you remember me to him and Bea.

Madeline Green wrote a card from Paris, I'd have answered, but lost it.[4] Dutch gentleman came, raving queer: Frenchman too, extraordinary charm, with beautiful ½ Vietnamese wife. Read <u>Torrents of Spring</u>, surprised how much more I liked it than when I read it first, also <u>Felix Holt the Radical</u>, odd

---

3 Refers to *The Manila Rope*, published in the US by Knopf in 1967.
4 Madeline and John first met in New York shortly after his arrival there in February 1966. Patrick Gregory was a childhood friend of Madeline's, his parents living near her father in Snedens Landing.

good bits and flashes:[5] also Jean Santeuil, extraordinary, the few themes over and over, the terrible pound the individual imagination must circle and circle, do you know the Ven. Bede and the bird in the lighted room.[6]

Hoping I can get used enough here to work again.

As always
John

Patrick Gregory
[Madeline McGahern]
[39 Church Hill Road]

16 March 1967

Dear Patrick,

Anu was growling about the note on the dustcover, and I told her to write to you, she's said nothing since, so it may have let the steam off.

---

5 Unknown whether *The Torrents of Spring* is the Turgenev novel of 1872 or the Hemingway novella of 1926. McGahern comments further on George Eliot's *Felix Holt, The Radical* (1866) in a letter of 16 March 1967 to Gregory.

6 *Jean Santeuil* is an unfinished novel by Marcel Proust written between 1896 and 1900, and published after the author's death. The first French edition was published in 1952 by Gallimard. The first English version, translated from the French by Gerard Hopkins, was published in 1956 by Simon & Schuster. The reference to the Venerable Bede relates to an event that took place in AD 625 when Paulinus had been sent from Rome to preach Christianity to the English-speaking Northumbrians. With the help of a divine vision he wins the conversion of the Northumbrian king Eadwine. Eadwine then feels the need to consult his leading men, to see if they will agree to adopt the new religion. The chief of his priests, Coifi, speaks first, urging an open mind to Paulinus's preaching. Then 'Another of the king's chief men agreed with this advice and with these wise words and then added, "This is how the present life of man on earth, King, appears to me in comparison with that time which is unknown to us. You are sitting feasting with your ealdormen and thegns in winter time; the fire is burning on the hearth in the middle of the hall and all inside is warm, while outside the wintry storms of rain and snow are raging; and a sparrow flies out through the other. For the few moments it is inside, the storm and wintry tempest cannot touch it, but after the briefest moment of calm, it flits from your sight, out of the wintry storm and into it again. So this life of man appears but for a moment; what follows or indeed what went before, we know not at all. If this new doctrine brings us more certain information, it seems right that we should accept it." ' See Bede, *Historia Ecclesiastica Gentis Anglorum*, Bk. II, ch. 13; the translation above is taken from L. C. Jane trans., *Bede's Ecclesiastical History of the English People*, ed. and trans. B. Colgrave and R. A. B. Mynors (Oxford: Clarendon Press, 1969).

I have no complaints. It's a beautifully produced book, I wish I felt as easy with the text, reading through. Wishing Meri was some good, wishing the translator was some good, wishing both to the devil.

Who got the N. B. award? Percy's second novel came out here, it got respectful notices.[7]

The novel with good bits was Felix Holt the Radical by George Eliot; some of the language, especially slang, which doesn't seem to have survived in England, some of the words, are in common use in Ireland, they'd be now termed Irish. There's very much preachifying though. Read, from a stall in the market, The Victim by Bellow, it would exactly drive you to borrow money to find out more, but apart from an embarrassment of an end, it was honest work compared with some of the later stuff I saw.[8]

Have you any exact plans for London?

The Great Russell is a lovely hotel.[9]

Do you go then to France?

If you wish, when you've business finished, and it'd suit you, there's plenty of room here, it's not like last year, the outside is pretty grim.[10]

What happened to your nephew? He didn't leave an address, I meant to invite him out, if he'd come.

Murphy asked me to put him up for an Arts Council Award; he's written thanking me for offering to put him up, and accepting. [I told him to find out if I'd be any good, hoping, when he asked] I'll do it but I don't know what the devil to write. Completing a great epic, historical; in dire poverty in palatial house by the sea, necessary no income tax to the work.[11]

Lehane sent a charming letter today & a St. Patrick's Day card/ May the good saints protect ye and the devil neglect ye. I've never seen the things

7 Walker Percy (1916–90), an American author known for his philosophical novels set in and around New Orleans. The novel referred to here is The Last Gentleman (New York: Farrar, Straus and Giroux, 1966).

8 The Victim was Saul Bellow's second novel, published in 1947 by the Vanguard Press in New York and by John Lehmann in London the following year. McGahern likely picked up the 1966 paperback published by Penguin.

9 Likely the Russell Hotel, Russell Square, London.

10 Gregory did not stay, as is clear from a letter he sends, dated 19 May 1967: 'I am tempted by your kind offer to put me up for the night, but I daren't quite accept it. [. . .] I'd like to drop by your place on Saturday morning around ten. Then we can conspire together on the best way to kill the day with all the proper sacrificial rites.' Knopf, HRC.

11 Richard Murphy was, at this time, working on his long historical poem The Battle of Aughrim. It was published by Faber the following year.

before. It used to be the Railway Cup at Croke Park and the pubs closed, unless you wanted to go to the Dog Show.

Nothing else. A programme about <u>Barracks</u> on Irish Television. A warning on faith and morals (Lehane) to selfstyled intellectuals by the Archbishop. Usual howl of the city going up round closing time.

Sick to death of the dogslife in this school.

All drifting out to sea apparently.

> How are you?
>
> > Your father and mother?
> >
> > > John

> > Michael McLaverty Archive
> >
> > 39 Church Hill Road

18 March 1967

Dear Michael,

We've changed from where we were, the man who owned the flat came back; it's east of London and dreary.

I've been wondering if it'd be possible for me to teach in the North of Ireland.

I have two years primary school training, which is not recognised here: I've a B.A., which is.

Will you forgive me for asking you to find out for me (a) whether my qualifications are acceptable (b) if they'll allow me increments (c) if it'd be possible to find a position.

I've been offered a number of jobs both academic and schools of writing, by American universities, but I don't want to go.

> > Can you find out for me?
> >
> > John

Patrick Gregory Papers

[*39 Church Hill Road*]

15 May 1967

Dear Patrick,

Saturday seems the best for the long day, if you like you can book out of the hotel that morning, sleep here, and go from here to the aeroplane on the 11th for Greece. Decide yourself what suits you best, the hotel or not.

It's the same with the evenings. I teach in the day, till 3.45 p.m. So whatever times if any after that is easy (suits with your other appointments); decide what's easy for yourself; and you'll need some time on your own.

Can Knopf send a <u>Dark</u> to

> Ivan Rosanov
> Gen. Secretary Friendship Society
> 14 Kalinin Ave
> Moscow K-9[12]

for translation consideration. Bring me a few copies of <u>Dark</u>, my account; or post it.

Any decent book you can get hands on, preferably paperback.

This is only to say do what's easy for you, I'll be glad to see you when it's that.

> John

Michael McLaverty Archive

39 Church Hill Road

22 May 1967

Dear Michael,

So relieved and happy that you're out. How are you?

I applied Stranmillis, good references, rejected by return.[13] Think I'll stay in London until this book is in more secure shape, but we'll move then, if you

---

12 In a letter of 19 May, Gregory confirms that he has sent a copy to the Russian.

13 Stranmillis is a teacher training college in Belfast. Charles Monteith had written a very supportive reference on McGahern's behalf on 27 April, describing him as '<u>the</u> most promising young Irish prose writer at work today', but to no avail.

find out there's a real possibility of getting a job, preferably in State school, under the real name. It's impossible to hope that they'd appoint me without knowing. It wouldn't be fair either.

Annikki says the particular writer is useless, a great beauty though, wife of the Esthonian Ambassador to London.[14]

What happened in the school before you left? Write and let me know.[15]

I wrote to O'Connor too about a school.[16] Do you want any books or anything from London?

John

Patrick Gregory Papers

39 Church Hill Road

27 May 1967

Dear Patrick,
This is a difficult place to get to, even by London: and I suggest I pick you up at the hotel about 9–10 a.m. and we can move this way for lunch, and make our way back to town in the evening.

Does this suit you? If you'd prefer to adventure say so.
It looks like change again, then we leave here July, but it's not certain.

Pirandello wrote a novel: a cinema operator confusing his life and the films he projected, is it available in America?[17]

Tony White gave me Gunn's new poems in Faber proof, and they didn't even badly exist.[18]

---

14 Refers to Aino Kallas (1878–1956), a Finnish-born writer of prose fiction who lived much of her life in Estonia. From 1922 to 1934 she lived in London where her husband, Oskar Kallas, was ambassador to the United Kingdom.

15 McLaverty retired in the face of mounting work-related stress.

16 Probably refers to Belfast writer Patrick Joseph O'Connor who wrote under the pen name Padraic Fiacc.

17 Luigi Pirandello, *Shoot! The Notebooks of Serafino Gubbio, Cinematograph Operator*, translated from Italian into English by C. K. Scott Moncrieff in 1926.

18 The collection in question is *Touch* by Thom Gunn, published by Faber in 1967. McGahern had met Gunn in the company of Tony White and the Shakespearean actor Sheila Ballantine on 5 April 1967 in the Salisbury, a public house in Covent Garden. See Thom Gunn Diary 1966–70, Carton 2, Folder 37, Thom Gunn Papers BANC MSS/235, Bancroft Library, University of California, Berkeley.

Reading a charming Borrow, Lavengro.[19]
Kindest regards,
John

Tony Whelan

43B Grove Road
[*should read Gore Road*]
London E9
[*hereafter 43B Gore Road*][20]

Thursday [*July 1967*]

Dear Tony,
I am sorry about the conversation on the telephone.
I still feel the work falls into some limbo.
Rather than ring you at a time I think it's better to post it, and if when you think of it I can be of any use, I'll be grateful and glad.[21]
John

19 George Borrow, *Lavengro: The Scholar, the Gypsy, the Priest*, first published 1851 in three volumes in London by John Lane. Its unnamed protagonist is born the son of an officer in a militia regiment and is brought up in various barrack towns in England, Scotland and Ireland. After serving an apprenticeship to a lawyer he becomes a Grub Street hack, an occupation that gives him ample opportunities to observe London low-life. Finally he takes to the road as a tinker.
20 Still in East London, further away from his place of work in Chingford than his Church Hill Road address, but a more handsome flat overlooking Victoria Park, Bethnal Green.
21 Whelan had writerly ambitions that McGahern's criticisms blunted. He describes the relationship in the essay, 'Working at the mill', *The John McGahern Yearbook*, vol. 2, 28–41. The two had met to talk about Whelan's draft novel in their usual meeting place of Dirty Dick's public house in Bishopsgate.

18 July 1967

Dear Patrick,

I hope that last half pint, jibbed down your throat, didn't put the kibosh on
your holiday; the only reason for my clumsy ringing the morning you left.

We're about settled here. Long red curtains up: a big solid beech table: 6
black bentwood chairs with cane seats: a bed: an oaken writing desk with
drawers down to the floor and brass handles, that I bought in the market:
and much empty space, the best of all: and books along the wall in two
rooms, candlesticks, one of them brass with an electric bulb, the small green
chestnuts showing in the leaves across the road.[22]

I read Pierre.[23] The one thing always clear about Melville is that he's a
poet, some of the early parts magical: but often the impression of a moral
elephant beating a mouse's go cart into moral shape, especially towards the
end, chapter after chapter, some kind of more angelic cross between Lewis
and Lawrence hectoring goodow.

I like the Carpentier, but haven't finished.[24]

Murphy came, on one of his P.R. visits, I get more and more embarrassed at
being left along with him, those doing eyes looking out in vacancy, but he's
indomitable, and that's something.

Anu spends most of her time with a friend at a sociological conference, to
end the system of oppression and being oppressed.

Can you send the stories? I've another finished but want to go over it.

John

---

22 The flat overlooked the west end of Victoria Park.
23 *Pierre; or, The Ambiguities* (New York: Harper, 1852), a novel by Herman
Melville that became a firm favourite of McGahern's.
24 Alejo Carpentier y Valmont (1904–80), Swiss-born Cuban novelist, essayist and
musicologist. Unknown which of Carpentier's works McGahern was enjoying.

Faber

43B Gore Road

26 July 1967

Dear Charles,
Thank you for the Letters, I was too moved to write till now by the generosity,
until I'd read them, I'd meant to buy them.[25]

I admire Joyce, but nothing near as much as, say in the letters of this
century, Yeats or Proust, I think you know this, and the letters confirmed
this more. Bucket in the well of my life, and many direct beautiful things,
Stanislaus more enigmatic and sympathetic [than] everything I read, and
much and much more.

Would you like to come here to dinner any convenient evening, and
Rosemary, and anyone you'd like to bring else?

Anu goes 11th August to Finland.
Love
John

Madeline McGahern

[43B Gore Road]

[Postmarked 18 October 1967][26]

Madeline,
I know you can understand I do not want to say anything except these slight
things, but I have to say that, out of utter care for you, and common courtesy.

The place to write
Miss Dymphna McGahern
23 Forest Drive West
London E.11

25 On 6 July Monteith had sent McGahern volumes II and III of the *Letters of James
Joyce*, edited by Richard Ellmann and published by Faber in 1966.
26 This is the earliest surviving letter from McGahern to Madeline Green, b. 1934 in
New York. Madeline had first met McGahern in New York in February 1966. Later
that year she moved to Paris where she worked in her father's recording studio. In
August 1967 she had moved temporarily to London with her father where she was
working in some of his business interests. She contacted McGahern and a love affair
quickly followed.

Either send it with <u>Rue Christine</u> on the back <u>to her</u>: or envelope to me, within envelope to her.[27]

I am conscious almost always of your absence, of putting hands out, and finding them empty, of re-enacting in my mind the simple and terrible things we seem to do ordinarily well together.

To walk in some eternal market full of meat and vegetables and eggs and cheese and wine, or the soles of our feet together, or to talk about your father, or when you winked at me Sunday over coffee and it was to tell me this particular confusion was a generality you were aware of. Will you sometimes remember me?

John

Madeline McGahern

[23 Forest Drive West]

[Postmarked 21 October 1967]

[To Madeline]
I love you and I miss you all the time.
    Will I see you in five weeks?
Do you love me at all?
    Why did you threaten me?

John

Madeline McGahern

[London]

[Postmarked 24 October 1967]

Dear Madeline,
I can hardly abide the wait of days.

I rang Aer Lingus. You can change the ticket for Belfast. Planes leave London at 5.50 pm and at 7.15 pm for Belfast, up to midnight.

---

27 Madeline Green lived in an apartment owned by her father – and later transferred into her ownership – at 1 Rue Christine in the sixth arrondissement. The apartment would remain an important property for the couple throughout the courtship, marriage and right to the end of McGahern's life.

I'll be met there, but will escape as soon as I can. I'll send you the name of my hotel as soon as I have it. Do you want me to book you into it?[28]

Where would you like to go to get out of the place on Friday, after I'm finished. Dublin (2 hours) or some of the towns by the sea?

I'll ring Saturday, either the morning or late evening.

> With my love
> John

Madeline McGahern

[*London*]

1 November 1967

Dearest Madeline,

I'm not calm enough to write, it's insanity all the time in the house now.[29]

It's all Thursday in my mind. Thursday, Thursday, and Thursday.

Send me some word. I love you.

> John

Madeline McGahern

23 Forest Drive West

[*Postmarked 14 November 1967*]

Dear Madeline,

Write to me all you can, as much as you are able, all I care is that it is about you in some way, that's the only way you spare me.

I only mean slight in the sense of our lives, there are no Importances, as the moon in a bucket of water is more real than in the sky, as if suddenly it's frail as our own flesh.

Why do you threaten me? – 'For these days at least'?

I do not know how to tell you of the torment of these last days.

There are many things more now I want to ask you about your own life.

I dreamt last night I climbed the stairs of the Rue Christine, with an empty milk bottle, and the bed was unmade, and no light except the streetlight, and

---

28 The couple were amused by the hotel room, which bore a sign with the legend 'no bedroom entertaining' over a picture of Adam and Eve.
29 As his marriage with Annikki fell apart.

I sat down to wait, and nobody came, only the mockery of drunks singing on their way home outside.

I go to Belfast Thursday 23rd November to Sunday the 26th.[30]

Will I see you then?

After I've spoken we can escape on some excuse to the sea.

Will you tell me?

John

Do you know who loves you?

Madeline McGahern

[*London*]

[*November 1967*]

Dearest Madeline,

I am so muddled after the flu that I cannot properly think.

I'll get the 10 am from Victoria: it gets in somewhere in the early evening. Which'd you prefer to meet me there or for me to ring or come?[31]

Don't worry about Friday evening if it's any way difficult or uneasy.

Where do you go in the evenings, outside the A.C.?[32]

John

Madeline McGahern

[*London*]

30 November 1967

Dear Madeline,

I am so sorry the days were so public and scattered and broken, but you were for me a rock of calm, though it must have been hard.[33]

---

30 McGahern had been booked to give a lecture and reading at the Belfast Festival.

31 McGahern travelled to and from Paris as much as possible through the autumn and winter of 1967–8.

32 American Centre, Boulevard Raspail, where Madeline went to play table tennis. Visiting lecturers could also be heard there – Madeline recalls one especially memorable talk delivered by Marcel Duchamp (1887–1968).

33 Refers to the couple's days together in Belfast when Madeline first met, among others, Charles Monteith, Richard Murphy and Seamus and Marie Heaney.

A confusion of warm and cold days, so I have this horrible cold, and I cannot think clear or work with it.

Can I ring you at ten on Sunday and I think of you and think of you, and follow grey coats and tall fair hair in the streets.

Will you think of me?

John

Patrick Gregory
[*Madeline McGahern*]

Whitehall C.P.
Normanton Park
London E. 4
[*hereafter Whitehall School*]

5 December 1967

Dear Patrick,

For a long time now things have been growing worse between Annikki and I.

If you want to write privately to me it's better

McGahern
Whitehall C.P.
Normanton Park
London E. 4[34]

If it's neutral it's alright to this place.

Will you come to London this summer?

You didn't send me Share's book, and a few promised[35]

John

---

34 This is the address of the Chingford school in which McGahern taught.
35 Gregory had mentioned a book entitled *Inish* by a new Irish writer named Bernard Share (1930–2013) being published by Knopf in 1967.

James Swift
[*Madeline McGahern*]

43B Gore Road

20 December 1967

Dear Jimmy,
I wondered if you knew what happened to Kavanagh or if he'd been ill long.[36]
I saw the Irish Times.

I went on the TV in Belfast for money. It was gruesome sitting there, drinking water, feeling you should have learned to dance or play the French fiddle, hearing the spontaneous conversation you heard a ½ hour before in the dressingroom, and then the embarrassment of being expected to talk.

Is Paddy coming for Christmas?
Would you be able to write sometime. I'd be glad. With kind wishes to your mother always.

John

36 Patrick Kavanagh b. 1904 died on 30 November 1967.

1968

Madeline McGahern

[*London*]

[*Postmarked 8 January 1968*]

Dear Madeline,
I send the books today. I hope they'll please you. The Muir is for Nancy.[1]

I am all the time in either confusion or disturbance.
Sometimes it seems round and round I turn.

I felt not able to say the things I wanted on the telephone, or if I tried it was plodding and awkwardness.

Tell Nancy and Sanche what I asked you. I am seldom that way, it is more self-hatred than anything mean.[2]

Will you forgive me?
It looks like snow this evening, I'll see Ian after the books. The birds are low over the football field.

> Believe me that I love you.
> John

---

1 Nancy Ryan de Gramont, a poet known to Madeline in Paris who wanted Ian Hamilton to read her work.
2 Sanche de Gramont b. 1932 in Geneva, Switzerland; moved to the US in 1937. Name legally changed to Ted Morgan in 1977; married second wife Nancy Ryan on 11 May 1968.

Madeline McGahern

[*London*]

[*January 1968*]

Dear Madeline,
I sent two books: they hadn't the others; I'll send them in some time. The Borrow I want to get in the Oxford edition.[3]

The snow came, all eight inches, rows of abandoned buses, cars, lorries.

Milling of crowds at Liverpool St. Wet concrete, drip from glass and girders, skeleton trains running.

'British Rail regrets owing to severe weather conditions . . .' – the loudspeaker. 'If they keep us here much fugging longer it'll have melted, it will,' a woman, market woman, who got off at the Broadway.

I'll ring at the same time on Sunday: is that all right?

Almost always you are in my mind

John

Madeline McGahern

[*London*]

[*Spring 1968*]

Dear Madeline,
I got back without hitches. They were almost the calmest and nicest days I've ever had.

I didn't get the Washington place. A rather strange letter came saying I'd been the alternative choice and the first choice had accepted it. So. That's that, with curses.[4]

The Paris girl stays till Friday.
Cold blue days and I'll ring on Sunday morning early and Ian's wife madder than ever.[5]

John

3 *Lavengro* by George Borrow, a favourite book of McGahern's. See letter to Patrick Gregory of 27 May 1967.
4 McGahern had applied for a position teaching creative writing at Western Washington State College in Bellingham, Washington.
5 Ian Hamilton's then wife Gisela Dietzel.

[*Spring 1968*]

Dear Madeline,
This will come either Friday or Saturday.

Magnolias have all come down, even the diehards, and this morning I saw children trying to make petal castles out of the fall of blossom; the old men pension out the days on the seats, and nobody lies on the withering crocus stalks, under the tree.

George came yesterday, it was he who blew at us on Bethnal Green Road, chairs and books and doors went wallop upstairs; we'd to go.[6]

He'd got the complaints, of that unfortunate September evening.

C. 'Grace has too good a job for me to see her go, with him she's the best of both worlds.'
B. 'He's made his choice and he can't get out of it. If she (you) does that now she'll do the same to him later.'

One curses, all that peasant fear.
Geo. 'We're all in ideal dog carts, coupled, and for anybody to jump out it's lynch law. The strawberry trifle in danger of melting.'

It looks more and more to get out it'll have to be for a time Paris.
One thing, it's an old bone among lovers, try not to talk too intimately about me to anybody, and I'll try the same or not to talk at all to anybody about you.

I wish I could walk over the park with you, and sit in the old part of the bridge, and talk of where we have choices of going and doing, and go across the Marshes, you'd drink Guinness and get stared at, we'd meet when I'd the cheque cashed, and eat 2 plates of cheese with beer, and fuck each other to rest.

I'm teasing you out of love
John

6 George Kelly, a Bethnal Green neighbourhood friend, eel and pie shop entrepreneur, and the first person in London to whom McGahern introduced Madeline. Known to McGahern as 'George Eels'.

27 March 1968

Dear Peter,[7]
Thank you for the contract, and kind letter.

I have only three things, two of them minor.

(1) I left Matson (Peters in America) in 1965, and since then Patrick Gregory has been handling all my work in America. I <u>cannot</u> now take this away from him nor do I want. So the American rights will have to be withheld.[8]

(2) I have 3 already foreign language publishers, and have been paying Intercontinental 20%, so in the circumstances it hardly seems fair that I should now pay more, though it's only 5%.[9]

(3) This is a query. I know authors who have got 60/40 for paperback, again it is small, but especially <u>The Barracks</u> has done well in paperback.[10]
Can I ring tomorrow, when you've seen this. It may be easier for me to go into the office and sign there, in a few minutes.

With kindest wishes

John

7 Peter du Sautoy.
8 Du Sautoy has written 'ok' after this point.
9 Du Sautoy has written 'ok' after this point.
10 Du Sautoy writes in margin: 'Subject to agreement when a contract is made'. In a letter of 1 April du Sautoy writes to McGahern: 'As for the paperbacks, there is an arrangement for a 60/40 division in special cases and I think we had better consider the matter when the actual offer is received. Usually the 60/40 division only applies when the advance is exceptionally large: that is to say for very large sellers in the region of 100,000 or 150,000. But we will certainly look at it when the moment arrives.'

28 March 1968

Dear Patrick,

I didn't write, because it's been a terrible year; and I seemed too unfit to write to you.

I have left Sissons. I have signed a contract with Faber. They'll pay me £500 over the next two years and the Arts Council may pay me a similar sum, I dislike it, but I owe them no money, and it is necessary that I leave this school.[11] I know that I am able now to write better than I've ever been, in my own style, if I am granted grace.

I have given Fabers the world rights, except the United States. I learned today that you are leaving Knopf. I'd already withdrawn the U. S. rights, to give or offer them to you at Knopf. But I very much want that you'll let me move with you, <u>if the new firm want the work</u>, and I want no contract or advance, since my work has never made money in America as it has here.[12]

I disliked the <u>Share</u> book, it seemed to me an exercise in aesthetics against life, rather than an attempt to live another way, when Beckett weakens he is close to this.[13]

There's a room, and it is big, for you to stay if you want when you come. I'll be glad, and I hope you will.

Can you write two letters, one with no hint of disturbance to 43B Gore Road; and the other to the school. Please forgive me for this.

Can you tell me how your father is?

11 This £500 was the advance for McGahern's next novel. The agreement, dated 15 March 1968, states that he is to be paid £100 on signature, £100 on 1 October 1968, £100 on 1 April 1969, £100 on 1 October 1969 and £100 on delivery.

12 Matthew Evans at Faber writes to Bill Koshland at Knopf on 13 May 1968 asking if Knopf would be prepared to let McGahern follow Gregory to Atlantic. Koshland appears to have agreed to this arrangement. McGahern's comment about his work's relative failure in the US remained a constant irritant until the late flowering of *By the Lake* (2002) and *All Will be Well* (2006) under the watchful eye of Sonny Mehta at Knopf.

13 Reference to Bernard Share's debut novel, *Inish*. See letter to Gregory of 5 December 1967.

Murphy has been here with a tinker valet.

Write if you can soon

John

Madeline McGahern

[*London*]

[*March 1968*]

Dear Madeline,

I rang an hour ago, and I'll try again early this evening or in the early morning.

I miss you continually, and in this missing I am continually defeated by the grimness of the smiling that I am able in the absence to manage too the days.

The crocus in the shortcut garden to the station at Bethnal Green have gone, ragged stems, except a few in the north shadow of the trunk, delayed flowering, delayed death, I remember the frigidity you spoke of till these last years, my egotistical timidity, and those northern diehards against the University buildings please me NO END. Life at last, for the time, the sun the other side of the electric railway, last to be put down. The stems at the back of the north side of the track will obviously outwear all the early talent of the south.

I got the contract from Faber; it goes to the Arts Council, soon I'll be free, I feel it against the tags of these brutal buds leaning into Gore Road.

John

Patrick Gregory Papers

43B Gore Road

5 April 1968

Dear Patrick,

There'll be no trouble here, I'd be hurt if you stayed some other place, and there's even toilets on each floor.

236

Can you come the 8th if it's possible instead of the 9th? The reason is selfish: there's a byelection, and I don't have to go to school on the 9th. You'll be here for the very end of the soccer season.[14]

The reason for the school as address is, among others, that if the letters appear personal, or to me, that Anu uses them against me; and she almost always gets and opens letters first. Neutral letters to here are alright. I don't want to go into it here, it seems close to illness, the whole business.

Can you tell me the time and date when you'll come?

Can I do anything for you here?

Read a very amusing and good novel The Master and Margarita by Bulgakov.

Such relief to have handed in my notice to that cursed school

John

Patrick Gregory Papers

43B Gore Road

22 April 1968

Dear Patrick,

I have checked the matches, and we can go the afternoon of the 11th of May, the Saturday after you come.[15]

The reason I delayed was that I thought it might be possible to wrangle tickets for the Cup Final, a week later, but it seems hopeless: the worst of these end of the league matches – and the London teams have had a poor season – is that since the result doesn't at that stage often matter, what you may get is a sleepy exhibitionism.[16]

I am looking forward very much to your coming.

---

14 The 1967–8 First Division title was won by Manchester City with Manchester United as runners-up. United had won the European Cup that season, the first English club to do so.

15 The game in question was almost certainly West Ham v Everton at Upton Park, which ended in a 1–1 draw.

16 Of the London clubs, West Ham finished twelfth, Tottenham Hotspur, the other London team McGahern kept an eye on, in seventh, Chelsea sixth, Arsenal ninth and Fulham bottom of the table and relegated to the second division. The Cup Final was played on 18 May 1968 and resulted in a 1–0 victory for West Bromwich Albion over Everton after extra time.

Tell me the aeroplane times when you can
John

24 April 1968

Dear Patrick,
Thank you for the flight information and I'll meet you there. There's no telephone. If anything should be wrong – it's not likely – the tube station is Bethnal Green; and a taxi comes less than 2 dollars from Victoria.

I wrote to Knopf about the soccer match, there's one on the 11th, the Saturday; and Matthew Evans said he'd like to come, apparently he goes to New York a few days afterwards. It's the last league game of the season, the trouble with this is that by that time the League is generally decided – the Champions, and the relegated teams. 2 teams go down each year, and the 2 top teams in the lower divisions go up. And you wind up with a kind of premadonnish kickabout, with appropriate irony from the working man, goodnatured if there's sun, sour in the rain.

Be certain to give my respect to your mother and father before you leave.

Has the nephew gone to Vietnam yet?
John

Madeline McGahern

[*London*]

[*Postmarked 7 May 1968*]

Dear Madeline,
Your letter came this morning, Tuesday; the Gron one, yesterday; the dinner seemed mean, and in a way competitive, how children try to be first to the lavatory.[17] 'You should be sorry because I've beaten you all these years to

17 Madeline invited her father Niels Gron and his young wife Kika to dinner at her Paris apartment. Madeline and her father had a difficult relationship and at the dinner party referred to in this letter Gron was very rude about the food. Gron (1913–95) was Danish-American, born in Norway, the son of a Danish politician and writer of

the lavatory, and since the lavatory is an indisputable fact, and I did get first, and since we all agree that getting first to the first lavatory is life, then I have lived a lovely life, and to convince me of that I need you; and since you didn't get first to the first lavatory you could feel sorry for yourself, because in order for me to enjoy having got first to the first lavatory, I need to feel you want to too, whether you have use for it or not.' I think it's as simple as that confusion.

I found, to my own confusion, that this translation is to be finished on the 15th. Patrick goes to Ireland about that time. I mention this because it'll be easier for you when I ring, whether or not Gron [15th], and I'll have more definite information when I ring. I'll ring on Thursday if I know at 10pm. If I don't know I'll ring as I said on Friday. If for any reason I can't on Friday I'll ring early Saturday.

Forgive me for this.

Mean cold weather here.

Blackie was made footballer of the year.[18]

I've finished the first shape of a story.

School is pretty desperate, I hate the people, I'd go postman if I wasn't going, almost anything.

Love

John

the same name. He was an accomplished musician who for much of his later adult life resided in Paris where he owned a number of properties.

18 Blackie was McGahern's nickname for his fellow Irishman George Best, the Football Writers' Footballer of the Year, winner of the European Footballer of the Year Award, and much admired by McGahern. John and Madeline had seen Best play for Manchester United against West Ham on 2 September 1967 – their first date as a couple.

Madeline McGahern

[*London*]

[*Spring 1968*]

Dear Madeline,
I have been at the banks, and I have a beat here away from the hot day.[19]
   They have music now, which is a curse, over which some one shouts for muscatel.
   I leave tomorrow at 8.30. I'll probably get the blankets on my way back.
   I miss you very much. You can probably use Dymphna on her way to check the outside room, as excuse.
   I saw Ian and White yesterday.[20]

As always, with my love
John

Faber

43B Gore Road

[*June 1968*]

Dear Charles,
Thank you for letting me know the marvellous news.[21]
   I am looking forward very much to Thursday.
      Balls Brothers
      465 Bethnal Green Road

---

19 This letter is written on the back of a blank Balls Brothers of London bill. This public house on Bethnal Green Road was a particular favourite of McGahern's when living at Gore Road and is described thus in Tony White and Martin Green's *Guide to London Pubs*: 'The walls are covered with old newspaper cuttings and Austin Balls' quaint inscriptions; port and sherry are served from wooden barrels and the original gas-lights still function.'
20 Ian Hamilton and Tony White were among McGahern's closest London friends, sharing his love of football and characterful public houses.
21 The news is likely to have been either that McGahern had been awarded a £500 Arts Council bursary (June 1968) or a £400 grant from the Phoenix Trust under the auspices of the Society of Authors (October 1968). Monteith had lobbied for both these grants on McGahern's behalf.

The 8 bus which passes close to Russell Square, going down New Oxford Street, drops you a few yards away.

But it'll obviously depend on many things how you'll want to travel.

So I'll ring at 11.30 to discover how it is for you.

Love

John

Madeline McGahern

Co. Galway

[*Late August 1968*]

Dear Madeline,

The sea is calm, and sun, and the gulls follow, without tossing.[22]

If you want to ring for any reason, Murphy Cleggan <u>13</u> (thirteen) will get me between next Sunday and Wednesday. It's probably safer to mark it personal.

I miss you, and I love you, or the other way round.

Sean [*with John scribbled over it*]

I signed my old name first.[23]

Patrick Gregory Papers

[*No address*]

3 September 1968

Dear Patrick,

At last I send this, the trouble is that several other stories started to creep in: it has three parts: train, rest, train. There's only one sentence that's a risk.[24]

I have Hearts of Oak and Bellies of Brass almost finished.

I doubt if it is publishable in America.[25]

---

22 Note written aboard the ferry to Ireland on British Railways Irish Shipping Services letterhead.

23 Madeline never knew McGahern as Sean.

24 The story in question is almost certainly 'Wheels', which opens *Nightlines*.

25 McGahern's worries about the story are well founded given Gregory's chariness over his use of 'F-U-C-K' on the opening page of *The Dark*. 'Fuck' and its cognates appear in various forms in what is a frank depiction of Irish navvies, alcoholism and

If you and or two others like it I'll be happy and think it well published. Write to me as soon as you can. Will you tell me when you come to London on the business?

I'll be back there in three days.

As always

John

Sudd Zeitung are publishing a series of three stories.[26]

The Image is appearing in 2 translations.[27]

Will you tell me how you are in Boston?

Patrick Gregory Papers

43B Gore Road

17 November 1968[28]

Dear Patrick,

Can you send me airmail the paperback Pirandello?[29]

The way I'm trying to avoid embarrassment or trickery at Reading is to read something and let them talk about it.[30]

---

prostitution on a London building site. The story, as McGahern feared, was rejected by the *Kenyon Review*, as Gregory tells him in a letter of 23 June 1969: 'It occurs to me that you might have better luck in placing the individual stories in England, where – perhaps – the magazine boys may have a somewhat clearer idea of what you are up to. The confusion here is tremendous. Never (in my memory) have the so-called literary magazines been less sure of their tastes, or less hospitable to foreign voices.' Knopf, HRC. 'Hearts of Oak and Bellies of Brass' finally appeared in America as the fifth story in *Nightlines* (Boston and Toronto: Atlantic Monthly Press; Little, Brown and Company, 1971).

26 Süddeutsche Zeitung, publishing house based in Munich. There is no evidence that such a publication occurred.

27 Appeared in French as the preface to *Lignes de Fond* in 1971.

28 First of McGahern's correspondence with Gregory addressed to The Atlantic Monthly Press, Boston.

29 Gregory had written on 20 November 1968 on Atlantic Monthly Press letterhead: 'I raced around to the local paperback marts yesterday evening in search of the Pirandello. No soap. BUT my secretary has located a copy by telephone at the Harvard bookstore.' Madeline McGahern Papers.

30 McGahern was a Visiting Research Fellow at the University of Reading in the 1968 autumn term and again in autumn 1971 thanks to the patronage of Professor D. J. Gordon. He had limited and untaxing teaching duties. See *Memoir*, 255.

I've put down <u>Soft Touch of Grass</u> for early and I've found I've lost my own copy, a few days ago, and it's not published here.[31]

I've sent the last of 'Korea'.

Affectionately
John

Will send soon <u>The Recruiting Officer</u>[32]

Patrick Gregory Papers
Whitehall School

[*Autumn 1968*]

Dear Patrick,

I got £800.

It reads and sounds a bum business, but I am grateful, we have to leave here, I'll use it to get some permanent place.

I am sorry, because I've never written so well continuously as this last run, and the change makes me afraid again.

There were 3 of £1,200; 12 of £800. The Reporter West got one. I was glad Higgins got one.[33]

Murphy's old house got burned down.

Hamsun didn't come.

When are you thinking of holidays?

Madeline Green wrote a card to give her Paris address.[34]

<hr>

31 'The Soft Touch of Grass' is a short story by Luigi Pirandello (1867–1936).

32 Gregory remarks in his letter of 20 November 1968: 'I look forward to receiving "The Recruiting Officer" [. . .] Could it be, John, that you are moving towards a book? [. . .] if the material continues to accumulate, we might want to think seriously of issuing a small collection of stories.' This exchange is the first germ of what would eventually become *Nightlines*, published in the UK by Faber in 1970 and by Atlantic Monthly Press through Little, Brown and Company in the US the following year. 'The Recruiting Officer' was accepted for publication by the *Atlantic Monthly* where it appeared in July 1970. See Gregory to McGahern (28 July 1969). Madeline McGahern Papers.

33 British Arts Council bursaries. Higgins is the Irish novelist Aidan.

34 McGahern had been seeing Madeline for over a year at this point, making regular trips to Paris throughout. Gregory was an admirer of Annikki's and McGahern was trying to keep vague the details of his personal life.

Dramatization of Tarry Flynn runs at the ABBEY.[35]
Dymphna teaches permanent here, likes it more than Dublin, my Leytonstone relatives able to booze steady in spite of freeze.

Did the drawing exhibition of the Jewish one come off in Paris?

What happened your nephew?

John

35 P. J. O'Connor's dramatic adaptation of Patrick Kavanagh's 1947 novel *Tarry Flynn* ran at the Abbey Theatre, Dublin in November–December 1968.

1969

John McGahern Papers[1]

[*No address*]

[January 1969]

[*To unknown, Colgate University*][2]
Thank you for your kind letter and I am looking forward very much to meeting you in February.

The books you've ordered are ideal, I am very grateful. Because of Christmas the mails have been very slow, and rather hurriedly I enclose this additional list. I would like them, subject to your approval, to be available to the students either through the bookshop or library.

One of the problems at Reading, I teach mostly European and American writers there, is that the students are already overloaded with compulsory reading – for instance the whole 19th century English Novel – and I have to be careful, as Visiting Fellow, to add as little as possible to this burden.

I'd be extremely grateful for any guidance you could give me.
Can you give me any rough idea of the days of my classes yet? And how many probable students?

I include Beckett and Kavanagh because of two different traditions in their continuance. Because of the haste I am not able to include the American publishers, and I am sorry for any trouble this may cause you, but it is hardly important if they are not all available at the very beginning of the course.

Did you get any letter concerning the formalities of the temporary work permit. Does this usually take long?

I hope to travel through Boston. The Atlantic Monthly Press will publish my next books in America and they want to give a small reception for me. I moved there with my former editor at Knopf, Patrick Gregory.[3]

1 This letter rests among the McGahern Papers at NUIG, P71/1177.
2 McGahern was preparing his teaching curricula for what would be his first stint as a visiting professor at Colgate University, Hamilton, New York in the spring of 1969.
3 This letter has the look of a draft, with multiple crossings out and insertions. It is followed by a more formal and finalised list in pencil of the books required by McGahern for his spring classes at Colgate.

[*Reading List*]
Traits and Stories of the Irish Peasantry by William Carleton (or in fact any Carleton)
The Real Charlotte by Somerville & Ross
The Big House at Inver by Somerville & Ross
The Great Hunger by Cecil Woodham Smith as social background to the 19th century
The Islandman by Tomas O Crohan translated by Robin Flower (O.U.P.)
Dubliner's Diary
My Brother's Keeper by Stanislaus Joyce
Letters of James Joyce editor Ellmann
Autobiographies W.B. Yeats
Murphy or Malone Dies by S. Beckett
All That Fall by S. Beckett
Tarry Flynn by Patrick Kavanagh
Collected Poems by Patrick Kavanagh

Madeline McGahern

Faculty Club
Colgate University
Hamilton, New York 13346
[*hereafter Colgate*]

6 February 1969[4]

Dear Madeline,
I hope it was all right when I rang, I was overtired and excited.

Did you ring the next day? Patrick and I had to go out to the editor's house for lunch, it was out the country, we left at ten, got back at four.

It is all snow, with hail, and old trees, the houses wooden or Greek, white triangle above pillars.

It is all right for you to come, but we may not be able to live in the Club, it may mean you in the hotel and me in the Club; the trouble is that [*illegible*] of going to Paris, but it seems increasingly difficult.

---

4 This is McGahern's first extant letter written from Colgate University where he would go on to work haphazardly as a member of the English faculty over many years up to 2001.

I am managing to write almost every day.
                    With all my love
                    John

                                        Madeline McGahern

                                        Colgate

[*February 1969*]

Dear Madeline,
I speak in Boston on Sunday the 2nd March. I finish lectures on Friday the
28th of February at 11.15 am. I can be in Boston at 6 pm that Friday.
    Which would you prefer, Friday or Saturday, I'd love to see you on Friday,
but you will get to Boston before me that day, at about 1 pm, so – ? my love.
    I get holidays from the 18th March to the 7th April.
    It is tough, but it will get less so, and the Chairman is a person of real
quality.[5]
    You'll have got letters certainly [*illegible*] this, this morning I am sorry,
I feared a death, and I could hear my own echo.
    This place is 2 days behind New York or Boston, so write your plans as
soon as you've got this.
                    And forgive me
                    Love
                    John

5 Bruce P. Berlind (1926–2014), Professor of English specialising in modern American
poetry. Beginning his teaching career at Colgate in 1954, he founded the English
Department's visiting writers' series in the 1960s when he began hosting readings by
US and British poets on campus; he devoted long service as department chair. Born
in Brooklyn in 1926, Berlind attended Princeton and Johns Hopkins universities. He
served in the US Army in intelligence, being stationed in Germany after VE Day and
then in Japan during the Korean War.

24 February 1969

Dear Patrick,
It's almost certain Madeline Green will be in Boston this week-end. If she comes, she'll probably not want to go to the reading; but I think she'd probably be glad to see you, and if you don't want it'll be easy to avoid.

Judith Jones wrote to Berlind, and apparently Kinsella will come in April.[6]

I finished the first draft of the new story this weekend. Three days I have to teach in the morning, and they are finished. After Yeats' Tower Poems I had headaches all day.

When I was an infant teacher I had to learn how to withhold all egotism in order to write afterwards, but at this level the students' demands and awareness make it impossible, it's no place for long for a writer.

I got paid today and it's easier for me to pay you now, in the sense that I won't have to remember. I can speak it openly since you let slip once you have the same disease.

John

Faber

Colgate

25 February 1969

Dear Charles,
Patrick is looking forward to seeing you in late April.

It's beautiful here, a village of Greek Revival Houses in the valley and the University on one of the surrounding hills; old avenues of trees from the village, the gold of the chapel tower against pine forest and snow.

I wasn't able to work after coming, but last week I began, and finished the first draft of a new story, but the 3 lectures are killing; they are in the morning, and the day is finished.

6 Judith Jones (1924–2017) was an editor at Knopf and was responsible for *The Diary of Anne Frank* being published in the US by Doubleday. McGahern admired Thomas Kinsella. He particularly liked the early poem 'A Lady of Quality'.

248

Yeats spoke here, mostly remembered because of the Chairman of the Trustees: when he heard the poet was coming rushed to the library, read all of Keats's Endymion, and congratulated the visitor at the Reception, with many quotations, on its authorship.

David Halliwell was offered Richard's and my place at Reading.[7] The Atlantic Monthly will publish the last story I wrote.[8]

All the days since the dead bird in the chimney is in my head.[9]

I speak to the Irish Boston Society in an old hotel next Sunday: as a Protestant Patrick is looking forward. They want me to read the new work out.

The Chairman, Berlind, is a very fine person, and there seems little of the Faculty Party.

There is great trouble getting my books here, the Knopf may be sold out, but the Macmillan is lost in a warehouse. I'll ask Madeline to get 15 copies of both The B. and T. Dark, can you send them airmail, since the students are complaining, to me, and charge it to an author's account.

Will you remember me to Rosemary.

Love
John

7 David Halliwell (1936–2006), British dramatist. His best-known play, *Little Malcolm and His Struggle Against the Eunuchs*, won Halliwell the *Evening Standard*'s Most Promising Playwright Award in 1967. McGahern admired him both as a writer and a friend.

8 'Korea' was first published in the *Atlantic Monthly* for October 1969.

9 Must relate to an anecdote told to McGahern by Monteith that he subsequently uses in 'Sinclair', his radio play adaptation of the story 'Why We're Here'. The eccentric and troubled Lord Oxford visits a Harley Street psychiatrist and is told: 'After careful examination of your cranium and long deliberation with my own I have eventually come to the conclusion, my Lord, that you have a dead bird in your chimney.' See McGahern, *The Rockingham Shoot and Other Dramatic Writings* (2018), 74.

Madeline McGahern

Colgate

[*February 1969*]

Dear Madeline,

The man in the post office, he was concerned with the image of the post office, and that the mails left N.Y. for days because of snow, but that it did not happen often.

Rather than hauling in and out to the Airport, you'll be tired if you continue in excitement, why don't you try and get some hotel some place near Copley Square, there's a service at the airport.[10] And meet me in the foyer of The Sheraton Plaza Hotel at 6.30, it's Copley Square; I think do not get that hotel, since it's always better to enter enemy country for such engagements, but someplace fairly near there – 15 minutes walk. Or get a place close to the market. Probably near S.R.H. The Sheraton Plaza Hotel is the one place I know, only because I looked at the map; it's a long ride to Airport under the river, and it's dreary. At that time we'd have to look for an hotel anyhow, and it makes sense for you to go to one immediately, with the bags, and I'll get a taxi at 5.45 from the airport to the Sheraton Plaza, and we can have a drink together or go to whatever hotel you've got by then. There won't be very much hours between your arrival at the hotel and when I come to the Sheraton.

The reason for all this is that I don't want to bring Patrick into it, I'll call him sometime after we've met.

It'll be very easy, since N. G.'s dramatic arrival at Palisades we've got the benediction of laughter, in its way it makes things easier or less initially tense.[11]

Also you'll have a room at the Faculty Club, it's rather beautiful. I managed it today.

Can you bring any copies of The Dark (Faber) in the flat with you, or any – a few, 2–3 – paperback Barracks. It doesn't matter if it's not easy.

10 McGahern was making arrangements to meet Madeline in Boston to coincide with his reading at the Sheraton Plaza Hotel for the Éire Society of Boston.
11 Niels Gron, Madeline's father, visited Patrick Gregory's parents in Palisades, Snedens Landing, New York casting doubts on McGahern's intentions in pursuing his daughter, and implying that he was dating Madeline for her money. The visit failed in its intentions and the Gregorys remained fond of McGahern.

Is there any MSS of Coming into His Kingdom? You'll need shoes, boots for the snow. Bring too the grey coat I like on you so much.

The party for Matthew will be on the 22nd: the next Friday I'll have holidays.[12]

John

Faber

Colgate

[*Early April 1969*]

Dear Charles,

Thank you for your letter, and the telegram, apparently Darks came, but were sent by airfreight, and were held up for clearance.

I am sorry about the Iremonger, a frantic letter came from Roger McHugh to cable you, why Iremonger couldn't get the stories himself before this I don't know. I met him once, for a boring three hours, and it was probably mutual.[13]

I'll be glad to be out of here, and to see you in London.

Apparently a West Indian, Hearne, an author of yours, will have this Chair next year.[14]

If you have time to write I'll be glad – I have finished 2 more stories.

Love
John

12 Matthew Evans of Faber visited when Patrick Gregory got engaged to Justina Winston.
13 Monteith had sent a telegram on 10 April telling McGahern that a selection of his short stories had been airmailed to Iremonger. 'Hearts of Oak and Bellies of Brass' was the favourite at this time of both McGahern and Monteith. Valentin Iremonger (1918–91) was an Irish diplomat, editor and poet of note. Monteith and Faber were encouraging Iremonger to revisit the anthology of Irish short stories he had edited for the company in 1960.
14 John Hearne (1926–94), a Canadian writer of Jamaican parentage. He had published five novels with Faber between 1955 and 1961.

Faber

Colgate

[Late April–early May 1969]

Dear Matthew,[15]
Thank you for the letter, and for the Berlind. I told him about your airport offer. He was sheepish.

I went to Maine for the break – Madeline's father has an estate there – and she has stayed on.[16]

I'm looking forward to the books o– and more than that – to seeing you in London and I enclose John Head's book, which is his gift to you, but he was diffident about sending it. It seems very good to me, for a history book.[17]

I hope you are well and if you write again I'll be delighted.

John

15 Matthew Evans (1941–2016) joined Faber in 1964 as assistant to its director Peter du Sautoy, and in 1971 was appointed managing director. After the retirement of Charles Monteith in 1980, Evans became Faber's chairman and managing director. In the 1998 Birthday Honours he was appointed as a Commander of the Order of the British Empire (CBE), and on 11 May 2000 was created a life peer as Baron Evans of Temple Guiting. In the House of Lords, he was a government whip from 2002 to 2007, and a spokesman for the Department for Constitutional Affairs from 2003.

16 Niels Gron had bought land and built a sprawling black mansion in Hancock, Maine. For this holiday the Berlinds drove John and Madeline up and John back while Madeline spent several happy days alone in this idyllic location.

17 John Head, a Texan, was an historian friend of McGahern's and an assistant professor with tenure at Colgate who later moved on to Boston University. The book in question is John Head, *A Time to Rend: An Essay on the Decision for American Independence* (Madison: State Historical Society of Wisconsin, 1968).

Patrick Gregory Papers

Department of English Language and Literature
University of Reading
Whiteknights
Reading RG6 2AA

[*Mid-June 1969*]

Dear Patrick,

It's safer to write to Paris and more likely I'll be there.

I am finishing classes here. It's hell in London. I get no work done. I almost finished My Love . . . in Paris but there's much to be done, to keep it from becoming farce/pornography.

My play is to go to Ireland for few days and then to Paris.[18]

Anu is busy spending her award on Harley Street analysis.

The tart's name is Hugh Leonard, did Stephen D. once, and several cheap hits.[19]

Did you get Brockway's book?[20]

Any news of Prestcott? Or the stories? Or yourself? When do you think you may be able to come to Europe?

John

---

18 A stage version of *The Barracks* adapted by Hugh Leonard and directed by Tomás MacAnna, which premiered at the Olympia Theatre as part of the Dublin Theatre Festival, 6 October 1969.

19 Hugh Leonard (1926–2009). Born John Joseph Byrne, Leonard was a successful Irish playwright and journalist. His play, *Stephen D.*, was an adaptation of Joyce's *A Portrait of the Artist as a Young Man* and the posthumously published *Stephen Hero* (London: Jonathan Cape, 1944). It was first presented at the Gate Theatre on 24 September 1962 as part of the Dublin Theatre Festival.

20 James Brockway (1916–2000) was an English poet and translator, who was born in Birmingham and lived much of his life in the Netherlands. In 1997 he was knighted by the Dutch government for his services to literature.

Madeline McGahern

Dublin

18 July 1969

Dear Madeline,
It finished last night and today, and I am finally broken.[21]
   I'll ring in a few hours, there is a long wait, but before you get this, long before.
I go to Murphy's at the end of the week, and then at the end of the next week to Boyle. I'll go back to London to wind up the flat then, and to Paris.
       Cleggan
       Co. Galway
is Murphy's address.
   If you want anything write to me there.
                    Love
                    John

Faber

1 Rue Christine
6e Paris
[hereafter 1 Rue Christine]

[July 1969][22]

[To Charles Monteith]
Please address or forward all mail to me at the above address until further notice.[23]
                    URGENT
              John McGahern

21 Refers to the final breakup with Annikki.
22 McGahern's first extant letter using 1 Rue Christine as an address. This apartment acted as a first home for John and Madeline and in later years was an important source of rental income.
23 Memo in Faber files.

Patrick Gregory Papers

1 Rue Christine

23 July 1969[24]

Dear Patrick,
It's about the safest address above.

Thank you for your letter to Richard's. I was more interested in the story than most things but it makes no difference.

I'd to leave Richard's because of Anu's breakdown, she is good as can be now, moving each day through all the parts from hell to heaven.[25]

Do you want to come to Paris in late autumn as you said you might?

I'll go back to see my father if Anu goes next week to Finland. Then I hope to stay in Paris for a time.

I was never more certain of my work and it goes past the finishing of the stories which I can do in a few weeks once I start. I do not intend to begin until Anu is all right.

John

Patrick Gregory Papers

[1 Rue Christine]

[Late July 1969]

Dear Patrick,
I hope Stina and you have many happy days, please tell her so from me, and thank you for telling me.[26]

24 Despite the address, this letter was posted in London.
25 Gregory was fond of Annikki and writes in a letter of 28 July 1969: 'I was sorry to hear about Anu's breakdown. It must have meant a great deal of hellishness for both of you. Since I spent some very good hours in Anu's company, she has a place of real affection in my memory.' Madeline McGahern Papers.
26 Patrick Gregory and Justina 'Stina' Winston married on 2 August 1969. McGahern first met Justina that year when she and Patrick visited Colgate before they married. John and Madeline subsequently stayed with them in Boston before they paid a return visit later in Paris. Justina's parents were Robert and Clara Winston, translators of Hannah Arendt, Franz Kafka and Thomas Mann. As Justina Gregory,

Gron says you can have one of his floors at the Rue Guisarde if you come to Paris, which would make it very much cheaper to come.[27]

I work every day here, it was impossible to work at all in the continual emotional violence of London.

I'll have to go back to see about abandoning the lease, I'll put it off as long as possible, and try to finish the first draft of the Spain story.[28]

This is by far the most continual address.

I was very glad of the Rec. Officer, and I want to go through Bomb B. for a last time.[29]

Madeline asked me to wish both of you happiness from her.

John

Faber

1 Rue Christine

4 August 1969

Dear Charles,

It has been a horrible summer, but I am here, and working each day on the last of the stories. The Atlantic bought the last long story for 600 dollars.

I'll be in London from the 20th to the end of this month to clear up about the lease and decoration. If you aren't too busy I'd like to see you very much then.

_____

she became Sophia Smith Professor of Classical Languages & Literatures at Smith College, Northampton, Massachusetts.

27 Niels Gron owned a large house on Rue Guissarde. He was friendly with Gregory's parents and knew Patrick Gregory from childhood.

28 'Peaches', the longest story in *Nightlines*.

29 In a letter of 28 July 1969, Gregory tells McGahern that he has managed to place 'The Recruiting Officer': 'Bob Manning has accepted "The Recruiting Officer" for the Atlantic [. . .] He was actually delighted with both the stories, and debated long on the choice . . . before deciding that "The Recruiting Officer" had more specific gravity than "The Bomb Box", and was thus somewhat more appropriate for the magazine. Two stories by a single author represents a real investment of interest by the "Atlantic", and I'm naturally pleased that the magazine is supporting the Press's enthusiasm in such a tangible fashion.' Madeline McGahern Papers. The other McGahern story published by the *Atlantic Monthly* at this time was 'Korea' (October 1969).

Madeline said if you'd like to come to Paris she'd be delighted and she has prepared the guest room which is on the same floor as the flat.[30]

Apparently Patrick was married last Saturday.

Love

John

Patrick Gregory Papers (TS)

1 Rue Christine

16 August 1969

Dear Patrick,

Thank you for so quickly sending the story, I've completely rewritten its opening and cut it.

I have almost finished the Spanish story in first draft, it stands 40 pages.[31] Also My Love My Umbrella, it's shorter. I'll finish these two and possibly write a third. Then I'll go back to the novel. I will not touch the novel until I've got these out of my head.

There's 90–100 pages written, I have not looked at it for 2 years. I'll begin by rewriting those pages.[32] I'll start in November.

I am anxious to get away from the short story, it's intolerable, it's worse than verse. The MSS of the Recruiting Officer is 600 pages.[33]

Unfortunately I have to go to London on Wednesday to end the flat, I have to redecorate it, and possibly, I am not certain, to see Anu, if she wants or needs. Getting out of the relationship is as much release as getting back breath, it seems so for her too.

I'll see Charles on Thursday, he's looking forward to seeing Stina and you in Autumn.[34] Will you remember me to her?

John

---

30 The apartment at Rue Christine was originally set over two floors, but in later years became just the small, top-floor garret.

31 'Peaches'.

32 'Rewriting' is circled.

33 The fragmentary drafts of the story held among McGahern's papers in NUIG give no indication of a story so sprawling, though it was not untypical for McGahern to rewrite and pare down obsessively.

34 Monteith had written on 6 August inviting McGahern to meet him for lunch in the upmarket Soho restaurant Kettner's on Romilly Street. Monteith visited the Gregorys in Boston in October 1969.

3 September 1969[35]

Dear Patrick,
I am sorry for the vagueness. I am a tenant of the Queen. I pay her 25 dollars
a week. In order to relinquish the honour, I have to 'rehabitate', which means,
since they exact their pound of flesh ruthlessly in formal fashion, around 500
dollars. Her other tenants are in H.M.R. jails. I sourly wonder if they have to
'rehabitate' their cells on leaving.[36]
   I work each morning but it is difficult.
The great Socio/Psychio communication with Anu has now reached the old
profession, three brass balls, of the lawyers.
   What kind of wedding had you? I had the two door porters as witnesses.
For some reason, in the sense of ceremony, I find it consolation.
   As soon as I finish with the lease etc I'll go back to Paris. I am trying to
hurry it. For the time I am too disturbed here. There's no need to write to me
c/o Madeline, since it goes as easily direct to 1 Rue Christine.
   Is Stina well? Do you intend to come to Europe? Charles is very much
looking forward to seeing you in autumn.
                              John

14 September 1969[37]

Dear Patrick,
I've cleared up all the London business, flat/furniture, and I am going back to
Paris today – Anu has started the divorce. I am tired but it's good to wake up
in the morning without the certitude of some violence before night.

---

35 This letter was sent from London.
36 The flat at Gore Road formed part of the Crown Estate.
37 This letter was sent from London.

The Barracks goes on in the big production in October.[38] They are now trying to involve me, they think it'll be a hit, which is how they probably always think, and I am trying to stay clear.

I'll be in Paris at least until I finish the stories.

Is Stina well?

Charles is looking forward to seeing both of you in the next weeks.

John

Joe Kennedy

1 Rue Christine

21 September 1969

Dear Joe,

I got your letter a few weeks ago, it missed me at a number of addresses in a displaced summer, and came long after your visit, and I'd be glad if you'd tell Margaret that it wasn't my fault that we didn't meet.

I was in Dublin for a day and rang the Herald but since you weren't there didn't want to leave my name.

I am finishing the book of stories here, and I'll be glad to get back to the novel. I'll be here, I think, until Christmas.

John

38 A reference to Hugh Leonard's adaptation of *The Barracks* that was put on at the Olympia Theatre, Dublin from 6 October 1969 as part of the Dublin Theatre Festival, directed by Tomás MacAnna. McGahern did not attend, and Kevin Lehane wrote to him of the opening night: 'Play not bad enough to assault him [Leonard], not good enough to murmur approval.' Madeline McGahern Papers. In a letter to Susanna Capon of 22 June 1971 in the BBC Written Archives Centre, John says that his dislike of the play led him to attempt a dramatic adaptation himself; this was produced on BBC radio in 1972.

Dympna McGahern
[*Madeline McGahern*]

1 Rue Christine

[*October 1969*]

Dear Dymphna,
Thank you for the letter, and I got the bags from [*illegible*] today. Take whatever it cost you, it must have been trouble too.
   Only interesting thing about the D business is[39]
   (a) The complete self-love
   (b) Grudge against the world that it does not give him the same attention as he gives to himself.
   (c) When lack of attention – actual attention would have the same result since he is the only legal heir – results in boredom cause trouble.
   (d) Since the feelings of others don't exist the only care in causing trouble can it rebound on him.
   (e) Since it would with me let off poison on Margaret.
   (f) The luxurious illness of neglect/misunderstanding, Ingratitude/Abandonment.
   (g) Take to bed. The timelessness of having stayed up so long (70 years)
   (h) Hot water bottle. Hot oranges and lemon drinks. O God O God what's that door banging for can there never be peace in this house (repeat of ora pro me)[40]
Sorry for the scribble. Pressure to go to Dublin but staying put.
   There's only one more story to write.[41]
   Peculiar letter from B. Friel saying that his advice unasked was that I shouldn't let Barracks go on stage for 10–15 years.
         Write soon
         Keep ticket for time being
                   Love
                   Sean

---

39 D. is Daddy; a comical description of Frank McGahern's behaviour follows.
40 A Latin invocation: pray for me.
41 To make up the first collection, *Nightlines*.

7 October 1969

Dear Brian,
Thank you for your kind letter, and for returning the story. I am sorry after all your care there was, on their part, poor behaviour; but my gratitude to you for its consideration is the same as if it had gone through.[42]

I signed over the novel on the agent's advice.[43] I've not seen the script but I suppose in some days notices will come. I looked on it as much the same as signing translation rights away.[44] Leonard wrote me a very nice letter, but I did not want to go to the festival, I am having troubles with the last story in the book, and it's a too easy distraction.[45]

I have one contact in the French theatre, as far as I gather it's almost impossible, but I'd be glad to be of use to you or to try.

I've read and liked your stories. And I hope your work that you do now is well for you.

John

[*Stamped 'rec'd 27 October 1969' by Gregory*]

Dear Patrick,
I hope you like it, it was hell to write which means nothing to the work, and it seems more that way with everything now. I think the movement is slower than anything I have written.[46]

---

42 Possibly refers to the number of the Belfast-based literary magazine *Threshold* of which Friel was guest editor for Winter 1966–7.
43 See preceding letter of October 1969 to Dympna McGahern in which John complains about unwanted advice from Friel about the wisdom of theatrical adaptations.
44 Refers to the stage adaptation of *The Barracks*.
45 Hugh Leonard, who had adapted *The Barracks* for the stage. The final story in *Nightlines* is 'The Recruiting Officer', though McGahern is more likely referring here to either 'Peaches' or 'My Love, My Umbrella'.
46 The letter is sent with a typescript of 'My Love, My Umbrella'.

The longer story – about twice or more – will follow in a few days. It is finished but I want to go through the typescript.[47]

I may do one more story, I think it won't take long, to get it out of my head, before I go back to the novel.

Encounter don't want either to give a firm date for My Future at my Back (can you think of a better title?) or to return it though they accepted it a year ago.[48]

Bomb Box is far better now, I think it'll be broadcast on the B.B.C. and published in the Listener.[49] Manning was very kind about the first version.

Could you send a copy of The Atlantic Korea to Kevin, and if it is easy I would like 2 extra copies. We can settle it when we meet.

When do you think to come to Europe?

I do not envy Stina, she probably has a great deal of useless pedantry to do to honour and obey her examiners. Won't you tell her that I wish her well with them.

Read a translation of Lucretius by a Rolfe Humphries which would make sleeping pills obsolete if it could be put in general circulation.[50] Also Jonson's masks, the language very beautiful, but the introduction fit to sink a battleship.[51]

I have been working in 2 or 3 sittings each day for six weeks and all I read is Swift and Byron's prose in the indulgence the tired look for in old friends.

Richard says he'll come here in late November.[52]

I was very glad that a real poet at long last has been offered the Nobel.[53]

> I hope you can write soon
> John

Never liked Gide very much, seems always to me caressing his various qualities.

---

47 'Peaches'.

48 An early title for what is eventually published as 'Wheels'.

49 'Bomb Box' was published in The Listener of December 1969.

50 The Way Things Are: The De Rerum Natura of Titus Lucretius Carus (Bloomington: Indiana University Press, 1968).

51 Ben Jonson wrote a number of masques with stage design by Inigo Jones. Their works are usually thought of as the most significant in the form. It has not been possible to identify which edition McGahern was reading.

52 Murphy did not stay with John and Madeline in Paris.

53 Samuel Beckett.

6 November 1969

Dear Charles,
Patrick wrote what a marvellous evening he had with you in Boston.

I've sent him the long story 4 days ago and today a story that was not planned. I have to butcher an early weak story (3/4 days) and then it is for worse or better finished.[54]

I'll have to go to London in December.

Do you think I should send in the typescript or are the publications enough.

Panther say they want to see an MSS. So do the Germans.

I am unfamiliar with this. If you can tell me I'd be grateful.

Or can we fix it up together in December?

The last three stories were written here.

Do you know anything of property law?[55]

> Love
> John

Faber

1 Rue Christine

10 November 1969

Dear Charles,
There are two things.

If any phrases in the book strike you harshly will you please tell me? Also if you have ideas about the sequences will you tell me? I think the simple <u>To</u> is the most dignified style of dedication.[56]

---

54 The long story is 'Peaches'; the story that was 'not planned' is likely 'Lavin'; the story he needs to 'butcher' is probably 'Strandhill, the Sea', which he never fully got right to his satisfaction.
55 Monteith has written in pencil on this letter: 'Answered verbally when I saw him in Paris Nov. 8.' McGahern was presumably seeking advice on Madeline's behalf as she attempted to secure her ownership of the Rue Christine property.
56 *Nightlines* is dedicated 'To Charles Monteith'.

I had a letter today from Fred Busch saying you are about to read his novel and asking me to act as advocate.[57]

All I can honestly say is that he has certainly verbal facility and is quite desperate to be published.

If you do not decide to publish the book it would be a temporary kindness to write him about it.

Berlind and Busch are mutual admirers of each other's work.

Richard will have the O'Connor Chair there in Spring.[58]

Love
John

Dympna McGahern
[Madeline McGahern]

[1 Rue Christine]

[*November 1969*]

Dear Dymphna,

Thank you for writing – did you go to Dublin – and I'd be very glad to hear if you did. Can you find out anything exact about the letter Margaret burned. She reminds me of a Female Cardinal giving advice to her flock before she [*illegible*] to the moon. I got a very horrible letter from him, I have not answered, and in his own very good words 'I'll attend his funeral if I hear of it.'[59]

I've finished the book.[60]

There was a story in the Atlantic October.[61] There'll be one soon in the Listener and Encounter.[62]

---

57 Fred Busch (1941–2006), American novelist, was one of the first people with whom McGahern became friendly at the English faculty in Colgate. He went on to have a long publishing career, though never had a book published with Faber.

58 McGahern was the first person to hold the O'Connor Chair at Colgate, an endowed position that rotated between departments, which used it as a vehicle to attract visiting talent. Richard Murphy held two visitor's appointments at the English Department over the course of his career as well as teaching in nearby Syracuse University for a period.

59 Referring to his father. Contents of letter unknown.

60 *Nightlines*.

61 'Korea' was first published in the *Atlantic Monthly* (October 1969).

62 'Bomb Box' was first published in *The Listener* (December 1969); 'Wheels' was first published in *Encounter* (April 1970).

Can the Atlantic be got in London?
It's lovely here, and the cold frosts are beginning, and we may go to London in December.

As always love,
John

Faber

1 Rue Christine

28 November 1969

Dear Charles,
Madeline got a lawyer through going to the Embassy and she is very grateful.[63]
  We'll be now definitely in London from the 10th until Christmas.
Patrick approved of Peaches finally, though he said it made his blood chill in places, and an important change he asked is a definite improvement, it was my own instinct at first that I failed to trust; but he still hangs over Lavin, which is the reason I haven't sent the stories in. It's probably easier to bring them with me now.[64]
  It'll be marvellous to see you in London.

Love
John

Patrick Gregory Papers

[1 Rue Christine]

4 December 1969

Dear Patrick,
I'll go to London next Wednesday 10th and will be there until Christmas.
  I've had the flu, and the weather is cold and wet.

---

63 On 19 November Monteith wrote to McGahern suggesting that Madeline contact the American Embassy about finding a property lawyer.
64 Monteith and Faber had no such hesitations about 'Lavin', with Monteith writing to McGahern on 19 November: 'I've now read the three stories you gave me in Paris – as has Matthew; and Rosemary is reading them at the moment. I think they're absolutely stunning, and of the three the one that – rather to my surprise – made the greatest impact on me was Lavin.'

Richard Murphy was here for 3 days. There's no concealing the homosexuality anymore, it rampages in the face. As always he was more fun in his absence than presence. I get guilty: renewing the future fun with slow doses of the presence. And the strangeness is that I grow fonder of him, admittedly in the absences.

Charles wrote he liked <u>Lavin</u>, to my surprise, best of all the later stories.[65]

> 23 Forest Drive West
> Leytonstone
> London E. 11

is the safest address until after Christmas. I record <u>Korea</u> there on 13th and then I may go to Ireland to see my father. The old bastard wrote a horrible letter over the breakup of my marriage to Anu.

I hope Stina and you have a good Christmas. I hate the season. Though in <u>The Three Blackbirds</u> everybody gets so paralytic that it becomes seasonless.[66]

> John

> Patrick Gregory Papers
>
> 23 Forest Drive West

20 December 1969

Dear Patrick,
I had lunch with Charles/Rosenthal Thursday.[67] Charles wanted the stories badly. He wants to publish in autumn and apparently the production people are howling because of overcommitment or something and he's had difficulty keeping a place open.

The copies I want with your questions are
1. Lavin, 2. Peaches, 3. Recruiting, 4. Christmas, 5. My Love
I saw 4 people in 3 months in Paris so it's wild here.

---

65 Patrick Gregory was not a fan of 'Lavin' as he wrote in a letter of 20 November 1969: 'Lavin still baffles me a bit, but I haven't reread it carefully yet and will have to do that before I can talk to you about it.' Again on 1 December Gregory argued vociferously for the exclusion of 'Lavin' from the collection: 'The piece strikes me as tight and true at every turning: there isn't a false note in it, and the writing maintains a concentration and intensity throughout. And yet John, I don't feel that it works at all as a short story [. . .] it's the only story of yours that I have yet encountered that doesn't seem to chrystallize around a central image.' Madeline McGahern Papers.
66 The local pub in Leytonstone. See letter of late April 1965 to Gregory.
67 They dined at Kettner's.

I've had to see Berlind, he's giving Richard the O'Connor 1970, and it's more depressing than I even imagined. I wait for the flesh to fall off the bones before my eyes.

After Christmas I'll go to Ireland. I'll go back to Paris from Dublin.

Bomb Box comes out next week.[68]

I'll be grateful, extraordinarily, if you can suggest some sequence or shape for the book.[69]

Is Stina well?

You send no news of your visit. I'd be glad of any news of your visit. I'd be glad of any news of Ann Holmes.[70]

I am going to a football match.[71]

John

68 Short story that was first published in *The Listener* (25 December 1969). Also appeared under the same title in *Nightlines*. An amended version of the story appeared under the title 'The Key' in *The Collected Stories*.

69 In response to this request, Gregory wrote a somewhat exasperated letter dated 5 January 1970: 'I am now in a state of sweet confusion, but I am a bit hamstrung from my side because 1) I don't have copies of two of the stories listed in your table of contents ("Coming into his Kingdom" and "Strandhill"), and I now have no idea whether some of the stories I possess are in their final form. [. . .] The point is this, John: I want to be able to say to my people here, "This is it, take it or leave it." And I don't want to show any material that hasn't received your final approval. [. . .] The order that I came up with, for the ten stories in my possession, goes like this: 1) "Wheels" 2) "Why We're Here" 3) "Christmas" 4) "Hearts of Oak" 5) "The Bomb Box" 6) "Korea" 7) "Lavin" 8) "My Love, My Umbrella" 9) "Peaches" 10) "The Recruiting Officer". I would be hard pressed to explain why this order imposes itself on my imagination, but a number of rational considerations do play a role [. . .] it seems to me important – since almost all the stories are first-person narratives – to present a pattern that discourages the reader's tendency to view the collection in terms of an autobiographical sequence.' Knopf, HRC. Gregory went on, in this lengthy letter, to argue that the collection ought to be prefaced with McGahern's short manifesto, 'The Image'. In publishing *Nightlines*, McGahern did not take this last piece of advice but largely followed Gregory's suggestions for the order in which the stories should appear, inserting 'Coming into his Kingdom' after 'Why We're Here' and 'Strandhill, The Sea' after 'Hearts of Oak and Bellies of Brass'. When *Nightlines* was translated by Pierre Leyris and published by Mercure de France the following year as *Lignes de Fond*, it was prefaced by 'The Image' and 'Peaches' was dropped.

70 A publishing friend of Patrick Gregory's.

71 The day he wrote this letter, McGahern was on his way to watch Tottenham Hotspur at home to West Ham, a game Spurs lost 2–0. Ian Hamilton, one of John's best London friends, was a Spurs fanatic and John had become increasingly keen on the club.

Madeline McGahern

[23 *Forest Drive West*]

[*December 1969*]⁷²

[*To Madeline*]
Margaret rang Sunday – he, Pop, wanted pronto 23 attitude to the fact he was going to sue me over Bomb Box.⁷³ Probably boredom and threats but it just added to the general jigs.

Saw Ian. Drinking tomato juice since he'd come from long lunch, 2 people, going on from me to see more. A strip band serenades you up to his office.⁷⁴

Will go to B.G. baths after the Traveller's.⁷⁵ Monica rang to see if we could put her up in Paris at Easter.⁷⁶

Beginning to feel the effect of all the tension, will long for one secluded room, and I miss you very much.

Love
John

Madeline McGahern

[23 *Forest Drive West*]

[*Late 1969*]

[*To Madeline*]
Charles asked very affectionately after you. Can you write me the number of the [*illegible*] (is it 78) to 23. I'll probably leave for Paris next Tuesday

72 This letter comes with a Christmas card signed 'To Miss McGahern, From Simon Cooper'. Possibly one of McGahern's students.
73 At the centre of 'Bomb Box' is a hypochondriacal policeman very clearly based on Sergeant McGahern.
74 Ian Hamilton edited *The Review* and later the *New Review* from an office on Greek Street, Soho. A local pub, the Pillars of Hercules, acted as a de facto headquarters with Hamilton having a legendary capacity for alcohol and cigarettes. Soho was then the heart of London's red light district.
75 The Bethnal Green Baths, located in the York Hall on Old Ford Road in Bethnal Green, London, a legacy of the large Jewish population of Russian and Polish origin. 'The Traveller's' is probably a reference to the gentlemen's club on Pall Mall of which Charles Monteith was a member.
76 Monica McGahern spent an enjoyable Easter 1970 break in the Paris flat.

morning (or else on Sunday). Seeing Davison Thursday night in the Thorpe Garden restaurant in Covent Garden.[77] Rosaleen has got much worse.[78] Why don't you ring Friday at 8.30 in the morning.

Writing before leaving the baths, orange peel and Senior Service and baths and the ladies' husbands' obscenities in the background.

Love

John

77 Peter Davison (1928–2004), senior editor at Atlantic Monthly Press to whom Gregory had passed on the MS of *Nightlines* in order to bring it to publication. He and Gregory did not have a good working relationship, such that Gregory left the Press before the publication of *Nightlines*. Gregory writes in an undated letter from this period: 'Naturally, I'm disappointed. I had hoped to stay here forever, and to watch over the growth of a set of projects that have now been nipped in the bud. The point is that it takes <u>years</u> to make one's case quite clear in this business . . . But I am also deeply relieved by the final rupture, free at last of a nagging anxiety.' Madeline McGahern Papers. This parting of ways did not affect the coming to press of *Nightlines* with Atlantic Monthly Press in the US, and Gregory moved to Gambit, another Boston-based publisher.
78 McGahern's sister who lived at 23 Forest Drive West.

1970

Faber

1 Rue Christine

10 January 1970

Dear Charles,
I am going back to Paris today. I hope it's not too late, and it's not to cause
too much trouble. I'd like to change the stories of Nightlines to this order.

    1. Wheels
    2. Why We're Here
    3. Coming into his Kingdom
    4. Christmas
    5. Hearts of Oak and Bellies of Brass
    6. Strandhill, the Sea
    7. The Bomb Box
    8. Korea
    9. Lavin
    10. My Love, My Umbrella
    11. Peaches
    12. The Recruiting Officer

It's the last interference. The reason is to take the emphasis off adolescence.
And to break up Hearts and The Rec. Off.
    If there's any trouble can you write to Paris or ring Medici 2767.
              With love
              John

12 January 1970[1]

Dear Patrick,
Almost the only thing I don't agree with you on is Lavin.

What I'll call the book is <u>Nightlines</u> (an image from <u>Korea</u>) in this order (1) Wheels (2) Why We're Here (3) Coming into his Kingdom (4) Christmas (5) Hearts of (6) Strandhill, the Sea (7) Bomb Box (8) Korea (9) Lavin (10) My Love (11) Peaches (12) The Recruiting.

If you think it's too short I'll write another story for the American edition.[2]

I didn't get your December 1st letter until now because some one enclosed a rejected story by P. Troyal with a label which was stuck on and sent to Iowa City. It came by the boat rate.

I was glad to leave Ireland, there's a real cold feel of the spray of the parish pump.

I think the only way <u>The Image</u> can be used, if it can, is as a blurb. Otherwise, in an inverted way, you play their game. It is possible though as blurb. Kevin was admiringly appalled by your sister's energy and intelligence.[3]

Macmillan want an anthology story, they read <u>Bomb</u> in the <u>Listener</u>, would you give them it or some other?

Did you show any of the stories to the Atlantic or should I try them elsewhere as I've got 2 offers to print something but I think it's fair they should have first refusal.

I can't thank you enough for all your care and help. I think I'll write better now. When do you hope to come to Europe?

Can you also thank Stina for her nice Christmas card?

John

---

1 Mistakenly dated 1969 by McGahern.
2 This was the published order of the stories in *Nightlines* in both the British and American editions.
3 Kevin Lehane.

Faber

1 Rue Christine

26 January 1970

Dear Charles,
Macmillan wrote for a story for their <u>Winter Tales</u>, but they do not want it to clash with the volume. I wonder if you could give me an approximate date so they can make up their minds.[4]

Can you also send me a photostat of <u>Peaches</u> and <u>My Love, My Umbrella</u>? There's been trouble with Madeline's father. The lawyer secured the upstairs for her after he tried to seize it. He wants us to stay here but it's apparent now he wants to involve M. in the Seafield case and to use the apartment as bargaining & we may leave Paris altogether.[5] Last week was quite horrible.

Are you well?

Will you be in London all spring?
With love
John

Dympna McGahern
[*Madeline McGahern*]

1 Rue Christine

26 January 1970

Dear Dymphna,
I wrote to Kelly today to tell him that you'll write to him and that I'll be grateful to him for any help he can give.[6]

4 Monteith replies on 29 January that the book will likely be published in late October. McGahern did not appear in the Macmillan anthology of short stories, *Winter Tales*.
5 Neils Gron, Madeline's father, had been having an affair with Nina Studley-Herbert, 12th Countess of Seafield (1906–69), a Scottish aristocrat. At her death in October 1969, she was the second richest woman in Britain after the Queen. Gron had profited enormously from the relationship – chiefly through the acquisition of Parisian property – and there was a real possibility that he would be pursued through the courts by her son, Ian Ogilvie-Grant, 13th Earl of Seafield.
6 Lionel Kelly b. 1937, an American literature scholar at the University of Reading.

When might Breege be fit to travel? Has she definitely put it out of mind? If so when is the earliest? I ask because of the present uncertainty of our movements.

I have not been able to work all week with this nuisance of M's father. Horrible man.

Your letter came. Kelly would also be the best person to tell you what to ask. Also I'd go guarantor, for what it would be glad. It's Gordon is the Professor.[7] They'll certainly help you.

Don't worry, I'll be only too glad to give any help at all.[8]
Forgive any distracted note and blame it on last week which is too much a saga to tell.

Love
Sean

Faber

1 Rue Christine

2 February 1970

Dear Charles,
I agree with the contract offered, I'll be in London in 2 weeks for about a week, and perhaps it may be simpler to sign it then.[9]

We moved upstairs today. It was very dirty and disturbing and now we are being courted with invitations to the Ritz etc., which is the final pornography.[10]

I enclose the revision of Peaches. I want the previous chapter I sent cut out, and this to replace it. I know this must be a great irritation for you.

I'll be in London about from the 17th–25th. If you have time it goes without saying how much I'd like to see you. Unfortunately you have only until after Easter to come here, which Madeline would love if you can.

John

7 Donald J. Gordon d. 1977, Professor of English Literature at the University of Reading. A Yeats scholar much admired by McGahern.
8 Dympna graduated from UCD in 1967 with a Bachelor of Commerce degree while working in the Central Statistics Office. She went on in the early 1970s to take a degree in English Literature at Reading.
9 For Nightlines McGahern agreed to an advance of £350 with 10% royalties on the first 2,000 sales, 12½% on the next 4,000 and 15% thereafter.
10 'Courted' by Madeline's father.

The enclosure should begin from the now EN of Ch. 2 to the beginning of Chapter 3. It now ends Ch. 2.

Patrick Gregory Papers

1 Rue Christine

9 February 1970

Dear Patrick,
I'd be glad to hear from you.

I am in the first draft of this new thing and it seems to get longer. I've no idea what length it'll be but it'll be certainly longer than <u>Peaches</u>.[11]

Terrible trouble from that madman Gron, who wasted a whole week. It seems he'll be centre of a case in London in the summer, very scandalous, and to him very dangerous. Madeline owns a very small flat in this house, which he tried to seize, I think to have her in his imaginary power in the case, perhaps too the obsession with property, but she got a lawyer. Howls. In the fracas she mentioned that she knew all about his visit to your parents.[12] Came around with 2 bodyguards to call me liar and troublemaker. I told him to calm down and we ended with handshakes (all an unfortunate misunderstanding). Then advised me, man to man, that M. was crazy, though I was the last person he should tell. The servants come round with hair-raising stories. Also in the most sordid way profoundly comic.

We have decided to leave Paris but in our own time. It's too much to even see him twice a year. Where we'll go we [*illegible*] Ireland but there's nothing certain.

I'd be very glad if you'd write to me.[13]

---

11 This piece was the earliest version of what would become *The Pornographer* nine years later. Gregory writes on 12 February 1970: '<u>What</u> exactly are you writing at now? I assume that the new story, "even longer than 'Peaches'", is not intended for inclusion in NIGHTLINES . . .?' Madeline McGahern Papers.

12 Madeline's father had visited Horace and Marya Gregory in Snedens Landing to warn them off McGahern.

13 In a letter of response, dated 12 February 1970, Gregory writes: 'Certainly the whole affair must be awful for Madeline, and she has my very real sympathy and concern. It seems to me important that she be allowed to lead her own life, free from the fantasies and obsessions of her very remarkable father.' Madeline McGahern Papers.

Is there anything definite from the Monthly?

John

Patrick Gregory Papers

[*1 Rue Christine*]

[*Early March 1970*]

Dear Patrick,

It was bad news for me. We moved upstairs today, out of Gron's world; it is small but very beautiful and with the roof glass windows – it is snowing now – I often feel I'm in a ship.

I go to London in about 2 weeks to clear up some money business, I am hoping to see Peter Davison too then; and I think we'll close up this place, and leave, it's not certain to where yet, perhaps to Barcelona. Neither of us wants to stay in Paris and besides Gron appears to have started conciliation which I am even more wary of than his attack.

Madeline thinks not to sell until a definite place of living has been decided on. Would it interest you and Stina if it's not in use in the summer?[14]

What advance do you think fair for <u>Nightlines</u>? Peter suggested negotiating with Faber, but is there point in paying Faber 15% for something I can do? Or do you think it's clearer that way? I'd be grateful if you'd write me what you think.

I hope to be around for Richard's old age, it'll obviously grow ever more comic, and I am very fond of him. Never met Freyer, but Richard and he sound a fair pair, as they say in Galway.[15]

Anu sounds wildly happy and is about to be married again. I often go over in my head how our relationship became the terrible thing it did, but never much sense.

When do you leave for Europe?

John

14 The Gregorys were planning a June trip to Paris.
15 In a letter of 27 February 1970, Gregory had described a visit by the Irish writer and potter Grattan Freyer (1915–83), 'who is barnstorming the country on lecture assignments'. The letter went on to recount an anecdote about Freyer meeting Richard Murphy at Ballinasloe Horse Fair.

Faber

1 Rue Christine

16 April 1970

Dear Charles,
The reason I hadn't answered your previous letter was that I was waiting for a move, if any. I got an abusive letter 2 days ago so it seems that will be all. Incidentally, he got the allusions completely wrong, but for certainty can the doctor's name be changed to <u>Neary</u> and the policeman Cannon to <u>Bannon</u>? (this won't interfere with type).[16]

In the dust, sweat and cursing of trying to make this place habitable. Madeline goes to London this week and stays with the Evans for a day or 2 and then my sisters and then in Surrey with a terrible old related fool who founded the Consumers Guide and who apparently has now just finished a novel on the effect of a nuclear war on supposedly consumers.[17]

Do you ever think to come to Paris again? Patrick says he'll be here in the beginning of July.

I had a very good evening with you and Rosemary and the Heaneys. We had a drink later at Victoria with my sister, which was fortunate, since the first person I met on the train was Madeline's father and I was sufficiently ablaze to give him a stiff talking to and to later set him imbecilely drunk on his own good Glenlivet in mid-channel: I was going into the nature of morality; and he trying to make a couplet in which BEER and QUEER rhymed.

I hope you are well.
Love
John

16 McGahern had come under attack from his father over the content of 'Bomb Box' and was worried about possible legal repercussions. Monteith consulted with Peter du Sautoy and they felt there was no real cause for concern.
17 Madeline's relation in Surrey was Dexter Masters (1909–89), a first cousin of her father. He was a novelist and editor, and director of the Consumers' Union in the US from 1958 to 1963.

[*April 1970*]

Dear Patrick,

This is above all to wish you well at Gambit. Fabers (Ch & Mat) spoke extraordinarily well of Lovell Thompson.[18]

It was for me an uneasy evening with Peter. His own lack of confidence makes it hard to start with. I'd been reading a lousy book The Listener gave me beforehand in the Turkish baths in Bethnal Gr.[19] He took me to a pretty awful place called The Garden out of desperation and boredom. I'm afraid I set out in egotistical fashion to entertain myself; and when Peter put me into a taxi – I didn't want to go – to see poor Kannon in a pub in Chelsea I started to blaze.[20] I'll write to Peter to tell Kannon.

It was not all by any means. I ran into Pops Gron on the nightboat back. I gave him a long harangue on the nature of morality and who the hell he thought he was anyhow – interlarded by large doses of flattery to keep the patient awake – had him rhyming beer and queer. Went to his cabin for 15 y.o. Glenlivet. More beers and queers, watched over him so that he drank more Glenlivet than he wanted and left him in much worse shape than I was. I saw his wife try to get him out of his train when she met it at Nord. She hadn't a pram unfortunately.

If you and Stina wish I can ask him, since the lovely place we used live in is empty downstairs, if you can use it in July. It'd be no trouble and he'd probably love that. Madeline refuses to see him. What do you say? Or would you rather stay completely clean?

When do you come in July?

18 Lovell Thompson (1902–86) joined the Houghton Mifflin publishing company in 1924 and was head of the General Trade Division for most of his forty-two years there. After retiring from the company in 1967, Thompson co-founded Gambit to publish books of high literary and artistic quality. Gregory joined the firm from Atlantic Monthly Press.

19 The book that McGahern so disliked was *Being Geniuses Together* by Robert McAlmon and Kay Boyle (London: Michael Joseph, 1970). He wrote a dismissive review of it in *The Listener* for 23 April 1970, concluding of the authors that 'neither of them writes well'. See *LOTW*, 290–3.

20 Joseph Kanon b. 1946 in Pennsylvania. Harvard-educated, then a senior executive at Houghton Mifflin and subsequently a spy novelist.

Wheels is in the April Encounter[21]

John

Madeline says to be sure to tell you that it doesn't disturb her if we ask Gron. And it might be nicer to stay in the flat, which is being wasted, than in the hotel.

Faber

1 Rue Christine

5 May 1970

Dear Charles,

Thank you for your letter, and the copy. My one fear after reading was that you may have placed too much importance on my work, and he may resent that. Wait and see is all that can be done. The whole situation was a stumble. And I want to say how very grateful I am to you.[22]

Madeline has been saying that in the short time she has known you she's never seen you look so well as the evening at the Russell.

Nothing but dust and work since we came back. A phrase of Byron 'dust, sweat and universal swearing' is continually in my head.

Is there any text or pretext on which Faber can send me £100 (Chase Manhattan, 41 Rue Gambon)?[23] On the strength of their loot my Portugese plasterers have bought a secondhand car and are pressing. If there's no text they'll have to wait on the slow wheels of the Bank of Ireland.

I hope I'll see you in July.

Love

John

---

21 'Wheels', the opening story of *Nightlines*, was first published in *Encounter*, vol. XXXIV, no. 4 (April 1970).

22 Refers to a certain awkwardness about which American house should publish *Nightlines* as Patrick Gregory had just moved from Atlantic Monthly Press to Gambit. Monteith and Matthew Evans agreed that it ought to stay with Atlantic and met with McGahern in London in late April to explain the decision.

23 Monteith arranged this transfer immediately on the strength of the advance owing to McGahern for *Nightlines*.

[*May 1970*]

Dear Patrick,

Gron seems to be away. (If there's case against him it's probably about the time it should come to Chambers).

Madeline talked with me about it. She had this proposal.

Downstairs is very lovely. Gron is unlikely to get round to it for 2 years. We use it all the time for its lavatory/shower anyhow. So she says if there's no word you simply use it. All we'd need to give you is linen.

If there's change before you come we'd get you a hotel.

If there was a hotel emergency we can put you up until you'd find or we'd find you one, there's no risk of stranding.

It makes perfect sense to me. It'd be certainly nicer. It'd save you money. We'd be glad to have you so near. You could come or go as you pleased. It cannot affect our position with Gron. He's out. He'll stay out.

My only reservation is that you may have distaste for the arrangement. In that case tell me.

Madeline is well and looking forward to your coming. Her beauty seems to me to have grown calmer and richer. In odd moments it causes me to catch my breath. I am happy, which induces more panic than gratitude, since I find it an extraordinary perilous way to be. My feelings over Atl/Ga is of great gratitude to you for the much Nightlines owes you, and regret out of a depth of waters . . .[24]

Give Stina my sympathy (for exams), my good wishes (for everything) and how I'm looking forward to the arrival of – as Mr Lehane puts it – your good self and your fully accredited wife and scholar in July.

John

---

24 For background, see McGahern's letter to Monteith of 5 May 1970.

1 Rue Christine

1 June 1970

Dear Giles,[25]
I wonder if I could trouble you to get the exact text from a good early edition of Book Four of Milton's Paradise Lost. It is early in the book, the serpent overhearing Adam and Eve discourse of their first vision of each other. The line as I remember it is, 'And I will bring you where no shadow staies thy coming.'[26] If you could find this, could you also get me the lines around it. I hope you'll forgive me for troubling you so, but I remember with great gratitude how accurately you corrected my poor rendering of Horace in The Dark.

  Also could you tell Miss Brooksbank that while her letter and the last sixteen pages of Nightlines has come for proof correction, there is still no sign of the 160 pages that were apparently sent beforehand.

  If for any reason you come here I'd be glad to see you. Also I think I owe you belated congratulations on your directorship, which pleased me.

                    Yours
                    John McGahern

                    Michael Hamburger Papers
                    1 Rue Christine

14 July 1970

Dear Michael,
It was kind to think of me, and to write. The book of short pieces Nightlines will come out in October, a novella and 11 stories, so that is no use then to Mrs Taylor.[27]

25 Giles de la Mare, then working as a director at Faber.
26 McGahern was checking this because he was having a ring engraved with these words to give to Madeline in Paris. John thought this was followed by 'Where no false reproaches are', but he was wrong and de la Mare told him so.
27 The first of several references in letters of this period to an approach from a small publisher wishing to produce a bespoke volume of a McGahern story or stories.

I'm on the 2nd writing of a short novel (15,000–25,000) – I'm not sure – and I hope to have it finished in September.[28]

Would that be of use?

I'd send it to you then (to see if you'd like it). It's been awful mostly since the long time we met last but it seems now calm and I am working.

I'll finally leave here for good when I finish what I've said. One of the things I'll look forward to when I come to England is getting your book of poems.

Are you well?

If you come here you know how glad I'll be to see you.

Why don't you write to me sometime?

John

Faber

1 Rue Christine

22 July 1970

Dear Charles,

The Patrick visit was disturbing, but at least there was no open breach.

Can a proof of Nightlines be sent to Mrs. Elisabeth Schnack, 8032 Zurich Breutisveg 3? She is the German translator.[29]

I was approached on behalf of a Mrs Taylor, who is starting a press to print fine limited editions of 250 copies, for a prose work. The other person she plans to open with is Ted Hughes.

Do you advise offering her the novella which I'm ½ way through the first draft, or would you prefer to see it first? The copyright would remain mine but a prose work may be different, from your position, than verse?[30]

28 No such novel exists either in published or draft form. The work may have been early sketches towards what becomes *The Leavetaking* in 1974.

29 Swiss-born Elisabeth Schnack (1899–1992) was McGahern's most important German translator. She also translated plays by Brian Friel, and fiction by Elizabeth Bowen, Edna O'Brien, George Moore, Sheridan Le Fanu, Benedict Kiely, Liam O'Flaherty, Frank O'Connor as well as a host of American writers.

30 Faber was not keen on this idea, and on 26 July Monteith wrote to McGahern suggesting he offer Mrs Taylor some of the stories from *Nightlines* once it had been published, with 'Peaches' possibly making a good standalone book. No such publication happened.

I'll be glad to go back to the novel, when it's finished, but in some dread
as well.
The flat looks rather lovely now.
It'll be great fun for us if you can manage to come.

Love
John

Faber

1 Rue Christine

11 August 1970

Dear Charles,
Thank you for the telegram and letter. I rang the Ir. T. They seemed confused.
And are ringing this evening again. All I said was that I'd consent to no
changes.[31] They gave me a lot of information on travel by tube in London.
    Certainly the Panther cover deserves banning.[32] We'll leave here the 17th,
next Monday.
    17th–24th at Claude Duneton, Meyssac 13, Correze.[33]
    24th–3rd Sept. or so American Express, Barcelona.

---

31 Monteith had cabled McGahern on 7 August to say that the Irish Censorship
Board was lifting the ban on *The Dark* provided McGahern made some textual
changes, and that he should contact the *Irish Times*. On 11 August Monteith wrote
to apologise for the misleading cable: 'What happened, apparently, was that the Irish
Censorship Board announced that there was to be a variation of the original order
banning THE DARK. By this they meant that from today they're going to allow the
sale in the Republic of the Panther paperback edition – though not, as yet, our own.
Someone misunderstood the word "variation" and thought that the Board meant by
it textual changes.' Monteith's letter crossed with the letter from McGahern above.
32 Panther produced *The Dark* in two different 1960s paperback editions, the first
(1967) bore a very odd, psychedelic cover of a man's staring eyes tinted in blue light
on the bottom half of the cover and the blurred face of a young woman alongside a
dramatic mask on the top half. The second (1969) is more likely the one to which
McGahern is referring here: clearly meant to titillate, it consisted of a cartoon-like
drawing of a priest standing over a scantily clad young woman.
33 Claude Duneton (1935–2012) was a French actor, playwright and screenwriter,
and occasional visitor to the McGaherns' Paris flat. He became best known for the
films *Three Colors: Blue* (1993), *The Double Life of Veronique* (1991) and *Betty Blue*
(1986). McGahern first met Duneton through the playwright David Halliwell. John
and Madeline stayed with him for three or four days on their journey through France.

Rather than Morocco I think we'll go someplace by the sea for a few weeks—do you know of any such place? – and come back by way of Madrid to here on Oct. 1st.[34]

We'll stay here a week, let this place, and come to London.

Though we may decide to go to Morocco, depends how the days go.

Do you think should I accept invitations to speak at the Universities of Dublin and Galway in November, soon after the book?[35]

Very tired after the novella, almost afraid to see it in type.

Benziger, the German publisher, complain they got no proof copy of Nightlines, though I left clear instructions that they were. They had a small success with The Dark and are anxious to follow up.

With my love
John

London Magazine Papers
Barcelona

26 August 1970

Dear Vivienne Lewis,[36]

Thank you for your letter and the proofs, they are unfortunately late as I had left Paris. I hope you'll find the corrections all right.[37]

I was born in Dublin in 1934. I have published 2 novels The Barracks and The Dark. Nightlines is the title of the new book. I have been living outside Ireland since 1964, and in Paris for the last year.

I hope the proofs reach you in time. Until 1st October I'll be out of Paris and c/o Faber will be the safest address.

Yours sincerely,
John McGahern

---

34 John and Madeline very much enjoyed Barcelona, before moving on to Madrid where John fell ill. They returned to Barcelona, then back to Paris.
35 Monteith encourages McGahern to take up these invitations in a letter of 12 August and reminds him how impressed he was by his lecture on Melville's 'Bartleby, the Scrivener' delivered at Queen's University Belfast in November 1967. McGahern read in Galway in December but does not appear to have taken up a Dublin invitation.
36 Then working in an editorial capacity at the London Magazine.
37 McGahern is referring to the proofs of 'My Love, My Umbrella'. The story was first published in the London Magazine, vol. 10, no. 7 (October 1970).

19 September 1970

Dear Peter,[38]
My heart fell at the sight of the cover.[39]
    1) Impression: a schoolgirl's book (11–15)
    2) A chocolate green or green chocolate of the pig in the kitchen.
My prose stands against everything the cover says. Surely Yeats, Joyce and Beckett gave Irish letters some universal dignity.
    I might let it pass if I thought it would find its readers.
My experience is that people likely to buy a book are people who enjoy the language. A cover like that is the same as selling cheese under a sugar label.
    MacMillan published <u>The Barracks</u> with an Irish cover.[40] It got sensitive Irish reviews. It sold 750 copies.
    Knopf published <u>The Dark</u> in typographical cover. It got tough wide reviews as literature. It sold 3,500 copies and with a little luck could have done much better. Irish except Joyce/Beckett wasn't mentioned in the reviews.
    That hankering after the little old homestead is played out. Grove have no need of it. The cover is lazy, unimaginative and it stereotypes, since whoever designed it thought it a cliché, a long dead one at that. Why can't it just get decent type and red and black, if nothing can be better thought of.
    The only justification of a picture is that it's a good picture, a painting or a print.
That cover is DEATH to the book. Gregory wouldn't have let it through. I don't want to hear the viciousness in his laugh when he sees it.
    And you as a poet as well as a publisher must be able to see it's a disaster.
    That kind of Irish cover has been literally played to death, and is as dead as the literature (?) it symbolised.
    Lovely mists that do be rising on the bog. Top of the morning.
    I'll be back at 1 Rue Christine on 1st October.

38 Peter Davison, senior editor at Atlantic Monthly Press to whom Gregory had passed on the MS of *Nightlines* in order to bring it to publication.
39 The proposed cover for *Nightlines* that so infuriated McGahern depicted a drawing of a peasant woman wearing a shawl and carrying a stick walking down a path away from a thatched cottage.
40 The 1964 Macmillan edition of *The Barracks* featured a forest green dustjacket with a picture of a bicycle in black.

Can you write to me?
 Forgive any mistakes. I am disturbed.[41]
  John

BBC Written Archives Centre

1 Rue Christine

2 October 1970

Dear Susanna Capon,[42]
Thank you for your kind letter of the 9th September.
 The story <u>Why We're Here</u> first began as a play I never finished. I think I could make interesting radio of it, using it simply as a base.[43]
 I'll be in London from the 9th of this month. If you thought it worth commissioning perhaps you'd leave a note for me at my sister's
23 Forest Drive West
London E. 11
What time would be easy for you that week to meet to discuss it further.
 Yours sincerely
 John McGahern

41 McGahern won this argument and the book was published with a plain black cover bearing the title of the book in quadruplicate in varying shades of purple.
42 Susanna Capon b. 1944 in Sonning, Berkshire, growing up in London. She had written to McGahern in her capacity as commissioning editor for BBC Radio 3 drama, where she had been hired by Martin Esslin (1918–2002), best known for his critical treatise *The Theatre of the Absurd* (New York: Anchor Books, 1961). The controller of the station at that time was P. H. Newby (1918–97), the English novelist and inaugural winner of the Booker Prize in 1969 for his novel *Something to Answer For* (London: Faber, 1968) – he suggested to Capon that she try to commission something from McGahern, whose work he greatly admired.
43 McGahern made the radio play *Sinclair* from his *Nightlines* story 'Why We're Here'. It was first broadcast on BBC Radio 3 on 16 November 1971 with Cyril Cusack playing Boles and Norman Rodway as Gillespie. The play was produced by Ronald Mason.

Faber

1 Rue Christine

3 October 1970

Dear Charles,
I'll be in London in less than a week.

Can you please hold all letters for me (<u>not</u> to have them forwarded to Paris).

I'll probably stay at my sister's (LEY 1229) if for any reason you should want me. Otherwise I'll ring you at Faber's early in the week.

I thought the production of Nightlines fair. Its shape is better than either Barracks or Dark, but the printing – after the proofs – was a disappointment; and all these Improve-yer-provincialism ads on the back.[44]

It'll be very nice for me to see you in London.

Love
John

Joe Kennedy

23 Forest Drive West

16 October 1970

Dear Joe,
Thank you for your letter to Paris. I have left it for a time.

---

44 When McGahern met Monteith in person on 12 October he complained to him about the quality of the paper used in *Nightlines*. The advertisements on the back of the first edition dustjacket are all for Irish Faber authors: by Julia O'Faolain, the novel *Godded and Codded* and short stories *We Might See Sights!*; by Tom MacIntyre, the novel *The Charollais* and short stories *Dance the Dance*; and by Kevin Casey, the novel *The Sinners' Bell*. The overall production values of the dustjacket are poor, with badly misaligned print both on the spine and on inside leaves. A second, much-improved, impression quickly followed in 1971. The errors in alignment on the dust-jacket are corrected, though the back cover still lists both MacIntyre volumes and Casey's novel. In a contorted effort to leaven the charge of provincialism laid by McGahern, an extract of Kathleen Nott's *Observer* review of MacIntyre's *Dance the Dance* is included: 'His stories are all brilliantly and consciously Irish . . . As we all know, the educated Irish write the best English. Irishness, however, does not limit his range and depth.' The inclusion is unlikely to have pleased McGahern.

I am staying for some days with my sister.

I don't think it makes much difference – the interview – but if you want we could possibly concoct some harmless nonsense.[45]

If I go to Ireland we can have a drink then.

> Remember me to Margaret
> John

Faber

23 Forest Drive West

20 October 1970

Dear Charles,

It looks certain now that we'll go to Cleggan for the winter, Richard has found us a house across the bay, I am hoping it'll be a good place to work.[46]

Ian Hamilton said there should be a very good chance of getting an Arts Council grant if we drew up a new contract for the novel, as <u>Nightlines</u> would cover the last award. What do you feel?[47]

I am sorry I used 'forced' in the inscription when 'persuaded' would be more accurate. Would you like me to change it?

We'll probably leave in 2 weeks.

> With much love
> John

---

45 Kennedy travelled to London in late 1970 to interview McGahern for the *Evening Herald*. This frank and very interesting interview took place in a pub near the National Gallery but was suppressed by the *Herald* (McGahern was still in bad odour in certain quarters in the wake of the banning of *The Dark* and his dismissal as a teacher). Many years later, after McGahern's death, it was published in the *Sunday Independent*.

46 John and Madeline had finally decided on a move away from Paris. They chose Cleggan, Co. Galway as their new home under the sway of Richard Murphy, who had lived there on and off since the early 1960s. Ted Hughes and Sylvia Plath had similarly lived there for a brief period, prompted by Murphy's entreaties.

47 Monteith agrees in a letter of 28 October that he will look into the possibility of applying to the Arts Council for the novel as suggested by McGahern and Hamilton. This scheme worked, the money was awarded and led, ultimately, to a house hunt in Leitrim and purchase of the Foxfield property that became the McGahern home for most of John's life.

Cleggan
Co. Galway
[*hereafter Cleggan*]

8 November 1970

Dear Rosemary,

Thank you for such a nice letter. And I hope too it'll be before May.

I asked Jennifer to send them the information (the enclosed) but apparently since then it's reached hysterical proportions. I don't understand exactly what they want. According to Charles Faber commissioned the book and because of that there were no need of acknowledgements.

I've written to Bragg. He keeps sending me his books and it's embarrassing (certainly no fault of Fabers).[48]

Richard has got us Miss Brown's cottage and we move in at the week-end.[49]

Would you remember me with affection to Matthew?

Love

John

PS. Would it be use to the traveller that Hughes is opening College week in Galway on 28th and I am closing it 4th, with readings?[50]

48 Melvyn Bragg had at this point published four novels, all with Secker & Warburg: *For Want of a Nail* (1965); *The Second Inheritance* (1966); *Without a City Wall* (1968); and *The Hired Man* (1969).

49 Cleggan was known to Goad as she and Monteith had both visited Murphy there previously.

50 McGahern gave a reading at the Aula Maxima, UCG under the auspices of the university's Arts Society to a packed audience on the evening of Friday 4 December 1970 as the closing event of College Week. The original intention of the Arts Society was to have Ted Hughes open the Week and he was advertised in local Galway newspapers to do so. The Hughes reading did not come to pass and instead the Week was opened by Hughes's good friend Richard Murphy.

12 November 1970

Dear Charles,

It's allright about £600: the only reason I asked for £700 was for benefit of Arts C.

On Saturday we move to Miss Brown's cottage across the bay.[51]

Owen Goff did a favour for us; so can a copy of <u>Nightlines</u> be sent to him?[52]

Do you think it would be right to send a copy to Samuel Beckett; I'd rather, if you think it good, if Faber sent it, because he might feel <u>he had</u> to read it if the author sent it.[53]

Do you know anything, very roughly, of the sales? It's simply curiosity.[54]

I have finished the play, the final draft.[55] I have started a commission for BBC2, which fortunately is part of the novel. They shoot it about February.[56]

Forgive this clumsy pen.

Madeline sends you her love.[57]

Love

John

Cushatrough
Claddaghduff
Co. Galway

51 This house was the home of the wealthy Twining tea merchant family for the second half of the nineteenth century. The house was inherited by Julia Holberton in 1902. Mrs James Browne was an elderly lady who rented out the house, complete with a wonderful collection of books.

52 Eoin Goff was part of an eclectic group of writers, artists and outsiders who had settled in Cleggan in this period. An expert sailor, he owned a boat of his own in which John and Madeline regularly sailed.

53 Monteith, in a letter of 19 November, agrees enthusiastically to send a copy to Beckett with a cover letter from himself.

54 Monteith replies on 19 November that sales are over 1,000, pointing out that short stories never sell as well as novels.

55 Refers to 'Sinclair'.

56 'A Matter of Death' focuses on a dying woman and her husband's decision to empty her house of its furniture and their children. The scene will be familiar to readers of *The Leavetaking* or *Memoir*. There is no archival evidence that this piece was ever produced for the BBC.

57 Monteith's reply asks for his love to be sent to Madeline, Richard, Mrs Coyne, Eileen O'Malley and everyone else in Cleggan.

17 November 1970

Dear Susanna Capon,

The above will be a permanent address for some months. I am anxious to know where I stand with you; and if you still want <u>Sinclair</u> what rate you are prepared to offer me.[58]

I am working on a story for BBC 2 and when I finish that I am anxious to go back to the novel I am writing, as soon as possible; and once I start I don't want to interrupt it. So can you please tell me one way or the other about <u>Sinclair</u>, and if you want me to finish it the rate you can offer.

Sincerely

John McGahern

Faber

Cleggan

2 December 1970

Dear Rosemary,

Thank you for sending me the reviews. Could a review copy be sent to:

Lionel Kelly
English Department
University of Reading

He did a long review of <u>The Barracks</u> and <u>Dark</u>.

And a copy from me to:

Mr. T. Davey
111 Friern Barnet Lane
London N. 20[59]

58 Capon was enthusiastic about commissioning McGahern and he was offered £85 for his thirty-minute radio play.

59 Tom Davey was a friend McGahern first met in the King's Head pub, Chingford when he was teaching in East London. He was a dentist from Belfast and a graduate of Queen's University. His wife Claire was also from Ulster. McGahern was a regular guest in their North London home and occasionally turned to Tom for dental care.

The roof leaks. The cows in the surrounding stables moo us awake. Eileen O'Malley gave headline gossip about us to the Irish Press (I have paranoiac visions of relatives descending from Roscommon) and now journalists have started to pursue Richard's phone.[60] If I stay certainly O'Malley's will get the boycott treatment.[61]

Never worked so easily but I don't know how long we can stay now.

Love always
John

Faber

Cleggan

5 December 1970

Dear Charles,

Thank you for your kind letter and the Fuller review. Can you send me 2 copies of Nightlines.[62]

I was amazed at the dullness of the Irish Times today, it was as if Faber was trying to tone down the review the Irish Times gave the book.[63] Who manages this business in Faber?[64] It wouldn't matter if there weren't so many better reviews. As an ad for sleeping pills it would be fine though.

---

60 Much to his annoyance, on 30 November 1970 the *Irish Press* ran an article on McGahern's move to Cleggan. Titled 'McGahern Takes a Cottage in Connemara' and written as part of Mary Kenny's weekly column, the piece described McGahern's move: 'He has hired a cottage there with his Anglo-American wife Madeleine, and leads a quiet, industrious life in the area. He meets his old friend the poet Richard Murphy in the Pier Bar almost daily, and next Saturday he'll be going in to Galway University to speak at a literary society there, but otherwise he seems to be content to be far away from people generally. Cleggan people recall his being there nine years ago when he wrote his first novel "The Barracks" so he is well integrated in that spot.' The article was problematic for McGahern in several ways, not least the fact that his father knew nothing at this point of the existence of Madeline.

61 O'Malley's Pier Bar.

62 On 27 November 1970 Monteith had written to McGahern alerting him to Roy Fuller's glowing review of *Nightlines* in *The Listener*.

63 Bernard Share reviewed *Nightlines* for the *Irish Times* of 24 October 1970, concluding that it was 'a formidable collection: formidable in its assurance; formidable in its uncompromising view of our condition; formidable in its promise of even better things'.

64 The advertising manager at Faber was John Bodley.

I'd also love to know what 'in the great tradition of Irish short-story writers' (Listener ad) means. It's the sort of book I'd run a few miles from.[65]

If the academic dullness of sticking to one review is kept surely the end of the Fuller review is a natural.

All went well in Galway.[66]

Love

John

PS. 6th. I saw the Fuller ad in the S.T. today. Do Faber think respectable/dull quotes sell books? Obviously the same person is picking the quotes. If it's like Dubliners then the sensible thing to do is read Dubliners (same way of dull thinking as 'great tradition'). The end of Fuller is the obvious quote.[67] I know ads possibly don't sell books and I'd much rather not be advertised at all than in this way.

I feel like some suburban tea-cosy.

John

Joe Kennedy

Cleggan

6 December 1970

Dear Joe,

I was looking out for you in Galway; and I thought you might be coming here for the week-end??? Madeline had a bed ready.

I was disturbed by the Kenny/Irish Press. Apparently it happened through a 2nd cousin of hers who owns a village bar, who gave the interview, almost

---

65 A phrase used by Share in his *Irish Times* review of the book. Such a description of his work inevitably irritated McGahern, who saw any such categorisation as provincial. See his letter to Monteith of 3 October 1970 on the subject of the *Nightlines* dustjacket.

66 McGahern's packed reading at UCG was reported in the *Irish Times* of 5 December as 'a triumphant return'.

67 Roy Fuller's review of *Nightlines* in *The Listener* compares him to Joyce: 'Reviewers confronted suddenly by an author of this quality are apt to make wild and perhaps unhelpful comparisons, but it is worth saying that for me the present book constantly recalled *Dubliners*.' The closing sentence of the review, preferred by McGahern, describes 'An exciting blend of penetrating realism and sad lyricism, and a sympathy with and understanding of great stretches of human life extraordinary in a young writer.' See *The Listener* (26 November 1970), 755.

all inaccurate.[68] I have asked Coogan to publish a letter (no published letter/ no answer).[69] And now other papers are ringing up Murphy. Some of my friends didn't know I was in Cleggan.

We'll probably leave rather soon.[70]

I may go to Drogheda at Christmas.[71]

Are you well?

John

Fran O'Rourke

Cleggan

8 December 1970

Dear Fran,[72]

I want to thank you for your courtesy and all you did for my reading on Friday evening.

I wondered if it'd be any use to you to invite David Halliwell after Christmas (his most famous play is Little Malcolm and His Struggle Against the Eunuchs) and his company Q.U.I.P.U. is putting on a play – it's running in London now – on James Joyce at next year's Dublin Festival.[73]

I think he would come while I am here for his expenses, without fee. I'd be glad – it doesn't matter much – if you'd tell me as soon as possible as I may go back after BBC make a film here of something I've written.

If you'd want it and give me dates I'd write to him. If it's uneasy it makes no difference. And thank you for organizing so well the evening.

John

68 Eileen O'Malley of the Pier Bar.

69 Tim Pat Coogan, editor of the *Irish Press* (1968–87).

70 Despite the upset of the article, John and Madeline in fact stayed in Cleggan until October 1971.

71 John and Madeline spent Christmas 1970 with his sister Monica and her family in Drogheda.

72 Fran O'Rourke was then an undergraduate student at UCG and auditor of the Arts Society. He had approached McGahern in Paris in the summer of 1970 to ask if he would consider giving a reading at the university. O'Rourke went on to a distinguished academic career as a philosopher at UCD.

73 In 1968 Halliwell set up a company called Quipu, which operated until 1973 at the Arts Theatre, Lamda, the Mercury Theatre in Notting Hill and the Little Theatre, off St Martin's Lane, central London. No play by Halliwell ran at the Dublin Theatre Festival and he was not invited to speak at UCG.

28 December 1970

Dear Charles,
Thank you for your letter and for the great kindness of the telegram of the Arts Council Grant.[74]

I am sorry but I still think the quotes <u>extraordinarily</u> inept.
Take the Irish Times.

a. It got a 'rave notice' in the Irish Times.

b. The Irish Times is probably the most influential Irish newspaper.

c. If the idea that the book was widely reviewed was wanted to be conveyed (and English quotes carry more prestige in Ireland than England) surely a number of short quotes (Observer, Daily Telegraph, New Statesman were to name a few definitely available) would cause more excitement than a long and middling good from the Guardian.

d. It makes no advertising sense as it had got a <u>long</u> and excited review in the I. Times already.

e. It makes no sense holding them back because after a few weeks another long quote will look exactly like the previous one.

f. After Christmas the money will have fallen out of the buyers' pockets anyhow.

g. The use of the one quote would have the opposite effect of what was wanted to be conveyed; it would seem it was the only quote you had.
Any fool would see (Listener ad) that the Fuller quotes used are idiotic.

a. The ending is obviously the most favourable.

b. To use <u>Dubliners</u> outside the full context of Fuller must be close to damaging, as it has already been used well past saturation point.

c. It would seem to have made sense to have used The New Statesman in the Listener rather than Fuller again.
I know a book will finally have to live or die on its own quality.

But I do think some imagination should be used to try to sell it at publication (or why bother at all, just sit back).

<hr>

74 Monteith had written to McGahern on 14 December trying to assuage his worries about the advertising of *Nightlines*. On 18 December he had sent a telegram telling McGahern of his success in securing an Arts Council Grant for the writing of his next novel. The amount awarded was £750.

I don't believe in the BIG WORDS (NATURE SCOPE etc) and they certainly don't apply to the Irish Times, since they'd already been finally gone into. The whole effort seemed dismal and grey and tired and safe.

John

1971

5 January 1971

Dear Charles,
The fair reasonableness of your letter makes me feel a garrulous old bastard,
and I am sorry to have been so tiresome; it was the wishywash of the Guardian
quote hurt me.[1] There was nothing personal either against John Bodley, in
fact I didn't know who was responsible for the quotes.[2]

I let the Mercure editor have my reviews so I'll have to use memory to
choose.

1. <u>End</u> of Fuller review.[3]

2. Quotation about rhythm in T.L.S.[4]

3. P. J. Kavanagh B.B.C.: world we see on our very worst days, and he
writes about it beautifully. Or there may be a better one there.

4. Something from Maurice Leitch's Ulster review.

5. Last sentence of Janet Burroway in New States.[5]

---

1 Monteith wrote a placatory reply on 1 January 1971 suggesting that McGahern
choose which quotes to use from the reviews for the next advertisement for *Nightlines*
to be placed in the *Irish Times*.

2 John Bodley (1930–2004), born in Brixton, London and worked all his life for
Faber from the age of seventeen, eventually rising to the position of director in 1986.
At the time of the drafting of this letter he was working as advertising manager.

3 A Faber memo of 19 January 1971 selects four quotes from reviews to use in the
next advertisement for *Nightlines* as follows, above, beginning with Roy Fuller in
The Listener.

4 'McGahern's piercingly accurate eye for resonant minutiae, his ability to project a
world which, though richly darkened by the novelist's imagination, is yet convincingly
inhabited and furnished, his very delicate ear for the resources of prose rhythm:
these qualities, which place him almost on his own among the younger novelists, are
abundantly present in his new book.'

5 '. . . at a time when Ireland seems less and less of a charming joke, his relationships
ring chillingly true.'

6. End of Daily Telegraph.[6]

7. Cork Examiner – One must say that all the themes are sick and one of them, Lavin, is downright offensive, whatever the merit of the writing.[7] Jebb is writing a long review for the London Magazine. I know all these can't be used, I'd choose from them though. It depends on what effect is wanted. What you say about the buying makes sense. And it is a matter of impression.[8]

The Guardian review, for instance, enraged the Dutch editor. Probably the day will come when I'll be lucky to get that good of review.

Richard left and gave a party, it had its ghost, Eoin Goff appearing at the window; he wanted 'to offer the greedy poet a glass of vitriol on his departure.' It disturbed me, awful to see some one getting so constantly into such extreme conditions of pleasantness or violence, though they are close, that they are no longer taken seriously, drunk or sober; and the one way out is to kill oneself.

Tony White is laying the foundation of his cottage in Aughris.[9] We went to Clifden on Sunday and played handball, the alley is in the middle of the town dump, so we had it all to ourselves.

The Third seem excited by the play, it is a long elaboration of Why We're Here. I have to confess I used your dead bird in chimney story.[10]

6 The *Telegraph* review was by Michael Maxwell Scott: 'All the stories here are beautifully complete and satisfying, with no sentimentality or pat endings – only a quiet compassion, edged with humour, for those caught in circumstances beyond their powers.'

7 John Bodley felt aggrieved by McGahern's criticisms and was especially unwilling to use the highly critical Cork Examiner quote, as he writes to Monteith in an internal memo of 15 January: 'His idea of quoting the Cork Examiner strikes me as very perverse. How could we hold them up to ridicule for what they said when we ourselves sent a copy of the book for them to review?'

8 In his letter of 1 January, Monteith had written: 'In the case of books of high literary quality such as yours it has always seemed to me that the chief practical function of advertising is to remind people about them. Book buyers – or at any rate buyers of this kind of book – don't, I'm certain, buy books simply because they see them advertised.'

9 Tony White's simple cottage stood alone by the sea near Cleggan. White was a close friend of Richard Murphy's; a useful map of various locations around Cleggan, including this cottage, is provided in the opening pages of Murphy's memoir, *The Kick*.

10 See letter to Monteith of 25 February 1969.

BBC2 have accepted the TV story, but apparently there's a budget that has to get past several people.[11]

I am slowly getting my teeth into the novel, it's like cutting iron.

Was there any offer from Panther for Nightlines? Have you heard at all from Patrick Gregory?

I hope you'll have a marvellous New Year.

Love
John

BBC Written Archives Centre

Cleggan

5 January 1971[12]

Dear Susanna Capon,

Thank you for your kind letter. And I am very glad you liked <u>Sinclair</u>.

I had thought of writing a play, about a woman's attempt to communicate she is dying and all the people about her refusing to accept it except as a joke. It would be long.

As far as the commission is concerned I want to be honest. My first allegiance is to the novel I am writing.[13] I would only work on it if I had a block with the novel or when I finish it. So any time limit would only be of contractual interest.[14]

David Halliwell said how much he enjoyed meeting you at Christmas.

Yours sincerely
John McGahern

11 Most likely refers to 'Swallows'. See letter to Monteith of 12 November 1970.
12 Mistakenly dated 1970 by McGahern.
13 The novel, which eventually became *The Leavetaking*, had as one of its central passages the lonely death of the narrator's mother, a scene that haunted McGahern throughout his career and which resurfaces in his final *Memoir*.
14 Capon had written to McGahern on 17 December 1970 thanking him for *Sinclair* and soliciting new dramatic work.

Joe Kennedy

Cleggan

20 January [*1971*]

Dear Joe,

Madeline says it's fine on Monday. I don't know if Margaret can come because of the children but of course she's welcome if she can.

My advice is: avoid Galway, because of traffic chaos. The Clifden road is on the Dublin side.

After Clifden avoid Coast Road.[15] Once you see CLEGGAN take first right around bay (at galvanized cottage). The house is in trees across bay.

We can see about story when you come.[16] I didn't yet get official confirmation from Arts Council. Did I tell you Nightlines has gone into 2nd printing.

See you soon
John

[*over*]

[*On reverse of this note McGahern draws a map of Cleggan with the following instructions:*]

Come through Cleggan village. Past Coastguard Station (white and black building). Next hill. A large house on top. A small house in furze below it is where we are.

Joe Kennedy

Cleggan

31 January 1971[17]

Dear Joe,

I'm sorry you had such a journey and the doctor and the back. They probably can't get much worse, though that's a poor comfort.[18]

I enclose the play.

15 'After Clifden' is underlined twice.
16 'Swallows', which appeared in Kennedy's paper, the *Evening Herald* (20 December 1971).
17 Mistakenly dated 1970 by McGahern.
18 Written in the wake of a visit to Cleggan by Joe Kennedy.

If they don't want it, it doesn't matter. I wouldn't offer it except for you being at the paper and in a sense of luck.[19]

Can you send it back if they don't want it?

It looks as if Madeline has to go to Paris tomorrow. Tenants vamoosed, probably with everything of value in the flat.[20]

No harm can come of the record business.[21] I'll send the news when it comes, perhaps you'll drop a line soon.

John

Patrick Gregory Papers

[*Cleggan*]

13 March [*1971*]

Dear Patrick,

I was very glad to get your letter. I hope everything goes well for Stina and you at the end of May, and that it'll be all happy. I have mixed feelings, it's like arriving at a party, it takes a long and painful time to learn a little of the language and what's going on, and when you do your teeth and hair fall out, bones rattle, and they throw you painfully out again into [*illegible*] night.[22]

The cover is a jewel compared to their first offering, it was a shawled working out of thatched whitewash into a vomit of green.[23] At least it'll get one very beautiful edition, in the Mercure de France, minus <u>Peaches</u> but with <u>The Image</u> as introduction.[24] It's gone into its 2nd Faber printing; because of the dedication I was doubly glad it made a profit.[25] After horrible grappling I've got at last the final <u>shape</u> of the novel, so it's <u>safe</u> at last. Or at least as

19 Kennedy was deputy editor at the *Evening Herald* at this point – the paper did not publish the play, though later in 1971 it did publish the short story 'Swallows'.

20 The tenant had, indeed, left the flat in very poor condition, the first of a long run of misfortunes with the property over the years.

21 A reference to Kennedy's close ties to the folk group The Johnstons, all siblings of his wife Margaret. See letter to Joe Kennedy [14 December 1966].

22 Referring to McGahern's move to Cleggan.

23 McGahern is describing the first mooted cover for the Atlantic Monthly Press *Nightlines* that angered him so much. See letter to Peter Davison of 19 September 1970.

24 The Mercure de France edition of *Nightlines*, published as *Lignes de Fond*, had a plain, light green card cover with elegant black typeface.

25 *Nightlines* was dedicated to Charles Monteith.

safe as I am. There's a comedy <u>Sinclair</u> for BBC, based on said character from <u>Nightlines</u>. And a story <u>Swallows</u>. For a change I can work almost every day.

Politician Murphy has arranged that he and I split next year's Colgate loot. So Madeline and I might see the whole Gregory family at Christmas. It's a month longer than the last time. I suppose you'll hardly be in Europe this year?

We'll probably stay here until Christmas. Madeline loves it here, and may have to be eventually dragged away. We've had a freak winter of summer weather (probably the usual summer of winter weather is on the way). The birds and cattle, particularly 2 legged, bore me but I get fierce comfort from the sea and a few trees.

Love to you and Stina, and wishes for your joy in May.

John

Faber

Cleggan

13 March 1971

Dear Charles,

Thank you for your letter.

Can you send me £50 direct and the rest to my current account:[26]

Bank of Ireland
College Green
Dublin

Madeline had trouble with her tenants and had to go to Paris which upset our immediate finances.

We also had trouble over our lease here, because of a transfer of ownership.[27]

After long grappling I've got the final <u>shape</u> of the novel. So it is safe at last. Or as safe as I am.

How is Queen Square and more especially yourself?[28]

With my love
John

---

26 The 'rest' amounted to £150.

27 Mrs Browne's relatives decided to renovate the place so John and Madeline moved to a more modern and comfortable house across the bay offered for rent by Dorothea and Conrad Ormond.

28 Faber had moved to Queen Square from Russell Square earlier in March 1971.

Cleggan

19 March [*1971*]

Dear Luke,²⁹

You are welcome to come, and we can put you both up.³⁰

By a fluke we have a car for a week or so.

I'll meet the 10.15 bus, leaving G., from Galway in Clifden. There is a cheap weekend return (33/-)

If you come later and wish to be met perhaps you could leave a telephone message with Mrs O'Malley at Cleggan postoffice.

I'll look forward to seeing you
John

Faber

Cleggan

24 March 1971

Dear Charles,

Can I have a little time to think about your offer? – whether I'll do it or not.

As it stands I think the fee you offer is abysmally low.

If I am to do an authoritative book, and it would upset a few old apple carts, there'd be much reading, correspondence, possibly translation from

29 Luke Gibbons b. 1951, a native of Keadue, Co. Roscommon, was then studying for an undergraduate degree in Philosophy at UCG. He went on to have a successful academic career, serving variously as director of Graduate Studies for the Keough-Naughton Institute for Irish Studies at the University of Notre Dame, Indiana; and Professor of Irish Literary and Cultural Studies at the School of English, Maynooth University. He is the author of, among other books, *Gaelic Gothic: Race, Colonization, and Irish Culture* (Galway: Arlen House, 2004), *Edmund Burke and Ireland: Aesthetics, Politics, and the Colonial Sublime 1750–1850* (Cambridge: Cambridge University Press, 2003) and *Joyce's Ghosts: Ireland, Modernism, and Memory* (Chicago: Chicago University Press, 2015).

30 'Both' meaning Luke Gibbons and his undergraduate friend and housemate Tadhg Foley, who had been closely involved in the UCG reading of 4 December and had written about it for the *Irish Times*. Like Gibbons, Foley went on to have a successful academic career.

Gaelic, and the need to write an introduction (as well there'd be expense of correspondence).

More importantly, if all this care results in a commercially successful book, it is only fair that I should have some interest in it i.e. some royalty interest.[31]

The only news is Richard Murphy has rigged it that we share the O'Connor Chair (he seems to be half-running the externals of my life) for next year. I have mixed feelings about it but I couldn't afford to turn down the money offered for 5 months.[32]

For that reason I'll stay here till Christmas so as not to run the risk of disturbance. Is there any hope you may visit us?

Love

John

Luke Gibbons

Cleggan

28 March 1971

Dear Luke,

The name was <u>Letters to Milena</u> published by John Lehmann.[33]
Rather similarly it and Malthe Laurids Brigge, Hogarth Press are brilliantly translated while Rilke degenerates into another author once Spender gets his grey political hand on the texts.[34] There are marvellous translations by McIntyre in the University of California Press though (Poems).[35]

---

31 Monteith had written to McGahern on 19 March asking if he might be interested in editing a new Faber book of Irish short stories to supersede the earlier 1960 volume edited by Valentin Iremonger, poet, critic and then Ireland's ambassador to India. A flat fee of £250 was offered with the editor expected to deal with all copyright clearances. On 2 April Monteith wrote again to say that, for sound commercial reasons, the offer could not be improved.
32 McGahern spent the spring semester of 1972 in Colgate.
33 *Letters to Milena* is a book collecting Franz Kafka's letters to Milena Jesenská from 1920 to 1923. She was the translator of sections of his work into Czech with whom he fell passionately in love – she ultimately met her fate in a Nazi death camp.
34 Rainer Maria Rilke's only novel, *The Notebooks of Malte Laurids Brigge*, was issued by the Hogarth Press in 1930 (reissued in 1950) in a translation by John Linton. The Hogarth Press issued Rilke's *Duino Elegies* with English translation and commentary by J. B. Leishman and Stephen Spender in 1942.
35 Rilke's *Fifty Selected Poems* with English translations by C. F. MacIntyre was published by University of California Press in 1947.

Dithering, it is a usual state, whether to do the Faber Book of Irish Short Stories, It's tempting. I'd throw over a lot of old apple carts. The first short story would be Yeats' Purgatory.[36] Lived too long under the O'Faolain obscenity.[37] It's very nice for Madeline and me that you and Tadg could come and I hope it'll not be the last time.[38]

Thanks too for the Mao.[39]

'I am old and they are young
And I speak in a barbarous tongue'.
To misquote.[40]

I'd be glad if you'd remember me to your Mother and Father at Easter.[41]

John

36 *Purgatory* was the Yeats play most admired by McGahern and he was insistent that it ought to appear in any anthology of Irish prose. See his letters to Charles Monteith of 10 and 22 November 1980.

37 McGahern disliked Seán O'Faoláin's work as a writer and what he saw as his – and Frank O'Connor's – control of the Irish writing scene. See letter to Michael McLaverty of 9 March 1960.

38 Tadhg Foley, Gibbons's undergraduate friend and housemate in Galway.

39 The Mao refers to an essay condemning McGahern's 'bourgeois pessimism' that appeared in a publication circulated by a lively Maoist group in Galway at the time, probably in relation to McGahern's visit to UCG of December 1970. Gibbons sent it to John who was amused, saying he agreed with a lot of it, at least where the pessimism was concerned.

40 The misquotation is from the final lines of W. B. Yeats's 'To a Child Dancing in the Wind'. The actual lines read: 'But I am old and you are young,/And I speak a barbarous tongue.'

41 Gibbons's mother Josephine 'Josie' Lee (1917–87) came from Cootehall and made an impression on the young McGahern when she came home from nursing in London during the Second World War. McGahern always spoke warmly of Hugh Gibbons (1916–2007), who had been a star on the Roscommon senior men's gaelic football team that won back-to-back All-Ireland titles in 1943–4. A respected general practitioner, he went on to serve as a Fianna Fáil TD (member of parliament) for Roscommon/Leitrim 1965–77.

Joe Kennedy

Cleggan

2 April 1971

Dear Joe,

Madeline and I were in Dublin for 2 days & I had a car for that time – and meant to try to see you and didn't. Time started to run out on us almost as soon as we arrived when I discovered an old friend Tom Jordan was very ill in hospital we walked then into the Capitol to see Lehane – he tempted us to the races – and that was that.[42] We almost had to stay overnight in Galway on the way back with tiredness.

It's to tell you we're moving into a new house a week after Easter, other side of village, and that anytime after that would be a good time to come.

Write if you can

John

Luke Gibbons

Cleggan

7 May 1971

Dear Luke

Thank you for your letter and Criterion.[43] I liked Snow especially its dialogue though it is closer to a sketch for a novel, for in that space you have to make

---

42 Tom Jordan was one of McGahern's dearest friends. A native of Kilrush, Co. Clare and a former Christian Brother, he became a schoolteacher on leaving the Brothers. The two men worked in Belgrove alongside one another. They remained close friends for the rest of Jordan's life, with John and Madeline frequently staying with Tom and his wife Blainid in Raheny and the Jordans coming for summer stays in Foxfield. Alas, no letters to Jordan survive.

43 Criterion, named in homage for T. S. Eliot's influential little magazine, is an annual literary journal and organ of the UCG (now NUIG) Arts Society. Luke Gibbons was editor for the 1971 issue that published McGahern's 'My Love, My Umbrella', the story he had read on his campus visit of 4 December 1970, leading to considerable trouble for Gibbons with university authorities.

up your mind which you want to <u>see</u> – either the night in its casualness or the girl or boy or the weather.[44]

The only things in the magazine I thought unprintable were J.C. Garvey and Reynolds.[45]

Do what you want with Murphy as long as you don't apologize. For he'll complain if he's allowed, in that way he's a child and a very old woman. If the situation is <u>obviously</u> without possibility of complaint he'll blissfully accept.[46]

I am curious of your impression of Montague.[47] I met him first when I was very young. And I see him and his work increasingly as a very frail, and sincere, fraud.

The reason Fran was complaining was obviously he felt upstaged, 'better to smile on all who smile'.[48]

We have moved across the bay and will be here till October, if you'd like to come sometime we'd be glad, only let me know a week or so beforehand. Remember me with affection to Tadg.

John

Faber

Cleggan

12 May 1971

Dear Charles,

Can the <u>Anthology</u> decision be delayed until we meet? I'll be in London early October, at the latest. And perhaps you may be here before then?

44 'The Snow' was a short story by Luke Gibbons that appeared in *Criterion*. A slice of rural Roscommon life, one might describe it as McGahernesque, replete as it is with a garda sergeant, a barracks and locations such as Carrick and Drumboylan.

45 J. C. Garvey was a Franciscan friar who taught in the Department of Philosophy, UCG; his short essay 'Art and Society' appears pp. 51–3. Lorna Reynolds was then Professor of English at UCG; two Reynolds poems appear on p. 30: 'The Violet Plucked and Burnt' and 'The Traveller'. On Reynolds, see letter to Charles Monteith of 24 October 1964.

46 What Richard Murphy's possible complaint was remains unknown. His poem 'Saint Gormgall's Well' appeared on p. 31 of *Criterion*.

47 Irish poet John Montague.

48 Fran O'Rourke who had issued the original invitation to McGahern for the UCG event. See letter to O'Rourke of 8 December 1970.

Is it true that all such books, for instance Auden's Faber book of Aphorisms, come under the same house rule? I'd feel easier – one way or the other – after I'd seen you.

I think publishing changes, and that the Faber rule encourages amateurism (19th century translation was often an intellectual substitute for embroidery, often no worse for that) or vanity. Either the author uses the publisher to advance himself or his friends.

Or he prepares a dish for friends.

Or he includes what his vision of a tradition is (this is the best) with a few polite sentences.

Since he has no stake in the book it is not worth his while to argue his choice at any length or scrupulosity.

If he has any reputation better to do it for an American magazine or write his own book.[49]

Gavin Miller was here to go over the screenplay of <u>Swallows</u> and to search out locations.[50] They hope to start shooting in June. He seemed to be serious and very clever and he was also good company.

Do you have holiday plans?

Love
John

49 Monteith, after conferral with du Sautoy, still felt that Faber could not improve the offer, and wrote on 21 May that royalties *were* generally paid to editors of poetry anthologies, and of the Auden anthology mentioned by McGahern in his letter. But short story anthologies were seen as more straightforward: 'Since we've maintained this rule for a very long time, we don't feel that we could possibly alter it now however strongly we're tempted to do so in particular cases. It would be terribly inequitable to all the other editors [. . .] Overall justice, I'm afraid, does depend on precedent!'

50 Gavin Millar b. 1938 is a Scottish film director, critic and television presenter. Millar was a film critic for *The Listener* from 1970 to 1984. With the film director Karel Reisz, he co-authored *The Technique of Film Editing* (London: Focal Press, 1968). On television, he wrote, produced and presented *Arena Cinema* for the BBC from 1976 to 1980, and wrote and presented numerous other cinema and visual arts documentaries. Millar, who headed up the *Review* series of which 'Swallows' was to be part, had written in an internal BBC memo on 30 April: 'If it is decided that his rate can now be raised to £10 per minute, in view of his comparative literary eminence, we are prepared to go to £300 for all work on the story, including the screenplay not yet finished.'

18 May 1971

Dear Niall,[51]
I'll be here till sometime in next September and I thought before to write to tell if you or Mrs Walshe were near here how glad I'd be if you would call.
John McGahern

26 May 1971

Dear Niall,
Come for lunch or dinner if you can, whichever the more suits you.

I don't know what arrangements you usually have but the children will be welcome if they come.

If you were to come from Achill you'd leave the Westport/Clifden Road at Moyard and the house is a mile past Cleggan village.[52]

---

51 Having moved back to the west of Ireland, McGahern resumed contact with Niall Walsh, a doctor with whom he had been friendly in Dublin of the early 1960s. This is the first piece of correspondence in the NUIG collection of letters from McGahern to Walsh. Born in Tullamore, Co. Offaly on 28 September 1930, Walsh studied medicine at UCD and qualified in 1956. He spent four months as a ship's doctor, did some general practitioner's work and then trained as a pathologist in the laboratories of UCD. He was appointed as consultant pathologist in Portiuncula Hospital, Ballinasloe in October 1964 and spent the remainder of his career there. Walsh replied four days after this letter was sent: 'I was delighted to hear from you after all these years though I have kept track of your movements via the press since you left here. Shouldn't you be lecturing to starry eyed co-eds in the States or drinking wine under olive trees in Spain instead of being in Cleggan?' Madeline McGahern Papers. Thus began a warm correspondence that would endure until McGahern's death. Walsh died on 5 November 2018.
52 The Walshes had a holiday home in Achill, Co. Mayo that they lent to John and Madeline in 1973 and in which McGahern completed writing *The Leavetaking*, which he dedicates to Niall Walsh.

My marriage finally ended 2½ years ago and I've remarried.[53]

It'll be fine to see you again.

John

There's no telephone but Mrs O'Malley – Cleggan 1 (post office) will take any message for me.

Faber

Cleggan

5 June 1971

Dear Charles,

I have decided to accept the offer to edit the book of Irish Short Stories.

I have realized that the book I had in mind would not be a book of short stories.

It would have contained short stories but it would have pushed past to the novel, letters, autobiography and dramatic verse to search for a more catholic tradition. Emphasizing style and personality it would have questioned the false separateness of The Irish Short Story and placed it in style.

As this book would have to be backed by argument, even long, of course I would have to demand royalty. Perhaps I may yet find a publisher some day for the idea.

In its limited context I am hoping The Faber Book will be a move in the right direction.

Would it be possible to have a look at the out-of-print Iremonger book?

I'd be grateful to discover from Frank Pike the paperback position of Nightlines and the reprints of Barracks and Dark and how long is Panther's lease.[54]

We are both hoping very much to see you in July.

Love

John

<hr/>

53 Madeline and John did not marry until 3 February 1973 in Paris.
54 An internal Faber memo from Frank Pike to Monteith of 9 June 1971 suggests that Panther intends to publish *Nightlines* as it has done well out of its paperbacks of *The Barracks* and *The Dark*. Internal bureaucracy in the Granada group, of which Panther is part, is blamed for the delay.

12 June 1971

Dear Mr Ross,[55]
Thank you for your letter of the 28th April 1971, asking to reprint <u>My Love, My Umbrella</u> without fee.

I am glad to give this permission and want to thank you for its original publication.

The letter came only a few days ago by way of different addresses.

Yours sincerely,
John McGahern

BBC Written Archives Centre
Cleggan

22 June 1971

Dear Susanna Capon,
Thank you for writing to me. I am still working on the novel, and see no end to it soon; so it would be useless to give a date for the play. I'll work on it as soon as I finish or if I get a serious blockage before then.

I interrupted it to do a version of <u>The Barracks</u>. I am sending the finished script in this week, to Belfast. The BBC in London refused the contract for the Belfast idea as I was already under contract. I took a chance on its acceptance as I dislike the successful Hugh Leonard stage version of it. I believe its final acceptance or rejection rests in London.

I'd be glad if you'd let me know the date for <u>Sinclair</u> as soon as it is known, as the <u>Listener</u> would like to print it just after the broadcast.

I'll be in London from October – I do a day a week at the University of Reading – and I wonder if the Third would be interested in me reading?

---

55 Alan John Ross (1922–2001) was a British poet, writer, editor and publisher. A contemporary of Philip Larkin and Kingsley Amis at St John's College, Oxford, he served in the Royal Navy during the Second World War and in the 1950s became cricket correspondent for *The Observer*. He edited the *London Magazine* from 1961 until his death in 2001.

Anyhow it'll be nice if we can meet then.

With good wishes

John McGahern

BBC Written Archives Centre

Cleggan

28 June 1971

Dear Susanna,

Our letters crossed.

I read Tolstoy's play and admired it, but it was several years ago.[56]

I have done one such similar work for Knopf, a translation of the Finnish novel <u>The Rope</u> by Viejo Meri into Irish dialogue.

I'd have to read it again and if I thought it possible to do well I could attempt to do it in the evenings.

As my hands are more than full it is only fair to say I'm not terribly anxious for it.

As it is the most difficult form of translation outside verse – rhythmically it needs to be deadly exact to avoid parody – I would need to be very well paid for it.

With good wishes

John McGahern

56 Leo Tolstoy, *The Power of Darkness* (1886). Susanna Capon, who was expert in nineteenth-century Russian literature having studied for her degree at the University of London's School of Slavonic and Eastern European Studies, had encouraged McGahern to consider adapting the play for radio. Though hesitant at first, McGahern quickly became deeply interested in the play and wrote the adaptation that played over almost two hours on BBC Radio 3 on 15 October 1972 at 7 p.m. McGahern returned repeatedly to the play for the rest of his life, most notably when it was staged in the Abbey Theatre in 1991.

London Magazine Papers

Cleggan

5 August 1971

Dear Mr. Ross,
If you thought this story good enough to print in the <u>London Magazine</u> I'd be glad.[57]

Yours sincerely,
John McGahern

Faber

Cleggan

13 August 1971

Dear Peter,[58]
Thank you for your very kind letter, and the computer explanation.

I'd be grateful if the payments situation for the next book could be cleared as quickly as possible – I think Faber owe me about £300 or £400 – I cannot be certain as my papers are in London – and as I leave for at least a year in 7 weeks or so I want to appear in good standing with the income tax clearance i.e. to show I can live off my work.[59] This is important as the £750 Arts Council Award is synonymous with the Faber contract.

I'll be at the University of Reading in the autumn and it'd be nice if we could meet then.

John McGahern

57 Refers to 'Swallows', which appeared in the December 1971–January 1972 issue. On 19 June 1972 Joyce Carol Oates wrote to Ross to compliment him on the quality of this issue of the magazine, reserving special praise for 'Swallows': 'McGahern so moving I had to reread it immediately'. Alan Ross Papers, Brotherton Library, University of Leeds.
58 Peter du Sautoy, then chairman at Faber.
59 McGahern left to teach at Colgate in January 1972.

18 August 1971

Dear Niall,
Saturday is fine.
Why don't you both try and come for lunch Saturday? We would wait till two and it would break your journey.
Mary Hutchinson came last night.[60]

> Looking forward to seeing you Saturday,
> John

31 August 1971

Dear Charles,
Thank you for today's kind letter.[61] I'd like the balance or at least the greater part of it.
It's that I bought a small property and would like to clear it financially up before leaving.[62]
I hope you have a wonderful holiday.

60 Mary Hutchinson (1889–1977), a member of the Bloomsbury Group, was a key supporter behind *X*, the magazine that saw McGahern's first publication in 1961. A friend of Samuel Beckett and well connected in the arts both in London and Paris, she was also largely responsible for the publication of *Nightlines* by Mercure de France. She stayed in Cleggan for a week, gifted John a copy of Vincent Van Gogh's *Letters* and offered John and Madeline the use of her daughter's Little Venice house in London to which they moved briefly in the autumn. She also presented them with a bottle of champagne to celebrate their purchase of the Foxfield property.
61 Monteith had written on 26 August to clarify that the agreed advance for the next novel was £500 and that initially it was to be paid in instalments. McGahern wished to change this arrangement to get the advance as a lump sum. Monteith was agreeable but urged McGahern to act quickly before he left on annual summer vacation.
62 Refers to McGahern's purchase of what would become his home from 1973 for the remainder of his life in Foxfield, Co. Leitrim, near the village of Fenagh.

Both of us are looking forward very much to seeing you in London.

Love
John

Joe Kennedy
Cleggan

[Early September 1971]

[To Joe Kennedy]
We leave here soon. It'd be nice to have a drink in Dublin – we'll pass through round end of month – if we do not see you here before we leave?

    <u>Sinclair</u> will be printed in the <u>Listener</u> the week of broadcast so it's just as well the way it fell out but it'd have been fun your way.[63]

    Madeline asks to be remembered. Remember me to Margaret

John

Faber
Cleggan

21 September 1971

Dear Charles,
I am leaving here in a few days and will get to London around October 1st. My address will be:

27 Blomfield Road
London W. 9[64]

---

63 McGahern and Kennedy had discussed the possibility of publishing the play in the *Evening Herald*. *Sinclair* was broadcast on BBC Radio 3 on 16 November 1971 and published in *The Listener* – then under the editorship of Karl Miller – two days later.
64 This large house in the Little Venice area of London was lent to John and Madeline by Mary Hutchinson. It was the home of Hutchinson's daughter Barbara and her husband, the Greek artist Niko Ghika, whose short essay 'A Pine Tree' appeared in *X: A Quarterly Review*, vol. 2, no. 2 (August 1961). John and Madeline moved into this address on 1 October 1971. There was some unfortunate acrimony at the end of the stay over telephone and utility bills. See letter of 24 April 1972 to J. D. Langton & Passmore, solicitors to Hutchinson. Monteith replies on 28 September to say that he is especially pleased that the McGaherns will be living so close to his own home

314

I'll be grateful for any mail to be sent there rather than Cleggan from now on.

Thank you for the cheque of £400.

Both of us look forward very much to seeing you. We hope you've had a good holiday, in Greece.

I've finished the first rough of the novel, which makes it seem unfortunately that real work has started on it.

With my love

John

Joe Kennedy

Cleggan

[*September 1971*]

Dear Joe,

Thank you for your letter.

We have more or less decided to leave next Friday or Saturday (24th or 25th) or even Sunday.

If you were to come down before we leave the best for us would be Thursday or Friday or Saturday and we would go back to Dublin with you the next day on the understanding that we would pay the expenses of the journey.[65]

If it's not easy don't think further about it.

We can easily get to Galway to the train. Only it would be a pleasant way to go back if it suited you.

I teach an hour a week in Reading for the autumn. Madeline says not to bother with the magazines as there's not time.

Perhaps you could leave a telephone message Yes or No at Cleggan 3?

John

---

at Hamilton Terrace, a fifteen-minute walk away. Monteith visited the house on a couple of occasions for dinner.

65 Joe Kennedy drove John and Madeline to Tom Jordan's house in Raheny where they stayed before going on to the Holyhead ferry the next day. They drove through Leitrim to get a sense of the sort of landscape they would eventually return to in Foxfield.

Madeline McGahern

Faber and Faber
3 Queen Square
London W.C.1

14 October 1971

Dear Sirs,[66]
I am very disturbed to learn that the last paragraph was cut out of my The Image in the preface to Lignes de Fond.
  As the last paragraph brings together all the threads of the argument, and reveals the image as possibly something concrete – a yard of lead piping – the piece as a whole is nonsense without it, and while I dislike interfering with a publishing house I admire as much as the Mercure de France, I have to insist in this instance that the paragraph be restored.[67]
Yours sincerely
John McGahern

Joe Kennedy

27 Blomfield Road
London
[hereafter 27 Blomfield Road][68]

Tuesday [19 October 1971]

Dear Joe,
The owners are still in the house, their latest date for going is next Monday, but they have changed dates so often we have given up.

---

66 McGahern is writing to Mercure de France, which was issuing a French translation of Nightlines.
67 The paragraph in question was restored: 'Religion, in return for the imitation of the formal pattern, promises us the eternal Kingdom. The Muse, under whose whim we reign, in return for a lifetime of availability, may grant us the absurd crown of style, the "revelation" in language of this private and unique world each of us possess, as we struggle for what may be no more than a yard of lead piping we saw in terror once.' See LOTW, 6.
68 Frequently misspelled 'Bloomfield' by McGahern.

If they have gone you're welcome to stay. If they have not it'd be nice to have a drink.

The Herald is fine with me if they give a fair fee but I'll have to clear that it's all right with Alan Ross of the London Magazine who has the English rights.[69] I'll write him today. I don't expect difficulty but it is a usual courtesy.

Madeline sends her kindest regards to Margaret and you.

It'll be nice to see you in London
John

London Magazine Papers

27 Blomfield Road

19 October 1971

Dear Mr. Ross,

I have been offered a sum of money from an Irish newspaper for Swallows. The newspaper has no English circulation, its reputation is based on its horseracing pages; but I would give it to them for the money, with your permission.[70]

If you did not wish it to appear there before the London Magazine publication could you let me have a date after which they could publish it?

The offer surprised me – and I feel awkward writing to you – but if you do not wish it to appear at all I'll tell them so.

Yours sincerely
John McGahern

Niall Walsh Papers

27 Blomfield Road

20 October 1971

Dear Niall,

We were glad to get your letter, and that you enjoyed Paris.

---

69 'Swallows' was republished in the *Evening Herald*.
70 Ross granted permission for 'Swallows' to be published and it appeared in the *Evening Herald* on 20 December 1971.

For us it's been a mess since leaving Cleggan, due to this neurotic woman.[71] It was the 1st October – then the 10th – definitely the 15th – we moved in on the 17th – she's still here, and now it's definitely next Monday. We live on the top floor, and treat it as a hotel but it's impossible to work. I do not blame her for not moving but for involving us in her confusion. It's a lovely house and we hope you'll stay here when you come.

To mark time between 10th and 17th we went to Paris. Leyris said how sorry he was not to meet you but it is a hard time for him as his only daughter has gone crazy. Lignes de Fond comes out in November.[72]

We notice how high prices have gone in London, and house prices sky high.

Has the shooting season started yet?[73]

I hope you'll write soon and I'll write when things are settled or more so. When do you hope to come?

I teach each Monday in Reading, which is fine, but the amount of academic socialising expected is wild.

Madeline asks to be remembered to you and Phil, with affection, as I do.

John

---

71 Barbara Ghika, Mary Hutchinson's daughter.

72 French translation of Nightlines. Pierre Leyris (1907–2001) was a friend of Mary Hutchinson who brokered the translation. One of the most celebrated French translators of the twentieth century, Leyris translated, among others, Shakespeare, Melville, Milton and Jean Rhys. His four-volume translation of the works of William Blake, published by Aubier & Flammarion, remains the most complete in French and earned him the 1974 Prix Valery Larbaud.

73 Niall Walsh was a keen hunter and brought a brace of pheasant to Blomfield Road when he visited. McGahern hunted with Walsh for a period but eventually stopped shooting completely in the wake of his killing of a hare about which he felt deep remorse.

BBC Written Archives Centre

27 Blomfield Road

[Autumn 1971][74]

Dear Susanna,

Thank you for your kind letter. I admired Ronnie's production – some of his interpretations improved the script – and I owe a great debt to him and to you for its production.[75]

I've been looking through the Tolstoy. It certainly has possibility.

The real problems are (1) what you can offer me to do it and (2) since the novel is my first allegiance I can give no promise of date of delivery, until the novel is finished.

I want to say as well that the Sinclair production showed me how exciting a medium radio can be and chastened a snobbish and stupid view I held of the theatre and especially actors.

With good wishes

John

---

74 This letter is written on Department of English Language and Literature, University of Reading notepaper. McGahern taught at Reading on Mondays through the autumn term of 1971.

75 Ronnie is Ronald Mason (1926–97), a director and producer of drama for the BBC over many years. A native of Ballymena, Co. Antrim, he was a BBC executive in Northern Ireland and was head of BBC Radio Drama as successor to Martin Esslin. Mason produced and directed Brian Friel's earliest plays, *A Sort of Freedom* (16 January 1958) and *To This Hard House* (24 April 1958), for the BBC Northern Ireland Home Service on radio and later brought Friel's stage work to the BBC's national networks. The production McGahern is referring to here is his radio adaptation of *The Barracks*.

27 Blomfield Road

[Marked 'acknowledged' 25 October 1971 by Monteith]

Dear Charles,
At dinner with Ghika Friday evening I mentioned we'd lunched with you and
that you'd said you liked his work and 'would have liked to have a Ghika but
they were too expensive for me.'[76]

He said that he had special prices for anybody who liked his work and
came through private contacts.

I gathered these were about ¼ of gallery prices (£100–£150).

He leaves on Wednesday for Athens. I think you'd be welcome to come
round to see pictures if this interested you, and you could ring them or me at
the above if it did.

Ignore this note if it doesn't.
John

Joe Kennedy

27 Blomfield Road

27 November 1971

Dear Joe,
Thank you for the letter.

I'm glad you liked the broadcast.[77]

The copyright is mine.

Is it £50 they'll pay me?

Can you change Mrs Gilboy in the next to Mrs Kilroy as I realize there is a
Mrs Gilboy among the Cootehalls.

It'll be very nice to see you in London.

76 Nikos Hadjikyriakos-Ghikas (1906–94), also known as Niko Ghika, husband
of Barbara Hutchinson, was a leading Greek painter, sculptor, engraver, writer and
academic. His works are featured in the National Gallery (Athens), the Musée d'Art
Moderne de la Ville de Paris, Tate Gallery (London), the Metropolitan Museum of
New York and in private collections worldwide.
77 *Sinclair* was broadcast by BBC Radio 3 on 16 November 1971.

I may have to go to cursed Belfast 8th Dec. over the Barracks.[78]

         Madeline sends her best wishes

         John

                            Faber

                 27 Blomfield Road

[Early December 1971]

Dear Matthew,

Thank you for ringing this morning. I'll ring when I get back from Belfast.

    I wondered if it would be worth meeting separately for this, either at lunch or for a drink after work.

    1. If Jason Epstein would be interested in a paperback of <u>The Dark</u>, with a revised text, as I dislike the ending.[79]

    2. To go over the whole American position.

If you think there's no point I won't mind.

    I have a very poor idea of the American position.

If you do it'd be necessary to go over the whole idea privately. Perhaps you'll tell me when I ring.

         Love to Elizabeth

         John

                       Joe Kennedy

                 27 Blomfield Road

[Early December 1971]

Dear Joe,

The proofs came this morning.[80]

    The only changes I made were

                Biddy into Mary

                 Kilboy into Gilroy

78 *The Barracks* being McGahern's radio play – the Troubles were at their height and travelling to Belfast made McGahern nervous.

79 Jason Epstein b. 1928, then at Random House, was one of the most powerful figures in American publishing.

80 Refers to the appearance of 'Swallows' in the *Evening Herald*.

The lines are sometimes faint but I suppose it's usual in news paper. Can you keep a special eye on above in final?[81]

We leave 3rd January.

I go to Belfast in the morning (Wednesday) and I'm not looking forward. I'll be there till the weekend.

We could raise a glass in the Old Wine Shades if you come before January.[82]

John

Niall Walsh Papers

[*27 Blomfield Road*]

[*December 1971*]

Dear Niall,

There's a phrase of M. – it takes 2 to tango; and it was a great pleasure for us that you came.

I have written to Pierre Leyris

> 63 Rue de la Republique
> 92 Meudon
> telephone: OBS 21-97

saying you'd telephone him to see if he was free. His wife is English.

I have written to Robert Rothchild

> Ambassade de Belgique
> Paris[83]

---

81 These changes are made as requested when the story appears in the *Herald*. The final version of 'Swallows' as it appears in *Getting Through* (1978) and in subsequent collections reverts to 'Biddy' and 'Kilboy'.

82 The Olde Wine Shades on Martin Lane, off Cannon Street, was a favourite London haunt of McGahern's. Opened in 1663, it was one of the few buildings in the area to survive the Great Fire of 1666. In *That They May Face the Rising Sun*, Joe and Kate Ruttledge have their first date there. Tony White and Martin Green describe it thus in *The Evening Standard Guide to London Pubs*: 'the atmosphere is redolent of Dickensian times, with its darkened oil paintings and political cartoons harking back to a more robust age of journalism.'

83 Rothschild was then seeing an old American friend of Madeline's, Nancy Newhouse. Newhouse was editor of the *New York Times* travel magazine, the *Sophisticated Traveller*, and had visited Cleggan with Rothschild. In 1992 she commissioned McGahern's essay on Co. Leitrim, 'The Plain Ways of Leitrim', for the magazine: see *LOTW*, 19–26; and in 1997 his essay on Morocco was also commissioned by Newhouse. See 'Morocco, the Bitter and the Sweet', *LOTW*, 52–9.

saying you'd leave a note or telephone message at the Ambassade giving the address of your hotel and its telephone number so that he could contact you if he was free. Both will be in the telephone book. Probably say a letter of introduction was written and you wanted to leave your name and hotel with his private secretary. I hope you have a marvellous time.

We leave the same day as you via Dublin and Leitrim and look forward to seeing you both in London.

Perhaps drop a note

c/o Ghika
27 Bloomfield Road
London W. 9

John

Meudon is to Paris as Howth say to Dublin[84]

---

84 Pierre Leyris lived in Meudon. This PS appears in a different pen to the rest of the letter.

1972

6 January 1972

Dear Niall,

Madeline was surprised and delighted, as I was, that you rang us. It was a poor swop, on all sides; the flowers for the spilled British sherry. (The man who stole the flowers)

I came here the 3rd. Madeline went direct to Los A.[1] She'll come here the 11th.

It depresses me already, even more than the last time, this morality of <u>success</u>, bright hopefuls of all ages or bewildered hopefuls of later age searching for the absent next move.

I suppose it works though, it is their phrase.

I have already started my own work and will let nothing stop it.

The carrot is: if you're a nice fellow they may have you back.

There was a snow storm all day and with the hills and trees it is glittering and beautiful.

The house is a kind of Motel. There's neither pan nor kettle. And I am rather looking forward to Madeline's reaction as she arrives with cookbooks.

Remember me with affection to Phil and I hope you'll write us.

John

1 Madeline was visiting her mother, Frances Katherine 'Kate' Delafield (1913–95), for the first time in sixteen years.

7 March 1972

Dear Matthew,

Thank you for your letter. I am sorry for the delay in answering but I approached someone whom I trust who has been on the inside of the book-trade here for long. When I asked him about the possible change I mentioned only the name of Random House and not Jason Epstein.[2]

The answer was that Random is probably the best publisher in the States for an author to be with for their kind of books but with this proviso: if you don't make a lot of money, which is always a lottery, they'll probably drop you at once. He went on to say that though the Atlantic is not the house it was it has a reputation for caring for its quality authors. The final advice was that unless Random House made a very good offer that the kind (?) of writer I am might be better off with Atlantic. It would also in my case probably mean severing with Bob Manning and the magazine as well, and the unenviable history of having four U.S. publishers with four books.[3]

I spoke at Boston College last week. I met the Atlantic people. They were greedy about the novel but I was noncommittal. Certainly Upton Brady had already sensed some outside interest, it was very obvious during lunch.[4] They asked me to let them know if I needed money.

The novel in the sense of the risk of the journey is finished. The opening fifty pages or so are publishable. In this final writing I am going through it from beginning to end. All the rest of the novel, from fifty or so pages on, has to be rewritten; and probably two important scenes have to be written in, as well as some link passages.

2 McGahern was considering a change of US publisher away from Atlantic Monthly Press. See letter of 10 April 1972 to Jason Epstein.

3 Robert Joseph 'Bob' Manning (1919–2012) was an American journalist. He worked as London bureau chief for *Time* from 1958 to 1961, and editor of *The Atlantic* from 1966 to 1980. McGahern's first three books had been published respectively in the US by Macmillan, Knopf and Atlantic. Atlantic-Little, Brown eventually published his fourth book, *The Leavetaking*.

4 Upton Brady (1939–2008), a Harvard graduate, was then a senior editor at Atlantic Monthly Press, which he had joined in 1965 after spells with Knopf and McGraw-Hill.

I would on no account want Jason to make a blind offer. What I suggest is that I show him the finished pages and give him an outline of the rest; or for him to wait to see more finished prose, whichever he prefers.

I liked him and Barbara the evening we met and I would hope for a hard straight answer.[5] I've done far too much moving in the U.S. and I have to have a good reason to move again.

Do you wish me to contact Jason with this offer? Or will you? I saw Gregory in Boston, and Stinaberger.[6] Your sweet self came up but I prefer to leave it to an evening of wine and a certain promise of laughter.

I envy you the football mornings in Hyde Park.[7] We are both longing for the end of May. I finished the modern adaptation of Tolstoy here (The Power of Darkness) but it is only in the last week that I have managed to take up the novel again with the fierce harassment of here. We are to sail on the <u>France</u> on the 25th of May.[8] We may stay a year or so in Paris as it's a good place to work. I don't suppose there's much chance of you having another ride around up in these parts courtesy of Brucy Baby Boy.[9]

Madeline sends her love and please remember us to Elizabeth.

[unsigned]

Niall Walsh Papers

Colgate

25 March 1972

Dear Niall,
We sail from New York 2 months from today.[10] I'll be glad. It's not that the work is too hard but with it and trying to put names on faces and the social demands it's almost impossible to get enough calm to do my own work. It's as if one's real life was put away with camphor balls in boxes like summer clothes until May. Even the huge monthly pay checks increase the unreality though they are the only reason to be here.

5 Barbara Epstein (1929–2006) was then Jason Epstein's wife and another influential figure in the American publishing scene.
6 Patrick Gregory and his wife Stina.
7 Evans was a sportsfan who enjoyed playing football, but more especially cricket.
8 John spent the voyage reading Coleridge's *Biographia Literaria*, while Madeline played a great deal of table tennis, winning the cup for best player aboard.
9 Bruce Berlind, chair of the department.
10 John and Madeline sailed to Europe aboard *The France* on 25 May 1972.

I spoke to the Jesuit University in Boston, young Jesuits all swingers, dress closer to Carnaby Street than the round collars of my youth, stiff whiskeys before dinner & wine – cigars and brandy. The two generations detest one another so much that they have two Community Houses on opposite ends of the Christian campus. I had dinner with the younger before the lecture. It's a brutal business to be expected to eat/dine and talk to several strangers from five thirty to shortly before the lecture at 8.

I doubt if there ever was any sense of religion in this country as we came to know it. All social and moral, likeable good fellow, pure American girl, harlot with heart of gold, get your head above your neighbours, upstanding citizen, business contacts. A useful and good business.

TV and newspapers are full of the North. Brian Friel has suggested that Nero and his fiddle should be hired for a long Irish season.

Saw a cock pheasant on the road Thursday. The deer have come out of the forest on to the hills, as the snow melts. There are warm spring days mixed with days of snow and wind. The trout season, which is good here, starts today.

I wrote to McGarry and I am sure he'll help you.[11] His brother in law McKiernan who is an auctioneer is a rogue.[12] McGirl was the one I dealt with, more interested in machine guns in coffins.[13] With the North so near it might be a good time to buy.

Madeline is well, goes to sewing class, reads [*illegible*] Davis.

Remember me with affection to Phil.

I hope you'll write soon,

John

11 Emmet McGarry was a first cousin of McGahern's on his mother's side and involved in local Leitrim house building.

12 McKiernan, a local Leitrim auctioneer, married to McGahern's first cousin, Rose McGarry.

13 John Joe McGirl (1921–88) was a local publican and auctioneer in Ballinamore who brokered the sale of the Foxfield property to John and Madeline. Devoted to the unification of Ireland and overthrow of British rule on the island, he was for many decades a leading figure in Irish republicanism who was elected to the Dáil on a Sinn Féin abstentionist ticket in 1957. He is memorialised today on a large Ballinamore monument as 'An Unbroken and Unbreakable Fenian'.

Jason Epstein
[*Madeline McGahern*] (TS)

Colgate

10 April 1972

Dear Jason,[14]
Here is the first part to page forty-two, and the opening to the third part which comes in between pages seventy and eighty; it is practically rewritten but another twenty pages – the father's dramatization of the real death since he doesn't have to suffer it now and the ceremonies live through the boy/man's imagination – would add nothing one way or the other to what you have to go on. The reference to the cancer child is to the sex act in the second part, where the father impregnates the woman against the doctor's advice so that the cells flow from the breast into the whole bloodstream.

I attempted to put down for you the movements of the day – the comedy of the father looking for a new woman, the aunt, Lightfoot and his friend onto the sacking and to the women's remembered life to the love act before sleep by the sea – but it was too complicated.

I enjoyed very much your company and the meal on Friday, and want to thank you.[15]

> Sincerely,
> John McGahern

Faber

Colgate

10 April 1972

Dear Matthew,
I got your letter today after coming from New York, where I lunched with Jason on Friday.

---

14 Jason Epstein, then a vice-president at Random House.
15 Epstein replied on 4 May 1972 that, while wanting to see more of what was becoming *The Leavetaking*, the commercial possibilities did not look good and that American readers would not buy books that failed to give back mirrored fantasies of themselves. Despite this personal enthusiasm, Random House did not publish *The Leavetaking*.

I told him the plan and I am sending him the first 50 pages – tomorrow.

I suppose we can only wait and see, to see what Jason will offer, if anything, though he seemed to me very keen. My friend – he's Peter Prestcott the book editor of Newsweek – said I should get $10,000 at least, if Random really want it.

I'll be grateful if you handle the dealing. I'll let you know – or he will – when he decides, one way or the other.

What is the contract position with <u>Atlantic</u>?[16]

Can we protect ourselves if the worst happens with Jason?

Madeline sends her love, as I do

John

J. D. Langton & Passmore Solicitors

[*Madeline McGahern*]

Colgate

24 April 1972

Dear Mr Passmore,[17]

Thank you for your letter and the enclosure. My own trouble was apparently the same as yours, as I had no definite accounts to go on. As Mrs Ghika did not leave until almost the end of October she asked me to be only responsible for the months of November and December. As she also returned in November for some days it made the telephone charges more complicated still. So what I did was try to estimate fairly my own use of the telephone for November and December, and thought that use was probably within four pounds for each month. I wrote this to Mrs Hutchinson and of course told her that I would be glad to pay more if this estimation seemed inadequate.

Mrs Ghika gave me fifty pounds to cover incidental household expenses. Of this I used only four pounds – fifty pence to the boiler mechanic and three fifty for a book I ordered for Mrs Ghika at her request. When I wrote to Mrs Hutchinson I sent a check to her for fifty-four pounds which was made up of forty-six pounds that wasn't used for the incidental expenses and the eight

---

16 Evans replies on 25 April to say that he cannot find a copy of McGahern's Atlantic Monthly Press contract, and asks him to send a xeroxed copy to Faber if possible.

17 Letter to J. D. Langton & Passmore Solicitors, 8 Bolton Street, Piccadilly, London W1Y 8AU concerning a dispute with Mary Hutchinson over perceived monies owing in the wake of John and Madeline's stay at the house in Blomfield Road, Little Venice.

pounds I estimated my telephone bill to be. It was at Mrs Ghika's request that I gave this money to Mrs Hutchinson.

I'll be glad to pay the electricity bill for November and December when you learn what it comes to. My address after the end of May will be c/o Faber and Faber, 3 Queen Square, London WC1.

Yours sincerely,

[unsigned]

Faber

Colgate

[*Late April 1972*]

Dear Charles,

I have asked for the pages to be sent to you from Ireland.[18] There should probably be a link sentence at the beginning of Ch. 2. The <u>abed</u> chapter is now finished. <u>A</u> will start in the novel about p. 80. I was reluctant to send it as it's only beginning to develop.

I have showed it to Jason Epstein, as I wanted him to see what he was letting himself in for. Random has a reputation for extreme ruthlessness – sell or else! I am waiting to see what offer he'll make – if any. There's no hurry.

I am glad Seamus is coming. Colgate are lucky. Richard will be at Bard that year.[19]

We sail from New York on the 25th May. I'll be glad. It's very hard to get my own work done here.

It'll be marvellous to see you again.

Madeline sends her love.

Love

John

18 Refers to opening pages of what was becoming *The Leavetaking*.
19 Monteith had written to McGahern on 21 April to say that Seamus Heaney would visit Colgate in 1974. He came along with his great friend David Hammond, and the pair made a very favourable impression, particularly on Bruce Berlind.

2 May 1972

Dear Matthew,
Thank you for such a clear letter about the Random.

As far as I can remember the contract is in the black bag in your house. I cannot be certain; but you are certainly free to look.[20]

It is not in the separate contract but as an addendum to Nightlines contract. It says, as far as I remember, that they will pay $3,250 on receipt of an as yet unnamed novel.

Our plans are slightly changed. We sail still on the 25th but to Southampton and will stay for a few weeks in London. It'd be very pleasant to see you then.

Her ladyship has turned to martinis (dry with olives) on the rocks and holds forth volubly on life and art.[21]

Love
John

If you reply please reply by more or less return as we leave here about the 16th–18th.

20 Evans had written to McGahern on 25 April saying that once they had a considered opinion from Jason Epstein of Random House about the section of the novel he was reading, McGahern would have to answer two questions: whether he actually wanted to move to Random House (clearly he did) and whether it was going to be possible to get out of his agreement with Atlantic Monthly Press. It will not have helped that neither McGahern nor Evans appear to have had a copy of the Atlantic contract to hand at this point.

21 Referring to Madeline.

Patrick Gregory
[*Madeline McGahern*]
Colgate

16 May 1972[22]

Dear Patrick,
We leave in a few days.
   We'll be in London some of June and then we'll go to:

1 Rue Christine

Paris 6e

There's a telephone there <u>3262004</u> and it'd be nice to see Stina and you if you do come.

   I am tired out now and have done no work of my own for a month. I am glad to be leaving.

   I want to thank both of you for such a nice evening you gave us in Boston. I'll send <u>Lignes du Fond</u> when I get to Paris.

With good wishes
John

22 This rather valedictory letter is McGahern's final extant one to Gregory. Gregory's final letter back was sent two days later and addresses the progress McGahern was making with *The Leavetaking*: 'I am eager to learn that your novel approaches completion. I can well understand that it is a difficult book to write: you are at that stage in your work and life when one's old ideals tend to seem a bit stale, one's credos sound a bit tinny – and the new ones assume strange and frighteningly impersonal forms. It is of course the toughest stage of all for a writer, especially for a writer like yourself whose sensual responses have always formed an intimate part of his style. It is a stage when most poets drop out of the picture. But if the work can be forced into shape it must be a triumph, and the way to future is opened.' Madeline McGahern Papers.

24 June 1972

Dear Seamus,[23]
My sister told me you rang, after I'd come home to leave. I had no way of contacting you.
    I'll be at the above for some time and I hope you'll come.[24]
    Remember me with affection to Marie and with good wishes
                John McGahern

Susanna Capon

1 Rue Christine

11 July 1972

Dear Susanna,
We thought both you and Barry were wonderful company and we miss you since you left.[25]
    The flat was horrible, dust and dirt, coruscations – like sugarstick – of unflushed piss in the shower and bidet, and everywhere signs of the sexual battlefield. We were very lucky to get out of the adventure so lightly.
    It's clean now, and ready for you when you next come.
I finished the Joyce today. It was far more difficult than I thought.[26]

23 Seamus Heaney (1939–2013), Irish poet, playwright and man of letters, awarded the 1995 Nobel Prize for Literature. *Death of a Naturalist* (London: Faber, 1966) was his first major published volume, produced by Faber in close cooperation with Charles Monteith. American poet Robert Lowell described him as 'the most important Irish poet since Yeats'. Heaney and McGahern knew each other first through Faber and across more than three decades. They are generally regarded as the most important Irish poet and fiction writer of the post-war years.
24 Heaney did not visit the McGaherns in Paris.
25 What had begun as an entirely professional relationship had blossomed into friendship between John and Madeline with Susanna Capon and Barry Hanson whom she had married in 1971.
26 Refers to McGahern's adaptation of 'The Sisters', the opening story of James Joyce's *Dubliners* (London: Grant Richards, 1914).

Can Denys H. let me know as soon as he can whether he wants me to come to London or not?[27]

Duneton came round looking for you. We had lunch with him. The price was having to read his play. He showed us a letter in which Admiral Halliwell had summoned him to Falmouth, offering to pay fare and hotel, for a consultation.[28] He was impressed but couldn't go because of his school.

I hope we meet. Madeline sends her love, as I do

John

Faber

1 Rue Christine

16 July 1972

Dear Matthew,

I am meeting Mrs. Beck of the Atlantic M. P. on the 24th of this month. I thought to let you know because of the Jason business. I suppose it's best simply to say nothing?[29]

The flat was filthy after the tenants but it's habitable again.

When do you and Elizabeth hope to come?[30]

Is there any gossip?

Please remember me to Elizabeth and her ladyship sends both of you her love

John

27 Denys Hawthorne (1932–2009), Northern Irish actor and director. Born in Portadown, Co. Armagh, he read law at Queen's University Belfast and developed an interest in the stage. He found a natural home in the BBC radio drama repertory company and was much in demand as a radio actor throughout his career. His vocal skills brought him work reading poetry on air. In 1962 he took part in a reading of Richard Murphy's poem 'The Cleggan Disaster' with the poet on the BBC Third Programme. He became the leading interpreter of Louis MacNeice's poetry after the poet's death in 1963. In 1972 he was appointed producer of BBC Northern Ireland radio drama, a position he held for eighteen months.

28 McGahern had first met the playwright David Halliwell through Susanna and Barry.

29 Refers to the ongoing negotiations with Jason Epstein at Random House about McGahern's possible move from Atlantic Monthly Press. Wendy Beck was John's editor at Atlantic.

30 The Evanses stayed in Paris with the McGaherns on a couple of occasions.

BBC Written Archives Centre

1 Rue Christine

9 October 1972

Dear Susanna,

Thank you for your kindness to me in London, it was too late to ring by the time I was finished with Frears. Actually he was very good to work with.[31]

I don't know if the enclosure augurs well or ill for the production but it certainly is Irish thumbs down all the way. Don't bother to return it.[32]

My sister came over and we had a lovely day at the races yesterday except we all lost money.

The place is still a depressing mess but there's now some end in sight. Both of us are very much looking forward to your coming. Do you have yet any dates?[33]

Please remember us with affection to Barry

Love

John

31 Stephen Frears b. 1941, British film and television director. Cambridge-educated, he began directing TV programmes in the late 1960s and has been nominated for two Academy Awards for best director: for *The Grifters* (1990) and *The Queen* (2006). He directed McGahern's adaptation of 'The Sisters' in 1972, broadcast on 17 February 1973.

32 With this letter McGahern encloses an uncompromising rejection note, dated 28 September 1972, written by Lelia Doolan, artistic director of the Abbey Theatre, in which she sets out the company's reasons for considering *The Power of Darkness* unsuitable for their needs. Extracts from the two anonymous readers' reports are included and can only have been bewildering for McGahern to read: 'The grim and primitive life of the Russian peasant in the mid-nineteenth century, the ignorance and superstition does not at all translate to Ireland at any time'; 'the excesses – the murder of the child especially – here as depicted, would cause laughter even if well done. A great disappointment this from an established writer'; 'The dialogue is flat and uninteresting, and only carries the plot forward, not illuminating anything of the human spirit.' Capon, in her 16 October reply to McGahern, writes that 'The Abbey Theatre's letter is really stupid and the comments totally invalid'.

33 Capon replies that she hopes to stay in Paris from 23 to 26 or 27 November where she was making a programme about expats in Paris in advance of the UK's impending entry into the European Common Market.

Neill Joy
[*Madeline McGahern*]
1 Rue Christine

10 October 1972

Dear Neill,[34]
It was so nice for us to get your letter and to know you are happy in London.[35]

Did you try to contact Mindlin at all?[36] For apparently an eye fell out and he was a long time in hospital and the last I heard was that he was back in hospital, the other eye having fallen out as well.

We are ruining ourselves by getting in a bathroom. We are living in dust and mortar. We have quarrels with the architect of the building – it is a historic monument – who doesn't care a curse about history but wants to be wildly bribed for every concession.[37] It'll be such a relief when it's finished. Sometimes I wonder if it ever will.

I hope you and Mary can come to Paris. We'll make a night of it if I get to London but I am not certain. I have to spend 2 weeks in Dublin for the shooting of Joyce's The Two Sisters starting from the 20th November and I am behind with work but we'll see. It is lovely here, blue autumn weather; and we had an indian summer day for the races last Sunday but we all lost money.[38]

I hope we'll meet before long and Madeline sends her affection to Mary and you, as I do.

John

34 Neill Joy b. 1929, a colleague of McGahern's in Colgate. Now William Henry Crawshaw Professor of Literature, Emeritus, Colgate University. He began life in Colgate as an Instructor in 1963 and spent the remainder of his academic career there, retiring in 2002. This is the earliest extant letter to Joy in what became one of McGahern's longest runs of correspondence.
35 Neill Joy, his wife Mary and their two sons (Matthew Joy was born in London) spent five or six periods over the years in London with Neill heading up the Colgate English Department's study groups or on sabbatical. McGahern and Joy had a shared love of the city.
36 Murray Mindlin, anti-censorship campaigner. See postcard to Rosemary Goad of 6 May 1964.
37 Completed in 1607, Rue Christine is named for Christine de France (1606–63), second daughter of Henri IV of France and Marie de' Medici.
38 Refers to horseracing at Longchamps.

20 December 1972

Dear Susanna,

Thank you so much for enquiring about the fee, they didn't tell me it had come in Clifden; but that is typical.[39]

It's a pity we didn't meet in London. Though it'll probably be pleasanter when both of us has more leisure. I found myself dead tired at the end of each day in Ealing. I grew to like Frears very much and to admire the care with which he worked.

It was very nice to have you here. Our only regret is that the flat and ourselves are in such poor condition with the workmen that we didn't make you properly welcome.

Remember me with affection to Barry and I hope both of you have a marvellous New Year.

John

Niall Walsh Papers

1 Rue Christine

24 December 1972

Dear Niall and Phil,[40]

Thank you for the lovely card from London.

It looks if we can be married either Saturday the 27th January or the first Saturday in February. Of course we'd love if you could come. If you can, do any of the days suit you better than the other?[41]

---

39 Capon had written on 14 December to say that the BBC had lodged £83.50 into McGahern's Bank of Ireland, Clifden account in payment for his extra work on *The Power of Darkness*.
40 Mary Philomena 'Phil' Walsh (1929–92), the Dublin-born wife of Niall Walsh. She studied radiography but changed to medicine after a year and went to the Royal College of Surgeons, Dublin. She qualified in 1956, worked in general practice for a period in Dublin, then trained in psychiatry and was given a consultant psychiatrist's position by the Western Health Board in St Brigid's Hospital, Ballinasloe in 1968.
41 John and Madeline were married on Saturday 3 February 1973 in La Mairie at Place Saint-Sulpice, Paris. Nearby is the Café de la Mairie, a favourite haunt of

I told Madeline what you said about one of us being around about the time of the doing of the house, which makes sense.

What we are considering is moving totally from here in April to Achill, I can work on the last of the novel there, keep an eye on the house from there, and move in when it's finished. Also we could look after the tillage field ourselves.

But you must be very honest and tell us if this would inconvenience you in any way.[42]

We'd probably buy a car in London to move our possessions.

I hope you'll write soon. I hope you can come. You can stay with us when you come if it suits you.

Madeline sends her love and write soon.

John

Madeline's, so frequented by her that she came to call it 'the office'. This café, in turn, was a very short walk from Niels Gron's main Paris residence on Rue Guissarde. The Walshes could not attend the wedding.

42 The idea of the move to the Walshes' Achill cottage was greeted with great enthusiasm by Niall in a letter of 3 January 1973: 'I would say that you would both fit into the island life very well and you could start fishing again. There are plenty of pubs around and really good walks everywhere.' Madeline McGahern Papers.

1973

4 January 1973

Dear Charles,

I want to thank you for such a lovely Christmas card and for the evening we had together.

A friend of ours, Robert Rothchild, who has been Belgian Ambassador here, is to go to London as Ambassador on the 16th of this month. I took the liberty of giving him your name at the Faber address. I hope that was all right. I like him very much and I think you might find him good company.

Is there hope of seeing you here?[1]

   Love

   John

30 January 1973

Dear Niall,

Thank you for telling me about the possibility of the herring lorry.[2] I actually don't know whether they collected the trunks or not.

---

1 Monteith replied on 8 January that he had no immediate plans to visit Paris, but goes on to say: 'I met Sam Beckett a couple of times last week, and he told me that he's read and admired your books. If I do come across, we must certainly bring about that meeting at last. He's one of the nicest men I've ever met – and I'm sure you'd like him.'
2 McGahern was discussing means of moving furniture and other possessions from Paris and London to Achill. Eventually he did, indeed, use a fish lorry, procured via his Paris-based friend and only witness at his wedding, Paddy Hogan.

We sign the papers this Friday in the old Town Hall. The translations etc. unfortunately cost, for what they are, the earth; and the red tape cost hours. What is interesting was to see that the whole ceremony is basically about property, which is carefully obscured from young love by the Romance industry.

My father had a heart attack, and lost his speech, which apparently he is regaining. All my sisters <u>hared</u> home, and one of them is still nursing him. It's hard to see anything through the female DRAMA except he's like the devil in the mornings. I'd be very interested to know what you think happened medically, and its likely course.

We hope to leave in about 5 weeks. It'll be marvellous to have weekends together in Achill. The Yugoslavs are still with us.[3] If you can come over from London you can stay with us. There's a weekend boat/train return for about £8 and it might be fun if you can save the time.

Madeline sends her love to you both, as I do.

John

Niall Walsh Papers
1 Rue Christine

23 February 1973

Dear Niall,

Thanks for such a good letter. My father was paralyzed, also he can't write; and apparently had another 'turn', but there is such cursed female hysteria that it's impossible to tell the wood from the trees. He's always had high blood pressure. One of the more serious exhibitions of the hysteria was an attempt to cause trouble between my brother and myself, which fortunately didn't work.

We have rented the flat. We go to London next week, do a few things there, pick up the Tin Lizzie we have there, and drive to IRELAND. There's a small chance that the herring lorry may arrive on your doorstep instead of Dick's.[4] I hope that is all right, but I'll believe it when it happens. The entrepreneur in question is on the run from a wife and child in Dublin, where 'a few possees

---

3 Workmen who were doing up the apartment and putting in a bathroom thanks to Colgate money.
4 Dick Walsh, Niall's brother, a Co. Leitrim planning officer who then lived in Carrick-on-Shannon. Paddy Hogan arranged for the herring lorry that picked up the McGaherns' belongings in Paris, travelled on to Forest Drive West, then on to Ireland.

await me'; and the result of the herring arrangements so far have been limited to a few bad hangovers.[5]

The Joyce film went out in LONDON on Saturday night, it must have been well received, since on Monday the phone was busy with offers.

There's a good chance I may be given the Visiting Professorship next January at Boston University. It's already ½ way there, but with the Nixon cutback on education it may collapse like a pack of cards at the last minute. If it does go through I won't have to worry about money for years.[6]

I am impatient to be away and find it hard to concentrate enough to work well. I am looking forward very much to seeing you and Phil soon. Madeline sends her love to both of you, as I do.

John

In a recent British popularity poll of the professors, politicians with real estate agents – shades of McKiernan – were at the bottom of the list.

If you want us to do anything for you in London the address is

23 Forest Drive West
Leytonstone
London E. 11
Tel: 539 1229

Faber

23 Forest Drive West

[*Late February 1973*]

Dear Charles,

I rang and was very sorry when your secretary told me you were not well. I hope you are better soon.

---

5 Paddy Hogan was a friend of the McGaherns whom they met through the Irish painter Michael Farrell in Paris and who worked for Bord Iascaigh Mhara, the Irish Fisheries Board, in Paris.

6 John Head, one-time Professor of History at Colgate, had tried to arrange a job for McGahern at his then place of work, Boston University, but it never came to pass. In a letter of 9 October 1973 he writes to John: 'The fact of the matter is that the word on your appointment or non-appointment rather, became official this week – the Office of the Vice-President simply would not approve the funds.' Madeline McGahern Papers.

I am finishing that recording and on my way to Achill, in ten days or so. Madeline is finishing up odds and ends in Paris and will join me here. The address will be:

Keem Road
Dooagh
Achill[7]
With love and good wishes
John

BBC Written Archives Centre

Keem Road
Dooagh Achill
[*hereafter Achill*]

1 March 1973[8]

Dear Mr Travers,
Thank you for your letter and I enclose the signed contract.[9]
    I'd be very grateful if you'd notice my change of address to the above.
                    Sincerely
                    John McGahern

7 Monteith replied on 1 March to say how much he hoped to visit Achill: 'I used to go to Achill a lot just after the war when I stayed in a mad hotel run by a dotty man called Major Freyer. The place itself was absolutely lovely – it was called Corrymore, and overlooked Keem Road where I see you're going to be staying.'
8 This letter was sent from London – the McGaherns did not move to Achill until 17 March.
9 The contract was for a thirty-minute television drama to be titled 'A Matter of Death', to be produced in Birmingham by Barry Hanson, drama producer for BBC English Regions Television. The theme is described on the contract as follows: 'A man, afraid of the reality of his wife's death, moves the children and furniture out of the house. Workmen move in to dismantle everything and their world impinges on the leavetaking of the children.' McGahern was to be paid £400 for his work but I have failed to find archival evidence that any such piece was ever produced. See letter to Charles Monteith of 12 November 1970.

20 March 1973[10]

Dear Niall,

This is only a note – as it's not easy to be accurate on the phone.

Both of us are delighted with the house and I have been working every day since you left, and well.

I have scraped at the gate but what it obviously needs is a blowlamp. Could you enquire if a preparation should be applied before the application of paint?

It would be a relaxation to do the lawn but you have first to think of Mrs English's hens: they scrape each morning; and to dig and seed it would be a laying of the table, without wiping it off.

Madeline has tried the washing machine but it seems seized up so she'll wait for Phil.

If it suits you better ring around seven on Thursday, as we seem to go early to bed, though it makes little difference.

Both of us are incredibly happy and grateful.

John

The coal came today.

The sea yesterday was fine – a few Pollock – and sore muscles today from the rowing: but the bonhomie – in spite of the best will in the world – was even more crushing than the rowing.

[Spring 1973]

Dear Niall,

Thanks for telling me this morning about the likely virus. I was troubled by my desire to get back to work or fear that to do so I'd do it too soon.

---

10 The first letter from Achill where the McGaherns lived in Niall Walsh's cottage. They moved in on St Patrick's Day 1973 when they witnessed a little parade to mark the day.

I'm glad you liked the pages. These places might be fun to visit if you have time in London.[11]

> Love to Phil
> John

Since there are so many places in a small area it's better to give it a whole morning and afternoon. Pick the first fairly fine looking morning, as the easiest way round it is walking, and it's miserable trudging in the rain and being poked by umbrellas. If you get stuck or late or tired take a taxi: the distance is too short for public transport.

I'd first book lunch in the Boot & Flogger

> 101 Borough High St
> Hop 1184 (this is now changed)

Get off at Bank Station and walk up Cornhill: to Leadenhall Market about 3' or 4 minutes, it's on your right but easily missed. Stroll back towards the Monument – 4 or 5 minutes – toward Billingsgate, the streets around it are charming, and there's a marvellous knife shop across from the Market House. Beside it there is The Olde Wine Shades on Martins Lane between Cannon St and Uppr Thames St. curved by Arthur St. This is one of the loveliest wine bars as well as one of the best. It's probably worth it to take a taxi across the river to The George, the old coaching inn, probably busloads of Germans there for 2 minutes. At the back is Guys Hospital, some of it beautiful. 4 or 5 doors from the George is The Boot, the entrance is easily missed, black and small; the tourists do.

After lunch if you cross the street you can walk by The Borough Market down Clink Street to the river and walk west you'll come to the house Wren lived in when he was building St Paul across the river.

Bethnal Green St, very interesting branch of the V & A beside station: Furniture, Materials, odds and ends, 17th C. Shoes, dolls etc. Brocades.

Up Bethnal Green Road under railway br. away from Wren Ch. Balls Bros, a lovely old pub, which serves good lunches very cheaply, and they only charge you corkage on wine.

11 McGahern regularly sent work to Walsh for comment. Here he is referring to what becomes *The Leavetaking*.

Etoile in Gerard Street is expensive but worth it. Rely for everything but the main course on the trolleys. I like especially the marinated herring but you can't go wrong with anything there except your wallet. Choose from 3 or 4 cheapest wines.

Everywhere round Greenwich is worth it but you probably show it with the children.

Courtaulds Gallery have a small marvellous collection. Woburn Sq. shared by the Warburg Inst N. W. Corner.

Wards Pic Circus corner of Shaftesbury Ave. Wheeler's Fish Old Compton Street. Very good house Chablis and sole.

York Minster, Dean St, good bloodsport at lunch, lots of artistes loving one another.

Faber

Achill

15 April 1973

Dear Charles,
It is very lovely here and I was able to work almost at once.

The cottage is in the village and looks out over the bay. Sometimes I walk to the other village of Keel, which is two miles away; and Keem Bay is as beautiful as you described it.[12] They started to shark and salmon fish with nets there last week. The people are obviously used to tourists for generations, which makes it much easier than Cleggan.

Both of us very much hope to see you here. I'd be grateful if you'd, when you know, tell me what dates approximately you may be here. It is only to make sure to keep them free.

12 Monteith had written enthusiastically about Achill's beauty in a letter of 1 March.

I'd send you the greater part of the novel, but my typewriter was stolen coming through customs, but I can give it to you when you come. I am waiting for a new typewriter.

As always with my love
John

Faber

Achill

25 April 1973

Dear Matthew,
I am curious about any information you brought back from the States, even if it is unpleasant?

The cottage is quite lovely, it's in a small village, it's 100 yards from the shore, and looks out on the bay. The mountains are behind. It's eleven miles from the Sound, where the bridge crosses to the island. We both like it – the people are used to strangers and aren't near as vicious as in Cleggan – and I've been able to work well. I'm farther on than I thought I'd be now in the novel.

We half thought you might break your journey in Shannon and come up for a restorative few days. How is Elizabeth now?[13] Please remember me to her with affection.

John

Faber

Achill

21 May 1973

Dear Matthew,
I am curious about whether you got my letter enquiring whether you'd had any clearer information about the U. S. people and the novel.

You told me once to ask if I needed money. I am in the odd position of being owed £900 or so – mostly BBC and German money – but for some reason it's being slow in coming, though it could arrive in the morning; and

13 Elizabeth Evans had suffered from flu that spring.

346

my own money is going very low. If Faber could advance me £300 I wouldn't have to worry about it and I am in the last stages of the novel. Faber runs no risk. The typed part of the novel is no longer than <u>The Dark</u> and it'll be finished within 6 months, when almost £2,000 comes through Faber.[14]

But, Matthew, if it's awkward for you in any way don't worry, for I'll scrape by all right.

How is Elizabeth?

It'd be nice to hear from you
Love
John

Is there any likelihood of you coming to Ireland?

Faber

Achill

14 July 1973

Dear Matthew,

Thank you so much for sending the telegram. Madeline and I were delighted that both Elizabeth and the boy are well.[15]

Charles was here for 2 days. I gave him 210 pages of the novel to take back. Do you want me to ask him to give it to you or will you do that yourself? I would offer you a copy for yourself, but it would mean that much extra typing on Madeline; and C. can get it photstated at Fabers. I hope it doesn't disappoint you. I'll hand the rest of it over about October. I haven't finally finecombed through any of the prose (the 210 pages as well).

Is there any trouble over the £300? Actually most of the monies I was expecting came and I am out of the red. If there is difficulty I can approach <u>Atlantic</u> directly?[16]

It'll be nice if you can write soon and even nicer to have an evening together when the horrible discipline this work imposes is over.

Love to Elizabeth
John

14 McGahern needed financial assistance with work on the house in Foxfield which his builder cousin Emmet McGarry was carrying out.
15 Evans had telegrammed the McGaherns to announce the arrival of a son to himself and his wife Elizabeth.
16 See letter to Matthew Evans of 21 May 1973.

22 July 1973

Dear Charles,

Thank you for such praise and for such a useful letter. All of the reservations are to my mind justified. The 'Duchess' has become ridiculous already, as has the woman's language in the working – it is 30 pages on, and in about another week I will have left London completely – grown quieter. It is strange that when one is unsure of tone there seems always exaggeration. Rather than any 'crossness' I am indebted and grateful.[17]

What I intend to do is go ahead and finish the novel. My feet will be more certain then, and then come back. All of the novel has to be combed through a last time anyhow. The mother will almost certainly go completely, and your idea of the man's first time in the hotel suite is marvellous.

I have noticed that all my serious mistakes have been made when I have copied life too closely. Its obviously a great deal more bizarre than the poor imagination.

It was a great pleasure for Madeline and myself to have you in Achill and we miss you. The next day was fine and we walked again on Keel Strand. A strong wind was blowing from the golf links and fine sand was moving like smoke across the strand into the curl back of the spent waves. The Menawn cliffs were clear and beautiful and you were very much in our thoughts. We were in fact inaccurately rehashing your marvellous telling of the 'her chum' story. Both of us would obviously have dearly loved to have delivered that sermon.

Madeline sends her love. I do as always.

John

17 Monteith had stayed with the McGaherns earlier in July, enjoying his time with them in Achill despite the drizzle and mist, and taking with him a 210-page MS of what became *The Leavetaking*. On 19 July he wrote at length to McGahern praising the novel as 'stunningly good, easily the best you have ever written'. But he then went on to point out what he felt were some serious flaws, chiefly that the character of the 'Duchess', though drawn from life, was unbelievable, and that the American love interest in part two of the MS needed to be toned down, particularly in her speech. He also felt that the central male character needed to respond with more surprise to the American's account of her life.

Faber

Achill

9 August 1973

Dear Matthew,

Thank you for your letter and I am so glad you liked the writing, and grateful for your praise. Charles was right: but all that London passage has now been finished – there's about 50 pages after what you saw – and that has been completely revised. I hope you'll like it. In a few days I'll begin the last passage, it's in Dublin. I'll be glad when it is over.

The monies I was waiting for came, so there is no hurry. As far as I can recall there was an agreement for $3,250 advance, with Faber getting 10%, but of course if I get all the money it will be even better still. What do you think we should do? And I am all right for money for the time being.

Poor Sissons makes the old mistake: the equation of life with sensation.[18] He must live in terrible private insecurity and fear. I wonder what he'd make of Beckett's phrase, 'a mug's game, and tiring into the bargain'.[19]

It is very lovely here but it has been the worst summer for years, which makes it marvellous for work.

I was very glad Elizabeth and the child are well and I am looking eagerly towards seeing you both soon

Love

John

18 Michael Sissons, McGahern's sometime London agent. Matthew Evans had mentioned to John in a letter that he had been playing quite a bit of cricket with Sissons who was claiming to have multiple girlfriends.

19 A slight misquotation from Samuel Beckett's *Molloy* when sex is described by Molloy as 'A mug's game in my opinion and tiring on top of that, in the long run. But I lent myself to it with a good enough grace, knowing it was love, for she had told me so.'

12 September 1973

Dear Matthew,

The novel is completed, and I'll send it in later this week, when it is typed. There are 70 or so additional pages to what you read and that is much altered. I hope very much you'll like it. Perhaps Peter might wish to see it.[20] He was very kind to me on my first day at Faber.

I'd be very grateful if you'd send me the 4 volumes of Sir Thomas Browne (I want to give it as a present to the man who loaned me this house) and Auden's paperback of Dryden's poems.[21]

Would it be possible to have a copy of the novel photostated and shown to William Miller?[22] I promised this to him a long time ago. Has Frank Pike any news of the Panther Nightlines?

I hope we'll have some good hours together so. I feel tired and a bit emptyhanded and depressed after the novel. Madeline sends her love to Elizabeth and you, as I do

John

20 Peter du Sautoy, whom McGahern always remembered fondly as having been the first person to greet him at Faber in the spring of 1961. See letter to Charles Monteith of 25 April 1961.

21 Sir Thomas Browne (1605–82) was an English author in diverse fields including science and medicine, religion and the esoteric. Faber had published a four-volume edition of his works in 1964. McGahern wished to make a gift of them to Niall Walsh. Faber's *Choice of Dryden's Verse* was selected and edited by W. H. Auden in 1973.

22 William Miller (1934–2009), editor, publisher and literary agent. His first job was as an editor under Frank Rudman, the pioneering paperback publisher, at Four Square. From there, in 1962 he joined John Boothe as joint managing editor at Panther Books, at the time an independently owned middle-range paperback publisher and the first to bring McGahern out in paperback. In 1965 Panther was bought by Sidney Bernstein's Granada Publishing and the drive to challenge Penguin continued. In 1972 Miller and Boothe resigned from Granada and, along with Ken Banerji and Brian Thompson, launched Quartet Books. The unique vision of Quartet was to publish both hardback and paperback editions under the same imprint, which at that time was unknown. The company published a paperback of *The Leavetaking* in 1977, selling at 95p.

2 October 1973

Dear Charles,

Thank you for reading through the MSS with such care. All your changes seem improvements to me. And the Erse is certainly better in italics.[23]

I made the other big change by transposing p. 35–p. 46 to p. 159. It seemed to break the early narrative flow too much, and to fit more logically into p. 159. I'd be grateful to learn what you think of the change. I also made some technical changes in dialogue because of the transposition.

A whole era seemed to close down with Auden's death. I felt my own dislike of his later poems petty and ungenerous in the face of a life's work that had given me so much pleasure and instruction.[24]

The Finance Committee cut down the Boston appointment.[25] All I regret is the loss of the money and I am thinking of going to London for the winter when I finish a short novella I am writing.[26]

Madeline sends her love, as I do

John

Do you think The Leavetaking is a good title or should I try to search for a better? It seemed right when I found it.

23 Written in response to a letter of 26 September in which Monteith writes that the toning down of the American woman's past experience makes the novel 'infinitely more credible'. He also encloses a marked-up copy of the MS with some minor comments, and suggests that the Irish-language sections ought to be italicised rather than capitalised.
24 Auden died on 29 September 1973 and Monteith attended his funeral in Austria. He writes in response to McGahern on 10 October: 'I went out to Austria to Auden's funeral – which was a very simple, dignified and moving occasion. It was exactly, I'm certain, what he would have wanted. Thanks to the ecumenical spirit that is now in the air the service was conducted by the parish Priest and the Anglican Chaplain in Vienna – and Wystan was buried in the village churchyard. It was a golden Autumn morning – I'm certain it's something I shall remember all my life.'
25 McGahern had hoped for a teaching appointment at Boston University.
26 This 'novella' appears to have been stillborn.

Faber

21 Forest Glade
London E. 11 1NU
Tel: 989 4760
[*hereafter 21 Forest Glade*]

15 October 1973[27]

Dear Charles,

We are closing house in Achill, and moving to London sometime next week. I'll stay with my brother for a while, I've put his address above.

Atlantic are delighted with the novel, but strongly question the title. Perhaps we can go over their letter when we meet?

Thank you for telling me of Auden's funeral. I read your tribute in the N. S. and thought it exactly right, with just the one private and very moving image of the slippered feet.[28] Poor Spender, it seems, is unable to resist making an exhibit of himself on any occasion.[29]

I have written to Matthew over the U.S. advance, saying that while I do not want to interfere with house protocol my worry is that if the cheque goes through the Faber accounts it may land me in the British tax net, being in London over the winter. I have exemption here.[30]

Madeline sends her love, as I do.

John

PS. The old boneshaker blew up last week as if it knew our stay was at an end.

27 John and Madeline lived at this address with John's brother Frankie and his wife Mary from October 1973 to spring 1974, when John took up a Northern Arts Fellowship at the University of Newcastle upon Tyne. This letter was composed on, and posted from, Achill.

28 When McGahern attended a writers' conference in Berlin in October 1964 he had admired Auden above all others and was struck by the image of the great poet moving about the hotel in slippers.

29 The *New Statesman* of 5 October 1973 carried tributes to Auden from, among others, Monteith, Philip Larkin and Stephen Spender.

30 Irish-based writers, musicians and visual artists are exempt from paying income tax on their earnings under Irish tax law. The tax exemption was introduced by Charles Haughey when he was Minister for Finance in 1969.

16 October 1973

Dear Matthew,

Madeline and I are more or less closing house here and we'll go to London sometime next week. We are looking forward very much to seeing you and Elizabeth again.

Atlantic wrote that they are delighted with the novel but that they are sending the cheque directly to you. I have no desire to interfere with Faber protocol but my worry is this: I have tax exemption here, but not in Britain. I am thinking of taking a job in London for the winter while the house is being finished. And I am afraid that if the dollars pass through the Faber/sterling it may get caught in the British tax net. Result: hasty exit for McGahern from G.B.

I'd be grateful for any advice.

I am already living in the streets of London. And I wish I could see the match tomorrow.[31]

Love
John

31 The match in question was a World Cup qualifier at Wembley between England and Poland. It became an infamous game in English football history with the result a 1–1 draw, thereby denying England a place at the 1974 World Cup in West Germany. Jan Tomaszewski, the Polish goalkeeper who had been dubbed a 'circus clown in gloves' by Brian Clough on TV before kick-off, conceded just one goal in a one-sided match that saw England take 36 shots to Poland's two, force 26 corners, hit the woodwork twice and have four efforts cleared off the line.

Niall Walsh Papers

21 Forest Glade

4 November 1973

Dear Niall,

I am well and Madeline is though it has been wear-and-tear after Achill.

We were about 20 minutes in the house when Hamilton rang up and since then it has been a progression of lunches and dinners and people.[32] Charles was in marvellous form, and enquired after Phil and yourself; he has now become the soon-to-be Chairman of Faber, ganging up with his rival – who becomes Managing Director – in a night of knives and platitudes.[33] His homosexual tormentor has directed his attentions to Lord Hailsham, which probably appeals to the crassest side of C's snobbery: 'Even if the man is mad he continues to show good taste'. We are lunching with him in All Souls on the 18th.

I am handing on the novel tomorrow for the last time. I have severely cut the woman's past, and it is lighter. They have a copy editor at Fabers now, since it is too expensive to have authors meddling with proofs.

Madeline got what seems a pleasant job at The Observer, but there is a chance it may fall through, because of the Aliens Law.[34] Anyhow she says she's writing to you soon.

After next Wednesday I'll be more-or-less out of the Social wood. I am not sure what I'll do yet, as I'm fairly certain to get an Arts Council Award; and I want to write again.[35]

My brother's house is vast, and we are happy here, and no problems have yet come in sight. Also I think it's unlikely any will.

32 Madeline writes in a typed letter to the Walshes postmarked 8 November 1973: 'Ian seems to be more at the center of power than ever. The feeling is that the enlargement of The Review – the first special issue appears in April – will be the literary magazine of its period. Five extracts from The Leavetaking will appear in it.' Niall Walsh Papers, NUIG.
33 Matthew Evans.
34 In a letter from Madeline to the Walshes, postmarked Walthamstow, 8 November 1973, she says: 'I'm now an Irish citizen no less, and can come and go and work as I please.' She describes the job: 'John spotted an advertisement in an agency window. [. . .] It was a lucky fluke. It consists of working for a pool of reporters.' Niall Walsh Papers, NUIG.
35 Madeline writes in the same letter (8 November 1973): 'Roy Fuller proposed an Art's Council Award and John will almost certainly get it. A handy thousand.'

The Boot and Flogger is closed, to be torn down. The place has moved towards the river but its spirit decided not to travel. It was some consolation to me that Phil and you restored yourselves so well there before it closed.

The most we miss in this great city is that it's unlikely that we'll see you for so long but we'll be glad to do things for you here. I asked Margaret to look out for the clock for you and she'll ring you when she buys one.

I am curious how it went with Emmet and your house on St John's lake.[36]

　　　　　　　With love to Phil and yourself
　　　　　　　John

　　　　　　　　　　　　　　　　　　　Niall Walsh Papers

　　　　　　　　　　　　　　　　　　　21 Forest Glade

21 November 1973

Dear Niall,

I am so glad you stuck to the idea of a solid house. There's something ridiculous about a holiday house on 20 acres but perhaps that's all those dead peasants living again in me.

Madeline is delighted with the job on The Observer. She has the rights of an Irish citizen everywhere except in the U. S., where she has the rights of a U. S. citizen. Her passport remains American. She had just to make a declaration and pay £5.75.

I'm almost 2 weeks on the pills and back almost to normal. Feverish and tired initially, pains in fingers, toes, ankles, ears; but that is what you said they'd do. It's the first time since the attack in Hemill that I can put my full weight on the left foot.[37]

I've to see the paperback editor tonight and that's most of my business over. I don't have to teach but I probably will, certainly for the money but as much so for the discipline of the grind that it is. It'll probably quickly restore to me the sense of the luxury it is to be free to do the work I loathe and I suppose love.

It is very pleasant in my brother's house. I've come to a financial arrangement with him, we have our own kettle etc. and I foresee no problems.

36 The Walshes had a house built not far from the McGaherns in Leitrim but never lived in it and quickly sold it on.
37 McGahern suffered from occasional, debilitating bouts of gout.

Francie came last week from Clifden. We had a lovely Chinese meal with him the night after he came and a too lovely day with him on Monday in Brighton that ended with Frankie Vaughan numbers at Tottenham Court Road Station.[38] We had a fine lunch – whitebait to begin, a bottle of claret, pheasant in chestnuts, a cheese soufflé, coffee and a cognac – in All Souls on Sunday. Charles showed us round the Colleges, a beautiful blue Wren sundial, 'time is passing and will be accounted against you!'[39] He asked to be remembered to both of you.

I'm looking forward to hearing about Leitrim and with love to Phil and yourself.

John

Niall Walsh Papers
21 Forest Glade

14 December 1973

Dear Niall,

I enclose the enclosed, for the sake of information or amusement, but not to seek a sale, which it is designed for. About 5,000 words of The Leavetaking will appear in April or May.[40] I'll send it to you then.

I had an irate letter from the farmer up the lane, saying that the 'traffic' – at least he restored the word, knowing the desolation round the lake, to its original usage – to my site had made it almost impossible for him to get in or out and demanding restoration.[41] I have asked advice from Emmet and Dick.[42]

---

38 Francie Mannion, from Clifden. John and Madeline had become friendly through buying meat in his Clifden butcher shop during their Cleggan sojourn. They dined in the Good Friend, a Chinese restaurant in the Stratford area of London, and visited Brighton Pavilion the next day.
39 This sundial, attributed to Sir Christopher Wren, can be found in All Souls College, Oxford where Monteith was a Fellow.
40 What was enclosed was a subscription flyer for the New Review, advertised as 'a new literary monthly' to be edited by Ian Hamilton and launched in April 1974.
41 Mattie Early was the neighbour in question. He lived up the lane behind the McGahern property leading from Laura Lake with his wife Agnes and daughter Mary.
42 Emmet McGarry, McGahern's first cousin, a local builder; and Dick Walsh, Niall's brother, who was planning officer for Co. Leitrim.

I work every morning, and have almost finished the novella. The tiring part of London is the travel and so many people. Madeline is still delighted with the job, she says it's more fun than work, and in her luncheon hours wanders in the city markets or goes to galleries. The most recent thing she's set her eye on is a butcher's block. Heads of sovereigns will undoubtedly roll. We hope to go to Paris on St Stephen's Day.

All else are questions. Any news of Achill? Your house and mine? It reminds me of that old phoney civil servant who wrote your father. The old Vauxhall? And if there's anything Phil and you want us to do here?

Madeline sends her love to you and Phil, with the Seasonal greetings, as I do.

John

1974

Niall Walsh Papers

21 Forest Glade

2 January 1974

Dear Niall,

We got back last night. We ate a stupidly frozen and defrosted turkey here Christmas, and had food poisoning for ½ of the time in Paris, it was nasty.[1] It was Saturday before we could eat or drink anything other than milk.

Madeline saw Pop on Saturday. He played the abused father, but they had it out, and all is friendliness. Both of us had a four hour lunch – it <u>was</u> heavygoing – in the house on Monday. It was all friendliness and it's amusing to witness the difference 'the married state' makes still in so many 'emancipated' quarters. She is pleased with the return to the veneer of social normality.

I was sorry Loughnane had such misfortune in Leitrim, and he was lucky to have you with him. They had to go down 200 ft for water – £477 – but at least they got the rig in, which at one time was doubtful.[2] The house must be finished or almost so but I have got no certain news yet. It's marvellous news about your house and I thought you must be glad to have sold the stocks and shares when you did.

Madeline says that if Phil or you want her to get stuff for you that she has time to do so in the middle of the day in the city – either to post or to leave here for you to take back on the 20th when you come.

I have finished a fairly long story and work every day on a new work.[3] It's a toss up whether to teach or not. It wouldn't be worth it if they caught me for tax. Though if they didn't the money would be useful in Leitrim.

---

1 By 'here' McGahern means Paris.
2 The McGaherns had a well dug at the Foxfield property, a decision they quickly regretted having realised that it would have been much easier and cheaper to pump water from the lake below the house.
3 In a letter to Niall Walsh of 25 January 1974, Madeline writes: 'John is in fine fettle. In high song. At this rate, he'll have another book ready by the time the novel

I was thinking of Ballinamore after you wrote. It must be the dreariest town in Ireland or thereabout. Still there's Mohill and Drumshanbo.

We had only one marvellous meal in Paris, at the Coupole on Sunday night. The spectacle of gorgement there is extraordinary and the food was good.

Fortunately we had Hogan's – the fishman – flat which is very comfortable while we were ill.[4] He was whoring in Cologne.

Just now I got confirmation of the Arts Council – it's a £1,000.

It'd be nice to hear from you and even better to see you round the 20th February.

I hope Christmas was all right and that all the house is well.

With love to Phil and yourself,
John

Susanna Capon
[*Madeline McGahern*]
21 Forest Glade

16 January 1974

Dear Susanna,

Madeline says Sunday – the 27th – is fine with her: it might be fun to go to the <u>Hollands</u> beforehand and eat about 2?[5]

––––

comes out. He's completed four stories and today begins a novella. The arrangement with Frankie has worked out fine and it's peaceful with the sisters. Our social life has been very low-keyed, with a slight lapse yesterday with Ian Hamilton and wife, lots of wine and a very good meal at the Hostaria Romana, Ian was full of malice and very good company. It looks like the magazine will cause quite a stir. He said he's getting a lot of advertising. We went with Donald Gordon to the Chinese Exhibition. He disappeared after the two of us had finished and John guessed rightly that there was a bar somewhere, and there he was "resting" over a very large gin and tonic. Charles is in great form, telling us about how Faber hours are effected by the energy crisis: they work from 8-4.30, or until the light is gone, all this over a £28 lunch at the Etoile. A fascinating bit of news from Peter Lennon: Anna has left the radio and is training to become a psychiatrist.' Niall Walsh Papers, NUIG.

4 Paddy Hogan.

5 Holland's was a public house beloved of McGahern and David Halliwell. The Tony White and Martin Green pub guide describes it thus: 'Its low wooden ceiling, period fireplace, brewers' mirrors, old photos and prints, fringed lampshades and warm, subdued lighting make this one of the most attractive pubs in London.' Opened in

I think The Stoat might suit Denys better but I enclose a copy of both new works.[6] I am finishing a third, and then I hope to begin the play.

Nightlines has just come out in paper – the cover is not too objectionable – and I hope you like it.[7]

> With love
> John

BBC Written Archives Centre

21 Forest Glade

17 January 1974

Dear Miss Dyson,[8]

Thank you for your letter. I enclose the signed form. I came here from Achill for a visit.

I am having trouble with the BBC. Last summer they stopped £102 and though I have gone through the proper processes still haven't recovered it. To go through this for a small sum isn't worth it.

I am domiciled and resident in the Irish Republic where I have tax exemption on all my writings which makes it still more annoying.[9]

> Yours sincerely
> John McGahern

1843 as the Exmouth Arms, it was located at 9 Exmouth Street, Stepney. It closed in 1997.

6 Denys Hawthorne, radio actor.

7 The cover of the Panther paperback bore a photograph of a lit candle in a candlestick and a gold watch.

8 Kathleen Dyson worked in the copyright department of the BBC.

9 Dyson had originally written to McGahern in Achill on 14 December, a letter he had not received. She then sent a follow-up letter on 15 January to the Forest Glade address. Both letters sought permission to broadcast a four-minute segment from *The Dark* for a BBC Radio 4 Schools programme in Northern Ireland as part of the *Explorations* series, for which McGahern stood to make about £9. Paragraph two of the 14 December letter is doubtless what so irked McGahern given that relatively tiny amounts of money were at stake: 'Under the United Kingdom Income and Corporation Taxes Act 1970 the BBC is required to deduct United Kingdom income tax at 30 pence in the £ from all royalty payments made to persons resident abroad. There is however a Double Taxation Convention between this country and the Republic of Ireland and if you apply to your local tax office for a Form "K" this can be filled in and sent to the Inspector of Foreign Dividends at New Malden House,

Joe Kennedy

21 Forest Glade

24 January 1974

Dear Joe,

Would you know of anyone interested in the enclosed? Also if you'd know of anybody who'd call at Easons or the Eblana or Hodges Figgis just to enquire if they'd stock it?[10] The Oxford people should do that but you can never be sure with such a large publisher. The magazine is extremely well backed but for the meantime they don't have the kind of money needed to send a representative of their own to Ireland.[11]

I'm going over to Ireland in 4 or 5 weeks. If you're not over here before then it'll be nice to meet then.

John

Madeline McGahern

Dublin

[*5 March 1974*]

Dear Madeline,

Can you send the photostat of The Beginning of an Idea
    Joe Kennedy (Editor)
    The Sunday World
    Creation House
    Ballsbridge
    Dublin[12]

I had a wonderful steak and salad with him in the National Gallery a few hours ago. His Lordship has returned safely to Dublin and I am seeing him

---

1 Blagdon Road, New Malden, Surrey, KT3 4BB, asking him either to authorise the BBC to pay without deduction of tax or if the payment has been made to refund to you the tax deducted by the BBC in the first instance.'

10 Refers to the *New Review*.

11 The *New Review* was distributed by Oxford University Press.

12 The *Sunday World* was the first Irish tabloid newspaper, appearing in March 1973 with Joe Kennedy as editor. 'The Beginning of an Idea' was first published in the *New Review* (August 1974).

in about an hour.[13] Tom and Blanaid were delighted with their presents. Tom is ill with his chest and does not look well. I took a cabin for myself (£3.50) and slept the sleep of the dead all last night. I'll ring Emmet this evening and I'll be more certain of my movements after that. I'll ring you Friday at 8 pm.

I'm afraid I solved my clothes – for better or worse – this morning. A blue tweed/wool suit, 2 trousers for £53. And a brown jacket for £25. I think you'll like them.[14] With all my love.

John

Susanna Capon
[*Madeline McGahern*]

21 Forest Glade

17 March 1974

Dear Susanna,
Thank you for your letter. I've just got back from Ireland and I have to report – to my cost this time – that everything is in the usual good disorder.

I am delighted that Denys Hawthorne will be able to read The Stoat. Madeline and I were just listening to him one evening by chance in The Dark Tower and thought his performance quite extraordinary.[15]

I hope we'll meet soon. And maybe Barry would like to come to a match before the season's end.[16]

We have decided to go back to Ireland in May.

John

13 Kevin Lehane.
14 McGahern, while not particularly interested in fashion, liked to dress smartly.
15 *The Dark Tower* (1946) is a verse drama by Louis MacNeice.
16 Barry Hanson (1943–2016), film and television producer, married to Susanna Capon from 1971 to 2012. Born in Bradford, he read English at Newcastle University and is best known for producing the classic British gangster film *The Long Good Friday* (1980). He was friendly with the playwright and fellow Yorkshireman David Halliwell and the director and producer Stephen Frears – all loosely members of McGahern's social and professional circle in the 1970s. Christopher Hampton, in his *Guardian* obituary for Hanson, describes him as having 'a keen nose for metropolitan bullshit and a healthy mistrust of authority', qualities that would have endeared him to McGahern.

Susanna Capon
[*Madeline McGahern*]

21 Forest Glade

27 March 1974

Dear Susanna,

I am so sorry you've been unwell and I hope you'll be well enough to come on Friday.

Vogue are going to print The Stoat.[17] I enclose the BBC offer and I'll be grateful if you'll look at it. Of course I'll sign it but it seems the lowest I was ever offered by the Copyright Dept. and I'd be glad of any advice.

I'll be the Northern Arts Fellow at Durham and Newcastle for the next 2 years. It came completely out of the blue and it still seems strange to me but I am glad.[18]

I hope you are better already and I want to say again how grateful I am for your having Denys's reading of The Stoat accepted.

> Love
> John

Faber

21 Forest Glade

[*Late March 1974*]

Dear Charles,

I hope this is all right. Change or add whatever you wish.[19]

> Love
> John

17 The *Vogue* publication came about through McGahern's friendship with the Belfast poet Derek Mahon (1941–2020) who at the time was working as features editor at the magazine. The magazine paid McGahern £200.

18 The Northern Arts Literary Fellowship, valued in 1974 at £2,100 per annum, was funded jointly by Northern Arts (£1,600), University of Newcastle upon Tyne (£500) and University of Durham (£250). The fellowship for 1974–6 was first offered to Seamus Heaney, who declined.

19 What follows is a typed blurb written for *The Leavetaking* by McGahern at Monteith's request. A number of changes are made in pencil by Faber. What I record here is McGahern's original.

'I watch a gull's shadow float among feet on the concrete as I walk in a day of my life with the bell, its brass tongue in my hand, and think after all that the first constant was water.'

The teacher on schoolyard duty is to be dismissed at nine of the actual day of the novel by the authorities for, in their eyes, his immoral relationship with an American divorcée.

As the novel moves through the day of dismissal, the early shaping influences of both the man and woman are traced through memories and imaginings: his life in Ireland, his primal love mixed with guilt for his dead mother; her early life in New York, her guilty desire for her rich and domineering father expressed in a confusion of hatred and love; and the shackles of these patterns carried by both the man and woman into their early sexual relationships to their breaking free of them towards a longing for an adult love.

From these very different pasts they come to meet by chance in London, there the first days of their love take place. Against her father's opposition they marry in a registry office there and go to Ireland to face his almost certain dismissal.

In the final recognition of their love – the prolonged leavetaking – they move from the first constant of water through the broken girdle of faith to the last constant of being true to one another till they meet the first death.

BBC Written Archives Centre

21 Forest Glade

4 April 1974

Dear Mr Gower,
Thank you for your letter, altering the fee for The Stoat from £30 to £55.[20]

I have now done a great deal of work for the B.B.C. and my rate has hardly gone up at all.

Since The Stoat is a difficult work – and the B.B.C. were given first rights to it – I do not think it unreasonable to ask for a somewhat higher fee.

---

20 Gower had written to McGahern on 29 March apologising for suggesting a fee of £30 for 'The Stoat', a piece he originally thought ran to just fifteen rather than thirty minutes. He suggests an increased fee of £55.

I do not want to be in any way difficult but I think in this instance I have a fair case.

> Yours sincerely
> John McGahern

Niall Walsh Papers

21 Forest Glade

8 April 1974

Dear Niall,

I want to thank Phil and you for your kindness to me in Ballinasloe, and for the bloodtest.[21] Apparently one of my youngest sister's kidneys – she is 31 – is permanently damaged, which forced the Sisters to look into the pills.

We are going home at the end of the month. I'll ring my Uncle tomorrow to tell Tony that. If he has nothing done I'll go even earlier and camp in the place.

We were at a party for Ian's venture – 300–500 people 6 to 8: 60 to 80 for dinner afterwards. ALL the old whores and young, and a few decent faces! He looked tired to death but he did carry it through with great dignity.[22]

All the finished work since The Leavetaking has been bought, some of it several times over; and I'd have, as the cards have fallen, lost money by schoolteaching. It doesn't alloy the guilt; neither would the other: our minds must have come out of a desperate inheritance.

We are a bit harassed now with people, and it won't change till we get away. And we are longing to leave. And I hope we'll see both of you soon.

> John

---

21 McGahern had been diagnosed with gout, a recurring condition for the rest of his life.

22 Ian Hamilton hosted a lavish launch party for the *New Review*. The inaugural issue was of an exceptionally high quality, featuring work by, among others, Robert Lowell, Edna O'Brien and George Steiner.

11 April 1974

Dear Niall,
Thanks for the 2 letters, I have written to White on impressive notepaper.

Madeline has handed in her resignation. I have to see the American editor on the 19th and I can go soon after that.[23] Probably it is best for me to go before Madeline.

I wish you a marvellous Easter, I don't know if I told you that Finito has been published in Stubbs.[24] I'd love to be in Achill, if only to see Sonny in his seasonal plumes.[25]

> With love,
> John

Is there anything I can bring either Phil or you from London?

10 May 1974[26]

Dear Niall,
We've been here since Saturday and it's been more or less building site conditions – inside and outside – since then but we are very happy.[27] We had the ESB and have now got water but Tony has vamoosed for the last two days

---

23 The American editors for *The Leavetaking* were Wendy Beck and Peter Davison at Atlantic Monthly Press.
24 Finito was a conman of their acquaintance. Actual identity unknown. *Stubbs Gazette* lists bankruptcies.
25 Sonny had the pub next to Niall's cottage. John once asked him what he liked to drink: 'To tell you the truth John, whatever gives me the injection.'
26 The earliest surviving letter written from Foxfield, the McGaherns' home for the rest of John's life.
27 The previous Saturday was 4 May.

and he's still plenty to finish.[28] I'll leave the rest till we meet. There's a spare room and double bed if Phil and you can manage to stay.

The one serious mistake – and it was unforeseeable – was that if we had taken the lake instead of drilling we'd have had better water and saved £600.

My uncle drove us over to your site last Sunday. It was very lovely and the skeleton of the house impressive. I'd say Tony needs a shove.

If you remember when you come bring some Allopurinol and tell me what they cost.[29] I have more than 50 left.

We see and hear pheasants all the time and duck and a hare, brown thrushes and bats diving over the water in the evening.

Give my love to Phil and Madeline sends you both her love.

As always
John

Faber
Foxfield

13 May 1974

Dear Charles,

I write to confirm the address and to ask about <u>The Leavetaking</u>. If it is to be published in October I should be getting the page proofs very soon.

I asked about this before leaving London and the Production Manager said that the delay was due to 'this unexpected offer from the American Publisher, and how best to take advantage of it,' and that I'd be informed of the details, which I wasn't. As Davison seemed to imply the delay was Faber's; and Rosenthal of Secker, who asked me only in the social sense about it at a party, said that the delay surprised him even in terms of the printing difficulties, I'd like very much to know.[30] I am in no way clamouring for immediate publication: on the contrary I consider timing to be totally within

---

28 Tony Walsh, a nephew of the former postman in Fenagh and a workman of dubious quality. McGahern kept finding what he called 'Tonyisms' in the house, though he was generous in lending John and Madeline his car.
29 Generally used to treat kidney stones or gout.
30 Tom Rosenthal was an editor at Secker & Warburg. See letter to Patrick Gregory [early September 1966].

the publisher's domain – but it's not pleasant to be left so much in the dark. I'd be grateful as well for any information about the cover.[31]

A few good days and since then the usual fool weather. We have water and electricity but still live partly among the builder's rubble. I hate to think how little we'd have got done if we hadn't turned up. Obviously the builder spends his life flitting between one point of harassment and a greater. He tells me if he 'got started, it's not one but twenty books I'd have to write about the people and troubles I have to put up with.' Since he's got the water going he's vamoosed again – more harassment required.

Madeline and I want very much to thank you for the last lovely day in London, for the lunch and the tour of the charming cottage.

With love
John

BBC Written Archives Centre
Foxfield

24 May 1974

Dear John,[32]
It's only a note to tell you that your commission of The Barracks is going out in German from Stuttgart on next Sunday the 26th May.

I hope you are well and with good wishes.
Yours
John McGahern

31 Monteith replies with an apologetic letter on 17 May explaining that Atlantic Monthly Press originally suggested that they would set The Leavetaking themselves, but subsequently changed their minds, and hence the delay and confusion. On the issue of the cover, Monteith writes: 'I've spoken to Shirley Tucker about the jacket and she hopes to start work on designing it in the next week or two [. . .] if you've any particular ideas in mind – about colours, lettering etc. don't hesitate please to let me know.'
32 John Scotney, BBC producer, teacher and broadcaster. He was the BBC's head of Drama in Ireland and later head of the BBC TV Drama Script Unit. He has written books and articles about literature and the media, and written and directed numerous programmes for the BBC, many on Irish themes. He was briefly acting chief producer and editor of the world's longest daily radio soap opera, The Archers. Altogether he produced about 300 programmes of various kinds, and scripted about 100 plays, classic serials, dramatisations, dramatised features and actuality features. He stayed with John and Madeline when they lived in Cleggan 1970–1.

24 June 1974

Dear Charles,

Thank you for your kind words about the parts of The Leavetaking.[33]

We've been backbroken since coming, but the place is fairly habitable now; and you'll be always welcome to stay with us when you can come.

I was afraid I'd have to go to Birmingham for the tv film next month but it's now postponed until 7th October. We'll probably leave at the end of September. The weather is fiercely hot now and the first meadows are coming down. Can a copy of Nightlines be sent to John Fox, McManus's Garage, Ballinamore, Co. Leitrim? He took the boat up from Sligo for me and asked for a book when I offered him money.[34] He's a mechanic there.[35]

We've seen nobody other than the locals and my uncle and the Doctor (Achill) since coming. The Doctor's house across the lake is now ½ finished.

Madeline sends her love to you, as I do

John

33 Monteith had written to congratulate McGahern on the extracts of The Leavetaking published in the second number of the New Review (May 1976) over eight pages as the opening piece after the 'Greek Street' editorial, 5–12.

34 The McGaherns kept a rowing boat for fishing eels and perch, usually moored on the inner lake, behind the McGahern home, Lough Drumlaheen.

35 John Fox was the trusty assistant to McGahern's uncle Pat McManus in his Ballinamore garage. Having worked there from boyhood, after Pat's retirement he took over the business.

Joe Kennedy

Foxfield

28 June 1974

Dear Joe,

I enclose a copy of the other story – if your friends are still interested in buying it.[36] The Beginning of an Idea was bought for the Autumn by The New Review.

We have been doing nothing but attempting to make the place ½ habitable since coming.

We are almost always here but if you are coming and want to make sure, write and give a telephone number to ring. If for any reason we'll be away I can go into the village and phone you. Otherwise just come.

It's 2 miles from Fenagh, between Mohill and Fenagh, and the sign is Lough Rowan.[37]

Madeline sends her love
John

James Swift
[*Madeline McGahern*]

Foxfield

25 July 1974

Dear Jimmy,

Madeline and I will be here till September, till about the 24th, and if you'd like to come down you'll be very welcome. It is past Longford, 6 miles the Fenagh side of Mohill, and you turn at the sign Lough Rowan and go all the way to the right round the lake.

36 The story is 'The Stoat' and the potential buyers were the backers of a new and shortlived Irish men's magazine, *Man Alive*. The story was published in vol. 1, no. 4 (October 1974).
37 Lough Rowan is more commonly known by locals as Laura Lake.

If it is not easy for you to get down perhaps we could have a meal or a drink together in Dublin in September.[38]

                    With good wishes,
                    John

                                        Susanna Capon
                                    [*Madeline McGahern*]
                                        Foxfield

4 September 1974

Dear Susanna,
Thank you for your kind letter and I look forward very much to hearing the Reading.

We had a great time with Barry and Bob Kidd.[39] He probably told you about the cottage. I'll take time to get it habitable. Barry slept at the end of a shaky ladder above our bed.

I have to be in Newcastle the 2nd October. So we'll leave in about 3 weeks. On our way we'll be in London for a few days so I hope we'll meet. I'll ring as soon as I get into London.

It rains here and it rains and rains. You can hardly walk in the fields. We're almost looking forward to leaving.

                    With much love and hoping to see you soon
                    John

38 Jimmy Swift became a regular visitor to Foxfield over a number of years.
39 Kidd and Hanson visited Foxfield and stayed there to discuss plans for a film adaptation of 'Swallows'. This was eventually directed by Kidd, produced by Hanson and aired on BBC2 on 27 March 1975 as a thirty-minute TV drama for the *Second City Firsts* series, an anthology of half-hour plays produced by BBC English Regions Drama at Pebble Mill in Birmingham from 1973 to 1978. Alas, no recording of this play appears to have survived. Robert Kidd (1943–80), a Scottish theatre and television director, is best known for his work at the Royal Court, London.

Flat 2
Marris House
Upper Claremont
Newcastle Upon Tyne NE2 4AJ
tel 29939
[*hereafter Newcastle*]

29 September 1974[40]

Dear Niall,

Thank you for the card from London. On the Monday after you came to the house Madeline had to leave for Paris – (the tenant had to leave, and wanted to sublet it) – and she is still there. I closed up the house in Leitrim and came here on Friday. She expects to be here later in the week. My stint begins the 2nd.

The flat is enormous, a floor of the Chancellor's old house, and it goes without saying how welcome you'll be if you come up from London.

No other news, since I've laid low since coming, but a few of the Fenagh locals got inspired (in Ellis') and painted their family gravestones with used car oil, much to popular indignation and my delight – nothing like the desire for permanence.[41]

With best regard to Phil and the children.

Love
John

---

40 This is McGahern's earliest surviving letter from Newcastle. He arrived on Friday 27 September.

41 Ellis's was one of two pubs in Fenagh that were in business in McGahern's time. The other was Quinn's. The former pub was seen as a Fianna Fáil stronghold, the latter, Fine Gael. Both were frequented by John and Madeline.

30 September 1974

Dear Charles,
I had hoped – and Madeline had – to see you in London but she had suddenly to go to Paris and I had to close up the Leitrim place on my own and had the wrong few days in London. I hope though that you had a marvellous holiday.

Can Faber send me a proof of The Leavetaking as I have to pick as soon as possible the extract the Irish Press want to use for the publication, and I have nothing to check their suggestions against.[42] Also, can you tell me if it was entered for the Booker, as Ian Hamilton wants to know.[43]

The feeling is that with the late November publication it will need to be pushed unusually hard if it is not to be lost among the Christmas stockings. Already some people who liked the extracts have promised to do what they can.

I have seen no one here since coming on Friday but I like the feel of the city and the flat is quite beautiful. Madeline hopes to get here in about a week.
   Love
   John

42 An extract from *The Leavetaking* was published in the 'New Irish Writing' page of the *Irish Press*, edited by David Marcus, on 4 January 1975, two days before the novel's publication. The extract chosen by McGahern comes from early in Part One of the novel, as the protagonist faces into his final day as a teacher.

43 Monteith confirms in a letter of 9 October that *The Leavetaking* has been entered for the Booker Prize but tells McGahern not to get his hopes up because there will likely be a particularly strong field. Ultimately the prize for 1974 was jointly won by Nadine Gordimer for *The Conservationist*, published by Jonathan Cape, and Stanley Middleton for *Holiday*, published by Hutchinson. Also shortlisted were Kingsley Amis, *Ending Up*; C. P. Snow, *In Their Wisdom*; and Beryl Bainbridge, *The Bottle Factory Outing*.

James Swift
[*Madeline McGahern*]

Newcastle

4 October 1974

Dear Jimmy,

Madeline and I had looked forward to seeing you in Dublin. Then, suddenly, she'd to go to Paris. I had to close up the cottage in Leitrim and came here. Because of the [*illegible*] I went through Dublin.

We have a large and very lovely flat in the centre of the city. It'd be a great pleasure if sometime you could come and stay with us here.

I have hardly any duties in the position. It's been already made clear to me that they expect my first responsibility to be to my own work, and so hardly ever does what's outside seem to agree with the private that I don't believe it.

Madeline came 2 days ago and asks to be remembered to you.

John

Faber

School of English
University of Newcastle Upon Tyne

10 October 1974

Dear Charles,

Thank you for your kind letter. I have written to Ian to say The Leavetaking was entered for the Booker. I have no illusions about it at all. Remembering your Lenten Election Party on this day I'd quote it about the Ladbroke odds on Thorpe for Prime Minister.[44]

Madeline came here a few days ago. It all went well in Paris.

44 Jeremy Thorpe MP was leader of the Liberal Party. 1974 saw two General Elections, one in February, the other in October. One possible outcome in February was a Conservative–Liberal coalition government. Labour, in fact, formed a minority government. The idea of Thorpe – who subsequently left politics under a cloud of sexual scandal – becoming Prime Minister was wildly unlikely but perhaps worth a small punt.

There's a story this month in <u>Vogue</u> that will be read on the Third and published later in the Irish version of <u>Playboy</u> called <u>Men Only</u>.[45] I've been asked to read from <u>The Leavetaking</u> to the University about the 19th of November.
With much love
John

Faber

Newcastle

18 October 1974

Dear Charles,
I am disappointed, not about the Booker, but about the whole long handling of the MSS, especially when I think that books handed into other Houses after mine have appeared already. It always seemed to me that the weeks just after Christmas were a dead time, in which books the Publisher had no real confidence in were slipped into the market in the hope they'd be noticed because of the scarcity law. After the Christmas stocking comes the graveyard. I suppose we can only hope it's wrong.[46]
Love
John

Joe Kennedy

School of English,
University of Newcastle

[*Autumn 1974*]

Dear Joe,
Tom Jordan wouldn't want to do anything public; I'm too long out of it all, and no longer have much contact with teachers.

---

45 The story is 'The Stoat'. The Irish magazine was in fact called *Man Alive*. McGahern's brief involvement with the magazine later became in part an inspiration for the plot of *The Pornographer*.
46 Monteith had written on 15 October to say that *The Leavetaking* had not made the Booker shortlist. This, in turn, meant that the novel did not have to appear in 1974, and Monteith writes of Faber's intention to put off publication until January 'when reviewers are really looking round for serious books'.

Coughlan should have told either you or me what he was up to – he could have got me into copyright trouble – and I'll be grateful if you can get the £100 without much trouble from him.[47]

It's very lovely here. I like it as much as any city I've been in.
I think you can dial direct for Dublin when you're coming and with good wishes[48]

John

Joe Kennedy

Newcastle

[Autumn 1974]

Dear Joe,
Thank you for your letter. There are regular flights and it is only 3½ hours by fast train from London. It is a marvellous city with a great covered market and fine stores and [*illegible*] – Madeline is going this evening to The Magic Flute – and very lively bars and restaurants. We live in a very large flat. And you can stay here if you come. If you want perhaps you could tell me (1, 2, 3, 4 . . .) what information you want for the article.

Don't worry about The Stoat. My bank manager will be glad of the money. It is in this month's Vogue as well and will be broadcast on BBC 3.

If you decide to come suddenly dial direct from Dublin and it'll almost certainly be alright if I have not to be in Durham on that part of the fortnight.
With best wishes to Margaret
John

I'll be here for 2 years and I'm delighted with the city
John

47 John Coughlan (1943–2013), Cork-born journalist and editor. He began his professional life at the *Cork Examiner*, leaving in 1963 to establish *Spotlight*, which quickly became Ireland's most important showbusiness magazine. In the 1970s he cooperated with Hugh McLaughlan's Creation Group where Coughlan came up with the idea for the colourful and edgy tabloid the *Sunday World*, poaching Joe Kennedy from the *Evening Herald* as its first editor. Coughlan was publisher of *Man Alive* and the later, more successful, *Holiday* magazine. He worked as a travel writer with both the *Sunday Independent* and the *Sunday Tribune*. A larger than life character, he is in part an inspiration for aspects of Maloney in *The Pornographer*.
48 Kennedy never managed a visit despite several efforts, tempted by invitations to High Table at Durham.

26 October 1974

Dear Charles,
You wrote me to Leitrim that the jacket would be black and white, the same as all my other books, and I was happy; but this is not the same. All my other jackets used the fine Faber style of lettering. <u>Nightlines</u>, for instance, had a lovely jacket.

It is not in my style to have such an enormous photo of myself on the back; and, besides, I don't think it is a good photo. If it is too expensive now to redo the whole jacket to the traditional style – lettering – please take that photo off, and if necessary put the bird on twice. I can't stand that photo.[49]

I wonder, also, why the same quote (TLS) is used twice? Surely it'd be better to vary them, say use the Roy Fuller instead in one place. Especially since the TLS is used for <u>The Barracks</u>.

I hate to write 2 complaining letters but I was dismayed to see that enormity of a photo.

> But with my love
> John

11 November 1974

Dear Rosemary,
Thank you for you letter. There was obviously misunderstanding about the photos.

Ian Hamilton chose the photos for the N.R., out of I think 3, all of the tunnel. I had no choice, which seemed fair enough to me, as it was his magazine.

---

49 The jacket marks a break with the previous very plain lettering on monochrome background used for McGahern's first three books. Ultimately, no author photo appears on the jacket of *The Leavetaking*, though there is still the shadow of one gull (to chime with the opening of the novel), not two.

Later Mrs. Godwin asked me if she could approach Fabers with the photos. Naturally I said yes, since I thought it went without saying, and thought no more of it other than a courtesy on her part. I am sorry if she interpreted this as in 'preference to all others'. That I would not say, since I'd consider that Faber's domain, and I was very happy with the Bauer. But if Faber wanted to bring the photo up to date, and wanted to use Mrs. Godwin what I did expect was to be asked about the choice of photo, as was done with the Bauer, which is a good photo. When I heard no more I thought Faber had simply decided to retain the Bauer, and not use Mrs. Godwin.[50]

I don't like any of the tunnel photos, but blown up on the jacket it looked worse than I imagined, and to belong far more to the cinema than to photography.

When Mrs. Godwin very kindly offered me a present of some photos I chose 4, all taken sitting at a table in her house.

I liked Mrs. Godwin very much and feel sorry there was this confusion.

If you are near hand or passing through, we'd love if you'd call us.

Love

John

Faber

Newcastle

[*Mid-December 1974*]

Dear Charles,

Thank you for your nice card and Madeline and I wish you a happy Christmas in Ireland.

I'll not, unless I need to, go to London. I am working on a new novel and trying to live as quietly as I can. And I feel disturbed with <u>The Leavetaking</u>

---

50 Fay Godwin (1931–2005), born in Berlin to a British father and an American mother, was a photographer best known for her landscapes of the British countryside and of literary figures. At the *New Review* she worked as director of photography and picture research. She had taken a series of black and white photographs of McGahern for use in the magazine including one of him posing in a London railway tunnel, which is used as the image for this book's dustjacket. Jerry Bauer (1934–2010), American photographer best known for literary portraits, particularly of Samuel Beckett.

coming out. Somehow I never can get used to it. The old nuisance, I suppose, of 'the virginity of the soul.'[51]

With much love
John

Niall Walsh Papers

School of English,
University of Newcastle

26 December 1974

Dear Niall,

Thank you for your letter. I am glad you liked the book. And I hope Phil and yourself and the children have a Happy New Year.

The Murphy saga grows even here.[52] 'His wife with the emotional problems' was first married to the now Professor of Philosophy here, who is in turn married to the lady above. As the Newcastle version is that Mr M. filched the Prof's former wife there is a certain frost on all things Irish – Murphy's story is that she, hearing of his homosexual fame, set her cap at him and stormed his defences. He is also well known at the University of Durham but that for another day.

I suspected for a long time he'd try Phil. He's been trying to stop the tinker's drinking for a long time, and became the first person ever to be barred from Coyne's in Cleggan in the process.

The book is on the 6th January. It's the critics' choice of the week on the Third Saturday 4th – Tom Stoppard, Drabble, Lambert – so it may well open

---

51 A reference to the comment reputedly made by W. B. Yeats to the Oxford literary scholar John Sparrow: 'The tragedy of sexual intercourse is the perpetual virginity of the soul.' McGahern's source for this is most likely *Letters on Poetry from W. B. Yeats to Dorothy Wellesley* (London: Oxford University Press, 1940), a favourite book of his.

52 McGahern has drawn an arrow to the name Barbara M. H. Strang, the Professor of English Language and General Linguistics named on the letterhead. Her husband, Colin Strang, was head of Philosophy at the university. In 1948 he married Patricia Avis who subsequently had affairs with Philip Larkin and Richard Murphy. In 1955 Strang divorced Avis and married Barbara Carr, Professor of English at Newcastle. McGahern felt anxious about the Murphy visit to Newcastle because of these entanglements and their potential to disturb what had thus far been a happy equilibrium. For more on this, see Murphy, *The Kick*, 154–61.

its career with a good drubbing.[53] I got word last Monday, a letter out of the blue, that I am to be given the Society of Authors Award for 1974 of £500. It was marvellous to get for Christmas, but if the news gets out before the 6th it may well add muscle to the blows.

I am working on a new novel, and have got past the worst part, when one isn't sure if it can be written at all or not.

Newcastle, I think, is a very interesting and exciting city, almost exotic to my eyes.

It might be an idea if both of you were able to take the car across and drive up through the Lake District. It is closer to Dublin than London is. As well as some of the old city and the Victorian City and T. Dan Smith's city it has branches of all the big London stores like John Lewis, Harrods, Marks and Sparks etc.[54] The fish from South Shields is fresh and plentiful.[55]

My uncle is involved in tree planting, but while elaborate preparations have been made, no trees have been planted.

I am delighted the house is finished and I am hoping to turn up on the doorstep with some offering to placate the household gods when I get to Aughaboniel.

With all good wishes to Phil and yourself and the children and maybe ORA PRO me on the 6th.[56]

Love
John

53 *The Leavetaking* formed part of the subject for *Critics' Forum* on BBC Radio 3 on Saturday 4 January 1975 with Margaret Drabble and Tom Stoppard as the 'critics' for that week.
54 Thomas Daniel Smith (1915–93) was Leader of Newcastle City Council from 1960 to 1965. He was a prominent figure in the Labour Party in north-east England, such that he was nicknamed Mr Newcastle.
55 The Black Gate restaurant in Newcastle, with its simple, black and white elegance, was a particular favourite where McGahern relished its dover sole, its tripe and a house speciality of jugged hare. Balmbra's, a pub and music hall, was another favourite haunt and is described with great affection in McGahern's essay 'An Irishman in Newcastle', *LOTW*, 60–4.
56 Pray for me.

[*Late December 1974*]

Dear Charles,
I hope you've had a very happy Christmas in the North. At least, I read, it had the odd grace of peace.[57]

I am writing to say that I've just been given the Society of Authors Award of £500 for 1974. Perhaps you know this already, or indeed may have been instrumental in the award.[58]

I am a little nervous now that the date is so near. Publication is a horrible time.

Love
John

57 Monteith spent Christmas 1974 with his brother in Castlederg, Co. Tyrone, just miles from the border with Co. Donegal. The Provisional Irish Republican Army (IRA) observed a ceasefire between midnight on 22 December 1974 to midnight on 2 January 1975. The ceasefire was called to allow the British government time to respond to proposals put by the IRA to Protestant clergymen on 10 December 1974. 58 The award McGahern won was intended to permit the author to travel. Monteith congratulates McGahern in a letter of 2 January and makes clear that he played no part in securing the prize.

1975

11 January 1975

Dear Niall,

Thank you for your letter.

Since Sunday there has been 4: the T.L.S. (a love), New Statesman (attack), Guardian (love), The Times (good). I'll bundle a pile up and send them off when more come in. Anyhow it's more that ½ over. It's been a nervewracking business. What a bloody trade it is.

I only met De Vere White briefly and politely once. He's been complaining for a long time that my reputation was caused by the banning/sacking etc, and hasn't a strictly literary base: and he is a quite shameless pusher of his own work, using his position.[1] So? But others will attack it the same way, the N. S. says it is adolescent, and that's fair enough. His came close to personal abuse, which just isn't very clever. What can I do but bow?

Madeline was offered a job in the Economics Department, she took it, and she likes it. It is much the same as The Observer, except she gets a day off for study, to 'improve her skills'. She is starting a course at the Polytechnic. She has only to walk 5 minutes from here.[2]

---

1 Terence de Vere White (1912–94) was literary editor of the *Irish Times* from 1961 to 1977. His stinging review of *The Leavetaking*, titled 'The Sack Race', appeared in the paper on 4 January 1975. 'When Mr. McGahern is not consciously polishing his prose', complains de Vere White, 'he lets a good deal that is slipshod pass through the critical net'. Almost exactly a year later he returned to pick at the carcass: 'This week I will write about the disappointments of last year. They began with John McGahern's "The Leavetaking" [. . .] If this was the first novel by an Irish country boy about his experiences in a wicked city, it would be understandable; but Mr. McGahern is within a few years of the age at which Balzac died. I was disappointed, because I had hoped from "The Dark" Mr. McGahern would advance.' See Terence de Vere White, 'The Lights That Failed', *Irish Times* (3 January 1976), 10.

2 Madeline was the fourth secretary under an affable head of department. Her office was on campus, a pleasant walk down a tree-lined avenue from the apartment.

It was very good of Dick and Ursula to look in on the house.[3] Maybe, when you see him again, you might mention about the grants. The £1,000 must have been a sinking feeling. I had it over the well, and the road repairs, which they caused to have done. I know Tony's 'views' too well.[4] The funniest thing is that he imagines he's been very nimbleminded and devious while delivering those elephants. Still the house will be wonderful there.

I had a long and interesting letter from Emmett explaining how he was forced into bankruptcy. He's managed to pay for his house, stay out of private debt; and start up again, in a small way.[5]

Nobody has had any word from Murphy for a long time, not even Charles, who is an old friend.

Whether we'll go over at Easter depends very much on holidays, will they be long enough to make it worth it. The trouble with planting is that you have to be there to tend them as well.

We'll love it if you both can come. It's very hard to describe. I've never seen anything quite like it. Almost exotic in a harsh way. We plan to go to Edinborough some Saturday. It is 2 hours away.

The book will be out in the U.S. any day but that doesn't seem real. Anyhow I couldn't go through the cursed stress again.

With love to Phil and yourself,
John

Niall Walsh Papers
Newcastle

27 January 1975

Dear Niall,

These may amuse you, if you haven't seen them. There must be 60/90 other dead men floating around by now, as it has been the most heavily covered (a good country word) of all books by now.[6] You have to pay for the service,

---

3 Dick Walsh, Niall's brother who lived nearby in Carrick-on-Shannon. Ursula was his wife.
4 Tony Walsh, the tradesman who had worked on the Foxfield house.
5 Emmet McGarry.
6 A batch of reviews and previews (*The Listener*, *The Guardian*, the *Sunday Telegraph*, *Publisher's Weekly*, *Newsweek*, the *Times Literary Supplement*, the *Houston Post*) all largely positive, some very powerfully so. Christopher Wordsworth in *The Guardian* compares the book favourably with Joyce's *A Portrait of the Artist*

which I've done. The Charles letter is private to you and Phil, as I've never seen him so openly censorious.[7]

The American things are previews, not reviews, as it doesn't come out there till the 4th Feb.

I am almost back to myself, and both of us are well.

To cap the whole affair we had a film producer, who invited himself for a week, and had to be kicked out.[8]

I'll write soon. Love to Phil and yourself.

John

Faber

School of English,
University of Newcastle

11 February 1975

Dear Charles,
Thank you for your letter. I wrote to David Higham, saying that while I may well need an agent at some future point I do not need one now.[9]

The publication, for some reason I cannot fathom, took more out of me than I thought it would; and only now am I getting back to my work.

---

as a Young Man and writes that 'Few living authors can describe the terrible gravity of carnal love so faithfully'. Julian Jebb in the *Times Literary Supplement* writes that '*The Leavetaking* represents an achievement of a very high order and substantiates the belief that its author is among the half-dozen practising writers of English prose most worthy of attention.'

7 A typed letter from Charles Monteith of 20 January 1975 sending on two reviews of *The Leavetaking* and commenting as follows: 'Congratulations in particular for having scored three dead-on bull's eyes in the Sunday papers. I read the Irish Times review – though very belatedly. So far as sales are concerned it can't, I'm sure, do anything but good. And it can't do any good at all, I'm quite certain, to poor old Terence.'

8 Cathal Black b. 1952 was the Dublin-born film maker in question. In 1976 his adapted short film of 'Wheels' was shown on Irish television and in 1995 his feature-length film adaptation of McGahern's story 'Korea' was released.

9 David Higham (1895–1978), literary agent and founder of David Higham Associates, a major London literary agency working at the time out of offices on Dean Street, Soho. He had lunched with Monteith in January and expressed his interest in representing McGahern. At this point McGahern was representing himself, having parted company with Michael Sissons.

Beckett's description of sexual intercourse – 'a mug's game and tiring into the bargain' – was how I felt most of the time.[10]

Normally I'd go to Leitrim in early June, but it's uncertain. Madeline has a job she likes in the university. So it depends whether she wants to keep it or give it up, and how I'm working then. I'll definitely be there in July. Madeline is a bit disturbed. She used work for David Wilson at The Observer, who was killed last week.[11]

Is it too early yet to have any idea of sales? Is there any way Faber can sell foreign rights?

Is there any likelihood of you coming up to Newcastle? They say it was the finest of the Victorian cities, and there's just about enough of it left to believe it.

> With much love
> John

Niall Walsh Papers

School of English,
University of Newcastle

27 February 1975

Dear Niall,
Some more salvos; and it got an extraordinary notice on BBC TV on Tuesday night.

We've now definitely decided not to go home for Easter and Phil and you will be welcome here if you can come.

An 1890's scholar, a Dr Thornton, may use the place. I suppose if we were Mr Murphy we'd charge him for the discomfort.[12]

Thanks very much for the information. I am working well again. It was a lousy old experience though.

> Love
> John

10 A favourite phrase of McGahern's from Samuel Beckett's *Molloy*. See letter to Matthew Evans of 9 August 1973.
11 Labour correspondent for *The Observer*, killed in a traffic accident.
12 Robert Kelsey Rought Thornton b. 1938 worked in the School of English at Newcastle University. Among his scholarly interests was the life and work of Gerard Manley Hopkins, a poet much admired by McGahern.

School of English,
University of Newcastle

3 March 1975

Dear Charles,
I enclose the <u>Newsweek</u>.[13]
   If the Quartet cheque doesn't bounce perhaps Faber would send my share
of it to

> The Manager
> Bank of Ireland
> Westport
> Co. Mayo[14]

   I hope all goes well in Dublin
>   And with much love
>   John

20 March 1975

Dear Charles,
It's first to say how much we are looking forward to seeing you in April and
to wish you a happy holiday.
   The second is a disturbing query. Several people – more than a dozen –
have complained to me how difficult it has been to order <u>The Leavetaking</u>
compared to Nightlines. 2 to 3 times longer, from libraries as well as book
shops.

---

13 Peter Prescott reviewed *The Leavetaking* in *Newsweek* of 17 February 1975.
Writing for an American audience, the opening sentence of the review reads: 'I doubt
there is another practicing writer of fiction in English as good as John McGahern who
is so little noticed in this country.'
14 Quartet Books bought the paperback rights to *The Leavetaking*, though it did
not appear until 1977. McGahern would have been using a Westport bank since his
sojourn in Achill.

While in London over the weekend Madeline asked about it in Foyles. They had one copy left. When M. thanked the girl and said she didn't want it just now the girl said it would be 30 days before they'd have more in. It now took 30 days to order a book from Faber.

I had heard earlier that there was trouble between Faber and the bookshops over credit but to not have a book in a bookshop a few streets away from Queen Square while it is getting attention must amount to perversity. It is now too late to make much difference to The Leavetaking but can it be true? If it is, surely it's a mixture of Heath's Social Contract and the Miners as a way certain to get everybody's back up.[15] Empty bookshelves can't be any good for even Fabers.

I hope all this is just speculation on my part but with all the complaints and the Foyle's incident there seems something wrong.

Love

John

Michael Hamburger Papers

Newcastle

21 March 1975

Dear Michael,

Thank you for your letter and your kindness to the novel. You are welcome here if you can come and there is plenty of room. I approached them here about an invitation, and they'd very much like to invite you, but for this term they'll be beaten down with the exams. Next year will be fine – anytime? I am divorced, and married again, and I suppose there's no more to say. Like in a Hardy poem I remember too well 4 of us going to a Chinese restaurant in Whitechapel. Anu is in Finland now. I'll hardly be down before June. In July we will go to a small farm we have in Ireland. So come if you can. It's a marvellous city. Does your own work go well? And Anne? Remember me with love to her.

And as always

John.

---

15 The reference – not fully historically accurate – is to fuel shortages and the so-called three-day-week under Edward Heath's Conservative government of 1970–4.

20 April 1975

Dear Brian,
I cannot thank you enough for such a generous letter.

A writer can only hope for such a letter from another writer he respects once or twice in a lifetime.[16]

I'll be here for another year and, if you are ever near, my wife and I will be delighted if you'll come to see us. Then we hope to be able to go home to Leitrim for good. I'll be in Belfast and Coleraine on the 8th/9th May and hope to go down for a few days then.

> With best wishes for your own work
> Sincerely
> John McGahern

21 April 1975

Dear Niall,
It must have been a horrible time with the L. C.[17] What compensation will they give you? Still you have by far the best part. It's much the same size as Aughaboneil, and I couldn't manage more. They have started planting the trees there. I am recording for the BBC in Belfast the 8th May, I'll speak in Queen's that night, in Coleraine the next night – a kind of one man showband

---

16 On 11 April Friel had written an admiring letter to McGahern on the subject of *The Leavetaking*: 'and still in the heat of the read want you to know how impressive I think it is. It was very right for you to return to the territory you staked out & claimed in the earlier books; because it is your territory where your unique memory-imagination becomes quickest. And the deliberation of that return is important to all of us. The only review I saw was in the I. Times & any poor bastard who is apparently immune to the image & experience you offer is to be pitied. I think it's your best book & this note is a gauche congratulations & thank-you.' Madeline McGahern Papers.
17 Referring to some trouble Walsh had with the Land Commission.

– and if I escape the usual crowd there hope to get down to Leitrim for a few days. I have to be back here for the 15th.

Charles Monteith came up a week ago, in 'splendid form' after a week in Istanbul. They have all but sold out the first printing (4,000) of *The Leavetaking* and it's reprinting. The first foreign language rights – Dutch – have just been sold. There's an account of Auden's funeral in this issue of the London Magazine, in which Charles figures, as well as an account of Ackerley.

It's extraordinary how late the spring is here. The daffodils have only just come, and the leaves only beginning. We were at the sea yesterday, a stark North Sea beach, but somehow very English and cosy, plump horses galloping, leisurely golf swings, dogs and flasks of tea. Some of the stone villages are incredibly calm and beautiful. Everywhere is the Norman influence. The land is very rich. Durham is said to be the finest Norman cathedral. Architects describe it as a great night storage heater.

> I hope Phil is well again soon
> and with love
> John

Alan Ross Papers

Newcastle

22 April 1975

Dear Alan

Thank you for your kind word about The Leavetaking and for your invitation.

I feel I'd be no use to the series. Over the past eleven years I've lived in too many places, more places than the number of the years, and never long enough in any one place for any serious degree of familiarity. All of the dislocations were due to accident or financial need and were never real choices.

I'll be in Newcastle for another year and if you are ever here I'd much enjoy meeting you again.

> Yours
> John

Joe Kennedy

Newcastle

16 May 1975

Dear Joe,
Would the enclosed be of use to <u>Man Alive</u>? I'd prefer if they used this new work rather than <u>Christmas</u>. They'd be free to use it from <u>July</u> onwards.[18]

They'll give me the <u>Society of Authors Award</u> at a party in London on July 1st and I hope to go home immediately afterwards. It'd be nice to think of seeing you then.

The Faber <u>Leavetaking</u> has sold out and is reprinting. They're now thinking of reprinting in the States as well. It went very slow at first there, and now it's started to sell quickly. Even the publishers are completely puzzled. Because it's wrong way round. It seems worse than the horses.

With affectionate regards to Margaret
John

Seamus Heaney Papers

Newcastle

20 May 1975

Dear Seamus,
Thank you for your letter, and I send you two congratulations. On <u>North</u>, I found it rich and powerful work, and the public poems – though I still dislike Whatever You Say, Say Nothing – seem largely absorbed into the richness around them now.[19] And the wholeness and solidity of the book gave me so much pleasure that I should not pick and mix such poems. And

---

18 The story is 'A Slip-up', which appeared in vol. 1, no. 6, the Summer 1975 special issue of *Man Alive*.

19 On 4 May 1975 Heaney had written to McGahern from Glanmore Cottage about *North* (London: Faber, 1975): 'I remember you not liking some of them, but as far as I'm concerned, publication of them is one way of exorcising this pressure to "say something about the north". It has cleared my head already.' Madeline McGahern Papers.

on the E. M. Forster Award.[20] Davey Hammond told me in Belfast. I was delighted. It was nice to see Davey again and the Muldoons, to see how intelligent and tough Paul Muldoon is behind the manner.[21] He'll need it all there. In a different coinage I got caught by Fiach or O'Connor in a train for 2 hours. It was like being doused in soft warm shit.[22]

I am working, but only on short works. I haven't the strength back to return to the novel. The publication disturbed me. It's had a strange career for itself in the States. It sold hardly anything in its first 2 months, and then started to sell steadily, it has the publishers completely puzzled, but as it's still continuing they're talking of reprinting.[23]

It's a fine town here, and we like it. Especially round the river and the markets is quite marvellous.

We go home in early July. We are looking forward to it, and to meeting Maria and yourself again. Maybe you'd like to come down to Leitrim for a time as well?

So until we meet, and with all good wishes.

John

Niall Walsh Papers

Newcastle

6 June 1975

Dear Niall,
I want to thank Phil and you for your kindness to me in Ballinasloe.[24]

---

20 Heaney was awarded the E. M. Forster Award in 1975. Administered by the American Academy of Arts and Letters, the award amounts to $20,000 and is given annually to an Irish or British writer to fund a period of travel in the United States.
21 Paul Muldoon b. 1951 in Moy, Co. Armagh, Irish poet, critic and academic. McGahern and Muldoon became friendly in this period, with Muldoon visiting the McGahern home in Foxfield. He remembers the house's idyllic Leitrim setting in his poem 'The Wood', which he dedicates 'To John and Madeline' in *Mules* (London: Faber, 1977). At the time of this letter's composition Muldoon was working for the BBC in Belfast. His debut collection, *New Weather*, was published by Faber in 1973 and he first met McGahern through Charles Monteith.
22 Padraic Fiacc (1924–2019), *nom de plume* of Patrick Joseph O'Connor, Belfast poet.
23 *The Leavetaking* was published by Atlantic-Little, Brown in the US in 1975.
24 Niall Walsh had arranged for a number of medical tests to be run in Portiuncula Hospital, including a test of the thyroid gland, on uric acid levels and on cholesterol.

The flat in Paris falls vacant in July. And we don't intend to rent it till September. Would it be any use to you both or the children – I thought of the 2 girls doing French – during those 2 months? If it is I'll be grateful if you'll let me know as soon as you can.

The Society of Authors 'do' is on July 1st and I go to Ireland after that. Madeline, it seems now, will go direct from here, as she wants to avoid the London sharkpool.

There's a good review of the novel in this month's <u>Encounter</u>.[25]

        With love to Phil,

        John

Faber

Department of English
University of Durham
Elvet Riverside, New Elvet
Durham DH1 3JT
[hereafter Department of English, Durham]

6 June 1975[26]

Dear Charles,
Thank you for calling me Monday. The Society of Authors is now definitely fixed for July 1st, Martine Terrace, New Zealand House 6.30–8.00. I'll probably do down on the Monday and stay on a few days afterwards before going to Ireland.

'So the stress associated with the publication of the book', writes Walsh in a letter of 5 July 1975, 'is over'. He suggests that John have his blood pressure measured in Newcastle, but that 'I would not get involved in more elaborate "check-ups" as they are mainly useless and tend to breed neurosis – heresy in certain Americanized ears!' Madeline McGahern Papers.
25 The review, titled 'Exiles', is by Jonathan Raban b. 1942 and compares McGahern favourably with James Joyce. Raban considers the opening half of the novel exceptionally well done: 'McGahern has a genius – and that word does not overstate what he does – for mediating between the deep currents of feeling which belong to myth and history and the exact texture of the moment, seen so freshly that it comes off the page in a vivid cluster of sensations.' The second half of the book he considers a failure: 'McGahern, so brilliant on the familiar, turns out to be surprisingly clumsy when it comes to dealing with strangers.' Encounter, vol. XLIV, no. 6 (June 1975), 78.
26 McGahern is using Durham University notepaper, but may be writing from Newcastle. This is the case for all following letters using Durham as an address.

I am having lunch with Higham on the day of the party, simply because he's been pressing me to, but I have made it clear that I do not feel I need an agent now.

Knopf just wrote to see if I was interested in going back to them, and I suppose it's just as well to have in reserve, knowing how fickle American publishing can be.[27]

I am looking forward to a first hand account of the Poet's goats.

With my love
John

Michael Hamburger Papers
Department of English, Durham

6 June 1975

Dear Michael,

Thank you for calling. The Party is on July 1st 6.30–8.00 Martini Terrace New Zealand House. It'd be terribly nice to see you both there.

Can I ask you? If it's an embarrassment ignore it and I won't mind at all.

Do you know of any decent German Publisher who might be interested in doing The Leavetaking?

I've had a bad relationship with Benziger of Zurich and their translator for long and I've broken with them now. So I have no publisher at all there. If you have any ideas I'll be very grateful and I won't mind at all if it's difficult.[28]

Love to you both
John

27 The Knopf interest (which came to nothing) was prompted largely by Jonathan Coleman's presence at the press. Coleman b. 1951 is an American author of literary non-fiction who worked for a period in publishing with both Knopf and Simon & Schuster. He assisted Ian Hamilton at the *New Review* through 1974 where he met and admired McGahern.

28 Despite his unhappiness, *The Leavetaking* had the same German-language translator as the previous McGahern work – Elisabeth Schnack. It was published as *Abschiednehmen* (Frankfurt am Main: Büchergilde Gutenberg, 1984).

[*June 1975*]

Dear Joe,

Thanks for your letter. I asked the Society of Authors to write you though I know you're unlikely to be able to come. I don't care one way or another about the publicity. If it's any use to you use it.

If they don't mind Man Alive might acknowledge in small print first published in Stand after A Slip Up. If they do it doesn't matter as I own the rights. So let them please themselves.

There was a very good review in the May Books and Bookmen and in this month's Encounter.

Madeline and I will travel to Ireland on July 9th.

Looking forward to seeing you soon and with good wishes.

John

Niall Walsh Papers

Department of English, Durham

26 June 1975

Dear Niall,

This is just to confirm that the dates are fine (any dates would be). Mostly the flat will be empty.[29] We liked August best there, because the city is less crowded.

Madeline and myself get into Dublin about 12.30 on Wednesday the 9th, by plane, from Newcastle. We have to see some people so we might as well get it over with that day and go to Leitrim on Thursday. It'd be very nice to go down with you but if it's awkward in any way don't worry about it.

I go to London for the award next Monday and will spend the week there. I'm not looking forward to it.

Shopping is very easy in Paris. The Buci market is 3 minutes away. It has an enormous supermarche as well as all the stalls. Also the Samaratine is just

29 The flat at Rue Christine.

across the river, which has <u>everything</u>. Madeline knows the places better than I do.

She also says you must call Pops, if he's not in Brittany.[30] Apparently he loves to hear about his daughter and is concerned, committed etc., the ideal 'family man'. With love to Phil and yourself.

We hope to see you both soon,
John

The American visit is now completely settled. They agreed to my terms and we go in January 1977 for 5 months.[31]

Seamus Heaney Papers
Newcastle

[Late June 1975]

Dear Seamus,

Madeline and myself get into Dublin Airport from Newcastle around 12.30 on Wednesday the 9th July. It'll be nice to see you and Marie then but if it's awkward any way don't worry about it. We'll be in Leitrim for a whole week.

I suggested to Durham that they invite you to read and they are anxious to have you in the autumn. If it suits you, you can name almost any date you want (say sometime you think you may need to be in England).[32] They'll pay your expenses from Ireland but I'm sure the fee won't be very large, though I'll try to get the most I can. You can, of course, stay with us.

With all good wishes to Marie and you
John

---

30 Madeline's father had a house near Tréguier in Côtes-d'Armor.
31 To Colgate.
32 Heaney replied on 1 July 1975: 'Thank you for the Durham reading arrangement. Early or mid-October would be grand: although I'd rather not fix the exact date just now. The fact is, I've applied for a job in Carysfort College of Education and if I get that, I'll not just be as free.' Madeline McGahern Papers. Heaney was successful in his job application.

Faber

Foxfield

7 July 1975

Dear Matthew,

The young Knopf editor who wrote me is Jonathan Coleman.[33] The way I see it is that there is no hurry, and it may be useful to have. I don't know how I am with Atlantic and I don't have a contract with them anymore.

Madeline was delighted when I told her I met you and sends you both her love.

Con remembered the hot day long ago on the cricket field. He was glad to see me at first, but soon I saw I just became part of the everyday of his pain, an exasperation, as everything is to him now. My sister can't sleep now either. It puts our minor cares or ills into savage perspective.[34]

We be at the above till August 6th and then we'll be here in Newcastle

2 Marris House
Newcastle Upon Tyne NE2 4AS
Tel (0632) 29939

Love
John

Joe Kennedy

Department of English, Durham

12 August 1975

Dear Joe,

It was great fun to see you and Margaret and the children that long, lovely Sunday, in spite of aristocratic rabbits, property affairs etc.

I meant to ring you but we were over-run the last week, especially with the sisters. As well the neighbours were going crazy, since they installed the

---

33 Jonathan Coleman was then working as an assistant editor at Knopf (1975–7). From there he went on to Simon & Schuster (1977–81). Coleman was unsuccessful in his attempts to convince Robert Gottlieb, his boss at Knopf, to take on McGahern.
34 Refers to the final illness of Con O'Brien, husband of McGahern's sister Breege.

father in a café in Mohill. We've been recovering since coming back. The simplest way in the end was to take the gun back with me.[35]

I saw the <u>Man Alive</u> illustrations, a good demonstration in how to crack an eggshell with a sledge hammer. Can they send the fee to the Bank of Ireland, Westport, Co. Mayo.

We have to go to Paris on September 5th but we'll be here till then. We'll be back the 16th.

Perhaps you'll come sometime this winter.

With affection to Margaret and yourself
John

Niall Walsh Papers
Newcastle

4 September 1975

Dear Niall,

It's just a note to thank Phil and you for your calls. The phone gave the impression of ringing, and not being answered: and the imagination, as I said on the phone, often an ally, became the enemy. It's so nice for us to know it wasn't too uncomfortable.[36]

We go ourselves tomorrow to Paris. I'm not looking forward to it, will be there till the 12th, mostly to see a lawyer, maybe rent the flat. Maybe I'll see Pops as well.

Well Dev, by now, must be drinking cold tea with all his true blues up in Flaitheas na Naomh.[37] I'm sure you've had your fill of the 'chief' all last – and this – week. Tom Jordan was here. He was hoping Dev'd last out till school opened. He is planting some fruit trees for me in October. If you want his help in your place I'm sure he'd be glad to go down with you, and he knows his trees and flowers well. His Dublin No is 311638 (56 Ennafort Park).

I begin my few morsels of duty on October 1st. I hope you'll both be able to come here.

35 McGahern had a shotgun that he took good care of especially during the period of the Troubles. In this case he thought it best not to leave the gun in Foxfield while nobody was living in the property.
36 The Walshes had stayed in the Rue Christine flat from 12 to 22 August and enjoyed themselves despite the lack of a phone and electricity.
37 Éamon de Valera, statesman and sometime Taoiseach and President, died on 29 August 1975. 'Flaitheas na Naomh' translates, roughly, as 'heaven'.

By the way the phone is now working in Paris (the electricity is a long story, of a new meter, and an old, that they had been reading in our favour, but if they make a mistake they just switch it off) and if you've forgotten anything, or want anything brought back or done, ring us here (326 2004).

We both send our love to Phil and you.

John

Joe Kennedy

Department of English, Durham

[*September 1975*]

Dear Joe,

According to the Bank Manager – who isn't always right about his own bank – Man Alive (or Sunday Newspapers) didn't put money in the account. Maybe you'd check with them for me? There's no urgency.

The brother-in-law died, in terrible pain. He went mad before he died.[38] There'll be new work in The New Review (October) and Encounter (November).[39]

Does <u>M. A.</u> want work for Christmas? Or are they caput?[40]

Do you have any news?

Love to Margaret

John

---

38 Con O'Brien, Breege's husband.

39 'Faith, Hope and Charity' was first published in the *New Review* (October 1975), and was reprinted in the *Irish Press* (20 November 1976). 'All Sorts of Impossible Things' was first published in *Encounter* (6 December 1975), and was reprinted in the *Irish Press* (8 May 1976).

40 *Man Alive* pubished nothing more of McGahern's beyond 'The Stoat' and 'A Slip-up'.

[*September 1975*]

Dear Seamus,

We, too, had a marvellous time. Thank you for the card and book. I found it moving, the poems and some of the things he said quite wonderful; but it was to some extent spoiled for us by my dislike of the wife's – the writer's – personality. And I find no guff more tiresome than literary guff, whether it's up or down.[41]

If you can give me a more or less firm date for Durham I'll try to arrange a Morden Tower (£25).[42] It has to be on a Friday. That is, of course, if it suits you.

We half-expected to see Marie and the children, but maybe she'll come with you here.

I hated closing down the place and leaving.

> With love to Marie and yourself
> John

41 Heaney had given the McGaherns a gift of Nadezhda Mandelstam, *Hope Against Hope: A Memoir*, trans. Max Hayward (Harmondsworth: Penguin, 1975), inscribing it with a quote from Shakespeare's *Timon of Athens*: 'Our poesy is as a gum which oozes. From whence 'tis nourished . . .'

42 A thirteenth-century tower in the old walls of Newcastle upon Tyne. The Morden Tower has been a major centre for poetry readings in the North East since 1964, with McGahern himself reading there on at least one occasion during his time as Northern Arts Fellow. While Fellow he invited Heaney, Paul Muldoon, Michael Longley and Derek Mahon to read there: Heaney, Muldoon and Longley travelled to Newcastle while Mahon wrote back to say he had given up readings for the time being.

22 September 1975

Dear Niall,

Thanks for writing, and Madeline asks that the girls be thanked for writing her their kind letters from Athlone.[43]

We had a hard week in Paris. We found out where we stood in law. The lawyer's advice was to close up the flat (because of outside investment space in that area is getting like gold) unless we found some one we could let it to without contract. Strictly we are not allowed to let it until the building is done up; and work is starting this October. We cannot sell it for another 2 years. We were about to close it, and leave, when an American girl showed up – her marriage – Catholic – to a French nobleman on a trial separation, and we gave it to her.[44] She's going to Harvard to complete her doctorate next June, and the flat will probably be empty again, if it can be of any use to you next summer. I'm tired of it, but we should be well placed to review it when we come back from the States in '77, and we can sell it then, or let it properly. We had an amicable drink with Madeline's stepmother.[45] The old monster was in the States, routing caravans that had parked on his shore front in Maine.

The day after we came back – a week today – my brother-in-law died. [. . .][46]

If you're driving here the best way is Larne/Stranraer. Just as passenger Liverpool is best.

There are direct flights to/from Dublin/Newcastle on Mondays, Wednesdays, Fridays. It's cheaper than to London and takes 50 minutes. It's the best way if you haven't much time.

43 Susan, Oonagh and Maeve Walsh went to The Bower (then a boarding school) in Athlone.
44 Linda de Nazelle, a Seattle woman who had married a French nobleman, le Conte de Nazelle, with whom she had two children. This was one of a few happy lettings of the Rue Christine property over the years and de Nazelle remained a friend of the McGaherns after leaving.
45 Frederique 'Kika' Gron b. 1939.
46 In the interests of family privacy, I have chosen to redact a short section of this letter recounting the events around the death of McGahern's brother-in-law Con O'Brien.

I saw Charles down in London, who is more alarmingly himself every time we meet, having a dangerously good time, and making – I suspect – lots of enemies. Lennon managed to get his paranoia into harness even down in Achill this good summer.[47] Hamilton got some nervous disease, with the result that all his hair suddenly fell out. It's growing back in patches, but snow white. I have to say he handled it with great dignity, even humour. He was marvellous company but he smokes and drinks so constantly that he doesn't seem to eat. He sipped at the juices of a minestrone and picked at a plate of whitebait. Seamus Heaney reads in Durham in October. He has taken a permanent job in Carysfort Training College.[48] Charles told an amusing story. Seamus was having his breakfast when his next door neighbour burst in 'You were on the wireless this morning in what the papers say,' she said in great excitement.

'What did they say?' he said, expecting something nice had been said about his book.[49]

'That you're on the U.D.A. death list.'

Apparently he nearly choked on his egg but to his relief he found she'd mistook it for Seamus Twomey.[50]

I suppose it'll take me a week to get working properly and the damned teaching starts then.

With our love to Phil and yourself
John

47 Peter Lennon had visited the McGaherns during their Achill stay. Other visitors included Maurice Leitch and Richard Murphy.

48 Heaney worked at Carysfort teacher training college in South Dublin from 1975 to 1981.

49 The book in question was *North*, which, though critically acclaimed for the most part, was heavily criticised by figures such as Edna Longley, Conor Cruise O'Brien and Ciaran Carson who saw it as politically suspect.

50 Seamus Twomey (1919–89) was an Irish republican activist and twice chief of staff of the Provisional IRA.

7 October 1975[51]

Dear Paul,[52]
As it's about the correct length I wondered if this'd be of any use to you. If it's not I won't mind at all.[53]

Term is beginning here and I am hoping they'll invite you here. It'd be useful to me, if you could tell me what time of year suits you best to come (maybe a time you'd want to come to England anyhow.)

With good wishes to Anne Marie and yourself[54]
John

Jonathan Coleman
[*Madeline McGahern*]
Newcastle

14 October 1975

Dear Jonathan,[55]
Thanks for your letter. There's no trouble. I went to Ireland July/August. My brother-in-law died in London in September – 41, bone cancer: Term has just started, and I am trying to get back to working every day. I had dinner with Ian in London. We'll go back to the smallholding in Ireland at the end of May. I finish up here then – and take all our belongings with us, and be

51 Earliest McGahern letter in the Paul Muldoon Papers, Rose Library, Emory University, Collection Number 784, Box 4, Folder 2.
52 Paul Muldoon has published over thirty collections of poetry and won a Pulitzer Prize for Poetry and the T. S. Eliot Prize. He held the post of Oxford Professor of Poetry from 1999 to 2004. Now at Princeton University, he is both the Howard G. B. Clark '21 Professor in the Humanities and Founding Chair of the Lewis Center for the Arts.
53 Probably refers to the short story 'A Slip-up' that Muldoon produced for BBC Radio 3.
54 Anne-Marie Conway was Muldoon's first wife.
55 Jonathan Coleman, American publisher then working with Knopf. See letter of 6 June 1975 to Charles Monteith. McGahern had first got to know Coleman when he worked as an editorial assistant at Ian Hamilton's *New Review* through 1974.

settled in one place. Madeline, as well as I, is tired of climbing other people's stairs. It's eleven years of having no place now. We'll not move until we go to Colgate the following January. I find as I get older I can only afford violence or excitement like holidays. Otherwise there's no energy of calm left for the work, only surfaces.

I enclose a short list of the published stories. Also I mentioned your interest to Matthew Evans when I was in London, so if he brings it up you'll know from where it came. Of the published work I'm best pleased with next month's Encounter, which was the most difficult.[56] There are also 2 love stories that I haven't had typed up yet. So in a way (if the author stays alive a little longer) that book is safe.[57]

The novel (wasn't it Fitzgerald called the short story a sharp cough but the novel a long groan). I was working every day on the novel, was totally involved in it, emotionally had forgotten The Leavetaking, and there it was one horrible evening – published. It was partly the long delay between handing it in, and publication; and being at 2 universities. The textual provos were really out. They must have read every review. Now that it has been – in a manner, for a term – elected, it's as easy now as it was difficult before, but what use is that, if you have imagination. I didn't write at all for a while, and then the Encounter story (it took almost 3 months) and since then have been practicing the Cough, but am almost ready for the Groan again. I'm dreading the winter.

What's written is scattered but the shape is clear. The male character is a Civil Servant, who makes a lot of money writing hard porn for a blue magazine. At the beginning he's being mocked and pressed by the editor to give up the Civil Service (He's the first of my characters to have more money than he needs).

He's been brought up by an Aunt and Uncle, simple decent people. The Aunt is dying of cancer in the city hospital, and he all the time through the action, till she dies, brings her in bottles of brandy, since she doesn't trust 'the auld drugs'. The Uncle comes up to see her now and again – he owns a garage – inarticulate with pain in the face of death.

The pornographer has a place in the country. Only one of the women has been there, the one he'd hoped to marry. He goes to considerable lengths to prevent any one else going there, except his Uncle, and the Porn editor.

On a level it's the City and the Country clashing in the Psyche. After the failed idyll – a bid for sexual order – he meets – the opening of the novel

56 'All Sorts of Impossible Things'.
57 The book in question is *Getting Through*.

in Time Present – a journalist – 38 (he's 29) – she gets pregnant, refuses an abortion, puts pressure on him to marry. The chickens have come to roost. She's basically an eternal full of brightness, says he's sick. One of these terrible instincts without mind, all is black and white.

She has the child in London while he attends the funeral in the country. He's just come from London, a last bid on his part to get rid of the child – adoption – and she to get him to assume responsibility. And he's beaten up by a protector. He's black and blue for a wedding as well as for a funeral.

What I haven't worked out is the resolution but you can see it's the usual hopeful brew.

Why I tell you this is for both of us[58]

Brian Friel Papers

Newcastle

14 October 1975

Dear Brian,

I'll be grateful if you'll read the enclosed.[59] Seamus Heaney was here at the weekend. And he agreed that you and Paul Muldoon would be ideal and the three of us enough.

The idea, if it got off the ground, would be to do a very small number of selected texts, that a person at the outset of their life would not normally have, except for these?

Would it interest you at all?

Of course if the idea pleases you, and you choose to come in, I'd be delighted.

The idea would be not to gain from the venture, but not to lose money either.[60]

Yours

John McGahern

58 Only two pages of this letter survive in Madeline McGahern's papers.
59 A note in the margin reads here: 'It's not very accurate'.
60 Friel responds on 24 October from his home in Muff, Co. Donegal: 'I think the idea is very good & I'd be very happy to join you in it. Naturally there are problems – finance, distribution (a big one), the right choice of books etc. – and the distance between Belfast, Newcastle & Muff. But I'm sure these can be overcome. And with Seamus H's help in Dublin & Paul Muldoon's in Belfast, this should be made easier.' Madeline McGahern Papers.

[*Enclosed with this letter is a typed letter to Mr Colm O'Briain, Director, Arts Council, 70 Merrion Square, Dublin*]

Dear Mr O'Briain,

I am writing to see if you may be able to help me.

For long I have been pressing my publisher, Faber, to reissue Forrest Reid's finest novel <u>Brian Westby</u>.[61] Eventually they refused saying though they admired the work that it'd lose them money (now his centenary will go by almost unnoticed) but that they would not charge for their rights if I could find a publisher. I don't agree with them but their overheads are high and these are bad times in the trade.

I was hoping to find some one when I came across a remarkable case here in Newcastle.

Jack Common is the only early 20th century writer from these parts with a claim to permanence. He was well thought of among writers, and kept alive by battered copies, and word of mouth (he died 1953) but no publisher would touch him, and this year he's been issued by a private person, with the help of Northern Arts, and it is moderately successful, as well as necessary.[62]

The figures are open to me but I want to see if there's enough interest before going into them.[63] What I thought of was that there was a place for a small press, watched over by writers, that would make available good works of, primarily, the neglected dead. (Reid's trouble was that he wrote rubbish towards the end of his life, which was moderately successful, and tagged him.) And I thought <u>Westby</u> an ideal starting point.

I put this to Michael Longley in Belfast, and he is putting it to his own committee.[64]

61 Forrest Reid (1875–1947), Irish novelist and memoirist much admired by McGahern, who made several unsuccessful attempts over the course of his writing life to have Reid's 1934 coming of age novel *Brian Westby* republished. See McGahern's letter to Michael McLaverty of 13 September 1966.

62 Jack Common (1903–68) was a Newcastle-born writer and socialist activist. McGahern reviewed his books, *Kiddar's Luck* (London: Turnstile Press, 1951) and *The Ampersand* (London: Turnstile Press, 1954), in the *Times Literary Supplement* of 13 February 1976. The two autobiographical novels had been reissued in 1975 by the small Frank Graham press in Newcastle and McGahern is here encouraging the Irish Arts Council to consider backing the republication of certain lost Irish classics. McGahern's review of Common's books is republished in *LOTW*, 298–301.

63 In margin here McGahern has written in his own hand, 'a touch of a secretary'.

64 Longley joined the Arts Council of Northern Ireland in 1970, working in literature and the traditional arts as Combined Arts director before taking early retirement in 1991.

If it was lucky it could go on to Somerville and Rosse's The Silver Fox, Roy Campbell's translations of De Quieroz, O Cadhain . . . but that would depend on others as well as me.[65]

If it goes any further I'd thought to ask Brian Friel and Paul Muldoon if they'd have interest in joining me.

Yours sincerely

John McGahern

Seamus Heaney Papers

Newcastle

[*October 1975*]

Dear Seamus,

Thank you for your letter. Madeline and I had a marvellous few days with you, and have to thank you. I'm sorry not to have seen you off – Excess suddenly caught up with me on the railway platform.[66]

I wrote to the Director of the Arts Council, and to Friel. Muldoon has agreed to come in.[67]

They want me to speak in Belfast and if I do I'll speak on Brian Westby. The trouble is I can't lay my hands on a copy.

I read the poems. I was surprised how good the Muldoon is, 4 or 5 poems above anything in the first book.[68] And a definite voice. It's extraordinary.

65 The desire to include Roy Campbell translations in the series is puzzling. *The Silver Fox* (London: Lawrence & Bullen, 1897), a novel by Somerville and Ross, makes more sense, as does Máirtín Ó Cadhain whose Irish-language short stories, published in translation as *The Road to Brightcity*, were a particular favourite of McGahern's.

66 Heaney writes of this visit to Newcastle in a letter dated 13 October 1975: 'That was a delightful intense couple of days, and if I left shaken by excess it was my own fault.' Madeline McGahern Papers.

67 Of this proposed venture, Heaney's letter of 13 October states: 'why don't we aim at publishing Brian Westby this time next year, or early November? (I wonder, by the way if Longley could get Blackstaff Press in Belfast to handle the new imprint?) (He would jump to your instructions quicker than mine, so I'll not mention that to him yet).' Madeline McGahern Papers. Heaney also mentions William Steuart Trench's *Realities of Irish Life* (1868) as another title for the proposed series.

68 Muldoon's first book, *New Weather*, was published by Faber in 1973. This letter possibly refers to some of the poems that would eventually appear in the second

They're beginning the process of appointing my successor. The local verse trade union has called out: 'We don't want another prose writer.'[69] No wonder the country is in such a state.

With love to Marie
John

22 October 1975

Dear Charles,
Thank you for sending the books to Paris. Does the new price (£2.90) mean that it has limped into the 2nd printing or just inflation?

As my tax position during the Fellowship is uncertain can any payments due to me be withheld until further notice? Perhaps the accounts can tell me what they paid me 1974/75, April to April.

Seamus was here for 2 days. He drew an enormous crowd and read marvellously. He came with Madeline and myself to a wedding the next day.[70] He'd to go but only the next morning because of a class he had to take in the Training College.

Madeline sends her love, as I do
John

24 October 1975

Dear Niall,
Thanks for calling. And many happy years to you and Phil on your new acres. I hope they don't turn Leitrim into a white elephant.

---

collection, *Mules*. Heaney writes on 13 October 1975 that he left behind batches of poetry by Muldoon and by Seamus Deane for McGahern to read.
69 McGahern lobbied unsuccessfully for W. S. Graham (1918–86) to be his successor.
70 The wedding of a secretary in the Department of Economics who arrived at the church in a silver Rolls-Royce. Heaney was, recalls Madeline, 'the best company imaginable'. The packed reading referred to took place in Durham.

Both of us are looking forward very much to seeing you both, and this is why I'm writing: Do you have any idea of the dates you may be able to come?

I have to give an address in Queens this term, and to record; and I have to give them dates soon. I don't want to be in Belfast while you are both here.

Try to be here on a Friday evening. It's formal high table in Durham, with the cellar open, and the master of the wine in attendance.[71]

No news, like the haircut gentleman – thank God. Except English Income Tax are showing an unhealthy interest in my sojourn here.

Madeline sends her love, as I do

John

Faber

Newcastle

1 November 1975[72]

Dear Charles,
I am very grateful to you for Brian Westby.[73]
   I have copied it and return it herewith.

Love

John

Ernst Honigmann

[Madeline McGahern]

Newcastle

[Autumn 1975]

Dear Ernst,[74]
Thank you for your note.

---

71 Niall and Phil Walsh visited in November and happily availed themselves of high table at Durham.
72 Mistakenly dated 1 October by McGahern.
73 Monteith had sent the book on 28 October, regretting that he would not be able to attend McGahern's lecture at Queen's University Belfast and asking if he could borrow the script of the talk at some future point.
74 Professor Ernst Honigmann (1927–2011), then head of the School of English at Newcastle. A leading Shakespeare scholar, born in Breslau, Germany (now Wrocław,

I was only anxious to meet him in the sense of natural courtesy, he being the previous fellow. And I can do that by attending his reading.[75]

As chance has it I'll be in Belfast and Coleraine the same week. I hope to get back in time – and intact – for the 15th.

If I don't succeed I'll be grateful if you'll offer my apologies.

John

Perhaps these will interest the young Powys scholar![76]

Faber

Newcastle

6 December 1975

Dear Charles,

Thank you for your letter of the 14th November. I am sorry for not answering before now. I was here and there – classes, readings, mostly uselessly.

The stories published are: I've also told Jonathan Coleman this:

Swallows – London Magazine

The Stoat – Vogue

The Beginning of an Idea – The New Review

The Slip Up – Stand

Faith, Hope and Charity – The New Review

All Sorts of Impossible Things – Encounter

Most of this has been republished. These are first publications.

I've just finished Along the Edges (a story) and I am working on 3 stories, in some way all connected.

I haven't gone back to the novel. There's 15–20 thousand words written. It's clear in my head but I won't go back until I am certain I won't have interruption. That'll probably be soon.

Poland), Honigmann arrived in England in 1935, age seven, as a refugee from Nazi Germany.

75 Paul Bailey b. 1937, the British novelist, biographer and critic, was the previous Northern Arts Fellow from 1972 to 1974. On completing his fellowship, Bailey gave a gift of a photo of the Marx Brothers to McGahern which he kept in his Foxfield study. See review of Bailey's An Immaculate Mistake (London: Bloomsbury, 1990) in LOTW, 354–6.

76 This letter was found inside the Powys Newsletter, 2 (1971), among McGahern's books in Foxfield.

The poet rang. Long, accusatory pauses. 'Are you sure this isn't costing you too much Richard?' 'No John, it's a great pleasure . . .' 'Where are you?' Long pause. 'London. I'm staying with my – '.

I'm obviously due for a Reading Lesson before too long. In definite bad books. God knows why.

As always, with my love, and I suppose it's the accident of Happy Christmas too once more.

John

Brian Friel Papers

Newcastle

10 December 1975

Dear Brian,

Thank you for the Forrest Reid memorial. Forster mostly always makes sense. What a buffoon old/young Gilbert is.[77] (By the way, I am not certain whether you wish me to have the paper, or not. Only tell me if you'd like it back).

The idea has fallen through.[78] They wanted Peter Waring.[79] I think it was a proper thing to do, or try to do: but in all other ways I am relieved. I am writing an essay on Westby for the centenary, and I'll feel I've done my stint. I'll always be grateful to you, though, for the offer of your voice.

I'd like to wish you and your family a happy Christmas. (though privately I think it's a dreadful time of year: all the more reason, I suppose, for wishing happiness).

John

77 Stephen Gilbert and John Boyd co-edited a special Forrest Reid number of *Threshold* magazine for Spring 1977 which Friel had sent to McGahern and which forms part of his library.

78 See letter of 14 May 1975 to the Arts Council of Ireland.

79 *Peter Waring* (London: Faber, 1937) is a full-scale revision of Forrest Reid's earlier *Following Darkness* (London: Edward Arnold, 1912) in which Peter, a sensitive boy with literary inclinations, grows up unhappily in the household of his father, a cold village schoolmaster in Newcastle, Co. Down, and among his Belfast relatives whom he finds intolerable.

1976

Dónal Cleary

Newcastle

1 March 1976

Dear Donal,[1]

I want to thank you for your kind invitation to visit the school, which Tom relayed to me.[2] I had decided not to, as unfortunately it might be misconstrued; and meant to call instead to see Dolores and yourself, but this time old time caught up with me. As well, I want to congratulate you on the Principalship and to wish you long and happy years in it.

It may amuse you, after the whole unhappy tumult, that part of The Dark is now a text on BBC Schools Program for the 12–16 age group – God help us.

With best wishes to Dolores and yourself[3]
Sincerely
Sean

1 Dónal Cleary b. 1930 was a colleague of McGahern's at Belgrove School, Clontarf, with whom John remained friendly. He went on to become principal in September 1975 and had written to John inviting him back for a visit to the school.
2 Tom Jordan, then still teaching at the school.
3 Dolores Cleary, Dónal's wife. McGahern spent many hours visiting in the Clearys' Raheny home while he was a teacher in Clontarf and was very fond of both Dónal and Dolores.

411

[*Spring 1976*]

Dear Madeline,
I was glad to get your letter today – I stayed with the Davey's last night, after coming from Newcastle.[4] All sent you their best wishes. Ernst said: 'Madeline was the most satisfactory British Northern Arts Fellow we had, er, I mean you and Madeline, I mean . . .'[5]

Why don't you just send some photo to Kilkenny or send it to McDermott.[6]

There was a big crowd at the Tower, including Shit Silkin and Garfitt.[7]

At the very earliest I'll leave Wednesday night, at the latest Thursday night, but most probably Thursday morning.

I am very tired even though I've been extremely careful.
I'll be glad to be home, but most of all to see you.

> Evans's hope to come the 12th/13th August.[8]
> With all my love
> John

---

4 Tom and Claire Davey, John's London friends.
5 Professor Ernst Honigmann.
6 Philip McDermott worked promoting Faber books in Ireland. He established the Poolbeg Press in 1977. The reference to Kilkenny refers to plans for an appearance by McGahern at the Kilkenny Arts Festival.
7 Jon Silkin (1930–97), poet and founder editor of the literary magazine *Stand* which was the first place of publication for 'A Slip-up' in June 1975. McGahern disliked Silkin, hence the insulting sobriquet. Roger Garfitt b. 1944 is an English poet, critic and magazine editor.
8 Matthew and Elizabeth Evans visited Foxfield on a number of occasions over the years.

29 March 1976

Dear Paul,

Thank you for your poem and the honour of the dedication.[9]

We'll be here on the 21st (in fact we leave exactly 2 weeks later) and it'd be very nice for us to have you. Michael Longley is very welcome to stay with us, though he'll probably want to stay in Gateshead.[10]

If I was certain you'll be coming I could try to see if other readings are open. That's if it'd suit you. Maybe give me a ring?

Maybe you'd ask Tony McCauley if the programme for schools fell through or not, since he rang me up.[11] It's been ½ in ½ out of my head.

We both hope to see you soon and with best wishes to Anne Marie.

John

1 May 1976

Dear Niall,

Thanks for your letter.

Our plans are settled now.

I've hired a van and go Stranraer/Larne on Saturday the 29th. Kelsey Thornton – he stayed in Leitrim – last Easter a year ago – is driving me and taking the van back. Madeline will fly to Dublin on Friday the 18th June after the 'Exams.'[12]

9 The poem in question is 'The Wood' in which Muldoon recalls the McGaherns' idyllic Leitrim home and which he dedicates 'To John and Madeline' in *Mules*.

10 Longley's brother lived in Gateshead.

11 Tony McAuley (1939–2003) was then a schools unit producer at the BBC in Belfast.

12 Robert Kelsey Thornton was a colleague of McGahern's in the School of English at Newcastle who helped McGahern move back to Foxfield. Madeline stayed behind in Newcastle to take secretarial exams offered by the university.

Is there anything Phil or yourself wish me to bring across in the van? It'd be no trouble.

The girl in Paris said she'd be very grateful for Achill in August but are you sure that's all right?[13]

The Poet Murphy was here and surpassed even himself in a kind of shamelessness – I'll keep it till June. Since he left there's a phrase of Keats in my ears: 'The worst of men are those whose self interests are their passion – the next those whose passions are their self-interest.' I'm afraid M. swept both, as surely as he did the orphans out of the Orphanage.

I'm looking forward to seeing the land in Ballinasloe. As well as my own hedges, especially now when the social nonsenses are beginning to apply to their parting guest.

With love to Phil and yourself
John

Faber

Newcastle

1 May 1976

Dear Charles,
Thank you for the Joyce letters, and I was very moved that you should think to send them to me.[14] It doesn't matter at all about the readings – if any come up, well and good; and if they don't, well and good too, – but of course I'm grateful.[15]

The poet was here and he read well, and behaved well, and yet I found him curiously depressing. It's as if all the old manias have now become a real blindness.

I am sort of clearing up the book of stories. The later stories turned out more difficult than I had bargained for. I am hoping to steep myself in the novel before going to the States. I have a feeling that it'll go rather quickly once I go back to it.

13 Linda de Nazelle, the Rue Christine tenant.
14 Refers to Faber's *Selected Letters of James Joyce* (1975), edited by Richard Ellmann.
15 Monteith had been trying unsuccessfully to set up readings for McGahern at American universities in spring 1977 when McGahern was committed to teaching at Colgate.

I leave here for Leitrim on the 29th May. I am in some <u>minor</u> trouble with the tax people here but there's no knowing how it will go yet. The most that's involved is £400–£600.

Madeline enjoyed 'gorgeous popery' as much as I did and she sends you her love, as I do

John

Paul Muldoon is reading in the Morden Tower on the 21st May, with Michael Longley, and it'd be nice to have the same arrangement with his books, as they are not on sale here, and he has a certain following, especially among the young.

Yours
John

Faber

Newcastle

24 May 1976

Dear Charles,

Thank you for your letter and Madeline and I will look forward very much to your visit. There's only one time I expect to be away, and that's early September, when I'm supposed to teach with Seamus Heaney at the Arvon place in Devon, and that's for only 5 days.[16]

I leave late this Friday (28th May) by Stranraer and Larne. I'll be grateful if all mail can be sent to:

Foxfield
Co. Leitrim

Madeline follows me in mid-June.

Paul Muldoon read extraordinarily well and all his books were sold.

I gave your name to a Durham student – he got his first degree at Oxford, he's from Edinburgh, his father a biologist there – in the sense of Faber <u>Introductions</u>. He'll send poems. They are by far the best work I came on here, but whether or not they're fit for book publication, is, of course, a different matter: but I do think they are worth looking at.

Please forgive the haste of the note.

16 Totleigh Barton, the first of three Arvon creative writing centres to be opened in England, is a sixteenth-century manor house in rural Devon.

I'm in the dust and cursing of packing, and its peculiar sadness.

With my love

John

Madeline McGahern

Foxfield

8 June 1976

Dear Madeline,

Thank you for your letter, and the contract. I was very glad.

After Val and Kelsey left I just worked at getting seeds down.[17] Niall came late on Thursday – he found me in the back garden as the light was beginning to fail – and we had two drinks in Mohill, and afterwards sat by the fire for an hour or more (The reason we went into Mohill was the fear of visitors, I had escaped so far, and I was right. For Ursula must have come, she arrived next morning with a child and a bottle of wine 'as repayment for all the wonderful hours of reading, what thoughts these authors get up to', and was a great bore.)

I went into see Pat that evening, he hadn't heard I was home, and he left me out to the house. He was a delight, and abrim with prejudice. He is coming out with the man 'about the wood' this Thursday: 'we can throw him the odd lock of petrol.'[18] Jerome comes daily.[19]

Jonathan came Saturday, it seems almost certain that I'll go back to Knopf now, with a 2 book contract of about $4,000 for each book, but it has to be, of course, ratified when he goes back to New York: but he foresaw no difficulty.[20] Even to me the book of stories are finished, once I counterpoint Along the Edges with the story of the day.[21] So another private act is becoming public, another nail visible in the wood; but of course there's the great luxury of the choice and, by [illegible], there's the money.

---

17 Val and Kelsey Thornton.
18 Pat McManus, McGahern's uncle.
19 Jerome Donnelly, a near neighbour.
20 Jonathan Coleman stayed in Foxfield for a few days – the plans to go to Knopf came to nothing.
21 Referring to what was published in 1978 as his second collection of stories, *Getting Through*; 'the story of the day' probably refers to 'The Wine Breath', which precedes 'Along the Edges' in the collection.

I came with Jonathan as far as Mullingar. Niall met me. I'll be in Ballinasloe for 2 days. All weathers are fair.

If you can do these things, my love, I'll be grateful.

1. Get 3 or 4 Habitat lamp shades for Pat – his own request, much to my amusement – and maybe 3 more for us.

2. Send a clean copy – or Photostat – of <u>Sierra L</u> and <u>Getting Through</u> to Jonathan Coleman, c/o The New Review, to reach him before the 18th.[22]

3. Send S. L. to Mary D. Kierstead

> Dear Miss K.
>
> I'll be very grateful if you'll consider the enclosed.
>
> Sincerely[23]

4. Maybe book Jetsave to New York on the 24th December, unless you've heard something to the contrary from Colgate. Jonathan says he hopes we'll stay with him in New York over Christmas. I found the place opposite Curry's the most efficient. They said they could open book us for coming back mid or late May, but make sure – after the Co-op bungling with the ticket for the crossing.

The only thing that sticks out in the house is the extra bed, and the Walshes want that.

I'll write again at the weekend

> So my love, with all my love, and my longing to see you.
>
> John

Madeline McGahern

Foxfield

11 June 1976

Dear Madeline,

It's a day like winter, rain spitting, the lake wild, and the trees blowing, the air damp in the house.

Niall left me back yesterday. They go to Achill next week, so he cannot meet you. Unless I hear differently, I'll meet the bus at the end of the lane.

---

22 'Getting Through' was one of several working titles McGahern used for the story that was ultimately published as 'Doorways'. Coleman had worked at the *New Review* as an editorial assistant through 1974.

23 Mary D. Kierstead was then an editor at the *New Yorker*. The magazine accepted 'Sierra Leone' for publication.

Tom's number is 311638. You might wish to ring him, and he might like to come in to see you at the station.[24]

Coffee and dried milk are all I think that might be useful and light, and anything you think yourself. I enclose a cheque.

The one thing we forgot was the lawnmower. It would have been useless here. It's only worth about £3–£4 and my own feeling is that it's not worth troubling about it.[25]

Have a look at the letter to Linda before posting.

Also enclosed 1. Barclay's book 2. A card to you 3. A cheque request for postage to Wexford.

I've been going from Billy to Jack since coming.

I am longing for you to be home.

And with all my love
John

PS. Close down Barclay's account before leaving.

Madeline McGahern
Foxfield

12 June 1976

Dear Madeline,

There was no discourtesy in the delay, only the long haul with Kelsey, the two different bank holidays – I didn't get your first letter until Friday – and the hard weekend's work with Jonathan: for nice as he is, he is, in the good American fashion, totally immersing himself in the role of publisher; and every poor sentence, every tentative plan, had to be lifted out, and shook.[26]

I wrote and posted the letter the first chance I got – Tuesday morning, the morning after the Holiday.

Dick and Ursula were here last night, Ursula a great pain, loud noises that she was footloose etc. I concentrated all my attention on Dick, and Ursula

24 Tom Davey, the McGaherns' London friend.
25 Refers to final arrangements for leaving Newcastle.
26 Jonathan Coleman has fond recall of these few days spent alone with McGahern in Foxfield. Among his firmer memories is their attendance at a gaelic football match where there took place an involved discussion about wandering cattle with neighbours. The match was almost certainly the Connacht senior men's gaelic football semi-final between Leitrim and Galway held at Páirc Seán MacDiarmada in Carrick-on-Shannon. Galway won easily on a scoreline of 3–21 to 0–8.

began to rummage among the books. Anyhow, Dick seemed grateful. He volunteered to come round and plan the back addition, though I hadn't mentioned it all evening.

Naturally I'm disappointed that you're not coming on Friday, but I'll look forward even more to Monday.

They want me to open the Sligo Festival the following night – the 22nd – the damned note was in the door when I got back with Niall. I'll try to get out of it but if it's too late I may well have to do it.

If you see a stick-on rubber sole for a size 7 shoe in Woolworth's I'll be grateful if you'll buy it for me.

There's no news except I saw the 'wood'. It may well be useful, but it's certainly a fine example of how expansive Pat's imagination is about himself, even as it diminishes the light of others.[27]

I hope all goes well at the exam. I am so sorry to have had to give you the typing so close to it.[28]

I love you
John

PS. I hadn't closed this. It's now 3.40 and no sign yet of Weedy's van.[29] So . . . You may well be lucky to get this before you leave.

Sunday
Weedy's van blazed past at 4.15, without stopping. So I'm sending this with Nancy D., who'll post it tomorrow in Sligo, where she is supervising exams.[30]

Kelsey wanted this, having courageously ventured out to the match.[31] Maybe you'll let him have by internal post if you're not seeing him. They mentioned something about a 'dinner'.

With all my love
John

27 Refers to a scheme to cut some local trees and make into a supply of firewood.
28 Madeline typed up all of John's manuscripts from early in their relationship.
29 Muiredach 'Weedy' Walsh was the McGaherns' postman for years, living in nearby Fenagh.
30 Nancy Donnelly was the sister of Jerome Donnelly and daughter of the McGaherns' neighbour Anna Rose Donnelly. She was a teacher in Mohill.
31 McGahern was sending on a copy of the local newspaper, the *Leitrim Observer*. On 30 May Leitrim had defeated a traditionally much more powerful Mayo team on a scoreline of 2–8 to 0–10 in the Connacht senior men's gaelic football quarter-final after a replay, leading to great local celebration. The game was played in Páirc Seán MacDiarmada, Carrick-on-Shannon and was attended by McGahern and Thornton.

Tell K. that I had to wait for Donnelly's Observer, as all the Observers were bought up at once in euphoria of the historic success.

Leitrim lost 29–8 to Galway in the 2nd Round.

J.

Paul Muldoon Papers

Foxfield

15 June 1976

Dear Paul,

It's a note to say that the Paris situation hasn't changed, and that we'll be glad if you'll have it for the last two weeks of August.[32]

Madeline comes home on Monday next. The place should be running properly by early July. Maybe Anne Marie might like to join you in Dublin, and both of you come down for a weekend then?

I cook and mullock round the house, having arranged a sort of truce within pending Madeline's arrival. The farmer – he is 27, Jerome is his name – comes round out of loneliness. Over mugs of tea and slices of bread and of long silences that no one seems to mind and such punctuations as, 'Do you think, John, is this writin a good payin business?' or 'You wouldn't know whether a man'd be better off with these women or without them?'

I can read now early in the morning or late at night but I haven't tried to write yet.

Remember me to Anne Marie
with good wishes
John

Playing at half back that day was McGahern's distant cousin Liam Kelly, then a seminarian at Maynooth and a friend of McGahern's for many years. In 2006 he celebrated McGahern's funeral mass.

32 Muldoon did not stay in the Paris flat but stayed in Foxfield for short periods over three summers, occasionally helping to save the hay.

Robert Woof

Foxfield

6 September 1976

Dear Robert,[33]

I want to thank you and Pamela for your kindness to Madeline and myself during all the time we were in Newcastle.[34]

I am about to hand in the book of stories, and I wonder if you'll accept the Dedication. It'd be simply <u>To Robert Woof</u>.[35]

If for any reason you'd prefer not to have it, just tell me, and I won't mind at all.

I'm just about to go to Devon. I hope not to move from here after that till we leave at Christmas.

I'd a great deal of revision, some of the stories had to be rewritten completely; and the farmer was all the time catching me for work.[36] I am hoping to restore myself in Devon.

Madeline sends her best wishes.

Yours

John

---

33 Robert Woof (1931–2005), scholar, writer and academic. He was best known for his dynamic leadership of the Wordsworth Trust at the poet's former home at Dove Cottage, Grasmere in the Lake District, for thirty years. From 1971 to 1992 he was a reader in English at Newcastle University.

34 Woof's wife Pamela, also a Wordsworth scholar, is central to the continued success of the Wordsworth Trust.

35 Woof was happy to accept this honour and became the dedicatee of *Getting Through*, reflecting for McGahern the importance of the years spent as Northern Arts Fellow at Newcastle and Durham.

36 Jerome Donnelly would ask for help with chores.

Madeline McGahern

23 Forest Drive West

[September 1976]

Dear Madeline,
I got home yesterday evening. I spent the Monday night in Dublin, saw Mr Lehane – Embassy Cinema, Pearse Street – who was in great form, and hopes you'll call on him in Dublin.

Stayed with the Jordans, they too were hoping you'd stay. I found the same depression, definitely some poor idea of self-reflection, but it may be different with you.

Came on the morning boat, with Paddy Morahan, crowded because of the football international – England v Ireland – but there was a cautious gaiety with Paddy.[37]

Walked from Euston to Soho, a lovely balmy evening, the streets empty, and I felt you all the time as an absence, in the sense of the many evenings together in the same streets. Jermyn Street, Goodge Street . . .

I have to ring the Baron now, and the Agent, and begin the day.[38]

May sends her best regards, disappointed you didn't come, and the house and children are quite lovely.[39]

Mark is an even stronger candidate for our old predictions.[40]

> With all my love
> John

---

37 Likely refers to the international of 8 September 1976, which ended in a 1–1 draw. Paddy Morahan was a friend from schooldays in Carrick-on-Shannon whom McGahern liked and admired. He lived in Sligo, supported Sligo Rovers Football Club and was a devoted football fan. See *Memoir*, 200–1.
38 The Baron is Charles Monteith, a reference to Proust.
39 May McGarty, a much-loved Foxfield neighbour.
40 Mark McGarty, May's youngest grandchild.

22 September 1976

Dear Miss Kiernan,[41]
Thank you for your kind letter.

Naturally I'd be glad to publish at <u>The New Yorker</u> and some time ago sent <u>Sierra Leone</u>, a story, to Miss Kierstead there. I've had no decision on it yet.

It is the last story, and maybe the most perfect, in the collection; and I'm afraid if it goes down I can have very little hope of luck with The New Yorker.[42]

> With good wishes
> Sincerely
> John McGahern

Neill Joy
[*Madeline McGahern*]
Foxfield

2 October 1976

Dear Neill and Mary,[43]
We were delighted to get your letter. I was in London 2 weeks ago, on my way back from Devon where Seamus Heaney and I gave a course, and wondered if you were there yet. (From your letter, you were probably coming in from Italy at that time).

---

41 Frances Landau Kiernan b. 1944, editor and author, worked at the *New Yorker* from 1966 to 1987 as an editor in the fiction department. Later she was a senior editor at Houghton Mifflin and has written widely about literary matters. This is the first of several extant letters sent by McGahern to Kiernan.

42 McGahern had had bad experiences with the *New Yorker* in the past. See his letter to Charles Monteith of 16 November 1963 in which he complains that 'Summer at Strandhill' (later 'Strandhill, the Sea') was 'much spoiled by editors'. The magazine had also rejected other stories, such as 'Christmas' (c. 1962), 'Bomb Box' (1969) and 'The Beginning of an Idea' (1974). It published 'Sierra Leone' on 22 August 1977, thus beginning a fruitful relationship between McGahern and Kiernan.

43 Neill Joy, a Colgate colleague, and his wife Mary. See letter of 10 October 1972.

Charles Monteith of Faber was here 2 days ago, and took the MSS back with him, a book of stories, but now I have to go back to the novel, horrible work, and I don't intend to move for the next few months.[44]

I have only one engagement, on the 9th December, in the University of North Wales; and I may well go up to London then. We leave from London for Colgate on the 1st January.

Now, if you wish to come to Ireland for Christmas, and if it'd be of any use to you, you'd be welcome to this house. It might save you London rent in January, and you could close it up for us when you are ready to leave.

It's small, but it is comfortable enough, and there are books.

And there's plenty of time to think about it.

Either way, it cannot be long until we meet, and we look forward to that. Madeline sends her love, as I do.

John

Faber

Foxfield

8 October 1976

Dear Charles,

Thank you for your telegram, and for Lady Dufferin's invitation. I have written to her, to thank her, and to say how sorry I am that I cannot come.[45]

Telegrams, for some unknown reason, are <u>Gorvagh</u>, while letters are <u>Foxfield</u>. They are both almost equidistant from here, but they pursue a hard bureaucratic line with strays, which achieves nothing but to delay letters for 3 days, and telegrams for nearly a day. I believe they return both to Carrick-on-Shannon for redirection. You can't beat efficiency.

I'd have liked to have gone, but I have so little time till I go to Colgate. And it takes me a week to write after such 'excitements'. Perhaps she'll write me again at a better time. Devon took a month away.

---

44 The stories that became *Getting Through* in 1978; the novel is *The Pornographer*.
45 In the telegram of 6 October, Monteith, on behalf of the Marchioness of Dufferin and Ava (1941–2020), invited McGahern to a literary discussion at her Clandeboye Estate in Co. Down on the 16th. Iris Murdoch and John Bayley were already confirmed as participants. Lady Dufferin especially admired *The Dark*.

It was such a great pleasure to have you here that I cannot begin to tell.[46]

Madeline sends her love, as I do

John

Faber

Foxfield

3 November 1976

Dear Charles,

Thanks for your letter. There seems a long delay – going on the postmarks – in the post of late. I'll be grateful for any help with the order, or anything else you may notice either.

When we get the order right we can make a clean copy, and the 2nd copy. The £600 seems fair enough to me.[47]

The state of play in the States is uncertain and tricky as far as the publication of the stories goes.

I'll write about it when sending the clean copies or perhaps I can see Matthew about it before I leave for Colgate.

One thing: there's no rush.

Hoping to hear from you soon

and with my love

John

P.S. I got a big parcel from Harlow, which I had returned, not wanting to pay the tax. I ordered 2 Nightlines and 2 Leavetakings. Much more came. Would you secretly be able to check, as there was some mistake, either on my side or theirs. I'd be very grateful. John.

46 Monteith, in a letter of 6 October, thanked John and Madeline for their hospitality on a recent visit to Foxfield: 'What an absolutely marvellous day that was I spent with you in Leitrim. I think your house is delightful – and I can't tell you how much I admire the soft, green, peaceful countryside all round it. A very safe distance away from Dublin too!' McGahern handed over a full typescript of *Getting Through*, stressing his strong preference for a plain dustjacket with bold lettering in the manner of *Nightlines*. His wish was granted.

47 The terms offered by Monteith for *Getting Through* in a letter of 14 October were an advance of £600, 10% on the first 2,000 sales, 12½% on 4,000 and 15% thereafter.

Faber

Foxfield

4 November 1976

Dear Charles,
Thank you for your generous praise. I suspect it's far too generous.

I cannot tell you how grateful I am for the criticism. It's all that's of any use at this stage, and I'll be grateful for the other notes as well. I'm certain you are right about the order.[48]

I'll add the acknowledgements to the corrected copy.[49]
I feel a little like the Poet, when I offered him the fiver: 'It'll be a great help, John.'

         With my love
         John

48 Monteith had addressed the question of the order in which he felt the stories should appear in a letter of 2 November: 'It's always good strategy, I think, to begin and to end a collection of short stories with two absolute stunning ones – and to my mind, the two complete stunners here are THE BEGINNING OF AN IDEA and SIERRA LEONE. SIERRA LEONE, of course, is already the final story – and I wouldn't want to change that at all. But I would suggest that you start the book with THE BEGINNING OF AN IDEA. Quite apart from being a superb story in its own right, it's got the odd "merit" of not being an Irish story – and to make it your "lead" would, I think, startle reviewers into realizing that these stories have got to be judged as stories, not as "Irish stories".' The order that Monteith went on to suggest is the order in which the stories were eventually published, with the exception of 'The Wine Breath', which McGahern sent at the last possible moment.
49 Monteith had suggested McGahern include acknowledgements, though he was under no legal obligation to do so.

426

Faber

Foxfield

26 December 1976

Dear Niall,
The saw, with some oil, and fuel – it's already mixed – is under the pine table in the kitchen.[50]

Gus Guckian of Quinn's in Mohill will give you a file holder and file. You'll need it after about a day's cutting. I had the same cleared 2 weeks ago.[51]

You can cut all round there. The name of the forestry man is <u>John Harte</u>. I meant to cut more for you but the flu and Wales and poor weather caught up with me.

All is a rush now.
I hope Phil and yourself and the children have a very happy year.

John

The key fits but must be pressed hard

J.

50 A chainsaw that McGahern was lending to Niall Walsh.
51 At this point in the letter McGahern draws a picture of a house, cut timber and trees.

1977

Joe Kennedy

Colgate

7 January 1977

Dear Joe,
I am sorry.

Madeline and myself want to send Margaret and you our deep sympathy.[1]
I'll be speaking in Toronto the 8th and 9th of March, at O'Driscoll's place
and at York Uni.[2]

We have a spare bedroom and you are very welcome to stay with us.

Airports are Syracuse and Utica.

With all good wishes

John

Faber

Colgate

21 January 1977

Dear Charles,
Thanks for your kind letter.

The New Yorker is buying The Wine Breath (they rang up the day before
yesterday): and it'll appear in Hamish Hamilton's book of ghost stories this
summer.[3]

---

1 Joe Kennedy's mother died in January 1977.
2 Robert O'Driscoll (1936–96) was a Canadian with strong Irish connections. At the
time McGahern wrote this letter O'Driscoll was a Professor of Literature at Memorial
University in Newfoundland and key to the setting up of an Irish Studies network in
Canada.
3 The story appeared in *Irish Ghost Stories*, ed. Joseph Hone (London: Hamish
Hamilton, 1977).

Can this last sentence be changed in <u>Doorways</u>, the last sentence in the story to

And the real difficulty was <u>that the day was falling into its own night</u>.

The poet has swung another job. There was a call from a university near here, Syracuse, for a character reference. It's for 1978. 'It'll be a great help.'

He rang a few nights ago, rather shaken. Apparently Aer Lingus' St. Brigid bearing himself and his beloved nearly went down with all aboard. He and she are to come here in February.

I am able to work on the novel every day, the first time I have been able to work here.

Madeline sends her love.

It's so nice to be able to look forward to seeing you in May

Love

John

Old sentence: And the real difficulty was <u>fast coming into sight</u> (change underlined).

Frances Kiernan Papers

Colgate

28 January 1977

Dear Miss Kiernan,

Thank you for your kind letter. I was waiting for the other proofs.

I am delighted with the proofs and grateful for your work.

It'll be the last story in a volume <u>Getting Through</u>, a collection of my stories, that the British publishers will be bringing out next Winter or Spring.[4] Can I assume that it is alright for them to do that, and to use it in an anthology they are planning just before? (I was reading the back of the check)

With thanks and good wishes

Yours sincerely

John McGahern

4 Refers to 'Sierra Leone'.

1 February 1977

Dear Mr Henry,[5]
Thank you for the copies of <u>Ploughshares</u> and for your kind letter.[6]

I'd gladly offer you work but all the stories in the book have been placed in the sense of first acceptance and I have turned back to the novel I've been working on.

There is one story that Peter has, <u>A Slip Up</u>.[7] It's been published in the small Newcastle Upon Tyne magazine <u>Stand</u>, but this may not cross your readers. If you like it and wish to publish it I'll be glad. If Peter hasn't a copy I can find you one.

> With all good wishes
> Sincerely
> John McGahern

5 DeWitt Henry b. 1941 in suburban Philadelphia. A graduate of Amherst College and of Harvard University, he is a founding editor of *Ploughshares*, a Boston-based literary journal with which McGahern published, and served as its editor and director from its inception in 1971 to 1995. He currently holds Emeritus status at Emerson College, Boston.

6 *Ploughshares* had been established by DeWitt Henry and Peter O'Malley in O'Malley's Cambridge, Massachusetts public house, the Plough and Stars, in 1971 as an antidote, in part, to the fashionable turn towards postmodern experimentation in fiction then prevalent in American letters – McGahern was exactly the type of 'traditional' writer favoured by Henry. Initially run from the basement of the pub, the magazine grew sufficiently in stature over the years to eventually become associated with Emerson College in downtown Boston, where it is still based.

7 'Peter' is Peter O'Malley, an Irish entrepreneur, publican and patron of the arts with whom Henry founded *Ploughshares*.

DeWitt Henry,
Ploughshares Papers

Colgate

16 February 1977

Dear Mr Henry,
Thank you for your kind letter. I am very glad you liked <u>A Slip Up</u>, and that it'll appear in <u>Ploughshares</u>.[8]

I am grateful, too, for the gift of the 3 volumes. I had much enjoyment of them. Of the writers I hadn't met before, I was surprised how good Debus is.[9]

It'd be nice to meet you if I can get to Boston?
Do you think it is possible to find a reading there as an excuse to go? I haven't approached anybody there.[10]

I may well go down anyhow.
With good wishes
Sincerely
John McGahern

Niall Walsh Papers

Colgate

18 February 1977

Dear Niall,
I hope the key reached you, and that you found the saw and the wood all right.

I've had one easy month, and I got real work done on the novel – it's the first time I've worked here – but now the grind has started. I work by getting

---

8 'A Slip-up' appeared in the Spring 1977 issue of *Ploughshares*.
9 Andre Dubus (1936–99), an American short story writer and essayist. He studied creative writing under Richard Yates at the Iowa Writers' Workshop and was much admired by DeWitt Henry, who published his work regularly in *Ploughshares*.
10 McGahern was not to know that this passing request would lead to the single best-attended reading of his life, alongside Robert Lowell (1917–77) at Harvard University on 30 April 1977.

up very early in the morning but it is a losing battle. I count out the weeks. Some new work will come out in <u>The New Yorker</u>, March or April.[11]

Murphy was here a few weeks ago, with his fiancée, a Miss Barnett, about 30, pretty, and needless to say private-incomed. She's a potter. The family own the deep sea docks into Belfast and a Grand Uncle won the Epsom Derby in 1929.[12] They are to be married in the summer. High Island or an English Lawn?[13] Anyhow, 'it'll be a great help.' They are both flying back for the Inishboffin Arts Week in April. I was glad to have a solid excuse not to go – Inish B. seems to have lots of money – but I'd like to go invisibly there.

The students are very different. Self expression is OUT. Explanatory writing is in. All are worried about grades, about law and medical schools. And heaven has provided the usual quota of clowns.

I hope to be home by the end of May. We must work out then what I owe you.

> Madeline sends her best wishes to Phil and yourself, as I do.
> John

Frances Kiernan Papers

Colgate

[*Spring 1977*]

Dear Miss Kiernan,
Thank you for your letter and for reading the prose so carefully.

What I was most afraid of was that the rhythm might be broken and it has not been disturbed at all.[14]

I've had it retyped as I seem to have taken only the copy with me in the rush of leaving Leitrim.

If there's anything you're still worried about write or call me.

I am very much looking forward to meeting you in April.[15]

11 'The Wine Breath' appeared in the *New Yorker* of 28 March 1977.
12 Trigo won the Epsom Derby of 1929, trained by Dick Dawson, owned by William Barnett. The horse was not considered a serious contender for the race and started at odds of 33/1 in a field of twenty-six runners.
13 Richard Murphy had purchased High Island, off the Connemara coast, naming his 1974 collection of poetry in its honour.
14 Refers to 'The Wine Breath'.
15 McGahern met Frances Kiernan for the first time in the offices of the *New Yorker* in April 1977, thus beginning a warm friendship. Kiernan wrote to him on 26 April:

I am hurrying to get this in the post but with all good wishes.
                    Sincerely
                    John

                                            DeWitt Henry,
                                        Ploughshares Papers

                                                Colgate

2 March 1977

Dear Mr Henry,
Thank you for your kind letter.

I rang just after it came, after I'd looked through the proofs, but it wasn't easy to talk on the phone, as people were coming and going in the office.

I don't mind at all reading with Montague. I haven't met him for years. I thought he felt I didn't value his work highly enough. It's not an unusual state. And what harm! It's his state. To each his own.[16]

What would be best of all is a reading that might benefit Ploughshares as well as myself or any other of its writers.[17] I think it's marvellous that there should be such a solid small magazine in Boston.

The story The Wine Breath will come out in The New Yorker within the next month or so. I only mentioned it in the sense it might be of use towards the reading.

I have to say how grateful I am that you'd think to go to so much trouble for a reading for me. When I mentioned it, I did mean it as any old excuse to go to Boston.

'You were thoroughly entertaining [. . .] Are you always so full of stories, or do you simply have an unerring sense for an audience that thrives on gossip? Somehow I expect you do.' Madeline McGahern Papers.

16 DeWitt Henry and Peter O'Malley were planning a joint reading with McGahern and John Montague as a fundraising benefit for *Ploughshares*. It quickly emerged that Montague was out of the country and unavailable. At this point Henry approached Robert Lowell who agreed to the idea.

17 The Lowell–McGahern reading was a great success, attended by 1,200 paying audience members and raising $4,000 for the magazine. It proved to be Lowell's final public reading – he died on 12 September 1977 having suffered a heart attack in a New York taxi.

Now I'll go to Boston whether I'll read there or not. And I'll look forward to meeting you.

With good wishes

John McGahern

Faber

Colgate

28 March 1977

Dear Matthew,

Thank you for your letter.

The Davison rejection was not a surprise, and while a rejection is never pleasant, I am in many ways glad of it.[18]

Jonathan Coleman has read the book. He has very little power at Knopf, in fact he is not even an editor. Gotlieb was interested – he read the stories – but only in the sense of first seeing the novel.[19] That takes care of Knopf, at least until the novel is finished.

Richard Murphy rang a few weeks ago that Fran McCullough of Harper & Row is interested – her husband is doing an article on the books – and would want the novel if she is. She should be probably offered the stories, and see what she says.[20]

I have no knowledge at all of Godine.[21]

Are you likely to be in the States at all now?

18 The end of McGahern's association with Atlantic Monthly Press, which declined *Getting Through*. McGahern had never felt easy with Peter Davison, then the powerful and influential poetry editor with the *Atlantic Monthly*.

19 Robert Adams Gottlieb b. 1931 is a New York-born writer and editor. He has been editor-in-chief of Simon & Schuster, Alfred A. Knopf and the *New Yorker*. Gottlieb joined Simon & Schuster in 1955 and within ten years became the editor-in-chief. In 1968 he moved to Knopf as editor-in-chief and soon after became president. He left in 1987 to succeed William Shawn as editor of the *New Yorker*, staying in that position until 1992. After his departure from the *New Yorker*, Gottlieb returned to Knopf as editor ex officio.

20 Harper & Row was then Richard Murphy's American publisher. Frances 'Fran' McCullough b. 1939 is best known as an editor and cookbook author. She began her career at Harper & Row in 1963, moved to Dial Press in 1980, and on to Bantam Books in 1986. She has worked with authors and poets including Djuna Barnes, Donald Hall, Ted Hughes, Sylvia Plath, W. D. Snodgrass and Robert Bly.

21 David R. Godine is an American publishing house, founded in 1970 in Boston.

Madeline goes home the 23rd of April and I'll follow her a month later.
With love to Elizabeth and yourself
John

Faber

Colgate

8 April 1977

Dear Charles,
I'm flying direct to Ireland on the 23rd May.

Madeline goes home in 2 week's time. She'll be in Leitrim from May 1st. Proofs can be sent there anytime now.

I got a great deal of work done on the novel in the spring break, and I'm writing still, but I feel so tired with the teaching now that I know it won't last long.

Will you be able to come down to us this year?

I hope you had 'a great time' in Florence.

I read a poem, Xenia of Montale, in translation: it seemed quite extra-ordinary, 'a small glass of inferno'.[22]
With my love
John

Faber

Colgate

12 April 1977

Dear Charles,
I go home by way of Shannon on the 23rd May.

---

22 *Xenia*, a poetic sequence in Italian by Eugenio Montale originally published in 1966. The first English translation appeared in limited edition in 1972 and was published more broadly in 1976 by Chatto & Windus. McGahern was likely first exposed to the work of Montale through his friendship with Professor D. J. Gordon at Reading University, who was a personal friend and admirer of the Italian's work. Later he came across *Xenia* as a result of his association with *Ploughshares* magazine where it was translated by Jonathan Galassi in vol. 2, no. 4, edited by Frank Bidart (1975).

Madeline goes home very soon. She'll be in Leitrim from May 1st.
The proofs can be sent to Leitrim then.

The New Yorker has just bought Sierra Leone.
I read with Lowell in the Sanders Theatre at Harvard on the 30th April.

The latest news is that the poet isn't to be married after all 'for income tax reasons'.

I got a great deal of work done on the novel during the break but I'm not able now – as well as the teaching there's now the hot weather the imagination loathes.

Love
John

Madeline McGahern

Colgate

25 April 1977

Dear Madeline,
The electricity is up to its old tricks tonight, on and off.

I was so tired that I holed up for the week-end. DeWitt Henry rang. Sanders is almost sold out.[23] I'm introduced: read 40m; Lowell introduced, read 40m.

Wil met me at Utica. He was drunk as usual. I was grateful for the truck, eyes off the road, jerks, and a lecture on Matthew Arnold.[24] His mother and sister were to come up 'for the prodigal's birthday.' He is 'the prodigal.' 39.

Barbara rang. She forgot to phone Wreszin. I phoned Wreszin. He sounded chastened and accepted my apology.[25] Perhaps it was the equilibrium of poor fortune (or confusion). Barbara was very pleasant.

23 The Sanders Theater, Memorial Hall at Harvard. The reading was followed by a reception, sponsored by Paddy and Murphy's Whiskey of New York, in Harvard's Lamont Library.
24 Refers to Wilbur 'Wil' Albrecht (1938–2017), a Professor of English at Colgate. A graduate of Brown, Johns Hopkins and University of Pennsylvania, he was hired at Colgate in 1967, specialising in the Pre-Raphaelites, Romantic poets and essayists. He retired from teaching in 2003 and is the dedicatee of The Pornographer.
25 Mike Wreszin was a friend of John Head, McGahern's one-time Colgate colleague and best friend in Boston. Wreszin is best known for his biography A Rebel in Defense of Tradition: The Life and Politics of Dwight Macdonald (New York: Basic Books, 1994).

I've written to Peter Woods, to see if he can fix the pump before you come. It may, of course, not be as bad as Mr. Ballinamore says.[26] It has to be fixed or a new one put in. I hope you don't have too much trouble.

Guy Martin just rang.[27] There's some question of going out to them Sunday – I arranged to see them at the shindy Saturday.

Forgive this old [*illegible*] of a letter. There was a long class today and I wish this week was over and I was with you in Leitrim.

With all my love
John

Remember me to Blanaid and Tom.

He seems a kind of Berlind, an obvious self-promoter, and not much more competent.

Madeline McGahern
[Boston postcard]

29 April 1977

[*To Madeline*]
Friday evening. Came yesterday on the bus. Head apartment is in the old Vendome.[28] Had lunch with Ploughshares. Out for a walk, on a lovely cold evening.

May well be 1,200 people tomorrow. Am a little nervous. Lowell threatened to cancel, because of I.R.A. connections, but has been reassured. Will read end of Wheels, Korea, end of The L., Slip Up (40 m.)

No risks and none intended.[29]

All my love
John

26 'Mr. Ballinamore' is McGahern's Uncle Pat. He also carried the nickname 'The Shah' because of his control over the petrol pumps in his Ballinamore business.

27 Guy Martin was then Dean of the Divinity School at Harvard and had previously worked at Colgate. He hosted McGahern in the Harvard Faculty Club at the time of the joint reading with Robert Lowell. In later years Martin and his wife Marilyn visited Foxfield.

28 John Head, McGahern's old Colgate colleague who had moved on to Boston University.

29 A play on the closing words of Samuel Beckett's Watt (Paris: Olympia Press, 1953): 'No symbols where none intended'.

2 May 1977

Dear Madeline,
I came back only last night, with the Berlinds leaving Boston at four. The Joys stayed on, 'there's so much in this great goddamned wonderful town.' I'd have preferred to have gone back with the Joys but Brucie was pathetically anxious for a piece of the cake <u>and</u> they were leaving early. Actually, it turned out a smooth journey, even interesting. I have to have dinner with them Wednesday, and see Nixon on tv.[30] I have dinner with the Slaters tomorrow, before the reading.[31] On Thursday I go to Oneonta for the day at 8.30.[32] The N.Y. proofs came, 13½ pages, $2,700, if they pay same as the last time.[33] After Harvard it'll be all easy enough.

It was one of the worst days I ever had. Ploughshares people came round Friday, and it brought this horrible excitement.

Their energy is O'Malley, 32, ex Clongowes, a lawyer, who owns bars and hotels in Boston, tall and enormously handsome, who'll either wind up in jail or rich and powerful. He is married to Richard Wilbur's daughter, who was lovely in every way.[34]

He outlooked, outdrank, outtalked, outcharmed Head, which was a terrible trauma for Head, who was drunk all the time. Alberta showed painfully what she is, an overgrown cheerleader, and decent enough and well-intentioned. It was actually painful to watch her in Harvard.[35]

The Berlinds looked like 2 stricken white mice. The Joys continued having a wonderful time.

I checked the reading in the morning and timed it, 36 minutes. And I walked.

---

30 Former disgraced President Richard Nixon (1913–94) appeared in a series of interviews conducted by British journalist David Frost. They were recorded and broadcast on television and radio in four programmes in 1977.
31 Joe Slater was a Ralph Waldo Emerson scholar at Colgate admired by McGahern.
32 State University of New York at Oneonta, forty-six miles south-east of Hamilton.
33 The *New Yorker* published 'Sierra Leone' in its issue for 22 August 1977. 'The Wine Breath' had been published there the previous April.
34 Richard Wilbur (1921–2017), celebrated American poet and translator.
35 Alberta was John Head's wife.

Earlier I'd gone and got shirts and underwear in Filene's Basement with Alberta and took her to Jake Worth's for a beer.[36]

Suddenly there was 6 hours to go to the reading, and then 5, and 4, and 3½, and 3, and next 2.

I was put in a back room, crowds milling round in the hall, with a dirty glass jug, and one dirty glass. I washed them and got talking to the janitor and started to drink water. There was an enormous hall one side of the room, an examination hall and where people sometimes now give blood, dusty too, with at least a hundred marble heads of dead worthies along the walls. You could play football in it, it was so large.[37]

Lowell was late. I read first, having to walk across a whole bloody long stage. I think I won the audience over, after beginning nervously, an old story.[38]

Lowell began strangely, saying there should be no competition between the speakers, which immediately introduced precisely that. Somehow he bungled it all, which didn't displease me.

I'll leave off.

I sent a card from Boston, and a letter a few days earlier.

I write to P. Woods about the pump. If it's burst we'll just have to get a new one.

I hope all is well. I envy you there. And I miss you.

With all my love
John

36 Jacob Wirth's is an historic German-American restaurant and bar in downtown Boston.

37 Neill Joy spent a period alone with McGahern backstage before the reading and recalls 'never before or since' having seen John 'in such a high pitched nervous and agitated state'.

38 One audience member present that evening recalls McGahern and the audience reaction: 'standing like an abashed schoolboy on the stage in Memorial Hall, still holding his story at his side, and listening as the rapturous applause swells to nothing short of acclamation.' See Anthony Glavin, 'Small is Beautiful: Some Thoughts in Praise of the Literary Journal', *Irish Independent* (2 May 2012).

7 May [1977]

Dear Madeline,
I was glad to get your air letter. Don't worry about the planting or anything.
It doesn't matter all that much. I hope you had some time of your own to
enjoy Paris and London.

I read here on Tuesday night. I spent Thursday in Oneonta, it was a long
day, but the place was very beautiful, a mountain city encircled by mountains.
The people were nice and unpretentious and paid me $225. There was the
usual problem of the failed writer, whose niche was disturbed by the outside.
You can wheel death anywhere/in his invalid chair.[39]

I had dinner last night with Hap Clark, crab meat and a dried-out brown
trout, but he was very pleasant, and went to a lot of trouble.[40]

Bruicy and Mary went to Hungary on Thursday. Their clothes drier went
on fire to honour the occasion. Busch is apparently back.

It's parents' weekend and it's strange how sad it is to watch them traipse
about in the sun.

I cleaned the flat, and I'm tired, but it's nearly over now.
I should go down to New York next week but I don't want to. I gave Jonathan
a fairly savage description of the situation from my point of view early in the
week, and he rang more flunkey than ever yesterday.[41]

Judging the time the letters take, there's probably little likelihood of any
letter reaching me before I leave. Ring me if you need anything.

I'm having lunch with Rexine Monday.[42] Joe Slater recommended I be
offered $25,000.

Janet and Wil ask after you and with affection.

I love you and you owe me nothing; but I'll be grateful for your love
                    With all my love
                    John

39 From W. H. Auden's 1929 poem 'The Questioner Who Sits So Sly': 'Will you
wheel death anywhere/In his invalid chair'. See Auden, Collected Poems, 42.
40 A member of the English faculty at Colgate.
41 Jonathan Coleman at Knopf, soon to move to Simon & Schuster. It was still up in
the air at this point which US publisher McGahern would move to after his time with
Atlantic Monthly Press and Little, Brown.
42 John E. Rexine was a Professor of Classics at Colgate.

Madeline McGahern

[*Colgate*]

Wednesday night, 11th [*May 1977*]

Dear Madeline,

I'd hoped a note might come today, and I know the mails are slow. I hope everything is all right.

I gave the last class today. All the papers won't come in till Friday, and I won't do much till then. I'll try to do most of it over the weekend.

I'll try to go to New York the 19th and to Boston on the 21st.

The plane is scheduled to get into Shannon at 10.20 on the 24th.

Dinner at Busch's was pleasant, but he's obviously been quizzing the students about me, and finding it awkward. He's doomed to the pattern.

I go to Albrechts to dinner on Sunday and to the Readings on Monday.[43] Doug rang up last night, changing it from Saturday to Monday.[44]

There was a sudden snowfall Monday, weighing and breaking some of the branches, but it's gone today. For me it was like a sharp farewell of white.

I miss you constantly, and I am longing to be home, and to see you.

> With all my love
> John

Frances Kiernan Papers

Foxfield

2 June 1977

Dear Frances,

I enclose the proofs. They just came as I was leaving. My father died and I'd to leave suddenly.[45]

---

43 Wil and Janette Albrecht, good friends of the McGaherns at Colgate.
44 Douglas 'Doc' Reading was a member of the History faculty at Colgate.
45 McGahern's father, Frank, died on 12 May 1977 and was buried in Ardcarne churchyard near his home in Grevisk, Co. Roscommon.

I think you're right about the last paragraph. It doesn't work here. Without the bitter-sweet spaces of the original bar scenes it is too much. Everything else seems right.[46]

I hope you had a good holiday. Write me a little about it. I'll be grateful.

There's scorching weather here. People are already driving cattle to the lakes and complaining that there'll be no grass in the meadows. I am a bit depressed, but the Lord knows that it's a sure sign of intelligence etc. God help us.

With good wishes
John

Dear Frances
Sorry about the envelope. Everything is upside-down here yet.
John

Russell and Volkening Papers
[Foxfield]

24 June 1977

Dear Mr Seldes,[47]
Thank you for your kind letter.

<u>England</u>
Faber has always published me in England. Charles Monteith is my editor. While he is there I would not wish to leave. They have acted as part agents, but I have told them I feel I need an agent, and wrote into the book of stories – GETTING THROUGH – that unsold rights would become the domain of an agent, should I acquire one. Panther used to publish me in paperback, but

---

46 Refers to 'Sierra Leone'. Frances Kiernan had written to McGahern about the story and the aesthetic stance of the *New Yorker* in an undated letter of early summer 1977: 'The major change was shifting the opening section back to the body of the story. Everything else comes to toning down writing that for our pages would not be acceptable. As you know from our work on THE WINE BREATH, our taste runs to a kind of writing that has a spoken, rather than a literary sound.' Kiernan Papers, NYPL.

47 This is the first of several letters to Tim Seldes (1926–2015), an American literary agent who then worked for the Russell and Volkening agency in New York. The company's archives are held by the New York Public Library. Seldes worked with Doubleday for many years before becoming an agent in 1972 and represented, among others, Anne Tyler, Nadine Gordimer and Annie Dillard.

Quartet bought THE LEAVETAKING, and are bringing out the early novels later in the year. Many of the literary magazines are anxious for my work, but – as I am sure you know – they do not pay very well.

Foreign

Various books have been published: <u>The Dark</u>, Germany-Benziger; Holland-Contact; Finland-Tammi; NIGHTLINES, France-Mercure de France; THE LEAVETAKING, Holland-Contact. Faber does not have much interest in selling foreign rights; they all came from enquiries or private contacts.

U.S.

I left Knopf to go to Atlantic-Little Brown with an editor who has since gone out of publishing, and I was never happy there. I could have taken THE LEAVETAKING to Random House, but didn't because there wasn't a great deal more money offered ($4,000) and out of loyalty because Atlantic lost money (1,000 copies) on NIGHTLINES. Anyhow, Atlantic rejected the book of stories, and I don't have an American publisher now.

I have a fairly solid relationship with The New Yorker now.

Ploughshares, which published one of the stories in their last issue and are anxious for my work to be better known in the States, think that Seymour Lawrence might take me up, and even bring out the early novels in paperback, but that is recent, and speculation.[48]

I am working on a novel. It is all thought out – the movements, the people. And parts of it are in finished prose. I hope to complete it this winter. After that I want to write a novella that's in my head, which, I feel, won't take long.[49] I could start it now, except for the novel.

I have to go to London sometime this autumn. It'd be nice if we could be there at the same time.

I hope this information is what you were looking for. I'll be glad to answer anything else you may feel you need to know.

With good wishes.

Sincerely

John McGahern

48 Seymour Lawrence (1927–94), New York-born, Harvard-educated independent book publisher in New York City and Boston for almost thirty years who brought the first works of many important writers to the public. His most notable success was with Kurt Vonnegut's *Slaughterhouse-Five* in 1969, which had been widely rejected by mainstream publishers. McGahern did not work with him.

49 There is no archival evidence of McGahern having written a novella in the same period or just after the publication of *The Pornographer*.

10 July 1977

Dear Niall,

Thanks for writing. It was forwarded from Colgate a few days ago. They let me go for the funeral, and I've been here since.

It was the heart my father died from, but he sank slowly, fighting each inch. Madeline was home in early May to open the house and saw him. The sisters seem calm enough. The prospect had been dramatized so that I suspect the real thing was a let down.

We bought 4 in-calf cows, and they've had 4 calves, all heifers. One of them got joint ill, but was treated, and seems all right, if a little shaky. We've started to put up a shed, and seem owned as well by the acres. I haven't written a sentence, and there's pressure to deliver the novel around the beginning of the year.

They've planted the wood, and wired it off.[50] I asked John Harte about your timber, and he said it'd be all right to take it out, as long as we don't damage the young trees. I'll help you some day you're up.

Have you started the Ballinasloe house?

A field across the lake, hardly an acre, was sold to a Dublin doctor for £2,400 while we were away.

Thanks for the enclosures. Mary Hutchinson was an interesting woman, but certainly nothing the notice written – probably John Mortimer – said she was.[51] All that vanity gone . . .

I hope you'll be up soon and Madeline sends her love to Phil and you, as I do.

John

50 A wood of oak, larch and maple planted on the McGaherns' land.
51 Mary Hutchinson, an early admirer of McGahern's work and important patron of the magazine in which he was first published, *X: A Quarterly Review*, died on 17 April 1977. See letter to Niall Walsh of 18 August 1971.

19 August 1977

Dear Joe,
Thanks for today's letter.

We've been here since May. My father died in May, and I'd to come home early. It's been a disjointed summer.

We'll be very glad to see you. Next week-end (27th) is about the one week-end that's no good, and I'll probably be in Dublin a few days after that. If we don't meet then, why not when you come back from the States!

I've gone back to work on the novel. It's always hell, but worse after an absence. The concluding story Sierra Leone from Getting Through will be in next week's New Yorker.

We're looking for a VW or some banger for the winter.

> With good wishes to Margaret and yourself
> Sincerely
> John

[*August 1977*]

Dear Frances,
Thank you for your letter.

And, of course, I'm deeply grateful for the care you've given to Sierra Leone from the very beginning. I mean more than that, but I don't know how to say it outside the convention.

I've just started to write again after an idle summer. It's always hell, but worse when you've been away.

I'd be grateful for 6 copies, and one copy of The Wine Breath. I left my copy behind in the confusion of leaving the States.

I'll write better soon.

> What's New York like now?
> With all good wishes
> John

445

27 September 1977

Dear DeWitt,
Thank you for your cheque and kind letter.[52]

Forgive me for asking for Revolutionary Road. I intended to buy it, but had to leave without warning. I'll make reparation in some way. They'll forward it.[53]

Faber will publish the stories in the spring. I've done nothing about it since in the States, and am getting an agent. I'm working all the time on the novel now. I'd be grateful to have it finished before the stories come out, to avoid any disturbance. The New Yorker took the whole bitter sweet pause out of Sierra Leone but I don't care.

Thank you for publishing The Slip Up, and for your's and Peter O'Malley's kindness to me in Boston.

I hope we'll meet before too long.
And I'll write again when Revolutionary Road comes.

> With all good wishes
> John

It's real spiritual relief not to have to think of Davison in any relationship with the work I do.

> J.

---

52 McGahern would have been paid a very modest fee by *Ploughshares* for 'A Slip-up', perhaps $50.

53 Henry had been taught by Richard Yates (1926–92) at the Iowa Writers' Workshop in the late 1960s where he studied in part to avoid being drafted to serve in Vietnam. Yates became his mentor and Henry, in turn, enthused to others about Yates's work. McGahern particularly admired Yates's best-known novel, *Revolutionary Road* (New York: Little, Brown, 1961), and chose to teach it at Colgate.

Faber

Foxfield

26 November 1977

Dear Charles,

Thank you for the good news, by telegram and letter, and of course for putting me forward in the first place. That was a real part of the pleasure.[54]

Seamus and Marie told me their pleasure in seeing you and of a very fine literary minuet you danced with Terence.[55]

We went to Enniskillen for the first time. It's such a handsome town it made me sad at how the South have ruined all their county towns. Sometime, we must meet in the Royal Hotel there, and bring you here.

Had a long letter from the poet, very studied. He may well be resuming attempt at nuptials.

> With love and gratitude
> John

Joe Kennedy

Foxfield

28 November 1977

Dear Joe,

Thank you for the note.

15th Dromod 9.20 a.m.

Dublin 11.20

Leave for Cork 1 p.m. 16th. Come back sometime the 16th.

17th Take morning train to Dromod.

---

54 Monteith had sent McGahern a telegram on 21 November telling him that he had won an Arts Council Grant of £3,000.

55 'Terence' is Terence de Vere White, then in his final year as literary editor of the *Irish Times*. White had written probably the most damning review McGahern ever received – for *The Leavetaking* in the *Irish Times*. See letter to Niall Walsh of 11 January 1975.

They wanted me to change it to the 10th, as Montague won't be there, but it wasn't possible for me, so we might as well take the hotel, though it doesn't matter, as the University will put us up somewhere anyhow.[56]

Ring me <u>Quinn's</u> of Fenagh 6 p.m. next Saturday.

Thanks, too, for the cheque. I got a British Arts Council Award of £3,000 since but I don't want to have it around.

It was a great pleasure to have you here.

Yours
John

Brian Friel Papers
Foxfield

19 December 1977

Dear Brian,

Thank you for your kind invitation. I've been looking forward to it for a long time, and was often hoping you might call and stay, the both of you, on your way to or from Dublin.

For going to Donegal, we have even a Volkswagen now. The difficulty is animals. Having committed the self-indulgence of acquiring them we have in the usual turn of the wheel wound up being owned. That'll change too, and then we'll go to you, but it maybe March. Is there any chance you may come this way? What I'll do is ring, I'll ring soon.

I was in Dublin Saturday, and ran into Davy Hammond, who gave me the bad news.[57] I am deeply sorry, especially for Mrs Friel. In the face of that we are all the one person, and all owned.

Madeline sends you the good wishes of the season, as I do.

Love
John

---

56 Kennedy, McGahern and Madeline travelled together to Cork where McGahern read at the University College. The trip was paid for by the *Sunday World*, which Kennedy was editing at the time.

57 David Hammond (1928–2008), Belfast folk singer, music collector, broadcaster, and eventually a director of the Field Day Theatre Company.

20 December 1977

Dear Matthew,

Tim Seldes of Russell & Volkening will act for me in the States. He likes the work and has agreed to act for me without strings other than his take from whatever he sells until we see how it goes.

I've felt for a time that I needed an agent in the States, especially for shorter pieces, but was reluctant to move, mainly because of the amount of work you'd done for me there.

What decided me was the last business at Knopf, and Coleman's move to Coward McCann and G.[58] If it had gone through I'd have been in the same position as with Gregory long ago.

Coleman was decent and indeed recommended Seldes, saying that with such a changing trade I needed some one person on the ground. And I got the same advice from elsewhere.

I know you'll probably feel only relief at not having to trouble there with an author that has had such a poor record but I want to explain it because of my gratitude.[59]

> I hope we can meet again soon
> And with good wishes
> John

58 A medium-sized publishing house founded in 1927, Coward-McCann was joined with the firm G. P. Putnam's in 1936 to publish titles such as playwright Thornton Wilder's *Our Town*. In 1959 John Geoghegan joined Coward-McCann as editor-in-chief. Two years later, he was named president, then chairman. In 1971 the company was renamed Coward, McCann & Geoghegan. Jonathan Coleman has no recollection of any discussions with the company and moved from Knopf to Simon & Schuster in July 1977.

59 Evans replies on 29 December to say that he thinks the decision to go with Seldes is entirely sensible, especially given the uncertainty as to which American publisher will take on McGahern's work in the wake of his break with Atlantic Monthly Press.

1978

Russell and Volkening Papers

Foxfield

6 January 1978[1]

Dear Tim,
Thank you for your kind letter of the 2nd Nov. and for the copy of Frances McCullough's letter.[2]

Within the next few weeks I'll send you the opening 25–30,000 words of the novel.

I was very glad after I'd met you. It was a pleasure for me as well.

With all good wishes
Sincerely
John McGahern

Russell and Volkening Papers (TS)

Foxfield

18 January 1978

Dear Tim,
Thank you for the memo, which must have crossed with my note.

I enclose the opening part of the novel and a synopsis of the rest. I hope it is the amount you had in mind for me to submit when we talked in London.

---

1 Mistakenly dated 1977 by McGahern.
2 Frances McCullough of Harper & Row had written to Seldes on 7 November 1977 in praise of the stories in the Faber-published *Getting Through*: 'These are wonderful stories but I think to publish them all alone, with no preceding or closely following novel, would be to drop them into the ocean.' She hopes to hear from Seldes again soon about the progress of a possible novel. Seldes had forwarded this letter to McGahern.

I suppose it's only fair that Jonathan Coleman should have his chance, if he is able to make an offer, and wants to, but I leave you to judge that best.[3]

I should have the novel finished by summer, or by the time I go back to Colgate at the latest, but I want to be sure of it before letting it go.

With all good wishes

John

Brian Friel Papers

Foxfield

15 February 1978

Dear Brian,

We want to thank Ann and yourself for a lovely time.[4]

I enclose Walking Slow and Madeline's book.

I'll have to face into a tax form soon. Could you give me some rough idea what you put down for expenses you claim for? I'll be very grateful.[5] I hope you have a good time in the States. I've written to Mary Fitzgerald.[6]

With good wishes

and our love

John

3 Coleman was then at Simon & Schuster from where he rejected the novel on the basis of the opening section in a letter to Seldes of 21 March 1978.

4 The McGaherns visited the Friels in Muff and Greencastle several times, as the Friels visited Foxfield.

5 Friel responds on 27 February: 'Since my only income is from writing, I make no claims at all (because as far as I know they're not allowed). I just stick down what I've earned in the year and claim no allowances.' Madeline McGahern Papers.

6 Then an academic at Fordham University, subsequently at University of New Orleans and University of Missouri, St Louis. Among her numerous publications in Irish literary studies were an edition of Selected Plays of Lady Gregory (Gerrards Cross: Smythe, 1982) and the Cornell Yeats edition of the MSS of Yeats's play The Words Upon the Window-pane (2002).

15 February 1978

Dear Tim,
It's eight o'clock (change on page 33).

I had another letter from Jonathan. I suppose the best thing is to let it lie until I hear from you?[7]

I gave your name – very reluctantly – to an English agent, David Higham, a rather odd man, who has wanted to act for me for a long time. When he learned I had a U.S. agent he pressed me very hard as to who it was. I saw no harm in telling him your name but I want to let you know. I'm under no obligation to him. I've been just putting him off.

There are consecutive pages that bring the MSS over the 100 but I don't suppose they're any use to you till you get them with the finished novel. If they are, I'll send them.

> With all good wishes
> John

29 March 1978

Dear Tim,
Thank you for your kind note, and the enclosure.

I think, in view of the introduction, it was the correct thing to let Jonathan see it first, and I'm almost glad about the way it turned out, outside the need for some eventual contract.

The ending now seems to have changed again. The darkhaired girl, who only appears as a nurse in the first part, took up more room than I had allotted her in my mind, took it up in the writing: and now the end is her

---

7 Refers to negotiations with Jonathan Coleman at Simon & Schuster.

beginning – so it may be even 'hopeful' now 'life-enhancing' or whatever those lying words may mean for a time.

With all good wishes
John

Joe Kennedy
Foxfield

10 April 1978

Dear Joe,

I'm very sorry about your father.[8] I didn't mind at all about the Montrose, it was very kind of you to have the girl ring.

I won't be in Dublin till the 27th, the Trinity Festival.

The book comes out May 15th.

I haven't seen Heaney for ages but I'll ask him about the Ledwidge when I do.[9]

Madeline is in Paris, I don't know when she'll be back.

Remember me with affection to Margaret.
With all good wishes
John

Faber
Foxfield

20 April 1978

Dear Charles,

I was very glad to get the Allard card.[10] Actually, around Easter, I'd been thinking of you, just in simple affection, remembering seeing you off to Ulster

---

8 Joe Kennedy's father Frank, a veteran of the Anglo-Irish War, was unwell, and died in May 1978.

9 Kennedy, then living near Slane, Co. Meath, Francis Ledwidge's homeplace, shared an interest with Seamus Heaney in the war poet, killed in action in 1917. Heaney's 'In Memoriam Francis Ledwidge' appeared the year after this letter in *Field Work* (London: Faber, 1979).

10 Monteith had sent McGahern a postcard from Paris describing a dinner at Chez Allard on Rue Saint-André des Arts, a favourite restaurant of both men.

8 or so years ago, and I wondered how you spent Easter now. So the card came.

I don't mind at all about the postponement. It gives me a slightly better chance of finishing the novel before publication.[11]

I may go through London to the Newcastle Festival around the end of June. It'd be a pleasure to think of seeing you then.

And I hope you'll be able to come down here if you come to Ireland.

I intend to stay put as much as possible for the summer. I go to the States at the end of August.

Madeline sends her love
and with my love
John

Brian Friel Papers

Foxfield

3 May 1978

Dear Brian,
We have to get a few things in Enniskillen on Saturday and I'll probably be watching the Cup Final in William Blake's bar between 3.00 and 4.30.[12]

If it'd suit you we could meet there otherwise just come straight here.

We're both looking forward very much to seeing you and Ann.

With our love
John

---

11 Monteith had suggested, in a letter of 6 April, that the publication date of *Getting Through* be moved from 15 to 30 May in order to give Faber's Dublin agent, Philip McDermott, more time to promote advance sales in Ireland.

12 The bar became a great favourite of the McGaherns. See McGahern's posthumously published essay 'Blake's of the Hollow' in *LOTW*, 41–4. The FA Cup Final took place on 6 May 1978 at Wembley. The underdogs Ipswich Town beat Arsenal 1–0, still their only FA Cup victory.

Neill Joy
[*Madeline McGahern*]

Foxfield

7 May 1978

Dear Neill,

Thanks for the long and kind letter.

We're both looking forward to returning, to seeing you and Mary; and I'm depending on the handball.[13]

As I've never been in the States in Fall, can you tell me when term begins – or maybe Nancy can – and when – ideally – I should be there. (the first Monday in September?)[14]

Madeline has just come from Paris. She tells me to give you

> Hotel de Bretagne
> Rue Raymond Losserand
> Paris 14e

It's off the Avenue du Maine, above the Montparnasse tower.

It's very good, and it's cheap, a hard thing to come on in Paris. We'll be here all summer. I'll be in Newcastle and London for about a week June/July and that'll be it.

Is there any likelihood of you coming to Ireland?

Any news of Dean Head?[15]

Give Mary my love, and my friends in the Department.

It'll be great to see you soon, either there or here.

> Love
> John

---

13 McGahern and Joy generally played handball three times a week at the Colgate gym, usually three games in an hour.

14 Nancy Sastri was the Irish-American secretary in the English Department at Colgate. She and McGahern got along well together.

15 McGahern's Boston-based friend John Head, formerly of Colgate.

Faber

Foxfield

2 June 1978

Dear Matthew,
Tim Seldi has sold Getting Through and the novel to Harper and Row. Fran
McCullough likes both books and Seldi seems especially pleased that Erwin
Glikes is very excited by the novel.[16] It's finished now except for getting some
scenes here and there right.

I'll be in London in late June or early July. It'd be nice to meet then. At the
end of August I go back to Colgate for a year. I suppose it's unlikely that you
and Elizabeth will be in Ireland but you'll be welcome here if you are.

Seamus and Murphy were on tv here about Getting Through. Seamus was
very generous and Murphy was Murphy.

I hope you don't mind the enclosed list for passing down and I'll be grateful
if you'll do it.[17]

> With good wishes
> John

Faber

Foxfield

4 June 1978

Dear Charles,
Thank you for Tom Paulin's review, and The New Fiction. I didn't know that
they'd picked it.[18]

16 Erwin Glikes (1937–94) was a Belgian-born and Columbia-educated author,
scholar and publisher. He began his career as a lecturer of English and Comparative
Literature at Columbia, 1960–2. He was president and publisher of Basic Books for
seven years in the mid-1970s, before going on to become vice-president of Harper &
Row, 1975–9. From 1983, he became the president and publisher of the Free Press, a
subsidiary of Macmillan Publishing Company. Glikes had begun working at Penguin
USA a few weeks before his death.
17 A list of people who were to get complimentary copies of Getting Through. The
list does not survive.
18 Tom Paulin's admiring review of Getting Through appeared in Encounter for June
1978: 'Running through McGahern's work is a fusion of sex, death and hopelessness.

Harper and Row have bought the 2 books. They are very excited by the novel. It is finished but there's some rewriting and I want to make sure of it. I hope you'll like it.

Seamus was very generous about Getting Through on tv. The Poet was Ponderous.

Faye Godwin took some photos for The New Review 4 years ago, has been selling them. I don't like them and would prefer if Faber didn't use them for sending out. I'll send in a new photo if the Jerry Bauer are out of date but the Jerry Bauer are fine.[19]

Can I be sent 6 extra copies of Getting Through, to be charged to me. Can these be sent trade copies:

1. Julian Jebb
BBC tv
Kensington House

2. Professor Roger McHugh
U.C.D.
Belfield
Dublin

But maybe Rosemary has sent Julian a copy already.

I want to say again how much in your debt I feel myself to be. It's not for me to say how good or bad it is but I do know it would be a poorer work without your care and watchfulness.[20]

And with much love
John

They are the presiding trinity of his imagination and are revealed in a series of epiphanies. [. . .] McGahern's imagination is intimately bound to a terminal condition where "all life turns away from its own eventual hopelessness, leaving insomnia and its night to lovers and the dying", and he writes of this condition in a prose which always possesses an astringent purity and delicacy.' The New Fiction Society chose Getting Through as one of its books of note.

19 See letter to Rosemary Goad of 11 November 1974.

20 Monteith replied to this letter on 12 June alerting McGahern to further excellent reviews for Getting Through in the Sunday Telegraph and The Observer.

8 June 1978

Dear Tim,
Thank you for the good news. I am very happy with the outcome.[21]
   The novel is now finished. I am revising it, and trying to make sense of it. I think it's the best work I've done.
   Faber bring out <u>Getting Through</u> on the 12th June. The early reviews have been exceptionally good but that generally lends virulence to the attacks. It's a choice of the New Fiction Society.
   I begin teaching at Colgate on the 4th September.

> With good wishes
> and thanks
> John

Faber

Foxfield

20 June 1978

Dear Charles,
Thanks for the kind letters, and the reviews.[22] There was a good review by John Fowles in <u>The Irish Press</u> and a better one by a good young writer Neil Jordan in <u>The Irish Times</u>. <u>The Sunday Indo</u> had a full page.[23] The scorchers are late this time.

---

21 Refers to a deal that had been brokered with Harper & Row for a two-book deal taking in the story collection *Getting Through* and the novel that would become *The Pornographer*. Seldes wrote on 26 May that the firm was offering $7,500. If the novel were to sell more than 10,000 copies within the first six months McGahern would get an extra $2,500.
22 Monteith had sent McGahern a telegram on 12 June to mark the publication of *Getting Through*. It ended: 'It is an honour to be your publisher'.
23 John Fowles (1926–2005) in the *Irish Press* of 15 June, confessing to this being his first encounter with McGahern's work, comments on a marked Irish penchant for pessimism but writes of *Getting Through*: 'I haven't admired a short story collection so much for a long time.' On 11 June the *Sunday Independent* ran a complimentary

I read at the Newcastle Festival Friday the 30th. I'll probably go to London Tuesday or Wednesday 27–28th beforehand, go up to Newcastle for a day or two, and come back to London for another four days. It'd be a great pleasure to see you.

My brother's (01 9896740) will take any messages. If there's none, I'll just ring.

> Madeline sends her love
> and with my love
> John

> Frances McCullough Papers
>
> [*Foxfield*]

20 June 1978

Dear Frances,[24]

I don't know how to thank you for such a kind letter.

I hope I won't disappoint you.

The novel took its own ending in the finish. It turned away from the ending I had foreseen for it, which never happened me before. I think it's my best work, but then I know that authors are as untrustworthy as lovers.

I start classes in Colgate on the 4th September. I'll be there for the whole year.

Does The Pornographer sound like a possible title?

It's a pleasure already to think that we may be able to meet before too long.

> With gratitude
> Sincerely
> John McGahern

---

and serious interview with McGahern conducted by Ciaran Carty. Neil Jordan's review in the *Irish Times* of 17 June, titled 'A Rural Irony', comments that 'one can see something changing and not only in McGahern, in the whole of Irish writing. The Sligo boarding-house could be on America's east coast, the Leitrim farms could be set in provincial France. The weight of association that has too often crippled these familiar landscapes has fallen off for good.'

24 This is McGahern's earliest surviving letter to Frances McCullough. All subsequent letters address her as 'Fran'. At this time she was an editor at Harper & Row, US publishers of *The Pornographer* and *Getting Through*.

Madeline McGahern

21 Forest Glade

[*Late June 1978*]

Dear Madeline,
I saw Ian for an hour or so on Tuesday, after getting in. He's getting divorced, has a new flat, near Baker Street. I'll see Matthew and Elizabeth this evening (they're going to Ireland August 7th) and I'll go on the train to Newcastle tomorrow, come back to the Daveys Sunday, see Ross Tuesday, Charles on Wednesday.[25] I saw Jimmy and Rosaleen – and B-R-EE-D-GE – last night, and managed to get ½ of the Colonel & Mavis scene done this morning. I'll be glad to finish with it.[26] The plan is to leave Thursday morning, Thursday evening at the very latest.

Getting Through got another first in The Listener and a rave by Nye in the Guardian.[27] There was a smokes of an attack by Arnold (the telegram) I saw going up in the Irish Indo.[28]

Forgive the paper.[29]
It's just a sort of report.

25 Ian Hamilton; Matthew and Elizabeth Evans; Tom and Claire Davey; Alan Ross of the *London Magazine*; Charles Monteith.
26 Refers to a comic pornographic scene in *The Pornographer*. McGahern found it difficult to write and had relied on Madeline to purchase pornography on his behalf when they lived in Newcastle upon Tyne and he was making serious inroads into what would become *The Pornographer*.
27 The *Listener* review was written by John Mellors and appeared on 22 June: 'It is a bleak world, coolly and lucidly presented in strong, economical prose.' On 15 June Robert Nye wrote of *Getting Through* in his *Guardian* review that 'for all the harping on the illusive nature of love, the repeated winter of landscape, the almost Jacobean insistence on darkness as the natural habitat of man, McGahern is an exhilarating writer. Why? Because he uses words so well.'
28 The Arnold review, titled 'Has John McGahern lost his way in this new collection?', is by far the harshest received by *Getting Through*: 'the stories are all marking time. They could as well not have been written, and some of them – "Faith, Hope and Charity" for example – should not have been written. They do not matter.' It appeared in the *Irish Independent* of 26 June.
29 This letter is written on the back of a contract issued by Radio Telefís Éireann (RTÉ) for a broadcast of the story 'A Slip-up' to be aired on the night of 30 June 1978 for a fee of £60.

I'm looking forward already to seeing you on Friday next.
And with all my love
John
The Mails seem very slow. Don't post anything after this week.

Frances McCullough Papers (TS)

[*Foxfield*]

30 July [*1978*]

Dear Fran,
Thank you for your letter of the 18th July. I tried to call you but the phone system out of this place is extraordinary.

We have no private phone but Quinn's in Fenagh (Ballinamore 15) will take a message.

On the Fenagh-Mohill road, one mile from Fenagh, seven from Mohill, there's a sign Lough Rowan. Follow the sign until you reach the water. At the water you turn 150° right, onto a dirt road. Across the lake in trees is a black, slated cottage. That's the house.[30]

Round August 14th will be fine. I'm supposed to take classes in Colgate on 4th September. I'll probably fly to New York 1st September, though my visa hasn't yet come.

Thanks very much for sending me The Mutual Friend.[31] I'm finding it hard going which I can't quite understand, for I admire the energy.

Clean copies of the novel's final shape are almost typed, but I haven't found a title. I hope it doesn't disappoint you. I think it's my best book.
Sincerely
John

30 McCullough did not visit Foxfield.
31 *Our Mutual Friend* (London: Chapman & Hall, 1865), the last published novel by Charles Dickens.

Faber

Foxfield

8 August 1978

Dear Charles,
I hope it pleases you.[32]
    I didn't come on a title yet.
                        With all my love
                        John

Frances McCullough Papers (TS)

[*Foxfield*]

23 August [*1978*]

Dear Fran,
Jim Kalett was here and shot and shot and talked.[33] His wife was quiet and lovely. Their son drank Pepsi and played in the bales of hay.
    I start in Colgate on the 4th September. I'll fly from London on the 2nd. The home telephone number in Hamilton is, 824 0937.
    Fabers have just read the novel. They've never been as excited by any work of mine. They've even offered a decent advance.
    I hope we'll meet soon.
                        And with every good wish
                        John

32 Refers to the typescript of the as yet unnamed new novel. Monteith reads it quickly and enthusiastically, sending a telegram to McGahern on 17 August: 'novel is magnificent'.
33 American photographer regularly retained by Harper & Row.

Madeline McGahern

Colgate

5 September 1978

Dear Madeline,

I'm not certain where to write to. I'll write to Paris as the safest. I'm still kind of dazed. I'll have my first serious class in the morning.

I saw Ian H. in London. Rosaleen and Jimmy were lovely and drove me to the airport.[34] I got a stand-by on the last plane to Syracuse Saturday night and stayed that night and Sunday night with the Albrechts. They are looking forward to seeing you, and will even go down to New York to meet you if you'd want that. Probably see how it goes in Paris. It may tie you down too much.

I'm writing to Matthew to get you on my account the Gardening Book to bring to Janette or he may send it.[35]

The flat is the same, but much nicer – done up, new fridge, freezer etc. Luxurious even.

The place is green and summery and rich, tomatoes and corn and squash on sale by the roadside farms; the trees are green and huge, with the first whispers of yellow.

I've got a pile of books out of the library, and it'll be a hard few weeks.

And I'll be waiting for you, with a constant love.

John

We were 3½ hours getting through Kennedy because of Labour week-end.

---

34 John's sister Rosaleen and her husband Jimmy Craig.
35 John Seymour, *The Self-Sufficient Gardener: A Complete Guide to Growing and Preserving All Your Own Food* (London: Faber, 1978).

[*Early September 1978*]

Dear Matthew,
It was a real pleasure to have you all those few days in Aughaboniel.[36]

And always I'll be deeply grateful that you should read the novel so immediately and speak so directly and generously about it in Donegal. My own 'shuffling' responses was out of fear that Brian Friel might feel in shadow because of the same openness.[37]

Can a xerox copy be sent to me and a copy of the Gardening Book, which should be charged, by post or with Madeline, whichever you think easier?[38]

It's very hot and lush here, the greenness of the huge trees beginning to turn, incessant crickets, big rough tomatoes and squash, and sweet corn for sale on wooden planks by the roadside farms. And, of course, the people are amazing.

I have given the first classes. It'll be hard work but I think it'll be all right.
With love to Elizabeth and yourself – and the pair of boys.
John

Madeline McGahern
[*Colgate*]

20 September 1978

Dear Madeline,
Thanks for today's letter, dated the 11th. I'll have rung you before you get this.

36 Matthew and Elizabeth Evans had spent some of August in Donegal, renting a cottage from the artist Derek Hill. While in Ireland they visited the McGaherns for a few days, and the McGaherns visited them in Donegal.
37 On 19 September Evans replies: 'I didn't actually register your "shuffling" response over the novel. I just put it down to excessive modesty! As Brian clearly has such a high opinion of you I think he was very pleased that I liked the book.'
38 See letter to Madeline of 5 September 1978.

Seldes described the novel as 'a fine work' and sent the check $6,750.[39] I haven't heard from McCullough yet. I had a waffling letter from McHugh.[40] £24 tax for paperbacking of <u>Wine Breath</u>, German offer of same. Golden wrote from Notre Dame.[41] <u>Wells</u> rang up via <u>Ploughshares</u> and I go there the 28th for $200.[42]

Mostly I see the Albrechts, who are fine company, and they look forward very much to seeing you. I have their tv but except the news not much I find to look at.

Outside I've been to the Berlinds once (a neutral evening. He's aggressive now and more a fool than ever, with a grey beard). To Kistlers (a ghastly evening).[43] To the Joys (the usual). It's easier and I drink hardly at all. The work is much the same and hard enough.

Wil lost his pilot's licence temporarily because of his state of health – fat, alcohol, blood pressure. He has to go for regular check-ups.

I wish I could have seen Scuts come up the avenue.[44]

I was at dinner next door. Very civilized and the table separate at working. Very French bourgeois. Decent and probably very usual.

They seem to know Leyris over a long time and publish him at the University Press. They live in Versailles.[45] Blackmore is their contact here.[46]

The first maples have started to turn red, the weather hot and wet and miserable.

---

39 The reaction of the American agent Tim Seldes to what was becoming *The Pornographer*.

40 Roger McHugh, the UCD academic and friend of McGahern's.

41 McGahern was looking for opportunities to raise some money via public readings and was most likely put in touch with Notre Dame by Roger McHugh at UCD.

42 DeWitt Henry at *Ploughshares* had put McGahern in touch with Professor Bruce Bennett at Wells College where McGahern had agreed to do a reading. Wells is located on the eastern shore of Cayuga Lake in central New York State, about fifty miles south-west of Syracuse.

43 Professor Jonathan Kistler – a member of the English faculty at Colgate – and his wife Patricia.

44 A much-loved Manx cat of the McGaherns'.

45 Michel Gresset was the visiting French academic. Gresset (1936–2005) was Professor of American Literature at the Institut d'Anglais Charles V of Université Denis Diderot (Paris VII), specialising particularly in the work of William Faulkner. For a time he was a consultant for Mercure de France, the company that published McGahern's *Lignes de Fond* in 1971.

46 Robert L. 'Bob' Blackmore, Professor of English at Colgate and co-founder of Colgate University Press, which specialised in publishing reprints of, and work on, John Cowper Powys and his family.

I hope it's not too hard in Paris, that the flat will not be too difficult.
                              And with all my love
                              John

I wrote Matthew Re Gardening Book for Janette. Leaving it up to him whether to send it with you or post it.

                              Madeline McGahern

                                  [*Colgate*]

24 September 1978

Dear Madeline,
There's no news other than I'm looking forward to seeing you soon.
   Parts of the trees are turning, a bright red, rust and raspberry.
I've got several lectures ahead of the class by this – in reading – and it's easier now.
   I'm having dinner tonight with the Albrechts. They are looking forward to seeing you. I've seen the Kistlers AGAIN – at Slater's last night – and they are barbarous.[47] I find the same seeping loneliness here that has always puzzled me. It grows clear that it has something got to do with the denial here of solitude, silence, all failure – the whooping crowd. And so it seeps and rots from everywhere.
   D. Reading rang up a week ago, and spoke for 40 minutes.[48] Janey left a bag of crab apples outside the door. I haven't seen them. Both now – I now as well as they – are plainly putting off meeting. Apparently he's got much worse. I passed the house yesterday, walking to Slaters for dinner, and I heard her call to Pablo, who was barking; but I didn't look back.
                              With all my love
                              John

47 Professor Joseph Locke Slater (1916–2001) was a graduate of Colgate University who returned to his alma mater to head its Department of English. He retired from its faculty in 1986 as Edgar W. B. Fairchild Professor of American Literature. Slater was a distinguished scholar of the work of Ralph Waldo Emerson and editor of *The Correspondence of Emerson and Carlyle* (New York: Columbia University Press, 1964); he was married for sixty-two years to Vivien Harvey Slater, pianist-in-residence at Colgate. Slater and his work were admired by McGahern.
48 Douglas Reading.

3 October 1978

Dear Charles,

I think the advance is very generous. And I am grateful and hope it repays it. Tell Rosemary please I'm sorry I overlooked it and that I want to thank her for the kindness of her letters.

Outside coming here, and starting to teach, I was putting it off in the hope of finding a title. I've never had so much trouble. I must have gone through 500 titles.

How do these look?

   1. This isn't Grenoble[49]

   2. Good People

   3. Nothing But the Usual

If you can think of anything I'll be only too grateful. The first, Grenoble, is Maloney's reply to 'How were the Blooms?'

I've always regretted not having gone to Greece in '65. It sounds wonderful.

I took the liberty of giving Matthew's name to the bookshop manager. I read here on November 7th and none of my books are in print in the U.S. And he was confused, ordering from England.

     All my love

     John

49 Refers to a moment in the book when Maloney scolds the unnamed pornographer for having Stendhalian delusions. In an internal Faber memo, Monteith rejects this title as 'far too esoteric' and is unconvinced by the other two suggestions.

6 October 1978

Dear DeWitt,
Thank you for sending me the Magazine all this time, and for introducing me to Bruce Bennett.[50] I spoke for him at Wells last week.

I'll be here for the whole of the year and I'm looking forward very much to seeing you.

I finished the novel in late August, just before getting here, but I haven't been able to find a right title for it yet. Faber brought out Getting Through in June. They'll do the novel in the Autumn of '79. Harper-Row will bring out both books here but there are no dates.

How does your own work?

And how are you?

Should you see Richard Yates, I'd be grateful if you'd remember me to him.[51]

> And to Ellen and Peter O'Malley
> With all good wishes
> John

[*Autumn 1978*]

Dear Fran,
Thank you for the photos and the kind letter. The photos seem all good to me, the subject less so. Do you want them returned?

I'm hoping to go into New York for a couple of days after classes end on the 5th December. It'd be nice if we could meet then.

---

50 Bennett b. 1940, Harvard-educated poet and academic, was involved in the foundation of *Ploughshares*.
51 McGahern had been introduced to Yates in Boston via the *Ploughshares* circle. See letter to DeWitt Henry of 27 September 1977.

Do you think is <u>The Pornographer</u> any good for a title? I've never had so much trouble with a title. Do you have any ideas?

> With good wishes
> John

James Swift
[*Madeline McGahern*]

Colgate

21 November 1978

Dear Jimmy,

I was very glad to get your letter. They sent it on from Foxfield. It'd be a pleasure to meet soon again, anywhere; but I'll be here until the end of May. Madeline will probably go home in April.

Many times I thought to write in the hope we could meet, and then would start to think in that useless way that it might be an imposition. And of course it slid, and grew more difficult.

Did you ever think of coming to the States? With the weakened dollar and the airfares war it is very inexpensive now.

Madeline asks to be remembered to you with affection. And please remember me to your mother and Tony.

Do you have any news?

> Maybe you'll drop me a note before too long.
> With all good wishes,
> John

28 November 1978

Dear Joe,
I've ordered the Hemingway/Fitzgerald book for you. Shall I send it or hold it or bring it?

I'm glad you got such a good handshake.[52] It seems a lot of cash to me but all things are relative.

The novel will come out next autumn.

Probably the easiest is to go down and find

> Peter Woods
> Arrody
> Foxfield
> Co. Leitrim

or write re. Alder saplings.[53]

Anyhow there'll all over the place, especially on the lake shore.

> Madeline sends her best wishes to Margaret and yourself as I do.
> A happy Christmas
> John

DeWitt Henry,
Ploughshares Papers

Colgate

6 December 1978

Dear DeWitt,
Thanks for the kind letter.[54] I hope all goes well with the novel's ending. And congratulations on Ruth Kathryn, and the Ploughshares grant.

52 Kennedy's departure from the *Sunday World*.
53 Kennedy had moved to rural Co. Meath and was tree planting on his land.
54 McGahern had sent Henry an MS of *The Pornographer* to read and then pass on to John Head. Henry wrote to him of the novel: 'It's an important book, beautifully articulating the edges of life choices I think most of us live and know and don't want to or can't admit easily.' Madeline McGahern Papers.

I put the December issue on the spring course, with <u>Revolutionary Road</u> – it'll go through the bookshop.

There's a very young Irish writer, Neil Jordan. Would you like me to ask him to offer you work? I think his work has real promise.

We have an old beat-up car. Do you have a phone no. in case we take a flitter towards Boston?

With all good wishes
And a Happy Christmas
John

Faber

Colgate

14 December 1978

Dear Matthew,

We've been ½-expecting you these past few week-ends. Did plans change?

I saw Frances McCullough in New York this week. She plans to do <u>The Pornographer</u> this coming autumn, and the stories the following spring (1980).

Tim Seldes said he enjoyed meeting you. I liked him a great deal. He looked very tired. He never got the 3 copies of <u>Getting Through</u> or copies of the reviews. And the German translator tells me that registered parcels have been returned to her from New York or have gone astray there.

Can trade copies of Getting Through be sent to:

Mrs. Frances Kiernan	Mr Peter Prestcott
The New Yorker	81 Benedict Hill
25 West 43rd Street	New Canaan
New York N. Y. 10036	Conn (of Newsweek)

I hope it's not an imposition. They both asked for copies. I'll be very grateful.

Kiernan asked to see <u>The Porn.</u>, since she'd wanted work and I hadn't been sending any in. Of course they couldn't print it but she said she liked it so much that she was sorry to finish it. I was very glad because she speaks only her own mind when it comes to what she reads.

Thanks for the Kissy Dicky.[55] The note was great fun. I come on more M. stories here, all of them amazing, all of them in character. He must have no idea of this dossier that's in wide circulation. It's quite dispiriting.

55 'Kissy Dicky' was the nickname for Richard Murphy used between Evans and McGahern.

A Happy Christmas to Elizabeth and yourself, and the boys.

Write soon. Tell us when you expect to come.

I had a nice letter from William Miller saying he was away to the ricefields (Tokyo).[56]

Love

John

I'll be very grateful if you'll pass 297 (enclosure) to the Copy Editor.

<hr>

56 Miller was a key figure in publishing McGahern's works in paperback. After a successful career in London, in 1979 he moved to Tokyo and co-established the English Agency Japan to sell the translation rights of British books to Japanese publishers. McGahern retained affection for Miller and met him for drinks during his November 2005 visit to Tokyo. For more on Miller, see letter to Matthew Evans of 12 September 1973.

1979

14 January 1979

Dear Charles,

I am not surprised at Philip McDermott's request.[1] I saw his publicity person, a young girl, when I spoke in Trinity last year; and you are quite right. What they like is the paperbacks covers, especially the cover of The Leavetaking, a naked pair of clowns who look likely to get their death of cold.[2] I think, as well, they're confusing the 2 very different audiences, paper and hardback.

Leaving out personal preference, I think by choosing The Pornographer as title we have gone a great distance in Philip's direction, and – as well – limited our cover room. Here comes The Porno Man.

Only people who have read the book will see it as a true title. The initial reaction to it, I am sure, will be 'Ah-Ha'. It would be mine. Dress it in an appropriate cover and that would be that. It may well be banned. And that'd be no use to Philip. I'd think primarily of England. If it gets an English audience the Irish will follow.

But I have no objection to using stronger colours, the other side of the palette to grey. Or even picture and design. But because of the title I think we have to be extraordinarily careful.[3] I'd prefer to think of it as our book.

Did the sales of Getting Through get anywhere near 2000?

1 Founder of the Poolbeg Press with David Marcus in 1976 and prominent figure in the Dublin literary scene who, among other things, helped to promote Faber books in Ireland at this time.
2 *The Leavetaking* in Quartet paperback (1977) does, indeed, have a particularly ugly cover bearing a childlike drawing of an embracing nude couple with a seagull overhead.
3 Ultimately the Faber cover shows a Dublin street scene, the dome of Mary Immaculate, Refuge of Sinners Catholic church, Rathmines in the background, entirely devoid of human figures or indeed of any kind of titillation.

Do you think might <u>The Pornographers</u> not be a slightly better title, or leave it be? It's slightly less solemn.[4]

Has the copy editor any questions? There's just a very few things I want to add?[5]

> It's hard work here but I get well paid.
> With much love
> John

Faber

Colgate

14 January 1979

Dear Rosemary,

Many thanks for your note. Rosalie Swedlin rang the Department, and left an L.A. no. I rang her back. Got this automatic voice: 'The number you've just rung has been changed to an unpublished number.' If she gives this number around she could start feeling ignored.

Anyhow, I'm sure it wasn't important. I'll be delighted if she sells anything but I'll be even more surprised. And that's no comment at all on her abilities.[6]

Did you ever come across the 17th century ballad.

> Correct your maps: Newcastle is Peru.[7]
> > With all good wishes for the New Year
> > Love
> > John

4 Monteith replies in a letter of 26 January: 'I hesitated for a long time over your extremely interesting suggestion that we might vary the existing title slightly and call the book "The Pornographers"; and opinions here were very divided. In the end, however, I've come down – as have we all – in favour of sticking to "The Pornographer" in the singular. It's a bit more striking and, moreover, it's more accurate.'

5 Monteith's reply makes it clear that no more changes are possible.

6 It is not known which of McGahern's works this Los Angeles film producer was interested in discussing, though there is evidence of interest in *The Pornographer* later in 1979 and into 1980.

7 Goad had been on holiday in Peru. 'England's a perfect World; has Indies too. Correct your Maps; Newcastle is Peru' goes a 1653 ballad imputing New World barbarism to north-east of England. The longtime Newcastle resident, poet Tony Harrison b. 1937, titled his 1969 collection *Newcastle Is Peru* (Newcastle upon Tyne: Eagle Press, 1969).

I hope you don't mind me enclosing this order.

John

Russell and Volkening Papers

Colgate

27 January 1979

Dear Tim,
Thank you for your letter of the 25th. That's fine with me.

Can I ask you about this?
When I first came here I had a friend in the History Department, a Texan, John Head. He has since gone to Boston University, where he is a Dean at one of the colleges.

When I visited him recently in Boston, he had started a book on Jesus, with 2 other people, one from the Dept. of Philosophy, the other from Theology, both at B.U.

Their aim: to bring Jesus up to date, in popular form, in the light of the most recent evidence.

Head wrote a book on the War of Independence, A Time to Rend. I can't speak of it as history but it was unusually well written.[8]

Do you think it's a wild goose effort?

Would it interest you at all?[9]

With all good wishes

John

8 John Head, *A Time to Rend: An Essay on the Decision for American Independence* (Madison: State Historical Society of Wisconsin, 1968). See letter to Matthew Evans [late April–early May 1969].
9 In a letter of 2 February Seldes asks McGahern to send on whatever exists of the book on Jesus.

James Swift
[*Madeline McGahern*]

Colgate

28 January 1979[10]

Dear Jimmy,

Thank you for your letter. Europe seems to have got the sort of weather this part of the State expects every year, and gets. There's over 4 ft of snow now, and that's low.

I am, indeed, grateful for your advice. I know it must be unpleasant. If I can impose this one thing more, do you have any idea of the boy's position, as such: does he feel he should have a father like others, rights to assert, see the actuality or whatever?[11]

There was no formal request previously. This woman – a Mrs Capon – had been told the story by Joan, and approached me herself.[12] From what she said, I understand that Joan was pushing for the boy's recognition, at that time, 8 years or so ago. When Joan elected to keep the child, as opposed to having it adopted, I told her that this situation was likely to arise. And when it did that I would be unavailable. It was considered part of my brutality at the time.

From my point of view, for what it's worth now, there is just the chance of a concessionary lie to the boy OR wait in the knowledge that anybody can call on any of us at any time, with the usual hazardous consequences. As you say, there is some time still to think it out. Either way it will have to be faced.

10 Mistakenly dated 1978 by McGahern.
11 Joan Kelly and McGahern had a brief love affair in 1962, with Joan becoming pregnant and giving birth in England to a son, Joseph. At the time of the affair she was involved in writing the 'Darina' gossip column for the *Irish Press* and subsequently went on to work as an information officer with the Royal Navy. See 'Man's world virtuoso', *Irish Press* (10 October 1969), 11. A fictionalised version of the affair forms a central plotline in *The Pornographer*. At the time of the writing of this letter, Jimmy Swift was acting as a go-between.
12 Edith Capon, Susanna's mother, hosted a party in her Highgate flat c. 1972 at which she confronted McGahern with the information about his son and what she saw as the unfair abandonment of mother and child. Mrs Capon had been told the story by a neighbour who had grown friendly with the boy's mother, Joan Kelly.

I won't get out of here much before the end of May, it depends on exams. Madeline goes back in late April. When she's passing through Dublin maybe you'd meet for a drink.

And I'm sorry you've had all this trouble.

With all good wishes,

John

Faber

Colgate

[February 1979][13]

Dear Charles,

I am sorry. As usual, it was later than I thought.

Can this dedication be added:

To

Wil Albrecht

In haste

Will write soon

The Pornographer is the better title. It was a sort of backsliding on my part.

Love

John

Faber

Colgate

[February 1979]

Dear Charles,

Change it if you can in the catalogue.[14]

---

13 Marked 'acknowledged', 12 February 1978, but has to be 1979 given the context.
14 Refers to the blurb for *The Pornographer*. The enclosure reads: 'Everywhere in this rich novel is the drama of opposites: the country and the city, scurrility and decency, fear and longing, love and loathing. Above all, sex and death are never far from one another. The narrator, a writer of pornographic fiction, creates an ideal world of sex through his two stock athletes, Colonel Grimshaw and Mavis Carmichael, while he bungles every phase of his entanglement with an older woman who has the

Writing in haste, on my way to Montreal.[15] Will send following letter, in a day or so. I thought the blurb too judging. That the reader should be let make up his own mind about the characters.

Thanks for the letter and the Poet's book.

Love
John

Faber

Colgate

2 March 1979

Dear Charles,

I hope you didn't mind the rewrite. It was done very quickly, and I'll be glad to add or take out, if you don't find it satisfactory – or to try again.

Thanks for the Poet's opus. I'd thank him for the pointed inscription, except for the postal strike. It is fine work.[16]

I was in Montreal, at McGill. The Faculty Club is all wood and solid splendour, an old fur trader's mansion.[17] I never saw so many restaurants. There are many lovely parts in the old city, the mountain and the great frozen waterway. It was nice to see the French names sans the French.

I took the liberty of giving your name to a nice man from here, a George Hudson, who was interested in inviting you to speak, knowing you could refuse. They liked your speech very much, the once before – though I remember you seemed not to like it.

I feel tired. I seem to do little but prepare classes, read papers, teach. Madeline leaves the 19th April. I should get away sometime round 23rd May.

---

misfortune to fall in love with him. His insensitivity to this love is in direct contrast to the tenderness and care he brings to his attempts to make his aunt's slow dying in the hospital tolerable. Over this broken world, Maloney, failed poet and comic king of the pornographers, comes gradually to preside. Sometimes appallingly funny, more often deeply moving, this is the work of a writer whose power has become more assured and authoritative with each book.'

15 To read at McGill University.

16 Richard Murphy's *Selected Poems* was published by Faber in 1979.

17 McGahern was hosted by Professor Joseph Ronsley, who was keen to support the teaching of Irish literature in Canada. Ronsley was from Chicago and went to Harvard where he studied for a PhD on Yeats under Richard Ellmann. On this visit to Montreal, McGahern met Denis Sampson for the first time. Sampson went on to become one of McGahern's most important critics, publishing widely on the work.

Please forgive another enclosure.

Madeline sends her love, and with my love
John

DeWitt Henry,
Ploughshares Papers

Colgate

12 March 1979

Dear DeWitt,

I am deeply grateful, – and dismayed I put you to so much trouble. What you said I did is what I tried to do. For a few moments your words gave me back the first impulse. A writer can't expect anything, never certainly that luck and generosity. I feel ½ my luck is spent already. I am deeply grateful.[18]

I taught Ploughshares and Rev. Road, which I admired even more than on first reading, and yet something nags, maybe that old unfairness: 'it is so good it should be better'. And that's not right. I tried to stay outside on Ploughshares, just told some of the history of magazines, their function, and let them make up their own minds about the stories. For what it's worth, Neugboren was their favourite.[19] Rev. Road upset some of them, which was fine.

I've read little Moore but enough to admire his skill and energy, enough – too – to tell me I'd find no sustenance, which is for me a poor comment on myself than anything else. But I respect him and wish him well.[20]

I'll be in Ireland by the 26th May, I hope. I hope to leave here the 19th. Before then, maybe I'll steal into Boston, and we can have a drink or walk together.

With all good wishes
John

18 Henry had written to McGahern in admiring terms about *The Pornographer*.
19 Jay Neugeboren b. 1938 in Brooklyn, New York is an American novelist, essayist and short story writer.
20 Brian Moore (1921–99), Irish novelist admired by DeWitt Henry.

Denis Sampson

Colgate

14 March 1979

Dear Denis,[21]

Thanks for the typescript.

   And I was deeply moved that you should read the novel so carefully and so generously.[22]

   It was mostly what I tried to do, what I ½-hoped for.

AUGHABONIEL

FOXFIELD

CO. LEITRIM is the Irish address. I'll be there from the end of May. There's no phone.

   If you are in Ireland in the summer, I'll be glad to see you there.

I am tired, my head wooden with students' papers. I'll be glad to be away.

> Please remember me to your wife
> And with all good wishes
> Sincerely
> John McGahern

21 Denis Sampson b. 1948 on a farm abutting the River Shannon in Whitegate, Co. Clare. He was educated at UCD (BA and MA) 1965–70, subsequently taking his PhD at McGill University, Montreal. Sampson was an important early champion of McGahern's work within the academy, spending most of his academic career at Vanier College, Montreal. He is author of the first monograph on McGahern's oeuvre, *Outstaring Nature's Eye: The Fiction of John McGahern* (Washington DC: The Catholic University of America Press, 1993), and the later short study of McGahern's genesis as a writer, *Young John McGahern: Becoming a Novelist* (Oxford: Oxford University Press, 2011).

22 Sampson had interviewed McGahern at the McGill reading – much of that interview was subsequently published in the *Canadian Journal of Irish Studies*. Before McGahern left Montreal he asked Sampson to read a typescript of *The Pornographer*. Sampson subsequently visited Foxfield in the summer of 1979 at McGahern's invitation.

21 March 1979

Dear Matthew,
Thanks for writing, and for sending out the copies.[23]
    We didn't know what had happened in December. We thought you mightn't have got to the States at all.
    I hadn't heard about Quartet.[24] I suppose that means that Panther etc. turned it down. William Miller wrote me that he was leaving for Japan.[25]
    We didn't see Seamus but he'll [be] here on the 11th of next month. He's busy and making lots of money. He's planning to spend the summer in Boston.
    Madeline goes home on the 19th – she'll fly direct to Paris – and she should be in London for a day or two a week after that.
    I'll get away about May 20–22nd.
        I'm just horribly tired.
                With love to Elizabeth and the boys
                Love
                John

2 April 1979

Dear Charles,
I hope they'll delay the tv programme until I get home. I'm sure it'll be fine. And it must be fun to give Castlederg a fright after those years in useless Oxford and wicked London.[26]

---

23 Evans had replied to McGahern's letter of 14 December 1978 on 13 March 1979 saying, among other things, that copies of *Getting Through* had been sent to Frances Kiernan and Peter Prescott, as requested.
24 Evans had written in his letter of 13 March that Faber had made an arrangement for *The Pornographer* to be published in paperback by Quartet.
25 On Miller, see letter to Matthew Evans of 14 December 1978.
26 Monteith had written to McGahern on 22 March of his involvement with a BBC television programme: 'I am I fear appearing on T.V. but, happily, since the

Thanks for asking the production people to send Fran McCullough a camera copy of The Pornographer. She wants, as well, copies of the Reviews of Getting Through. I hope John Bodley won't mind too much. I'll be very grateful.

I enclose the title page and letter for G. W. Taylor. Actually it was a copy of mine – the defective copy.[27]

It'll be marvellous to see you again. Will you be in London towards the end of May?

Love
John

Frances Kiernan Papers
Colgate

28 April 1979

Dear Frances,
Thank you for the kind note about Getting Through.

It was a great pleasure for me to be able to send them. It would be that just in meeting you and beyond that there is my gratitude for all the care you showed the work.

I've never taught for a full year before, and I am so tired I hear my life echoing most of the time. It is strange, depressing and – worst of all – ½ pleasurable.

I worked on 2 stories, but have put them aside. There is one of them I like. It's close to the material of Sierra Leone.[28] I'll finish it over the summer. I'll go to Ireland the week of the 21st May, and I can be in New York then for a couple of days. Is there any hope of seeing you?

I hope you are well and happy.
Yours
John

---

programme is only going out on B.B.C. Northern Ireland, it won't be seen by any of my friends over here! I flew over to Belfast one Sunday morning, recorded it and flew straight back to London the same evening, but it won't I gather, be televised until May, June or even early July. It is in the series called, somewhat pompously, Lifetimes. Ah well. Yet another reminder that the shades are gathering.'

27 McGahern had come across a defective copy of Getting Through in Colgate and worried in case it was one of a batch. It proved to be a one-off.

28 Probably what becomes 'Parachutes'.

Frances McCullough Papers

Colgate

13 May 1979

Dear Fran,

Thanks for the kind letter. The jacket is lovely.[29] Our letters crossed.

I'll be grading papers all this week.

I hope to leave here Friday evening and I have to speak in Albany at 2p.m. Saturday 19th.

I could come down to you that evening or on Sunday morning, whichever would suit you best.

But don't let me cause you any trouble.

I'm hoping to head for Ireland around the middle of the week. Madeline went home 4 weeks or so ago, so I'm on my own. If I don't hear from you I'll call during the week.

With all good wishes,
John

Frances Kiernan Papers

Foxfield

11 July 1979

Dear Frances,

The postal strike is over at last, after 19 sweet weeks.

I hope you like the story. It turned out different than I'd planned.[30]

The poor Pornographer has already run into gunsmoke here. The Irish Independent, the popular daily, described me as a 'fine writer who must have temporarily taken leave of his senses' and that it's 'blue not black' (comedy).[31]

---

29 The jacket of the Harper & Row edition of *The Pornographer* is plain and handsome, bearing just the title of the novel in cursive script and the legend 'A Novel by John McGahern' over a teal background with orange trim.

30 The story that becomes 'Gold Watch'.

31 *The Pornographer* got slated by Peter Donnelly in the *Irish Independent* of 13 October. While admitting that McGahern can only be equalled by William Trevor in the contemporary Irish canon, McGahern's prose is compared unfavourably with Nashville country and western mawkishness – the whole review has a rather

They shouldn't have reviewed it till October. It's a sort of nuisance as everybody reads the paper round here and are On The Alert.[32]

Thanks for the lovely few hours in New York. I hope August is not too hard. Write and tell me any news, and I'll write.

With love
John

James Swift
[*Madeline McGahern*]

Foxfield

15 July 1979

Dear Jimmy,

Madeline wonders if you'd like to come down to lunch some day. Almost any day is good for us; and if by any chance it should be difficult we'd ring you back the day we got word. We can meet you at Dromod, if it's easier to come by train.

I'll be in London this autumn, and I can go down to Portsmouth to see the boy then. But another time or place is all right, if that turns out not suitable for him or Joan.[33]

I was horribly tired after America, and it seemed to take longer to recover. I was in Dublin for a tv business but it was too hurried and I just came back the same evening.

I'll be in Dublin before very long, but it'd be nice to see you here before then.

Madeline sends her best wishes – and thanks you for your kindness in Dublin.

With all good wishes
John

---

adolescent, prurient quality. None of this negativity prevented the book going to number one in the Irish hardback charts two weeks later.

32 'On the Alert' was a phrase much mocked by John – it came from a Mohill bartender.

33 Joan Kelly was working for the Royal Navy in Portsmouth.

Joe Kennedy

Foxfield

28 July 1979

Dear Joe,

Thanks for the letter and I'll offer the cheque to Woods as soon as I see him.[34]

Read the book. The character alluded to isn't a caricature of anybody.[35] Very little of him exists in 'real life'. Of the characters I have drawn, with the possible exception of Elizabeth Reegan, he is the person I like best.

We'll be here all of the summer, except for a couple of days in early August, around the 6th. The Muscadet is gone but you'll be welcome with or without sea trout, as you always were.

I'm sorry you didn't like the interview. If it was poor it was no fault of Mary Holland's.[36]

Madeline sends her good wishes
John

34 In payment for alder saplings.

35 Kennedy had asked McGahern if the character of Maloney, the eccentric editor in *The Pornographer*, was based on him. The similarities between fact and fiction led to a temporary cooling of relations between the two.

36 McGahern had done a television interview with the prominent journalist Mary Holland (1935–2004) for the RTÉ programme *States of Mind*, broadcast on 13 July.

Susanne Dumbleton

[*Foxfield*]

16 August 1979

Dear Bill,[37]
Thank you for your very kind letter, and for Sue's and your kindness to me
in Albany.[38]

My only regret was that it fell while I was rushing between places. And I
am sorry for all that rush and haste on my part.

It'll be a pleasure to see you here in Foxfield or in the States and, either
place, it will be not too far away.[39]

Please remember me to all at that lovely morning lunch, and especially to
Bill Kennedy.[40]

>With good wishes to Sue and You
>Sincerely
>John

37 William 'Bill' Dumbleton (1927–2016), then Professor of English, University at
Albany, New York. Born in Troy, New York, Dumbleton earned a BA and MA in
English at the University at Albany; a PhD in English Literature at the University of
Pennsylvania; and an additional MA in Irish Literature at UCD (1970–1). He was
Professor of English at the University at Albany for more than forty years (1953–94),
during which he taught English and Irish Literature. His publications include *Ireland:
Life and Land in Literature* (Albany: State University of New York Press, 1984) and
James Cousins (Boston: Twayne, 1980). He was married to Susanne 'Sue' Murphy
Dumbleton.
38 By 1979 Bill Dumbleton was teaching *Getting Through* at Albany in a course on
the Irish Short Story, and taped McGahern reading 'All Sorts of Impossible Things'.
Also in that year, Dumbleton gave a series of lectures sponsored by the Capital
District Humanities Project in Albany, which was subsequently turned into the book
Ireland: Life and Land in Literature, in which the final chapter is titled 'Growing Up
in Ireland: Joyce and McGahern'. In it Dumbleton compares *A Portrait of the Artist
as a Young Man* with *The Dark*. The chapter's final sentence is: 'McGahern's strength
arises out of his ultimate theme, that while perhaps not lonely, everyone is alone in
the world, in his own world, in solitude. To grow up in Ireland is to grow up into this
isolation and solitude.'
39 The Dumbletons visited Foxfield at least twice.
40 William 'Bill' Kennedy b. 1928 was born and raised in Albany, New York to
an Irish-American family. Kennedy has had a distinguished career as a writer and
journalist and won the 1984 Pulitzer Prize for his novel *Ironweed* (1983). Many of
his novels feature the interactions of members of the fictional Irish-American Phelan

23 August 1979

Dear Charles,

I enclose the letter as a curiosity. It's not untypical of Dublin, I sent the questions back. Some of them were peaches, i.e. 'are you cashing in on the new wave of sexuality?' He is the literary editor of the Indo and has already attacked The Pornographer (in his book news), so it's nicely two faced. I don't remember ever meeting him.

I was afraid – when I write you – that they'd take juicy bits out of context.

I have no objection to excerpts, but only one that'd make sense. As it'd be difficult, it'd take a hefty fee to justify it, and maybe not even then.

Ordinarily we'd love to go to Seamus' reading, but because of The Pornographer coming out at the same time, and my own unease in Dublin, I'll probably stay away. But I'll be wishing the evening and Field Work a long life.[41]

I thought you were fine on tv, the chum story as always especially splendid, and I have to thank you for the kind mention of myself in the roll call.[42]

Madeline sends her love. She goes to Paris next week for two weeks or so.

With my love

John

---

family in Albany. Kennedy's works include *The Ink Truck* (New York: Dial Press, 1969), *Legs* (New York: Coward, McCann & Geoghegan, 1975), *Billy Phelan's Greatest Game* (New York: Viking Press, 1978), *Roscoe* (New York: Viking Press, 2002) and *Changó's Beads and Two-Tone Shoes* (New York: Viking Press, 2011). Kennedy founded the New York State Writers' Institute at the University at Albany in 1983 where he invited McGahern – to whose work he had been introduced by Bill Dumbleton – to be a guest speaker.

41 Seamus Heaney's Dublin launch of *Field Work*.

42 On 31 August Monteith writes to McGahern apologising for not speaking about *The Pornographer* on television as he got cut off before he could get to the final book in his list of three to look forward to. The first two were Seamus Heaney's *Field Work* and William Golding's *Darkness Visible* (London: Faber, 1979).

3 September 1979

Dear Tim,
I sent the story <u>Gold Watch</u> to Frances Kiernan at the <u>New Yorker</u>.[43]
My own feeling is that they're unlikely to take it but there's never any real knowing.
I've asked her to send it to you, for passing on to Fran McCullough.
If they don't take it, and you can place it elsewhere, naturally I'll be grateful and glad.
Do you think would any paper or magazine be interested in an Insider's view of the Pope's visit to this island at the end of this month? It sort of interests me in the sense of the long history and the sudden disintegration it marks.[44]

With all good wishes
John

James Swift
[Madeline McGahern]
Foxfield

26 September 1979

Dear Jimmy,
I thought I'd have to go to London before the book came out, which is the 15th October; but now it turns out that I don't have to go till after publication, around the end of October, the 27th.

---

43 'Gold Watch' was initially rejected by the *New Yorker* and subsequently published after revision.
44 Pope John Paul II (1920–2005) visited Ireland from Saturday 29 September to Monday 1 October 1979, the first trip to Ireland by a pope. Over 2.5 million people attended events in Dublin, Drogheda, Clonmacnoise, Galway, Knock, Limerick and Maynooth. In a reply of 20 September, Seldes suggests that McGahern's best bet for such an article is the *New Yorker*. No such article was ever published.

That's when it would suit me best to go down to Portsmouth, but it's no real hardship to go earlier, if you suspect expectations of an earlier visit have been aroused for any reason.[45] I could go over specially around the 6th.

Is there any hope of you coming down before too long?

Madeline told me how much pleasure it was to see you on the way to Paris.

With good wishes,
John

Faber

Foxfield

1 October 1979

Dear Charles,

It'd be a pleasure to see you here. The trains from Dublin to here leave Dublin (Amiens Street) 9.00 13.55 18.25.

It's 2 hours to Dromod, where I can meet you.

There's a spare room.

Also we can leave you to Cavan or to Enniskillen, where there's a choice of buses to Belfast. Cavan 12.15–Belfast 14.55. Cavan 13.15–Belfast 15.42.

A RTE crew did a film for Folio here last week, which should please Philip McDermott. It's a real ordeal though, as you know.

I read in Belfast on the 25th, Derry on the 12th. I'm sort of restless. I have much that I want to write but I can't settle to it. I dread these publication times.

The New Yorker bought the work I finished over the summer. It's the only work I've managed to finish since The Pornographer.[46]

Madeline sends her love,
And as always
John

---

45 To visit Joan and Joseph Kelly.
46 'Gold Watch'.

Madeline McGahern

23 Forest Drive West

1 November 1979

Dear Madeline,

I got the plane over, and I'm booked back round 2pm Dublin on the 14th. I'll just wait at the Airport till you have lunch with Margaret finished.[47]

I saw Tom and Claire Davey last night. I'm booked for long dental sessions with Tom on the 5th and again on the 13th. Tom says you can arrange any 2 weeks to suit yourself.

I go down to Portsmouth on the Saturday morning for the day.[48]

I see Charles for lunch today. Jimmy had hurt his back, but I met Tony, who left me at the Airport.[49]

I left in the suede coat. It was 11.50. They are a little afraid of the mildew. I'll get it out on the 12th. I'm not certain if you want me to leave it at 23 or bring it home.

I'll write again if I have any news. I'll probably come back from France Sunday 11th.

With all my love
John

Frances Kiernan Papers

[*Paris*]

10 November 1979

Dear Frances,

It seems a wonderful editing job to me and I am very grateful.

Anything I left alone or put OK to I agree with. The last paragraph should go but I'd like – if possible – to keep its last sentence, slightly changed now.[50]

---

47 Margaret McGahern, John's sister, who lived in Dublin.
48 To meet his son, Joseph Kelly, and the boy's mother, Joan Kelly. See letter to Jimmy Swift of 18 November 1979.
49 Tony Swift was Jimmy Swift's younger brother, and the first of the family John befriended in Dublin in the late 1950s.
50 Refers to 'Gold Watch', which was first published in the *New Yorker* (17 March 1980). The story also appeared in the US edition of *Getting Through* published by

I came here to give a lecture, an excuse to see Paris again.

It is beautiful, in clear light.

The story, it was forwarded here, but it took 9 days to get to Ireland. I'm not worried about the English publication. They can do without it.

With love
John

James Swift
[Madeline McGahern]
Foxfield

18 November 1979

Dear Jimmy,

I hope you are able to be about again.

I spent most of a day with Joan and Joseph Kelly in Portsmouth. They were very hospitable and kind and I think the day may have went as well as it could have. I found Joan as beautiful and as impossible as before. The boy was very nervous, which wasn't surprising, but I suspect he may be that way by temperament as well.

They both spoke extraordinarily well of you, with affection as well as gratitude.

I asked my sister about the prostate. She has worked for years in a hospital theatre.

She told me that there is a new technique for the operation, that enables men in most cases to avoid surgery, is painful for hardly ever more than 24 hours.

The danger of not having it done, outside the continuing discomfort, is that it can turn malignant.

Would you like to come down some day? It'd be a great pleasure for Madeline as well as for me.

Harper & Row in 1980 and the British edition of *High Ground* published by Faber in 1985. Kiernan had written to McGahern with the proofs on 24 October: 'With regard to my editing you are free as always to select what you care for and to discard the rest, always bearing in mind that at some later date Mr. Shawn will be raising those old questions of just what it is you mean and our proofreaders will be insisting on complete sentences, as well as straightforward attributions for speech.' Madeline McGahern Papers. William Shawn (1907–92) was a legendary editor at the magazine from 1952 until 1987.

I'll be at home at the time except for weekends in Galway and the week of 3–8 December.

Otherwise we must meet in Dublin before Christmas.

With best regards to your mother
Sincerely
John

Michael McLaverty Archive

Foxfield

17 December 1979

Dear Michael,

I was very sorry not to have met you at the affair at Queens, even though it would have been a poor way to meet after all these years.

I had always thought to call you the few times I've been in Belfast over the years, but then again would think you might prefer not to be bothered, and time itself makes it increasingly difficult.

What has been best of all over these years was to have been able to re-read your work, and to see how securely it stands against the same 'time'.

I'll be in the States until the end of May, at Colgate University, Hamilton, New York 13346.

Should you ever be near here in the summer, and would like to call, it would be a great pleasure to see you.

And a very happy Christmas and New Year to Mrs McLaverty and yourself.

Sincerely,
John McGahern

18 December 1979[51]

Dear Frances,

I'll be at the above on January 2nd, not long after the proofs, which I'm posting today.

I am very grateful for the check and proofs. I knew in Paris that it was marvellous editing, and my only objection is the 'spray' at the end. Keep 'in the water' if it's necessary for explanation but I'd prefer it to be done without.[52]

I'm hoping and looking forward to seeing you soon.

A Happy Christmas and New Year
John

On one of the printer's sheets for The Pornographer there was a space for comment. It contained the one word: FOUL.

23 December 1979

Dear Anne & Brian,

Thanks for the kind notes and thanks especially for coming to Galway.

Writing cannot be taught, was how the course began. To have that reaffirmed at the end may even have been useful. I didn't mind at all.[53]

---

51 In fact, this letter was composed in Foxfield, but McGahern is giving Kiernan the address at which he can be reached in the New Year.

52 Refers to 'Gold Watch'.

53 The National Writers' Workshop at UCG that McGahern directed in autumn 1979. Among those writers to speak were Nuala O'Faolain, Seamus Deane, Paul Muldoon and Frank McGuinness. A young Paula Meehan was one of eleven students to attend and writes an interesting account of the experience in 'Inside McGahern's Workshop', *John McGahern: Authority and Vision*, eds. Željka Doljanin and Máire Doyle (Manchester: Manchester University Press, 2017), 180–90.

I AM sorry for missing you in the morning. We just weren't able to get up. Which was a sort of punishment for having such a good time, Blackbushing it away in the corner, and it was more out of pure relief that the whole course was over than at the fine tensions throughout.[54]

We were in Enniskillen on Friday. William Blake's was even more lovely than ever, mistletoe and balloons and holly scattered carefully among the barrels and pewter. I hope we'll risk it in the early summer.

And thanks for the books, I've been already savouring the stories, and have reread the Foundry House. I thought all the lights in the house should dim.[55]

Madeline has cut her foot fairly badly with a bottle of Guinness, which shows the grave danger of taking a single bottle of stout for 'cooking purposes'.[56]

It'll be nice if a visit invalidated this note.

If not, I wish all the Friels a Happy New Year, and that I'll see Anne as beautiful again in that same lovely dress.

With much love
John

54 The workshop ended with a dinner and late night drinking session at the bar of the Skeffington Arms Hotel in Eyre Square, Galway.

55 'The Foundry House' is often seen as Friel's finest published story. It recounts the decline of a well-to-do Ulster Catholic family in melancholic terms reminiscent of James Joyce's 'A Little Cloud'.

56 Madeline was making a porter cake and dropped a bottle on her foot, injuring it badly.

1980

[January 1980][1]

Dear Paul,

Thanks for coming to Galway, though getting that taxi was so beyond the call of duty to be close to flagellation.[2]

Peter O'Malley's address is

21 Sparns Street
Cambridge
Mass T. (617) 876 2053

I'll ring him, and tell him as I pass through Boston, and it can do no harm, even if you are acting through Seamus.[3]

Madeline has written out information about Oscar. If you need anything else, please write.

A good hotel very close is

HOTEL RECAMIER
Place St. Sulpice
Paris 6

He is fairly deaf, but speaks clearly, in both English and French. He can lip read. And you can write out complicated questions for him.[4]

---

1 The Colgate address is handwritten – this letter may have been sent from Foxfield.
2 Muldoon had agreed to give a reading in Galway as part of the UCG writers' workshop being run by McGahern. He got sidetracked by the poet and academic Brendan Kennelly and the two men spent longer than intended in O'Neill's public house on Dublin's Suffolk Street, leading Muldoon to miss his train. Feeling guilty about the whole thing, he took a taxi from Dublin to Galway at his own expense.
3 Peter O'Malley was founding editor of the Boston-based literary magazine *Ploughshares* and part owner of the Plough and Stars pub, Cambridge, Massachusetts.
4 Oscar Nitschke (1900–91) was the German-born, Swiss-raised architect father of Kika, Madeline's stepmother. He is best known for the part he played in designing the United Nations Headquarters in New York and was on good terms with many of the

I was talking to Friel and the mischievous information re The Pornographer was blamed on our old stand-by 'Mr Thought'.[5]

I am looking forward very much to your new work. I thought some of the new poems you read were extraordinarily fine.

A very happy Christmas and New Year from Madeline as well as myself.

    Maybe we'll meet in the States!
                  Yours
                  John

Enclosed the small cheque from the English Society
                  John

Frances Kiernan Papers

Colgate

[*Early 1980*]

Dear Frances,

Everything seems all right. And I've agreed to almost everything. I think it should be 'time <u>that</u> does not have to run to any conclusion.'[6] 'Which' is awfully awkward on the tongue.[7]

And many thanks for all the work, especially the work sent to me in Paris. It was good to see how clear and true it was when I went through it a last time for Harper & Row.

               With all good wishes
               John

---

famous artists of his generation; he was particularly friendly with Alexander Calder (1898–1976).

5 McGahern was clearly irked by something he believed Brian Friel had said about *The Pornographer*, but it has not been possible to trace the lineaments of the story.

6 'That' is underlined four times in the letter.

7 Refers to the final words of 'Gold Watch'. When it was published in the *New Yorker* and in all subsequent publications of the story, it closes: 'time that did not have to run to any conclusion.'

2 January 1980

Dear Fran,

Many thanks for the good, funny letters, and for the kindness, all the kindnesses to the poor old PORNO MAN as well as to my dancing self, more dead than dancing after Galway.

I am writing 2 stories but they won't be ready for Getting Through. And I want to begin a novel. I'd like one more go at GOLD WATCH (a day). There's also a mistake in the Faber edition of Along the Edges that I'd like to correct.

I sent back the final N. Yorker proofs of GOLD WATCH yesterday. They are running it fairly soon.[8]

We'll fly straight to Hamilton. January is an easy month and I can come down to New York almost any time.

I'm looking forward very much to seeing you, and you ALL must come sometime this time to us in [*missing end*]

James Swift
[*Madeline McGahern*]

Colgate

10 January 1980

Dear Jimmy,

Madeline and I hope all goes well with you in the hospital.[9]

We watched the road for you the Friday after Christmas; but when 2 o'clock came, we knew the driving must have been too hazardous or you weren't well.

I'll be here until late May but Madeline goes home in early April.

We'd be glad if you'd tell us when you are well. And perhaps you'll enclose Joan Kelly's address. There's no urgency, it's just a small thing I promised to

---

8 There are a number of small, relatively insignificant differences between the *New Yorker* and *High Ground* versions of 'Gold Watch'.
9 Swift was having a prostate operation.

send, and it hasn't come out yet. In the rush I left all my addresses behind, and except for old addresses, I cannot trust memory.

> All our good wishes
> Sincerely
> John

Faber

Colgate

12 January 1980

Dear Charles,
I ran the writing course in Galway last autumn.

Very few of the people had talent, but there were one or two – just possibly.

Have Faber still the Introductions series? They might be worth looking at, if that is so.

There's no snow here, the first time in ½ a century, which is a disaster for the Winter Olympics.[10] All the graffiti mention Iran, and the newer cars are smaller.[11] Mostly I find it difficult to believe I'm here again.

Thanks for the lovely Christmas card and many happy returns.

> Madeline sends her love
> and with my love
> John

10 The 1980 Winter Olympics were held at Lake Placid in New York State from 13 to 24 February.

11 The US was in a period of recession and the major political controversy of the day was the Iran hostage crisis, a diplomatic standoff between Iran and the United States. Fifty-two American diplomats and citizens were held hostage in Iran for 444 days from 4 November 1979 to 20 January 1981.

22 January 1980

Dear DeWitt,
Thank you for the kindness of sending me <u>Ploughshares</u>. Heaney looks as if he's signed for the Pittsburgh Steelers.[12]
   Do you have any news?
I'm here 2 weeks now and will be here until the end of May.
   In that time, I am sure to get to Boston, and this time we must have a meal or drink together.

> I hope you are well
> Affectionately
> John

28 January 1980

Dear Frances,
It was so kind to write me.
   It was the first I heard of it, though there was a note from Tim Seldes in the same post, and Fran McCullough rang on Saturday. She is very fine.
   There's a row going on about <u>The Pornographer,</u> though I'm not very clear about it. It seems one of McCullough's main enemies was the head of the marketing division (it must be like a small country in there). And before the

---

12 The edition of *Ploughshares* being referred to here is vol. 5, no. 3 (1979), which has a rather bizarre, Bacon-esque monotype of Heaney on the cover by Michael Mazur and contains an interview with Heaney by James Randall as well as two Heaney poems, 'A Kite for Michael and Christopher' and 'Near Anahorish'. The Steelers were then the dominant team in the National Football League having won back-to-back Superbowls two days earlier, defeating the Los Angeles Rams at the Rose Bowl, Pasadena.

firing, there was a move to withdraw advertising from all her books. And the depressed Pornoman didn't even get a dollar.[13]

This should have killed it but not so and the sales have taken them by surprise, 550 sales for that one week in the week before last, and they sold 750 last week alone. That's without any advertising and Seldes is furious. It was very bad luck and I like Fran McCullough very much.

I am hoping to get down to New York before too long. It'd be a great pleasure to see you again.

Did Gold Watch come from Ireland? Is it possible for me to get a copy of the MSS from you? I don't like to trouble McCullough for it at this time.

With all good wishes
John

Faber
Colgate

30 January 1980

Dear Charles,

Thanks for both letters. We flew here New Year's Eve. January is an easy teaching month. The stint begins next week.

The people in Galway were all ages, selected from all over the country, and their work was mostly honourable and dull and sometimes just plain dull. There were 2 possible exceptions, a Colm Flynn, a young Cavan schoolteacher, certainly showing influence of Hughes and Seamus; and Annette Ferguson, a housewife, whose work was less technically sure, but more individual, and seemed to me to have some touch of genius. She was trained as a biochemist, and worked before her marriage in hospitals in Belfast. I'll ask them to send work to Robert McCrum.[14] I'll not encourage any great hopes of acceptance.

I am interested in the Anthology. There is a need for some standard work. And I feel it has to be a 2 volume work, beginning at Carleton with Beckett as probable watershed between the 2 books. A few years ago I did some work towards such an anthology, but inflation and indecision left it there. There is now just too much work for an anthology like Iremonger's. It would be just

13 Fran McCullough was fired by Harper & Row in January 1980 just as *The Pornographer* was due for publication.

14 Robert McCrum b. 1953, English writer and editor. McCrum served as editor-in-chief at Faber from 1980 to 1996.

another personal anthology. The Bodley Head are bringing out a one volume anthology next autumn.

I'll wait until I hear what you think of this and you may prefer to wait until we see one another in the summer.

My editor at Harper and Row, Fran McCullough, was fired last week. She really fought to have The Pornographer noticed. And that was without any advertising, because before she was fired they started to direct advertising away from her books. And so far a bare dollar hasn't been spent on the Porno Man.

Apparently it should be dead by now but last week alone it sold 750 copies and is 3 on the Washington Post bestsellers but that must soon come to a stop without an editor.

That's the third editor I've had here who has gone that way.
On that cheerful note I must sound like a private Alistair Cooke.[15]

> Remember me with affection to Seamus
> and with much love
> John

DeWitt Henry

Colgate

[*Late January 1980*]

Dear DeWitt,
Thanks for the kind letter and the fiction issue.[16] The McKenna evening sounds dreadful – a star of evening or hoots and squeaks?

I gave Grennan a story from Getting Through. He has to get S. H.'s approval.[17]

I'm not sure when it'll be released now. My editor got fired last week. Before they fired her they directed all advertising away from her books. So there wasn't a bare dollar spent on the old Porno Man. That should have

---

15 BBC correspondent in the US who presented a very popular weekly 'Letter from America' on BBC Radio 4.
16 The fiction issue McGahern mentions was vol. 5, no. 4 (Winter 1979), edited solo by DeWitt Henry.
17 Eamon Grennan b. 1941, the US-based Irish poet and academic, was helping Seamus Heaney edit the upcoming issue of *Ploughshares*, vol. 6, no. 1 (Spring 1980). The story McGahern submitted and Heaney included was 'All Sorts of Impossible Things'.

killed it but last week alone it sold 750. It has had the most wide and various reviews. (Did you see the curious long Updike piece in the New Yorker of 24th Dec.?)[18] There's even a row within Harpers about it now. It's been steadily climbing in sales and has now sold more than all my books put together here (which is far from splendid) but that can't go on much longer without even an editor. It was 3 on the Washington Post best sellers 2 weeks ago.

So there you are! I hope your own work finds a less troubled life when it comes out into the world.

New work will come fairly soon in The New Yorker. For some reason I've never been able to write and teach. If you could get a reading at any of the institutions you mention I'd be grateful (except B.C. where Sweeney and I don't get on).[19] But I don't want you to go to any trouble. It'd be just a nice excuse to get to Boston.

With all good wishes
John

Frances McCullough Papers

Colgate

7 February 1980

Dear Fran,
I got it retyped, there were too many changes.

I saw the Dean. The University will put you up at the Inn, it's a lovely old colonial place, anytime you feel like a break. So I hope you'll all come. I'd want you to come anyhow.

I go to London (Ontario) from the 3rd–7th March.[20]

I'll probably go down to New York soon after that.

18 John Updike (1932–2009) had reviewed *The Pornographer* in the *New Yorker* (24 December 1979) under the title 'An Old-Fashioned Novel', and while praising McGahern for writing 'entrancingly, with a lively pace and constant melody', he disliked the central character's 'deadly coldness', favouring 'Josephine's credible, vital, naïve humanity'. Reproduced in Updike, *Hugging the Shore: Essays and Criticism* (New York: Alfred A. Knopf, 1993), 388–93. Fran McCullough wrote to McGahern calling the review 'a priggish, grudging piece of work'. Madeline McGahern Papers.

19 Father F. X. Sweeney, the organiser of all things literary in Boston College at the time.

20 McGahern drove up with Madeline for a reading at the University of Western Ontario.

Frances Kiernan said they are putting G.W. into their next scheduling.[21]
She also said, 'Apparently Fran McCullough's only crime was in publishing good books. Several houses, who just don't go by the bottom line, will want her.'[22]

> With my love
> John

> Russell and Volkening Papers
> Colgate

26 February 1980

Dear Tim,
Thank you for your kind note of the 21st.[23]
I am hoping to go into New York for a few days about the beginning of April.
Are you likely to be in town then?
It'd be a pleasure to see you again.

> With all good wishes
> John

Gold Watch is scheduled for the 17th March New Yorker. I sent a revised version of it to the Harper & Row copy editor. They are shooting for May.
Ploughshares may want to use a story that was originally published in Encounter.[24] I told them to contact you, should they decide they want it. They have not much money.

> J.

---

21 'Gold Watch' and its imminent appearance in the *New Yorker*.
22 McCullough went to Dial Press after Harper & Row, and then subsequently on to Bantam.
23 Seldes had written to say that a contract for a French translation of *The Pornographer* had been secured for the sum of 10,000 French francs, roughly equivalent to £1,060. The book was translated by Alain Delahaye and published by Presses de la Renaissance in 1981 as *Le Pornographe*.
24 'All Sorts of Impossible Things'.

31 March 1980

Dear David,
I am sorry that this report of the Writers Workshop in Galway is so late in reaching you. I've tried to write it a few times already but it always grew more complicated. This time I'll try to keep it as simple as I can.[25]

When the Workshop was finished, I met the students to say goodbye and to discuss the actual course. All of them were there, with the exception of Geaney, who had left the course the week before. His dissatisfaction was ostensibly about the size of the grants. They told me that they had found the course extremely useful, were grateful for it, and that they hoped very much if it could continue in the years ahead. These are the suggestions for future courses that they asked me to put on their behalf.

1. That the format of the course be retained. They felt that the three weekends round the central week were far better than the two full weeks of previous courses.

2. That the University or Arts Council should help more with the provision of accommodation. This was a constant anxiety for some. They felt there should be, at least, some register.

3. That the grants be reviewed because of inflation.
They asked that their gratitude be expressed for the supplementary grant they received during the course. There was a demand by some for a magazine, in which they could show their work. I was against this. It would be expensive and serve no useful purpose.

This last is my own suggestion. I think some consideration should be given to reserving a few places for students of the University. It would have the obvious advantage of drawing the course more immediately into the University, without in any way endangering its present emphasis.

25 The National Writers' Workshop was inaugurated by Professor Tom Kilroy at UCG in 1976 (before his appointment as head of the English Department at UCG and when then head of department Professor Lorna Reynolds was on sabbatical). In 1977 Anthony Cronin was director; 1978 was Eoghan Ó Tuairisc; McGahern in autumn 1979.

Galway seems to me ideal for the Workshop. It has many of the amenities of a big city and yet the whole atmosphere is intimate. The only other such course I conducted was in Totleigh Baron in Devon and it was far too isolated.

The rest is all thanks. To the President of UCG, Colm O hEocha, for his reception and welcoming speech. To Seamus O Grady and Tom Kilroy, who were unstinting in their help, often at great inconvenience to themselves, though they never made it seem that way.[26] To the five people who visited the Workshop, Brian Friel, Nuala O Faolain, Seamus Deane, Paul Muldoon and Neil Jordan. They are all distinguished. They came for meagre honorariums and gave generously.

I want to thank yourself for several kindnesses, and particularly for your support and tact during the fracas over the grants.

I'll be home in late May. It'd be a great pleasure to see you then.

> With good wishes,
> Sincerely,
> John McGahern

Faber

Colgate

10 April 1980

Dear Matthew,
I had dinner with the Bessies and they spoke with great affection of Elisabeth and yourself.[27]

He is my editor now.
And I have a feeling that I owe a great deal of my precarious permanence among the dust clouds to your good self.

Seldes may write to you – just to find out who – if anybody – in the States has the rights to the other books.

He liked Robert McCrum and was going to write to him but I persuaded him you'd know that better. So it is my fault.

If it is troublesome I can find out myself when I get home. My own feeling – for what it is worth – is that the rights may have lapsed.

---

26 Seamus O'Grady, who oversaw extramural provision at the university, played an important administrative role in making the workshop happen and became friendly with McGahern.
27 Michael and Cornelia Bessie, both major figures in American publishing, then both associated with Harper & Row.

Madeline left for home last week but I'll be here till near the end of May.
Remember me with affection to Elisabeth and the pair of boys.
John

Madeline McGahern
Colgate

17 April 1980

Dear Madeline,
I was delighted with your letter.
Classes here, papers, some rain and that's almost all.
I spoke in the Library yesterday. Many people asked to be remembered to you with what seemed real enough affection. I liked Mrs Ryder and the Librarian very much. It seemed to go all right. I was sort of nervous. Most of them ate their lunches while I spoke.
There was a fairly long review of The Porn in the N.Y.R. of Books, a professor at Stoneybrook, neither favourable nor unfavourable, sort of puzzled.[28] And an extraordinarily nice note from Updike.[29]
A request from the Library for your Odes of Pindar but I couldn't find it anywhere.

---

28 The review by John Thompson appears in the *New York Review of Books* dated 1 May 1980. It is, as McGahern says, rather conflicted. On the one hand Thompson writes that 'As in his stories, loss is the theme and the method is poetic. Images and themes are juxtaposed, with the modern poet's sharp ear for speech and sharp eye for oddities of character and scene.' On the other he is frustrated by the sexually tormented Ireland presented: 'Author and narrator are obsessed with the conjunction of birth and death. Strange Emerald Isle! I doubt that even the transplanted Micks among us will recognize themselves in these tortured celibates.' Thompson (1918–2002) was a Professor of English at the State University of New York at Stony Brook from 1965 to 1983 and was the author of an acclaimed text on the history of British poetics, *The Founding of English Meter* (London: Routledge & Kegan Paul, 1961).
29 In a letter of 15 April 1980, Updike had written to McGahern: 'Just the other night I got to thinking about the brief scene where the pornographer is beaten up by a pious lout and wondered at your tact in describing it, and if that wasn't all the retribution a reader could want. Your short stories, which I read afterwards, are magical, and honest with a purity rare on all five continents.' Madeline McGahern Papers.

If you feel like it, I'll be only glad if you'll go up to the Friels. I don't think one can be too careful with Big B. The more I think of the Muldoon incident, the more I think its real name is ENTRAMPMENT.[30]

Wil seems to get worse by the week. He was telling me how he taught Neill J. everything N. knew about handball. He played N. once and was hardly able to run, never mind play or teach anybody anything.

Classes end 6th May.

I'll start papers on the 14th. So I should be finished round the usual time.

> I miss you a great deal
> And with all my love
> John

We might go to Belfast on the 16th?

Madeline McGahern

Colgate

19 April 1980

Dear Madeline,

Your letter came an hour ago. I posted a letter through the University yesterday, but the mails seem unreliable, they may reach you together.

I was delighted that the calving went so well, especially since it goes to the long bead of legendary triumphs. 'A man's fame is nothing but the account of his deeds,' Paolo wrote.[31] Francie is such a delight.[32] Bring him a bottle or some present. Blame it on Mr.

Terence and Ann called last night. She was collecting her things, driving out to Santa Fe. It was unpleasant. His stupidity and greed is even more obvious. She got hurt, but I thought her questionable too. She's after her glitter, vanity

---

30 See letter to Paul Muldoon [January 1980].

31 Refers to Paolo Vivante's book *The Homeric Imagination* (Bloomington and London: Indiana University Press, 1970), much admired by McGahern. Vivante (1921–2004) was an Italian classics scholar whom Madeline had first met as a young woman in Siena. At the time of the composition of this letter he was teaching in McGill University, Montreal where the McGaherns had visited him. He, in turn, had visited Colgate where he gifted the couple with his book.

32 Francie McGarty, the McGaherns' beloved Foxfield neighbour who had helped with the calving.

and middle class security, icing and cake – and to that end, anything goes. Ordinary human dignity is as nothing. I wish I hadn't seen them.[33]

Talking of greed, I have the prospect of the Busch's tonight 'Just the three of us.'

And there's a real <u>war</u> atmosphere in the country as a whole. It must be a very dangerous time. I suppose all times are.[34]

If Francie will give you a hand at the actual sowing, let him. You'd certainly learn more from him than me, the distances between the seeds, depth, that sort of thing, but of course he may not want to be so much in the open.

Thanks for finding the money figures. I will have to try to fill in the tax forms.

Should you want anything, write by return – or call me collect. With the slow mails, the time is very short now.

Classes end the 6th of May. I can't demand papers till the 12th, but my own feeling is that I'll get home around 22nd–23–24, that time. I'll have to see Bessie again, and Kiernan, maybe Prestcott.[35] I might try to do some of it between the end of class and the 12th.

And so with all my love
John

33 Ann Geneva was leaving Terrence Des Pres, a creative writing colleague of McGahern's at Colgate.
34 By April 1980 the Democrat President Jimmy Carter was in deep trouble as that November's presidential election loomed. On 25 April 1980, Carter's ability to use the Tehran hostage crisis to regain public acceptance was destroyed when his high-risk attempt to rescue the hostages ended in disaster with eight servicemen dying in an air crash en route to Tehran. The Republican candidate Ronald Reagan went on to win the election in a landslide.
35 Bessie is Michael Bessie (1916–2008), legendary figure in the American publishing world, then at Harper & Row.

10 May 1980

Dear Michael,
Thank you for your kind and too, too generous letter.[36] It'd be great pleasure to see you in Foxfield in September.

I may be in Belfast June 16th – to give a talk to teachers. Maybe we can meet then . . .

Classes are over here. I am just tired. I shall have the papers finished by the end of next week and I hope to be home by May 20th.

> With all good wishes,
> John

Alain Delahaye

Colgate

14 May 1980

Dear Alain Delahaye,[37]
Thank you for your kind letter, which was forwarded from Ireland. I go home next week.

I have asked Faber to send publicity. See Harper & Row on my way home in New York next week and will ask them to do the same.

I'll send the biographical information soon as I get home.

---

36 In a letter of 12 April 1980 McLaverty had praised 'Gold Watch' as 'truly beautiful' and compared its artistic integrity to the stories of Joyce's *Dubliners*. See Killen (ed.), *Dear Mr McLaverty*, 48.

37 Alain Delahaye (1944–2020) became McGahern's most important French translator. At the time of the composition of this letter he was translating *The Dark*. It would appear as *L'Obscur* with Éditions de la Sphère later in 1980. Delahaye also translated Patricia Highsmith, John Updike, Roald Dahl, Brian Friel and Oscar Wilde among others. He worked extensively in dubbing and subtitling films such as *Billy Elliot* (2000) and *The English Patient* (1996), and television shows such as *Game of Thrones* (2011–19) and *The Tudors* (2007–10).

I enclose the answers.[38] I'll be glad to give any help I can.

I am sorry that I do not know French, my wife does. I'd be very glad to see the poems and versions.

Forgive the handwriting.

And thank you for the trouble you are taking with the book.

With good wishes

Sincerely

John McGahern

p. 11 The postoffice would be the only shop, keeping all sorts of goods – newspapers, tea, butter, chocolate, lemonade etc. Even if it was Sunday, people would knock on the back door

p. 12 Two pikes – collective meaning

p. 12 Their = seagulls. The island of bare rocks was where the gulls lived. They were screaming because of the disturbance of the boat

p. 14 A description of a usual night, what was to be expected. Then the match flaring is a description of one particular, dramatic night. If it is too confusing it may be as well to leave out the first winding of the clock.

p. 30-31 Mountjoy is the main prison in Dublin, like the Sante. Pierrepoint was the state hangman

p. 40 S.A.G. Saint Anthony Guide, used by pious peasant girls on letters home

p. 42 grace (typo)

p. 51 bird (typo)

p. 56 Lying to the priest, to make the boy appear more in control than he was, more flattering

p. 67 Shoes are always sold in draper's shops in country towns in Ireland. E.S.B. Electricity Supply Board, a semi-state body. Quiet office job.

---

38 See answers provided by McGahern below to queries about *The Dark* included with this letter in a separate, typed list with occasional emendations in pen.

27 May 1980

Dear Charles,
I'm delighted that Coleraine should honour you so, we both are, and it seems to me happy and well earned. Very many congratulations.[39]

   I can easily drive or take the train on either of those two days, for lunch or just for drink should your schedule be too full.[40]

   It'd be lovely to see you again, to toast the new Doctor.

                              Madeline sends her love,
                              and with my love
                              John

                                             Alain Delahaye
                                               [*Foxfield*][41]

[*Late May–early June 1980*]

[*To Alain Delahaye*]
Thank you for the beautiful books, the extraordinarily beautiful L'Etre Perdu.[42] They'll wait for you like sentinels.

   Madeline liked/admired your poems, very much, wishing her feeling for the language was more true. I heard her speak a number of times of de visage en memoire.[43]

39 Monteith had written to say that he was to be conferred with an Honorary Doctorate of Letters by the University of Ulster in Coleraine on 3 July.
40 Monteith had suggested possibly meeting in Dublin on 30 June or 1 July.
41 Postcard of Achill Island scene with no postmark or stamp – presumably originally enclosed in an envelope. Probably sent from Foxfield.
42 *L'Être Perdu*, a book of poetry by Delahaye with illustrations by Jean Bazaine (Paris: Maeght, 1977). This book formed part of McGahern's library at his death. The other book was *L'Éveil des Traversées* (Paris: Mercure de France, 1971).
43 This is the title (or first line) of the third poem of *L'Éveil des Traversées*, a poem written in memory of Delahaye's friend the Swiss sculptor Alberto Giacometti, who had died in January 1966.

Some people called La Presses de la Renaissance have bought The Pornographer.[44]

Do you know of them?

Had minor accident in New York but will write soon & properly and have books sent, dreadful ugly to look at.[45]

Thank you for the kindness, all the care

John

Good luck with the grant.

Alain Delahaye (TS)

Foxfield

20 June 1980

Dear Alain,

Thank you for both your letters. I was handing my return reply to the postman when I noticed he had your second letter.[46] Madeline's family live in Paris and she has noticed that the mails to there are just as slow as to Valenciennes.[47]

It'd be nice for me if they haven't already assigned The Pornographer.[48] It was sold by an agent, who owns the rights, and not by Fabers, who sold The Dark. I hope the translation has not taken too much from your own good work. If there's any way I can be of use, please tell me.[49]

I'll be here all August. Old friends are coming for two days at the very beginning of August, but otherwise we're free. We'd be glad to put you up for a night or two, and help you with addresses, etc. We'd invite you to stay for longer than that but the cottage is just too small.

I was at the University of Lille last November – for two days – and I liked the centre of the town very much. It doesn't seem far from Valenciennes.[50]

---

44 Presses de la Renaissance went on to become McGahern's main French publishers.
45 McGahern fell through an open trap door in Frances Kiernan's Tuxedo Park home.
46 There are two short lists of answers enclosed with this letter, one typed, the other in pen. See below.
47 Delahaye then lived in Valenciennes.
48 McGahern liked working with Delahaye and was pleased when he became translator of The Pornographer as Le Pornographe (Paris: Presses de la Renaissance, 1981).
49 This sentence is added in pen.
50 Lille and Valenciennes are just sixty kilometres apart.

I'm fine again, and thank you for your kind wishes,
                    With all good wishes,
                         John

Ireland's Own, peasant magazine, horoscopes, lonelyhearts, serials, with a green cover.
Cathal Brugha, school where young girls are taught 'Domestic Science', cookery, nutrition, hotel management.
Interfere is very vague, implying the father's fear of sex; attempted rape is even too strong. It's almost legalistic or doctrinal. Inflict himself sexually on her in any way.
p. 80. Harm vague again. Did he hurt her, have intercourse and – worst fear – get her pregnant? The vagueness or timidity goes hand in hand with the violence. If he had, it might be cause of murder.

[*Separate, handwritten note*]
p. 104 Jeffrey Farnol was a popular English author of steamy adventure/ romances in the early part of the century
p. 99 They did bring the potatoes in on a cart.
p. 90 To walk, slightly stilted, formal . . . to walk in the shadow of i.e. to live with, pass days with.

                                   Neill Joy
                              [*Madeline McGahern*]
                                   Foxfield

24 June 1980

[*To Neill Joy*]
Thank you for the lovely card (it is a favourite of Madeline's) and the generous words about Getting Through.[51]
  Janette drove me to Syracuse and I wound up in a very strange place, Tuxedo Park, some of the people even stranger than the place (one man lived alone in a ballroom; another woman, whose great-grandfather had been Washington's envoy to France, lived in a 42 room mansion on one of the lakes, with enormous bones for her dogs everywhere over the carpets) –

51 Getting Through was first published in the UK by Faber in 1978, and in the USA by Harper & Row in 1980.

                                                              513

but it was beautiful. Except I had a lucky or unlucky fall I could have been seriously hurt and wasn't. I fell through a sort of trap door (left open for cats to come and go). It was horrible but no bones were broken.[52]

It resulted in me becoming a big social success: a wildly distinguished limp, slow grace of movement (an inch with effort every few seconds), interesting paleness, a sense of extreme fragility, extraordinary attentiveness (I could stand with head bowed forever if necessary. Several distinguished ladies in their late seventies seemed disappointed when they heard I was married. In short, I was 'just the sort of person we like to see in Tuxedo Park.' So, Neill, if you ever have a favourite candidate at Colgate, make sure you throw him down the stairs before the interview and social rounds.

The only people I felt sorry for were my host and hostess, who got a real fright. He turned out to be as fine as she.

I was like an old crow round the garden, hopping, for several weeks but am now back to my unsociable self.

Fortunately, the tv river film was postponed, doesn't start till July 7th. I was in Belfast, saw Paul, but not our song and dance man.[53]

Alain Delahaye

Foxfield

10 August 1980

Dear Alain,

Our station is Dromod, on the Dublin to Sligo line (trains from Dublin at 9.00, 13.45, 18.10 approx – check). A bus takes you to Lough Rowan (20 km from Dromod). It meets the train. I can meet you at Lough Rowan. Certainly stay the first 2 nights here when you come.

It might be worthwhile staying the first night in Dublin, there are many Bed and Breakfasts, going into the C.I.E. office (State Travel) in O'Connell Street, and enquiring about their Rambler ticket, (unlimited travel for a fixed sum).

There are many beautiful places, especially along the Atlantic, and in some of them we have friends, who will be useful.

---

52 McGahern had been visiting the home of Frances Kiernan.
53 McGahern was visiting the BBC offices in Belfast. 'Paul' is Paul Muldoon. The 'song and dance' man is likely Tony McAuley who ran the schools unit, though David Hammond is another possibility.

Quinn's of Fenagh (telephone: Ballinamore 15) will take a message for me if you need to telephone.

We're looking forward to seeing your wife and daughter and self.[54]

With all good wishes

John

If I do not hear to the contrary I'll telephone 321.20.03 at 18.00 on August 19th

Brian Friel Papers

Foxfield

21 August 1980

Dear Brian,

Thank you for your card and kind invitations.

It's very hard for us now to make the 28th and both of us had looked forward to seeing <u>Faith Healer</u> run again. If it's all right with Anne and yourself, can we put ourselves down for the 23rd in Derry?[55] Then this muddle of a summer should be over.

What makes it so difficult is my brother is to be home all next week and he seems intent on forcing my stepmother to go to court. If it's not settled by the end of next week, in fact, it has to go to the courts.[56]

We both wish you all luck on Thursday.

With much love

John

---

54 The Delahaye family spent a very happy few days in Foxfield later in August, Alain helping John to save the hay.

55 Friel's play premiered on Broadway in 1979 in a poorly received production starring James Mason that ran for a mere twenty performances.

56 John was executor of his father's will. The Grevisk property was left to Frankie who wished to take ownership, but the law would not permit the McGaherns' stepmother Agnes to be turned out of the homeplace. Ultimately the court ruled that Agnes inherit the house and an acre of land, Frankie getting the rest of the land.

14 September 1980

Dear Brian,
Thank you for having us sent the Invitation for <u>Translations</u> on the 23rd.

I'm looking forward to it. I liked the piece of it I read in <u>Ploughshares</u> very much.[57]

We want Anne and yourself to forget about us that night. You'll both have many things to look to. I think we are old enough friends to ask that.

We'll easily find some place around Derry. Or we may head home afterwards. And we can arrange a better time to meet.

We had a lousy summer.
To start with I nearly performed a Public Service by falling down a trapdoor outside New York.

We're both looking forward to Tuesday and to seeing you both in a more leisured time not too long after that.

With much love to Anne and yourself
John

Alain Delahaye
Foxfield

5 October 1980

Dear Alain,
Congratulations on the house. Madeline and I wish the three of you many happy years of its enjoyment.[58]

And thank you for the beautiful book. It was far too much to send. And the photographs.

I was glad you seemed to like Lehane. He is my oldest friend, a dear person.

---

57 An extract from *Translations* appeared in the Spring 1980 issue of *Ploughshares*.
58 The Delahayes had found a house in Buire-le-Sec and were beginning the move from Valenciennes.

We were, of course, intrigued by your account of Oscar's party, of Niels sudden attack of Pietas; and grateful to Pascale and yourself for taking the Black Bush.[59]

I'm afraid I don't like Powys very much, that large 'genius' gesture; but, at least, if you do take him, you won't have to worry about work for some time.[60]

I enclose the paperback. It might be useful for a grant. Maybe the title is good after all – no bungs, no tits, no flowers . . .[61]

Madeline asks to be remembered with love to Pascal, to Florence, and to yourself.[62]

I go to speak in Newcastle and London at the end of the week, and I'll be away for two weeks.

With all good wishes, and love
John

James Swift
[*Madeline McGahern*]
Foxfield

22 October 1980

Dear Jimmy,

I was in England for a few days and saw Joseph and Joan Kelly.[63] They told me you were unwell. I had hoped to see you on my way home but got flu and had to come straight through.

---

59 The McGaherns sent a bottle of Black Bush whiskey with the Delahayes as a gift for Oscar Nitschke's birthday. In a letter of 13 September, Alain tells John of a pleasant meeting with Kika and Niels Gron at the birthday party and of Niels's comment that he would like to hear from Madeline more regularly.

60 Delahaye had mentioned in his letter of 13 September that Hachette had asked him to consider translating the sprawling John Cowper Powys historical novel *Owen Glendower* (New York: Simon & Schuster, 1941). He did not take on the work.

61 *The Pornographer* – McGahern had struggled to find a title. See his letter to Charles Monteith of 3 October 1978.

62 Delahaye's wife was Pascale, his daughter Florence.

63 One of half a dozen such meetings in this period between McGahern and Joan Kelly, the mother of his son Joseph.

I'll be in Dublin before long, probably around the 12th, and it'd be a pleasure for me to meet. I know Joan dramatizes everything but she had me anxious and I'd be grateful for any word.

Madeline sends her best regards.
With all good wishes
John

Neill Joy
[Madeline McGahern]
Foxfield

8 November 1980

Dear Neill,
Thank you for your letter.

This is to say that the third week in January is fine, and that we'll look forward very much to seeing you. Madeline goes to Paris just after Christmas but she expects to be home well before then. And if it's any use to you, you're welcome to the old 1973 VW.[64] It runs. Tell me if I can be of any use on this side before you come.

I'm very glad for Wil, and grateful for the review.
I'd be grateful, too, if you'd give Bruce warmest congratulations for me.

I miss the handball.
I cut hedges, shoot pheasants, go on the lake, very seldom go to the pub; but the usuals are in amazing steam every time I go.

Give Mary my love, though after so many courses a case of good wine, I am sure, would be much more in line.

We are looking forward very much to seeing her, and Theo, and your good self.

With much love
John

64 A Volkswagen Beetle, driven for many years by the McGaherns, bought from a garage in nearby Rooskey.

10 November 1980

Dear Charles,

Thank you for your letter and the lovely lunch in the Garrick.[65] I conveyed your message to Richard, into a white-frost atmosphere, but was informed that he had already rung you. We were all redundant.

I'll take your suggestion and give a quick outline of the book I have in mind. It will be in two volumes: Volume 1, 1860–1920; Volume 2, 1920–1980. In the final arrangement the shape of the work would be more important than the dates. The first volume could stop short of 1920, or go some years over.

I'd begin with Carleton, the first important writer working in English whose base was Gaelic. He is as obvious as Lawson would be to an Australian.[66] It will not be a short story anthology, though it will probably have to lean heavily on that form, because of space, and its strength in the tradition.[67]

The book would claim its place as literature beside the Faber or Oxford Book of Verse, but it would stay outside their territory. It would include the novel, drama, autobiography, and even criticism, if such that looked permanent could be found. The one work of verse to be included is Yeats's Purgatory, since I see it as a key work, and whose rhythm is half prose anyhow. The immediate figures are Carleton (short story), Green (Autobiography of a Landlord's Agent),[68] Somerville and Ross, George Moore, Yeats, Joyce, Forrest Reid (the novel), Beckett, Corkery, Kavanagh (the novel), O'Connor, O'Crohan (from The Islandman), O'Cadhain (if he can be translated), O'Casey, Synge, Behan (perhaps), McLaverty.

I won't go into the 'moderns' at this stage, which may even include myself, and the problem will be that of exclusion. I will need to do a great deal

65 Monteith and McGahern had dined at the Garrick Club in London's West End on 13 October.
66 Henry Lawson (1867–1922), one of Australia's most prominent writers of the colonial period.
67 As early as 1971 McGahern and Monteith had been discussing the possibility of his editing a Faber collection of Irish short stories to replace an earlier collection edited by Valentin Iremonger. This new mooted prose anthology was something McGahern worked hard on for several years but, like the short story project, it never saw the light of day.
68 McGahern may mean W. S. Trench, Realities of Irish Life. Trench was a land agent.

of reading and re-reading, and names will be added to, maybe even taken away. Shaw and Wilde will be a real problem but I cannot see them being included now.

I will attempt to define a separate tradition which is large enough to make it worthwhile, still small enough to make it possible. I'll be glad to add to anything, or clear up any haze, but I feel that may be enough for now. There would be an Introduction to both volumes.

With much love,
John

Faber

Foxfield

17 November 1980

Dear Charles,
Thank you for your kind letter.

I want to wish you long and happy years in retirement, and good years in your new office.

I owe you too many, and too deep, debts of gratitude and affection to want to name them here. The dedication page in <u>Nightlines</u> tells more about the seriousness of my feelings than anything I can say here. And that you accepted it is a continuing source of pleasure for me.

So with love, and gratitude, and all good and dear wishes
John

Frances Kiernan Papers

Foxfield

[*18 November 1980*]

Dear Frances,
You may well be right about the story. I'll leave it aside for a while, and maybe try it again, beginning at the meeting in the bookshop. And see what happens.[69]

69 Refers to what eventually became 'Bank Holiday', which changed radically over the years of its composition. The story was never fixed to the satisfaction of the

I've finished another story. And I'll send it in a week or two.

I've done nothing at the play, putting off ever taking the money for the commission. I have ideas, maybe too many ideas, and I'd like to work in the theatre, but I keep putting it off. I may go up to Dublin for a few weeks and just fool around the theatre.

There's another novel it seems I'll have to write. And that's dismaying. Some of the scenes I can't get away from, which is probably some of the trouble with the play.

I remember Tuxedo Park with extraordinary vividness, and am very grateful to you and to Howard for having me there. I thought it a beautiful, an amazing place. I often think about it. I've never met anyone insecure in the same way as your John seems to be.

And of course I'm ashamed of myself for falling down the stairs. What a lousy fright I must have given you! I hope it's not just the start of a late talent. The French edition of The Dark (L'Obscur) arrived last week with a whole graveyard on the cover, complete with plastic flowers. I'd certainly not want such a person in my house.

With affection
and all good wishes
John

Faber

Foxfield

22 November 1980

Dear Charles,
The title is Irish Prose.[70]

<New Yorker despite repeated attempts. On 15 October 1980 Kiernan had written to McGahern about the story's flaws: 'To be sure, I can piece together a story that makes sense to me of a man untouched by all that happens to him, even the scene in that hotel bedroom, who looks for meaning in books and who finds instead this lovely young woman. But for all I know I have it all wrong.' Madeline McGahern Papers.

70 Discussions between Faber and McGahern had originally revolved around the idea of an anthology of short stories. Over lunch in the Garrick on 13 October and in the subsequent letter of 10 November it became clear to Monteith that McGahern had a much more ambitious Irish prose anthology in mind. McGahern is here replying to a letter of 14 November in which Monteith questions the presence of Yeats's play Purgatory in a prose anthology.

It's extremely unlikely I'd include criticism.

I'd include Purgatory even if it were pure verse, because it is so important that I couldn't afford to hold verse against it. As it is, it's ½ prose, verse crossed with a prose rhythm (see A General Introduction to my Work).[71]

Yeats himself began his Ox. B. of Mod. Verse with a very good piece of prose (Pater), much better than a lot of the verse that followed. There are other precedents. It's the only verse likely to be included.

I'm not quite certain if that's what you wish to know. I'll be only too glad to try to make anything else clear.

Love

John

PS. Is there to be an Introductions this year?
Is there a closing date?
I was asked the other day by a Colm Flynn.[72]

J.

Neill Joy
[*Madeline McGahern*]

Foxfield

[*December 1980*]

Dear Neill,

While we are disappointed not to be seeing you in a few weeks, we think that to come with the rates as they are would have made poor sense. Outside that January can be a bitter month here. You'd be better to settle into London. And there are all kinds of 'Winter Deals' between Dublin and London. My own favourite route is the day crossing, leave Euston 10 a.m. to Holyhead 2 p.m. Dublin.

I ran into Monsieur Longley on the opening night of a good Friel play Translations in Derry (It'll transfer to London in the spring). He seemed to want to recover some imagined loss of dignity, and sent a number of shots in my direction during the intervals, and at the party afterward. Anyhow I think he ran into a few late uppercuts. I seem to remember my own voice at

---

71 Refers to W. B. Yeats, 'A General Introduction for my Work', a key, and revealing, late manifesto written for a complete edition of Yeats's work that was never produced.
72 A writer from Arva, Co. Cavan who had attended the National Writers' Workshop in UCG in autumn 1979 and whose work was admired by McGahern.

the theatre bar: 'Heaney will get what he asked for, but you, Longley, will get who you deserve, which is the smallest of small measures.' At that stage, it was probably as rewarding as attempting to slow a swinging door.

I go to Dublin for a recording on the 17th and we'll probably turn it into the Christmas spree. Madeline goes to Paris on the 27th.

The political situation here is lousy. Haughey's a pure rogue and looks as if he may hang on to power for a long time. There's certain to be an election soon. The Northern business grows more bitter and farcical by the hour.[73]

The Pornographer is slated to come out in France in May or June. So we may meet you in Paris or Dijon.

And we hope very much that you'll be able to come here.

A very happy Christmas and New Year to all the Joys
and with love to Mary and Yourself from Madeline and me
John

---

73 Charles J. Haughey (1925–2006) was the dominant Irish political figure of the day. Leader of the Fianna Fáil party, he was Taoiseach on several occasions through the 1980s and 1990s. The early 1980s was a period of particularly marked instability in Ireland, both due to economic recession and to the ongoing Troubles. Haughey had a track record of support towards Irish republicanism with which McGahern was unsympathetic.

1981

30 January 1981

Dear Peter,[1]
Thank you for the beautiful book. It is fun.[2]

We'd be very glad to see you here. Or if you knew the day – to give you lunch or dinner.

Otherwise, we'll call before February is out. Are you in Loughcrew most of the time? Or days in Dublin?

Madeline sends her thanks and all good wishes, as do I
      John

30 January 1981

[*To Frances Kiernan*]
Thank you for both letters, for all care, and kindness.

I've finished another story, a country story, and I'll send it in a few days.[3]

I'll look at the razor story again then. It's a real problem. It'd be nice if it could be got right. Maybe it can't.[4]

---

1 Peter Fallon b. 1951, Irish poet, editor and founder of the Gallery Press.
2 The book in question is Paul Muldoon, *The O-O's Party, New Year's Eve*, linecuts by Tim Engelland (Loughcrew: Peter Fallon/The Gallery Press, 1980). Limited to one hundred copies and signed by the author, it was sent to John and Madeline on 25 January 1981.
3 Probably 'High Ground'.
4 Refers to the story that was eventually published as 'Bank Holiday' – then called 'The Natural Process' – in the *Irish Times* (9 August 1985). First collected in *High*

I'm glad you liked the other story. I'd have been surprised if it was taken. I was going to say that when sending it. It may not be quite as bad as saying that 'this is a terrific story,' but it's still the ugly oar.

I've been smiling over the Jonathan news.[5] It's certainly wiser to say nothing but I'm sorely tempted.

Madeline has been in France with her family. Myself and Charley, the black cat with four white paws, have been sort of lighthouse keepers here. The other cat, a male, has disappeared. Sometimes it used to be away, for as long as 10 days, on Byronic adventures, but he's weeks gone now. It's thought locally that 'he got in with some old woman or a fox got him.'

I'm so glad you've had such a happy winter. It should be lovely in Tuxedo Park. You should plant a few pear trees, if only for the blossom.

With every good wish
John

Faber (TS)

Foxfield

31 January 1981

Dear Charles,
Thank you for the very kind letter, and the clear terms. They seem fair to me. And I am happy to go ahead.[6]

Ground. McGahern had sent to Kiernan a second draft to which she replied on 5 January: 'I would very much like to say that I thought that the story was improved by this revision. By all rights it should be improved. Its form has a shapeliness that was lacking. McDonough is altogether a more sympathetic figure. Yet, for some reason, we continue to see him at a distance, and now, too, the girl seems remote. [. . .] I feel as if I'm being all too matter-of-fact and literal, and it is my hope that you'll forgive my obduracy and thick-headedness and credit it to my belief that a marvellous story will one day come of THE NATURAL PROCESS. The trouble is, I keep wanting it today, not tomorrow.' Madeline McGahern Papers.
5 Kiernan wrote in her letter of 5 January 1981 that Jonathan Coleman was looking for a job in television.
6 Refers to McGahern's agreement to edit what was to be called *The Faber Book of Irish Prose* to be published in two volumes. Monteith had written on 15 January with terms: 'we'd like to give you not simply a fee – as is usual with anthologies – but a royalty. If the book goes on selling for a long time – as I anticipate it may very well do – I think you'll find this quite a useful addition to your income over the years. The royalty we have in mind is in fact the highest we have ever paid on an anthology and

There are just a few things. I think your dates are far too optimistic. There'll be much reading and rereading to do. I'd want to do it as scrupulously as I can, but at the same time do my own work. I'd say 1983 for Volume I and 1986 for Volume II, though naturally I'll do my best to deliver before then.[7] In fact, it's in my own interest to do so – in all our interests.[8]

I'm prepared to do the work of the permission/fees/rights, but I think I should be reimbursed for any expenses, postage, etc. With the way inflation is going, they could come to more than the advances before all is over.

Thanks, too, for the very nice card.

Please forgive this hurried note. I'm a bit shaken with flu but want to get the answer to you.

With much love

John

PS. The Auld Sock has just got an award for its translator in France.[9]

Russell and Volkening Papers (TS)

[*Foxfield*]

9 February 1981

Dear Tim,

Thanks for the note.

It wags not too badly. I suppose, at this stage, that it wags at all is a virtual triumph of sorts.[10]

---

is a straight 10% on the hard cover edition; and a straight 7½% on the paperback edition (which we'll do in our own paperback series). On that royalty we'd be happy to pay you an advance of two thousand pounds.'

7 The plan was for Volume I to end with Joyce and Volume II to begin with Beckett.

8 Monteith had suggested that Volume I be delivered on 30 June 1982 and Volume II a year later. In his response of 18 February to the above letter, Monteith accepts McGahern's suggested dates.

9 Refers to *The Dark*, translated as *L'Obscur* by Alain Delahaye (Paris: Éditions de la Sphère, 1980). *The Dark* features scenes of the boy narrator masturbating into a sock.

10 Seldes had opened his letter of 28 January by asking 'How wags the world with you?' He went on to complain about what he saw as Harper & Row's continuing bad behaviour in failing to reply on whether it would bring *Nightlines* out in paperback. Michael Bessie of Harper & Row eventually did reply on 7 February to Seldes to say that, with regret, the company felt there was not a sufficient American market for such a book. There is a marked coolness in the exchange.

I sent the enclosed story to The New Yorker a few weeks back. Frances Kiernan said she liked it very much but that it wasn't their story.[11]

I wonder if you'd be interested in trying it elsewhere. I won't mind at all if you think it'd not likely to go.

The American Poetry Review wrote, looking for a contribution. I suggested they try you for Peaches, from Nightlines, which was never published in a paper or magazine, but I suppose nothing came of it.[12]

More recently David Evanier wrote looking for a manuscript for the Paris Review, but I haven't answered.[13]

Two new stories have just gone for consideration to The New Yorker and I have written some scenes of the novel.[14]

With every good wish

John

Frances Kiernan Papers

Foxfield

20 March 1981

Dear Frances,

Thank you for both letters. I'll let the other story lie for a time, and then write it for a last time. What harm if it's not taken! And it is very nice to be appearing again. It's like being back on the racetrack.

I've let nearly all the editing stand. Some of the small changes are quite beautiful.[15]

I think I've done the best I can with the 'explanation' (p. 13). It seems extraordinary especially in the view that all art is 'suggestion'. The word danger, though, may be useful.

What was your holiday like?

I'll be in Ireland all next year and it'll be lovely if you can come.

I'll write soon.

I am anxious to get the story to you.

11 The story is 'Parachutes'. Seldes writes on 18 February to say he agrees with Frances Kiernan and that the story stands little chance in the US market.
12 Seldes has marked 'sent' beside 'Peaches'.
13 David Evanier, American biographer, novelist and short story writer. At the time of this letter's composition he was fiction editor at the *Paris Review*.
14 Likely 'High Ground' and 'Bank Holiday'.
15 'High Ground' appeared in the *New Yorker* for 22 March 1982.

How is Howard? And John? And all the parents?
With all dear wishes,
John

Alain Delahaye

Foxfield

24 March 1981

Dear Alain,

It was lovely to get your letter.

Madeline is writing to thank you both for the Delacroix.[16]
The queries were no trouble. I enclose the answers.

I've signed the contract for the Faber Book of Irish Prose, 2 volumes. I'll probably rue the day, especially when I come to Volume II, due in '86. The Leavetaking and 2 of the stories are being made into tv dramas.[17] I have nothing to do with them. I myself – like Julius Caesar – have been in the Abbey Theatre, supposed to be working.

We bought a house in Dublin, ½ share, with my sister Margaret. It's small but in the centre of the city, the markets area.[18] We'll be glad for you to use it if you come. It's in the markets, fish and fruit and corn, and tell Florence it's not far from the zoo. I may go to look at the Buffalo now and again – to steady up.

I am working, but slowly, and it's hard. Mostly I fail.

Are you writing verse?

I'm looking forward to seeing the house some day. I hope it brings much pleasure to you three.[19]

16 The Delahayes made a gift of French romantic painter Eugène Delacroix's journals in two volumes to Madeline, a gift she greatly valued and returned to repeatedly.

17 A section of The Leavetaking was dramatised under the title The Lost Hour (1982) as a television film directed by Seán Cotter, adapted for TV by Carlo Gébler. Only one story, 'The Key', was adapted for a short TV film in this period under the same title as the story. It was directed by Tony Barry and adapted by Carlo Gébler; it was screened on RTÉ in December 1983.

18 The house is in Stoneybatter; McGahern eventually bought out Margaret's share.

19 McGahern visited the house several years later for lunch.

Do you think will you come to Ireland this summer? We'll be delighted if you do.

> With love to Pascale and Florence and yourself.
> John

Russell and Volkening Papers

Foxfield

12 April 1981

Dear Tim,
That would be good news. I'd be very glad.[20]

Michael Sissons of A. D. Peters handled The Barracks and The Dark. Macmillan did The Barracks and Knopf The Dark. They are long out of print in the States.

Selected Stories might have a better chance of going than Nightlines. (Nightlines + Getting Through + New Stories are coming out next year in German in a single volume).[21] But I am very happy to leave it to your judgement.

A few weeks back The New Yorker bought the most recent story. It's called High Ground.

> With all good wishes
> John

20 Seldes had written to McGahern on 3 April 1981 to say that Penguin had expressed an interest in publishing The Barracks and The Dark, both of which were out of print in the US. Seldes proposed writing to Faber to suggest that Russell and Volkening would handle it. He also proposed pitching Nightlines at Penguin. Penguin eventually reissued The Dark and The Leavetaking, in addition to being first American publisher of High Ground (1987) and Amongst Women (1990).
21 No such book was published.

2 June 1981

Dear Brian and Anne,
Thank you for your kind invitation, and we look forward very much to being
there, to wish Mary happiness on that day.[22]
    What do you think of that Aosdan thing? Are you likely to apply?[23]
       And many congratulations on the new Award.[24]
              Madeline sends her love
              With my love
              John

8 June 1981

Dear Seamus,
I'm writing to ask if I can put your name down as sponsor when I apply for
the Aosdana.

22 The McGaherns attended the wedding of Mary Friel, daughter of Brian and Anne.
23 The Irish Arts Council established Aosdána in 1981 to honour artists whose work
has made an outstanding contribution to the creative arts in Ireland, and to encourage
and assist members in devoting their energies fully to their art. Membership of
Aosdána, which is by peer nomination and election, is limited to 250 living artists
who have produced a distinguished body of work. Members must be (or have been)
resident in the Republic of Ireland or Northern Ireland for five years and have
produced a body of work that is original and creative. There are certain exceptions
where artists resident outside of the island of Ireland may be eligible if the body of
their work is deemed to significantly benefit the arts in Ireland. Both McGahern and
Friel became members, with Friel eventually rising to the highest position of Saoi (or
wise man) in 2006.
24 In 1981 *Translations* was awarded the Ewart-Biggs Peace Prize. Named after
Christopher Ewart-Biggs, British ambassador to Ireland who was assassinated by the
IRA on 21 July 1976.

I was very glad to read about the Harvard appointment and I hope it'll suit you.[25] I'd certainly like to be able to head down to the harbour there, on some idle Saturdays.

Please give my love to Marie, and the live boys and lady.

John

Alain Delahaye
Foxfield

1 August 1981

Dear Alain,

Thanks for the kind letter and I'm very sorry that you've been unwell. I hope the house will be settled soon and that you'll have strength for your own work. Give our congratulations to Pascale. Her parents seem the sort of parents everybody should have – my old peach in the graveyard would look on such generosity as positively subversive.

We've had a wonderful spell of weather. So all the hay is saved. I thought of you as I brought it into the shed yesterday. Madeline's ½ sister, Rose, is staying with us. Her mother won the appeal against the father and was given the Paris house. Rose is a very pleasant passive girl, more child than girl.[26]

I was tempted to go to Washington D.C. next spring but I have just too much work to do. We go back to Colgate from 1983, September to the May of '84. It'll be quite enough if we last that long.

No author's copies of either L'Obscur or Le Pornographe came. I promised a schoolgirl who is studying French a copy of L'Obscur. I'd be grateful if you'd enquire but there's absolutely no hurry. They may well be on their way via Faber even now.

Francie, the man across the lake, his brother came from England 2 weeks ago and died. I and a crazy chemist from Dublin had to lay him out. He, the chemist, kept adjusting the mouth.

'You'll never get it any better than that,' I said after the 16th attempt. 'They're wondering already what's keeping us. This is your very last chance.'

---

25 Heaney began teaching at Harvard in 1979 where he was elected the Boylston Professor of Rhetoric and Oratory (1984–95). He also served as the Ralph Waldo Emerson Poet-in-Residence, a post he held from 1988 until 2006.

26 The large house on Rue Guissarde and main residence of Niels Gron. Gron moved to another of his Parisian properties, a beautiful studio in the heart of Saint-Germain overlooking the famous café Les Deux Magots.

I knew this pursuit of perfection could go on all night. The murmurs outside the door were rising, people restless to start drinking, which they couldn't do decently until they had viewed the Departed. 'O we'll have our critics. Never you mind,' he said resentfully. 'We'll have our critics.'[27] So much, I thought, for the literary racket.

> Our love to Florence and Pascale and your good
> self
> John

Alain Delahaye

Foxfield

20 September 1981

Dear Alain,
Sydney B. Smith asked me for your address.[28] I gave him your old address at Valenciennes so that you can take avoidances if you want to. Unfortunately, such dance steps are sometimes necessary. I hope you do not mind.

Byron, after a long journey through storms, wrote down his age in the Italian hotel register as 101 (a hundred and one). I remembered it when reading about the move to Buire le Sec.

There's a chance, a small chance, that we may go to Paris for a few days around or before Christmas.

Montale died.[29] Do you know his Xenia?

> 'And Paradise? Is there a paradise?
> I think so, ma'am, but no one drinks
> sweet wines anymore.'

It's lovely golden weather but Francie across the lake came by and said, 'It's winter. Winter. Depressing all the football games are over.'[30]

---

27 This story forms the basis for the laying out of Johnny in *That They May Face the Rising Sun*.

28 Sydney Bernard Smith (1936–2008) was a poet and playwright, born in Glasgow and raised in Portstewart, Co. Derry. He studied at Oxford University and lived for twenty-five years in the west of Ireland, mainly on Inishbofin.

29 Eugenio Montale (1896–1981) died on 12 September. Italian poet, prose writer, editor, translator, and recipient of the 1975 Nobel Prize for Literature. See letter to Charles Monteith of 8 April 1977.

30 For many years up to 2018 it was traditional to play the All-Ireland inter-county senior men's gaelic football final in September. Often seen as a marker of the end of

I hope it's easier now in the house. Madeline sends her love to you there.

as do I

John

Faber

Foxfield

12 October 1981

Dear Matthew,

Thanks for your letter of September 29th.

I'd be happy if Fabers did the paperbacks, though that was the last thing in my head when I forwarded the letter from Alison & Busby.[31]

My own feeling is that they might be a bit much, together in the one volume. I think they'd be too much.[32]

There's a strong possibility that Penguin/Viking may do them in the States. They approached Seldes for the rights a couple of months back. The only thing holding up an agreement is the 'sorting out of some production difficulty' which may be just words for cold feet.

How nice to be going to France for a week! Do you remember the 1922 Champagne Cognac courtesy of M. Gron in Cromwell Road in the long

---

summer. On the day this letter was written, a dominant Kerry team defeated Offaly in the final by 1–12 to 0–8, thus winning their fourth All-Ireland title in a row to the dismay of most neutrals, Francie McGarty among them.

31 Allison & Busby is a publishing house based in London established by Clive Allison and Margaret Busby in 1967.

32 Presumably McGahern is referring here to a possible collected stories, a volume that eventually came to pass in 1992.

ago?[33] He's divorcing now. Madeline's ½ sister was here in summer, 14 years old, 6 ft. She's a nice girl.[34]

We've heard that The Porno Man has been a success of sorts in France. It even got into the Canard last month. I'm glad if it is so. The Dark sank without trace there last year.

There's a chance we may go to Paris for Christmas. I came across some very fine work by a Canadian Mavis Gallant.[35] It might be worth checking to see if she has an English publisher.[36]

It rains here, and it rains, and – it rains.

With our love

John

Frances Kiernan Papers

Foxfield

19 October 1981

Dear Frances,

I put this story aside after you returned it late last year, and it kept nagging me (that there wasn't enough of the love story to make sense, that there was too much of the Dublin crowd).[37]

33 Madeline lived at 17 Cromwell Road in the South Kensington district of London from spring 1968 to January of the following year, when she joined John at Colgate. She worked in an office as receptionist in an attractive redbrick terrace on Russell Square which acted as a business front for her father's orchestra, the Philomusica of London. John and Madeline were seeing a good deal of Matthew and Elizabeth Evans at the time, meeting in Charlotte Street in a small Greek restaurant or in the Good Friend Chinese restaurant east of Stratford for three- to four-hour lunches with them and others. Shortly before Christmas 1968 John discovered in the flat a case of exceptional brandy. There was no question of not opening it.

34 This is Rose, the youngest of Madeline's three half-sisters. She also visited the first summer the McGaherns stayed in Leitrim, 1974, before John took up his duties as Northern Arts Fellow at Newcastle.

35 Mavis Gallant, née Young (1922–2014), was a Canadian writer who spent much of her life and career in France. Best known as a short story writer, she also published novels, plays and essays.

36 At this point Gallant was being published in the UK by Jonathan Cape.

37 Refers to 'Parachutes', which was not taken by the New Yorker and eventually first appeared in Encounter (February 1983). It was then collected as part of High Ground in 1985. Originally titled 'Without Ceremony', Kiernan wrote to McGahern

It's so changed now that I'd love to show it to you again. I hope you don't mind. I admired a book of stories by Mavis Gallant. Many or all of them appeared in The New Yorker. There was a magical story called Irina.[38]

I'm told that The Pornographer has been a success of sorts in France. It was even in the Canard last month. Last year The Dark sank without trace, though it got an award for the translator.

The kittens have lovely silky winter coats, chasing the scattering leaves. I should sell most of the cattle but keep putting it off.

Is there any change in Mrs Kiernan? Have you closed Tuxedo Park?

Please remember me to Howard.
With all dear wishes
John

Russell and Volkening Papers

Foxfield

14 November 1981

Dear Tim,

Thank you for your letter of November 4th. I'm happy with the Penguin offer, and very grateful to yourself for arranging the business.[39]

Michael Bessie once spoke of his determination to see The Pornographer into paperback, if necessary into a Harper & Row paperback. I suppose that's hardly worth recalling, hardly worth the air into which it was spoken.

I hope you are well
and with all good wishes
John

---

about it on 12 January 1981: 'I liked WITHOUT CEREMONY, and for me the story never falters from first to last, so when I tell you that other readers did not share my feeling about this, I guess it's best to leave it at that. I have an idea that it is the bar-hopping that does them in or puts them off, or whatever.' Madeline McGahern Papers.

38 The book being referred to here is most likely Mavis Gallant, *From the Fifteenth District: A Novella and Eight Short Stories* (Toronto: Macmillan of Canada, 1981). 'Irina' is the closing story in that collection and first appeared in the *New Yorker* for 2 December 1974.

39 Seldes had written on 4 November to report that Penguin was making an offer of $2,000 against royalties of 6% for paperback rights to *The Dark*.

1982

[Early 1982]

Dear Frances,

I've gone through the proof and there are no problems.

If there had been a rush I'd have gone ahead and faked but I'd be grateful for help with the legal department.

Master Leddy and Senator Reegan are mostly based on real people, though they have fictitious names, and Reegan was never a Senator, and they are both dead. The place names are real. What do you suggest I change? I'll forward the proof as soon as I can.[1]

I'm very sorry to hear of Mrs Kiernan. My own suspicion is that it is more of character that's religion – Mr Kiernan's marvellous quality – though religion can, of course, be a part of character, and grow (but only if it is already there). And I am prejudiced anyhow.

I'd say Howard is wrong about the cat. There's an interesting proverb in Gaelic, referring to inherited traits – 'The very nature of the cat breaks through the eyes.' Is there hope of you still getting to Dublin? Or is that changed now? It'd be lovely to see you both.

With all good wishes

John

1 Refers to the story 'High Ground', which appeared in the *New Yorker* on 22 March 1982.

Alain Delahaye

Foxfield

28 January 1982

Dear Alain,

These were the confusions.

I drove Madeline to Dublin, meaning to come back here, and join her four or five days later to travel to Paris together.

We woke to find the roads impassable, the trains stopped, customers marooned in bars. My sister was running the emergency service and one bar, 40 customers aboard, rang in for sandwiches, when they heard on the radio the army helicopters were delivering food. Unfortunately there were no expectant mothers in that bar.[2]

After waiting three days, we travelled on the Liverpool boat, knowing that Francie would manage. The roads were almost as bad in England, and there was a train strike.

We went to Paris by Air France, and they lost Madeline's suitcase. We got it back but after three days trouble. It was during that time we telegrammed and rang Madame Martin.[3] Then we heard that pipes had burst and that the Dublin house was flooded. It was enough. We'd looked forward very much to seeing the three of you. Though we'd just have stayed a few hours. We know that your days must now be full.

Before leaving I left a native bottle inside Madame Martin's door. I'd hoped to leave it with the concierge, but there was none, and I noticed the door was open.

I think you and the Editor would have a better idea of which of the books would go in France. I'd say it's between The Leavetaking and the stories. If it were The Leavetaking I'd like to go through it before you'd start to translate; if it were stories, I'd like to show you some recent stories.[4]

> I hope Pascale is well, and little Florence
> and with much love
> John

2 On 8 January 1982 a severe cold spell began across Ireland that covered the country in snow until 15 January. The east of the country was the worst affected with twenty-five centimetres falling at Dublin Airport.

3 Madame Martin was the mother of Pascale.

4 Delahaye had mentioned in a letter of 16 December 1981 that Le Pornographe was selling well (2,500 copies) and Tony Cartano of Presses de la Renaissance was

Neill Joy
[*Madeline McGahern*]
Foxfield

28 January 1982

Dear Neill and Mary,
It was lovely to get your Christmas card, and thanks for sending the Rainsuit.
I couldn't find a price tag, so I'm taking pot luck with the cheque, and we can
make the adjustment in some bar somewhere some day.

What news?

The Government fell last night, the most decent Government I suspect the
State ever had. I'm sure Haughey and his crooks will come running back. The
election is on Feb. 18th.[5] Margaret wasn't happy with the Dublin house. So
we bought her share, and redid the whole house, which has put our finances
more or less on par with the country's.

The poet Murphy called, all smiles. He has got that girl you met pregnant,
got her to buy a house close to his own, visits her every day, looks forward to
being present at the birth, and has taken over the management of her potting
career. So-there-you-go.

I was made a member of the Aosdana, the state body you read about in the
Times, with 88 other writers and painters and composers. It was announced
just before Christmas. Nearly the whole country applied in the end. The most
distinguished member is Beckett. And there are a few turnips.

We were in Paris and London, and had some fine feasts, but I didn't enjoy
the travelling. Air France lost our luggage. We wasted 3 days getting them
back. The pipes were burst when we got back, the house flooded in Dublin.
But it was insured, so it makes no great difference, except the annoyance.

---

interested in publishing another of McGahern's books. Delahaye favoured either
Getting Through or *The Leavetaking*.

5 This government was led by Fine Gael's Garret FitzGerald (1926–2011) with support
from Labour and several independents. At 252 days old, it was the second shortest
government in the history of the state. The January 1982 Budget saw Minister of
Finance John Bruton's decision to introduce 18% VAT on clothing and footwear, with
no exemption for children's wear. Limerick socialist independent Jim Kemmy refused
to support the Budget, while Sinn Féin the Workers' Party's Joe Sherlock and Dublin
independent Seán Dublin Bay Loftus also voted against. The Budget was defeated 82–
81 and an election was set for 18 February. Charles Haughey of Fianna Fáil led another
weak coalition government after the election, with his government lasting just 279 days.

It's lovely being home and preparing to work.

I miss you often, and the handball.

Madeline sends her love, and will write herself before long.

And with my love to you all

John

Frances Kiernan Papers

Foxfield

[*March 1982*]

Dear Frances,

Thanks for your very kind letter and the story back. I hope I didn't trouble you too much with it. I'll look at it a last time and send it somewhere.[6] I am writing a good deal now but nothing seems to have any shape. That may come or it may not.

It must have been hard in Tuxedo Park, horrible when those doors blew open, but I was so glad it ended happily enough. It should be lovely in the spring, and spring is HERE (in Foxfield). Just yesterday I saw the black cat out on the stones [*illegible*] watching the amorous movements of the frogs in the water with a murderous intent.

The government fell here, and there was an election, an indecisive one, and it looks as if we'll have a crowd of crooks in power.

Nothing else much. Saw a delightful production of She Stoops to Conquer in The Abbey.[7] A few solid Australian movies. Re-reading Turgenev (what a wonder he is) and digging odd bits of the garden, the style desultory. I grow sort of fond of Dublin. Where the house is suits me, in the unfashionable middle of the city, near the markets, and the river, the dirty Liffey, with the old churches and the brewery chimneys on the hill. On the other sides stands the Zoo and the Main Lunatic Asylum – no nation needed it so much.[8]

With all dear wishes

John

6 'Parachutes'.

7 Oliver Goldsmith's *She Stoops to Conquer; Or, The Mistakes of a Night* (1773), adapted by Tom Murphy, premiered at the Abbey Theatre on 11 February 1982 and ran to forty-one performances.

8 McGahern's house in Stoneybatter was located near Grangegorman psychiatric hospital.

2 March 1982

Dear Eoghan,[9]
I meant to write a long time ago to thank you for your poems, and to say how
much I liked them, especially the later poems. I'm afraid it was the old story
of the intention becoming its own act. Forgive me.

Some one sent me the enclosed. Maybe you know about it. If not, it may
well be useful.

If you are ever near here maybe you'll call and we can bless that wagtail
again on dry land.

Please remember me to Rita with affection.

and with every good wish,

John

Alain Delahaye

Foxfield

14 April 1982

Dear Alain,
Thank you for your letter of March 31. I hope mother and child are, in a
phrase of Francie's, 'wonderful well'.[10]

I've relayed your message from Presses de la Renaissance to Hester Green
of A. M. Heath in London. She is very able and will have it dealt with. I'd like
to run through The Leavetaking before you begin to translate, as I'm hoping
you'll translate it. And if that is so, can you give me a few weeks warning
before you begin?

9 Eoghan Ó Tuairisc (1919–82) was an Irish poet and writer. In 1981 he published
The Road to Brightcity: and other stories (Dublin: Poolbeg Press, 1981). This is a
translation of nine of the best short stories written originally in Irish by Máirtín Ó
Cadhain. In a letter of 16 September 1981 David Marcus writes to Ó Tuairisc of
his delight 'that John McGahern praised your translation of O Cadhain'. See NUIG
Archives, G17/1995.
10 Pascale had given birth to a boy, Sébastien.

Random is a very fine house in the States, and that is probably the house style. I prefer Book and Verse, but my congratulations. I think it's a nice place to appear.[11]

Not much news in Foxfield. The cow had a bull calf the colour of café au lait on Good Friday. The early plum tree is in white blossom. There's fine weather, frost at night. The old woman up the lane – I was mowing her meadow when you were here – died in Sligo last Thursday, was buried in Fenagh on Sunday.[12] She broke her hip and died of homesickness. The postman scolded me and a few locals for standing on neighbouring tulips as we started to fill the grave. The postman is known as Weedy, from weeds in the garden, he is bad tempered and busy and small. The hunger for news is a symptom of a long oppressed people. It rages here. Francie hates to see you twice the same day – 'No good. Nothing new. No news. No news.'

Madeline sends her love to you all, as do I
John

Russell and Volkening Papers

Foxfield

27 April 1982

Dear Tim,
Thank you for your letter of April 19th.

I'm happy to accept, including the commissions you propose, which seem fair. I'd prefer, though, if the total British commissions should be 12½% instead of the superstitious 13% (7½ + 5½).[13]

Thanks for the very kind note about The New Yorker story.[14]

With every good wish
John

11 Some of Delahaye's poetry appeared in *The Random House Book of Twentieth-Century French Poetry*, ed. Paul Auster (New York: Random House, 1982).
12 Mrs Wrynn who lived at the top of the lane behind the McGahern home in Foxfield.
13 Refers to arrangements around a film option for *The Pornographer*. In his letter of 19 April, Seldes writes of a planned ninety-minute film: 'It may be a co-production between England's Channel Four and the Irish Film Board.' Kieran Hickey was the proposed director and Douglas Kennedy the producer.
14 'High Ground'.

31 May 1982

Dear Charles,
It was very nice to hear from you. No, there's no novel ready to enter lists, but it is going on. I'll be very happy if it's ready (or near ready) this time next year.[15]

We're delighted you're coming to Ireland and look forward very much to hearing from you when you're more certain of times.

> It'll be lovely to see you again
> with much love
> John

Russell and Volkening Papers

Foxfield

[*Summer 1982*]

Dear Hester,[16]
I am very grateful for the two cheques, the Dutch royalty and the film option.

I've read the treatment and I think it could work. It'd all depend on the images.

I saw Douglas Kennedy last night here in Dublin.[17] He says it is important to the Channel 4 people that I approve the treatment, and wanted me to write to that effect to his agent: Christie Dickson

---

15 Monteith had written on 6 May asking if McGahern might have a novel ready for Faber's spring 1983 list. In fact it would be another eight years before McGahern's next novel, *Amongst Women*, was published.
16 Hester Green who handled foreign rights at London literary agency A. M. Heath and whose professionalism McGahern admired.
17 Douglas Kennedy b. 1955, American novelist, journalist and travel writer. A New Yorker, Kennedy spent a year studying at Trinity College Dublin (TCD). In 1977 he returned to Dublin and started a cooperative theatre company with a friend. He was later hired to run the Abbey Theatre's second house, the Peacock. At the age of twenty-eight, he resigned from the Peacock to write full time. After several radio plays for the BBC and one stage play, he decided to switch directions and wrote his

London Management
235 Regent Street
Tel 734 4152

The next stage is the commissioning of the screenplay. I wouldn't want to stand in its way and I'd be glad if you'd do whatever is appropriate. He was very pressing and I said I'd prefer to do it through you.

Alain Delahaye, the French translator, wrote me that they want him to do The Leavetaking (there are some changes – revisions that I'd like to make in the text before he begins) but he tells me the go-ahead seems to be delayed by contractual difficulties.

I'll be in London early or mid September. It'd be very nice to see you again.

With every good wish
John

Neill Joy
[*Madeline McGahern*]
Foxfield

24 August 1982

Dear Neill,

Thank you for the long lovely letter, for the card, and to you and Mary for your great kindness to the Wrynns.[18] They were here to dinner last Friday night, and told us of your kindness, good company, how they liked you both. Pat's father is very ill in hospital.

Items:

1. I meant you to purchase the Bean suit. But this time next year we'll let it fly, with something more agreeable than rainwater.

2. Wilbur gave the Wrynns a short homily late one evening concerning the woe that is marriage and got reprimanded by Jeanette.

3. I got an offensive letter from F. Busch, inspired by The New Yorker, enquiries as to whether or not I had gotten his airmailed opus. Had to face up. Told him why I didn't like the opus. Have heard nary a word since. O my dears . . . how the heart turns cold . . .[19]

---

first book, a narrative account of his travels in Egypt called *Beyond the Pyramids* (London: Unwin Hyman, 1988). He has since become a bestselling novelist.
18 Neighbours of the McGaherns in Fenagh who had been holidaying in the US.
19 Fred Busch's novel *Take This Man* was published by Farrar, Straus and Giroux in 1981.

4. I go to Yorkshire next week to run an Arvon course, a short fling up to London, and then it's nose to the grindstone.[20]
We had great weather this summer. The hay was saved without trouble. The first plums are just now ready for picking, big Victorias. Madeline is in Dublin. The house now is quite lovely. We hope you and Mary will be able to enjoy it for a long stay one day before too long. We had lots and lots of the usual trouble with tradesmen.

Do you have any news of John Head? I know you dislike writing letters, but just scribble me a few such items, and I'll scribble back.

Madeline says she is writing to you both separately. She is so formidable these days that I tread about with the utmost caution. Gone are the days.

Please give my love to our friends
and with much love to you both
John

Madeline McGahern

[*London*]

Friday [*September 1982*]

Dear Madeline,
I found the tack cloth – tacky cloth they call them – in a lovely old wood shop at the bottom of Walthamstow market. They knew their trade. They did stock tung oil and were surprised I knew its name. It is too expensive to be used as an oil here: it would be different in a place like the States as it is native there. It is used here only as an ingredient in oil or paint, as a blender. For instance, it is used in Cuprinol. They told me that any of the good teak oils, Cuprinol for indoors, or linseed oil will give an identical finish. The small tin – the only size they stocked – that I bought in the city was £3.10.[21]

---

20 Since 1968, Arvon has offered writing retreats at three rural writing houses – in Devon, Shropshire and Yorkshire. The Ted Hughes Arvon Centre, Lumb Bank is an eighteenth-century mill-owner's house in West Yorkshire which once belonged to Ted Hughes. It is half a mile from the village of Heptonstall and two miles from Hebden Bridge. McGahern was struck by the dark beauty of the Yorkshire landscape and hoped to return with Madeline, but this never came to pass. He did, however, teach there again in 1989 with Tom Kilroy when they made a pilgrimage to nearby Heptonstall churchyard to visit the grave of Sylvia Plath.
21 Madeline wanted this oil for coating beehives.

Saw Tristan P. for lunch yesterday, and he was as miserly as ever, but he was very good about Julian, and seemed glad to talk.[22]

It is the long holiday weekend here. I decided not to contact Matthew or Faber and that is a fair excuse. Saw Rosemary looking mad in the distance and I ran for it.[23]

Tom Davey will be away for the weekend. I'll take Claire to lunch tomorrow. I'll make it my business to be close to the phone on Wednesday next between 6 and 7, should you decide to ring. That way it'll give you the choice of place.

I checked the VW vans. They are hard to get here because of the demand and more expensive than in Ireland. Cars are much cheaper.

I'll go to Lumb Bank on Monday and hope to go back by Liverpool on Saturday night. I should be home late on Sunday.

> I hope you enjoy Paris
> and with all my love
> John

Madeline McGahern

Hebden Bridge

8 [*September 1982*]

Dear Love,
It's all right here, no violently crazy people, but there's much work, some or most of a hopeless nature.

I saw Matthew and Elizabeth for a ½ hour. E. was pleased with the honey.[24] I'll stay with them on Sunday. They were painting the house, Matthew was charming.

Stayed at 23 with the Daveys. The house is lovely but unhappy. Tom took me out in his boat and did the teeth Monday morning.

---

22 Tristram (*not* Tristan) Powell was friendly with Julian Jebb and co-edited a book in his honour, *A Dedicated Fan: Julian Jebb, 1934–1984* (London: Peralta Press, 1993). Powell had, in 1966, directed a BBC television documentary on McGahern and his work. See letter to Patrick Gregory of 1 November 1965.
23 Rosemary Goad.
24 E. being Elizabeth Evans. Madeline had sent honey from her hives.

Jackie is pregnant and happy.[25] Jimmy and Rosaleen were good fun. Frankie is going round saying that Agnes and myself are liars and cheats and that papers are missing. He must be rattled.

I'll try and leave next Thursday morning.

Please don't worry about the house. I could just as easily have gotten Byrne. I did in a way. And the money is there. This time it should be ended.[26]

I'll go down on Saturday, if you are not in Dublin, when I settle over the house.

With all my love
John

Faber

Foxfield

30 October 1982

Dear Matthew,
Thank you for the Colgate piece, and to Elisabeth and yourself for two such pleasant nights in London.

I thought The Land of Dreamy Dreams extraordinarily good.[27] Housekeeping reminded me a bit of Busch – get hyped up and go.[28] Some one at Farrar must have a taste for it.

Horrible wet weather here. Will sell the few young cattle next week, and that's the real beginning of the winter.

Madeline sends her love to Elisabeth, and yourself, as do I

John

25 Breege McGahern's daughter.
26 Refers to some difficulties with the Dublin house.
27 *In the Land of Dreamy Dreams* is a 1981 collection of short stories from the American writer Ellen Gilchrist b. 1935. Her first book, it was published by the then recently founded University of Arkansas Press, sold more than 10,000 copies in its first ten months and won immense critical acclaim.
28 *Housekeeping* is a novel by Marilynne Robinson b. 1943, published in 1980 by Farrar, Straus and Giroux. The novel was a finalist for the Pulitzer Prize for Fiction (which Robinson would eventually win for her second novel, *Gilead* [New York: Farrar, Straus and Giroux, 2004]), and awarded the PEN/Hemingway Award for best first novel.

Alain Delahaye

Foxfield

31 October 1982

Dear Alain,

It's just a note to say that I've signed a contract with <u>Presses de la Renaissance</u> for <u>The Leavetaking</u>. Naturally I'm hoping you'll translate it.

I'd like to revise Part 2. Have you had any news? And when would you need the revision?

We've sort of battened down for the winter, working. Next week we'll sell the young cattle. Time seems to race and race.

Madeline sends her love to Pascale and you, as do I.

We hope all is well.

John

1983

Alain Delahaye

Foxfield

1 March 1983

Dear Alain,
I enclose Part II. I had a great deal of trouble with it.

We'd been hoping to hear from you and hope nothing wrong.

Madeline goes to Paris for a week or so on March 10th.

There's just one thing about Part II. Madeline's father thinks that there's a poor drawing of him in the original novel. It is very changed now and there's nothing in my eyes but it may be worth checking.

It's almost impossible there could be trouble but as he's <u>fairly mad</u> it is worth making assurance doubly sure.

Madeline sends her love to Pascale, yourself, and the children, as do I.

John

Alain Delahaye

Foxfield

26 March 1983

Dear Alain,
Our letters crossed. Did you get Part 2?

I'd very much like to see you and Pascale, to go to France, but it may not be easy. I have to go to the States at the end of August. I'll be there for the whole year, in Colgate University, teaching. I'm finding the new novel very hard. It won't be easy to get away, but I'd like to go. We'll see later. Thank you very much for the kind invitation.

Madeline was in Paris and left a note and small present for you with Madame Martin. She had a very pleasant stay.

I hope it gets easier with Sebastien. I saw where the male child is given the chemical equivalent of 30% more FEAR than the female in the womb.

Madeline sends her love to Pascale and yourself, as do I.

John

Alain Delahaye

Foxfield

20 April 1983

Dear Alain,

It was either my mistake – lightning/thunder – or the poor mother's, probably mine. Change it. It was a while on the bestseller list here and there was a big debate on the same issue. Fortunately I was out of the country and couldn't be found.[1]

Pin = Pioneer Pin – Temperance Badge – belong to Temperance Organization – small metal badge, heartshaped, declaring that they have foresworn the Demon Drink for life (Maybe Madame Martin would approve).

Modh múinte (literally Teaching Methods).

Pedantic Handbook for teachers, outlining the methods of introducing knowledge. i.e. Step 1 – you proceed by way of the known to the unknown.[2]

It is lovely to have the book. Thank you. Madeline is in Dublin. She'll write soon.

I'm writing this hurriedly because of the text.

Love

John

1 On p. 27 of *The Leavetaking* (1974) the mother tries to ease her son's fear of a thunder storm: 'You won't die and it's moving away. You can count between the clap and the flash. It's a mile away for every second you count.' Delahaye points out in a letter of 11 April 1983 that the counting ought to take place between the lightning and the thunder.

2 Answers to Delahaye's queries about phrasing in *The Leavetaking*.

4 May 1983

Dear Paul,

It was very nice to get your note. I slipped away from the meeting after voting.

I thought it quite awful.

There seemed just 2 choices: to leave the whole thing to its own devices or to try to form or join some decent group within it. As it is, it's tailormade for the Dublin pub crowd, who are already a solid group as far as everything outside themselves goes. I was amused overhearing some of the remarks – they felt their long overdue holy hour had come round at last.[3]

We are well.

I'm working but behind where I'd hoped to be.

I'll be in Colgate for the whole of next year, going there in August.

If you ever think of coming this way before then, we'll be glad, very glad to see you.

Love

John

14 May 1983

Dear Charles,

Thank you for your letter. I began to revise it, and found I had to rewrite almost all of Part 2. Part 1 is as it was. The translator, Alain Delahaye, thinks it makes it almost a new work.[4]

I feel ambiguous about it, a bit delinquent. One gets these chances at short stories but not at novels.

---

3 In reference to a meeting of Aosdána.

4 McGahern is writing here in response to a letter of 10 May in which Monteith asks for more detail about the new version of *The Leavetaking* to be published by Presses de la Renaissance in France. Monteith asks if it is something McGahern would like to see Faber publish.

I feel it might do as a paperback with a short preface but the last thing I'd want to do is push it.

I won't mind at all if you decide against it but naturally I hope it pleases.

With much love

John

Alain Delahaye

Foxfield

5 June 1983

Dear Alain,

Thank you for your letter.

'Pull-ups' – waterproofed legs of trousers, pulled up over trousers to protect them from rain and splashes while cycling.

Murdoch is dull, no feeling for words.[5] Several plots and ideas are used to flog puppets to a conclusion, but it may be the best sort of work for earning money. You'd not have to worry much about style.[6]

Do you know the work at all of Mavis Gallant, who lives in Paris?

I don't know about the summer. Only one of us can leave here because of the cattle and garden. I have to be in Colgate at the end of August – a year of lectures. I promised my sister to go to London for a few days. If I was to go over to France it could only be for a day or two and it might be better to wait till after the States when we both could go together . . .

In the sense of the house and meals and care, would you be tempted to meet in London for a few days in late July. You could stay at my sisters if you wished. Write and tell me what you think of the idea.

Horrible weather here, finding it very hard to work, bad dreams, disturbed – now and again I write well and it goes.

Madeline sends her love to Pascale and yourself, as do I

Write soon about the July idea.

Love

John

5 Iris Murdoch (1919–99), British novelist and philosopher.
6 Delahaye had been asked to translate Murdoch's *The Philosopher's Pupil* (London: Chatto & Windus, 1983) but was finding it boring and asked McGahern's advice.

Alain Delahaye

Foxfield

20 July 1983

Dear Alain,
Thank you for your letter.

If you should change your mind in August, and would like to come here, I'd meet you at the Airport.

I leave for the States at the end of August. Madeline will stay on for about 2 weeks to close the place up.

I like and dislike going. There is much about the States that I like, but the teaching will be hard, and I do not like leaving.

Faber will publish the new version of The Leavetaking but I have to write a short preface.

We've had wonderful weather. The hay is all saved. Francie sold his mule, bought a donkey, but the donkey wasn't able to pull the raker. He was quite annoyed. I gave a talk in the De La Salle College in Waterford in April and to my amazement was given a silver tray and a bottle of poteen (moonshine or illicit spirits) in a large Coca Cola bottle. Francie seemed to come every day till it was gone. 'Far, far better value than whiskey.' It was at least 3 times as strong.

Madeline sends her love to Pascale and you, as do I.

John

James Swift
[*Madeline McGahern*]

Foxfield

27 July 1983

Dear Jimmy,
My sister came by yesterday and told us she read of Paddy's death.[7] We are very sorry and Madeline and I want to offer you and all your family, especially your mother, our deepest sympathy.

John

7 Paddy Swift died at his home on the Portuguese Algarve on 19 July 1983.

29 August 1983

Dear Matthew,
After this week, the above will be my address. Madeline will close the place up here and come out in a few weeks. I'll be there for the whole year but I suppose there's very little chance you'll be able to come up. In March they are giving me a few weeks off to go to the Adelaide Festival.

I'm afraid it won't be easy to begin with anyhow for the paperbacks. I had the enclosed, in an open letter, from McDermott a while back, saying he was remaindering all the books, which he has done. He bought them from Quartet after William Miller left but he did pay the royalty until a year ago, which he said he didn't have to (The Leavetaking was the only book to sell out).[8] It is reported that he's in financial difficulty, but that's no comfort. I hope it doesn't damage your publication too much.

Please give my love to Elisabeth and the boys.

> And with all good wishes
> John

Alain Delahaye

Colgate

14 September 1983

Dear Alain,
It's just a note to say I'm here, giving classes already, a far cry from Francie and the lakes. Madeline is closing up the place at home. She'll come in a week or so.

There is so much wealth, the trees, the cut grass, white houses, the tanned beautiful young people in their energetic indolence. They continually wave to me. I feel like some stranded idiot, ½ believing that it's real.

---

8 On Miller and McGahern's paperback publishing history, see letter to Matthew Evans of 14 December 1978.

I hope Pascale, and the girl and boy, are all well, and with good wishes
and my love
John

James Swift
[*Madeline McGahern*]

Colgate

4 October 1983

Dear Jimmy,

Thank you for writing. I had already left for here and it was forwarded. I was going to call on my way through, but knew the house would be troubled, and was hesitant.[9]

I remember going with Paddy and, I think, Kathy one morning to a London square, where Paddy was having a portrait done by Tim Behrens.[10] We waited in the small park in the square, surrounded with a few benches and trees. Behrens came out with Paddy after an hour or two. We shook hands, there was some talk of us all going to the pub, but Behrens said he better go back to work. 'Is he any good?' I asked as we walked away. 'He's very good but he's so serious. The trouble I find with all these young men is that they are all so damned serious,' and he started to laugh.

The fall is amazing here now, with bright maple reds, and orange. The people are pleasant but sometimes the very force of the friendliness can be numbing, the ruthless practicality it hides.

Please give your mother our best wishes. I hope she's a bit better now.

With all good wishes,
John

9 Paddy Swift died on 19 July 1983.
10 Tim Behrens (1937–2017) was a student at the Slade School of Fine Art and formed part of the tightly knit group of artists and intellectuals who frequented the Colony Room Club, the Soho drinking establishment where Lucian Freud and others such as Francis Bacon spent much time during the late 1950s and early 1960s.

1984

Alain Delahaye

Colgate

17 January 1984

Dear Alain,

It was so nice to get your letter. I'd have been happy to do the interview if it could do the book any good but they didn't contact me.

We fly to California tomorrow to see Madeline's mother.[1] The old hard slog of teaching starts again in February.

I go to Australia (Adelaide) in March for 10 days. I hate the prospect of the air journey but it gets me off teaching.

It's snowing as I write, the vast hills all white. The trees are frozen. There's a skislope alongside the house, lighted and beautiful at night, the dark figures racing or climbing slowly on the lift as in a dream.

May from across the lake writes us very nice letters. My uncle feeds Charlie the cat. May had to scrape turkey grease off the floor. 'He's man and master round the place,' May writes but the cat thrives. We loaned the place to visitors from Dublin. My uncle was furious. As soon as they'd gone he disconnected the pump. All other visitors will have to haul water from the lake. Jerome on the hill got married in a hurry. 'All so secret,' May said.

Re. Murdoch there's a very nice anecdote in George Borrow (19th century) on his way to Spain. He noticed a man asleep in a field after reading a book of poems, the book on his chest. He guessed it was going to be a bestseller by the time he returned (2 years). He was right. The whole country was reading it when he got back (in order to get to sleep).[2]

---

1 Madeline's mother then lived in Atascadero, California.

2 Delahaye had mused in a letter of 12 December 1983 that the reason for his not being able to write his own poetry was related to 'the depressing effect of Iris Murdoch's laborious prose . . .'

Madeline sends her love to Pascale and yourself, and all wishes for your happiness this year, as indeed do I.

John

Faber

Colgate

1 February 1984

Dear Charles,

I was sorry not to get your telegrams till now. I was in California for the last 2 weeks. I had no idea that such a business – Top of the Irish – was afoot at all.

Much as I'd like to go to Dublin in May I fear it is out. I have 60 students here, and May is the very worst time, in the middle of the exams. Especially as they have given me 2 weeks off in March, to go to the Adelaide Festival (Australia).[3]

Did you go to Stockholm?[4]

I got the good news today that the new Leavetaking is doing well in France.[5]

By a lucky chance I got January free. The hard grind starts again this week, goes on till the end of May.

Did you see about the kidnapping and shooting in sleepy Foxfield? May from across the lake said it was a pity I wasn't there – I'd have had lots to write about. The boy from the post office was shot by mistake at a checkpoint. Some of the Irish soldiers are supposed to have thrown their arms away at the very sound of firing.[6]

With all good wishes for the New Year
And much love
John

3 This sentence has been underlined in pencil at Faber.
4 William Golding, with whom Monteith had developed a close relationship as editor beginning with his first book, *The Lord of the Flies*, was presented with the Nobel Prize for Literature in Stockholm on 10 December 1983. Monteith attended.
5 McGahern enclosed a cutting from *L'Express* which Monteith thanks him for in a letter of 7 March.
6 Refers to the kidnapping and escape of industrialist Don Tidey (November to December 1983) after a shootout between IRA volunteers, the Irish Army and members of An Garda Síochána at Derrada Wood, Drumcroman, Ballinamore, Co. Leitrim. One soldier and one garda were killed.

Madeline McGahern

Adelaide, Australia

5 March 1984

[*To Madeline*]
You'd love it here, 98°, dry; cold air blowing from the air conditioned stores, sea, clear skies.[7]
    I read well and am glad I came but I miss you.
                With my love
                John

Seamus Heaney Papers

Colgate

4 April 1984

Dear Seamus,
This is to give you the telephone, to say there's a room here, that I can meet you; but that you should do whatever makes the visit easy for yourself.
    Terence appears a bit het-up the last few days, and he may want you to stay with him, and if that's easier it is fine with me.[8] It may well be. Anyhow, you'll see what he says. The usuals are at work as well. There's a running feud between himself and Fred Busch but I am out of all that.
    I hope Seamus Deane's visit goes well. Please remember me to him.
              I'm looking forward to seeing you
              John

---

7 McGahern read at Adelaide Writers' Week. Other writers to appear included André Brink, Angela Carter, Bruce Chatwin and Salman Rushdie.
8 Terrence Des Pres (1939–87) was the author of *The Survivor: An Anatomy of Life in the Death Camps* (New York: Oxford University Press, 1976). In 1973 he joined the faculty at Colgate, where he held the Crawshaw Chair in English Literature. He ran a very popular course, which led to a certain degree of friction with Fred Busch.

6 April 1984

Dear Frances,
Thank you for your very kind note. I replied to the correspondent.

I sent you a card from Australia and had to rely on memory for the address.

I got a flu there, tried to walk it off, did to some extent – even went out into the bush to look at a GOAT FARM – but wound up in hospital soon after getting back.

Whether it was the fright I got or not I finished a story I've been with a long time. About how the middleclass Protestants disappeared in the New Ireland. I'll send it to you in a few days.[9]

It'll be lovely to see you again and classes will be at an end soon.

Please remember me to Howard.
Affectionately
John

Alain Delahaye

Colgate

16 April 1984

Dear Alain,
Thank you for your letter of March 18th.

I was in Australia, got flu there, tried to walk it off – they paid so much in airfares that I felt I couldn't just go to bed – got back here somehow (including 3 strange hours in a steaming Tahiti), found myself going for little walks on the ceiling, and wound up in hospital with pneumonia. I am completely recovered.

Madeline goes home on April 29th.
I should follow her a month later.

---

9 Refers to 'The Conversion of William Kirkwood', originally titled 'The Conversion of Andrew Kirkwood'.

We are hoping to get to France sometime in summer, and to see you. Is there any chance at all you'd like to take that holiday with us in Ireland? We'd be glad, very glad.

I liked California. San Francisco is a wonderful city. The hills everywhere drop into the sky. I spoke in Berkeley and we were very lucky in our hosts. Then we drove south to visit Madeline's mother, a small town Atascadero, the prison for the criminally insane, child molesters etc. She lived alone with an aged cat, feeding birds, and wild animals. She's a terrible person, almost worse than Madeline's father. It may be luck that we have no children.

Bonnefoy spoke here last week.[10] A nice man. John Naughton (teaches here) read his translations of each poem, then B. read in French, poem by poem, very <u>plainly</u> and beautifully.[11] Questions followed. Many of the questions were irrelevant or stupid but Bonnefoy handled them beautifully. He seemed to me to speak out of an enlightened commonsense. He'd plainly lived for long in that solitary place where poetry happens, and spoke clearly of its simple unchanging laws. It was a relief after the glittering nonsense that often travels on the same passport round here. There were 40–50 people. 700 cheered a drunken Dickey some months before.[12] I didn't go to the reception.

Summer will arrive in a mad rush any of these days, all haze, and then in three days the whole valley will be lushly, densely green. I've read that it comes to Moscow the same way.

Write if you find time.

Lectures end May 8th.

The exams end on May 19th.

I can leave whenever I hand in the results after that.

Madeline sends her love to Pascale and you, as do I

John

10 Yves Bonnefoy (1923–2016), French poet and essayist. In 1981 he became the first French poet since Paul Valéry to be elected to the Collège de France.

11 John Naughton, Professor in the Department of Romance Languages at Colgate. A leading Bonnefoy scholar, in the same year as this letter he published *The Poetics of Yves Bonnefoy* (Chicago: University of Chicago Press, 1984).

12 James Dickey (1923–97), American poet and novelist with a reputation for hellraising. Best known for his novel *Deliverance* (Boston: Houghton, Mifflin, 1970), which was adapted in 1972 into an acclaimed film of the same name directed by John Boorman.

1 May 1984

Dear Seamus,
Thanks for the generous words.

Several stopped me to say how fine <u>your</u> reading was. I felt like an Ambassador at large for a few days.

I'm sorry the whole surrounds were so prickly, and I was grateful for the ease and tact you waltzed through it all, and that glasshouse waltzing ain't easy. Both factions seem pleased which, not to [*illegible*] a point, is unusual.[13]

Madeline said before she left what a pleasure it was to see you again, and especially to see you in such great form, and looking so well. As so with me.

I'll call if I'm in Dublin and I'll look forward to seeing you in August.

> With thanks
> and love
> John

12 May 1984

Dear Frances,
Thank you for your letter. It would have been nice if the obvious ending had worked, but no good at all when it didn't.

I'll take it home. It'll be something solid to start with. My own feeling is that there are 2 separate stories, for the original was meandering into a novel.[14]

13 Heaney had read in Colgate earlier that month, moving deftly around some faculty divisions. For more on the different camps involved, see McGahern's letter to Heaney of 4 April 1984. Heaney had a professional relationship with Colgate going back to 1969; in 1994 he spoke at commencement and was awarded an Honorary Doctorate of Humane Letters.

14 Probably a reference to 'The Conversion of William Kirkwood'.

I have tentative plans to leave for Ireland Sunday evening, the 27th. I'll probably leave here in the middle of that week. There are a few things I have to do in New York.

I'm in the midst of student papers.

So perhaps you'd drop me a note about the best times for you. Or if it is easier to ring I'll be definitely in all Wednesday evening and all of Thursday.

(315) 824 2608

> It'll be lovely to see you again.
> With every good wish
> John

Robin Robertson Papers

Foxfield

2 June 1984

Dear Robin Robertson,[15]
Thank you for your kind letter, and Firebird.[16]

---

15 Robin Robertson b. 1955, Scottish poet and editor, then working as assistant fiction editor at Penguin Books.

16 Robertson was editing the *Firebird* series of anthologies for Penguin. He had written to McGahern on 22 May 1984: 'I am an admirer of your writing and I wondered if you would consider letting me see some new work – short fiction or a self-contained extract from something longer – with a view to publication in FIREBIRD 4? I cannot use anything that is scheduled for publication in book form prior to January 1985 – when FIREBIRD comes out – and would prefer to publish work that has not appeared anywhere previously. The deadline for submissions is the first week of July; the fee £125.' Robertson eventually included 'Like All Other Men' – the story that McGahern fears is 'too slight' – in the anthology *Firebird 4: New Writing from Britain and Ireland* (Harmondsworth: Penguin Books, 1985). He and his then wife Clare Reihill, who was from Irvinestown, Co. Fermanagh, subsequently visited Foxfield as part of a publishing project on *32 Counties: Photographs of Ireland by Donovan Wylie* (London: Secker & Warburg, 1989). One hundred copies of the book were signed by each of the thirty-two contributing authors. At this meeting, McGahern discussed his increasing unease at Faber, a situation that had been developing since the retirement of Charles Monteith. Robertson was then editorial director at Secker & Warburg and McGahern agreed to show him the MS of *Amongst Women* with a possible view to switching publishers.

I enclose Oldfashioned and Parachutes for you to look at. They will be published under the title Oldfashioned by Faber in the autumn of 1985.[17]

Parachutes appeared in Encounter, Oldfashioned in the small Belfast literary magazine Threshold. There are other stories that have been published in The New Yorker but I do not want to trouble you with too many.

The only unpublished story I have is too slight for publication on its own, and the concluding 2 stories of the volume will not be ready by July. I am sorry that this is so.

> With very good wishes,
> Sincerely,
> John McGahern

Robin Robertson Papers

Foxfield

21 June 1984

Dear Robin Robertson,
Thank you for your letter. I enclose 2 of the New Yorker Stories.[18] The 3rd has been reprinted in England, which rules it out for you. I am sorry I haven't my own copies to show. I've been away and cannot lay hands on them. Should you decide to print either of The New Y. stories I'd need to go through the prose again. It'd only take a day. I also enclose the manuscript of the unpublished story.[19]

> With best wishes,
> John McGahern.

17 This would seem to suggest that the book that became *High Ground* in 1985 was at one point being imagined under the title *Oldfashioned*.
18 The *New Yorker* stories are 'Crossing the Line' (1 August 1983) and 'High Ground' (22 March 1982).
19 McGahern is writing in response to a letter of 12 June from Robinson: 'Many thanks for letting me see "Oldfashioned" and "Parachutes". Of the two I preferred "Parachutes" but the fact that it's been published already by Encounter is a bit of a problem; I'd much prefer to use work that has not appeared in Britain. Could you possibly send me the stories published in The New Yorker and the unpublished piece that you think might be too slight?' The unpublished story is 'Like All Other Men'.

Neill Joy
[*Madeline McGahern*]
Foxfield

15 July 1984

Dear Neill,

I have to thank Mary and you for your kindness to us all last year, and for the good company.

I came straight back into the court case. My brother tried to bluff it to the last. The Judge had to work from chambers, where he agreed to retire, that he would start the trial if they didn't come up with a settlement within 5 minutes. My brother accepted what he was offered 4 years ago. And all the expense and anxiety his greed caused. So the old poisons run on.[20]

Then my aunt died, leaving my uncle the last outlying branch of that family. The three sisters all died in June.[21]

Amazing hot weather broke a week ago. The hay is saved. I bought a few cattle. Charlie the cat frisks around the place. I put out the eel line and have started to write.[22] I tried to smoke some eels but they didn't come out right. Tomorrow Madeline goes for a week to Gormanston, 20 miles North of Dublin, for a bee course.[23] Because of the hot weather the lake is low. 'Very sexy weather,' Francie shouts as he comes around the lake on the bike. Jerome got married. 'An old lady, a nurse, but good enough for him. She brings in the washers.'

I met your reference librarian and his wife in Galway. I go down again on the 25th. They seem to be having a great time. They are staying in a Gaelic speaking house, an old toothless fellow who blathers away. I doubt if they

20 Refers to the court case resulting from the will of Frank McGahern, John's father. See letter to Brian Friel of 21 August 1980.
21 Maggie (Breen), who had the shop in Ballinamore, died in June 1964. Her sisters Susan (McGahern) and Katie (McGarry) also died in the month of June. Jimmy, the oldest of the McManus siblings, had died on a visit to his daughters in England. Pat McManus of the garage in Ballinamore was the only one left when McGahern wrote this letter.
22 McGahern liked to fish for eel and perch from a rowing boat that he kept on the lakes in front of and behind the house in Foxfield.
23 Bees were kept at Foxfield for several years, and Madeline attended beekeeping courses in Gormanston on a number of occasions.

understand a word he says, but they are attentive, and what more does any man need! They have dictionaries GO LEOR.

We'll go to France for October.

We'll be here until then.

Write if you have time.

Madeline sends her love to you both, as indeed do I

John

Caroline Walsh

Foxfield

16 July 1984

Dear Caroline,[24]

Thank you for your letter and invitation.

I remember you well, and with affection.[25] I saw your wedding photo in the newspapers and was glad. I hope you'll find much happiness.[26]

Please forgive the enclosed typescript, but it is the only one I have here.

The story was published in The New Yorker late last year, but not on this side of the Atlantic.[27]

I won't mind at all if it doesn't suit you.

I have a small place here. If you are ever nearby, it would be a pleasure for me to see you again.

With every good wish

John

24 Caroline Walsh (1952–2011), Dublin-born daughter of the short story writer Mary Lavin. A graduate of UCD, she joined the Irish Times in 1975 as a news reporter, rising to the position of literary editor in 1999, a position she held until her untimely death in 2011.

25 McGahern first met Caroline Walsh in her mother's mews house at 11 Lad Lane Upper, Dublin in the early 1960s, when she was a child – she had fond memories of him reading her bedtime stories.

26 Caroline Walsh married James Ryan in October 1981.

27 The story is 'Crossing the Line', which was published in the Irish Times on 2 August 1984.

6 September 1984

Dear Frances,

I'm sending this back almost by return. I've had no problems. They almost all are improvements. Eddie Mac seems the right title.[28] If I come on better, which I doubt, I'll send it on.

The only thing I was sort of loathe to let go was 'No matter what their banks [?] looked like . . .' but it probably is too much.

I think at the end there should be some echo of the game – victory, triumph.

I hope what I wrote is clear and I am very grateful.

John

Alain Delahaye

Foxfield

1 October 1984

Dear Alain,

It seems we'll get to France late October, early November instead of when we planned. We'll go by way of London.

Madeline's ½ sister was here – she left today – and brought Liberation. It seems they went for local colour. Most of the quotes seemed wrong, or worse, ½ right – but I suppose it can do little harm.[29]

28 'Eddie Mac' appeared in the *New Yorker* for 3 December 1984. Kiernan had written to McGahern about the story on 30 August 1984: 'I've made some changes, which I've tried to mark on the proof and explain when necessary. I'm also suggesting further changes. The most important comes at the story's end, where we would like you to do away with any mention of the river. I'm always open to reason and suggestion and where I've taken out something you dearly love I want you to be sure to tell me. [. . .] The story has great power. Something about it reminds me of the novels of Thomas Hardy. We're very fortunate to have it, and we're mindful of that.' Madeline McGahern Papers.

29 Daniel Rondeau wrote the piece for *Libération*, which is a mix of quotes from McGahern and descriptions of the local Leitrim area, including a memorable description of Luke Early's bar in Mohill (misidentified in the piece as Dromod), a particular favourite of McGahern's. Rondeau b. 1948 was then chief editor of the

We hope Pascale is well and that the birth is happy.

Madeline sends her love

as do I.

John

Irish Academy of Letters

Foxfield

14 December 1984

[*To the Secretary, Irish Academy of Letters, School of Irish Studies, Thomas Prior House, Merrion Road, Dublin 4*][30]
I am writing to accept the offer of membership made by your President in his letter of December 7th. I'd be grateful if you could thank Mr. Kiely for his kind letter.[31]

Yours sincerely

John McGahern

---

book pages of *Libération*. Rondeau's piece on McGahern and the writer's Leitrim surrounds later appeared in his book of essays *Les Fêtes partagées: Lectures et autres voyages* (Paris: NiL Editions, 1994).

30 Sean J. White (1927–96) was Secretary of the Irish Academy of Letters in 1984. See 'Council Minutes: September 27th 1984', NLI MS 33,775 (Folder 2). White edited the literary magazine *Irish Writing* for ten years. In 1979 he was appointed dean of the School of Irish Studies and was later employed as a consultant to the Irish Studies Department at what was to become the University of Limerick. He was subsequently appointed professor there.

31 Benedict Kiely (1919–2007), writer from Omagh, Co. Tyrone, then serving as president of the all but moribund Irish Academy of Letters, an organisation founded in 1932 as a bulwark against the worst excesses of state censorship.

1985

Faber

Foxfield

24 January 1985[1]

Dear Charles,
I am deeply grateful for the extraordinary kindness of your private note, and the very generous offer of the 'Publisher's letter'. <u>High Ground</u> seems even now the right title, unless I can find something extraordinary over the next few weeks, which I doubt.

There is one very slight difficulty. Tim Seldes of Russell & Volkening has been acting for me for some time in the U.S. and he has asked for the contract to go through him as I didn't want to use his counterpart here A.M. Heath.

I have written to him that I am very happy with the offer, and have asked him to telephone Sarah Hardie so that there should be no unnecessary delay.[2] I foresee no trouble of any kind.

> With my love
> John

Russell and Volkening Papers (TS)

Foxfield

25 January 1985

Dear Tim,
I enclose the <u>Pornographer</u> and <u>Getting Through</u> contracts, Faber's offer (Monteith has been my editor there from the beginning but is in semi-

1 Mistakenly dated 1984 by McGahern.
2 Monteith had written earlier that week to say that the terms offered by Faber were a £2,500 advance and royalties that would 'certainly be at least as good as they were last time if not considerably better, since we've recently adopted the Minimum Terms Agreement proposed by the Society of Authors and the Writer's Guild'.

retirement now, coming in a day or two a week) and the manuscript. So far, High Ground seems the best title.

I think the advance offered is on the generous side for a book of stories, and I am happy with it.[3] I put down its generosity more to Matthew Evans than to Monteith. If you are happy with it perhaps you'd telephone Sarah Hardie and have her send the contract to you (01 278 6881 Faber tel).[4] I'll have written that you are acting for me.[5]

The U.S. manuscript has one story less than the British, the New Yorker story Gold Watch, since it was added to the U.S. edition of Getting Through, which was published a year or more later than the British. I am working on two shortish stories.[6] You could have them in a few weeks if the U.S. book needs filling out, but I think it's probably long enough. After that I'm going back to the novel.

I enclose an extra copy of Bank Holiday in case you might find a place for it. It has just been rejected by the New Yorker because there weren't enough difficulties and the man is too ordinary. I don't agree. It has not been offered elsewhere. They are at present considering The Conversion of Andrew Kirkwood, which has probably a much better chance, but you never know.[7] The N.Y. couldn't believe that the events in Like All Other Men could actually happen, which Penguin have just brought out in London, and The Yale Review will do over there.[8] I'll have Yale send you the contract.

All this sounds a bit longwinded.

I do hope the stories please you and it'll be a great pleasure to see you here.

> With all good wishes
> John

---

3 The advance offered for *High Ground* was £2,500.
4 Sarah Hardie was working at this time as assistant to Giles de la Mare who looked after contracts at Faber.
5 In the margin McGahern has penned 'I have written.'
6 'The Creamery Manager' and 'The Old Man'; the latter was eventually published as 'The White Boat'.
7 Later changes its title to 'The Conversion of William Kirkwood'.
8 The plot of 'Like All Other Men' involves a woman having a casual sexual encounter with a man on the night before she enters a convent.

23 February 1985

Dear Pat,[9]
Thank you for your kindness to me and Madeline in Waterford. It was lovely to see you again. I thought the classes were quite extraordinary in their attention and seriousness. Please remember me to the brothers I met, and your own Michael. Our only complaint was too much kindness.
There was snow to Kilkenny, and then a perfect run. We were home by seven.

I return Eamonn Barrett's prose.[10] It has something, a sense of pacing and rhythm, but I doubt if he has found his own themes yet. Some of the language is too vague and cliché ridden (where did he get all the Americanisms? TV?).[11]

I took the liberty of underlining in pencil certain phrases and sentences that he might look at again. Do they say anything vivid or exact as they stand? Could they be pictured differently? . . . But the work is still interesting. It may well become work.

> With every good wish
> Affectionately
> John

---

9 Pat O'Mahony was an English teacher at De La Salle College in Waterford City, Co. Waterford.

10 Eamon Barrett was then a sixteen-year-old student in Pat O'Mahony's Leaving Certificate class whose work O'Mahony admired. I am grateful to Eamon for permitting me to consult this letter.

11 Like many young readers in the 1980s, Barrett recalls being much under the sway of Stephen King.

24 March 1985

Dear Charles,
I took the liberty of playing around with your blurb, mainly because of epiphany and the association with Mister Joyce.[12] It might sink our frail vessel.

    Add to it or take away, if you think it needs it.
      Are you likely to be in Ireland this summer?
              With much love
              John

Faber

Foxfield

12 May 1985

Dear Matthew,
Have you heard of the 'Kerry Babies'?
    One mutilated infant was found in a plastic bag washed up on a Kerry strand.
    A Hayes girl gave birth to a child in an outhouse and buried it in a field. It was illegitimate. She already had an illegitimate child by the same man, who was married, and worked with her in the local sports centre. They were poor, with a small dairy farm, dim-witted except for this girl, alcoholic.
    The police forced confessions from the family, and charged the girl with the murder of the baby washed up in the plastic bag, which plainly was not hers. There was an outcry when the facts were reported. The murder charges were dropped, a tribunal of enquiry was ordered, which has been running for the last 6 months, and is about to end.
    A reporter from the Irish Times, Michael O'Regan, who comes from that area, has been covering it since it began. He will write a book on it

12 As much as McGahern admired James Joyce, he had a history of not wishing to have his name associated with *Dubliners*, knowing that no writer could benefit from such a comparison. See letter to Monteith of 5 December 1970.

with another journalist. He already has a verbal commitment from an Irish publisher he knows, Anvil, who are only interested in the paperback for the Irish market, and has been approached by Michael Joseph. I know and like him and am writing to see if it would interest you at all. He'd be well disposed if you were but I can see difficulties for you (a) the presence of the Irish paperback publisher (b) that it may be too sensational for Faber (c) of little interest to a wider public (d) how well can he write in book form. Perhaps you will let me know. [*several illegible words*] I am completely neutral. Once the tribunal ends the book will be written quickly.[13]

I was in Lumb Bank last week with Fay Weldon. She spoke of you with real affection. She was a marvellous teacher.[14]

Madame had lit out for Paris by the time I got back and is still there. 'Peaceable, middlin' peaceable', I heard a man say in the Enniskillen market. 'What you want . . . the sky above us.'[15]

With love to Elisabeth and the boys
John

Alain Delahaye
Foxfield

28 May 1985

Dear Alain,
Thank you for your letter and I am sorry for the confusion.[16]

---

13 Faber did not publish the book, which appeared in 1985 under the title *Dark Secrets: The Inside Story of Joanne Hayes and the Kerry Babies*. Published by the *Kerrryman* newspaper, it was co-authored by Gerard Colleran and Michael O'Regan.
14 Fay Weldon b. 1931, novelist, playwright and screenwriter. Her first novel, *The Fat Woman's Joke*, was published in 1967 by MacGibbon & Kee. Her work includes over twenty novels, five collections of short stories, several children's books, non-fiction books, magazine articles and a number of plays written for television, radio and the stage, including the pilot episode for the TV series *Upstairs, Downstairs*. Much of her fiction explores issues surrounding women's relationships with men, children, parents and each other.
15 'The sky above us' is later used as the subtitle of a frequently published essay by McGahern on Co. Leitrim. See *LOTW*, 19–26.
16 Delahaye had been sent a copy of Brian Friel's *Faith Healer* by an English literary agent minus the author's name, saying that McGahern would like his opinion of it. Delahaye eventually translated the play in 2009.

The play is by a friend, Brian Friel. He was worried about the translation, and asked me if I could get an opinion. I said I'd ask you if it wasn't too much trouble for you. It was supposed to be sent to me, and then I'd ask you before sending you the text (Since the text didn't come I thought they had changed their minds). They sent it to you instead. I am sorry. I saw the play in New York, with James Mason, and didn't like it but that could have been the production.

Does that mean that the whole family will move to Paris? I think a position in a business firm better than all the killing translation.

The book <u>High Ground</u> will be published in October. I'll of course send you and Pascale a copy. I've just been given the Award of the American Irish Foundation for 1985. It is 'confidential' until June 28th, when it'll be announced at a dinner in the Embassy. I'm very glad of the money but far from looking forward to the ceremonies.[17]

With every good wish.

Write me a note sometime you have time

Madeline sends her love to Pascale and yourself
as do I
John

Russell and Volkening Papers

Foxfield

12 June 1985

Dear Tim,

I enclose the promised stories that may be needed for a possible U.S. <u>High Ground</u>. <u>The Old Man</u> may still need something.[18] <u>The Creamery Manager</u> I am very happy about.

There is a sort of good news. I have [*been*] given the award of the American Irish Foundation for 1985. It is for $10,000 and will be announced at a luncheon at the American Ambassador's residence on June 28th. It is 'confidential' until then.

How are you?

17 The Irish-American Foundation Award brought with it a prize of $10,000, which was presented to McGahern at the American ambassador's residence in Dublin.
18 McGahern did not publish a story under this title – this story eventually becomes 'The White Boat', which was published in *New Writing 6: An Anthology*, ed. A. S. Byatt and Peter Porter (London: Vintage, 1997), but never collected.

Are you likely to come to Europe?
                    With every good wish
                    John

17 June 1985

Dear Tom,[19]
It was a pleasure to see Julie and yourself in Tuam.

I enclose the CNUAS circular. It may be of poor use. I've been billed for the award I got back in 1980 and I can see little option but to pay.[20]

Nothing to report but a rather unpleasant confrontation with the local F.F. politician who plans to dump the place out with guts. ELLIS is the name. ELLFAL the company. Get it: OFFAL. It's how they name racehorses. They must have sat up half the night. They are quite incensed there should be any opposition.[21]

Madeline sends her best wishes to you both, as do I
                    John

19 Tom Kilroy b. 1934 is an Irish playwright and novelist. A native of Callan, Co. Kilkenny, like McGahern he is the son of a garda. He studied at UCD in the late 1950s when he first met McGahern and they both attended Mary Lavin's literary salon. In his early career he was play editor at the Abbey Theatre, and in the 1980s he sat on the Board of the Field Day Theatre Company. In 1978 Kilroy was appointed Professor of English at UCG, a post from which he resigned in 1989 to concentrate on writing. McGahern worked closely with Kilroy at UCG when he convened the National Writers' Workshop in autumn 1979. See letter to the Arts Council of 31 March 1980.

20 Members of Aosdána are eligible to receive from the Arts Council a Cnuas – an annuity for a term of five years – to assist them in concentrating their time and energies in the full-time pursuit of their art.

21 Senator John Ellis, a businessman and politician from Fenagh, the closest village to Foxfield, had made an application with Leitrim County Council to build a pet-food refrigeration plant beside Laura Lake, in front of the McGaherns' home. McGahern is quoted in an article by Gerry Moriarty in the *Irish Press* of 13 August 1985 titled 'Author McGahern joins protest over pet food plant': 'The lorries drawing in the offal inevitably must create a stink and the soil is so thin that the raw material effluent would quickly flow into Laura Lake and cause pollution.'

10 September 1985

Dear Joe,
Thank you for the letters and enclosures. It'll be nice when the 'newspapers' are over and I can go back to the novel. I've always hated the days around a publication.

I'd be glad to meet John Boland and his wife. His review was too generous but no doubt others will correct that.[22]

I'd almost prefer if you published nothing <u>yet</u> about the Ellis business but I do not want to interfere. Whatever you do, don't mention the S.A. wine or we'll all be ruined afore tonight.[23]

It was very nice to see you again after all those years. I hope the next time will not be so far away. I was very sorry not to see you off in the morning.

With all good wishes
John

Seamus Heaney Papers

Foxfield

20 October 1985

Dear Seamus,
I want to thank you for the handsome and generous review of <u>High Ground</u>.[24]

I hope you are all well.

---

22 Boland wrote in the *Evening Press* of *High Ground* that 'literature of this sort doesn't need explication, merely gratitude'.
23 The drinking of South African wine would then have been frowned upon in some quarters as the Apartheid regime in that country entered its final years.
24 Seamus Heaney, 'A chronicle of middle Ireland', *Sunday Tribune* (6 October 1985), 21: 'we realise that John McGahern writes poetry as it was defined by Wordsworth – a history of feeling and a science of feeling. The history is in the terrific relish with which he chronicles those scenes of provincial life and records the craftily deployed, naturally weathered speech of Dublin and the countryside. The science is in his point of view, his vigilance and regret as he lays bare the subterfuges and consolidations that occur deep in the hidden growth rings of a life.'

It'd be very nice to meet sometime before you head back to America.
> Please remember me to Marie
> and with my love
> John

> Russell and Volkening Papers
>
> Foxfield

31 October 1985

Dear Gina,[25]
I am very happy with the offer and want to thank Tim and yourself for securing it.[26]

I know Tim met Seamus Heaney at Yaddo, and liked him.[27] The enclosed might interest him.[28]

Please thank Kathryn Court for her kind regards, and I return them warmly.[29]

> With every good wish
> John McGahern

---

25 Gina Macoby, then an employee at Russell and Volkening. In 1986 she became an independent literary agent.
26 Having read the *High Ground* stories, Viking had made an offer of $17,500 for a two-book deal on the stories and a subsequent novel.
27 Yaddo is an artists' community located on a 400-acre estate in Saratoga Springs, New York. Its mission is 'to nurture the creative process by providing an opportunity for artists to work without interruption in a supportive environment'.
28 Heaney's review of *High Ground*. See letter to Heaney of 20 October 1985.
29 Kathryn Court b. 1948, British-born, then married to Jonathan Coleman, who worked at Viking Penguin in New York. She joined Penguin Books in 1977 and became editorial director two years later. In 1984 she was named editor-in-chief of Viking Penguin and in 1992 senior vice-president, publisher and editor-in-chief of Penguin Books. She was named president of Penguin Books in August 2000, retiring from the company in January 2020.

Russell and Volkening Papers

Foxfield

1 November 1985

Dear Tim,
I've had a letter from Michael Bessie. He sounded upset.[30]

I've written him that while I was sorry – I understood his offer to be a business decision stemming from my poor sales. And that your decision to look for another arrangement was a similar decision regarding his offer, and that I could not interfere. I made no mention of any other agreement.

With all good wishes
John

30 Bessie held the senior position at Harper & Row. Seldes had written to him in September 1985 to say that McGahern would not be publishing *High Ground* with the company.

1986

Russell and Volkening Papers

Foxfield

20 January 1986

Dear Gina,
I had some one enquire at The Irish Times about the £200 fee and today they sent me a check for that amount.[1] I'll add the equivalent of £20 to the check when Faber send me your commission.

Did you get the 2 stories, and the note about Gold Watch being in the American edition of Getting Through? When are we likely to get a contract from Viking?

It was marvellous news about the Boston Globe taking Bank Holiday and I am very grateful to you.

> With every good wish
> John

Our equivalent of your Ed Meese made High Ground his book of the year. We may all get jobs yet.[2]

> J.

---

1 In payment for 'Crossing the Line', which appeared in *Modern Irish Stories from The Irish Times*, ed. Caroline Walsh (Dublin: The Irish Times, 1985).
2 John Rogers b. 1947 is the man in question. He was the Attorney General of Ireland from 1984 to 1987. He had been taught by McGahern at Belgrove primary school. Edwin Meese served as US Attorney General from 1985 to 1988.

Alain Delahaye

Foxfield

20 January 1986

Dear Alain,

We were delighted to get your note and thank Pascale and you for your kind wishes.

We haven't moved from here since I saw you in France and we have no plans to move. We bought the next farm.[3] Do you remember the poor old home boy who used carry the buckets of water up from the lake? They beat him up and drank the place out that we bought. The house is much bigger now. So if you and Pascale and the children would like to come you'll have plenty of room.

There was a good deal of disturbance round the publication of High Ground and it lasted up to Christmas, journalists, tv, too many faces – but that is over now. I am trying to write again now. It gets no easier. The Attorney General (head of the Legal system) made High Ground his book of the year – so best place of all could be prison.

Philip Larkin, whose work I loved, died before Christmas.[4] Another good poet, W. S. Graham, died last week.[5] Poor news.

I was very sorry you weren't able to translate the old Barracks but I understand completely.[6] You have your own work and life. I didn't hear from them about a translator but then I didn't ask. They sent me royalties from Journée d'Adieu before Christmas. I am deeply grateful for all the work you have done.

Can you write your own work now?

Have you still plans to go to work in Paris?

How is the house in Buire-le-Sec?

Would the family move to Paris?

---

3 John and Madeline bought the neighbouring Earlys' farm. See letter to Niall Walsh of 14 December 1973.

4 Larkin died on 2 December 1985.

5 Graham died on 9 January 1986.

6 Delahaye had written on 7 September 1985 to say that force of work meant he would not be in a position to translate The Barracks, a novel he greatly admired. Delahaye revealed to me in private correspondence that he had always been afraid of The Barracks, finding it intensely depressing, all the more so because it was so beautifully written.

We'd be glad of news.

We send you all our best wishes,
and our love
John

If I were called in
To construct a religion
I should make use of water.

Going to church
Would entail a fording
To dry, different clothes.

My liturgy would employ
Images of sousing,
A furious devout drench,

And I should raise in the east
A glass of water
Where any-angled light
Would congregate endlessly.

Philip Larkin, Water.[7]

Liam Kelly

Foxfield

25 February 1986

Dear Liam,[8]

I got word today that the BBC man hopes to come on the 8th and 9th March.[9] The 15th should be fine with us but is it too near St Patrick's day

---

7 This is the only instance in any surviving McGahern letter where he quotes a full poem – it is testament to the great regard and reverence he had for Larkin.
8 Liam Kelly b. 1952, a distant cousin of McGahern's, John's mother and Kelly's father being third cousins. He is a native of Aughawillan, Co. Leitrim. Trained as a Catholic priest at Maynooth in the mid-1970s and in the same period became friendly with McGahern after John and Madeline settled in Foxfield from 1974. Celebrated McGahern's funeral mass at St Patrick's church, Aughawillan on 1 April 2006.
9 Relates to McGahern's work on *The Rockingham Shoot*.

for you?[10] If it is – or if it is awkward in any other way – we can pick some
other Saturday.[11]

With all good wishes
John

Thomas Kilroy Papers
Foxfield

30 March 1986

Dear Tom and Julie,
Thank you for the cards. They were lovely to get. It all seemed like an idyll.[12]
   I liked <u>Double Cross</u>. Bits of Bracken did not seem to come to life on that
first night but the whole thing was fascinating.[13] Congratulations on it, and
congratulations on Aosdana.[14] I was at the meeting and worried when I saw
that the boulevardiers were out in strength. Sydney Bernard was canvassing
for Brian Lynch, and all were leaving for MacDara Woods.[15] Brian wrote
in a very good letter.[16] Jordan and Edward Maguire were very drunk and
provided light relief to some turgid goings-on.[17]

---

10 Kelly was teaching in the Comprehensive School in Cootehill, Co. Cavan and
living in Cootehill at the time.
11 Madeline needed a new sewing machine, which she knew could be got in Belfast.
John and Madeline drove to Cootehill, left their car there and Kelly drove them to
Belfast. The Troubles were at their height, Kelly was more familiar with Belfast than
the McGaherns and so he did the driving. There was much relief when they got back
across the border with the sewing machine. Saturdays suited Kelly because he had no
school teaching that day.
12 Tom and Julia Kilroy were in Bellagio, Lake Como on a Rockefeller foundation
for a month, staying in a beautiful villa.
13 The premiere of Kilroy's play *Double Cross* took place in the Guildhall, Derry, 3
February 1986. John and Madeline attended.
14 Kilroy had been approached by Seamus Heaney and Brian Friel to put his name
forward for election to Aosdána.
15 Sydney B. Smith; Brian Lynch b. 1945, novelist, poet, playwright; MacDara
Woods (1942–2018), poet.
16 Presumably Brian Friel.
17 Edward Maguire (1932–86), Dublin-born painter and member of Aosdána from
1984; John Jordan, poet and editor.

I'm finishing a tv play for the BBC. I've had to write to a mid-April deadline but it looks as if I'll be in on time.[18] Then we are going to London for a week around the wedding of a niece of mine. We'll be back late April/early May. It'd be great if we could meet then.

                    Madeline sends her love to you both.
                    Please remember me to Desmond.[19]
                    Love
                    John

                                        Thomas Kilroy Papers
                                              Foxfield

17 April 1986

Dear Tom,
We were glad to get your letter and we wish Double Cross all success all the way to London.[20]

I seem to have done nothing but fight off colds and write. I sent the play away today. It's an original God help us, one of three that must involve school/teaching (The other two are by Frank McGuinness and Anne Devlin).[21] Mine circles round the big pheasant shoot in Rockingham, when the British Ambassador used come as the guest of honour.

We go to London next Monday. We're taking the car across via Liverpool. We'd love to meet there but it seems that the dates are wrong. We have to be back by May 1st. So maybe when you get back from London and are rested we'll go over. What about the Races?[22]

Haven't heard from C.M. since before the publication of High Ground. I forgot to tell him that Seldes (the U.S. agent) insisted on drawing up the contract and I think he was annoyed. I don't expect to see him.[23]

If for any reason you come early to London 01 539 1229 will know where I am.

---

18 *The Rockingham Shoot.*
19 Tom Kilroy's son.
20 *Double Cross* played in the Royal Court, London from 8 to 31 May 1986.
21 *The Rockingham Shoot* was part of a three-part series for the BBC called *Screenplay Next.* The other two plays were *Scout* by Frank McGuinness and *The Venus De Milo Instead* by Anne Devlin. They were all produced by Danny Boyle.
22 Ballinrobe races, near the Kilroys' home.
23 C.M. is Charles Monteith.

We look forward to seeing you both soon. We wish good luck to Double Cross

> With love
> John

Faber

Foxfield

14 May 1986

Dear Matthew,

I want to thank you and Elizabeth for the lovely evening, though I felt guilty stealing it at the end of the working week. Madeline told me she'd a great time at Groucho's.

Thanks for Victory over Japan. I've read the first few stories and like them.[24] I liked the Paulin introduction. I didn't agree with much of what he was saying but it was said so spiritedly that it didn't seem to matter.[25]

It looks as if we'll go to Victoria on Vancouver Island for the first 4 months of 1987. I don't get anything like the Colgate money but I have little work to do, ½day in the week. I should be able to go on with my own work.

The German enclosure came when I was away. It should have been sent to Faber in the first place.

I'm not sure of the copywright position of Getting Through. McDermott has remaindered Getting Through in paperback and it is out of print at Faber, but I'd prefer if Faber handled it. I'd be grateful if you'd pass it down to the Departments that handle them.

Pat Mulcahy is the woman editor's name at Viking.

It'd be great if you could get down from Belfast. Madeline sends her love to you both, as I do

> John

---

24 McGahern gave a positive review to Ellen Gilchrist's *Victory over Japan* in the *Evening Herald* of 13 June 1986. The review opens in typically combative style: 'Ellen Gilchrist's first book, *The Land of Dreamy Dreams*, was a wonderful collection of stories. This was followed by a long novel, *The Annunciation*, the chief interest of which was how anyone as talented as Gilchrist had shown herself to write so badly.' 'New Victory for Gilchrist', *LOTW*, 308–10.

25 Refers to Tom Paulin's introduction to *The Faber Book of Political Verse*, published in 1986.

4 June 1986

Dear Michael,

It was kind of you to write and you would have been very welcome had you called. We have no telephone but mostly because the lines have not come this far. We live in 45 acres of poor land between two lakes close to the border. Enniskillen is the nearest big town and we go there almost every week. We have animals and trees, our orchard and garden, but it is all more happy go lucky/unlucky than efficiently run.[26] <u>Though</u> we are not the worst around. We'll be here all this year. Next January we'll stir and go to Vancouver for the Spring. We are unlikely to go anywhere much afterwards. I do not think that you have met my wife. She is American. We have no children. I hope you will call when you come to Ireland again. I often think of you and Anne and always in Herne Hill. Please remember me to her with affection.

> With all good wishes
> John.

[*20 October 1986*]

Dear Madeline,

The telegram came late Saturday. It's probably easier to ring the McGartys 078 42037.

A letter came from Jack Hodgkins with a real estate page.[27] With a bit of shock I realized I've only 10 weeks until I leave.[28] And I doubt if it makes

---

26 The reference to fruit growing would have appealed to Hamburger who himself lived in rural quietness in Suffolk and was a lover of orchards and rare apple varieties such as Royal Russet and Orleans Reinette.

27 Jack Hodgins b. 1938, a Canadian novelist and short story writer who saw the McGaherns a good deal during their stay in Victoria in the early months of 1987.

28 To take up a visiting fellowship at the University of Victoria, British Columbia.

sense to go to Paris. I'd love to be there with you for a few days but not if it just postpones the rush.[29]

The telephone poles are going up. They say the phone should be in around early November (our number will be 078 44528). The cattle were tested.[30] I haven't heard from the Hansons. Michael O'Regan is coming tonight.[31] I had Kitty & daughter Saturday night.[32] The cards for the cattle will hardly come for 10 days.

Woods brought his cattle over for the test, lost his temper with me and the cattle, rushed in and nearly got badly hurt.[33] That I saved him from being trampled on only added injury to hurt. I had sweet Jerome as well and a dazzling evening with Cafferty.[34] Father McCabe was here.[35] He was very interesting, and nice. Emmett wrote a very obvious careful letter, asking for £10,000.[36] I refused.

I kept thinking of Gron. The abuse has a ring of petty viciousness.

The weather has suddenly turned to winter. Charlie is staying even closer.[37]

I'll ring on Thursday about 5 pm.

I am hoping you may have got this [*illegible*] of going to Paris, and it seems increasingly difficult.

I am managing to write almost every day.

With all my love
John

29 McGahern changed his mind about this and went to Paris. See letter to Madeline of 28 October 1986.
30 The McGaherns never had more than a dozen head of cattle. They had up to fifty sheep at one point.
31 Michael O'Regan was parliamentary correspondent of the *Irish Times* who became a friend of McGahern's after a 1981 interview and later became a trustee of the literary estate. McGahern had tried and failed to persuade Faber to publish his co-authored book on the 'Kerry Babies' scandal. See letter to Matthew Evans of 12 May 1985.
32 Kitty Feeney was a teacher friend who lived in Ballinamore.
33 Peter Woods, a neighbour who, along with Francie McGarty, regularly helped with farm work.
34 Packie Joe Cafferty, a neighbour from around the lake, was a regular visitor to the house.
35 Fr Frank McCabe (1897–1994) was a native of Aughavas in Co. Leitrim. He was ordained for the diocese of Ardagh and Clonmacnois in 1924 and he was parish priest of Fenagh from 1957 until he retired aged eighty-nine in 1986.
36 McGahern's cousin Emmet McGarry was canvassing money for an investment scheme.
37 John and Madeline always kept a cat, sometimes several of them.

28 October 1986

Dear Madeline,

I hope you've had a pleasant birthday.[38] I didn't want to spend long on the telephone from Francie's. Mary and Tom were there.[39] I was waiting for the vet Gallagher, to help Francie hold the cattle. He was supposed to come in the morning but didn't come till 4 pm. Francie came with me to the mart in Drumshanbo. The big heifer, the one we bought off Cafferty, went the highest price of the day, £587; our Friesian, the black and white that used cause so much trouble, went a poor price, £352.

Hickey rang. They are sending the Porno scripts. I have to meet him, and possibly the Strongbow outfit, for a working lunch on Thursday November 6th. I don't intend to get too embroiled, and they have to pay me.[40]

I get into Charles de Gaulle at 10.35 am, Friday 7th. Eugene tells me there's a shuttle to the Metro, and I can go straight in.[41] So rather than haul you out, why don't we meet in the 6 Billiards at 12.[42] And if you're not there I'll go on to Rue Christine.

Charlie is as Charlie does, brought a live mouse into the room at 3.15 last night, was waddling around after the rich food of the Hanson visit, but otherwise rations have been Spartan, with the resultant howls.[43] Pat was out. The 1967 wine (£20) was opened for the Hansons, and though Suzanne protested it was fine it had definitely gone off. So much for £20 bargains. They just seem to live from meal to meal. I found it gross.

I am hoping to get back to my own work today.

I'm looking forward to seeing you on the 7th.

38 Madeline's birthday falls on 29 October.
39 Mary was the McGartys' daughter, Tom Ferris her husband.
40 Refers to the film director Kieran Hickey (1936–93), who went on to direct *The Rockingham Shoot*. Serious discussion had gone on for some time about the possibility of producing a screenplay adapted from *The Pornographer*.
41 Eugene Quinn of Quinn's bar in Fenagh. The McGaherns often used the telephone there and Eugene became a good friend. He and his wife Loretta visited the McGaherns in Colgate.
42 The 6 Billiards was a tabac, bar and restaurant frequented by John and Madeline.
43 A visit to Foxfield of Barry Hanson and Susanna Capon.

The ticket is booked for a week.
                    I send you all my love
                    John

At the end of the mart is a green VW without tax or insurance.

Susanna Capon
[*Madeline McGahern*]

Foxfield

24 November 1986

Dear Susanna,
Thank you for your kind letter. It was nice for me to see you here.

I was in Paris for a week. It was a week of strange warm perfect weather – in November! I was in Chez Allard, expensive and very mediocre.[44] I had to give an interview over the lunch, which must be the worst possible thing for both lunch and interview, but the food was still poor. The place was also ½ empty.

The publishers took us to the Recamier off the Rue du Four.[45] The prices were the same as Allard but the food was superb. Madeline said to tell Barry that the Sauvignon is as good as ever.[46] It is very close to the Recamier. We had a beautiful glass of Sauvignon on our way to the Coupole the last evening there.[47] The same couple still run it as on Talleyrand's afternoon long ago.[48]

I hope the Christmas and the holiday are merry (English) and happy (Irish).
                    With love to you all
                    John

44 Parisian gourmet bistro in the heart of Saint-Germain-des-Prés.
45 La Cigale Récamier, another high end Parisian restaurant, located on 4 Rue Récamier.
46 Au Sauvignon, a wine bar at 80 Rue des Saints-Pères, liked by Capon, Barry Hanson and the McGaherns.
47 La Coupole, famous Parisian restaurant, situated at 102 Boulevard du Montparnasse.
48 The reference to Talleyrand is a continuing private joke of obscure origin between Barry Hanson and McGahern.

29 November 1986[49]

Dear Colm,[50]
I have to be in Galway on Thursday the 4th. So the 12th is slightly the better day.

    There's a train at 5 p.m. and 6.10 p.m. There's also one at 1.30 p.m. I'll meet you at Dromod.

    Madeline is looking forward to seeing you. As I am.

With every good wish

John

49 Although this is the earliest surviving correspondence with Colm Tóibín, it is clear that Tóibín had sent McGahern a draft of *The South* on which to comment. In a letter of 8 October 1986 he writes: 'There are things you say in your letter I agree with. The Galway chapter was written as a first chapter and then placed towards the end. It should be abandoned. It has no place in the book. I did consider writing an opening chapter about what you call "the dull sense of money and class". I will certainly think about that. I agree about the Franco thing as well. Maybe they should just bring the painting home and leave it in the flat.' Madeline McGahern Papers. No 'Galway chapter' appears in the published book. Tóibín had first met McGahern at a reading of *High Ground* given by the latter in the Nuns' Island Arts Centre, Galway in 1985. For an account of that evening and the two writers' developing relationship, see Colm Tóibín, 'Out of the Dark: A Profile of John McGahern', in Tóibín, *The Trial of the Generals: Selected Journalism 1980–1990* (Dublin: The Raven Arts Press, 1990), 94–102.

50 Colm Tóibín b. 1955, Irish novelist, short story writer, essayist, playwright, journalist, critic and poet. Tóibín is currently Irene and Sidney B. Silverman Professor of the Humanities at Columbia University, New York and Chancellor of the University of Liverpool since 2017.

30 November 1986

Dear Matthew,

It was very kind of you to think of us when you were in Dublin. Seamus wrote and said how pleasant the lunch with you was, and the great time he had in Grouchos during the Eliot lectures.[51]

We were in Paris for a while. Madeline went about the flat, and I went there for a week. The Barracks had a surprising success there (I enclose 2 of the more important reviews: apparently Rinaldi is their most influential critic).[52] The Presses were delighted. They are going to do the Selected Stories and are hoping to get The Dark back from the small publisher who first bought it out there.

We are going to Vancouver in January. I have only to do one day in the week. And I'm hoping to get a good deal of my own work done.

Of course I'm very glad you are doing Getting Through.[53] RTE Radio are serializing High Ground after Christmas and it may sell some copies.

We have the telephone now. The wasteful poles come in all the way round the lake.

It doesn't look as if we'll be in London for some time.

> Madeline sends her love to Elisabeth and yourself
> As I do
> John

51 Seamus Heaney delivered the 1986 T. S. Eliot Memorial Lectures, which, along with some other pieces, were collected and published by Faber in 1987 as *The Government of the Tongue*.
52 Angelo Rinaldi b. 1940 in Bastia, Corsica is a French writer and literary critic. As a critic, he worked for *L'Express*, *Le Point* and *Le Nouvel Observateur* before becoming literary editor of *Le Figaro*, where he remained until his retirement and where he reviewed McGahern enthusiastically.
53 Faber was bringing out *Getting Through* in paperback.

Alain Delahaye

Foxfield

30 November 1986

Dear Alain,

Thank you for your letter and the Le Monde article. I was in Paris, and would have called you, but I was ill with flu most of the time.

Madeline was there because of the flat and told the publishers I was coming. Were it not Bank Holiday I would have got caught for publicity, flu or no flu. As it was I gave 2 harmless interviews, one in a good restaurant, a waste of food and drink and words. I saw Cartano, who spoke very warmly of you. In fact, he was quite delightful.[54] They are very pleased with the book's reception.

I wasted much time in the spring and summer on a BBC Film. I wrote the screenplay, a sort of high class furrier who delivers a few series they work on. I have lately done real work on the novel. I know it will be my last novel.

In January I go to Vancouver for 4 months. The city and University is Victoria. I have only to teach one afternoon in the week. I am hoping that I can go on with my own work, not so easy here, with the callers coming at all times, including midnight. But they are my own people. I'll look up and read Monkeys as soon as I get to Canada.[55]

There is no news. A very dear Dubliner, one of the most intelligent men in the world, just asks 'Am I standing properly today?'[56]

We have the telephone. The wasteful poles come in all the way round the lake. Write us some word if you can OR we might call. Madeline sends her love to you both

and with my love

John

The children are from the film.[57]

---

54 Tony Cartano b. 1944, French novelist and editor who was then literary manager of Presses de la Renaissance. Long an admirer of McGahern's work, he did much to promote his writing in France.

55 A novel by Susan Minot, published in New York by Dutton in 1986.

56 Jimmy Swift.

57 McGahern encloses a black and white still photograph of a classroom full of children from the film *The Rockingham Shoot*.

1987

Neill Joy
[*Madeline McGahern*]

Silverwood Inn
417 Quebec Street
Victoria B.C.
Canada V8W 2Y2

15 January 1987

Dear Neill,

We'll be home earlier than May, the 10th or 11th of April. My last class is on the 8th of April.

I was going to sell the sheep and cattle but when the neighbours found out I was going to be such a short time away they offered to look after them. They know when I'm coming home. Were I to stop off in London it could be a lynching matter.

Why doesn't Mary and yourself come over for Easter? There's a price war now in air fares. Ryan Air: Dublin/London, Belfast/London. We could meet you in Belfast or Dublin. You could use the car to go down to Clare. And you'd see how leaden the silver slippers are.

It's a very pleasant town. We live on the harbour. We can see the boats and hydroplanes leave for Vancouver and Seattle and Port Angeles. There's an enormous cavern of a hotel The Empress a few blocks away. The restaurants are varied and good. Even the hookers are friendly. When I mumbled my 'sorry' on Government Street last Saturday night she smiled and said, 'We could have had a real good time.' Mister Pound (poet) would be delighted with the politics of the local ruling party which [*illegible*] Social Credit. The local Safeway can take on the appearance of a geriatric ward. The weather is superb.

The University is 8 or 9 miles out. I go there on Wednesdays. I have 15 students.

Write us when you get settled in London. We'll have to arrange some meeting.

Madeline sends her love to Mary and yourself
with my love
John

Neill Joy
[*Madeline McGahern*]

University of Victoria
P.O. Box 1700
Victoria
British Columbia
Canada V8W 2Y2

10 March 1987

Dear Mary and Neill,
We want very much to see you both but it's easier for us to come and see you from Ireland than to stopover.

Outside the chores of home, the neighbours, promises, the luggage, the real reason is that we know we'll be no fit company for a few days for anybody but ourselves and the farm animals. There's a 10 hour time difference and the flight from Vancouver takes 10½ hours. As they say round the lakes, we'll be frigged. It makes a lot more sense to hop over from Dublin or Belfast.

By the way, your letter makes no mention of your visit to Ireland.
Madeline leaves on the 4th and I follow on the 8th.

It's gone like a dream here. I've even worked on the novel. I had hardly any work in the University. I speak in Vancouver on St. P's day. A turnout of the resident mafia is promised (Do you remember the St. Patrick's day long ago with Wilbur? Boastfulness and greed?) Then we'll go down to Seattle for a few days.[1] It is just 2½ hours by boat. We can see the boat from our window.

We get into Heathrow on the 5th and 9th at 12.40 and we leave for Dublin at 4 p.m. If you felt like a drink there either of us would like to see you but

---

1 In Seattle the McGaherns met up with a cousin of Madeline's, enjoyed visiting Pike Place Market and a few of the Seattle bars, and were struck by the relative poverty of the city's African-American population.

we both feel it is far too long a scamper for just an hour or two. We'll write or ring you from Ireland.

> Madeline sends you both her love
> And with my love
> John

Russell and Volkening Papers

Foxfield

6 April 1987[2]

Dear Miriam,[3]

Thank you for the copy of the contract and for your kind wishes. I leave Canada tomorrow for home. It was very pleasant here but I'll be glad to get home.

I wrote the enclosed very short story a few weeks ago and sent it to Frances Kiernan in The New Yorker.[4] She liked it but said it wasn't New Y. story for a number of reasons – one was its setting – but urged me to send it to Grand Street or The Atlantic.[5] I know it's fairly futile to send it to these places unless you have a contact there and I have none. [The reason I sent it first to Frances Kiernan is that Tim told me to keep my contact with The N. Yorker as it was before he took me on]

It is easy for me to publish it in the literary magazines that look for my work but do not pay much. And I do not like the idea of it kicking around for too long. So perhaps you'd ask Tim if he'd take a quick look at it and see what he thinks.

2 Addressed 'Foxfield' but sent from Victoria, British Columbia.
3 Miriam Altshuler began her career as a literary agent at Russell and Volkening, where she worked for twelve years. In 1994 she established her own agency, which she ran for twenty-one years until she joined DeFiore and Company in 2016.
4 Unknown story. Likely has not survived.
5 *Grand Street* was an American magazine that appeared from 1981 to 2004. Founded as a quarterly by Ben Sonnenberg, when Jean Stein became editor and publisher in 1990 the magazine's format changed to encompass visual art, and it began actively to seek out international authors and artists to introduce to its readers. Tim Seldes and his colleagues regularly, but never successfully, sent McGahern's work to the magazine for consideration.

I sent a story a long time ago <u>The Creamery Manager</u>. If it is still out – it's unlikely at this time – I'd like it withdrawn.[6] I sent another story with it <u>The Old Man</u> which is no good anyhow. I was looking at it a few days ago.

With every good wish
John

Liam Kelly

Foxfield

29 April 1987

Dear Liam,
Your kind letter followed us home from Victoria.

It was very pleasant there, and a little dull, full of very old people, strangely like children without futures. There was the ocean and good weather and the most magnificent trees, one which was still young when 'Europe was emerging from the <u>darkness</u> of the Middle Ages.'

We have a telephone now.

We were in London last week, but we intend to stay put now. We'd be delighted to see you.

With every good wish
John

Neill Joy

[*Madeline McGahern*]

Foxfield

30 May 1987

Dear Neill,
It was lovely to see you in London, and we both hope Edmund is better now. We'd be glad of news of him.[7]

---

6 Short story first published in *Krino*, no. 4 (Autumn 1987), the Irish literary magazine edited by Gerry Dawe, and subsequently in the *Canadian Journal of Irish Studies* (July 1991). First collected in *The Collected Stories*.
7 The Joys' son had been the victim of a hit and run driver.

It is back to the daily here, and hard to work in this good weather, much more pleasant in the garden or about the fields or out on the lake in the evening or viewing a bottle of chilled wine. And I'm afraid we had a bit of a skite on Thursday, with old friends at the Ballinrobe races.[8] We even won money and spent it all afterwards in Galway.

The TV film will be screened on BBC in September.[9] I'll send it as soon as I have a clean script. Haut-Terre comes out in Paris in September.[10] We may yet go, without a word of French at his command. It seems I'll be in Trinity next spring and summer.[11]

We had the bad news from Oneonta that Ed Kelly died while he was running. He was certainly difficult but I was fond of him.[12]

I enclose the Kavanagh, with an apology for subjecting you to so much guff on the subject around handballing hours.

Madeline sends her love to Mary and yourself. With my love as well to you both. Please remember me with affection to Edmund and Teo[13]

as always
John

Russell and Volkening Papers
Foxfield

28 July 1987

Dear Tim,

Thank you for your note.

I had hoped to have the novel almost finished by now and have not for two reasons. Last year I took a commission to write a tv screenplay The Rockingham Shoot. It cost me a lot more writing and rewriting than I had

---

8 Tom and Julia Kilroy.

9 *The Rockingham Shoot.*

10 The French translation of *High Ground* was published by Presses de la Renaissance in Paris, 1987, translated by Georges-Michel Sarotte. It was the third title in a series titled 'Les Nouvelles étrangères' under the direction of Tony Cartano.

11 McGahern was going to Trinity as Writer Fellow, a post established in 1985 as a joint venture between the Arts Council and TCD.

12 Kelly was a Daniel Defoe scholar at SUNY Oneonta and edited the Norton authoritative edition of *Moll Flanders* in 1973.

13 The Joys' sons. Teo was a diminutive for 'Matthew', a nickname picked up on the Joys' travels in Italy.

bargained for and stopped work on the novel for months. It'll be screened on BBC2 in September. I got back to work on the novel in Canada and worked well there and here since coming home until the summer work began on the farm. To justify the climate of violence in the novel I found I had to add an opening chapter which echoed the revolution of 1920/1921 and this affected subsequent chapters. This set me back too but I think it improves the novel greatly.[14]

I am accepting no other work until the novel is finished. Soon I'll be working on it every day again. My hope now is that I will have it finished early next year.

I'd be grateful if <u>The Country Funeral</u> isn't sent out any more.[15]

They are giving me a rather handsome award in Galway on August 5th.[16]

> I hope you are very well
> and with every good wish
> John

Neill Joy
[*Madeline McGahern*]
Foxfield

17 August 1987

Dear Neill,

I thought Mary and you might like to see the enclosed. It came out of the blue and was a shock to us but a real honour. We had a wonderful night in Galway.[17]

14 This new opening section of what becomes *Amongst Women* on publication in 1990 explains Moran's past as an IRA commander and deep disappointment with the subsequent fruits of revolution.

15 'The Country Funeral', now often considered McGahern's masterpiece in short story writing, and published by Faber as a standalone volume in 2019, had an unhappy history with the literary magazines. It was rejected in the US by *The Atlantic* ('McGahern is good, but this seems to us a set-piece'), the *New Yorker*, *Mother Jones*, *Harper's*, the *Paris Review* and *Grand Street* ('Mr. McGahern writes with authority, but story's just nothing new'). The story was eventually first published in *The Collected Stories*.

16 McGahern was honoured by the Galway Arts Festival in August 1987 – the festival's director, Ollie Jennings, presented him with a special award of £2,000 in recognition of his artistic achievements.

17 See letter to Tim Seldes of 28 July 1987.

The Rockingham Shoot goes out finally on September 10th at 9.30 BBC2. I'll send a clean script.

Next year, January through June, I'll be in Trinity College. I'll have rooms within the college. Is there any chance you'll be in Ireland next year?

It was a good summer here. All the hay is in. Most of the lambs are sold. I have now to get the head deep back into the novel. It was great escaping the novel in the summer's work.

We'd love news of you and Mary, and especially we'd like to know how Edmund is. It was a pure pleasure to see you both so well in London.

The one bit of bad news is that Faber have discovered that a rogue publisher here, Philip McDermott of Poolbeg Press has been pirating my books, printing a run, and selling them as ½ price remainders, putting it all in his own pocket. They are taking legal action. I'm hoping I haven't to go into the courts.[18]

Madeline says how nice it was to get your letter, and she sends you both her love,

and with my love
John

---

18 *Getting Through* and *The Pornographer* were the two pirated titles. McGahern did not have to go to court.

28 August 1987

Dear Joanna,[19]

Thank you for your letter and the books. The Heaney and Gunn were exactly what I wanted.[20] It was very kind to send me the 2 novels. They are lovely to look at. I really disliked Pubis Angelical.[21] I liked Machine Dreams very much but I feel she's recycling leftovers from the novel in Fast Lanes.[22]

It would have been lovely had you come here but I hope you'll come some other time. We are going to Aix en Provence in early October, to the Festival, for 4 days. I have to say a few words on landscape and literature to earn my presence there.

I'd be grateful if you'd give John Bodley a nudge over Forrest Reid's Apostate.[23] He was very keen to do it 4 years ago and has not done a thing, which is a more Irish than English approach.[24] Do you know the book? It is Reid's best book, a wonderful account of growing up in Victorian Belfast.

19 Joanna Mackle b. 1958, joined Faber in 1982 and held a number of roles starting as publicity assistant before being promoted to the Board as publicity director in 1987, thus becoming only the second woman to be invited to join the Faber Board. Mackle worked with a number of key authors at Faber including poets Ted Hughes and Seamus Heaney and novelists Peter Carey and Kazuo Ishiguro among others. She worked closely with McGahern on the publicity campaign for *Amongst Women*, which she describes as one of the most enjoyable and interesting times of her professional life. For an engaging account of her professional relationship with McGahern, see Mackle, 'The Publishing of *Amongst Women*', *The John McGahern Yearbook*, vol. 1 (Galway: National University of Ireland, 2008), 88–91.

20 Seamus Heaney, *The Haw Lantern* and Thom Gunn, *Moly*, both published by Faber in 1987.

21 *Pubis Angelical* is a 1979 novel by Argentine novelist Manuel Puig, published by Faber in 1988.

22 *Machine Dreams* (1984), a novel, and *Fast Lanes* (1987), a collection of short stories, by the American writer Jayne Anne Phillips, published by Faber.

23 *Apostate*, published in 1926, was the first of two volumes of autobiography from the pen of Belfast writer Forrest Reid, whose novel *Brian Westby* McGahern had tried and failed to have reissued by various publishers over the years. McGahern urged Faber to republish the out of print volume – this eventually happened in 2011.

24 '4' is underlined three times.

It was a pleasure to see you in Dublin and I hope we'll meet again soon.
With every good wish
John

Robert White
Foxfield

16 September 1987

Dear Bob,[25]
Thank you for Keats as a Reader of Shakespeare, and your letter. I'll look
forward to reading it and the little Oxford of Keats's letters. Congratulations
on it, and on the Chair in Perth.[26] I hope you'll have many happy years
there.

There's little new here. I'm behind on work with the novel, and under
pressure from the Americans because of the advance, and the writing speeds
like the snail. Next year (January) I'll be in Trinity. I'll have very little work,
and rooms within the College so that I can go and come between there and
here. In October I go to the Festival in Aix en Provence and there'll be a few
days in Paris for the publication of High Ground. Otherwise we'll be all
the time here if you felt like coming to Ireland before you leave. There's a
telephone here now.

I often think – why I'm not sure – of those strange days when you came
with Robin Graham.[27] Do you ever see him now?

Of course I'll send the books. And all good luck if I do not see you before
you go.
Affectionately
John

25 Robert 'Bob' White b. 1948 was Lecturer/Senior Lecturer in the School of English
at Newcastle University from 1974 to 1988. McGahern and he became friendly when
McGahern was a Northern Arts Fellow at Newcastle in 1974–6.
26 In 1988 White took up the Chair of English at the University of Western Australia.
The book McGahern refers to is (under the name R. S. White) Keats as a Reader of
Shakespeare (London: Athlone Press, 1986).
27 Robin Graham was a mature PhD student at Newcastle University in the late
1970s. He and Bob White visited Foxfield together while holidaying in Ireland.

[*Autumn 1987*]

[*Postcard to Michael Gorman*][28]
The gate still stands.[29] Halliwell wrote to say he'd be glad to meet you both, show you round Charlbury.[30]

I also sent the Hansons a card (01 741 2651) that you might call them.[31] Madeline sends her love and we hope you'll enjoy London.

John

Niall Walsh Papers
Foxfield

9 December 1987

Dear Niall,
I'll be in Trinity from January 6th. The nicest thing about the job is that I'll have rooms in the college. I'll write you when I have a number there. It'd be very pleasant if you could come in for a drink some evening, and then we could wander out somewhere.[32] I've kept the few cattle and sheep we have

28 This postcard represents the first surviving piece of correspondence from McGahern to Michael Gorman. Gorman b. 1952 in Sligo is a published poet. His books are *Waiting for the Sky to Fall* (Galway: Lighthouse Press, 1984), *Up She Flew* (Galway: Salmon, 1991) and *Fifty Poems* (Galway: Artisan House, 2019). He was co-director of the International Summer School at UCG for a dozen years at which McGahern gave a morning talk and afternoon reading on one day every year. This French postcard with an Irish postmark is addressed to Michael and Margaret Gorman, then living in London.
29 Gorman had helped McGahern erect a gate on his property in Foxfield. They had driven around the area inspecting gates before deciding on the best course of action and the whole process remained a standing joke between them.
30 David Halliwell, the playwright and friend of McGahern's, lived in Charlbury, Oxfordshire at this time and up to his death in 2006. See letter to Charles Monteith of 25 February 1969.
31 Barry Hanson and Susanna Capon, who then lived in Hammersmith, London.
32 McGahern spent a contented few months at TCD as Writing Fellow in the spring of 1988. He writes warmly about it in his essay '"What Are You, Sir?" Trinity College Dublin', *LOTW*, 35–40.

and I'll probably come and go a good deal between the two places. Only a few weeks before you wrote we were wondering idly where all the children were now, and what they were doing.

It was very kind to say what you said about The Shoot. They were a great crowd to work with – Hickey, the director, is intelligent – but it took more time than I had bargained for. All for an hour, and gone forever probably.

Madeline is well and she sends you both her love. Since this terrible season is almost upon us, I want as well to wish you all a happy Christmas.

Affectionately,
John

Faber (TS)
Foxfield

14 December 1987

Dear Robert,[33]
Thank you for your letter.

It seems to be a solid, rather predictable, very middle-of-the-road selection. I also think such selections have been overdone. I can count at least six in the past few years. I doubt if this one would turn out to be more than another addition.[34]

I have to confess an interest. In Charles Monteith's time I agreed to edit the Faber Book of Irish Prose. I have done a good deal of work on it but have put it aside for a time. It would take about six months more of fairly intense work to complete. I wanted to see for myself if a recognisable prose tradition could be said to have been established here. It includes the short story, autobiography, letters, bits of novels, even two translations from the Gaelic, anything that seemed to me to be good prose and able to make sense on its own. I am curious to see if what I am attempting will be superseded by the forthcoming Field Day book, but I want to try to finish the novel first.[35]

33 Robert McCrum, editor-in-chief at Faber from 1980 to 1996.
34 McCrum was presumably asking McGahern's advice about a proposed anthology of Irish short stories.
35 The three-volume Field Day Anthology of Irish Writing under the general editorship of Seamus Deane was published in 1991. It was heavily criticised for under-representing the contribution of women writers to the Irish tradition and two further volumes were published in 2003 under the general editorship of Angela Bourke to right this wrong.

I wonder if I could ask discreet help. One of the people I want to include is Forrest Reid. He has been discriminated against, I think, because he is outside the tradition. Three years ago John Bodley asked me about him. I recommended Apostate. He seemed very excited about it. I thought that he knew the book. I offered to write a short introduction if it was thought necessary. Three years went by. When Matthew and Joanna were over in the summer, I asked Joanna to look into the matter. John wrote me. He had not read Apostate. He was still interested and looking into it. I'm afraid another three years will go by.

Do you think that you could look into it? I believe that it is a small masterpiece of Victorian Belfast. There would be a grant from the Northern Arts Council. Its time could well have come round. I'd be grateful, and interested, in your reaction to a book I admire.[36]

> With every good wish
> Yours
> John

James Swift
[*Madeline McGahern*]

Foxfield

15 December 1987

Dear Jimmy,

I'm sorry to be late with this, and sorry for the quality of the only copy I can find, even if it is suitably black. I think it is legible just about.

I had to take my uncle to the new hospital in Beaumont in an emergency.[37] They weren't answering telephones so his doctor couldn't ring through for a bed. Casualty was locked. An ambulance with a coronary patient couldn't get in. Poundings. People appeared. Hand signals through glass. They didn't know where the key was. We'd to go through the back entrance. They tried to turn us away. He was too ill. We had to go down several flights, reaching the locked door at the bottom, the coronary retinue behind, the ambulance man swearing. We were 4 hours sitting in casualty before he was attended to. I left and he eventually got a bed towards midnight. The ambulance man

---

36 Faber did not reissue *Apostate* in McGahern's lifetime.
37 McGahern's beloved uncle Pat McManus.

was still there when I left wondering in the name of Jesus if they would ever get their tea.

Thanks for the evening and the very pleasant Cafe de Paris.

I hope we'll meet soon.

I'll phone when we get to Dublin.

Madeline is there now. She was thinking of phoning you to see if Danny or any of the family would know a jeweller who'd be able to value stuff she wants to sell.

With the season's good wishes
John

1988

Niall Walsh Papers

Department of Modern English
University of Dublin
[*hereafter Trinity College Dublin*]

[January 1988]

Dear Niall,

I am a week here now. My room is in the Rubric Building, which faces the main entrance. The house is 25, the door number 1.1. The phone extension is 1635. The room is very pleasant, even beautiful.

Many weekends I'll go down to Leitrim as I have a few cattle and sheep.

There's little news. My uncle from Ballinamore is dying in Beaumont. He'll be the last of that generation.

I hope I'll hear from you and that we can meet.

With love to you both,
John

Frances Kiernan Papers

Trinity College Dublin

22 January 1988

Dear Frances,

I am sorry you are leaving. I'll be grateful all my life for all the help you gave me, and all the kindness you showed me.[1]

I'd be very glad of any news of you . . . if you intend to work again . . . what of Howard and John . . . and the rest of the family. How are you now? Maybe you'd write me before too long?

---

1 Kiernan worked at the *New Yorker* from 1966 to 1987 as an editor in the fiction department. She later was a senior editor at Houghton Mifflin.

I'll be here until the end of June. I have a lovely high white room with six windows, three on the main quadrangle. I have little teaching and I am able to work here. I'm still wrestling with the novel and hoping to see an endlight soon. I wrote a film for the BBC last year. It did sort of well.

Are you likely to come to Ireland ever again? If you do ever come it'll be a delight for me.

With affection
John

Neill Joy
[Madeline McGahern]

Trinity College Dublin

10 February 1988

Dear Neill,

Thank you for your card. Is there any chance you may be able to come to Ireland in the summer? I'll have rooms here until the end of June. There's a literary conference in Dublin in mid-June that I have to attend. We'll be in London round July 21st for a niece's wedding. And somehow we'll have to save the hay as well.

I was sorry to hear of Terence's death.[2] How exactly did he die? I've had cards. Arnie Scio said 'passed away'.[3] It seems strange for a man not far from his prime.

Uncle Pat died of cancer here in hospital last Saturday, February 6th. We took him home on the Sunday and buried him under the mountains this Monday.[4] A light snow was swirling about the churchyard. The priest quoted from The Hound of Heaven.[5] Many of the faces in the enormous crowd looked ½ wild. Few had any notion what the priest was talking about. I heard them say they thought he'd never stop. We gave a dinner afterwards

---

2 Terrence Des Pres, McGahern's Colgate colleague, died on 16 November 1987 in Hamilton, New York.

3 Arnold Sio (1918–2011) was a Colgate Professor in the Department of Sociology and Anthropology.

4 Uncle Pat McManus was buried in Corraleehan churchyard, near the McManus family homeplace of Drumderrig.

5 A poem by the English poet Francis Thompson (1859–1907).

in the restaurant where Pat had eaten for 40 years.[6] For us a dear presence is gone. Mary and Theo may remember buying petrol at his garage.[7] 'This dying is a cunt of a business', he said to me in the last days. I fear that's more in my line than F. Thompson.

There's not much other news. There's a superb restaurant and cellar here and beautiful common rooms. People can drink as much wine as they like in commons but they are expected to take out no more than 6 bottles of any one vintage. I have hardly any work to do and I am able to write. Faber is taking an Irish Publisher, Poolbeg, to the Courts for pirating Getting Through and The Pornographer. The Porno Man was sold into Spain last week.

We were glad to learn that Edmund is recovered. I hope he gets lots of money.

> Madeline sends her love to you all, and with my
> love
> John

Thomas Kilroy Papers

Trinity College Dublin

28 April 1988

Dear Tom and Julie,
We were very glad to get your letter and to get such delightful word of Hannah May. She sounds a joy.[8]

Trinity is pleasant and easy. I have a beautiful room in Rubrics, with 6 light windows, 3 on the front entrance, 3 on the square behind. The work is light. Unfortunately I find it much better than Leitrim for getting my own work done. Madeline has been here a few times but it doesn't suit a couple and we don't like imposing too much on Francie with the animals. She may come up for a week on her own after Easter. There's a cupboard kitchen. The W. C. is downstairs and outside but it's all right if you hold your trousers.

My poor Uncle died. He was a dear presence about the place. We miss him very much. He had a rough passage in the end. I have the lousy executor's job again.[9]

---

6 McAllister's Restaurant, Ballinamore. Pat McManus dined there frequently, always in later years accompanied by his dog, 'Captain'.
7 Mary Joy and her son Matthew 'Teo' Joy.
8 The Kilroys' daughter.
9 McGahern had also been executor – much to his chagrin – of his father's will.

I had an extraordinary weekend in Renvyle: 2 Irish writers (Tom Murphy the other) 2 English, 2 French, Heads of Drama Granada TV, French TV, and 2 Irish cowboys. It was quite crazy. We all have to turn in separate 'treatments' by May 1st. We flew to Knock. It was all too much.[10]

What is the date of the Races? It'd be lovely to see you both again and to see Hannah May for the first time.[11] We'll both be in Foxfield over Easter. Did you notice Good Friday falls on All Fools Day this year.

Madeline sends her love to you all and with my love

John

Faber

Trinity College Dublin

1 June 1988

Dear Matthew,

Thank you for your very kind letter. I'd be very honoured if you brought out the Collected Stories.

From a practical point of view, I know that there are people who think it will be my most powerful book. It would probably have to be fairly carefully planned to stand much of a chance of getting true attention, but that after all is your business, and is very often a matter of pure luck.

This time I am writing the novel through from beginning to end and I'm now at p. 170. I hope it'll be close to the last time.

I wrote a sort of a fun piece for Liberation in connection with the European Cup. It'll come out there next weekend.

Would you know of a good film/tv agent? French tv/Granada approached me and others for films they will co-produce with a company called Gandon. They paid for the treatment and they want to commission it as a screenplay. They're having a conference in Paris the weekend of June 17th with the three writers – myself, a Julia Jones, a Michelle Letellier, the three they decided to go with. We'll be offered a contract that weekend and I feel an agent should see it. There could be a good deal of money involved and I don't trust them that much.

I'm afraid McDermott has still the half-price books on the market here. He's doing it to several writers.

10 Nothing came of this junket.
11 Ballinrobe races, not far from the Kilroys' Kilmaine home.

Sean O'Mordha, who did Joyce and Beckett, wants to do a tv film on my work that could go with the Stories . . . anyhow!

Madeline told me how much she enjoyed seeing Elisabeth.

> It'd [*be*] very nice to meet before too long
> With every good wish
> John

Russell and Volkening Papers (TS)

Foxfield

6 July 1988

Dear Tim,

I was commissioned to write a film treatment for a British/French co-production. I did so, and a week ago was asked to write a screenplay.[12] As there could be a good deal of money involved, I needed an agent who knew the business. Through a producer I know I got Stephen Durbridge. I told him you are my agent and he is writing to you to let you know what is taking place. Heath have let the film rights lapse in The Pornographer, and if you are agreeable Durbridge may take them over as well.[13]

Heath seem fine with the translations, but I felt it was useless to approach them with this business.

Up to now I felt uneasy mentioning the novel as I've had much trouble with it. I'm writing it through for what I believe is the last time and I've reached page 184. I am working on it all the time. I feel I'll have it finished by Christmas.

Fabers are talking about bringing out The Collected Stories next year.

How are you? Are you likely to get to London?

> With all good wishes
> John

---

12 Unknown, but possibly a treatment of Pierre Loti's 1886 novel *Pêcheur d'Islande* (*An Iceland Fisherman*). Pierre Loti (1850–1923) was the pseudonym of Louis Marie-Julien Viaud, a French naval officer and novelist, known for his exotic novels and short stories. McGahern's papers in NUIG reveal considerable work towards an attempted film treatment of 'Icelandic Fisherman' which came to nothing.

13 Stephen Durbridge is a London agent who specialises in representing writers for film and television.

Maguy Pernot-Deschamps
[*Madeline McGahern*]

Foxfield

16 July 1988

Dear Mrs Pernot,[14]
Thank you for your letter.

I taught Niall briefly, when he was 7 or so. His father taught me in the Training College for Teachers, where he was lecturer in Education.[15]

I was teaching in Clontarf. Niall came to me from a Montessori school. He was plainly very intelligent but because of the difference in the systems was behind the boys I had in certain subjects. The danger in such a situation is that the child will lose his confidence.

I had to send for the father to advise if Niall be placed for a time at least in a lower class. The father was inclined to be dogmatic and I remember I had difficulty with him but eventually he agreed and Niall was transferred to another class. So I taught him for no more than a few months.

I probably remember it so well because I had a run-in with the father when I was a student.

He selected me to teach an Exhibition Class, which was to teach a class in front of the whole college, very much like on a stage. It was considered a sort of honour but I thought the whole thing bogus and refused. He threatened me with expulsion. I had then no real choice. I taught the class but turned it into a skit. Everybody fell about laughing but Jordan was furious. He excoriated me publicly but there was little else he could do, since I had taken care to follow the rules, and in fact the students took my side, unusual in those days.

Our relationship had hardly been happy and here I was a few years later dealing with him over his son.

14 Maguy Pernot-Deschamps, a French academic who was researching the life of Irish author and film maker Neil Jordan b. 1950. She published her findings in *The Fictional Imagination of Neil Jordan, Irish Novelist and Film Maker: A Study of Literary Style* (Lewiston: The Edwin Mellon Press, 2009).
15 Michael Jordan, father of Neil Jordan, who lectured at St Patrick's College, Drumcondra where McGahern trained as a primary school teacher.

I hope this is of some use to you. For those few months I would have taught him a complete range of subjects.

With good wishes

Yours sincerely

John McGahern

1989

Mary Lavin Papers

Foxfield

26 January 1989

Dear Mary,[1]

I am very sorry you've had such a terrible time. I hope the New Year will bring you happier days.

Faber took McDermott to court on the 16th of this month.[2] I haven't yet heard what happened. It was expected that he'd seek time in which to file a defense. So far he has ignored everything, apart from ringing people up.

I was speaking in Belfast before Christmas. I heard that Michael McLaverty under pressure signed all rights to his complete works over to McDermott. The family had lawyers check it out but there is nothing they can do. McDermott owns the work.

There is nothing new here. I'm finishing a screenplay for another shady crew. Getting money from them is like pulling teeth though they can fly us all to Barbizon and pour champagne.[3] I'll have a month to go through the novel for what I hope will be the last time.

We've never had such a mild winter here but the land is sodden.

I hope you are better now
with my love
John

---

1 Mary Lavin, American-born Irish fiction writer whom McGahern had first met in Dublin in the late 1950s at her Lad Lane mews, a place that acted for several years as an informal literary salon attracting several of the younger writers of the day, including Elizabeth Cullinan, Tom Kilroy and Tom MacIntyre.
2 Philip McDermott had published two McGahern books under his Poolbeg imprint without Faber's permission. See letter to Neill Joy of 17 August 1987.
3 Barbizon is a town in the Seine-et-Marne department in north-central France near the Fontainebleau Forest.

Seamus Heaney Papers

Foxfield

30 January 1989

Dear Seamus,
Thanks for the word. I'll be in Galway that weekend and will go from there to the Academy of Music. It doesn't matter about the expenses.[4]
    Is Westland Row open to the public? I know a family who would like to attend.
The last of the Maxwells, Tommy, has left Woodbrook for a small house in Cootehall. He goes to the pub every night and sometimes sings.[5]

                With every good wish to the whole household
                Love
                John

Robin Robertson

Foxfield

16 July 1989

Robin,
Thank you for returning the MSS.

---

4 A memorial event to mark the first anniversary of David Thomson's death had been arranged for the Organ Room, Academy of Music, Westland Row, Dublin on Sunday 26 February 1989. In a card of 23 January Heaney writes: 'Maybe you'd read something from the work, and say four or five minutes worth of stuff? [. . .] Buswells afterwards, for a reception, for not too many persons.'
5 *Woodbrook* (London: Barrie and Jenkins, 1975) by David Thomson is an account of the author's time as a tutor in one of the last of Co. Roscommon's 'big houses' of the mid-twentieth century. It was admired by both Heaney and McGahern. The house itself still stands a few miles north of Carrick-on-Shannon. McGahern said of *Woodbrook* at the memorial event: 'It is strange in the English tradition of writing about Ireland. I know of no voice like it; there is no savage indignation, no exasperated tolerance, no dehumanizing farce, and no superior tone. It has a rare sweetness and gentleness.' See Julian Vignoles, *A Delicate Wildness: The Life and Loves of David Thomson 1914–1988* (Dublin: The Lilliput Press, 2014), x.

I was a bit depressed taking it from its envelope. Obviously I would have liked for you to have seen it into print. I'll be grateful to you always.[6]

What happened was this. Faber doubled your offer and, depending on its acceptance agreed to make an offer for The Collected Stories within 3 months. Seldes thought it a very good offer and he felt that nobody wanted a bidding situation.

I hope Claire and her sister and yourself will come here for lunch or dinner when you are [in] Enniskillen.[7] We'd be sad if you didn't. I'll even keep what's left of Blake's Special.[8]

I hope you are all well

John

Thomas Kilroy Papers

Foxfield

23 August 1989

Dear Tom,

We heard from both Anne and Brian. As you suspected, they have gone back behind the barricades of the 'good news' they received in Galway.[9] They were very gracious but they clearly want to look no further. I hope they are right.

I'm ½ way through the play.[10] The hard part was to get it started. It's strange how the framing device has changed the whole play. I begin with a priest at Maggie's hospital bed. End it with Maggie visiting Paul's cell. I think

---

6 Robin Robertson had come to know McGahern in the mid-1980s when he included 'Like All Other Men' in the anthology *Firebird 4: New Writing from Britain and Ireland*. See letter of 2 June 1984. McGahern, who had been increasingly uneasy at Faber since the retirement of Charles Monteith, agreed to show Robertson the MS of *Amongst Women* with a possible view to switching publishers to Chatto & Windus.

7 Clare (not 'Claire') Reihill was then Robertson's wife and worked for Faber.

8 Of this delicacy McGahern writes in his posthumously published essay 'Blake's of the Hollow': 'Blake's was selling "White Powers" then, a whiskey they bottled themselves, and it came from the time William Blake bottled beer and stout and spirits for the retail trade. It must have been fifteen or twenty years in the casks before it was bottled and it was the most delicious whiskey I ever tasted. Eventually, they only sold it to regular customers. I used to buy "White Powers" to give as presents. Now I wish I had kept some of those bottles for future occasions.' See *LOTW*, 41–4.

9 Friel had received good test results after a Galway medical examination.

10 Refers to McGahern's work on early drafts of *The Power of Darkness*.

it has taken much of the melodrama out and it has given me more control. I'm left with Paul, Maggie, Eileen, Peter, baby, Oliver and Paddy. I couldn't get rid of Paddy. I should finish it in about 2 weeks. Whether it ever goes on the boards or not, I needed to do it for my own peace. I'm very grateful for your letter: it was extraordinarily useful.[11]

R. Murphy was to come here from Sligo last Sunday for lunch. At one p.m. he rang and asked if he could come late and bring H. Vendler (It is completely in type). She was lively and very good company. She is spending these days in Clanmore.[12]

We heard in a roundabout way that Madeline's father has had a bad stroke. Clearly he doesn't want to see her. There seem few happy families.

I hope all goes well in Dublin

With love to Hannah May, Julie and yourself
John

Alain Delahaye
Foxfield

12 October 1989

Dear Alain,
A few weeks ago I learned that Tony Cartano is bringing out your translation of The Dark.[13] I learned it in this strange way.

I was picked as one of 10 Irish writers to go on a carnival called La Belle Epoque. I tried to get out of it. I see it as a hardship and embarrassment. I then came under a lot of pressure to go, mostly from the Foreign Ministry here, and also Brigitte Semler from the Presses rang up saying they were publishing The Dark then.[14] At least I hope you got money. I wound up

11 Kilroy, in a letter of 24 August 1988, had admired the play but suggested a scaling down and reduction in the number of characters. 'The real theatrical problem,' writes Kilroy, 'is how to set up this material and how to end it for the kind of theatre which we have today.' McGahern Papers, NUIG, P71/1184.
12 Helen Vendler b. 1933, Harvard professor and renowned literary critic. Vendler, as a W. B. Yeats scholar, was a regular visitor to the Yeats Summer School in Sligo.
13 Presses de la Renaissance published Delahaye's translation of The Dark as L'Obscur in 1989. It had originally been published by Éditions de la Sphère in 1980.
14 Brigitte Semler was then press officer at Presses de la Renaissance.

agreeing to go. I'm dreading it but it would be pleasant if I could see you there. The poor carnival will be in Paris 27th Nov–December 1st.[15]

I finished the novel. It will be published next May. It is my best work but several times I thought I'd never have the strength to finish it. I feel sort of worn out.

How are you and how is Pascale? What is it like living in Paris?[16] What kind of work do you do? Are you writing?

> Madeline sends her love to you both
> and with my love
> John

Colm Tóibín

Foxfield

14 October 1989

Dear Marsha Rowe,[17]

Thank you for your letter. I'm very sorry but I'm against the idea of endorsements. I think they have long since been devalued. Last year I was given one of the worst novels I have ever read in Proof and 6 months later the book arrived with glowing endorsements by Anthony Burgess and others.

I admire Colm Toibin's writing. His book on the Border was one of the best books of its kind I have read and it got less than its due here.[18] When I read

---

15 Les Belles Étrangères was a literary festival organised every year from 1987 to 2010 by the National Book Centre (Centre National du Livre) under the auspices of the French Ministry of Culture. It involved a group of writers from the same country or writing in the same language being invited to take part in meetings in November with readers throughout France. The Irish writers invited in 1989 were John Banville, Sebastian Barry, Nuala Ní Dhomhnaill, Jennifer Johnston, Thomas Kilroy, Derek Mahon, John McGahern, John Montague, Breandán Ó hEithir and Francis Stuart.

16 Delahaye and family moved to Paris in the autumn of 1987.

17 Marsha Rowe, an Australian then working in London publishing. The novel McGahern is referring to here is Tóibín's first, *The South*, published in London by Serpent's Tail in 1990 and in 1991 in New York by Viking.

18 *Walking Along the Border* (London: Queen Anne Press, 1987), reissued as *Bad Blood: A Walk Along the Irish Border* (London: Vintage, 1994). In the book Tóibín describes having a drink with McGahern in William Blake's bar, Enniskillen followed by attendance at a Seamus Heaney reading: 'Afterwards there was a big dinner for all concerned in Franco's Italian restaurant. I watched John McGahern getting into his car to go home. Big dinners weren't his sort of thing. He had become, over the

the novel in typescript I admired the same quality of writing, and above all its wonderful evocation of place, but I thought the people of the novel needed much more work.

I look forward to reading the published novel, and naturally I am hoping it will all have been made true. Then I'd want to help it in the way I have always done through telling people and trying to review it. I hope it will have great good luck.

With good wishes
John McGahern

Russell and Volkening Papers
Foxfield

6 November 1989

Dear Tim,

Thank you for the cash but the calls did not matter at all. We have arrived at that troubling stage when we have more money than life.

It was a real pleasure for me to meet Susan and to see you again.[19]
There was still a long way to go over the title after you left.[20] Faber didn't want The Family and tried to install Monaghan Day again.[21] It is settled now. Amongst Women. Blessed art thou amongst women.[22]

Will we do the same as the last time to avoid charges (currency charges) over payment. You had Fabers pay me and then I paid you your commission. Do you want it in dollars or sterling?

Madeline asks to be remembered to you both with affection,

And with all my good wishes
John

---

years, a connoisseur of quietness', *Bad Blood*, 80. There is a copy of the 1987 book in McGahern's library.
19 Seldes was married to the writer Susan Shreve and they lived in Washington DC. Shreve b. 1939 is a novelist, memoirist and children's book author. She co-founded the Master of Fine Arts in Creative Writing programme at George Mason University, Virginia in 1980, where she teaches fiction writing.
20 Tim and Susan had visited Foxfield.
21 As late as a letter of 24 October 1989 from Faber to Seldes, the book was being called *Monaghan Day*, with *The Morans* as another possible title until very late.
22 *Amongst Women* was suggested as a title to McGahern by Julia Kilroy and was immediately accepted.

Do you want a proof copy?
They should be out soon.

Alain Delahaye

Foxfield

22 November 1989[23]

Dear Alain,
I'll be in Paris all next week, getting in late Sunday evening, leaving for Strasbourg early Saturday morning.[24] Madeline is not coming. There will be 10 other writers. One is Derek Mahon who did a very fine translation of Jaccottet.[25]

I'll be at the Hotel Brea in Rue Brea which is very close to you.[26]
There seems many engagements and I'll get another list as soon as I arrive.

Would you like to drop into the hotel early Monday morning. Or phone it. If not I'll phone you.

I'm looking forward to seeing Pascale and you.

With my love
John

I enclose these. They came in a bundle. I would not advise attendance at anything.[27]

23 Mistakenly dated 22 December 1989 by McGahern.
24 The Strasbourg event was a meeting of Carrefour des Littératures Européennes.
25 Derek Mahon studied French Literature at TCD and at the Sorbonne. His translation of Philippe Jaccottet's *Selected Poems* (Harmondsworth: Viking, 1987) was the winner of the 1987 Scott-Manriet Translation Prize and the 1989 Moncrieff Translation Prize. McGahern was on friendly terms with Mahon as far back as the early 1970s when Mahon worked as features editor at *Vogue*. See letter to Susanna Capon of 27 March 1974.
26 Hôtel Jardin Le Bréa on Rue Bréa near Les Jardins du Luxembourg. Delahaye then lived on Boulevard Pasteur.
27 Flyers to the various events around the Irish writers' visit to France.

Alain Delahaye

Foxfield

14 December 1989

Dear Alain,

It was a real pleasure to see you and Pascale and the children – though Florence is hardly that anymore.

I'm ill and exhausted after the whole crazy business.

Larkin published only 3 slim volumes in his lifetime, but after his death they put in every bit of crap they could get their hands on. I took the liberty of marking some of the poems.[28]

Keep the video for me, or better bring it if you can come in the summer. Madeline thanks you for the tapes and sends you all her love.

> I'll write when I feel better
> with my love to you all
> John

28 It is not the case that Philip Larkin published only three volumes of poetry in his lifetime, but he was certainly sparing in his output, and the three books McGahern is referring to here are likely *The Less Deceived* (Hessle: Marvell Press, 1955), *The Whitsun Weddings* (London: Faber, 1964) and *High Windows* (London: Faber, 1974). McGahern was very angry about what he felt was the stupid and unfair treatment of Larkin after his death. He especially objected to the publication of discarded juvenilia. McGahern was sending Delahaye Larkin's *Collected Poems*, ed. and int. Anthony Thwaite (London: Faber, 1988). The poems that McGahern marked for Delahaye were 'Church Going', 'Mr Bleaney', 'An Arundel Tomb', 'The Whitsun Weddings', 'Talking in Bed', 'Sunny Prestatyn', 'Dockery and Son', 'High Windows', 'Annus Mirabilis', 'The Card-Players', 'Vers de Société', 'Cut Grass', 'The Old Fools', 'Money', 'Show Saturday' and 'Aubade'.

1990

Colm Tóibín
Foxfield

7 January 1990

Dear Colm,
Thank you for <u>Homage to Barcelona</u>.[1] I enjoyed it very much. I already loved the city and it brought much back to me.

I liked what was personal best and my one complaint is that there wasn't enough of it. The history was interesting and well written, as was the Miro/Gaudi/Picasso/Dali, but could be part of any brilliant thesis. It is a small complaint and I do not even know what brief they gave you.

I got an invitation to Barcelona May 9th–13th from Marta Pessarrodona.[2] I wondered if it had come through you. It will not be easy as the novel comes out May 8th.

I'd have written before this but was ill. I was in France for 2 weeks. It was a real punishment. I collapsed soon after getting home and am just about all right again.

We'd like to see you, and to see the new changed house, but it is not so easy for both of us to get away together at this time. Maybe if we just called for tea on our way home?

Will you be gone away by early February?

With every good wish
John

1 Tóibín's travel book looks at the city in which he lived for three years in the mid-1970s and was published by Simon & Schuster in 1990.
2 Catalan poet and literary critic.

Faber

Foxfield

10 January [*1990*]

Dear Joanna,
I enclose a list.
 I'll ring in with other writer/reviewers names that may cross like Ian Hamilton, on this list, who published part of the novel in Soho Bloomsbury.
                         Love
                         John

Brian Friel
Tom Paulin
Seamus Heaney
Richard Holmes
Melvyn Bragg
Hermione Lee
P. J. Kavanagh

We can talk about the list. I'll try to think as well.

Russell and Volkening Papers (TS)

Foxfield

15 January 1990

Dear Miriam,
Thank you for your notes before Christmas and for your very kind letter about Amongst Women (once The Morans). I was delighted that it pleased you.
 Robert McCrum rang a few days ago. He was in Viking and no one seemed to know or care very much about the novel. His fear is that it will be published with no conviction. I rang Amanda Vail when I was having trouble with the title but she did not return the call. Do you think I should write to her?[3]

---

3 Amanda Vaill then worked as an editor at Viking and was overseeing the publication of *Amongst Women*. In yet another stroke of bad luck for McGahern with American publishers, Vaill left the company just as the novel was published. Kathryn

When the New York Times rang for an interview about <u>High Ground</u> in 1987, they said that there was someone in Viking who was really keen on the work. I have no idea who that might have been. The woman who took me to Viking went to Random House soon afterwards.[4]

Fabers are excited about the novel and are making it their main book of the season. May eighth is publication date. McCrum is writing to the new head of Viking, whom he met in New York. The French are excited too and are doing a large print run. Their reprint of <u>The Dark</u> sold 7,000 copies in three weeks before Christmas and is being reprinted; and they also have sold it to a mass paperback market publisher. My critical reputation is very high in France, and the publishers feel that Amongst Women might win either the Prix-Femina or Etrangères. It may all come to nothing, as we know well, but at least they are running.

It looks as if <u>The Pornographer</u> will be made into a tv (90 m) film by the BBC. I will write the screenplay. I'm having Lemon & Durbridge (Bethan Evans) handle the deal. I told Tim about this arrangement and he agreed to it. He said there is a similar situation with Nadine Gordimer. Heath handled an earlier option on the novel, but that agreement lapsed.

Do you think should I write Amanda Vail or not?

With every good wish for the New Year
John

Colm Tóibín
Foxfield

18 February 1990

Dear Colm,
Thank you for the kindness and extraordinary generosity to the novel. I feel quite unworthy. All I can say in mitigation is that it was a pure pig to write. There were times when I thought it had me beaten and that I was finished as a writer. Many times in those 4 or 5 years it took to write.[5]

Court, with whom McGahern had a good working relationship, took over the reins. Vaill went on to have a successful career as a writer of non-fiction.

4 Pat Mulcahy was the woman who brought McGahern to publish with Viking Penguin. She had previously been at Farrar, Straus and Giroux. After Penguin she soon moved on to Random House and later Doubleday.

5 Tóibín, long an admirer of McGahern's work, recognised immediately on reading a proof copy of *Amongst Women* that it was a masterpiece and an important moment in the history of the Irish novel.

We saw Mr Brogan. He was charming and spoke of you with affection. He hopes to begin work on the house in 2 weeks.[6]

Would you be tempted to come down for a night? We'd meet you at Dromod. We intend to keep the lent and it'd be more fun if you came before Ash Wednesday.[7] But whatever suits you best.

With all good wishes
John

Seamus Heaney Papers
Foxfield

20 February 1990

Dear Seamus,

I was delighted that you liked the novel. It was a pure pig to write. There were a number of times I thought it had me beaten and that I was finished.[8]

There's not much news. The bonesetter died, helicoptered to Dublin in the end.[9] All the rest of us cling to the beds, some more shakily than others. The 'Rages' got put in a Home, and fought with everybody, and had to be taken out again.[10] She lives on her own up in the Big House. They take her in meals. Though she's bent double somehow she gets round with a walking aid. I called too early one morning and got her. I haven't been back since. The son got married to a 40 year old nurse. 'Bejasus you'd want to have something coming in besides farming'—and they had 3 sons in 3 years. The P. P. retired at 92.[11] They gave him a wallet of notes and a colour tv. The housekeeper got an automatic washing machine, which was wheeled on stage. The P. P.

6 Martin Brogan did all the work on the McGahern house in Stoneybatter at the recommendation of Tóibín.

7 John and Madeline, like many others in Ireland, occasionally stopped drinking alcohol during the Lenten period.

8 Heaney had been sent a proof copy of *Amongst Women* by Faber and wrote to McGahern on 22 January 1990: 'It is a work of heart-breaking purity and surety. Cello and honey, as Mandelstam said of bits of Dante. It wakened me and read me inside out.' Madeline McGahern Papers.

9 Boolie Woods, a favourite neighbour, from a family of bonesetters. Given to pithy remarks such as one of McGahern's favourites: 'Life is a shaky venture . . . if you think about it.'

10 Anna Rose Donnelly, a neighbour's mother. Nicknamed 'The Rages' by Heaney.

11 Fr Frank McCabe, parish priest in Fenagh with whom McGahern got along very well. Between them they arranged for Pat Conway, the 'homeboy' on a neighbour's

said if he'd got the washing machine early on he mightn't have needed the housekeeper. I couldn't get your line about praising the homemade bread out of my head for days afterwards. I suppose it's that whole lost world. My poor uncle died in the town. I miss him.

I hope you enjoy Oxford. I was delighted when I heard you were going, but it cannot be easy.[12] I hope the new work goes well. I read a lovely poem last year in the I Times.

It'd be nice to meet when you come home, either here or in Dublin.

John

Alain Delahaye

Foxfield

25 February 1990

Dear Alain,

I hope the play wasn't too hard for you. If it ever goes on in France I'd want you to have a proper share.[13]

There are 2 things at the beginning of A. Women:

p. 1 8 lines from bottom . . . 'Monaghan Day. He' Insert McQuaid came every year to the house on Monaghan Day.

p. 2 6 from bottom, as they wait [crosses out 'like taxes that have to be paid']

I'm ½ way through the screenplay of The Pornographer. It is more difficult than I imagined. I feed the sheep and cattle in the morning, and then work. March 7th I have to go to London to give a reading. The weather is terrible, storms of wind and rain. The fields are sodden. We'll not drink during lent. Ordinarily Francie loves going to town but he hates the town in Lent. There's nothing like logic. Ask Pascale.

We are dreading the publication in May and even that is ambiguous. We want the novel to do well but we are afraid of the publicity. It looks as if there is going to be a lot of it.

We are both looking forward to seeing you all in July. Madeline sends Pascale and you her love as I do.

John

---

farm, to be given sheltered housing in Carrick-on-Shannon, a story that is fictionalised in *That They May Face the Rising Sun* through the character of Bill Evans.

12 Heaney was Professor of Poetry at Oxford from 1989 to 1994.

13 *The Power of Darkness* was never published in French translation despite interest from Simone Gallimard at Mercure de France.

5 March 1990

Dear Tom,
I was delighted by the play, as was Madeline.[14]

When I went through it line by line you'll see that I found very little. I think the dialogue is so good that any small thing sounds grievous. I'm fairly sure about the 'Act'. And the words on p. 28. What I most fear about the girls is that they'd translate into whimsy on the stage. I would like more of the Sergeant and Greyhound and Pals. The Beckett may be all right on p. 35. I'm not sure. Madame MacAdam is great. I'd prefer a few of the speeches lightened, but it's hardly anything. Anyhow you'll test all this in your own darkroom.

I think it's your best play. It is extraordinarily pleasurable to read. You may well have a hit but that is a dangerous invocation.

I go to London on the 7th. I'll be back on the 9th. If you feel I can be of any help ring. I feel I have more than a bit of neck commenting at all I have so little experience of the theatre.

> With my love
> John

Adrian Munnelly, Aosdána
[*Madeline McGahern*] (TS)

Foxfield

12 March 1990

Dear Adrian,[15]
Thank you for your letter of March 7th.

The main work was the finishing and the cutting and revision of the novel <u>Amongst Women</u>. It will be published by Faber and Faber in May 1990 and

---

14 *The Madame MacAdam Travelling Theatre* was first published by Methuen in 1991 and first staged by the Field Day Theatre Company on 9 September of the same year.
15 Adrian Munnelly, then registrar of Aosdána. The letter that follows outlines McGahern's artistic work over the previous year.

by Viking/Penguin in New York. I wrote an original screenplay of ninety minutes for Gandon Films. This was accepted. Whether it is made depends on finance.[16] I wrote and appeared in a thirty-minute documentary profile directed by Sean O Mordha for BBC, to be shown later this year. I published the essay on Leitrim in Thirty-two Counties (Secker and Warburg). An essay was published on An tOileananch in the Irish Review.[17] In Galway in the Spring of 1989 I directed the Writers' Workshop and in September of '89 I was the keynote speaker at the convocation of university teachers of English in France at Chantilly. The following month I was the Irish representative at the Carrefour des Litteratures Europeennes de Strasbourg. In December 1989 I was one of the ten Irish writers invited by the French Ministry of Culture to take part in Les Belles Etrangeres in Paris and the French provinces.

This month I gave the opening reading in a series devoted to the short story at the South Bank Centre in London. Last summer I was made a Chevalier de l'Ordre des Arts et des Lettres by the French government.

> With all good wishes
> Yours sincerely
> John McGahern

Alain Delahaye

Foxfield

15 April 1990

Dear Alain,

Thank you for your kind letter.

August 6–19th is fine. The Dublin house will be empty, and you can stay here. You can come and go as much as you wish between the places. Are you arriving into Dublin or Rosslare?

I'll be glad if The Power of Darkness is staged or published in France, though I dislike that you have so much work without any certainty or payment.

---

16 McGahern's screenplay of *The Pornographer* was never produced.
17 The essay on Tomás Ó Criomhthain's *An tOileánach* (Baile Átha Cliath: Clólucht an Tálbóidigh, 1929; published as *The Islandman*, tr. Robin Flower, Dublin: Talbot Press, 1934), a favourite book of McGahern's, is reproduced in *LOTW* as "What Is My Language?', 260–74.

Bethan Evans
Lemon Unna & Durbridge
24 Pottery Lane, Holland Park
London W11 4LI

is the agent. The theatre company that were to do it here lost their state grant and a new contract is being sought, probably with The Abbey.

I would have had the screenplay of The Pornographer finished by now but I had to turn Amongst Women into 10 episodes for BBC's Book at Bedtime. It sends Britain to sleep each night during the week, it ranges from rubbish to Madame Bovary, and as it results in big sales there was much pressure to do it, and do it quickly. The producer loves the book and is easy to work with and I suppose if it should be done at all it was as well that I do it.[18]
Publication day is May 8th.
There's a reading and reception in Trinity College and another in London. There will be no peace till it is over. Already journalists have been here and more are on the way.[19] Francie won't come near the house without first making certain that all is clear. The one consolation is that many seem excited by the novel. And it is plain ordinary work. Not an elephant in sight.

It is very cold here too. The sheep have all lambed. 31 lambs. Some of the cows have been let out into the fields. Hailstones fell today.

If you have any difficulties with the agent just tell me or ask her to ring me. I'll write to her separately it is all right.

We are both looking forward to seeing you all in August.

> With my love
> John

18 Book at Bedtime (or A Book at Bedtime, as it was known until 9 July 1993) is a long-running radio programme that is currently broadcast on BBC Radio 4 each weekday evening between 10.45 p.m. and 11 p.m. First broadcast 1949. Pam Brighton was the producer McGahern worked with on this production. Amongst Women was broadcast over ten episodes and was read by Tony Doyle, who went on to play Moran in a four-part television production of the book.
19 There was a great deal more publicity around Amongst Women than for any previous McGahern publication. It sold well and brought McGahern into a wider public gaze without in any way altering his daily domestic life.

Nicholas Grene

Foxfield

22 May 1990

Dear Nicky,[20]

It was extraordinarily kind of you to write to me about the novel.

I've said before how happy I was in Trinity, and how grateful I was/am to you for my stay there, all the small things you went out of your way to do for me.

We had no idea how the novel would be received and are a bit taken aback by the reception. We had 2 strong lambs killed by dogs at the weekend, which only increased the [*illegible*].

Hermione Lee wrote a wonderful piece in the Independent on Sunday.[21]

If you and Elinor would like to call on your way to Sligo we'd be delighted.[22]

We send you all our love

John

---

20 Nicholas Grene b. 1947. Then a lecturer at the Department of English, TCD, in 1999 becoming Professor of English Literature, retiring in 2015. Taking his first degree in TCD (1969) and his PhD at Cambridge (1973), he lectured at the University of Liverpool for seven years before returning to Trinity in 1979. His main research interests are in drama, primarily on Shakespeare and modern Irish theatre, but he has also worked on Irish poetry and on Indian literature in English. He is the author of a number of books including *Synge: A Critical Study of the Plays* (Basingstoke: Macmillan, 1975), *The Politics of Irish Drama* (Cambridge: Cambridge University Press, 1999), *Shakespeare's Serial History Plays* (Cambridge: Cambridge University Press, 2002), *Yeats' Poetic Codes* (Oxford: Oxford University Press, 2008) and *Home on the Stage: Domestic Spaces in Modern Drama* (Cambridge: Cambridge University Press, 2014). He was the founding director of the Synge Summer School (1991–2000).

21 Hermione Lee's review of *Amongst Women* in the *Independent on Sunday* begins: 'From the first compelling sentence of John McGahern's superb novel [. . .] you feel that this is a writer who knows exactly what he is doing, and how best to do it.' The rest of the review continues in the same manner, and Lee continued to be a powerful promoter of McGahern's work for the remainder of his career.

22 Nicky Grene's wife Eleanor.

Frank McEvoy
[*Seán Sexton*]
Foxfield

25 May 1990

Dear Frank,[23]

Thank you for your very generous letter.

Viking Penguin will publish A.W. in September in New York and the Presses de la Renaissance will publish it in Paris next February.

By coincidence, I agreed to write about Apostate in the Irish Times series on neglected books in the hope of getting it back into print, and find I have no copy. Would you loan me your copy? I'd be careful and it would save me going to a library. I won't mind at all if it is difficult in any way for you.[24]

I may be in Kilkenny this summer. They invited me last year, I was finishing the novel, and said I'd go this year if it was of any use. I'll be even happier if they forget but it would be nice to see you there.

> With every good wish
> John

Alen MacWeeney
Foxfield

4 July 1990

Dear Alen,[25]

It was lovely to hear from you, and thank you for your good wishes, and the beautiful cards.

You'd be very welcome to come down when you're next in Ireland and there is a spare room if you'd like to stay overnight. I knew I'd like the

23 Frank McEvoy (1925–2012), bookshop owner and key figure in the Kilkenny literary scene where he helped to edit the *Kilkenny Magazine* (1960–70).
24 McGahern did not write about *Apostate* for the *Irish Times*. On his admiration for the book and attempts to have it reissued by Faber see his letter to Joanna Mackle of 28 August 1987.
25 Alen MacWeeney b. 1939, a Dublin-born, New York-based photographer whom McGahern had known as far back as 1964. See letter to Mary Keelan of 16 March 1964.

photographs. I saw some beautiful pictures of yours in a little French book on Ireland by [*illegible*]. The real difficulty is that I write so slowly that I'm always behind. There is a year of work ahead of me now before I have even a chance of catching up.

Madeline worked as a photographer when she was young (she'd say she went around taking pictures). She gave it up for years. About 5 years ago she started up again with a darkroom etc. She doesn't think of herself as a photographer. More like some one learning and she doesn't sell or show her work. I think some of her work is good but she might not ever want me to say that. Anyhow, that is her business. They had difficulty getting a photo from her for the publication.

Viking will publish Amongst Women in September in the States. I'd be surprised if it gets much attention there.

I remember vividly the day we spent around the Court, we have one of those small houses near there now.[26] Your mother and father, a nice English girl who was with you, and the Colonel who had espoused the [*illegible*].

It'd be lovely to see you again

I hope you are well

And with every good wish
John

Luke Dodd
Foxfield

4 July 1990

Dear Luke,[27]
Thank you for your letter. It was very kind to write so generously about Amongst Women.

We had a hard few weeks around the publication but it is all over now.

26 Presumably refers to Dublin's Four Courts in the Smithfield neighbourhood next to Stoneybatter, the location of the McGaherns' Dublin house.
27 Luke Dodd b. 1960 was at this time restoring Strokestown Park, the last of the Anglo-Irish 'big houses' to survive in Co. Roscommon. The stableyards were converted into a museum that commemorated the Great Irish Famine of the 1840s. Dodd and McGahern had first met at a reading in Lough Key Forest Park, Boyle, Co. Roscommon.

We'd love to see you, either in Strokestown or here – it's 25 miles, Rooskey, Dromod, Mohill, Gorvagh, and if you feel like coming over just telephone.[28]

We had 3 lambs killed with dogs this year, and we have to put them in the field beneath the house at night. The price of wool was so poor this year that it wasn't worth bringing it to Strokestown.[29]

Madeline asks to be remembered to you

and with all good wishes

John

Faber

Foxfield

8 July 1990

Dear Joanna,

Thank you for your letter and I think the poster is terrific.[30] Yesterday A.W. was back to No. 1 on the Irish list.

I'm glad you had a good time in New York and thanks for facing into Viking.[31] Scott Anderson wrote me a few days ago.[32] He seems to have an obsession with Shepherd's Pie. He says he'll eat nothing but Shepherd's Pie for a month if A.W. doesn't win the Irish Book Award.

Please tell Emma that I gave ABC that interview.[33] I should have taken her advice: there was a European Summit in Dublin and our link with London kept breaking down. The 10 minute interview took almost 2 hours.

I finished the screenplay of The Pornographer a few days ago. Almost certainly they will want rewrites.

Have you any plans to be in Ireland?

With my love

John

28 Dodd and the McGaherns met for dinner on several occasions over the years, both in Foxfield and in Strokestown.

29 McGahern annually sold his wool to a dealer in Strokestown, Co. Roscommon.

30 A promotional poster for Amongst Women featuring an image of the book cover dominated by the Irish tricolour.

31 McGahern was unhappy with the way Viking handled Amongst Women. He particularly disliked the cover, which showed a group of young women seated under a tree.

32 US assistant editor of Amongst Women.

33 Emma Bagnall was the Faber publicist for the paperback of Amongst Women.

4 September 1990

Dear Tom,

We were very glad to get your card.

I never heard of Snyder, but I'd be glad if you went to Colgate, and I'd give you every help.[34] They wrote inviting me for a year. M. had the next best thing to a fit at the idea of a whole year in Colgate. Nothing is settled yet but I may go for the Fall term of next year.

I promised different parties I'd read for them when I finished the novel. These are being called in now. I met your brother in Kilkenny, which was a late night shambles, and I couldn't even get him a drink. He said he used your house for the Galway Races and met Seamus Deane. I have Clifden[35] at the end of the month and the Patrick Kavanagh after that.[36] They waste at least 3 days. I met Matt Molloy in Galway and wasted more.[37] Still, like dear Beckett, it would have gone anyhow, I'm sure.

Pam Brighton sent the play to Chris F. at the Abbey.[38] He liked it. She and he and I went through it page by page last week. All the things they said made sense. I have to rewrite it and find a different title. He'll then recommend it, but he'll either have left or he'll be about to leave. Our feeling was that Hynes wanted him out.[39]

---

34 Don J. Snyder b. 1950, American novelist who taught for a period in Colgate. In 1987 he and his family lived for a time in Co. Wicklow while he wrote his second novel, *From the Point* (New York: Ivy Books, 1988). The Kilroys had met the Snyders in Maine and became friendly.

35 'Clifden' is circled and underlined three times.

36 Both arts festivals.

37 Matt Molloy b. 1947, an Irish traditional musician especially noted for his talents as a flautist. Proprietor of a public house named after him in Westport, Co. Mayo.

38 Pam Brighton (1946–2015) was a radical English theatre director best known for her work in Northern Ireland. She first went there in 1983 to join the Charabanc Theatre Company. In 1991 she formed Dubbeljoint with the actor Mark Lambert and playwright Marie Jones as a cross-border, cross-sectarian initiative – the company's name was a contraction of 'Dub(lin) Bel(fast) joint'. She produced *Amongst Women* for the BBC's *Book at Bedtime* in 1990. Chris F. is Christopher Fitzsimons, author, critic and one-time director of the Abbey Theatre.

39 Garry Hynes b. 1953, Irish theatre director. She was a co-founder of Galway's Druid Theatre Company in 1975 and was Druid's artistic director from 1975 to

Brian sent me his play. I liked the women and the whole situation but I felt he threw it away. I thought the Narrator was a feeble cop-out as was the curtain speech. I haven't answered and do not know what to say.[40]

Amongst Women comes out in France tomorrow. The sports editor of Liberation was here and offered me a seat in the press car on next year's Tour de France.[41] The American edition came. It looks dreadful. They plainly haven't a clue.[42] The business of the short lists has started. It is more like horseracing than anything to do with writing. Horseracing is fun as we know from Ballinrobe but not when you're the horse.

Have you any new news of the play? We both look forward to it very much, and wish Julie's launch great good luck.[43] I would have gone to London if I could.

> With much love
> John

Colm Tóibín

Foxfield

8 September 1990

Dear Colm,

Thank you for Homage to Barcelona. It is lovely to have. I enjoyed re-reading The South, the quality of the prose, the shining places, but I thought – though

---

1991, and again from 1995 to date. Hynes directed for the Abbey Theatre from 1984 and was its artistic director from 1991 to 1994. She and McGahern did not see eye to eye over the production of *The Power of Darkness* at the Abbey, not helped by the fact that McGahern had wanted Pam Brighton to direct the play.

40 *Dancing at Lughnasa*.

41 Daniel Rondeau and Carlos Freire of *Libération* visited Foxfield while putting together a supplement for the newspaper titled *Writers Speaking About Their Profession*. The idea of attending the Tour de France at close quarters would have appealed to the sports fanatic side of McGahern's character but it did not come to pass.

42 *Amongst Women* was published by Viking in the US with its dustjacket bearing a drawing of three young women sitting beneath a tree, giving entirely the wrong impression of the book. McGahern despaired of the image, which made him yet more determined to break with Viking.

43 Julia Carlson, *Banned in Ireland: Censorship and the Irish Writer* (London: Routledge, 1990) includes an interview with McGahern about his experiences of censorship.

it sounds schoolmasterish, maybe even churlish – you should have worked the characters more. I was hoping you'd give them the clarity all the way through that they took on late in the work.

We'd like very much if you came down. The next two weeks are not good. I have rewrites and people coming about the rewrites. Then I go to Clifden for 2 days on the 23rd. What about the days 26th, 27th, 28th or the early days of October?

With every good wish
John

Alain Delahaye
Foxfield

25 October 1990

Dear Alain,

Thank you for yesterday's letter.

I may have put my sweet foot in it but perhaps not.

Amongst W. won the Irish Award. It was presented by the President last Friday night at a ceremony in Dublin (19th) and Mr & Mrs Cartano came from Paris.[44] The next day (20th) the English publishers, Faber & Faber, gave a luncheon. At the luncheon I asked Cartano if he published plays. He said – 'No!' 'That's great,' I said. 'I can give it to the Mercure who published my first book in France.'

'How come?'

'Madame Gallimard wrote me. She heard about the play. She must know that you do not publish plays.'

'We'll have to talk about it,' he said and it was left at that.

I am writing by return to let you know what happened.

I am still tired after London and Dublin and interviews and interviews.

The Booker went down to two books <u>Possession</u> and <u>Amongst Women</u> and the votes split 3 to 2. My only surprise was that it went so close. Byatt (the winner) is part of the London Literary Establishment and I thought I had no

---

44 *Amongst Women* won *The Irish Times*-Aer Lingus Irish Literature Prize for Fiction, worth £10,000. The prize was presented to McGahern by Irish President Patrick Hillery at a ceremony in the Royal Dublin Society, Ballsbridge, Dublin on 19 October 1990.

chance.[45] I'm secretly glad. It is bad enough as it is but it would be almost impossible if I had won. The novel has now sold 30,000 copies which is more than the sales of all my other books <u>put together</u>. I don't understand it. Does anybody?

It'll be hard to get a quiet evening, but we will definitely meet. We have to go to La Rochelle and to the Festival in Cognac and there are two evening signings in Paris. Madeline is coming with me.[46] Please thank Madame Gallimard for her letter. I'll be glad to meet her in Paris.[47]

Madeline sends her love to Pascale and you.

> We're looking forward to seeing you soon
> With much love
> John

The play has to be gone through <u>once</u> more before it goes into publication.[48]

Paul Durcan Papers

Foxfield

3 November 1990

Dear Paul,[49]
Your letter was far too generous. But I respected and respect your wish not to have it answered. Prayers that cannot be answered . . .

---

45 A. S. Byatt's *Possession* (London: Chatto & Windus, 1990) won the Booker Prize in 1990. The remainder of the shortlist was made up of Beryl Bainbridge, *An Awfully Big Adventure*; Penelope Fitzgerald, *The Gate of Angels*; Brian Moore, *Lies of Silence*; Mordecai Richler, *Solomon Gursky Was Here*; and McGahern's *Amongst Women*. The judging panel was made up of Susannah Clapp, A. Walton Litz, Hilary Mantel and Kate Saunders, with Sir Denis Forman as chair.
46 The McGaherns enjoyed an especially memorable seafood meal by the port in La Rochelle. The fine hospitality continued in Cognac. In both towns there were readings, visits to libraries and sundry literary shenanigans.
47 Simone Gallimard was interested in publishing *The Power of Darkness* in France in the hope that she could also secure McGahern's future work. She confided in Delahaye that she regretted losing McGahern as an author after the publication of *Lignes de Fond*.
48 *The Power of Darkness* was published in 1991 by Faber.
49 Paul Durcan b. 1944, Irish poet. At the time of the composition of this letter, Durcan was at the height of his reputation as a public poet, with the *Irish Times* declaring him, in the wake of the 1990 presidential campaign in which he was closely

I hope you'll accept this in appreciation of your own work, it has just come from the publisher.[50]

If you are ever in this part of the country we'll be glad to see you.

With every good wish
John

Russell and Volkening Papers

Foxfield

6 November 1990

Dear Tim,

I am sorry about Thistledown. I had assumed you were going to go ahead and give him the rights for a nominal sum.[51]

A.W. went down to the last 2 in the Booker and lost by 2 to 3. Faber say they have now sold over 30,000, which is far better than getting a big advance, and not selling. I find it hard to believe it still. It is now 6 months in the top 3 on the Irish bestseller list. It's moving between 9–15 in Britain.

It was lovely to see Sara. Bill Hamilton was with her.[52] I met Roger Straus and his wife briefly.[53]

I came to like McCrum. Faber certainly did a great job.

I may go back to Colgate for the Fall of next year but it is not settled yet.

I go to France – Paris, La Rochelle, Cognac, Paris – for signings and readings next week.

------

associated with Mary Robinson, 'the nation's *de facto* Poet Laureate'. See 'Songs of a Successful Campaign', *Irish Times* (13 November 1990).

50 Durcan has written at the bottom of the letter that enclosed with it is a gift of *The Pornographer*. He has also written down directions to Foxfield as given to him by John over the phone. Durcan made several visits over the years that followed.

51 In a letter of 30 October 1990, Seldes had mentioned that Paddy O'Rourke of the Thistledown Press – a small publishing house in Saskatoon, Saskatchewan – was pressuring him for an answer on whether they could go ahead and acquire the rights to publish a high quality, limited edition volume of a McGahern short story. The idea appears to have come to nothing.

52 Sara Fisher and Bill Hamilton of A. M. Heath. Hamilton soon became McGahern's closest contact at the firm.

53 Roger Straus (1917–2004) was co-founder and chairman of Farrar, Straus and Giroux, a New York book publishing company. This company, along with Knopf, was being considered closely by Seldes as a possible good fit for McGahern as he prepared to leave Viking.

I am finishing the shooting script of The Porno man. I swear I'll never put couples into bed again. It's so hard to get them out.

I want to thank Miriam and yourself for all the kind words throughout the hurly burly.

Yours

John

Tom Paulin Papers

Foxfield

9 November 1990

Dear Tom,[54]

Thanks for the very kind card and I want to tell you how grateful I am for your support of the stories over all those years now. It's an awful way of putting it but it's true.[55]

It'd be lovely to see you here soon and I have no plans to go anywhere, this year or next or the next . . .

John

Seamus Heaney Papers

Foxfield

23 November 1990

Dear Seamus,

We were in France when your kind letter and invitation got here. We got back last night to find it.

I had already read the play and would have liked very much to have seen it played. What I enjoyed best in the reading was the marvellous freshness of the language. I wish it all good luck.[56]

---

54 Tom Paulin b. 1949, poet, critic and member of the Field Day Theatre Group.
55 Paulin had long been an admirer of McGahern's short fiction, and, in 1988, was the first to prompt Matthew Evans at Faber to publish a *Collected Stories*. For more on Paulin's interest in McGahern, see letter to Charles Monteith of 4 June 1978.
56 Heaney had written to McGahern on 9 November 1990 inviting him to an after-show party at his Dublin home on the last night of *The Cure at Troy* at the Abbey Theatre.

I was delighted to see you got that great barrowful of dollars from the California Foundation.[57]

It was a hard year. At its end I feel more like one of those advertising types excoriated by Auden than a writer. I have to say, though, that the Faber crowd could not have been better or more decent all through it.

Tommie Maxwell out of <u>Woodbrook</u> died 2 weeks ago. The old bonesetter went as well, proving how shaky each venture is, and my own dear Uncle, but enough! Only this morning Francie was saying that they'd sicken you with talk of dying round the lake, and the poor man is even off the drink for November.[58]

> Remember us with love to Marie
> With my love
> John

Gerard Smyth

Foxfield

3 December 1990

Dear Gerry,[59]

Thank you for your kind invitation and I'll be glad to serve as a judge on the International Fiction Prize panel.[60]

---

57 Heaney was awarded a Lannan Literary Award for 1990 valued at $25,000. The Lannan Foundation was then based in Los Angeles.

58 Giving up the consumption of alcohol for November is a common penance in Ireland, offered up for the intentions of the holy souls.

59 Gerard Smyth b. 1951 is a poet, critic and journalist whose role in the *Irish Times* for almost twenty years was as managing editor with responsibilities for the paper's arts and literary coverage. He has published nine collections of poetry.

60 McGahern had won *The Irish Times*-Aer Lingus Irish Literature Prize for Fiction in 1990 for *Amongst Women*. He was also on the International award shortlist, as was Alice Munro, whom he met at the Dublin awards ceremony in October 1990. McGahern retained an enduring admiration for her work. A. S. Byatt won the International award for *Possession*, which had also won the Booker that year. When McGahern judged the International Fiction Prize for 1991 it was awarded to the American author Louis Begley for *Wartime Lies* (New York: Knopf, 1991). McGahern served only one year, with the prize later losing Aer Lingus as co-sponsor, becoming *The Irish Times* International Fiction Prize.

I may be in New York for a time next autumn (Sept. to Dec.) but that is hardly a difficulty because of the Aer Lingus involvement.

With every good wish

John McGahern

Susanne Dumbleton

Foxfield

4 December 1990

Dear Bill,

It was lovely to hear from you, and I want to thank Sue and yourself for the very kind words about Amongst Women.

We both enjoyed meeting Patsy Murphy. She was full of life that evening. We hope we meet her before long again.[61]

It looks as if we'll be in Colgate next Fall. They invited me back for a year but Madeline felt it was too long to be away. I suggested the Fall term. I should hear from them any day now.

I've been involved with a screenplay of The Pornographer. There seems endless tedious meetings, and everything advances like the snail. Also we had trouble with a good Dublin entrepreneur pirating the paperback.[62] I've finished a stage play. It needs some work yet but it looks as if it will go on at The Abbey. I'd like to go back to write a few stories again.

We were in Paris last week. The city is as beautiful as ever and the enclosed might amuse you.[63]

And if you get to Ireland you'll be very welcome here.

Madeline asks to be remembered to you both with affection, as I do.

Yours

John

61 Patsey Murphy is Susanne Dumbleton's sister. At the time, she was editor of the Weekend section of the *Irish Times*.
62 Philip McDermott. See letter to Neill Joy of 17 August 1987.
63 The enclosure was probably a review of *Amongst Women* (published in French as *Entre toutes les femmes*) by Dominique Durand cut out from *Le Canard* which includes a cartoon depiction of McGahern playing with a paper chain of female dolls.

Robert White

Foxfield

15 December 1990

Dear Bob,

Thank you for your kind letters. It sent me back to the copy of Yeats's prose you so generously gave me all those years ago when I was leaving Newcastle, and your own books.[64]

The Booker was a hard evening. The judges were tied 2–2 and the Chairman gave Antonia Byatt his casting vote. A.W.'s success took us completely by surprise. It is now in its 6th printing, and has collected 4 Awards. The worst thing about it is that it eats away at private time. A play is being cast and goes on at The Abbey in March. I have to finish a screenplay of The Pornographer so there is little chance of a let up or real work for months. Next Fall I'll probably go back to Colgate. I've been invited to New Zealand for 1992 but I doubt if I'll go.

We have sheep and cattle still and the black cat Miss Charlie.

If you are in this part of the world and would like to call we'd be glad.

I hope you are happy in Perth.

We both wish you a happy Christmas
John

64 A copy of Yeats's *Autobiographies* signed by Bob White forms part of McGahern's library.

1991

Sophia Hillan
[*Madeline McGahern*]

[*Foxfield*]

19 January 1991

Dear Sophia,[1]
Thank you for your letter, and your articles, which I read with interest, and
your very kind words about my novel.

I gave you permission to quote the private letter I wrote to Michael
McLaverty for a paper you told me you were delivering to a Society but I
cannot extend that permission to allow you to use any quotations for Poolbeg
publication. I am sorry that you will have to paraphrase.

Daniel Corkery's friend was Donncha O Ceilleachair, who wrote in Irish.
He taught with me in Clontarf. It was he who encouraged me to write to
Michael McLaverty. He was a very charming man. He died young but some
of his work is still read. I'm sorry I can give no help with the train story.[2]

I think your thesis Corkery – McLaverty – McGahern is neat but other than
the fact that I admire the work of both writers it is in my case hardly true.
I suspect it may be equally tenuous in Corkery's case. I was an unpublished
writer when we first corresponded and met, and you can judge the distance
between us, that I cannot remember ever showing Michael any unpublished
work. All he would have read was published extracts from the unpublished
novel I wrote and The Barracks and The Dark. I moved in a circle in Dublin
that Michael would not have approved of. And they did not think much of
Michael's work when I tried to introduce it to them. We disagreed about
much contemporary writing the few times it was discussed. 'Poor Kavanagh',
he always said and the inference was that he had gone wrong along the

---

1 Sophia Hillan, Irish novelist and critic. Under the name Sophia Hillan King, she
edited *In Quiet Places: The Uncollected Stories, Letters and Critical Prose of Michael
McLaverty* (Dublin: Poolbeg Press, 1989) and published a monograph on McLaverty's
work titled *The Silken Twine* (Dublin: Poolbeg Press, 1992).
2 See letter to Michael McLaverty [23 January 1961].

way; though I would never agree he was always kind and gave me a copy of Kavanagh's first book, which I still have.[3]

I think that the difficulty of dealing with letters is that they are never quite honest. Often out of sympathy or diffidence or kindness or affection or self interest we quite rightly hide our true feelings. Anyhow I have no doubt about the end of the relationship. I was dismayed when he sent me The Brightening Day. I wished it had never been published as I saw it could only damage the work. I am sure I tried to put it as gently as I could, but there was no way I could give him the support he so much wanted for such a book (If it was to this book Patricia Craig was referring I'd agree with what she said) and that ended what was always a tentative, cautious relationship. He did not want to see me when I came to give a lecture in Belfast, it must have been 67 or 68.[4] I learned later from John Boyd and Seamus Heaney – Seamus can give an extraordinary imitation of McLaverty – that I had become 'Poor McGahern' but none of this has made any difference in my affection, then or now.[5]

With every good wish,
Sincerely
John

Russell and Volkening Papers (TS)

Foxfield

19 January 1991

Dear Tim,
Thank you for both letters. I am very sorry to be so late in replying.

Amongst Women picked up two more awards on both sides of Christmas, the last on January 15th (it now has four), and it went back to number one here on the Christmas bestseller list. This means TV dinners and interviews. Nothing much happens but it just seems to eat away the time. A few weeks ago Faber said the sales had reached 33,000. It is still number one this week here.

3 Patrick Kavanagh's rare first collection, *Ploughman and Other Poems*, signed by McLaverty in 1936 and by McGahern in 1964, formed part of McGahern's library at the time of his death.
4 McGahern's November 1967 lecture with Herman Melville's 'Bartleby, the Scrivener' at its core was delivered in Belfast as part of the Belfast Festival.
5 John Boyd (1912–2002), Belfast-born editor, radio producer, playwright and man of letters.

This is how things are. After a conference that should take place within the next few weeks I have to write the final shooting script for The Pornographer. I've had a lot of trouble with this as they have changed their minds so often and had new ideas that just put more work on me.

The Abbey Theatre are going to do the play The Power of Darkness (provisional title) as their main production for the Dublin Theatre Festival in September. I expect I'll have to work on the script in rehearsal. There will be a preliminary run-through with actors next month.

I want to write two or three new stories – I have already started one – for the Faber Collected Stories and to revise some of the published stories.

I have a new novel in my head, but I have to get the other things out of the way first. The enclosed is a rough draft of the idea, but it could change beyond recognition in the actual writing.[6]

I'd like to do the Faber Book of Prose sometime but I do not want to be tied to dates. As you can see, I have more than the full of my arms to contend with.

Madeline joins me in wishing you and Susan a very Happy New Year,

        Yours
        John

Thomas Kilroy Papers

Foxfield

2 February 1991

Dear Tom,

Thank you for your letter and the Marquez.[7] I was sorry to hear of the trouble with Stafford Clark.[8] Anyhow, the play is good enough to stand on its own, with or without him.

---

6 The rough novel outline enclosed came to nothing and in no way resembles McGahern's next novel, *That They May Face the Rising Sun*.

7 Kilroy had gifted the Gabriel García Márquez novel *A Hundred Years of Solitude* to McGahern.

8 Maxwell Robert Guthrie Stewart ('Max') Stafford-Clark b. 1941, English theatre director. From 1979 to 1993 he was artistic director of the Royal Court. There was a lengthy period when Field Day, Druid and the Royal Court were in negotiation to stage Kilroy's *The Madame MacAdam Travelling Theatre*. After a reading at the Royal Court, Stafford-Clark became uneasy about producing it.

I didn't like the Donoghue but it would have created an awkward situation to have said what I thought about the book as I had taken the place at the International Jury he had vacated in order to become eligible for the Irish award.[9]

Pam Brighton and myself have been smiling over the extraordinary performance in Wynn's. My poor entrance in answer to your call seemed to have the effect of a cattle prod on Friel. We never saw a man in our lives in such panic to get to his dinner. Pam says she thought she saw him peeping at us from behind a pillar earlier in the evening. What's wrong with the man or the situation?[10]

It looks as if the play will go on still at the Abbey but nothing is settled yet.

It doesn't look as if we'll get to Galway. Because of the animals we are tied and there still seems endless work on The Pornographer, and I'm trying to struggle back to my own sentences again. We are, as well, going back to Colgate in the Fall. It'll be strange to see it again after 7 years.

We hope one way or another we'll see you soon.

> With our love to you both and Hannah May
> John

Russell and Volkening Papers (TS)

Foxfield

14 February 1991

Dear Tim,

Thank you for your letter of 31 January. I'm depending on you for advice about the contracts: what best to do or not to do.

The reason I sent an account of the novel is that I thought you wanted a resumé in order to sell it to Sonny Mehta or Roger Strauss with the Collected Stories.[11] I was going on your previous letters. The stories would be a revised

---

9 Denis Donoghue's (1928–2021) book of memoir, *Warrenpoint* (London: Jonathan Cape, 1991).

10 Unknown, though this description is illustrative of a certain uneasiness sometimes evident between McGahern and Friel.

11 Ajai Singh 'Sonny' Mehta (1942–2019) was the editor-in-chief of Alfred A. Knopf and chairman of the Knopf Doubleday Publishing Group. Beginning a successful publishing career in London, he moved to New York in 1987 to head Knopf as president and editor-in-chief. Mehta was hand-picked by Robert Gottlieb, who was leaving Knopf to edit the *New Yorker*. Seldes, knowing that McGahern was

<u>Nightlines</u>, <u>Getting Through</u>, and <u>High Ground</u> with three new stories.[12] One is already written. A new long story is almost completed. The book will be ready by the end of the summer before heading off for Colgate.

I don't know what the situation is now with Viking or if they still own the rights of <u>High Ground</u> or how they stand with <u>Amongst Women</u>. My French publisher, Tony Cartano, was shocked by how little Viking seemd to value <u>Amongst Women</u> when he was in New York sometime before publication. I think Robert McCrum feels that the Collected Stories, or whatever they decide to call them, should be taken from Viking. I now get the odd friendly missive from Viking, mostly with reviews, but I haven't been answering them. What do you think about the whole situation?

Next Thursday I get my Chevalier's medal from the French. I get to wear a ribbon like thousands of old fellows.[13] Trinity College give me a doctorate in July and it is now settled that I go back to Colgate for the Fall term. Tell Susan that the delights of Fred Busch's prose awaits me.

I enclose this piece which was commissioned for a special issue of a magazine for young people, 'In Dublin'. 'The Telegraph' will publish it in London when the paperback of <u>Amongst Women</u> appears in May. I think 'Liberation' will publish it in France. I'm sending it in case Miriam might think of some place that it could interest in the States; but it may well be too local.[14]

> With all good wishes
> John

---

increasingly unhappy at Viking Penguin, was approaching other possible publishers – foremost among these was Knopf to whom McGahern moved next and with whom he happily concluded his American publishing career.

12 In fact, only two new stories appeared in *The Collected Stories*, 'The Creamery Manager' and 'The Country Funeral'. It may be that McGahern was still considering having 'The Old Man' (published ultimately as 'The White Boat') as part of *The Collected Stories*.

13 McGahern was presented with the award at the French Embassy, Dublin. Among those in attendance were his friends Liam Kelly, Gary Swift, Jimmy Swift and Joanna Mackle who had done much work on promoting *Amongst Women* at Faber.

14 The essay in question is 'The Solitary Reader', which can be found in *LOTW*, 87–95. It was published by *In Dublin* under the title 'Amongst Books' and by the *Daily Telegraph* as 'Those Dangerous Mirrors Reflecting Our Lives'. Seldes placed it with the *New York Times* where it was published on 28 April 1991 under the title 'Me among the Protestants: A Bookish Boyhood'.

23 April 1991

Dear Tim,

I wasn't bothered at all.

I think it had more got to do with bad luck and manners than rights or wrongs. Shakespeare came back off holiday to find a decree on his desk from The New York Times and he hit the roof. He was at the Faber table for the Booker dinner where the idea of the piece came up. He delayed the publication until May to coincide with the paperback publication. I wrote him a note today.[15]

The New York Times cleared it word by word over the telephone. A girl called Becker was helpful and nice but it must have cost a little fortune or a good lunch.

Amanda Vail also has come back off holiday and finds your proposal on her desk. Seemingly it is dangerous to go on holiday. I haven't answered.

I was in Dublin recording A.W. for the Irish radio in 24 episodes. I'd be grateful for the Times fee in dollars.[16] That way I'll have dollars in September. The Abbey has now signed a contract for the play and it looks as if it may go on in Paris as well.

> With every good wish
> Yours
> John

15 The *New York Times* published its version of the McGahern essay that has become best known as 'The Solitary Reader' the day after the *Daily Telegraph* of which Nicholas Shakespeare was then literary editor – presumably, from the tone of this letter, much to Shakespeare's annoyance.
16 McGahern was paid a fee of $500 by the *New York Times* for his essay.

2 June 1991

Dear Brian,

I'm sorry you were upset in any way. I did make that remark to Michael Colgan.[17]

He asked me to meet him about a number of projects. During the meeting he asked me about the play and I told him about it. I mentioned the great help Tom Kilroy had given me, and hence to the remark.

Before I received your letter, Tom rang me to warn me of the decision. He said he was very distressed, especially since he felt that it was the kind of play the Field Day should be doing. He said nothing in detail about what had taken place; he was the soul of discretion. I just assumed that because you were the other playwright on the Board your weight must have come down against the play. This assumption was reinforced when Tom Paulin, around the time of the Booker, said much the same thing to me as Tom Kilroy.[18] I also shared the popular belief that nothing went on at Field Day unless it was approved by you. When I made the remark to Michael Colgan, I thought I was just stating the facts.

I never took the rejection of the play in any way personally. I knew the play wasn't political. I also knew that plays by ageing novelists are, historically, a disaster zone. While I was, I suppose, disappointed, there were also reasons that made me feel, in fact, quite relieved by the decision. So all it seems to be, finally, is a misunderstanding, like the Muldoon business all those years ago, except this time our roles appear to have been reversed.[19]

17 Friel had written to McGahern on 29 May expressing his upset after Michael Colgan – then artistic director of the Gate Theatre and a leading light in Dublin theatre life – had reported to him that McGahern had claimed twice that 'Friel rejected my play'. He sought to assure McGahern that this was not the case, that the Field Day Board had rejected the play and that he had, in fact, argued that 'we try to set up a reading of the play, a proposal that was overruled'. Madeline McGahern Papers.

18 Tom Paulin, the Belfast poet, critic and public intellectual, was then a member of the Field Day Board alongside Tom Kilroy, Brian Friel, Seamus Heaney, Seamus Deane, Stephen Rea and David Hammond.

19 The nature of 'the Muldoon business' must remain, for now, unclear, though again this suggests some uneasiness between McGahern and Friel.

Your letter was the first news I had that the play is going on at the Festival.[20]
I hope that Anne and you are well and that we'll see you soon.
With love to you both
John [*handwritten signature*][21]

Niall Walsh Papers

Foxfield

28 July 1991

Dear Phil and Niall,
I rang but had no luck and I'll ring again.

I wanted to thank you for the meal and evening and I hope the news from the scan was good. It was lovely to see you both again and I hope I didn't wear you out by staying as long as I did.[22]

I sold ½ the lambs. They made just under £35. There was an interesting fellow here John Fortune in connection with a tv script.[23] He wrote many of On the Buses and The Establishment scripts all the way back in the 1960s and he played with Eleanor Bron in some of the shows.[24] I had to go up to The Abbey over casting difficulties – an actress has become pregnant. As a mere writer of prose fiction one never imagines these excitements. There was no repercussions over the shot cow.[25]

Everything seems to be moving toward closing the place down and they are even crowding in already though I do not leave till September 2nd.

20 In his letter of 29 May, Friel told McGahern that *The Power of Darkness* would be staged by the Abbey Theatre as part of the Dublin Theatre Festival.
21 In a cordial letter of 11 June, Friel thanked McGahern for his 'gracious and patient' letter, stating again that he had not personally rejected the play and that his power at Field Day was greatly overstated. Madeline McGahern Papers.
22 Walsh made a full recovery from the cancer with which he had been diagnosed, and lived until November 2018.
23 Born John Wood (1939–2013), English satirist best known for his part in the successful Channel 4 television show *Bremner, Bird and Fortune* (1999–2010). He stayed in the McGaherns' Dublin house. The project came to nothing.
24 Fortune was a regular member of the cast of the BBC TV satire show *Not So Much a Programme, More a Way of Life*, alongside Eleanor Bron.
25 Refers to a local incident in the Anglo-Irish War of 1919–21 recalled again in *That They May Face the Rising Sun*.

It looks as if Linda's daughter may be attending Galway on one of those exchange years within Common Market universities next year. Madeline says she is a nice girl and quite beautiful in a quiet way.[26]

> With our love
> John

Russell and Volkening Papers

Foxfield

4 August 1991

Dear Miriam,

I enclose The Country Funeral. I hope you like it. It's the longest story I've ever written.[27]

I suppose it is worth trying The New Yorker though I haven't much hope. Jeremy Treglown who is helping Jean Stein at Grand Street wrote me a short time ago from London, looking for a contribution. I suppose if you decide to try Grand Street I should send it to him directly but I'll wait till I see what you say.

Faber will publish the play. The Mercure de France will do it in French.[28] Amongst W. continues to sell and sell in paperback. I fly directly to Colgate September 1st. I'm very much looking forward to seeing you this Fall.

> Best regards to Tim
> With every good wish
> John

---

26 Audrey de Nazelle, daughter of Linda de Nazelle, a great friend of Madeline's who rented Rue Christine for several years.

27 The only previous story of comparable length was 'Peaches', written more than twenty years earlier.

28 This did not happen despite some initially positive overtures from Mercure de France. See letter to Alain Delahaye of 25 October 1990.

20 August 1991

Dear Tim,

I have been thinking a good deal about the contract for the novel, and I would like to put my hesitations about signing anything to you before we meet. When you were here, you thought that I should leave Viking – and I felt exactly the same – and that the easiest way to do it would be to submit a proposal for a new novel. It will be several years before I can hope to finish the novel, and I wonder, given the musical-chairs nature of American publishing, if we might not be tying ourselves into another Viking situation by signing with Knopf. The woman editor who took me on at Viking left for Random House.[29] Amanda Vail inherited me, and you and I know the result only too well. She would never return calls or letters until the novel started getting attention in Britain, and by then whatever small chance the book ever had in the States had been lost.

The collected stories will be published before the novel. With the long story, The Country Funeral, which I sent to Miriam, that volume is now probably completed. Naturally, I would like that whoever publishes the stories would publish the novel as well, and even more attractive still would be that the publisher would be interested in gradually bringing the backlist into circulation. Going on what Sonny Mehta told you, this would seem to be the agreement John Banville has with Knopf.

Because of the success here of Amongst Women, the backlist is now enjoying considerable sales. I know how hard the American market is, and I realize too that a comparable reception may well never happen to my work there, but since the advance is not large, and I am looking more for the right publisher than a contract, it is probably worth waiting and seeing people at Farrar-Straus as well as Sonny Mehta before signing myself into anything. This is especially so since I am not in need of the money.

We can go over all this when we meet, but I wanted to let you and Miriam know my doubts before then; it should be easier to sort out when we do meet. I fly to Colgate on September first. Madeline joins me the twelfth. We are both looking forward to seeing you and Susan again.

> With every good wish
> John

29 Pat Mulcahy.

Colgate
Home: (315) 824 4542
Work: (315) 824 7270

6 September 1991

Dear Miriam and Tim,
I am writing to let you have the home and office numbers and the address.

I go to Dublin for rehearsals on 19th–23rd September and on the 5th to the 15th of October, when the play opens.[30]

I've been getting regular royalty checks from Faber in sterling, 90% of the total, and I assumed the 10% went to you. As your last check was the first to come in dollars would you check that it is all right. I'm very happy with it as long as it is mine.

With every good wish
John

Alain Delahaye

Colgate

12 November 1991

Dear Alain,
I'm sorry to be so late writing. I was exhausted after Dublin. I'm still behind with the students here.

The play and production was savagely attacked by the Dublin critics. Fortunately the London critics were in Dublin for the Festival and gave it some wonderful notices. Now a whole bitter controversy is raging about the play in Dublin. The critics have been attacked. And the play will now reach the end of its run, playing often to full houses. When I left Dublin I felt it was doomed. Only the first Dublin notices had come in and they were terrible.[31]

---

30 The play ran at the Abbey Theatre from 16 October to 16 November 1991.
31 Eight of the ten reviews of the play were negative, with the *Irish Times* running the headline 'Sadly risible drama debut for author'. For a useful discussion of the play's reception, see Christopher Murray, 'The "fallen world" of *The Power of Darkness*', *The John McGahern Yearbook*, vol. 2, 78–91.

It was very hard. With a book you only expose your poor self. With a play you expose a whole crowd of poor people. And it is instant and public and bloody awful.

I leave here on December 17th. Madeline goes home on the 8th Dec. I'll telephone before I leave.

With love to Pascale
and your self
John

Peter Fallon Papers
Colgate

14 November 1991

Dear Peter,
It was very kind of you to write.

I had never wanted to shake off Tolstoy. I tried to be true to the spirit of what I saw and recognized well in the original play, but it became so changed in the many reworkings that it seemed wrong to say after or adapted from: but I'd hoped I'd made my debt clear in the preface.

I didn't mind the reaction all that much for myself, though I'd have preferred it otherwise. It was almost bracingly like old times. But in a play you expose so many other people, especially the players who have to go on night after night, and that first night was so instant and public and brutal.

Having to go back twice to Dublin screwed me up here, and I'm still behind with classes. It's just for the one term and we'll be home in Leitrim for Christmas.

I hope your own work goes well and with every good wish
John

18 November 1991

Dear Tim,
Thank you for <u>Whiskey Man</u>.[32] I enjoyed it, it has great energy, and it is strange he has not gone on . . . though he may be too intelligent to go on writing novels.

This is just to reconfirm my dates.

I can go down to New York at almost any time on the week of Dec 9th. I get into Kennedy at 3pm on Dec 17th and will be in New York that night and the next day. I leave for Dublin on the evening of the 18th.

Much to my surprise the play turned out to be a hit. An enormous controversy blew up. Even the critics got attacked, and it wound up playing to packed houses. I was grateful to be here.

Please give my apologies to Susan for troubling her about my blessed tie. It turned up in the pocket of Madeline's suit, where I put it.

John

Alain Delahaye

[*Colgate*]

10 December 1991

Dear Alain,
A number of dead babies were found in Kerry, a woman was accused of murdering her baby. The enquiry was much an enquiry into police attitudes and conduct as into the guilt of the woman, which was a national scandal in a society that tries to pretend sex doesn't exist outside marriage. I'll send you a book about it if you're interested.[33]

---

32 Presumably the 1977 Howell Raines novel of that name set in Depression-era Alabama, published by Viking in America.

33 Here McGahern is describing in rough terms the so-called Kerry Babies scandal, a notorious 1980s case involving hidden pregnancy, infanticide and a bungled garda investigation in Co. Kerry. These events inspired McGahern in part to adapt Tolstoy's *The Power of Darkness*. See letter of 12 May 1981 to Matthew Evans.

Washers is a low workman's word for money, derived from [*draws the circular head of a nail*] for nails [*draws a larger circle*] for roofs.

I've been going through all the stories for The Collected Stories. I rewrote The Stoat and I enclose the worst pages from the others. They are mostly deletions. If they are too difficult ignore them. I hope it's not too much. Reading them again is a bit like listening to the 'stupid bastard' in Krapp's Last Tape.[34]

I'm sorry to be in such a hurry. Phil the Fluther's Ball is just a drinking song, any old song will do. I'll send the words when I get back. He only sings a snatch.[35] They tell me they are still fighting about the play. It wound up playing to full houses.

Love

John

34 Beckett's 1958 play, particularly admired by McGahern.
35 Delahaye had asked for more information about this song which McGahern uses in *The Power of Darkness*.

1992

Alain Delahaye

Foxfield

29 January 1992[1]

Dear Alain,

I'm sorry you are not well.

Don't worry about the Presses and just get well.

Our old cat Fats is dying. She is 13 years. We've had her almost since we have been settled here. She is black, with four white paws, and a white breast, almost like a formal shirtfront. Though we know it is foolish, it is distressing. It is like watching a whole part of our life go. In a way, she was the playful heart of the house.[2]

I enclose a cleaner copy of The Stoat. I couldn't be sure if it worked or not. We'll be in Paris in June.

Love to you all and get better soon
John

Niall Walsh Papers

Foxfield

20 April 1992

Dear Niall and Phil,

We've often wondered how you are but knew there was your grandchildren on the way with the world and that long promised holiday and we were sort of writing to hear.

---

1 Mistakenly dated 29 February by McGahern.

2 McGahern loved animals and had a particular liking for cats, an aspect of his personality brought to the fore in his late story 'Creatures of the Earth'.

We were all the time here except for a few places I had to speak in, mostly dragging through mud after sheep and cattle, a welcome change from the Abbey and transatlantic travel. I did manage to get The Collected Stories ready for the printer and they'll come out in October and that'll be more trouble. A long time ago I promised to give a talk on the Catholic Church – it seemed safely in the distance then – and that's in less than 2 weeks and not a word in order.

I was also on the third floor of the Mater for most of a week for the prostate operation. They told me you hadn't been back and I took that for good news. I got wonderful care. I also provided the comedy of the week – and believe me it was painful – a very old Kerry nun, a great fan of Charlie H., a Sister Mary, got tangled up in my catheter, nearly pulled the works out, and then ran like a greyhound.[3]

Madeline will go to Paris at the beginning of June and I hope to join her for a couple of weeks towards the end of the month.

The old black cat Fats with the four white paws that we had for 13 years died in January. It was kind of silly but it was like watching a whole happy part of our life go.

We hope you are all well and send you our good wishes and love,

John

Alain Delahaye

6 Church Street
Enniskillen
Co. Fermanagh
Northern Ireland[4]

[May 1992]

Dear Alain,
There's a postal strike here and it looks as if it will be protracted.[5]

3 Charlie H. is Charles Haughey, the colourful and controversial leader of Fianna Fáil, who had been Taoiseach on several occasions through the 1980s and 1990s, most recently stepping down on 11 February 1992. McGahern was not an admirer.
4 This is the address of William Blake's, a favourite public house in Enniskillen occasionally used by the McGaherns as an address in time of postal strikes south of the border. See LOTW, 43.
5 Hence the use of the Enniskillen address, approximately twenty-nine miles from Foxfield, across the border.

Madeline goes to Paris on June 10th and I'll join her there on June 22nd. We'll be at 1 Rue Christine.

I was in hospital for a prostate operation. There was a possibility it could have been cancer, but it was benign. I'm glad it's over. It hung over me like worry for several months.

Faber bring out The Collected Stories in October. Knopf do them in the U.S.

Did the story of the Bishop of Galway and his lady and their son reach Paris?[6] One woman near here burned her house down lighting candles to try to get the scandal to go away. We are looking forward very much to seeing you.

With my love to you all
John

Michael Gorman

Foxfield

17 September 1992

Dear Michael,

Madeline and I were delighted to get your card and hope you and Margaret and Irene will come this way some day.[7] Your gate still stands against the lake.

I'll be in London next month to do publicity.[8] I'm not looking forward to it but Faber say times were never so bad in the trade and that it is necessary to do. It will be nice, though, to see Maura Dooley again.[9]

6 Eamonn Casey (1927–2017) served as Catholic Bishop of Galway and Kilmacduagh from 1976 to 1992. In May 1992 the *Irish Times* broke a story about a relationship he had with an American woman, Annie Murphy, in the 1970s that resulted in the birth of a son. Casey stepped down as bishop and moved to Ecuador. This was the first of a series of sexual scandals within the Irish Church that saw the rapid diminishment of its power over the next two decades.

7 A daughter, born 1991.

8 Publicity for *The Collected Stories*.

9 Maura Dooley b. 1957, English poet of Irish extraction. McGahern had worked with her at the Arvon Foundation at Lumb Bank, Hebden Bridge in the 1980s. At the time that this letter was composed Dooley was directing the Literature and Talks programme at the Southbank Centre (Royal Festival Hall), where McGahern had been invited to read from his *Collected Stories*. In later years Dooley sent Alistair MacLeod's collection of short stories, *The Lost Salt Gift of Blood*, first published in Canada in 1976 by McClelland & Stewart, to Michael Gorman who passed it on

I was in and out of Galway during the summer and they told me you were doing some work from Mayo.

I like Yates's work.[10] Probably his best book is Revolutionary Road.[11] I met him once in Boston. He was tall, elegant, with beautiful old-fashioned manners. I think he has struggled with alcoholism most of his life, with the attendant clinics and divorces. Though he was more real than most of the more solid citizens gathered in that Boston morning.

I hope we'll see you soon
John

Colm Tóibín
Foxfield

24 September 1992

Dear Colm,

I admired much of The Heather Blazing, and found many of the scenes quietly powerful, none more than law court scenes set in the Judge's mind, the wonderful old lady's house in Enniscorthy, the sense of the political, the scenes with the father, (though I thought the childhood delving should have been more compressed) the whole sense of place, and the ocean.[12] The difficulty I had was with the marriage. The scenes between the Judge and his wife never rang true to me, and this affected the daughter's drama. When the son visited the summer house the whole domestic scene came wonderfully alive, and I began to think maybe there should have been more of the son and his girl. I still thought it a much better – more ambitious, more difficult – novel than The South but what crossed over was the sharp real sense of place. And the same writer was at work. Without this nothing else much matters.

A week or more ago I drove to Rosslare on a Sunday to meet the Rosslare Ferry. I had time to spare and stopped in Enniscorthy.[13] It was a kind of happiness walking in the actual streets and seeing them against the depth

---

to McGahern for whom it became a firm favourite. His essay on the book, 'Terrible Tales from the Mart', appeared in the Irish Independent of 27 December 1997 and is reproduced in LOTW, 172–7.

10 Richard Yates, American novelist and short story writer. See letter to DeWitt Henry of 27 September 1977.

11 Yates's acclaimed debut novel, published by Little, Brown in 1961.

12 Tóibín's second novel, The Heather Blazing (London: Picador, 1992).

13 Tóibín's hometown.

of the imagined streets and then I came on your novel in a small bookshop window. As I made my way back to the car parked by the river I even ran into a teacher called Dea who was trained with me and he was rushing to catch 12 o'clock Mass in the Church on the hill.

With congratulations, and good wishes
John

James Swift
[*Madeline McGahern*]
Foxfield

6 October 1992

Dear Jimmy,
It was very kind to write to me and I owe you much over all the years – and they are all well out now, and will not turn.

I set down my memories of Paddy, mostly to see what they were and because they started to badger me. I have no desire or wish to publish them but they are formal and lean towards praise and I'll be glad to show them to you should you wish that.

Poor David W. is in the wars again. He gave Larkin a bad review and is described as 'that deaf cunt,' an advance on 'The deaf one even suggested I send out for another bottle.'[14]

I have a rough few weeks ahead. Dublin – Enniskillen – Dublin – Cork – Belfast – London – Trinity. I'll call when I'm in Dublin to see if you are free for an hour or two. The good news is that Faber have had to reprint before publication.[15] Madeline is talking of going to the Iceman when this thing is over and maybe we could go together and have supper afterwards?[16]

John

14 See Philip Larkin's letter to Robert Conquest of 5 October 1956 in Larkin, *The Selected Letters 1940–1985*, ed. Anthony Thwaite (London: Faber, 1992), 266–7.
15 *The Collected Stories*.
16 Eugene O'Neill's *The Iceman Cometh* ran at the Abbey Theatre from 10 October to 7 November 1992.

Kathryn Court

Foxfield

10 October 1992

Dear Kathryn,[17]
It was lovely to get your letter and even nicer to think of seeing maybe you and your daughter and her father here in the summer. Remember me to her.[18]

The stories come out on Monday and I have to face into 2 weeks of readings and interviews. The good news is that they sold heavily into the shops and are being reprinted. Amongst Women has been shortlisted for the GPA Award. John Updike will pick the winner on Dec. 4th.[19] It'll be nice when all this public business is over and I can go back to normal life.

Madeline asks to be remembered to you.

With affection

John

James Swift

[*Madeline McGahern*]

Foxfield

9 November 1992

Dear Jimmy,
I enclose the piece about Paddy.[20]

---

17 Kathryn Court had taken over responsibility for McGahern at Viking Penguin in New York after Amanda Vaill's departure. See letter to Gina Macoby of 31 October 1985.
18 Court had once spent a weekend in Foxfield with her young daughter Francesca.
19 The GPA (Guinness Peat Aviation) Award was briefly one of the world's richest literary prizes. The decision to float the aircraft leasing company on the stock market in 1992, during an aviation industry downturn following the 1991 Gulf War, proved disastrous and the Award ceased to be. McGahern won the 1992 prize for *Amongst Women*, which was presented to him by John Updike on the popular and long-running RTÉ television programme hosted by Gay Byrne, *The Late Late Show*.
20 'The Bird Swift' appeared in *PS . . . of course: Patrick Swift 1927–1983*, ed. Veronica O'Mara (Oysterhaven: Gandon Books, 1993), later reprinted in *LOTW*, 65–74.

Twice I refused to write it, for the reason that I hardly knew him, which remains true. Then that summer of 1960 started to nag at me like work and I wrote it simply to see what was there, if anything.

I have no desire to ever see it in print, but since you know it was written I feel it could be a discourtesy not to offer to show it to you, almost greater than not to bother you with it at all.

If you feel it too close or impertinent or poor just ignore or burn it and that'll be the end of the experiment.

It was grand to see you in the Iceman evening and thanks for its pleasant end in Nicos.[21]

John

Seamus Heaney Papers

Foxfield

9 November 1992

Dear Seamus,

It was a pleasure to meet Marie and yourself at Matthew's and thank you for the very kind words. Sometimes the head gets very low down here.[22]

I hope you both had a good time in Barcelona and Madrid and that I was wrong about Golden.[23] I loved Barcelona in the '60s. Voices of the Old Sea by Norman Lewis catches forever what it was like then.[24] It is unlike Woodbrook, but like it in that it is written out of deep immersion or love. Do you remember when we visited D. T. in London and the pint bottles of Guinness started to yo-yo out of the rolltop writing desk?[25]

---

21 Nico's is a popular Italian restaurant at 53 Dame Street, Dublin that has been in business since the 1960s. It was a favourite of McGahern's.

22 Heaney had written to McGahern from Magdalen College, Oxford on 21 October 1992 about how much he had enjoyed seeing him at a Matthew Evans get-together: 'And I just think I should reiterate to you also how your work makes us all carry our writing (and reading) heads a bit higher. The book of stories is a real landmark.' This last compliment refers to *The Collected Stories*. Madeline McGahern Papers.

23 Seán Golden was a Professor of East Asian Studies at Universitat Autònoma de Barcelona. He had a strong Irish background and had a particular interest in the work of James Joyce.

24 Lewis's book describes traditional Spanish life on what has become the busy Costa Brava in the years after the Second World War (London: Hamish Hamilton, 1984).

25 D. T. is David Thomson, author of *Woodbrook*, who lived at 22 Regent's Park Terrace, London NW1.

When I was leaving Hazlitt's the owner told me with good pride that Seamus Heaney was coming in that evening.[26]

With my love
John

Michael Gorman
Foxfield

20 November 1992

Dear Michael,

It was very nice to see you in Castlebar and I hope I'll see you both in Galway soon.[27] Nenagh was a 'pig's arse' that night and I got away early.

The psychologist wife of Niall Walshe, the Ballinasloe pathologist, died last week and was buried in a small churchyard at Ballymore, near Athlone, on Sunday last. It was strange meeting people I knew almost thirty years ago.

Thank you for the Granta.[28] I thought Hamilton was in good form. I haven't read it all, but much of it, including the Larkin, seems to be very close to pornography.[29]

Madeline asks to be remembered to you both, and with my love

John

---

26 Hotel on Frith Street, Soho in which the McGaherns regularly stayed.

27 Michael Gorman was writer in residence for Co. Mayo that year, having succeeded Dermot Healy.

28 The *Granta* in question is no. 41 (Autumn 1992) and is a special on Biography. It included an essay by Ian Hamilton on James Boswell's *Life of Johnson* titled 'A Colossal Hoard' and an essay by Andrew Motion on the writing of a Philip Larkin biography titled 'Breaking In'.

29 Though it is not immediately apparent why he should so dislike this issue of *Granta*, to describe writing as 'pornography' is always a sharp criticism from McGahern.

11 December 1992

Dear Tim,
My suggestion would be to go ahead and see what comes of the enquiry – if anything.

When I was in London for the Faber promotion, Durbridge had a serious enquiry for <u>Amongst Women</u>, and I met the people. They were serious and very keen on the book. They had made many films, the best known, 'Defence of the Realm'. Their plan was to make it into a four-part TV series because of difficulty in getting finance for feature films in Britain. They have been following up since, but they will not buy an option until they are fairly certain of going ahead. So far, they have not bought an option. I'd say it is about fifty-fifty.

I'm told <u>Amongst Women</u> has won the GPA Award. John Updike is the judge. He and the six finalists will be on a live TV show tomorrow night. The result is supposed to be secret, but it will be long over by the time you get this. I'm afraid I'll only believe it when I have the cheque in my hand.

In late February I may be speaking at Lit. Soc. Gala in Columbia near Baltimore.

We send our love to Susan and you, and our best wishes toward a Happy New Year.

John

1993

Colm Tóibín

Foxfield

6 January 1993

Dear Colm,
Thank you for your very generous words about the stories, and for arranging the whole business of <u>Christmas</u>.[1] I hope you'll help me spread some of it over an evening before long.

 There was a very nice man here over the Christmas from Waterstones in Manchester and he brought the good news that <u>The H. Blazing</u> was one of the few novels they had that was selling.

 I thought the Kaplan biography of <u>H.J.</u> was superb.[2]

With every good wish

John

Susanne Dumbleton

Foxfield

14 January 1993[3]

Dear Sue and Bill,
It was lovely to get your card. We'll be here all the time as I teach one day a week in Galway this term. We'd love to see you both if you change your plans and come to Ireland.

---

1 Tóibín greatly admired *The Collected Stories*, his favourite being 'The Country Funeral'. The reference to Christmas is about Tóibín arranging for a Christmas section from *Amongst Women* to appear in the *Sunday Independent*.
2 Fred Kaplan, *Henry James: The Imagination of Genius* (New York: William Morrow & Company, 1992).
3 Mistakenly dated 1992 by McGahern.

Amongst W. won the GPA award a few weeks ago. It took place on the Gay Byrne TV show. It was a horrible evening – except for the Award itself – and John Updike was stylish in a quiet attractive way and his words about the book were extraordinarily generous.

I'll be in the States briefly towards the end of February. I have to speak to the Howard County Literature Soc. on the 26th February in Columbia, Maryland. Knopf bring out The Collected Stories about that time.

Madeline is in London. She rang a few minutes ago and said she was going to see Branagh's Hamlet tonight. She asked to be remembered to you both with affection.

A very happy New Year
Affectionately
John

Robin Robertson

Foxfield

26 January 1993

Dear Robin,

Thank you for your kind note and Ghosts.[4] I enjoyed our meeting in Enniskillen.[5]

The TV has come and gone. Tony Knox seemed pleased with what they got. Ghosts didn't come up.

I had trouble with the novel. There were beautiful passages, even more so that Croke Now, try Croke until it has to meet Hatch, but the spaces between seemed to pause and wander and hesitate as if waiting for inspiration. Maybe it was John's aim but even after a 2nd reading I do not know what it is all about.[6]

I hope you have a wonderful evening in the Voicebox[7]
and with my love to Clare
John

4 John Banville, *Ghosts* (London: Secker & Warburg, 1993). Robertson was in his final year as editorial director before moving on to Jonathan Cape.

5 The McGaherns regularly met up with Robertson and his wife Clare Reihill around Christmas or New Year in William Blake's of Enniskillen.

6 Referring to Banville's *Ghosts*.

7 The Voice Box was a reading space next to the Poetry Library in London's Southbank.

28 January 1993

Dear Kathryn,
Thank you for your kind letter, and the covers.
I gave the GPA people your name as the U.S. pub. of A.W. but I didn't
expect you to come all that way.
I enclose John Updike's judgement though they may well have sent it to
you already.[8]
I'll be reading in Washington in late February and I hope to be in New
York for a few days. I'll call then. It'd be very nice to see you again.

With my love
John

15 February 1993

Dear Niall,
The enclosed came with a card from Linda.[9] She always asks after you and
Madeline told her at Christmas that Phil had died.[10]
For this term I teach on Fridays in U.C.G.[11] The teaching is fairly harmless
but I find it tiring. Tomorrow I go to New York and Washington for a week.
I'm hoping to get a couple of days to myself to just walk around the place.
Yesterday a fellow rang from the N.Y. Times. It's a disastrous medium for

---

8 Updike's thoughts on his judgement of the GPA prize appeared in the *Irish Times* of
1 January 1993: 'in the novel's weave of many brief scenes the novelist shows himself
everywhere knowing and tactful, in language that is both simple and subtle, austere
and affectionate. McGahern brings us the tonic gift of the best fiction, the sense of
truth – the sense of a transparency that permits us to see imaginary lives more clearly
than we see our own, a sight that cleanses us even as it saddens and frightens.'
9 Linda de Nazelle.
10 Phil Walsh had died on 13 November 1992.
11 McGahern taught two small seminar groups for the Department of English at
UCG through the spring semester of 1993.

interviews. He went on and on as to why there was so little happiness in my work. I don't see large stacks of it around. I made the mistake of trying to explain so no doubt I'll appear as a complete asshole and then it'll be forgotten by the next Sunday.

We're hoping you're keeping well and that it's not too hard a time.

Madeline sends her love

and with my love

John

Neill Joy

[*Madeline McGahern*]

Foxfield

2 May 1993

Dear Neill,

We were very glad to get your letter. It is sad about Johnstons, but after a lunch I had with them when I was in Colgate I am not surprised.[12]

I was in the States for a week, in Columbia, a dormitory town between Washington and Baltimore, a few blocks from where Wil's mother and sister live. Wil and Janette came down. I was in New York for a few days but it was rushed. The day I left I got away to the Oyster Bar in Grand Central and had a bowl of chowder, 12 oysters, a glass of Chardonnay and the whole passing show. Next week I go to Germany: Bonn, Cologne, Aachen, Dusseldorf. In October I go to Poitiers. Madeline will come. We'll take the car and drive around for a few weeks. Otherwise we'll be here on the farm with sheep and the ½ wild cows. I finished teaching in Galway last week but have weeks of grading in front of me when I get back from Germany. Is there any likelihood of finding you and Mary in Ireland?

We had a strange newsletter from Casey.[13] They are back in the U.S., in the South. It appears that all their moves since Oneonta have been disasters of one sort or another but the whole push seems to make them all look 'positive'. I liked Dan but I couldn't help remembering dear Ed's sour phrase, 'Casey's a pussylicker.'

---

12 Refers to a divorcing Colgate couple of McGahern's acquaintance.
13 Dan Casey, member of faculty at SUNY Oneonta.

The director Garry Hynes got the push at The Abbey.[14] The play is on the amateur circuit. I saw a Clare group from Mountshannon do a good production in the All Ireland Final. With distance I could see that the second half is not right. Some one at the BBC want to offer a commission and if it comes through I may have a final go at the thing.

Thanks for the cutting of the <u>H.G.</u> review. The reason for the publication is bad blood over the move to Knopf and a bad balls up by the agent.[15] I was delighted you liked the Knopf edition. Vintage will do it in paperback.[16]

Madeline sends you both her love. It'd be nice to think we could meet before too long

and with all my love
John

Russell and Volkening Papers
Foxfield

16 May 1993

Dear Tim,
Thank you for your note. I'd have answered before now but I was in Germany.

Knopf sent me some early reviews but none since I was in the States. The Y invited me to read next March and I put it through Bill Lovard who turned it over to Vintage.

14 Hynes b. 1953 was director at the Abbey Theatre, 1991–3, the sixth director in seven years. Early in her tenure she was heavily criticised for a production of Sean O'Casey's *The Plough and the Stars*. The *Irish Times* remarked on the 'palpable sense of disappointment that the high expectations generated by her appointment have been so poorly realised so far'. Criticism reached a crescendo after the opening of *The Power of Darkness* – the *Sunday Tribune* commented: 'To write a really dreadful play is easy. To have it put on in our national theatre should be difficult. The finger should be pointed at Garry Hynes [. . .] responsible for staging a recycled farrago of risible melodramatic nonsense.'

15 *High Ground* had its first US publication in 1987 with Viking. In 1993 a Penguin edition was published in the US just as McGahern was breaking his ties with the company to go to Knopf.

16 *The Collected Stories* was published by Knopf in hardback in 1993 and by Vintage in paperback the following year.

I had dinner with Sonny Mehta and two friends of his. It was a pleasant evening but there was no talk of the book other than that he was pleased with the reviews. I haven't heard from him since but I assumed that was his style.[17]

     With every good wish to Susan and yourself.

     Yours

     John

               Nicholas Grene

               Foxfield

8 August 1993

Dear Nicky,

I'll be glad to read for you in June though I'm trying to cut down on readings.

It's a scattered place. Foxfield is the post-office and church. Fenagh is the village, 2 pubs, 2 miles away.

I have 24 ewes and 11 cattle. All but 6 of the lambs have been sold. We are sick of the weather.

I have nothing against Synge.[18] I think the <u>Playboy</u> is a great farce and I taught <u>The Aran Islands</u> in Galway last term – it was very easy to see how directly they related to the 1890's and people like Pierre Loti.[19] It is the tragic stuff that makes me uneasy.

Una Walsh, Glen's wife, daughter of an old friend, got a lectureship in Southampton. She went for interview in a different field, which she didn't get, but made a good impression. A few weeks later their lecturer in Irish History committed suicide and she was offered the job. Her mother died last year.[20]

17 Seldes had written to McGahern on 22 April 1993 asking if Sonny Mehta had said anything about sales of Knopf's edition of *The Collected Stories*. Given the stellar reviews, Seldes was disappointed at sales of only 6,000.

18 McGahern had previously expressed his antipathy to J. M. Synge's plays to Grene, and his sense that the language was inauthentic.

19 The books that McGahern taught at UCG in spring 1993 included J. M. Synge, *The Aran Islands*; Tomás Ó Criomhthain, *The Islandman (An tOileánach)*; Ernie O'Malley, *On Another Man's Wound*; Alice Munro, *Friend of My Youth*; and Richard Ford, *Rock Springs*. McGahern admired Loti's 1886 novel of Breton life among fisherfolk, *Pêcheur d'Islande (An Iceland Fisherman)* and worked for a time towards adapting it for the screen. See letter to Tim Seldes of 6 July 1988.

20 Oonagh Walsh is the daughter of McGahern's great friend Niall, and her husband is Glenn Hooper, a one-time undergraduate student of Grene's. The man who committed suicide was Michael Hughes, an historian of Germany.

I've started to revise the play again (ostensibly for the French translator).
I saw it in a good amateur production but all its faults were on show. Either
the Abbey concealed them or I was too involved to see them.

I finished a long story/short novel but everything it contains is identifiable
so it can't be published. I'm trying to start a novel that has been in my head
for a long time.[21]

It was great to see that old fraud installed as your patron: you should hitch
him to Mother Teresa.[22]

Madeline asks to be remembered to you both

and with every good wish

John

Brian Friel Papers

Foxfield

9 August 1993

Dear Brian,

Thank you for your card and for sending me your play. I read it with great
interest and I'll go to see it in September.[23] Even I know enough now to
know a play is written to be played.

We're sick of the rain. The cattle come up to the house and boo when they
want a change of pasture. Our old friends across the lake have moved to the
town and we miss them.[24]

Madeline sends her love to you all

And with my love

John

---

21 The early germs of what would become *That They May Face the Rising Sun.*
22 Cyril Cusack (1910–93), the celebrated Irish actor.
23 *Wonderful Tennessee*, perhaps Friel's most Beckettian play, set on a Co. Donegal
pier.
24 The McGartys moved into Mohill from their small farm across the lake.

30 September 1993

Dear Charles,

We were very glad to get your note.

I almost certainly would never have seen Susan Hill's good words had you not sent the cutting.

I don't expect to be in London but if I have to go I'll tell you at once. It'd be very nice to meet.

We go to France in November. I have to speak in Poitiers and we'll take the car and use it as an excuse for a holiday. In March we'll go to New York. Vintage bring out the stories in paperback then and I speak at the Y.[25] They were a surprise success in the States – surprise to me especially – when Knopf brought them out last spring. The new streamlined Faber let them out of print a week before Christmas when they were 3rd here on the bestseller list and weren't able to get copies back in the shops till late January. It is, I suppose, like the trade itself, a luxurious complaint.

I'm rewriting the play for a French translation. I saw it in a good amateur production – they lost the All Ireland by a point – and all its faults were on full display. When I get it out of the way I go back to the novel I've started. I finished a long story, it has more the feel of a short novel, a few months ago but it can't be published as it deals in a fairly direct way with the 'Society' here around the locus.

I read a very good biography of Henry James by Fred Kaplan I feel sure you'd enjoy.

It was extraordinary to witness the spleen that followed Larkin into the grave. His work will outwear his own time and all its fashionable gases. 'Let it stay hidden there like strength.'[26]

We hope you'll come to dinner and stay overnight when you come next year and if that's not easy we can meet in Dublin.

25 The Y is the YMCA with a big auditorium on 91st Street, New York. McGahern spoke there with Alice McDermott, the author of *Charming Billy*, a novel he much admired.

26 Philip Larkin's work was admired enormously by McGahern, as it was by Monteith. The quote is from Larkin's 'Show Saturday', a poem that McGahern uses as a touchstone in *That They May Face the Rising Sun*.

With my love, and Madeline sends you hers.

John

Neill Joy

[*Madeline McGahern*]

Foxfield

10 November 1993

Dear Neill and Mary,

How are you both? We'd hoped you might come in the summer, but then we seemed to remember you had planned to go to Italy. For that, even we couldn't blame you, especially last summer, the worst summer we ever had. And then in this unpredictable climate we had the best autumn I ever remember, pure red and golden, dry leaves everywhere. I spent a lot of it rewriting the bloody play. I finished it last week. I saw it last spring in a good amateur production – it lost the All Ireland by a point, a penalty in overtime – and all its faults were on show. I was too involved and angry during the Abbey business to see anything. We go to France this week, and I'll hand it over for the French translation, and hope to be rid of it forever. Though there's no guarantee it's right even now, but it's probably as right as I can make it.

We'll be in the States for 2 weeks or so in March. I'll be at the $\overline{Y}$ in N.Y. of the 14th, Washington 16th & 17th, and Boston on the 22nd. Those are separate arrangements to Vintage, but as they are sharing expenses with the Y no doubt they'll be calling other tunes, but they can't do anything about those dates and it'd be very nice for us to think that we might see you then.[27]

We'll be having lunch in Paris this weekend with Madeline's father. It will be 23 years since I saw him last.[28] I was thinking of you when I heard J. Kistler's death and how even animosities disappear in 'Time's rolling smithy smoke'.[29] After Paris I have to speak in Poitiers. We'd planned to go back leisurely through France but I got caught for work in Bordeaux. We're already

27 Vintage was preparing to publish the American paperback of *The Collected Stories*.

28 This visit would be the final occasion for both John and Madeline to see Niels Gron alive. He and Kika had been divorced in the intervening years and he had spent his final years married to a Japanese woman named Yoshiko Kuramara.

29 Jonathan Kistler was a Professor of English at Colgate. The quote is from Philip Larkin's 'Show Saturday'.

crying <u>enormous inconvenience</u> and hoping to get a few good cases of wine out of the deal. After that we'll just stay put here and work until March.

Do you remember Ann Geneva? T. de Pre's old girlfriend who worked in publicity in New York? She lives in London and works for Yale. She just bought an old cottage on 2–3 acres about 10 miles from here, in the mountains. The site itself is quite stunning. She'll need to spend money but it could be very beautiful.[30]

Remember me with affection to Edmund and Matthew.

> Madeline sends her love to you both
> and with my love
> John

Colm Tóibín

Foxfield

[*December 1993*]

Dear Colm,

Thank you for the lovely book. I enjoyed it and Madeline, I think, enjoyed it even more. There was no need of any gesture re. Aosdana. I was glad to nominate you and relieved it succeeded. I hope you'll feel more ease there than I feel.

I'd postponed writing in the hope of seeing you in Dublin but Madeline's father has just died and she's on her way to Paris so it'll be even more disjointed than usual here into the New Year.

I hope you are well and wish you a very happy New Year

> John

30 Geneva sold the property on after a short period and was an occasional visitor to Foxfield.

1994

Michael Gorman

Foxfield

10 January 1994

Dear Michael,
Thank you for your card and good wishes and the 1963 programme.[1]

We had a scattered Christmas. Madeline's father died in Paris and was cremated there on Christmas Eve. She spent the Christmas with his widow, a young Japanese woman.

We go to the States for 2 weeks in March but other than that we'll be here with the sheep and few cattle.

If Margaret and yourself would ever like to call you'll be welcome though I know it cannot be easy with work and the children.

A very happy New Year to you all.

With affection

John

Alain Delahaye

Foxfield

10 January 1994

Dear Alain,
We want to thank you and Pascale for the good wishes.

It was a disturbed Christmas. Madeline's father died in Paris and was cremated there on Christmas Eve. She spent Christmas with his widow, a young Japanese woman, who sounds very decent and honourable.

---

1 Gorman had sent McGahern a Tottenham Hotspur match programme dated 1963 as well as a video of the 1961 Cup Final against Leicester City, which Spurs won 2–0, thus securing the first League–Cup double since Aston Villa in 1897.

I've only sent the play to one person, a woman producer, who was very interested in the original version, and so far I haven't heard. I do not want to press her because of the Christmas.

I get no ideas from those trips. Those unfortunates come from within the head. All those conferences are foolish but the people at Poitiers were pleasant. We stayed a night in Chinon and enjoyed the day there on our own.

Michael Gresset was talking to Simone G. and wrote to me. I gave him your suggestion that they do The Country Funeral in a single volume.[2]

Madeline joins me in wishing you and Pascale a very happy Year

and with my love
John

Kathryn Court
Foxfield

3 February 1994

Dear Kathryn,
This is just a note to tell you that Madeline and I plan to travel to New York on March 12th for the Y on the 14th.

I have to go to Georgetown on the 16th, Swarthmore 17th, Harvard 22nd, and FDU on the 24th.[3] We'll probably go home on the 26th.

We'd both love to see you.

We hope you are all well and
With every dear wish
Love
John

2 Michel Gresset, French academic whom McGahern first met when he was a visiting professor at Colgate in 1978. See letter to Madeline of 20 September 1978. Gresset lived for a period in Colgate, was a visitor to Foxfield and stayed in the McGaherns' Dublin house. Delahaye's suggestion for a standalone publication of 'The Country Funeral' in French came to nothing, though it was eventually published alongside 'The Creamery Manager' and 'Creatures of the Earth' in a volume titled Les Créatures de la Terre (Paris: Albin Michel, 1996), translated by Delahaye. The story was published alone in English by Faber in 2019 as part of a series of short stories from established and new writers to celebrate the company's ninetieth birthday.
3 FDU is Fairleigh Dickinson University in New Jersey.

Luke Dodd

Foxfield

2 May 1994

Dear Luke,
Thank you for your invitation and I'll take you at your word and hope to see the Museum at a more quiet time.[4] Having to go to Italy just after returning from the States was too much and I am finding it hard to get back to my own work.

Patsy Murphy rang and offered that I write up the opening for the I.T. I had time to think about [*it*] since the call came when I was out, and I realized I know hardly anything at all about Strokestown or Strokestown House. That I wish you and the whole venture well would not have to be faked, but all the other feelings or attitudes would almost certainly have to be, and the chances are that it would end up honouring nobody. This I told Patsy with regret.

I hope the opening is a great success and with all good wishes to Catherine and yourself[5]

John

Alain Delahaye

Foxfield

21 July 1994

Dear Alain,
Thank you for your kind letter and congratulations, and I offer you my sympathy and Madeline's on your mother's death.

It must have been strange to go to Lourdes for the funeral. Peter Woods – I think you met him, an old villain and actor always crying about dying, who lives at the corner of the lake – went to Lourdes this summer. During the flight he discovered the pilot's grandfather, one of them anyhow, came from Mohill. When the flight landed in Lourdes he insisted on entering the cockpit

---

4 Referring to the 14 May 1994 opening of a Famine Museum in Strokestown Park. See McGahern's praise for Dodd's work in 'County Leitrim: The Sky above Us', *LOTW*, 24.
5 Catherine O'Connor worked with Dodd in Strokestown Park.

to congratulate the pilot on his safe landing and no doubt to trace in more detail his Mohill origins. I wonder how in hell they got him off the plane.

A woman rang about the prize more than a week ago.[6] She spoke to me in poor English, to Madeline in French. I do not mind going to Bordeaux, but she mentioned some 'homage' in Trinity College Dublin in early September by French writers and intellectuals that is quite alarming. It may well be a hoax but it may also be true as it is financed by a bank and it may be the excuse for an expense/account frolic.[7] We asked her to write but so far she hasn't written and the whole thing may not be true.

They have put <u>The Barracks</u> on this year's C.A.P.E.S.[8] et Aggregation. I refused to go on a tour of France when the Publishers asked but then Academics and the Embassy started to telephone and write. It appeared they'd consider it a discourtesy if I didn't go as I'm the only LIVE writer on the course, a lone lobster in a restaurant tank before dinner. Anyhow it seemed easier to go than to continue to refuse. So it is Poitiers, Bordeaux, Montpellier, Lyons, Caen, Lille, Rheims in January.

25th July
Good weather came. I went at the hay, but the tractor broke down, it is now in the garage, and the rain has returned.

The woman rang again. Unfortunately, it wasn't a hoax. The only slight relief is that the Dublin business is taking place at the French Embassy instead of Trinity College, which is closed for September.[9] One of the writers is a Claude Duneton, a dreary self-promoting fellow from the Correze I knew slightly when I was young.[10]

I haven't done a single thing with the play. I am working on a novel – but not in the last weeks, . . . the hay . . . a degree in Galway . . . (The tinkers in Mohill told me I was a clever fucker as they saw I'll be taking blood pressures next) . . . too many visitors (Madeline calls this the silly season). I did finish a story that broke away from the novel.[11]

---

6 Prix de Littérature Étrangère 1994, presented as part of the Bordeaux Book Fair to recognise the achievement of a foreign writer and his translator.
7 The prize was financed by the Aquitaine Nord savings bank.
8 *Certificat d'aptitude au professorat de l'enseignement du second degré*, the diploma that allows one to become a certified secondary school teacher in France.
9 McGahern was presented with the prize at a function in the residence of the French ambassador, Dublin on 12 September 1994.
10 See letter to Charles Monteith of 1 August 1970.
11 A story that McGahern felt was too close to events in his Foxfield neighbourhood to publish.

It'll be very nice to see you in Bordeaux in October. Madeline is coming as well.[12]

> Remember me please to Pascale and the children.
> With my love
> John

Do you know anything about the Bordeaux award? Is it of any importance? Somebody told me recently that there are now 300 literary awards in Italy.[13]

> J.

> Liam Kelly
>
> Foxfield

14 August 1994

Dear Liam,

Thank you for your letter. What you say about the house makes sense, especially when given thought. It was there and we heard you express a wish.[14]

I saw Lar Cassidy about a year ago. He is Lit. Officer of the Arts Council. I was in Carrick and he was passing through and spotted me. I gathered there should be no problem about an Arts Council Grant except it would have to be to Lilliput or a similar approved publisher.[15]

I'd be inclined to go to Farrell now and be straight and, if necessary, blunt.[16] Remember you owe him no obligation until something is agreed upon. And that the relationship is in some ways adversarial, which is why

12 The McGaherns travelled to Bordeaux under the terms of the prize from 5 to 9 October.

13 The award helped to further boost McGahern's literary reputation in France – both he and Delahaye greatly enjoyed their time in Bordeaux.

14 John and Madeline had purchased a neighbouring house and land, previously occupied by the Earley family. John had offered for Liam Kelly to have it when he needed to escape from his work but Kelly, then a curate in Killinkere, Co. Cavan, thought better of it. Such generosity by John towards Kelly was typical.

15 McGahern was helping Kelly to get a collection of photographs published. The photographs had been taken by Leland L. Duncan in Co. Leitrim between 1889 and 1894. The book of photographs, *The Face of Time*, was published by the Lilliput Press in 1995 and McGahern wrote a foreword for it that is reproduced in *LOTW*, 17–18.

16 Antony Farrell, founder in 1984 of the Lilliput Press and still central to its successful operation.

agents make a living. Farrell will try to get the most advantageous terms for himself. Because of that you'll have to be clear about what you want.[17] Helen Lanigan Wood of the Enniskillen Museum was here and is interested in the project. She is a charming and intelligent woman. Do you think would it help for us to go to Enniskillen and go over the state of play with her. She is also very interested in a possible exhibition when the book comes and has published and written similar books herself.

When you think about this maybe give me a ring.

> Madeline sends her best wishes, as do I
> John

James Swift
[*Madeline McGahern*]
Foxfield

20 September 1994

Dear Jimmy,

I was very glad to see you in the French Embassy and Madeline was delighted to know that you are well.[18]

We plan to go to Bordeaux on Wednesday, October 5th, and wondered if Tuesday night, the 4th, would suit you to meet. We could eat something together or just have a drink, whatever is the easier. Gary and Nora, I think, mentioned something about joining us.[19]

Maybe you'd telephone sometime before then? We'll be here all along.
Madeline asks to be remembered to you with affection,

> With every good wish of mine,
> John

17 Kelly reached a deal with the Lilliput Press; it helped his case to have McGahern write the foreword.
18 McGahern was presented with the Prix de Littérature Étrangère du Salon du Livre de Bordeaux 1994 at a function in the French Embassy, Dublin on 12 September 1994. The prize was awarded in association with the Bordeaux Book Fair to recognise the entirety of McGahern's literary achievement.
19 Gary Swift, brother of Jimmy, married to Nora.

Frances Byrnes

Foxfield

20 October 1994

Dear Ms Byrnes,[20]
Thank you for your kind letter and invitation.[21]
  I am confused as to what could be meant by 'its backbone would be your prose', whether it refers to narrative or drama or something different. I'd be grateful for some kind of example or idea and I'd also like to know what rates of pay Mr Green would have in mind.[22]

> With every good wish
> Yours sincerely
> John McGahern

Thomas Kilroy Papers

Foxfield

11 November 1994

Dear Tom,
I saw your play for the first time last night and enjoyed it very much. I thought T. O'Sullivan and Yourself did near miraculous work with a poor format. I thought the actress very fine, particularly our wild friend.[23]

20 Frances Byrnes, a native of Sheffield, South Yorkshire, was a young BBC Radio Features producer in 1994, having completed a two-year BBC Radio Production Traineeship followed by a stint producing *Woman's Hour* on BBC Radio 4. She has continued to make radio programmes for BBC Radio 3 and Radio 4 and also, latterly, to write original radio dramas and adaptations for the networks. After McGahern's death in March 2006 she wrote an obituary of him in *The Guardian*.
21 Having been deeply impressed and moved by *Amongst Women*, Byrnes had written to McGahern seeking to commission a piece of writing to fit with a new series called 'Spirit of Place'. The series was to consist of newly commissioned work by writers with a powerful sense of place. Byrnes's idea was to record authors telling their stories in the place where they were set, evoking the sound of their world.
22 Michael Green, then controller of BBC Radio 4. In November 1994 McGahern was told he would be paid the drama rate: £55.90/minute for the programme's duration (twenty-five or thirty minutes). This is more generous than the short story rate.
23 A short television drama called *Gold in the Streets* directed by Thaddeus O'Sullivan. Acted by Alan Devlin (wild friend) and Derbhle Crotty.

I hope you'll enjoy your time in Trinity. I found it a pleasant place to live and work.[24]

> Please remember me to Julie and Hannah May
> and with my love
> John

James Swift
[*Madeline McGahern*]

Foxfield

16 November 1994

Dear Jimmy,

I hope the dental work wasn't too hard and that it's an easier time.

Madeline and myself expect to be in Dublin Nov. 30th (Wednesday). It'd be very nice to see you but if it's difficult in any way don't worry or bother about the idea.

I was sorry to read that David Wright had died. I was never able to talk to him and hardly knew him but I liked his work and was always grateful to him.[25]

It was interesting to see Bordeaux somewhat from the inside – Rich, extremely closed, formal. There was an extraordinary dinner in the Gallery of Modern Art, once a workhouse for storing Barrels of wine for shipping on the harbour, the stone polished white. There must have been 300 red roses in the middle of the Mayor's table (circular).

We missed the Italian summer here, and it's all rain and cattle lowing ever since we got home.

Madeline asks to be remembered to you with affection.

> John

---

24 Kilroy spent the spring of 1995 at TCD.
25 David Wright, with Patrick Swift the co-editor of *X: A Quarterly Review* (the first periodical to publish McGahern), died on 28 August 1994.

Liam Kelly

Foxfield

Thursday 24th [*November 1994*]

Dear Liam,

I'd say the book is safe, which is the most important thing.[26]

It's always safer to have your attitude to Bailieboro. My own feeling is that you should be saying prayers to your Uncle. From what I saw there, he was greatly disliked. It's far better to come after an eejit than a saint, things being always relative.[27]

We talked about going round to Laheen and decided to do so closer to the Christmas.[28]

We're having lunch with Helen LW on Saturday and will tell how things are with the photos.[29] Madeline asks to be remembered with affection.

John

26 McGahern is referring to *The Face of Time*, which was published by the Lilliput Press in 1995. Kelly wrote the introductory text and the captions for the photographs and McGahern wrote the foreword.

27 Kelly moved as curate from Killinkere to Bailieborough at the beginning of January 1995. Kelly's uncle Fr Micheál Kelly (1922–2011) had been a priest in Bailieborough parish from 1965 to 1980. He had been curate in the parish of Kill, near Cootehill, from 1950 to 1953 and, following the publication of *The Dark* in 1965, relations between Kelly's uncle and John deteriorated greatly. That animosity is evident in this letter. In general, Kelly's uncle was popular wherever he served as a priest.

28 Kelly's family moved from Aughawillan to Laheen, near Keshcarrigan, Co. Leitrim in 1962. McGahern is talking about visiting Kelly's parents.

29 Helen Lanigan Wood of Enniskillen museum.

1995

Colm Tóibín

Foxfield

2 January 1995

Dear Colm,
I heard some time ago that you were ill and didn't believe it but I've heard it a number of times by now. I was also reluctant to write since I naturally want you to be well and working and know how vain and useless hopes and wishes can appear.

What I was hoping to do was invite you out for an evening to thank you for The Sign of the Cross.[1] I enjoyed the writing very much – especially when it was in Enniscorthy, and wished it had stayed forever there. Outside, the writing was always good, and sometimes much more than that, but for me the net of travel was too wide. I fear I'd always lean towards the narrow focus of Walking Along the Border/Bad Blood.

I'd be grateful for a word. Madeline sends her thanks too and every good wish

and with much affection
John

Luke Dodd

Foxfield

28 January 1995

Dear Luke,
    Hotel Keltik
    15 rue d'Odessa
    Paris 75014 tel (1) 43209353
is the cheap hotel (230–300 f.f.)

---

1 *The Sign of the Cross: Travels in Catholic Europe* (London: Jonathan Cape, 1994).

Another hotel is

> Hotel Saint-Pierre
> 4 rue de l'École de Medicine
> 75006 Paris
> Tel (1) 46347880

Beside the Sorbonne. It is more comfortable and they speak English but it is about 375. I stayed there this week. You should probably book by telephone as they seem full all the time.

I got back last night after a long round of France. I feel fairly battered. The last thing I want to think about is another audience but we can talk about it another time. I just want to get you the information. I hope you enjoy your stay.

John

Kathryn Court

Foxfield

26 April 1995

Dear Kathryn,

Thank you for your letter.

I was very glad to learn that <u>A.W.</u> was reprinting. It would be nice if the cover could be changed but I don't suppose it sells enough to justify a new cover in commercial terms.[2]

Unfortunately, I have no date for a new book. In the last 12 months I was abroad too much. I am staying put for all of the rest of this year and most of next year. I work every day but the work goes very slowly.

I hope you'll be very happy in your new house.

With affection

John

---

2 McGahern deeply disliked Penguin's cover for the US edition of *Amongst Women*. See letter to Joanna Mackle of 8 July 1990.

Frances Byrnes

Foxfield

3 May 1995

Dear Frances,

Thank you for your letter.

When you learn for certain, tell me, and we can take it from there, or let it rest in peace.

I am well and work every day but the work goes very slowly.

It was hard in France after I met you.[3] As the train was getting into Lyons from Montpellier – and I had to face another set of people, another restaurant, another hall, another reception, another dinner – I found myself wishing the train to go on for days, which is unusual for me, since I dislike travel. There were many interesting things like speaking to a full house in the anatomy theatre of the Sorbonne with the glass dome above the tiers of students.

TV bought <u>A. Women</u> to be filmed by David Leach in 4 parts.[4]

I enjoyed meeting you, and very much your company at lunch, and I hope we meet again before too long.[5]

          With every good wish

          John

3 McGahern and Byrnes met for lunch in Dublin on 7 January 1995 where they discussed the possible commission – an original story conceived for radio. McGahern told her about a local woman who, shot by her husband, had died gripping a handful of currants she had just pulled from a jar.

4 *Amongst Women* was adapted into a four-part television series for BBC Northern Ireland and RTÉ in 1998. It was directed by Tom Cairns and starred Tony Doyle as Michael Moran. The screenplay was written by Adrian Hodges.

5 Their next meeting would be in Bristol on 18 March 1996 for the back-up studio recording of the BBC Radio 4 commission, which McGahern went on to write and which he would call 'Love of the World'.

Frances Byrnes

Foxfield

12 July 1995

Dear Frances,
I hope it interests or pleases you.[6]
  It'll almost certainly have to be cut.[7]
I do not want to say anything else about it until you have thought about it
for yourself.

With every good wish
John

Luke Dodd

Foxfield

18 July 1995

[*To Luke Dodd*]
Thank you for the card. Were the Paris hotels any use? Everything is quiet
here. I have a few deadlines to meet and a few summer tasks.
  I'm getting out of the sheep. In a few weeks time I'll be taking the last cargo
of wool to Strokestown.[8]

---

6 McGahern was sending Byrnes a story titled 'A Finished Man'. The story – at an
earlier period called 'The Old Man' – was eventually published as 'The White Boat'
in *New Writing 6: An Anthology*, ed. A. S. Byatt and Peter Porter (London: Vintage,
1997).
7 Byrnes replied to McGahern that 'The Finished Man' was not appropriate for the
radio series, it would not survive the necessary editing, and asked him to write instead
the tale that he had regaled her with over lunch in Dublin in January. The commission
was for an original piece of writing for radio. In a letter of 7 August 1995 Byrnes
wrote to McGahern: 'the story that we discussed in Dublin (about the mother who
had outlived her daughters, and about the particular death of one of the girls) would
be more appropriate for this project. Not only do I think that "A Finished Man"
would be ruined by excessive cutting, for its poignancy is in the waiting for his story
to unfurl, but I think that the first idea you gave to me had more varied and, in a way,
stranger qualities.'
8 McGahern brought his wool each year to a dealer in Strokestown, Co. Roscommon.
See letter to Luke Dodd of 4 July 1990.

If you are free maybe we can have a drink then.

> Please remember me to Catherine
> With good wishes
> John McGahern

Neill Joy
[*Madeline McGahern*]
Foxfield

24 July 1995

Dear Neill and Mary,
It was a real pleasure to have you here and I hope it will not be long until you come again.

We'd hoped to see you in Dublin.[9] Then the calf, a beautiful strawberry heifer, delayed and delayed her entrance. Family started to call and it became too difficult.

We've had the best summer for years. All the hay is saved. We have sold all the sheep to make the winter easier. Madeline calls this 'the silly season' in the sense that we are never quite certain what the days will bring, but that will be all over in another few weeks.

> We hope you are both well
> and with my love
> John

9 After their stay in Foxfield, the McGaherns had given the Joys use of their Dublin home. In a letter of 1 August 1995, Neill Joy thanks John and Madeline for advice on Dublin pubs: 'In Dublin we searched for and found Ryan's pub, which, sadly, is a good bit altered; the snugs are moved since we were last there with you both. [. . .] I shall never set foot in Davey Byrne's again; it is disgracefully changed. But thank god you sent us to the Longhall, the Duke, across from DB, and a couple of other pubs which sustain the historical past [. . .] Oddly, we didn't get inside Mulligan's.' Madeline McGahern Papers.

Frances Byrnes

Foxfield

20 August 1995

Dear Frances,

I know that what you say about <u>A Finished Man</u> is right.[10]

But I have real difficulty with your proposals for the other story.

In my opinion, no real people or even places could be used. The events are too recent and too shocking and compromise too many people – take the Mart Manager, for one – too deeply.[11]

People would clam up. We'd be watched like hawks for libel. The perfect spurious excuse of 'protecting the children' is to hand.

My own feeling is that if I were to write it that I'd have to be extremely careful that no real places or people could be identified. It would have to be a local everywhere. They would almost certainly be identified but since nothing could be purported it would stay in silence. Closer than that I see nothing but trouble.

I don't know where that leaves us. I won't mind at all if you think it is too difficult. Maybe call me when you think about it.

With every good wish

John

Neill Joy

[*Madeline McGahern*]

Foxfield

20 August 1995

Dear Neill,

The wine you generously left has been drunk. There was no need to leave any but it was enjoyed. It was, as I have said, a pleasure to have you both here.

---

10 See letter to Byrnes of 12 July 1995.

11 'Love of the World' leans for plot to some degree on a murder that had taken place in McGahern's part of Co. Leitrim in 1982.

I enclose a recent book. There's a blurb for Goldring's Pleasant the Scholar's Life at the back, which is provocative and very good.[12] J. C. Beckett's is almost certainly the short history.[13] Joe Lee is readable and good from the opposite side.[14] Nicholas Canny is best on the 17th and 18th centuries.[15]

After the Sligo ceremonies I was beside Anne Yeats at dinner.[16] She has her father's head, her mother's skin, and carried sticks because of her very swollen legs. I liked her very much. She told a story of crossing Italy by train at night with Mother and Father. Father was bringing back reproductions of Titian etc. The custom officials liked those and he had only to open a few but they forced Mother to open a parcel wrapped in a gold cloth despite her repeated protests. The cloth covered a birdcage of canaries who then sang throughout the night as the train crossed Italy and France. She had great spirit. 'Mr McGahern', as we said goodbye, 'I hope I'll have thrown away my sticks when next we meet'.

There'll be very little 'public man' from this on.[17] I plan not to move out and just work. Madeline may have to go to Paris for the winding up of her father's estate in October. There's no pressure on the Colgate decision.

12 Maurice Goldring, *Pleasant the Scholar's Life: Irish Intellectuals and the Construction of the Nation State* (London: Serif, 1993). McGahern reviewed this book in largely positive terms for the *Irish Times* (23 July 1994), reprinted for *Études Irlandaises*, vol. 20, no. 1 (Spring 1995). The review is reproduced in *LOTW*, 378–83.
13 J. C. Beckett, *A Short History of Ireland* (London: Hutchinson, 1952). Neill Joy had asked for advice on the best one-volume history of Ireland to read.
14 In a 1999 essay, McGahern describes J. J. Lee's *Ireland 1912–1985* (Cambridge: Cambridge University Press, 1989) as 'brilliant and provocative'. See 'Whatever You Say, Say Nothing', *LOTW*, 128–32.
15 Among Canny's publications are *The Elizabethan Conquest of Ireland: A Pattern Established, 1565–76* (Sussex: Harvester Press, 1976); *Kingdom and Colony: Ireland in the Atlantic World 1560–1800* (Baltimore: Johns Hopkins University Press, 1987); and *Making Ireland British, 1580–1650* (Oxford: Oxford University Press, 2001). Canny spent most of his career at UCG, subsequently renamed the National University of Ireland Galway in 1997 – where McGahern worked in the Department of English for the spring semester of 1993.
16 Anne Yeats (1919–2001), daughter of W. B. Yeats and Georgie Hyde-Lees. McGahern had opened the 1995 Yeats Summer School in Sligo. A version of his address can be found among his papers deposited in Galway – see McGahern Papers, NUIG, P71/1378.
17 McGahern is referring to a remark made by Neill Joy in a letter of 1 August 1995 in which Joy was trying to put pressure on the administrators at Colgate to offer McGahern teaching in the 1996–7 academic year by telling them that McGahern was a 'public man' and would need a decision soon. The McGaherns were in Colgate for the 1996–7 autumn semester.

Poitiers in France want to give me a degree. If I'm not going back to Colgate, they'll give it in Oct '96 (They need to know in October). If I am, it'll be in '97. I was reading a biography of Edmund Wilson. Mentioned is the <u>Fort Schuyler Club</u> in Utica, the <u>Savoy</u> in Rome, the <u>Hulbert House</u> in Boonville, the <u>Towpath Inn</u> in Turin. I wondered if they still exist.[18] It'd be fun to try them out with you and Mary.

The real news is that we've had the most amazing summer of continuous good weather. Madeline swims in the lake most days. I have sold the sheep.

Madeline sends you both her love, and with my love

John

Luke Dodd

[*San Francisco*][19]

[*Early September 1995*]

[*Postcard to Luke Dodd*]
To thank you and Catherine for your kindness to Tom Jordan and myself when we visited. I was delighted and a little amazed at what you've made of the place.[20]

With affection
John McGahern

Michael Gorman

Foxfield

14 September 1995

Dear Margaret and Michael,
I want to thank you very much for the whole of the pleasant evening you showed us in Galway.

---

18 Hostelries in upstate New York. Many are still in existence.
19 A postcard of San Francisco where John and Madeline were staying having earlier attended the funeral of Madeline's mother in Atascadero, California where she had settled in later years after a long, peripatetic life.
20 Referring to Dodd's work as curator of Strokestown Park and Famine Museum.

I'm sorry to be so slow in writing, and with the enclosed. I thought <u>Break on Through</u> superb work. In fact, all the stories of male violence had a poetry. I found the stories involving women poor or unconvincing.[21]

We went to California for the funeral of Madeline's mother, and have just got back. We were the only relatives present at the small funeral. Death is like another business deal there, more aesthetic than usual, formal, subdued, but still strictly business – The Chapel of the Roses.

I hope you are well and happy and that you had a lovely time with the children on Inishboffin. Madeline sends you both her love

And with my love
John

Tom Paulin Papers

Foxfield

30 September 1995

Dear Tom,
Thank you for your letter and the copy of the Review.

I enjoyed your poem and thought it a true celebration of Charles, and the only poem to address the Occasion.[22] It seems to me that the other two songsters sought to honour the Occasion by avoiding it. Or is that too Irish?

If you are ever in these parts and would like to call you'll be welcome.[23]

With good wishes
John

21 Michael Gorman had sent McGahern Thom Jones's collection of short stories *The Pugilist at Rest* (London: Faber, 1994).

22 Charles Monteith died on 9 May 1995. The *London Review of Books* for 21 September 1995 published three poems in memory of Monteith: Tom Paulin, 'Motoring'; Paul Muldoon, 'Burma'; and Seamus Heaney, 'Exile Runes', from *Beowulf*, lines 1117–40. See *London Review of Books*, vol. 17, no. 18 (21 September 1995), 8. McGahern did not attend the funeral service; Paulin found it emotionally overwhelming.

23 Paulin, along with his wife Giti and two sons Michael and Niall, subsequently called in at Foxfield.

1996

Frances Byrnes

Foxfield

3 January 1996[1]

Dear Frances,
I have written a prologue and epilogue to frame the story. You'll notice that they belong to silence.[2]

My own feeling is that all sounds should be muted, and kept to a minimum, to be effective. The voice will carry most of it, but certain sounds – the auctioneers in the cattle mart is an obvious instance, and it should be ritualised rather than realistic – can replace the voice.[3]

It's yours now.

Affectionately
John

THE VOICE IS A COMMUNAL VOICE [AS IN A.W.]
It shifts only ONCE to the first person – to bring Harkin and the voice into sharp focus.

1 Mistakenly dated 3 January 1966 by McGahern.
2 'Love of the World'.
3 'Love of the World' was ultimately recorded in Bristol (where Byrnes was then based) on 18 March 1996. Byrnes subsequently went with McGahern to Foxfield to record the 'real' version, and all its atmosphere, later that week, with a sound man named Iain Hunter. A cat answered back to John's voice as he read, causing many retakes. The piece was broadcast on BBC Radio 4 on 29 October 1996.

6 January 1996

Dear Donal,

Thank you for your card and the diary. It is very nice to have and to use the diary, and amusing in the light of the story.[4] I'll take it with me to the States when I go for the last months of the year in late August. I'm trying to lie as low as I can and work, though I have to go to France in March, to Berlin in April.

Tom was in very good form when he came last summer, and was a delight to have.[5]

A cousin of mine, a priest in his forties (he seems young to me now) discovered a remarkable collection of photographs taken in Leitrim between 1889 and 1894. I think they'll probably become a permanent part of the National Archive and are well worth looking at and even getting a copy for the school.

I hope we'll all meet in '96.

Please remember me to Frank O'Dea and Desmond.[6]

A very happy new year to Dolores and Yourself.

Sean

You are entitled to take out your <u>red</u> pencil to the enclosed. I enclose item for fun.[7]

---

4 A Belgrove school diary.

5 Tom Jordan.

6 Frank O'Dea was a teacher from Barefield, Co. Clare who started in the school in March 1956. Desmond Millett was from Clonmel, joined the school in 1949, and in the 1960s felt he had a late vocation to the priesthood, to which he was eventually ordained in 1971.

7 Two pamphlets enclosed: 'Madness/Creativity' and 'Creatures of the Earth'. Both published by La Licorne, UFR Langues Littératures Poitiers.

Joe Kennedy
Foxfield

17 January 1996

Dear Joe,

We were sorry to learn that Margaret had more ill-luck. We hope we will see her soon. I'll phone as soon as both of us see a way to get to Dublin together.

I'm glad Seamus got the Nobel. Nobody will enjoy it more.

I was hoping to stay here over the whole winter and spring, but it's not going to be so easy. Anyhow, that's my problem.

Give Margaret our love. A happy New Year to you both.

John

Michael Gorman
Foxfield

20 February 1996

Dear Michael,

Thank you for the books. I enclose some of [the] books and will return soon the others.

I thought the Brodkey fraudulent to the core.[8] I wouldn't compare it for a moment with AUBADE, or even Potter, who used his death to give dramatic edge to a powerful political statement.[9] MacAmhlaigh's piece is likeable and decent.[10] Years ago I read and liked a book by Richard Power Úll i mBarr

---

8 Harold Brodkey, *This Wild Darkness: The Story of My Death* (New York: Henry Holt & Co., 1996) is a compilation of essays written by Brodkey as he neared death from AIDS, many first published in the *New Yorker*.

9 McGahern was a great admirer of Dennis Potter, the English playwright and screenwriter. On 15 March 1994, three months before his death, Potter gave an interview to Melvyn Bragg, later broadcast on 5 April 1994 by Channel 4 in which he revealed that he had named his cancer 'Rupert', after Rupert Murdoch, who he said represented much of what he found despicable about the mass media in Britain. Philip Larkin's late poem 'Aubade' was also deeply admired.

10 Dónall Mac Amhlaigh (1926–89), a native of Co. Galway, is best known for his Irish-language works about life as a labourer in the post-Second World War era, as

an Ghéagáin.[11] What an abused/abusing generation Holy Ireland threw out without any preparation for the life they had to face.

I was under the impression that you had read and liked the Meschery which is why I asked for it.[12]

The recent J. A. Philips was a disappointment but the Graham gets better and better with rereading.[13]

Please remember us both with affection to Margaret.

John

Neill Joy
[*Madeline McGahern*]
Foxfield

Ash Wednesday [*21 February 1996*]

Dear Neill,
It was lovely to get your letter at Christmas, and I'd be glad to pay the postage increase if you just write on.

We've had the best summer in years, and a mild winter, very like a poor summer. We've had a very quiet time, just reading and working. But there's a lot of travel coming up, Paris tomorrow for a day, for a week in March, then Bristol, Aix-en-Provence, Berlin, St Malo, Palermo and I hope that will be that till Colgate.

---

part of the Irish diaspora in Britain. His first book, *Dialann Deoraí* (Baile Átha Cliath: Clóchomhar Tta, 1960), is his most widely known and has been translated into English by Valentin Iremonger under the title *An Irish Navvy: The Diary of an Exile* (London: Routledge & Kegan Paul, 1964). It is not known which Mac Amhlaigh piece McGahern is referencing here.

11 Richard Power (1928–70), *Úll i mBarr an Ghéagáin* (Baile Átha Cliath: Sáirséal agus Dill, 1959), translated by Victor Power as *Apple on the Treetop* (Dublin: Poolbeg Press, 1980).

12 Joanne Meschery b. 1941 had taken part in the UCG summer writing workshop. She is the author of three novels, all published by Simon & Schuster: *In a High Place* (1981); *A Gentleman's Guide to the Frontier* (1990), which was nominated for a PEN/Faulkner Award; and *Home and Away* (1994).

13 Jayne Anne Phillips b. 1952, an American novelist and short story writer. The book to which McGahern refers here is most likely her novel *Shelter* (Boston: Houghton Mifflin, 1994). The Graham referred to is W. S. Graham, *Selected Poems* (London: Faber, 1996).

Many close deaths in a few weeks. Francis across the lake died in Mohill (83).[14] Joe Conway (49) who worked in the bank, was from Clare, and drove Mary home all those years ago when she came with Dan Casey [out of the blue out of Vermont a progress report/card from Casey at Christmas] died watching TV.[15] The local doctor (65) came here with his wife for dinner 2 weeks ago and died the next day.[16] An old soak came up to me in the bar after the funeral: 'Take it steady, boys. I can't guarantee I'll be around much longer to see yez safe.' I have a feeling you'd like Selected Poems by W. S. Graham, Faber 1996. I thought them marvellous.[17]

Mild winter sun on the white of the house and the trees as I write this and love to Mary and your good self.

John

Caroline Walsh
Foxfield

25 April 1996

Dear Caroline,

I've been out of the country, and heard of your mother's death very late. I am writing to offer you my sympathy.[18]

My last contact with her was strange, a couple of long conversations on the telephone, and I invited her to lunch in Trinity.[19] She seemed to like that and we arranged a day. She never turned up. I telephoned your step-father and gathered then that she was no longer well.[20] The house near the canal

---

14 Francie McGarty, buried in Fenagh.

15 Joe Conway was a friend of McGahern's, manager of the Bank of Ireland in Mohill.

16 Dr Farley, who practised in Mohill. He and Francie McGarty drank together in Luke Earley's after Francie moved to the town.

17 McGahern had also gifted Graham's poems to Jimmy Swift in the spring of 1996. He had tried and failed to arrange for Graham to be his successor as Northern Arts Fellow in Newcastle and Durham in 1976.

18 Mary Lavin died on 25 March 1996.

19 McGahern had been a visiting fellow at TCD in the spring of 1988.

20 Lavin's first husband, William Walsh, died in 1954, little over a decade into the marriage. She married Michael Scott in 1969; he died in 1991 and she was once again a widow, remaining so until her death.

where I first saw you as a very young and delightful girl now seems another world away.[21]

I'd be very grateful if you'd convey my sympathy to Val and Elizabeth.[22]

And with my love
John (McGahern)

Colm Tóibín
Foxfield

24 August 1996

Dear Colm,

I'm writing to thank you for having Jonathan Riley write me. I'd be happy to go to Picador and I wrote him explaining exactly what my situation is.[23]

I work every day but it goes very slowly and it has never been much different.

I leave to teach the Fall term in Colgate on August 21st, and in case I don't see you before I leave I want to wish you great good luck in September.[24]

With affection
John

21 The mews house at Lad Lane.
22 Caroline's sisters, Valentine and Elizabeth.
23 Riley was then at Picador and moved to Faber the following year. Tóibín had been encouraging McGahern to move away from Faber, which he felt did not sufficiently appreciate the asset it had.
24 Refers to the publication of Tóibín's novel *The Story of the Night* (London: Picador, 1996).

12 October 1996

Dear Liam,

I meant to write before I left, mostly to wish you well on your new work, but all the days seem to crowd into that part of August.[25]

I have been travelling too much. I go to Arkansas this week – Chicago, Dallas – and after that I haven't very much outside the work here. I'll get home before Christmas. Madeline will probably leave earlier.

There's very little election fever. It is taken for granted Clinton will win. Dole hammers away at Clinton without conviction and Clinton doesn't either mention Dole or the election. He speaks about the good times and claims the credit.[26]

The weather is clear and beautiful, and it is beginning to get cold at night. The colours of the trees are amazing now and indescribably rich.

I hope you are happy in the new work. I am sending this to Laheen as I haven't another address. Please remember me with affection to your mother and father and all in the house.

With every good wish

John

14 November 1996

Dear Liam,

I was very glad to learn that you like your new work. I had a feeling that you would and I look forward to hearing about it when I get home.

---

25 Kelly had been moved from Bailieborough to Cavan the previous summer to work at Pastoral Renewal (the involvement of laity in the Church) in the diocese of Kilmore.
26 The US presidential election took place on 5 November 1996. Bill Clinton won re-election with a substantial margin in the popular vote and the Electoral College thus becoming the first Democrat since Franklin D. Roosevelt to win two straight presidential elections.

Madeline gets into Dublin on Wednesday, December 4th. She was just going to get the train down and get one of the neighbours to meet her at Dromod. She was reluctant to let me write you but I said you wouldn't have offered it unless you meant it. She insists <u>only if you are free that day.</u> She gets in from London at 10.15am on EI 153 from Heathrow (9.05). It's not hard to get a taxi to Connolly and get the midday train. I wouldn't want you to go to the Airport if it's in any way difficult and we will be grateful for your offer and twice so if you cannot because of difficulty.

It's winding down here. The students are even richer than they used to be if that's imaginable. I had a deputation this morning to see if I'd cancel all classes the week of Thanksgiving (There's a class the Tuesday before that doesn't cut into the holidays). I think I've had enough of teaching.

Please remember me to your mother and father.[27]

With every good wish
John

---

27 The blood relationship was between Kelly's father and McGahern's mother. Kelly's mother was Mary B. McNiffe, a native of Coraleehan, where John's mother came from. She had great affection for John, remembering him as a young teenager cycling to his mother's grave in Aughawillan.

1997

Colm Tóibín

Foxfield

4 January 1997

Dear Colm,
Thank you for sending us The Story of the Night.[1]

I was able to read it quickly and easily, and found the prose coldly exact. I thought the sex scenes often worked as poems, none more so than the extraordinary and moving scene with Susan Ford.

My one and serious hesitation is whether it worked as a novel because of the lack of a society – on the development of the corruption/espionage story for the night to feed on. I'm sure the last thing you need at this time is a discourse on how the night needs the day, and I have already much to be enormously grateful for.

I'm not long back from the States. Madeline came a few weeks earlier, and both of us have been ill with flu.

It'd be a pleasure to see you again.
Would you like to come down or would you prefer to meet in Dublin? Are you travelling now or staying in Dublin?

With gratitude
and every good wish
John

---

1 Tóibín's novel set in Argentina and New York of the final decades of the twentieth century.

Robin Robertson

Foxfield

3 March 1997

Dear Robin,

Thank you for A Painted Field.[2] The book is a delight and Random did you proud. Madeline as well as myself send you congratulations and wish the poems long life.

A few weeks ago there was a programme on RTE about Colum from the archives. He said that he came on She Moves . . . in Donegal and that the 3 lines around Her feet made no din were complete but he had to build the rest of the song with Landor and Browning as his models.[3] I'd say Lawn Tennison managed a phrase or two.[4]

Madeline said she had a pleasant time with Clare in Paris.

Please give her my love
John

Neill Joy
[Madeline McGahern]

Foxfield

4 March 1997

Dear Neill,

I was delighted to get your letter. And it was wonderful to have your company, and Mary's, all last Fall.

I have been here all along, writing at my usual pace, which makes the snail look like a sprinter. Madeline has been in Paris twice. She's been seeing if her father's estate can be settled and having her flat done up. If they cannot agree

2 Robertson's debut poetry collection, A Painted Field, was published by Picador in 1997 and won the Forward Prize for best first collection.

3 Padraic Colum (1881–1972) is usually credited with writing the very popular Irish love song 'She Moved Through the Fair'. Walter Savage Landor (1775–1864), English writer, poet and activist; Robert Browning (1812–89), leading English poet of the Victorian age. Robertson incorporated the song's verses in a poetry sequence, 'Camera Obscura', which was included in A Painted Field.

4 Alfred, Lord Tennyson (1809–92). The spelling is an old Joycean put-down.

on the estate before the end of this month it has to go to court. She went down to a friend in Bordeaux for one weekend. And Liliane and her husband came and stayed with her in Paris for another weekend.[5]

We both go to Morocco for 2 weeks in April. I have to write a piece. When the offer came in January I said NO and felt virtuous for a few days. After 5 days of foddering cattle here in the rain and looking for myself I said to hell with virtue and telephoned to see if the offer was still open. I also persuaded them it was necessary for me to stop in Paris on the way in order to check out a Moroccan restaurant I used go to in the early 1970's. Our itinerary is Rabat, Fez, Marrakesh, Taroudant, Paris. We pick up a car in Rabat.[6]

Thanks for the kind words about the story. As it was broadcast in a truncated version while I was in Colgate, and it is the locale (not the theme) of the novel I wasn't anxious to publish it but the agent felt otherwise and sold it to GRANTA. I'll not write any more stories until I finish the novel. And I have the selection of J. B. Yeats's letters to do for Corti.[7] And thanks for the button. There are so many buttons on that damned raincoat that 5 or 6 wouldn't be missed.

The I.R.A. are very isolated now, which is a good thing, though we had a Democratic Congressman over here from Syracuse, New York pleading their case.[8] A few days after he left they shot a young British soldier in the back and tied a 16 year old girl to a lamp-post, cut off her hair, and poured white

5 Liliane Louvel, McGahern friend and scholar, based at the University of Poitiers.

6 McGahern wrote a travel article titled 'Morocco, the Bitter and the Sweet' for the *New York Times Magazine* (14 September 1997), 18–20 and 32–4. Reproduced in *LOTW*, 52–9. It came about through Madeline's old friend Nancy Newhouse who worked with the magazine.

7 José Corti is a bookshop and publishing house founded in 1925 and located at 11 Rue Médicis, Paris. Its motto is *Rien de Commun*, or 'Nothing Commonplace'.

8 The only evidence of an American politician visiting Foxfield is of Tom Hayden in 1996. Hayden (1939–2016) was a social and political activist, author and politician, best known for his major role as an anti-war, civil rights and radical intellectual in the 1960s. In later years he ran for political office numerous times, winning seats in both the California Assembly and California Senate. At the end of his life he was the director of the Peace and Justice Resource Center in Los Angeles County. He was married to the Hollywood actress Jane Fonda for seventeen years. A Michigan-born Irish-American, he was sympathetic to the cause of Irish republicanism and interviewed McGahern as part of a book he was editing on the Great Irish Famine, *Irish Hunger: Personal Reflections on the Legacy of the Irish Famine* (Boulder: Roberts Rinehart Publishers, 1997). McGahern decided, ultimately, not to let his interview form part of the book.

paint over her.[9] There'll be British and Irish elections in the late summer. It looks as if they'll both bring a change of Government, though John Bruton has done well here.[10]

House prices have doubled in Dublin in the last 2 years.

The Murphy had no life and was sad or bad. I'd say he has to be very careful now. There have been several programmes about paedophilic rings working out of S. Lanka recently.

Please give our love to Mary

and with my love

John

P.S. I was very sorry to hear of V.'s bad luck. Please remember us to Joe and Herself.[11]

John McGahern Papers (TS)

[No address]

14 May 1997[12]

As writers associated with the Abbey Theatre we would like to contribute to the current debate about the future of our National Theatre.

It is our view that development should take place in the present building, incorporating the imaginative plans of Theatre Project Consultants and their associates which were placed before the Board of the theatre in 1995. It is time for these plans to be realized. They would transform the present building,

9 The last shooting of a British soldier in Ireland before the Good Friday Agreement of 1998 was of Lance Bombardier Stephen Restorick, aged twenty-three, who had been manning a vehicle checkpoint in Bessbrook, Co. Armagh when an IRA sniper struck in February 1997.

10 In May 1997 the Conservative government in the UK was swept out of power by Tony Blair's Labour in a landslide victory. In June the existing, so-called rainbow coalition government in Ireland, made up of Fine Gael, the Labour Party and Democratic Left, lost power to be replaced by a coalition of Fianna Fáil, the Progressive Democrats and a few independents. Bertie Ahern became the Taoiseach in place of Fine Gael's John Bruton.

11 'V' is Vivien Harvey Slater, wife of Joseph L. Slater, McGahern's Colgate colleague and an expert on Ralph Waldo Emerson. Vivien had had a fall and a hip replacement.

12 Appears to have started life as a letter to the press, Thomas Kilroy and Brian Friel having drafted it, with first drafts of the letter appearing on 4 May in the Abbey Theatre Archive at NUIG, P103/548(50). It was signed by a Who's Who of Irish writers.

inside and out, giving it two modern performance spaces and an exterior which would both enhance the whole surrounding area and be worthy of a National Theatre.

We believe that this is preferable to any other suggested development for the Abbey Theatre, for two reasons. One is historical: this is the site of the original foundation and continuity with that tradition is vitally important. Secondly, the present building, for all its faults (which are fully addressed in the new plans) enjoys an exceptional location in the city centre and this should not be easily surrendered.

We are now seeking public support for the renewal of the theatre building which is so important if we are to have a National Theatre of which we can all be proud.

John McGahern

Neill Joy
[Madeline McGahern]
Foxfield

24 June 1997

Dear Neill,

It has been a scattered, very scattered few months. Madeline has been much in Paris: it does look as if her father's estate is about to be settled at long last. We were in Morocco together. I wrote a piece for the N.Y.T. (Hotels like rich ghettoes, a beautiful countryside, great poverty, police everywhere, an air of desperate resignation). Then we went to Florence together and met Wilbur and Janette. I thought W. was in poor form. We had dinner in a restaurant in Fiesole, overlooking Florence, that hadn't changed since Madeline and her father were there over 40 years ago. I found the hordes of tourists depressing, and especially the knowledge that I was adding to their number.

There was a letter from Poitiers saying that the ceremony was fixed for Tuesday September 30th. I suppose it's very unlikely that Mary and you would be interested in going for a long weekend.

Next week I have to speak in Belfast. I'm not looking forward to it. It seems worse than ever there now.

Do you have any news or plans?

Madeline asks to be remembered.

Love to Mary and yourself
John

3 October [*1997*]

Dear Gerry,[13]
Got back last night.
   See you, I hope, at Tom's play on the 8th.[14]
                    Love to Dorothy[15]
                    John

---

13 Gerald Dawe b. 1952, Belfast-born poet and academic. Dawe was introduced to McGahern by Tom Kilroy when both Kilroy and Dawe were on the English faculty at UCG in the 1970s. When Dawe headed up the writers' summer school at UCG, McGahern was a frequent contributor. McGahern was encouraging of Dawe's poetry and the men shared an admiration for W. S. Graham. A joint reading at an early Arts Festival in Galway cemented the relationship. This short note is written on the back of a photocopied page 81 from Rainer Maria Rilke's novel *The Notebooks of Malte Laurids Brigge* with McGahern adding the following publication details in pen: 'The Notebooks of Malte Laurids Brigge, Rainer Maria Rilke, translated by John Linton, first published 1930, Hogarth Press 1959.' Dawe had mentioned to McGahern that he was considering calling his new collection of poems *Human Wishes*, but McGahern felt this might be too close to Rilke and sent on this photocopied page to confirm his point. The relevant passage involves some advice from Malte's mother: 'Ah! Malte, we pass away thus, and it seems to me people are all distracted and preoccupied and pay no real attention when we pass away. It is just as if a shooting-star fell and no one saw it and no one expressed a wish. Never forget to wish something for yourself, Malte. One should never give up wishing. I do not believe there is any fulfilment, but there are wishes that endure, that last a whole life long, so that, indeed, one could not wait for their fulfilment.' Dawe retained 'Human Wishes' as the title for the final poem in the collection, which was ultimately named *The Morning Train*.
14 *The Secret Fall of Constance Wilde* by Thomas Kilroy.
15 Ought to read 'Dorothea', Gerry Dawe's wife.

14 October 1997

Dear Neill,

Thank you for the letter, and all the news.

Three of us were given degrees, Orlo H. Clark, a professor of surgery at U.C.S.F., Nélida Piñon, President of the Brazilian Academy, and this ecrivan.[16] The ceremony was long, over 2 hours, and it was very hot. The plentiful champagne afterwards was a blessed relief.

Liliane was very pleased with your invitation. I think she thought you knew she couldn't attend. In France these territories are ringfenced. Not being a Conrad scholar she probably wouldn't even be given university approval to attend.

I reread the Heart of Darkness recently and thought it a strange great poem.[17]

Madeline was in Paris all September. Her father's estate is settled and will be settled formally close to Christmas.

They are shooting A.W. in the old stone cavalry barracks in Castlebar, four 50 minute episodes. I was there just once. I walked up the wrong stairs and discovered a soldier polishing a silver trophy. I found him much more sympathetic than the movie people.

We had a whole summer of political scandal. Haughey was discovered to be on the take for years, as assumed, and may even have to sell his island and

16 Refers to McGahern's award of an honorary degree at the University of Poitiers. Dr Orlo H. Clark is Emeritus Professor of Surgery at University of California San Francisco (UCSF). A graduate of Cornell Medical School, he joined the UCSF faculty in 1973. Nélida Piñon, celebrated Brazilian novelist, was born in 1937 in Rio de Janeiro of Galician immigrants.

17 McGahern's admiration for *Heart of Darkness* lasted his whole adult life. See 1960 letters to both Jimmy Swift and Dympna McGahern.

estate.[18] 'These are miserable times,' he said. The Government is shaky. We are ½ way through a grindingly dull presidential race.[19]

It was 80° in Poitiers. On a Sunday we went to a small town and bought oysters, sardines, bread, cheese, lettuce, tomato, artichokes and went back to a 5 hour lunch under linden trees in a big garden. A couple of 22, both handsome, sat through the 5 hours without a flicker of boredom, and discussed the food and wine as knowledgably as if they were 2 centuries old. The landscape is a little like Pooleville, but more cultivated, more populous, and very burnt.[20]

The Busches were in very good form. I never saw Fred in better form.

Madeline sends her love to you both, and with
my love
John

---

18 In 1997 a government-appointed tribunal, led by Judge Brian McCracken, first revealed that Haughey had received substantial monetary gifts from businessmen and that he had held secret offshore accounts in the Ansbacher Bank, Cayman Islands. Haughey faced criminal charges for obstructing the work of the McCracken tribunal. His trial on these charges was postponed indefinitely after the judge in the case found that he would not be able to get a fair trial following prejudicial comments by the then Tánaiste (deputy Prime Minister) Mary Harney. Also in 1997, it was revealed that Haughey had embezzled money destined for the Fianna Fáil party, taxpayers' money taken from government funds earmarked for the operation of a political party, and that he had spent large portions of these funds on luxury items, while preaching belt-tightening and implementing budget cuts as a national policy.

19 The presidential election was due to be held in November but it was advanced by two months upon the early resignation by the incumbent, Mary Robinson, to assume her new appointment as the United Nations High Commissioner for Human Rights. The turnout for the election was low, with 48% of the electorate casting their votes. In the final result, the Fianna Fáil candidate, Mary McAleese, easily beat Fine Gael's Mary Banotti, while Dana – social conservative and one-time winner of the Eurovision Song Contest – came third. Thus, Mary McAleese became the eighth President of Ireland.

20 Poolville, New York is a small village just south of Hamilton where the Joys lived.

14 November 1997

Dear Matthew,
I have completed a selection of the letters of J. B. Yeats, the father of the poet and painter, for the French publisher Jose Corti with a 30 page introduction. I did so because I have long admired the letters and because of the offer.

The introduction is new but the letters are taken from the volume Eliot published at Faber in the 1940's. It is much shorter than that volume. I have retained roughly half the letters.

In the present turns of the wheel of fashion here, John Butler has dropped more of less out of sight and it may be of no interest to Faber – but I thought I should tell you before mentioning it to any of the smaller publishers it may interest.[21]

Please remember me to Caroline with affection, and with my love[22]
John

Seamus Heaney Papers

Foxfield

19 November 1997

Dear Seamus,
I see that Deirdre Madden's nomination has got through to the General Assembly.[23]

If you can be there on the 26th I'd be glad if you'd speak for her.

21 Evans replies immediately and enthusiastically on Faber's behalf and the book begins to take shape.
22 Caroline Michel, b. 1959 in Harrogate, Yorkshire, has worked in publishing with a wide variety of prestigious presses and has been CEO of the literary agency Peters Fraser & Dunlop since 2007. At the time of this letter's composition she was married to Matthew Evans.
23 Deirdre Madden b. 1960, Irish fiction writer and a native of Toomebridge, Co. Antrim. This letter refers to Madden's election to Aosdána.

I know your speech would carry more weight and it would be good to see her elected. And it may be difficult with 14 people.

With good wishes

John

Faber

Foxfield

22 November 1997

Dear Matthew,

Thank you for your letter. I am very happy you'd want to do the letters. I enclose the introduction. I hope you'll like it.

I made the selections of the one photostat I had and sent it to Corti. I wasn't thinking at the time that there might be an English edition. I'll write today to Bertrand Fillaudeau at Jose Corti to see if he can send me a copy of the selection as quickly as possible.

Two things:

Would it be worth including a small selection of the pencil sketches with the letters?

Will Faber be able to do an index or will I have to do that?[24]

Conti isn't announcing a publication date until the end of the year. I imagine it'll be next autumn. Is there any particular reason to make haste on this side? Telephone me if there's any urgency.

Please remember me with affection to Caroline

With my love

John

24 Eight handsome pencil sketches appear in the book published in 1999 and Faber took care of the indexing.

Faber

Foxfield

4 December 1997

Dear Matthew,
I enclose a copy of the list of selections. They are from the 1944 Faber edition
by Hone. I am hoping you'll have a copy and be able to photostat it. Though
I'm happy to go to Galway or Dublin and have it done if that's necessary.

The selection is stringent. I had in mind a French reader who would know
nothing about JBY. The English reader is hardly much different by now. I kept
the letters I liked best or I thought would make the strongest impression –
and left out anything I felt repetitive or weak. I also left out the WBY letters.

I would have no objection to including more of the letters.[25]
Secker brought out a very poor reproduction for libraries some years
back. My copy was owned by Roger Senhouse and was given me by Mary
Hutchinson.[26] Do you remember the house on Bloomfield Road she got for
us when I was teaching for D. J. Gordon in Reading? All that marble. All
those years.

John

Denis Sampson

Foxfield

4 December 1997

Dear Denis,
It was very nice to get your letter. I enclose the McCourt. The translator
slanted it, changing farce to comedy right through, and leaves out things

---

25 Evans had written in a letter of 2 December if it might not make more sense just
to reproduce the 1944 book in full, replacing Hone's introduction with McGahern's.
Ultimately the McGahern-edited volume was substantially different to Hone's 1944
book, containing 134 letters to Hone's 251.
26 Roger Senhouse (1899–1970) was an English publisher and translator, and a
peripheral member of the Bloomsbury Group of writers, intellectuals and artists. In
1935 he became co-owner with Fredric Warburg of the publishing house that became
Secker & Warburg, rescuing it from receivership. Mary Hutchinson was very much
part of the same social and artistic milieu.

like – 'Its American focus shows' – 'a cinematic predictability invades the comic set pieces'.[27] I don't mind. It's not a great book, but it is good, which is enough, and deserves its notice. I read a better book recently, a Canadian, Alistair MacLeod. I thought some of the stories were superb.

There was a bad opera made out of My Love, My Umbrella/Gold W./ and Sierra L. They didn't know what they were doing. The players/singers were terrific. They gave it a great swing and partly disguised how bad it was. I felt sorry for them. They had to tour all over with the wretched thing.

They are still shooting A.W. and I am staying clear, which has the agent annoyed. I get all sorts of friendly shouts in the creamery. There has been advance publicity. Some of the remarks are funny.

Love of the World is coming out as a book in German and is being serialized in the Frankfurt newspaper.[28] I have to go there at the end of January. I have a number of things to do and hope to get them done in a week around that time. I'm delighted L of the W pleased you.

Jose Corti will do the JBY Letters in the spring of '99. Faber say they want to do it.

I'm sorry for all this humdrum. I work on the novel and look at the cattle every day, like the local priest who 'fodders and says Mass'.[29] Did I tell you they gave me a degree in Poitiers? Madeline came. We had a very pleasant time in scorching weather.

Madeline wishes you and Gay a very happy Christmas and New Year, as I do,

> with affection
> John

---

27 McGahern reviewed Frank McCourt's hugely successful memoir, *Angela's Ashes* (New York: Scribner, 1996), in *Le Monde* on 5 September 1997 in an article titled 'La comédie tragique des hommes d'Irlande'. An English version among the McGahern Papers at NUIG is reproduced in *LOTW*, 396–401.
28 'Love of the World' was published as a standalone title in German by Steidl in February 1998. It was titled *In einer solchen Nacht*, translated by Hans-Christian Oeser.
29 Fr Frank McCabe.

31 December 1997

Dear Robin,

I admired *Lost Salt Gift of Blood* by Alistair MacLeod that Cape published in 1991 and wrote about it in the I. Independent at some length, under the guise of writing about the countryside.[30]

Is it still in print? If it is, I'd be glad to get some copies. I'm probably owed a review copy but I'd be very happy to pay for 3 or 4 extra copies.[31]

We miss seeing you here or in Enniskillen and a very Happy New Year to you all.

John

---

30 'Terrible Tales from the Mart', *Irish Independent* (27 December 1997), 10. See *LOTW*, 172–7.

31 Cape had brought out the UK edition of *The Lost Salt Gift of Blood* in 1991, but it was out of print by 1997. McGahern and Robertson shared an enthusiasm for MacLeod's work that would eventually develop into McGahern writing a foreword to a collected stories titled *Island* (London: Jonathan Cape, 2001).

1998

27 January 1998

Dear Matthew,

Thank you for your letter and I'm happy with the offer.[1]

I'd have been happy, too, if you and John Bodley had decided to go with the original Hone, though I think what I have done may have a better chance of winning new readers. Hone did a marvellous job. I'd want to keep all his relevant notes. I think I should add a short note as well as go through the preface again before it goes to the printers.

What about the index?

Is it worth considering his pencil sketches? Or would they be too expensive?[2]

When do you plan to go to the printers? I'll be away from some days but will be back early next [*week*]. I hope this will be a very happy year for you and Caroline.

> With my love
> John

Frances Byrnes

Foxfield

25 February 1998

Dear Frances,

Thank you for the tape, and for sending a copy to Gudrun.[3]

---

1 The offer was for an advance of £2,000 against a royalty of 10%.
2 The pencil sketches are included.
3 Byrnes had sent tapes of 'Love of the World' to both McGahern and to Gudrun Boch of Radio Bremen, who had broadcast some work of McGahern's previously.

I was upset to hear that you were ill for so long. Are you well now? To me you always looked the picture of attractiveness and health, but I know illness falls where it will. Tell me how you are now.[4]

The daffodils are out here as well, and crocuses, and the primroses on the banks. I find it strange, too, disturbing. One day a few weeks ago a man at the garage told me that all the cars were covered with dust from the <u>Sahara</u>. I go to Newfoundland for 5 days at the end of next week. That should be free of all Sahara dust.

I'm going through what I hope will be the last or second last writing of a novel. The publishers badger, but I'm not letting it go until I can get it no better. I have finished a small selection of the letters of John Butler Yeats for a French publisher. What's nice is that Faber will bring them back into print next year. He must have been a terrible husband and father but he was also marvellous.

I enclose this small folly, as a token of love and gratitude.[5]

> If you are ever here we'd both love to see you here.
> With my love (and some anxiety)
> John

Frances Byrnes

Foxfield

2 April 1998

Dear Frances,
I was very gladdened that you are well again – though the phrase sounds so poor – in the light of all that you had to come through.

Reading your letter I was going over old thoughts: only through suffering can we grow, how many will it dishearten and break? Do you know the Patrick Kavanagh poem – 'A year ago I fell in love with the functional ward of a chest hospital/'.[6] These old thoughts can be too heavy. I'm just glad you have come through, and the way that you have.

---

4 Byrnes was diagnosed with cancer in April 1997 and had then undergone major surgery and chemotherapy, returning to work in November 1997.
5 A signed copy of the German publication of 'Love of the World', *In einer solchen Nacht*.
6 These are the opening lines to Kavanagh's 'The Hospital', first collected in *Come Dance with Kitty Stobling*, a book particularly liked by McGahern.

Do you have any plans to come to Ireland? I'd love to see you if you do, and you'll be welcome here.

I've come back from Newfoundland. It was very beautiful and stark, and incredible spaces. I liked the people very much. Waterford and Cork can be heard in some of the accents. The houses were like white boats on the edge of the sea. There's a writer from Nova Scotia, Alistair MacLeod, whose work I like very much.

It's bleak here still, very much the same as when you were here, but the days are getting warmer. The blackthorn and the plum are in blossom.

Are you staying put in Bristol or travelling much for work? Write to me when you have time.

I'm uneasy on the phone. I think it comes from having to 'mind' the phone when I was a boy in my father's police station, but maybe I'll try and call later.

> Madeline asks to be especially remembered to you
> and with all my good wishes, and love
> John

Joan O'Neill

Foxfield

6 May 1998

Dear Joan,[7]

Thank you for the Daisy Chain War.[8]

I'm writing this note as I have just got the book from Declan Kiberd's secretary – there was almost a month's break in classes, and they have had it for some time – and I am looking forward to reading it.[9]

It was a pleasure to see you again and to see you well and prospering.

---

7 Joan O'Neill had attended a writing course led by McGahern at the Tyrone Guthrie Centre, Annaghmakerrig, Co. Monaghan in the 1980s. He had said that what she had written was the beginning of a book and had been very encouraging generally about her work.

8 Book One in O'Neill's trilogy set in Ireland during the years of the Second World War, in which young Lizzie Doyle comes to terms with living with her fiesty English cousin Vicky, and the effects of the war on an impoverished Ireland (Dublin: Attic Press, 1990). The book was subsequently reissued by Hodder & Stoughton in 2002.

9 Declan Kiberd b. 1951 was then Professor of Anglo-Irish Literature at UCD. As a child he had been taught by McGahern at Belgrove Boys' National School, Clontarf, and was for a period co-executor of the literary estate with Madeline.

I hope the meeting in Galway went well.[10]

>And with every good wish
>Sincerely
>John McGahern

Please don't go to the trouble of getting the other edition. The very intention would be honour enough.

>J.

>Michael Prusse
>
>Foxfield

6 August 1998

Dear Michael Prusse,[11]

Love of the World was first published in Granta 1987[12] and broadcast BBC Radio 4. Creatures of the Earth was published in Granta 1995/Best Short Stories 1995/Best Short Stories 1985–1995/and with The Country Funeral and The Creamery Manager in Les Creatures de la Terre Albin Michel 1996. The White Boat was published in the Anthology of the British Council 1995 (I can't lay my hands on a copy or remember the title).

A. Women has just been broadcast as a 4 part BBC series with a screenplay by Adrian Hodges.

The Collected Stories was published by Faber and Knopf in 1992 and 1993.[13]

---

10 A writers' workshop.
11 Michael Prusse b. 1963, Professor of English Language Teaching and English Literature at the Zurich University of Teacher Education. In 1998 the *Dictionary of Literary Biography* commissioned him to write an entry on McGahern. In the same year he was appointed as lecturer for English Language at the Zurich University of Applied Sciences in Winterthur and continued to work on the article, which was published in *British Novelists Since 1960*, Fourth Series, ed. Merritt Moseley, *Dictionary of Literary Biography*, vol. 231 (Detroit: Gale Thomson, 2001), 135–45. Prusse later met McGahern in person when he came to Zurich in May 2005 to read from *Memoir*.
12 This date is an error on McGahern's part and ought to read 1997.
13 Prusse had asked in his letter for details of any stories published since *Amongst Women*.

There are errors and ommissions in Sampson's bibliography.[14]

I'll be glad to help you if you send me a list of what you require and thank you for your kind letter.

Yours sincerely
John McGahern

Mary Keelan
Foxfield

12 October 1998

Dear Mary,

Thank you for your card. It was very kind of you to write to me.[15]

I often think of you and always with affection.

I'm not sure if the address is precise enough to reach you or if you meant me to reply.

I hope you are well and very happy.

With affection
John McGahern

Michael Prusse (TS)
Foxfield

20 November 1998

Dear Michael Prusse,

Thank you for your letter and kind words about Love of the World. I have tried to answer your question as best I can.

1. Sampson's list isn't important. There are a few errors of dates and omissions Books have been published in German, Dutch, Sweden, Italian, Spanish, Greek, Portuguese, Polish.[16]

---

14 Prusse mentioned that he was particularly interested in bibliographical information not covered by Denis Sampson's outline in the *Canadian Journal of Irish Studies*, vol. 17, no. 1, 1991.

15 This is McGahern's first letter to Mary Keelan since October 1964. Keelan had been visiting Ireland earlier in 1998 and had sent McGahern a postcard from Howth.

16 See letter to Prusse of 6 August 1998.

2. Cootehall, Co. Roscommon.[17]

3. December 1992 Amongst Women was given the GPA Award by John Updike for the best book by an Irish Writer over the three previous years. 1993 D. Lit., Galway University; 1995 Prix Etranger Ecurieul; D. Lit. 1997 Universite de Poitiers. Publications of stories: Creatures of the Earth, The White Boat, Love of the World.[18]

4. Working on novel, That He May Face the Rising Sun.

5. The novel and stories create worlds, which people inhabit. They grow out of the words, not the other way round.[19]

6. Love of the World grew out of the detail of raisins being found in a dead women's hand during an autopsy, it seeks to make no point, political or otherwise unless the attempt to see and understand embraces the political and personal.[20] I'd be glad to answer the last three questions if I was able. The true answer is that I don't know.[21]

I write as well as I am able. The work will not live again unless it finds readers. It is up to them to decide what position, if any, I occupy. The writer may be the least reliable person in these matters. All she or he can do is offer the work.[22]

> With good wishes,
> Yours sincerely,
> John McGahern

17 Prusse asked for the correct location of McGahern's father's barracks.

18 Prusse asked for a brief biographical outline covering the years 1993–8.

19 Prusse's question was as follows: 'Many of your novels and stories analyse relationships – between parents and children, between lovers, between husbands and wives. Is this your most important source of inspiration?'

20 Prusse's questions about 'Love of the World': 'Did you write this story because the divorce issue was hotly debated in the mid-nineties in Ireland? And did you want to make a political or personal statement by writing this story?'

21 The relevant questions from Prusse's letter are as follows: 'Reading your first novel, The Barracks, I was struck by the many parallels with Le Mythe de Sisyphe and, to a lesser extent, L'Homme Révolté. Was Camus a big influence on you at that time? Or was it, rather, that these ideas belonged to the "spirit of the time"? Similar themes can, after all, also be observed in Beckett and some of your contemporaries. Am I right in comparing your work to Faulkner in so far as you create a very detailed locality in which all your stories are set? What do the stories you set in Spain and Finland mean for you in comparison to those set in Ireland?'

22 Prusse had concluded his letter with the following: 'Glenn Patterson once called you "the father of the modern Irish novel". Can you comment on that? How do you see your position among other (Irish) authors?'

Mary Keelan

Foxfield

[*Christmas 1998*]

Dear Mary,
There was no euphemism intended about health and happiness.[23] They were wishes, but probably badly phrased. I live here on a small farm with a few cows, 5 cats, and a dog. My wife and I are the same age and we have no children.

When I thought of you I imagined you as a Professor or Dean or President. We all have fantasies about the lives of others. Elsewhere is nearly always more seductive than Here. Fame or obscurity is relative, and unimportant. It's the spirit that is. Do you know the E. Bishop lines:

> ('O difference that kills,
> or intimidates, much
> of all our small shadowy
> life.')[24]

It's close to Christmas here in a deserted countryside. In a few days I'll pick some holly from the hedges. 'That's life,' our friend across the lake used to say equally cheerfully whether he brought us good news or bad.[25]

I want to wish you and your whole family a happy Christmas and New Year

> With affection
> John

23 This is an undated Christmas card but is almost certainly a follow-up to McGahern's letter to Keelan of 12 October 1998.
24 From Elizabeth Bishop, 'Song for the Rainy Season'.
25 Francie McGarty.

Neill Joy
[*Madeline McGahern*]
Foxfield

[*Christmas 1998*]

Dear Neill and Mary,
It was very nice to get your letter.

We were in Denmark together and M. was 2 weeks in Paris.[26] She brought back 2 Calders, one very fine, a naked clown pursued by black spots (abstract wasps or fate).[27] Here it is the worst winter since 1927. Endless rain. All autumn the place smelled of mud.

I go to U.C.D. in January, for one seminar a week, on Wednesday afternoons. M. didn't want me to take it but I was going to Dublin anyhow to work on the final draft of the novel. Now I'll have an obvious reason to be there.

By coincidence the J.B.Y. Letters will come out at the same time in Paris and London/Sept.–Oct. The Faber cover looks lovely.[28]

I heard the Conrad conference was a great success and was delighted. Liliane Louvel was here in the summer. She said how pleased she was with your invitation but in France you dare not step out of your territory.

Please remember us to our friends, especially the Slaters.[29] I hope you'll remember us over a good dry martini at the Inn.

We miss you and send you our love.

A very happy Christmas (I hate the word merry) and New Year
John & Madeline

---

26 Read at University of Aarhus with Michael Longley.

27 Paintings by the American artist Alexander Calder. See letter to Paul Muldoon [January 1980].

28 See John Butler Yeats, *Letters to His Son W. B. Yeats and Others 1869–1922*, ed. Joseph Hone, abridged and with an introduction by John McGahern (London: Faber, 1999). The front cover of the book reproduces John Butler Yeats's unfinished self-portrait in oil, 1911–22. The back cover bears a reproduction of a pencil drawing of W. B. Yeats by John Butler Yeats from 1886. Faber had wished to carry a photograph of McGahern on the front cover but he argued strongly against the idea.

29 Joe and Vivien Slater.

1999

Joe Kennedy
Foxfield

7 February 1999

Dear Joe,

Thank you for your letter and enclosure.[1]

What good news that Margaret is well. Madeline and I are both very fond of her.

The literary stuff doesn't matter. Literary reputations last as long as the body of work they represent remains useful, whether to one reader or to many, and will disappear into the long night like ourselves, eventually. What matters is the spirit to which they give utterance.

Like many things that come my way that I was once part of, the enclosure is both accurate and inaccurate.

I attended that party in O'Connor's flat.[2] I went reluctantly. Elizabeth Cullinan (Betty) needed an escort.[3] [. . .][4] It was the one time I met Frank O'Connor and he remained in bed throughout my stay, which wasn't long. The prize was the AE Memorial. The Barracks wasn't published then. The English man was almost certainly Philip Edwards, Professor of English at

---

1 Kennedy had sent McGahern an extract from *The Happiness of Getting it Down Right: Letters of Frank O'Connor and William Maxwell 1945–1966*, ed. Michael Steinman (New York: Alfred A. Knopf, 1996). O'Connor wrote the following to Maxwell on 6 January 1963: 'Betty came to a party with her boy, and who should be here but an Englishman who was on the committee that gave him a prize. "So sorry," he said as he left. "He shouldn't have got it, you know, but he was everybody's second best."'

2 Frank O'Connor (1903–66), born Michael O'Donovan in Cork. Short story writer, novelist and playwright – one of the most successful Irish writers of the mid-twentieth century. McGahern also liked to tell an anecdote of this soirée when O'Connor opined that 'nobody has the right to tell the truth'.

3 American writer. See letter to Michael McLaverty [21 March 1963].

4 I have chosen to redact a short section of this letter in the interests of its subject's privacy.

Trinity.[5] Thomas Kinsella was expected to win the AE. I had no hope and only entered at Charles Monteith's insistence.[6] Faber offered to pay the expenses if I lost. Typing 5 or 6 copies of an unfinished novel, having it typed, was expensive then, and it absorbed most of the £100 prize.

The edge to O'Connor's remark was due I imagine to a tv interview I gave on winning the prize.

I was asked, 'What do you think of O'C and O'F?'[7] It was like asking a young writer now, 'What do you think of Heaney and Friel?'

I replied blithely, 'I don't think about them at all,' thinking with a young person's conceit that I had adroitly avoided the question. Elizabeth C. told me that O'Connor had watched the interview and that I couldn't have said a worse thing. So much for conceit! I also said Beckett and Kavanagh were the 2 living Irish writers I most admired. Kavanagh had attacked everybody, including O Connor and O Faolain. I read a long sad attack by O'Connor on Beckett about the same time. My response was an unfair young person's response and I would prefer it to have been different. I think O'Connor's early work, particularly his first book, and the first parts of his autobiography is good work.[8] Too late, too little and it probably wouldn't have done them either.

I'm in U.C.D. on Wednesday afternoons the spring term. I didn't need it and was reluctant, as I'm trying to write the final draft of a novel from a number of drafts, but they couldn't have made it easier or more pleasant.[9]

---

5 Philip Edwards (1923–2015) held the Chair in English Literature at TCD from 1960 to 1966. A scholar of Renaissance literature, in his time at Trinity he became a powerful advocate for the Irish literary tradition and appointed Frank O'Connor to a part-time post. Edwards formed part of the committee that awarded McGahern the AE Memorial Prize in 1962, the same year in which TCD awarded O'Connor an honorary doctorate.

6 See McGahern's letters of 24 January and 10 February 1962 to Monteith.

7 O'Connor and O'Faoláin.

8 McGahern admired O'Connor's early collection of short stories, *Guests of the Nation* (London: Macmillan, 1931). The two volumes of autobiography are *An Only Child* (London: Macmillan, 1961) and *My Father's Son* (London: Macmillan, 1968).

9 McGahern was teaching a Master's in Anglo-Irish Literature course for Declan Kiberd at UCD. The works considered included Somerville and Ross, *The Silver Fox*; Kate O'Brien, *The Ante-Room*; W. B. Yeats, *Purgatory*; J. M. Synge, *The Aran Islands*; Tomás Ó Criomhthain, *The Islandman* (*An tOileánach*); and Primo Levi's *If This is a Man*. He was particularly taken with Alistair MacLeod's stories 'The Closing Down of Summer' and 'The Tuning of Perfection' – and gifted each member of the class a copy of MacLeod's book *As Birds Bring Forth the Sun and Other Stories* (Toronto: McClelland & Stewart, 1986).

I am anxious that it not be publicised, though it will be known anyhow. We can meet some evening.

I was very glad to have John Boland's news and look forward to his book.[10] I read and liked Gerry Dawe's forthcoming poems.[11]

Remember us to Margaret
John

Colm Tóibín
Foxfield

16 May 1999

Dear Colm,

Thank you for your book, and the very generous words about my work.[12] I had no idea whether I'd be included and feel honoured and grateful.[13]

The Burkes were here for lunch. They were a delight. They said how much they enjoyed meeting you again in Dublin.[14]

I hope your own work goes well.

Madeline asks to be remembered to you with affection.

With every good wish
John

10 John Boland's book of poetry, *Brow Head* (Newry: Abbey, 1999).

11 Gerald Dawe, *The Morning Train* (Loughcrew: Gallery Press, 1999). See letter to Dawe of 3 October [1997].

12 Presumably Tóibín had gifted McGahern a copy of his new novel *The Blackwater Lightship* (London: Picador, 1999).

13 This comment refers to *The Modern Library: 200 Best Novels in English Since 1950*, ed. Carmen Callil and Colm Tóibín (London: Picador, 1999). *Amongst Women* was one of the chosen novels. In an amusing letter to McGahern of 11 February 1998, Tóibín describes how extremely difficult he found the process of compiling the list: 'I read half of what I was meant to read; I was, mostly, never sure.' Madeline McGahern Papers.

14 Tom and Donna Burke, mutual friends from St John's, Newfoundland.

26 July 1999

Dear Joe,
Thank you for your kind letter.

Frank was 55 when he died.[15] He must have been about 16 when we put him on the boat.[16] There is a long wait in London between death and burial. It was hard for everybody.

I had more than my share of readings and speeches this summer and they are not quite over yet and I have been fighting to keep space for my own work. I read and liked John Boland's book and have been intending to write him. I thought the obvious influences – Larkin, Kavanagh, Stevens – were wonderfully ironed out in the completed versions.

Please remember me with affection to Margaret.

With every good wish
John

The date was correct

Colm Tóibín
Foxfield

5 October 1999

Dear Colm,
We were in France and only heard of your nomination at the weekend.[17]

I was delighted and offer my congratulations.

Whatever happens in the Guildhall – and I wish you all the luck – it'll make life easier for The Blackwater Lightship.

15 John's younger brother Francis 'Frank' Jude Anthony McGahern died in London on 9 July 1999. He was born on 4 November 1943.
16 McGahern and his sisters assisted Frank in leaving his unhappy boyhood home as an adolescent. McGahern had brought his brother aboard the Holyhead ferry and persuaded a purser to take charge of Frank's money.
17 Tóibín's The Blackwater Lightship was shortlisted for the Booker Prize in 1999. J. M. Coetzee's Disgrace (London: Secker & Warburg, 1999) was the winner.

I was about to write to thank you. I struggled with the opening, but found the Wexford pages very fine, particularly the marvellous portraits of the women.

Madeline sends you her congratulations and good wishes

Affectionately

John

Barry Hanson

[*Madeline McGahern*]

Foxfield

8 October 1999

Dear Barry,[18]

Thank you for your very kind words about Frank. He always spoke of you with affection.

While his death was sudden – driving home after taking his dog for a run in the forest – it was not unexpected, and that is almost the worst part. A year ago he suffered a mild stroke and was told he'd have to quit drink and lose weight if he wanted to live. His response was that he'd do neither. He wasn't about to change his life and he didn't care whether he lived or died.

He continued to drink, if anything more heavily. He was here 3 times in the last year. It wasn't pleasant to have a few drinks together anymore. There was a horrible feeling that you were taking part in something he shouldn't be doing and you should not be part of. But there was nothing that could be done.

Even still, there's a feeling of waste as well as loss.

Nothing much new here. I'm trying to finish a novel that should have been done by now. Madeline is well and asks to be remembered to you.

We were sorry that you have had such turmoil of your own. We hope it'll get easier and that you'll get better and that we'll see you soon.

With my love

John

18 Barry Hanson, husband of Susanna Capon, both old friends of John and Madeline. See letter to Susanna Capon of 17 March 1974.

21 October 1999

Dear Robin,
I enclose the piece and will be happy to go over it again.[19]

The Scott F. is definitely risky but is an attempt to steer it away from the provincial label J. C. O. managed to stick it with.[20]

Come to think of it: Carraway and Gatsby are as provincial as they come, but in the true sense.

I found it very difficult but it was an honour to do. These stories will be around for a long time.

Did you get to see The Rivers of Lapland (Pirandello)? If you have difficulty, I'll try and get you a copy.[21]

Please remember me to Caroline, with affection[22]
and with love
John

---

19 McGahern encloses his essay on Alistair MacLeod's stories, eventually published as an untitled foreword in Alistair MacLeod, *Island: Collected Stories* (London: Jonathan Cape, 2001), vii–xiv. See *LOTW*, 208–12.

20 McGahern opens his foreword to MacLeod's stories by stating that they 'have a uniqueness that is rare in the writing of any time. This quality is easily recognisable but is almost impossible to describe. A different kind of genius marks every magical page of *The Great Gatsby* and "The Rich Boy" and stories like "May Day", yet in much of Scott Fitzgerald's other work, where this rare quality is missing, the writing never rises above the level of competent journeyman.' See *LOTW*, 208. 'J. C. O.' is Joyce Carol Oates b.1938 who was on the University of Windsor faculty with MacLeod, and who wrote an afterword for *The Lost Salt Gift of Blood*.

21 A short story by Luigi Pirandello, first published in English as part of *The Horse in the Moon: Twelve Short Stories* (New York: E. P. Dutton, 1932). Pirandello's work was a long-standing interest of McGahern's.

22 Caroline Michel was then a colleague of Robertson's, running Vintage, the up-market paperback wing of the literary imprints of Random House.

Neill Joy
[*Madeline McGahern*]
Foxfield

16 December 1999

Dear Neill and Mary,
Thank you for your letter, and the very kind invitation: we'd love to go to see you both, but it's too difficult to get away together for any length (cats, cattle, getting somebody to take care of the place, the damned business of writing).

M. goes on her own to Paris and Bordeaux in January. In March we go to Nashville together, and it is just there and back.[23] In May we'll go to Washington for 4 days, and maybe New York, for 2 days at the most.[24]

The Foster review is typical of the academic/intellectual attitude to McCourt here (He has even managed to unite North and South in condemnation, always easier granted than in praise).[25] I think A.A. is a good, very strange book. It is primarily a <u>farce</u> (nobody in Limerick or anywhere else speaks like the McCourts) a kind of kick at humiliation and suffering, not all that far from Stan Laurel & Mack Sennett. There's also the clear evocation of the lanes of Limerick in the naturalistic American school. The weakest part is the literary pretensions. Anyhow, I liked it, and it'll make it more interesting when I meet him in May. He, William Kennedy, Jennifer Johnston (N. of I. novelist) and J. McG. read together in the Kennedy Centre.

There's not much else to report here. Plenty of rain. Plenty of work and money.[26] There's even a very unpleasant anti-immigrant lobby, in a nation that sent its sons and daughters to the four winds. I write about it in a newspaper

23 A colloquy on McGahern and Alice McDermott at Belmont University, attended by several members of faculty from the universities of Angers and Poitiers, some of whom became firm friends of McGahern's.
24 The Washington reading took place in the Kennedy Center.
25 A reference to Roy Foster's review of Frank McCourt's hugely popular memoir *Angela's Ashes*, 'Tisn't: the Million-Dollar Blarney of the McCourts', *New Republic* (1 November 1999), which Neill Joy had sent to McGahern in a letter of 14 November 1999. Foster charges McCourt with playing up to 'the complex attitude of the United States to what it expects the Irish to be'.
26 Ireland went through an economic boom from 1997 to 2007 known colloquially as the Celtic Tiger years. For many, McGahern included, the financial plenty seemed to bring with it a widespread and lamentable coarsening of manners.

essay and wasn't thanked for it in some quarters.[27] I read a marvellous novel set in a University that I've ever read, I think. Also marvellous classic stories by an <u>Alistair McLeod</u>, who teaches at the University of Windsor (Ontario). He has just written a disappointing first novel.[28] It seems art is almost as unpredictable as life, in the making anyway.

We were glad to hear of Edward and Matthew, and all of it such good news.[29]

We had Debbie Knath and Steven here, and John Naughton.[30]

We send you both our love

A very happy Christmas (Merry is never used in Ireland of Christmas, because of its association with 'stimulants', I suspect)

and many years of happiness

John

27 In 'Whatever You Say, Say Nothing', *Irish Times* (26 October 1999), McGahern wrote of Irish post-war migration to Britain: 'They were young, poorly educated for the most part, ill prepared. Names like Holyhead, Chester, Crewe were burned into the national consciousness; but this was a silent generation, and it disappeared in silence.' See *LOTW*, 128–32.

28 Alistair MacLeod's novel *No Great Mischief* was published in 1999 by McClelland & Stewart to critical acclaim but was never liked by McGahern, who was a great fan of MacLeod's short stories and wrote an admiring foreword to *Island: Collected Stories*. See *LOTW*, 208–12.

29 The Joys' two sons – 'Edward' should read 'Edmund'.

30 Deborah Knuth, a Colgate colleague, and her then husband. John Naughton was a Professor of Romance Languages at Colgate. See letter to Alain Delahaye of 16 April 1984.

2000

Neill Joy
[*Madeline McGahern*]
Foxfield

14 January 2000

Dear Neill,
Thank you for the generous and heartening letter about JBY and the Intro.
I'm delighted Mary and you liked the book.

I'll have the Luke [?] corrected for the French edition. It carried over from
the 1944 Hone edition.

Most Irish classics are in print in French, including such books like The
Islandman and On Another Man's Wound, so it was not as wide a field as you
imagined. W.B.Y. hasn't much of a reputation in France, probably because of
the high rhetoric, and France has mostly turned away from poetry.

Madeline says she'll try to get you and Mary a copy of The Swimmers.

Jack would have little to do with them. He maintained that he bullied
them. He was also notoriously tight with money. (Beckett wanted to buy a
painting but he wouldn't give it to them until he went home and returned
with the cash). Think of JBY with money. The most recent biography of Jack
– by Bruce Arnold – is both violent and derisive about JBY.[1] The feminists
also have been going to town on J.B.Y. (The Yeats Sisters and the Cuala).[2]
We are in unfashionable waters but I stick to that incomplete old man. It'll
be interesting to see what kind of reception it gets in France, if it gets any.

Madeline is in France, with a friend in Bordeaux, and she'll spend a couple
of days in Paris on the way home.

I'm working on nothing but the novel. The end is a good way off still, but
it's in sight.

1 Bruce Arnold, *Jack Yeats* (London: Yale University Press, 1998).
2 Refers in part to Gifford Lewis, *The Yeats Sisters and the Cuala* (Dublin: Irish
Academic Press, 1994).

As I wrote, we go to Nashville in March and Washington/New York in May. New York will be a very small affair.[3] They saw I was going to be in Washington.

We have had endless rain – what's new? – and I have never seen the lake so high. For the last few days we've had frost, wonderful clear ringing weather.

Madeline asked me specially to send her love to you both,

and with my love
John

Joe Kennedy
Foxfield

23 February 2000

Dear Joe,

Thank you for your letter, and the very kind words about the Piece.[4] I was reluctant to do it as I'm in the middle of what I hope will be the last section of the novel – after that there is much revision – but they seemed to want it badly.

Anyhow it hit some nerve. I've never had so many letters or calls, and invitation to address a fringe farming organization, a letter from a man in Wicklow who said he used play handball with me all those years ago in Drogheda when, as he put it, 'the sap was rising'.[5] Also from someone who said, 'a prod with a pitchfork would do a world of good.'

I haven't been in Dublin or anywhere recently. We go to Nashville in March where there's a Conference featuring the short stories. Otherwise I'll be just trying to work.

Please tell John Boland how sorry I am to hear about his father.

I hope Margaret will be all right and better soon. We are both very fond of her. Both of you must be very busy with the children and grandchildren.

With every good wish
John

Except briefly for Tony Doyle's removal.[6]

---

3 The New York reading took place at Ireland House, NYU on 18 May.
4 The article in question was 'Rural Ireland's Passing'. It appeared in the Weekend Review section of the *Irish Independent* of 29 January 2000. See *LOTW*, 166–71.
5 McGahern taught for a term in a Drogheda primary school in 1956. It was while living in a boarding house there that he first met Joe Kennedy.
6 Tony Doyle (1942–2000), popular Irish actor who died on 28 January 2000. He had starred as Moran in the BBC adaptation of *Amongst Women*.

Caroline Walsh/James Ryan

Foxfield

6 March 2000

Dear Caroline, dear James,[7]
Thank you for the lovely evening, and the superb dinner.[8] And it was a pleasure to meet your son and daughter.[9]

I enclose the MacLeod. I'm sorry about the marks as I used the copy for preparing classes. I hope they please you. I like The Tuning of Perfection best and I think them all good.[10]

> With every good wish
> Affectionately
> John

Caroline Walsh

Foxfield

14 April 2000

Dear Caroline,
Thank you for your very kind note. Of course the McLeod is yours. I was just sorry for the marks I made while making notes. I'll read the Wharton.[11]

Nashville was more a series of neighbourhoods than a city, and the motor car was king. The weather was 70°, with the great trees coming into leaf, and

---

7 James Ryan b. 1952 is the author of four novels: *Home from England* (London: Phoenix, 1995); *Dismantling Mr Doyle* (London: Phoenix, 1997); *Seeds of Doubt* (London: Weidenfeld & Nicolson, 2001); and *South of the Border* (Dublin: The Lilliput Press, 2008). He launched and directed the Creative Writing programme in the School of English, Drama and Film, UCD, 2006–16. He married Caroline Walsh in 1981.

8 The dinner involved lots of reminiscing about literary Dublin in the 1950s and 1960s, with Caroline Walsh providing many anecdotes about life in the mews at 11 Lad Lane Upper.

9 The children are Matt b. 1983 and Alice b. 1986.

10 The book in question is Alistair MacLeod's *Island: Collected Stories*.

11 Caroline Walsh was a particular admirer of Edith Wharton's work, completing an MA thesis (UCD 1974) on the writer. It is unknown which of Wharton's books is being referred to here.

the people were very open and friendly. There was a lot of Cajun cooking, all kinds of fish, including delicious catfish, and chicken. New York was just New York. It was a bit dull round the hotel – 58th St, between 5th and 6th – but 3rd Avenue was very lively.

As well that evening, I could not have been more glad to see you so happy in your own house.

With my love
John

Colm Tóibín
Foxfield

17 May 2000

Dear Colm,
Thank you for the lunch, and for the Anthology – which is very handsome.[12] I hope it wasn't trouble or expense. I thought the Publisher would just get me a copy. Also for the Gunn and Charming Billy. I found the personality that comes through the Gunn poems extraordinarily attractive.[13] Charming Billy is superb work. You'd think novels like that would put paid to the old vulgar chestnut about material, as if the writer has any choice. I suspect a great part is in discovering what his/her material is. What's marvellous is what A. McD. makes of it![14]

I hope you have a marvellous summer. Maybe you'll tell me when you get back to Dublin? And we can have a dinner to wish you well on your way to New York.

With every good wish
John

12 *Penguin Book of Irish Fiction*, ed. Colm Tóibín (London: Penguin, 1999). From McGahern it contained 'The Country Funeral' and an extract from *The Barracks*.
13 The Thom Gunn collection in question is *Boss Cupid* (London: Faber, 2000).
14 *Charming Billy* (New York: Farrar, Straus and Giroux, 1998) is a novel by American author Alice McDermott that tells the story of Billy Lynch and his lifelong struggle with alcohol after the death of his first love.

Caroline Walsh

Foxfield

9 June 2000

Dear Caroline,
It was lovely to hear from you, and it was very kind to think of me for the MacLeod novel.[15]

I'm glad it gave so much pleasure, and it has got similar reactions from others I trust and respect.

I liked it less than the stories (I read it in Canadian proofs and since then I know Robin Robertson has worked on it with MacLeod). Since I have written an Introduction for Vintage to the stories (there's difficulty over rights, and God knows when it'll appear) I think it's better not to review the novel because of the reservations, though there were true and marvellous bits, especially the opening.

Will James be driving to Italy soon? Will you be able to go?[16] I hope his work goes well and that all the house is well.
> With my love
> John

Belinda McKeon

Foxfield

2 September 2000

Dear Belinda,[17]
Thank you for your card. It reads as if your summer in Italy was a delight, and thank you, too, for the generous words about the TLS piece. I'm writing

---

15 Alistair MacLeod, *No Great Mischief*.
16 Caroline Walsh and James Ryan went to Italy almost every year from the early 1990s to 2010.
17 Belinda McKeon b. 1979, Irish novelist and graduate of TCD and UCD. From 2000 to 2010 she worked for the *Irish Times*, writing on theatre, literature and the arts. In 2005 she moved to New York City, where she completed an MFA at Columbia University. She is currently Assistant Teaching Professor in Creative Writing at Rutgers University. McKeon's first novel, *Solace* (London: Picador, 2011), won the Geoffrey Faber Memorial Prize. Her second novel, *Tender*, was published in 2015 by Picador.

the ending now. It's gone too long and when it's done I will have to cut and shape.[18]

I'd be glad to read your piece, if you'd wish that. I found it hard to concentrate in the hotel, not in the least because of you, but because of some comic goings-on at the end of the room.

I hope you'll be happy in U.C.D. Should you need any advice or help Declan Kiberd in English is a friend and could be very helpful.

If you'd like to come here for a drink or to eat something with Madeline and myself before you head for U.C.D. you'll be welcomed.

With every good wish

John

18 The opening of *That They May Face the Rising Sun* was published in the *Times Literary Supplement* of 30 April 1999 under the title 'Easter'.

2001

James Ryan
Foxfield

19 March 2001

Dear James,

Thank you for <u>Seeds of Doubt</u> and your kind letter.[1] I'm sorry to be so slow in responding but I wanted to be free of my own novel before settling to read.

I enjoyed the first section more than anything you have written, its quiet careful observant control, its life. I could see the 'idea' behind the second part but it ran me into trouble. I felt it broke the novel's flow, even though the writing was a pleasure. I was back in the familiar in the final part but felt something had been lost from the opening, its surefootedness, I think. All this may seem oldfashioned, and may be wrong. There was much I admired, and will reread it in a few weeks.

I saw but the one review, a very fine one by Liam Harte, and was glad.[2] I wish the novel luck and success.

Please remember me to Caroline with affection, and with every good wish, and congratulations

John

1 James Ryan's third novel, *Seeds of Doubt*, was published by Weidenfeld & Nicolson in 2001.
2 Liam Harte's review, titled 'One house, five sisters, one secret', appeared in the *Irish Times* of 10 March 2001. The review compared Ryan's work favourably with McGahern's *Amongst Women*, Seamus Deane's *Reading in the Dark* (London: Jonathan Cape, 1996) and Colm Tóibín's *The Heather Blazing*.

James Ryan
Foxfield

10 April 2001

Dear James,
I was very glad to get your letter, and manly and kind of you to write.
I thought I was too hard and blunt about what I felt didn't work, in spite of
all that I liked. What you say about Templeard is true, dangerously so.[3] Such
places give no quarter to 'postmodernism'. If allowed in at all it (the outside)
can only be let through in glimpses. Why? That leads into deep waters, too
deep for now, or me.

Thanks for the kind invitation. We'd love to see you both, but it's not easy
for the two of us to get away together because of the animals, cows, cats, a
dog. In May I'll probably go to Poland while Madeline is going to Lisbon
with a friend. I know we are very much out of the way but should business
or chance draw you near it would be a great pleasure to have you both here.

Please remember me to Caroline with much affection, and with every good
wish for you and Seeds of Doubt.
                              Affectionately
                              John

                                        Susanne Dumbleton
                                        Foxfield

18 April 2001

Dear Bill,
I meant to write before now to thank you for your card and note of Christmas
and was waiting to finish the novel: it was long, and mostly it was cutting and

---

3 The plot of *Seeds of Doubt* centres on the Mackens of Templeard, a Tipperary
family of five sisters who grow up in the 1930s and 1940s. The opening section is
narrated by Nora Macken who recalls her life from the point of view of the 1970s
and tries to deal with memories of her rape by a priest when she was an adolescent.
Liam Harte's *Irish Times* review of the novel comments that 'Templeard is the most
powerful presence in the novel, a superbly realised physical and figurative entity [. . .]
it acts as a vivid metaphor for the hardening of egalitarian ideals into exclusivist
dogmas in post-independence Ireland.'

editing, and took longer than I thought. It's gone now. Faber will publish it in the spring. They are going to make it their main book. I promised Colgate I'd go back when it was done and I'm going in the Fall. All that time I thought it might never be done but now I'm sort of looking forward to a quiet time there before coming back to face the music. I'm not looking forward to that. A very old friend of ours died in Colgate this year, Joe Slater: he edited, and wrote a very fine Introduction, to the Emerson/Carlyle Correspondence.

We had a very pleasant winter here, going nowhere. We had a very nice evening with Patsy in Dublin just as she was facing into the editing of her magazine.[4] That was well before Christmas and she must be busy.

I'm going on a skite to Poland in early May – they are bringing out The Pornographer – and Madeline is going to Lisbon for 10 days or so when I get back.

The cows are waiting for the clover, oblivious of the foot and mouth. We are hoping we'll escape.[5]

Madeline sends her best to Sue and yourself
And with my love
John

Susanne Dumbleton

Foxfield

28 May 2001

Dear Bill,
It was very nice to receive your kind card. I had a good time in Poland, though the publisher in Warsaw worked me like a borrowed donkey. The people were very attractive, Catholic, serious, from a long tradition of spirituality,

---

4 Patsey Murphy, Susanne Dumbleton's sister, and editor of the *Irish Times* Weekend supplement.
5 Ireland experienced its first foot and mouth disease outbreak since 1941 in March 2001. For three months the country's farming community and government watched as the disease took hold in Britain. Stringent control measures were put in place by the Irish Department of Agriculture, Food and Rural Development to try to prevent transmission of the disease from the UK, to limit the extent of the outbreak that did occur and to prevent its spread. These control measures had their greatest knock-on effects on the tourist and service sectors, particularly in rural areas, as much of the countryside was placed off-limits for the three-month period. The disease did not strike the McGaherns' cattle.

rigour, openness. A part of France may have been like that once. I spoke in a nineteenth-century mansion in the middle of Lodz, built for a Jewish textile manufacturer. There were 25,000 Jews in Lodz before the war. Now there are 200. In the weedinfested Jewish cemetery there was an unfilled trench, where they were still carrying out executions as Lodz was being liberated. I found the blackened streets very moving. Everywhere people were selling flowers, even small lilac branches.[6] Madeline is in Lisbon now.

I'm easy about Albany. I have to speak in Swathmore and Princeton in September and I have agreed to go out to Notre Dame though the date hasn't been fixed, probably in October. Bill Kennedy asked me to Albany when the novel is out.[7] I'm not anxious for too much running.

(Knopf) Sonny Mehta says he loves the novel – 'miraculous' was the strange word – but I know it's no more than a lottery. He's not sure about the title while Faber is very happy.[8]

I have heard South Africa is dangerous and very beautiful. There's a Sauvignon blanc Steenberg I like we get from a specialist shop in Temple Bar.

The cattle have no idea the disease is rampant.[9] They are spoiled. They come up to the house and boo in when they feel things are not in order.

> Are you coming to Dublin this summer?
> With my love to you both
> John

6 A number of Irish writers had been invited to Poland by the Polish academic Jerzy Jarniewicz and Irish poet Cathal McCabe. The group included McGahern, Bernard O'Donoghue, Justin Quinn, Harry Clifton, Deirdre Madden, Edna Longley and Gerry Dawe. Bernard O'Donoghue recalls McGahern being in terrific form and delivering a marvellous talk without notes, hands in pockets: 'I particularly remember how enthused he was by the agricultural terrain on the bus trip from Warsaw to Łódź. He was extraordinarily positive and genial throughout.'
7 By 2001 the Dumbletons had moved to Chicago where Susanne became dean at DePaul University; McGahern read there after his appearance at Notre Dame in South Bend, Indiana on 9 October.
8 *That They May Face the Rising Sun* was eventually published in the US under the title *By the Lake*.
9 Foot and mouth disease. See letter to Bill Dumbleton of 18 April 2001.

20 June 2001

Dear Seamus,
It was pleasant to hear from you, and very kind of you to write. I thought it showed the height of great good sense to absent yourself from the Dublin Carnival.[10]

The Naipaul evening went well and I was at Dublin Castle for the Macleod Award.[11] He was courteous, redfaced, and very suspicious looking – it probably stood him in good stead – and he had brought his wife and daughter and five sons. With pride he pointed out that 3 of the 5 were redhaired.

A few weeks ago I was in Poland and met a delightful man from Warrenpoint – Cathal McCabe – who spoke of you with great affection and admiration.[12]

Madeline asks to be remembered to Marie and you with affection
and with love, and every good wish
John

10 The Dublin Writers' Festival, June 2001.
11 V. S. Naipaul (1932–2018) and McGahern discussed their work at the National Gallery as part of the Dublin Writers' Festival earlier in June. Later in the year Naipaul was awarded the Nobel Prize for Literature. Alistair MacLeod's novel *No Great Mischief* was awarded the International IMPAC Dublin Literary Award for 2001.
12 Cathal McCabe b. 1963, a poet from Co. Down, lectured at the University of Łódź and worked as literature consultant with the British Council in Warsaw. From 2003 until 2009 he was director of the Irish Writers' Centre in Dublin. He and Heaney established the Ireland-Poland Cultural Foundation, and in 2010 both men were awarded the Polish government's prestigious Gloria Artis medal for outstanding services to Polish culture.

Frances Byrnes

Colgate

16 November 2001

Dear Frances,

How kind of you to write, and how generous, and I'm delighted it pleased you. Remember it was you who helped me find my way into that novel when you commissioned the story, and we made it together, the lake, the mart, the murder – 'I was in life, what else could I do?'[13] I then wrote it and it ran to over a thousand pages and was then cut down in many writings. I had become almost a master of avoidances.

I promised to return here when the novel was done and am here since August 25th. Madeline came on September 11th and the plane had to turn back and she was caught in London for a week.[14] She goes home in early December. I should get away about the 15th. It's pleasant and easy here and I'm savouring these last few weeks as I'll have to face the publication almost as soon as I get home.[15]

I'll be in London a number of times in January. Are you likely to be there at any time then?[16]

---

13 McGahern is responding to Byrnes's letter praising *That They May Face the Rising Sun*. She had read a preview copy of it and had immediately written. It is clear that the process of writing 'Love of the World' had been an important prompt towards what became the novel. On 11 January 2002 McGahern repeated the connection between the radio commission of 'Love of the World' and *That They May Face the Rising Sun* on BBC Radio 3's programme *Nightwaves*. It was subtitled 'A cultural map of Ireland: Enniskillen'.

14 On 11 September 2001 an Islamic fundamentalist organisation known as al-Qaeda murdered 2,996 people in an audacious terrorist attack on New York City and Washington DC using hijacked aircraft. Chaos ensued for some time across US and transatlantic air routes. As the letter indicates, Madeline's plane was in the air, heading across the Atlantic, when news of the attack reached the pilot and he turned back for London Heathrow.

15 McGahern used some of this period in Colgate to promote his new novel, to be published in December by Knopf under the title *By the Lake*. In October he read at both Notre Dame University, Indiana and DePaul University, Chicago.

16 McGahern and Byrnes met in London on 13 January 2002 at McGahern's hotel reception, Hazlitt's of Soho. They then went out for a meal nearby at Andrew Edmonds in Lexington Street where McGahern first told Byrnes the story of Jimmy

I have been smiling at the thought of your mother and her friends and Apollo's chariot.[17] In Carrick-on-Shannon I found her a FORCE.[18]

How are you now?

I often think of you and always with great affection.

John

Niall MacMonagle

Foxfield

14 December 2001

Dear Niall,[19]

Thank you for writing.

Your letter made me glad, and it was humbling in its generosity.[20]

Whenever I heard or read you over the years I always admired your integrity and independence and was very happy to meet you in Kildare.[21]

Maybe some day we'll drink tea or Powers together, depending on health and inclination, in Leitrim or in Dublin . . .[22]

A very happy Christmas and New Year

Sincerely

John McGahern

Gralton who was deported to the US from Ireland for his left-wing views. See letter to Byrnes of 2 April 2002.

17 Byrnes's mother and a friend had recently visited Versailles where they saw the Fountain of Apollo, depicting the Greek sun god rising from the sea at daybreak in his four-horse chariot. Presumably the prompt for some now lost joke.

18 Byrnes, her mother and McGahern had met for lunch at the Landmark Hotel, Carrick-on-Shannon on 29 August 2000.

19 Niall MacMonagle b.1954, teacher, critic, interviewer who contributes regularly to RTÉ Radio 1 and writes a weekly arts column in the *Sunday Independent*. He served on the Boards of the National Library and the estate of Seamus Heaney and was awarded an Honorary Doctorate of Letters by UCD for services to literature.

20 MacMonagle had written McGahern an admiring note about *That They May Face the Rising Sun*.

21 Probably a reference to the Kildare Readers' Festival.

22 Of commonly sold Irish whiskeys, Powers was McGahern's favourite. He especially liked a 'White Powers' bottling sold to select customers by William Blake's bar, Enniskillen. See letter to Robin Robertson of 16 July 1989.

Marie Reddan
[*Madeline McGahern*] (email)
Foxfield

8 January 2002

Dear Marie,[1]
Thank you for your very kind letter.

Over the years I have received a number of approaches, such as Trinity, and from dealers mostly in the States who had contacts with institutions, but in no case did I take the matter any further than to record their interest for a future time.[2]

When Seamus relayed your offer, I had no idea what the market value might be, and I made enquiries.[3] To my surprise, I was told that the offer was much too low. The £750,000 the National Library paid Brian Friel was quoted, and an English source placed the value on the papers as much higher, with the advice to wait. I was also told that it would reflect badly on the estate if I was to accept a low sum out of sentiment, and bluntly stated that in their opinion Galway did not have the funds at their disposal but that they were available elsewhere.

I have told Seamus all of this. He also knows my preference but agrees that it cannot be just a matter of sentiment.

I would be glad to meet, but this isn't a good time because of all the business and travel around the publication. I will be speaking in Galway on

1 Marie Reddan, Librarian, James Hardiman Library, NUIG.
2 As early as 1965, Howard Gotlieb at Boston University was seeking to acquire McGahern's papers.
3 Seamus O'Grady, McGahern's primary contact at NUIG whom he had worked with as far back as the late 1970s. The university brokered an agreement to purchase McGahern's papers the following year and they now reside in Special Collections of the James Hardiman Library, NUIG.

February 19th, and that would be a better time, since the publication should be all over by then.

> With good wishes
> Sincerely
> John McGahern

Niall Walsh Papers

Foxfield

22 January 2002

Dear Niall,

Thank you for writing and for your kind words about the novel.

I am sorry that Dick has died and was about to write to you to offer my sympathy and Madeline's. I had heard from Oonagh that he was very unwell – I have to speak for her in Aberdeen in April – and asked if there was anything we could do.[4] We would have been glad to, but knew it was unlikely that we could do anything useful. She said she'd convey all our good will and wishes.

We saw him last when he came to collect Niall in August.[5] He was very good company but looked ill. We asked him if he'd like to come for an evening but he said he'd prefer to wait till Christmas when we'd be back from the States and the book was out.

I was in London when he died and heard the bad news this weekend. We were fond of him, and he did us many favours when we were beginning here.[6] When I saw him in recent years I had a strange feeling that he was very lonely, but it wasn't something that [could] be spoken.

All our generation is in the waiting area now. I have always felt and feel it even more now that a lot of life is luck.

I hadn't seen Ian in many years – though would hear from him from time to time – but he was often witty and fun to be with. I thought his book Money was very fine.[7]

4 Oonagh Walsh, daughter of Niall and Phil Walsh.
5 'Niall' is Niall Walsh's son.
6 Dick Walsh was Niall's brother and a planning officer in Co. Leitrim who had been a great help to John and Madeline in their move to Foxfield. See letter to Niall Walsh of 14 December 1973.
7 Ian Hamilton, an important early friend and supporter of McGahern's, died on 27 December 2001. The book McGahern refers to was a collection of Hamilton's literary essays titled The Trouble with Money (London: Bloomsbury, 1998).

I'll be glad when the publicity around the novel is over, which should be soon now.

> Madeline sends her sympathy and good wishes
> with affection
> John

Frances Byrnes

Foxfield

27 February 2002

Dear Frances,

Thank you for your kind letters. I knew there was something wrong – though I had few symptoms – and got admitted to hospital as soon as the publicity circus was over. The bad news was that I had a cancerous tumour in the colon. The good news: it hadn't spread. Only one lymph gland on the edge of the tumour was infected. All the others were benign. The surgery was severe and all engagements had to be cancelled. I should get out of hospital in about a week. Then I'll have mild therapy over 9 months, coming in occasionally as an outpatient to clear up or attempt to clear anything that may have escaped the surgery. You have been through all this in a much more serious way. You'll know more about it than I. I'll be grateful for you to use your own discretion. I'd say it's useless telling the BBC lady as I never met her.[8]

I look saintly now, not a very desirable appearance, but I'm told I should be back to myself in 6–8 weeks. We can go over all your proposals in 3 or 4 weeks.[9]

8 Byrnes's radio unit's then editor, Elizabeth Burke. Byrnes was offering a suggestion to her that John write an edition of *Another Country*, a series of Radio 3 programmes in which writers wrote a non-fiction/memoir or 'personal journey' about a place that was fundamental to their life story. Byrnes asked McGahern for permission to mention his diagnosis to Burke, in case it impacted on his capacity to write to a particular deadline.

9 The proposals were: to write an edition of *Another Country*, a forty-five-minute written feature evoking a place that was integral to the writer's life for BBC Radio 3. This would be recorded in Foxfield. McGahern was the only suggestion Byrnes made and his name was accepted; a TV feature to BBC 4 – a portrait of McGahern – similarly set at Foxfield; the possible development of a feature or radio drama about Jimmy Gralton.

Please forgive this hospital scribble but I wanted to get you the news.
Madeline sends you her love,
and with my dear love
John

Frances Byrnes

Foxfield

2 April 2002

Dear Frances,

Thank you for your very kind letter. I am out of hospital, tending the cattle, going for the odd walk, drinking the occasional glass of wine – waiting to be called for chemotherapy, one hour a week in Dublin for 24 weeks. I had so resigned myself to a worse fate that I cannot believe it, as if it is unlucky to think I may be all right for a time.

I'm also carving up the novel for Book at B. An adaptation has been done, very skilfully getting all the material in, but taking the life out of the prose. I didn't want to do the adaptation, but they want me to do the reading, and there was no other way. It's set for May 3rd.

Your own proposals[10]

1. I see no difficulty. There is a script (done some years ago for The New York Times) that would have to be revised and brought up to date.[11]

2. The best short film on me was done by Ted Dolan, who used to work at RTE, but now has his own company. He's an intelligent, nice man, and would be easy for you to work with as producer. He'd be able to work with BBC technicians or get his own. We'd want to have something definite before approaching him. On the other hand, if they have a different director in mind or other ideas I am open.

3. – Gralton – we can talk it over. His nephew and an old I.R.A. man came to the house years ago and walked up and down the lane while I read about him and wouldn't leave until I agreed to open the first Commemoration

10 See letter to Byrnes of 27 February 2002.
11 Refers to an article he wrote for the New York Times on Co. Leitrim titled 'The Plain Ways of Leitrim' (May 1992). He recycled the article many times. See LOTW, 428.

of him in Effernagh.[12] 'I'll be home for Bonfire Night,' he wrote. 'I'll be home for Bonfire Night in Effernagh.'[13]

The novel <u>By the Lake</u> is getting some extraordinary reviews and coverage in the U.S., far more than for any of my other books.[14] There are complaints – the characters seem to have no purpose, there's no plot, no concessions to the limited attention span of the modern reader – but these are a minority.

I look forward to seeing you soon

With my love

John

Louis de Paor

Foxfield

10 April 2002

Dear Louis,[15]

I have written down Thursday June 20th. That day suits me well.[16] I was about to write to you, saying that I'd be able to do the cancelled evening anytime, but aware that this is probably a very bad time in the term – with the exams so close.

Did you ever get a copy of <u>By the Lake</u>, the U.S. edition? Why I ask is that I have a feeling that a whole list I sent in was lost or overlooked.

I'm looking after the few cattle, and around the fields. I have a feeling I was lucky insofar as anything at all can be said about such things.

---

12 Jimmy Gralton (1886–1945) from Effernagh, just outside Carrick-on-Shannon, Co. Leitrim became the only Irish citizen ever to be deported from the country when he was forcefully removed and put on a boat to America, accused of Communist agitation. In 2014 his story became the subject of a film directed by British director Ken Loach, titled *Jimmy's Hall*.

13 Bonfire Night is celebrated annually in Ireland – particularly in the west – on St John's Eve, 23 June.

14 Perhaps the most notable of such reviews was that written by Hilary Mantel in the *New York Review of Books* for 23 May 2002, which opens as follows: 'This is a novel about a private and particular world, which the reader enters as an eavesdropper. The writing is so calm that it seems the text is listening to itself. Its accent is a dying fall and its only tricks are tricks of the light.'

15 Louis de Paor b. 1961 is a Cork-born Irish-language poet and the director of the Centre for Irish Studies at NUIG.

16 De Paor had asked McGahern to give a guest lecture at NUIG on *The Islandman* (*An tOileánach*), Tomás Ó Criomhthain's account of life on the Blasket Islands.

It'll be a pleasure to see you again.

> With every good wish
> John

> Caroline Walsh
> Foxfield

26 April 2002

Dear Caroline,

Thank you for your kind and thoughtful letter. I'll be glad to do the O'Malley but would need a look at the new edition. How many words?[17]

We are such old friends that it's better to be plain about the illness. For some time I knew I had something wrong – though when I went to the doctor over a year ago he discounted the symptoms. When the publishing rounds were over I got myself admitted to the Mater. I had a tumour in the colon. All engagements had to be cancelled. There was an uncertain 36 hours while they discovered the cancer hadn't spread. I got great and instant care. The operation was successful but a small mistake was made with a catheter during surgery that led to all sorts of complications and prolonged my stay from 10 days to 5 weeks.

I am well now and go in as an outpatient for a course of chemo. Once a week, lasts an hour, four Thursdays at a time, then 3 weeks off, and it'll go on till November, when I'm told that I should be all right insofar as we can say anything about these things. My own feeling is that I was probably lucky.

I had a very nice note from Patsy Murphy. How is Patsy now?[18] We have had a few magical days, but weather soon takes away everything it gives. As I write hailstones are hitting the window. Are you going to Italy this summer? How are the kids? Though it's more lady and gentleman now.

Please remember us both to James with affection.

> And with much love
> John

---

17 McGahern reviewed Ernie O'Malley's memoir of Ireland's revolutionary years, *On Another Man's Wound*, in the *Irish Times* of 8 June 2002 under the title 'Return of the Revolutionary'.

18 Patsey Murphy was a colleague at the *Irish Times*. See letter to Bill Dumbleton of 4 December 1990.

Listowel Festival

Foxfield

26 April 2002

Dear Ms O'Connor,[19]
Thank you for your letter of April 23rd.[20] I'll be happy to arrive at the Arms Hotel before 5 p.m. As my wife will be travelling with me I will need a double room (and will be glad to pay any difference). That is on Wednesday 29th May.

I have this difficulty with Thursday May 30th, 12.30 p.m.
Very recently I had to enter hospital for surgery. The operation was successful and I am well again but have to attend for therapy. This is scheduled for May 16th, 23rd, 30th into June. We had planned to drive from Listowel early on Thursday morning to keep the appointment in the Mater on the 30th.

I would be honoured to read from the novel at 12.30 but am reluctant to ask for the therapy to be rescheduled to Tuesday or Friday unless I know I'll be required to read on Thursday. I feel very uneasy requesting this, not least out of respect to the other Finalists, the Judges, the Committee: but my position as regards the hospital and treatment is delicate. Any information you would choose to give me I would hold in strict confidence and would be grateful for the same concerning my medical situation.

Either way I look forward to seeing you on Wednesday 29th.

Yours sincerely

John McGahern

19 Maria O'Connor, administrator at Listowel Writers' Week Festival, Listowel, Co. Kerry. O'Connor had written to McGahern via Faber on 5 April to tell him that *That They May Face the Rising Sun* had been shortlisted for the Kerry Ingredients Irish Fiction Award worth €10,000. The judges were Eileen Battersby of the *Irish Times* and the author Eugene McCabe. The other shortlisted novelists were Fergus O'Connell, Monica Tracey, Eoin McNamee and Sean O'Reilly. O'Connor invited McGahern to attend the opening night in the Listowel Arms Hotel at which the winner would be announced.
20 O'Connor had written on 23 April setting out details for the prizegiving at Listowel, including a requirement for the winning author to read from their work on the day after the awards ceremony.

Michael Gorman

Foxfield

17 May 2002

Dear Michael,

It was very nice to hear from you, and please thank Skip for the enclosures if it was he who sent them.[21] I gave <u>Stoner</u> to Caroline Michel of <u>Vintage</u> in London. She loved the book and bought it together with <u>Augustus</u>.[22] The interview and cuttings will be useful.

I knew there was something wrong with me for about a year though a doctor discounted the symptoms and when the publicity rounds were done I got myself into the Mater. I had a tumour in the colon. There was an uncertain 24 hours or so until they discovered the cancer hadn't spread and was easily operable. This was a success but a mistake was made with a catheter during surgery that led to trauma and septicaemia and kept me in hospital for 5 weeks. My own feeling is that I was fairly lucky. I go in now for mild chemotherapy, an hour every Thursday, 4 Thursdays in a row, two Thursdays free, and it'll last till November. It's not pleasant but it's not too bad either.

I had to give some interviews from the broad of my back like a good courtesan when the book came out in the States [Knopf reprinted it 3 times in the last month which was a big surprise: that never happened there to any of my other books]. Everything had to be cancelled, but I am working normally again. I am speaking for Louis de Paor on June 26th and it'd be very nice to see you all then.

21 Arkansas author Donald Slaven 'Skip' Hays b. 1947 served as director of the Programs in Creative Writing at the University of Arkansas in Fayetteville from 1998 to 2013 and was regularly involved in summer writing workshops at UCG. Hays is best known for his baseball novel *The Dixie Association* (New York: Simon & Schuster, 1984).

22 Skip Hays, who, like the then neglected Texan novelist John Williams, lived in Fayetteville, Arkansas, had brought Williams's work to McGahern's attention. McGahern was immediately impressed, particularly with the novels *Stoner* and *Augustus*. He, in turn, brought the work to the attention of Caroline Michel and wrote prefaces for both books when they were published by Vintage Classics in 2003. For reproductions of these prefaces, see *LOTW*, 213–24. *Stoner* went on to sell tens of thousands of copies, becoming a publishing sensation.

I'm very glad to have the memoriam card. I remember vividly the visit to the house when your grandmother, and mother, and father were there.

Please give my love to Margaret and the girls.

With every good wish, and thanks again for the cuttings

John

Clare Reihill
[*Madeline McGahern*] (email)

Foxfield

24 May 2002

Dear Clare,[23]

Thank you for your letter. I am really sorry you were upset by remarks about the cover, and I want to assure you that there is nothing personal in those remarks.[24] It was all about business. I have been open about the cover from the beginning, perhaps sometimes too much so, and the last thing I'd want is to be covert or hidden about it, least of all to you.

The remarks in my last letter to you were occasioned by the new cover, with the highlighted print, which Jon sent.[25] As I wrote Jon, it is an improvement. The remarks really go back to the choice of image rather than the cover itself and to the beginning of the summer, when the selection of an image for the cover began. What I was expressing was regret that we couldn't have sat down then and come up with some agreed images to present to Pentagram, which would have avoided all that was to happen under pressure.

This is my experience of our dealings. At the beginning you presented me with three possible covers from Pentagram and told me you had picked the images yourself from a book of Irish art published by Lilliput. I thought they were too abstract and arty. The one you liked best was by Patrick Scott, a sort of abstract sun, which I saw as a weak, tasteful parody of the book. The only one I thought possible was an O'Connor, which you seemed to like least.

23 Clare Reihill then worked at Faber, subsequently at Fourth Estate and now with the T. S. Eliot estate. McGahern had known her since the late 1980s when he became friendly with her and her then husband, Robin Robertson.
24 McGahern was unhappy with the cover image on Faber's first edition of *That They May Face the Rising Sun*. The design by Pentagram features a black and white photograph of leaves by Paul Strand, titled *Leaves, Orgeval, France, 1965*. The cover of the proof copy featured a sepia image of a budding willow tree.
25 Jon Riley was McGahern's editor at Faber at that time.

It was then decided to try plain colour and print, but the results of that were thought too risky for a novel. I was beginning to feel at this stage that we should have been able to find an agreed image together before approaching Pentagram. The trouble was that I was not consulted. We then met at your request in Enniskillen. You said that Pentagram was complaining that they had already been put through too much work already over the cover. I suggested a detail from a Breughel, such as The Wedding, but you said that was out because it had been used on a Michael Frayn book. I offered to find an image, but the suggestion went unheeded. You told me that Jon Riley had put you in charge of the cover and that a decision had to be made before Jon came back off holiday, and you were making it. With some excitement, you said you were going to Dublin for a week or more, and would comb the galleries, and that you were certain that you'd find something for the cover. My dismay must have showed, or I said something. By way of reassurance you said that the book was so good that any cover with my name on it would sell. I wasn't reassured.

When I got home I picked the Sudeck and Strand's cornfield.[26] I was looking for something that would reflect honestly some aspect of the book and make it attractive to a potential customer. You then sent me an image of a boy in a boat out on a lake that you found in a gallery. There's not a sensitive boy in sight in the novel, and, again, it harks back to clichés of my early work. By this time, I felt that we were unable to communicate, and it was around this time that I talked to Joanna.[27]

I know the Sudeck couldn't be used, through no fault of yours. I had often wondered what happened to the suggestion of Strand's cornfield, and heard nothing about it until your last email. I assume that the choice of the leaves was yours as Madeline mentioned that during a phone call to the U.S. you told her that you had been going through a book of Strand's photographs and kept coming back to this one photograph that you felt was right. You also told me that Robin's friends thought it a wonderful choice, which I wondered at because I know they hadn't read the book. If I am wrong, I apologise.[28]

26 A black and white photograph suggested by Madeline. Josef Sudek (1896–1976), a Czech photographer, best known for his photographs of Prague. Paul Strand (1890–1976), American photographer and film maker whose image of the leaves was eventually used as the cover.
27 Joanna Mackle at Faber with whom John had worked closely on the production of Amongst Women. See Joanna Mackle, 'The publishing of Amongst Women', The John McGahern Yearbook, vol. 1, 88–91.
28 Robin Robertson, the Scottish poet, novelist and editor, was then married to Clare Reihill.

After my initial reaction to the cover, for weeks I hoped that I was wrong, but right across the board, when I was helping to publicize the novel, I discovered that people found the cover depressing and unrepresentative of the book's spirit. Among the Christmas books it looked especially funereal, if it could be picked out at all. Recently, Lindsay Duguid's husband told me that he used it in a class on book design as an example of a bad cover.[29] These are the facts as I see them. They do not involve our feeling for you and Robin. It was a business that went wrong through aesthetic differences and a lack of communication.

Beyond all that, I am enormously grateful to you for your appreciation of the book and your communication of that enthusiasm to people like Niall MacMonagle, who helped the book greatly – and I am sure to many others I don't know of.[30]

It will be lovely to see you in Listowel.[31] We'll be driving straight from there to Dublin, and should it suit you it would be a pleasure to have your company. We plan to leave early in the morning, 6.30–7.00, with this possible disruption: whoever wins the prize is expected to give a reading at noon on Thursday. Should that happen to me, we would obviously have to wait until after the reading.

Please give our love to Robin, and with love to you,

John

Niall Walsh Papers

Foxfield

27 May 2002

Dear Niall,

Thank you for your letter, and the response to the article. I'm glad it pleased you. I know of Being and Time but never attempted it, thinking it would be too difficult. What you attribute makes sense. That together with the pulse of

---

29 Lindsay Duguid was then fiction editor at the *Times Literary Supplement*.
30 On Niall MacMonagle see letter of 14 December 2001.
31 The Listowel Writers' Week Festival. *That They May Face the Rising Sun* was named as the winner of the €10,000 Kerry Ingredients Irish Fiction Award on the opening night of the festival, 29 May.

being could be a description of Homer's world. It's interesting that language loses that immediate power as well, as it expands.[32]

I think my Chemo must be very light compared to what you have been through.[33] It's unpleasant but very tolerable. It lasts until November. I have a number of public things coming up and I'm not looking forward to them as they are threaded through the treatment. I get some priceless encouragement like, 'HANG IN THERE' and 'DON'T GIVE UP,' as if I was suddenly part of a different process but I'm sure it must be all very familiar.

I hope it goes well with Niall in Budapest. I thought he was depressed when he was here last summer.[34] Drop a note or call when you get back and I'll look forward to that evening in Dublin. Madeline sends you her good wishes,

and with mine,
John

Joe Kennedy
Foxfield

7 June 2002

Dear Joe,
Thank you for your letter, and the cutting. Please give our love to Margaret. We are both very fond of her.

As far as I understand, Faber submitted the novel, at Listowel's request. It wasn't an easy position but I decided to go. Listowel is as worthy as any other place. I was by far the oldest, and the others needed the prize more than I did. These prizes are all lotteries, like most things. Enough said.

The novel was a surprise success in the U. S., both in coverage and sales. Knopf had to reprint 3 times in the last month. There were complaints: no plot, uncouth people, too much demands on the attention span of the modern reader etc. but they were in the minority, luckily.

I am slowly working again, doing an introduction to a neglected American writer I admire, John Williams, and I am to speak in public for the first time

---

32 McGahern had sent a copy of his frequently revised article on Tomás Ó Criomhthain's *The Islandman* (*An tOileánach*), titled 'What Is My Language?', to Walsh. See *LOTW*, 260–74. Walsh, in a letter of 23 May 2002, had commented on certain similarities between Ó Criomhthain's and Heidegger's worldviews.
33 Niall Walsh was successfully treated for cancer in the early 1990s.
34 Niall Walsh's son.

since the illness, in Galway, and Carlow. I have to go in for treatment but have a break now till June 27th.

Maybe we'll have that long delayed drink or meal with John Boland then?
Please remember me to them
With every good wish to you both
John

Caroline Walsh

Foxfield

10 June 2002

Dear Caroline,

Thank you for your kind congratulations and for giving the O'Malley such a handsome show.[35] It was a delight to get your letter, and we will look forward to seeing you and James in August. I hope you have a great time in Italy.

The fields here are like porridge. Matt and his tractor would disappear if he attempted to cut silage.[36] I remember hearing that Aidan Higgins was master of the 'revels' down in Nerja all those years ago.[37]

Patsy telephoned and I'm hoping to see her before too long.[38] I think my dosage is probably much less severe than Patsy's but it lasts till November. I have a break till June 27th, and am giving readings in Galway and Carlow (readings that were cancelled when I went into hospital). They'll be my first appearances since the Purcell Room at the end of January.[39] I'm not looking forward to them but I think I'll be all right. My dear Uncle, who treated his customers like minions and was upset if he got anything other than total

---

35 McGahern reviewed a reissued edition of Ernie O'Malley's *On Another Man's Wound* in the *Irish Times* of 8 June 2002 under the title 'Return of the Revolutionary'.
36 The reference to Matt and silage is to Walsh's son Matt's interest in farming, with which McGahern was fascinated.
37 Nerja, southern Spain. A number of Irish writers spent time there or in the general vicinity in the 1960s and early 1970s. See Aidan Higgins's *Balcony of Europe* (London: Calder & Boyars, 1972). Tom Kilroy was based there for a period during the late 1960s and into 1970, during which time Caroline spent some months with the family as a childminder.
38 Patsey Murphy, Caroline Walsh's colleague at the *Irish Times*.
39 The Purcell Room is a performance space in London's Southbank Centre. The late January event mentioned here involved a reading from *That They May Face the Rising Sun* followed by an interview with Professor Hermione Lee.

subservience, used to complain, 'You know, Madeline, you have no idea what it's like dealing with the public nowadays.'

> Please remember me to James
> and with my love, my dear Caroline
> John

> Frances Byrnes
> Foxfield

8 July 2002

Dear Frances,

It was a pleasure, a pure pleasure to see and to have you here.[40] Madeline says there was just a small error in the email address but that was enough.

I got through Galway and Carlow without difficulty, though it was a little strange to be so public again. People were talking about the characters in the novel as if they were real people. That was even stranger.

I found that the article wasn't of any use, and I have started from scratch in the first person. I don't think it will take long.[41] The trouble is that there is so much material that I have never faced in this way before, and to keep it to what's relevant. The first thing is to get it down. I'm now finishing the first part, the various schools I attended with my mother, schools in which she taught, all that old suffering that has to be to some extent partly concealed.

Your mother wrote me a very nice letter. I meant to answer and <u>may have</u> but it may also have slipped by in all the recent confusion. If I have not, would you please thank her for me?

There's not much news. The meadows are still not cut and the fields impassable. The novel is still selling in America.

> Madeline sends her love
> and with my love
> John

---

40 Byrnes had been recording with Michael Longley on 17 June 2002 in Belfast, and stayed in a B&B in Ballinamore, Co. Leitrim that night. McGahern fetched her from her accommodation on the morning of the 18th to bring her to Foxfield for lunch and talk with himself and Madeline. One of the matters discussed was what McGahern might write about for his edition of the series *Another Country*. They agreed that it would be about him coming home to, and living in, the place that he was from.
41 Refers to his essay 'The Plain Ways of Leitrim' (May 1992).

P.S. In the light of having too much material, would it be an idea to do a separate programme on the Catholic Church, its total power when I was young, its total collapse, and to tie it in with Gralton, using Gralton as a footnote. And to leave the Church as much as possible out of this script, confining it to place. As far as I can see it'll have to be that way anyway because of space. What do you think?[42]

John

The most competitive oncologist in Ireland is at present sunning himself in Spain, outswimming everyone.[43] The chemo is now biting, its effect seems to be cumulative, but it's still all right.

John

Frances Byrnes (email)
Foxfield

23 July 2002

Dear Frances,
I wrote the new Leitrim piece from scratch, without consulting the text you have, but, naturally, some of it is very similar and covers the same ground. I think you should see it before I go on, as this piece will take about 25 minutes. The last section should cover change in Leitrim and can include the Catholic Church. I'm not sure how much you want to keep for questions or textual readings. As I suspected, there is too much material.[44]

I wouldn't have any interest in dramatizing Gralton. There might be material for a short documentary, but it's not essential.

---

42 Byrnes agreed that McGahern should focus his *Another Country* script on place rather than the Church and Gralton, as the writer's relationship with a place was the series' subject.

43 Professor Des Carney who was treating McGahern for his cancer at the Mater Private Hospital, Dublin.

44 Byrnes had visited the McGaherns in Foxfield in late June 2002 and sent a follow-up email on 28 June trying to firm up plans for the BBC Radio 3 programme *Another Country*. McGahern sent on two pieces: the first is titled 'Leitrim Piece' and is very similar to the opening pages of *Memoir* about memories of his childhood in various places around Leitrim in which his mother taught. The second piece is titled 'The Fifties' and considers the existence of two sectarian Irish states, North and South, in the middle of the twentieth century.

The next few weeks are very busy with readings, starting tomorrow. I have a three-week break in the treatment. After Edinburgh, on August the 16th the calendar is fairly clear.[45] The chemo is unpleasant, but my dose is very light. I get no other drugs, and it's tolerable. I have to speak in Kilkenny just two days after treatment, and in Edinburgh the day after treatment, so there should be no difficulty recording in late August or early September.

I think that it's better to put the whole financial side through Bill Hamilton at A. M. Heath. I hope all goes well with all those programs you have on hand. 1965 was about the time when Eamon Keane was at his very best. I'm looking forward to seeing you soon, and with my love,

John

Niall Walsh Papers

Foxfield

4 August 2002

Dear Niall,
It was pleasant to see you in Boyle. I liked your friend, the vet, and Miss O'Reilly had great life, and a sense of fun.[46]

I'm back on the chemo this week for 4 Thursdays. I have to go to Kilkenny this coming Saturday, and Edinburgh the following weekend. Then it's clear for a while, and I'll call.

We'll go to Paris for the reopening of the Irish College on October 19th, and will go from there to Toronto from the 22nd to the 29th.[47] There's a break in the treatment then and we are turning it into a bit of a skite. I'll be coming back for the last four Thursdays. It's unpleasant but very tolerable.

> I'm looking forward to seeing you soon,
> With every good wish
> John

45 McGahern read at the Edinburgh International Book Festival.
46 Refers to Niall Walsh's friends Joe Connolly and Carina O'Reilly at a reading in Boyle.
47 John and Madeline travelled to Paris to officiate at the opening of Le Centre Culturel Irlandais, formerly the Irish College on Rue des Irlandais.

Frances Byrnes (email)

Foxfield

27 August 2002

Dear Frances,

I am sending this by return, as we'll be away for a few days. Naturally, I'm delighted that you liked it. I'll write out the North piece just in case, and we can go over it on Sunday, if you'd want that. I wasn't surprised by the Booker.[48] Once I saw the list of judges, I knew the novel had no chance.[49] Selwyn Jones gave it one of the few bad reviews in The Times, 'an out-of-date pastoral'; and Erica Wagner, another judge, is the literary editor there.[50] Jeannette Winterton is part of the same group, and she found it trivial.[51] The Chairperson is also in the same group.[52] I'd say they were making a literary point, as some of them were attacked for their views on the book. Everybody has an agenda. In fact, as I knew the book had no chance, I'm glad to be out of it early. Looking forward very much to seeing you soon.

> With my love
> John

---

48 *That They May Face the Rising Sun* did not make the 2002 Man Booker Prize longlist.

49 The judges for the 2002 Man Booker Prize were Lisa Jardine (chair), David Baddiel, Russell Celyn Jones, Salley Vickers and Erica Wagner. Yann Martel's *Life of Pi* (Toronto: Knopf Canada, 2001) won out over a shortlist of Rohinton Mistry, *Family Matters*; Carol Shields, *Unless*; William Trevor, *The Story of Lucy Gault*; Sarah Waters, *Fingersmith*; and Tim Winton, *Dirt Music*.

50 Russell Celyn Jones b. 1952, British novelist, opens his review of *That They May Face the Rising Sun* in *The Times* of 9 January 2002: 'John McGahern's big hearted, old-fashioned pastoral novel incorporates several deaths and entrances of men, women and livestock in rural Ireland and ends more or less where it begins, after one year's farming cycle.' Erica Wagner b. 1967 was literary editor at *The Times* from 1996 to 2013.

51 Jeanette Winterson b. 1959, Manchester-born novelist, broadcaster and academic.

52 Lisa Jardine (1944–2015), Oxford-born historian and broadcaster.

5 September 2002

Dear Frances,
Here is the revised part. The suggestions were very helpful. I have axed most of what you wanted, but kept a little of the train scene, as it's the single social outing and I have a feeling that it might be interesting to English listeners.[53] Anyhow we can go over that in a few minutes when you come. I have a copy of The Fifties and it's no trouble to include all of the Conboy scene.[54] I shortened it in the interest of brevity. I'll send you the second part tomorrow. The opening needs intellectual stiffening, and I'll need a few sentences to show how dominated by the Church the whole place was.

Love
John

6 September 2002

Dear Frances,
Here is the revised version. I found when I looked at it through your suggestions that it had to be changed drastically. I like and admire Stephen and would be very happy for him to read the passages, should you think that a good idea.[55] As you will see, he will have two more passages to read.

---

53 Refers to McGahern's account of the narrow-gauge railway that ran from Aughawillan to Ballinamore. Much the same scene is recounted in Memoir.
54 Byrnes was keen on the passage that tells the story of local entrepreneur Patsy Conboy who, having returned with money from America, opened a dance hall and later built a comically failed wall of death for motorcycle riders. Told again in Memoir.
55 In an email of the day before, Byrnes had suggested a few minor changes. She had also floated the idea of having the actor Stephen Rea read an extract from the story 'Oldfashioned' which formed part of the piece. McGahern would read his own script.

I think it's a big improvement, and the last section ties in with the opening.[56] Anything left out can be included in the conversation piece. See you soon.

Love
John

Frances Byrnes (email)
Foxfield

17 September 2002

Dear Frances,
I was puzzled when you told me you were talking to people in the shop about the book, telling them what you were doing here, and I'm sorry that you would want to include that in the program. If I had any hint that this was in question in the commission, I would not have agreed to write what I wrote. I've made many programmes here, both for radio and TV over the years, and the people I care about wouldn't want to appear. They'd see it as too obtrusive, and I'd see people I hardly know as intrusive as well. I hope it's just an idea that you are floating.[57] It was a pleasure to have you here and to work with you. I'm sorry I won't see you around Cheltenham.[58]

With my love
John

56 Refers to two passages from *That They May Face the Rising Sun*. McGahern now proposes to end with a favourite moment of his from the novel when, after watching the All-Ireland Senior Football final in Jamesie's house, Ruttledge muses on the nature of happiness as he walks home, and concludes that 'happiness could not be sought or worried into being, or even fully grasped; it should be allowed its own slow pace so that it passes unnoticed, if it ever comes at all'. Byrnes is delighted with the proposal and makes final arrangements to record in Foxfield on 9 September.

57 In an email sent earlier on 17 September, Byrnes had mooted the idea of interviewing locals about their reaction to *That They May Face the Rising Sun*. Such interviews did not occur.

58 McGahern read at the Cheltenham Literature Festival, October 2002.

Belinda McKeon

Foxfield

12 November 2002

Dear Belinda,

Thank you for your invitation, and your generous, far more than generous, response to the novel.

I am sorry to say I have hardly read a new book all year.[59] I promised Colgate University, who gave me badly needed work when I was younger, that I'd return for a term when I finished the novel. When I was there this time last year I knew there was something wrong with me though the doctors said No. Faber rushed the novel out and I came home into the pubicity mill. As soon as it was over I got myself into hospital.

The bad news was that I had cancer. The better news was that it hadn't spread and was operable. Then an error was made during the surgery that kept me a long time in hospital. When I got home I tried to read – an old favourite, Mansfield Park – and found my attention was gone after 3 pages. I'm almost back to normal and I'm in light chemotherapy ever since. The treatment ends in 2 weeks time. It's unpleasant but very tolerable and I have no complaints as I feel I may have been lucky. To be with the people in the Treatment Centre is chastening and strangely uplifting.

I have read some of the pieces you have written and thought them good. They were felt and thought out and true. They were heartening.

So maybe next year, dear Belinda, I hope I'll have read at least one good book and maybe we can do something then, but I hope we'll see one another before then.

> With affection
> John

---

59 McKeon, in her role as a journalist at the *Irish Times*, had asked McGahern to pick his books of the year for 2002.

Frances Byrnes (email)

Foxfield

19 November 2002

Dear Frances,

Thank you for your e-mail, and I was delighted to hear that things went so well with Stephen. Please thank him for me.[60] Paris was pleasant but busy – they are publishing the novel there next March; and the Toronto Festival was well-organized, with large audiences.[61] But I am very glad to be home. I'm finding the chemotherapy a bit hard this time round. I'm not sure whether this is the build-up of the drugs or because the end of the treatment is so near. I hope you are well and that the ending isn't too stressful.[62]

With my love
John

Louis de Paor

Foxfield

25 November 2002

Dear Louis,

Thank you for your letter.

Wednesday March 5th would suit me best of all but if that is difficult then the next Wednesday March 12th, is fine.

It will be interesting to speak about O Cadhain, and translation.[63] His widow was from Cloone, a few miles away from here. I remember reading about her death in the Leitrim Observer which mentioned all the priests and

---

60 Byrnes had emailed on 14 November, describing the studio production of *Another Country* and mentioning Stephen Rea's enthusiasm for the piece and his part in it.

61 Published in France as *Pour qu'ils soient face au soleil levant* by Albin Michel, translated by Françoise Cartano.

62 *Another Country* was broadcast on BBC Radio 3, 1 December 2002 at 5.45 p.m.

63 McGahern was long an admirer of the Irish-language writer Máirtín Ó Cadhain on whose work de Paor had completed his PhD thesis.

nuns she was related to, and as an afterthought, her late husband M. O C., Professor of Irish in Trinity College.

With every good wish

John

Frances Byrnes

Foxfield

12 December 2002

Dear Frances,

It's to tell you that I got a number of letters about your programme, all laudatory. 'Bravo Radio Bristol and Bravo Frances Byrnes,' Sean O Mordha the documentary film man wrote. 'It was like listening to the best of the old third programme,' a lecturer in Dublin. The poet Dennis O'Driscoll said there was much laughter in the house, and he wanted the text. Also my sisters and others. I haven't yet braced myself to listen to my own voice but I will.

That They May Face has just won The Novel of the Year Award, and is now 5 weeks at No I in paperback.[64] The occasion was a hard evening in Dublin Castle. Interestingly, in a reversal of the Booker, Banville was shortlisted and Trevor only made the longlist.[65] The novel has also been shortlisted for The South Bank Show Award (January 19th) in London.[66]

Would it be possible to send a tape of the programme to

Bill Hamilton (agent)	to Professor M. Wreszin
A M Heath	243 W, 99th St. Apt. 6B
79 St Martin's Lane	New York N.Y. 10025
London WL2N 4AA	

and an extra tape to myself, but if this is difficult don't worry.

64 An annual prize for best Irish novel inaugurated in 2000 and then sponsored by Hughes & Hughes bookshops.
65 John Banville's *Shroud* (London: Picador, 2002) made the Man Booker Prize longlist for 2002 while William Trevor's *The Story of Lucy Gault* (London: Viking, 2002) was shortlisted. *That They May Face the Rising Sun* failed to make the longlist. Yann Martell's *Life of Pi* won the prize.
66 Ian McEwan's *Atonement* (London: Jonathan Cape, 2001) won the South Bank Show Award for Literature in 2002; in 2003 it was won by Sarah Waters for *Fingersmith* (London: Virago Press, 2002).

I hope you have a lovely Christmas and a happy New Year.
With love, and gratitude
John

2003

Caroline Walsh

Foxfield

4 February 2003

Dear Caroline,

I admire an American writer John Williams, who died in 1995. He is unknown here, and little known in his own country, though his best known novel <u>Augustus</u> in 1973 won the National Book Award. I only know him through his work.

More than a year ago, I told Caroline Michel of Vintage about them. Straightaway she read the novels, loved them, and bought <u>Augustus</u> and <u>Stoner</u>, the best novel I know set in a University. They'll be published soon, and I'm writing to see if you'd look at them when they come into the Office, and, if you like them, give them space.

I wrote the Introductions. I didn't want to do this but Caroline insisted and I was glad to do it in the hope it might get them attention.[1]

We are looking forward to seeing Patsy and James and Yourself soon.

      With much love,

      John

---

1 On 5 April 2003 Eileen Battersby published an article in the *Irish Times* under the title 'Rediscovered US Master in Vintage Form', warmly endorsing the revival of John Williams.

Frank Shovlin
Foxfield

15 March 2003

Dear Frank,[2]
The first thing to be said is that I think you can write, which is rare, and then that none of the stories worked for me, though they contained brilliant bits. The one that interested me most was <u>Tyres</u>, but I thought the focus should be on the sisters and mother and then, if necessary, linked to the man, rather than the way it is. <u>Non Recyclable</u> was the story I thought worked least.

The form, while it looks easy, is in fact as restraining as a straitjacket, and I have a suspicion that the novel might suit you better.

There are small technical things that we could have gone over if you were here but these are not important as they can always be fixed.
It was a pleasure to see you again[3]
With every good wish
John

Janette Albrecht
[*Madeline McGahern*] (email)
Foxfield

4 May 2003

Dear Janette,[4]
Madeline thinks it's best for me to write to you. As you already know, I went for a colonoscopy, and was given the all-clear. David Legge, who

2 Frank Shovlin b. 1970, then a lecturer of Irish Literature in English at the Institute of Irish Studies, University of Liverpool. Shovlin had been taught by McGahern for a semester in his final year as an undergraduate at UCG in the academic year 1992–3 and had sent McGahern three short stories for comment.
3 Shovlin had attended a reading given by McGahern at the University of Central Lancashire, Preston with some of his students on 19 February 2003. McGahern suggested to his appreciative audience that they all ought to read John Williams's *Stoner*.
4 Janette Albrecht b. 1939, a psychiatrist and wife of Wil Albrecht. She was a long-standing Colgate friend of both John and Madeline.

is a friend, decided to run a liver scan before I left the hospital the same afternoon.[5] Within the program, I wasn't due a liver scan for another six months. Immediately, a node was spotted. It seems that the cells hid in the blood and attacked three or four months ago. David says the chance of this happening was two per cent, but that's all water under the bridge now. I went in to hospital last Monday, and was put through all sorts of tests and scans. At first, they were thinking of liver surgery, but the six small nodes were scattered in such a way that it made surgery too hazardous: I'd have no recourse if the cancer appeared again. So, my condition is terminal. There is no cancer in the stomach or the lungs or anywhere else. The blood tests are all clean, and the liver is functioning normally. Natural symptoms wouldn't have shown up for a long time. Because it was caught so incredibly early, and the nodes are still on the surface, a number of procedures are open to them, and they are starting with new drugs for three months; then they'll review or decide whether or not they're to burn the nodes – with lasers? They say the drugs aren't severe. They are all containments and not a cure, of course, but they said I could have a number of years. They were so blunt and straight about everything that I sort of believe them.

The whole thing was a rollercoaster for two weeks, but I feel very calm now, and I'm working every day. Madeline was terrific throughout, as was my sister Rosaleen, whose own husband has terminal prostate cancer. The other sisters were all off the wall and no help at all. We are trying to keep the above confidential as possible, without telling lies. Please give my love to Wilber and great good wishes for his retirement function on the 7th. I would have liked to have been there.[6] 1969 seems both very far away and very near, and with much love,[7]

John

5 A consultant radiologist in the Mater who had a house in Foxfield and was friendly with John and Madeline.
6 Janette Albrecht replied to this email by return, commiserating with McGahern and commenting on her husband's retirement: 'Wil has no nostalgia upon retirement. He really only agreed to the retirement functions on the 7th because I insisted. Rituals are important and adults need to acknowledge this.' Madeline McGahern Papers.
7 McGahern's first stint in Colgate took place in spring 1969.

Michael Gorman

Foxfield

14 June 2003

Dear Michael,
Thank you for your letter, and the too tempting truffles, and the Sligo photos.
I love those old photos – they look at you out of a depth of time – but there
was no dear Paddy Morahan. He would be with Sligo Rovers, and the old
ban seems to be in operation.[8]

There is not too much difference here, other than the adjustment to a
different reality, a reality we always knew was there, and unavoidable, but
is still different when it comes. I used to have ways of avoiding going to the
room to write, disliking the intensity and total absorption, but now I'm glad
of it, it belongs more to now than when we felt free in acres of time; and
that too was necessary, and is. I find I have to be socially more careful: all
society excludes this knowledge, in order to function. There was a do for
an old friend of mine, Alf Rowley, a barman in Mohill, two years ago.[9]
He was dying, and the function was to help pay bills. He lived less than a
week afterwards. He had a fine singing voice, and at the end, before The
Soldier's Song, he rose and thanked them, and then sang I Bid You All a Fond
Goodbye. There wasn't a stampede for the door, but it was the next best
thing, and mutterings about the poor man not being in his right mind, the
Leitrim way of describing a lack of tact.

I'll be glad to go to Galway for the school, depending on the chemotherapy.

The enclosed is one of the nicest paperbacks they ever made for me.[10]
After 2 months it has gone into 3 printings, at a terrible time for book sales
in the U.S.

Madeline sends her love to you all
And with my love
John

8 Sligo Rovers are a leading west of Ireland association football club. The ban was
a rule of the Gaelic Athletic Association that prohibited its members from playing
'foreign' games such as soccer. On Morahan's enthusiasm for the sport, see letter to
Madeline [September 1976].
9 Alf Rowley worked in O'Callaghan's shop and bar, Main Street, Mohill.
10 The American paperback of By the Lake bore a cover photograph of a wooded
island in a lake at twilight.

24 August 2003

Dear Caroline,

I am very sorry to learn of Elizabeth.[11] Please give her <u>my love</u>, and every dear wish. I may very well see her in the Mater, as I go back there for treatment. How is Valdi?[12] And Patsy? There are so many of us.[13]

    I was reluctant to accept the Nomination for a number of reasons, but we haven't the right to complain if we aren't willing to do something, and it is our country.[14]

Madeline says she'd be delighted if you and James would like to come for lunch sometime, and so would I. We also know that both of you are busy and you must feel under no pressure.

We go to Paris in a few weeks for the French translation. I'm not looking forward to it but we'll have a few days to ourselves when the interviews are over.

Did you and or James ever manage to look at Stoner by John Williams?[15] Much to my surprise, it has been reprinted.

                With much love

                John

11 Elizabeth, Caroline's sister, had been diagnosed with cancer.
12 Caroline's eldest sister, Valentine, who had cancer in her thirties and again in her sixties, this time terminally.
13 Meaning friends who are undergoing treatment for cancer.
14 Refers to McGahern's election to the Board of the Arts Council of Ireland.
15 Both Caroline and James admired *Stoner*.

Frédérique Roussel
[*Madeline McGahern*] (email)
Foxfield

3 October 2003

Dear Frédérique,[16]
I don't have a 'favourite' writer, but there are many writers I enjoy and admire. The one you ask about is the English poet Philip Larkin, who said that he'd like to go to China if he could come back in the same day. I think I was referring to the cliché that Irish writers had to go abroad – like Beckett and Joyce – to become writers. I couldn't imagine certain French writers, like Proust or Baudelaire, having to go abroad to become French writers; or certain English writers, like Evelyn Waugh or Philip Larkin . . . They could go abroad if they wanted to, but that is another matter.

It was a pleasure meeting you, and I'll send you the book I spoke about when it comes out.

With every good wish
John

Niall Walsh Papers
Foxfield

26 October 2003[17]

Dear Niall,
Thank you for your letter, it was very nice to hear from you. I'm just back from Toronto and New York. When we were in Toronto last year I was asked to speak at one of those endowed events at the U. of Toronto. A few of the people were very interesting. Madeline went straight to New York, spent a few days on her own, and we met up after Toronto. We stayed at the old Gramercy Place.

---

16 Frédérique Roussel, a journalist at the French daily newspaper *Libération*. She had met McGahern in Paris to interview him on the publication of *That They May Face the Rising Sun*.
17 Mistakenly dated 26 April 2003 by McGahern.

The cancer news is bad. I had the colon check last April, which was perfect. A scan wasn't due for another 3 months and so convinced were they that I was all right that it was only at David Legge's insistence that a scan was done then. 7 lesions showed on the liver, and there was no cancer elsewhere then or since. The statistics were 98% in my favour. The original tumour was very slow growing, and those cells were able to hide from the chemo, and 2% became my case.

Since then I have been in chemo. It's rough for a few days but all right after that. I'm in the battlefield of a mild turf war between your old friend Des Carney and 2 young radiologists trained in a new laser treatment last year in the U.S. After the first 3 months of the chemo the results were unusually good – 3 of the lesions had disappeared – to where? – and the other 4 were reduced – and D. C. insisted on another 3 months. The laser people wanted to operate then. The treatment will end next month. New scans. New decisions. I feel I should be interested but am not since it's completely out of my hands. I have cut down on engagements, just keeping promises like Toronto, and I write almost every day. I used always look for ways to avoid writing but now I find it's there like hidden strength or those obdurate cells. It was probably always that way but it was more obscured. What is but trying to deal with reality? I try to keep as quiet about it as possible, without caring too much as I know such news always gets out, but there's no duty to help it on its way.

We were in Paris in September for the French publication, which got an extraordinary critical reception. Galway made a handsome offer for the papers, more than I needed or ever wanted. I am happy they are going there without trading or hawking. Amusingly, I have been getting a number of letters, commending me for my 'patriotism' in 'donating' my papers to the 'nation' especially after the way I was treated.[18]

I suppose you saw that my dear friend Dick Walsh died.[19] He should have died many years ago but somehow survived through will and spirit as much as medicine. Tom Jordan, who taught with me in Clontarf, died. I'm

18 McGahern sold his papers to NUIG in 2003 – they are housed there in Special Collections of the James Hardiman Library. Issues around payment details were kept ambiguous.
19 Dick Walsh (1937–2003), a Co. Clare-born journalist and writer, associated primarily with the *Irish Times* during the 1980s and 1990s during Charles Haughey's various periods as Taoiseach. Also the author of two books, *The Party: Inside Fianna Fáil* (Dublin: Gill & Macmillan, 1986) and *Des O'Malley: A Political Profile* (Dingle: Brandon, 1986). McGahern wrote the foreword to *Dick Walsh Remembered: Selected Columns from The Irish Times 1990–2002* (Dublin: TownHouse, 2003). See *LOTW*, 79–84. He died on 11 March 2003.

fairly sure you met him here. My sister Breedge died suddenly on a holiday in New Zealand. It is that season, like that charming late ode of Auden's to the cuckoo.[20]

You must have enjoyed Trieste. Did your sister come to Ireland this year? I suppose Una and Glen and all the rest are well.[21]

Madeline says if you'd like to come to dinner some evening you'll be welcome or if it's easier we can meet in Dublin after Christmas.

With affection

John

Neill Joy
[*Madeline McGahern*]
Foxfield

16 November 2003

Dear Neill and Mary,
It was lovely talking to you both today, and I'm looking forward very much to seeing you in May.

I was planning to send you <u>Stoner</u> for Christmas with brief medical explanation of the long silence, and I'm sending you these 2 other books as well. I hope they please you. Dick Walsh was a marvellous man, who died this year. I didn't want to write the Williams Introductions but was told I'd have to if I wanted them published. <u>Stoner</u> did very well commercially, and continues to sell. They are bringing out <u>Augustus</u> in a Rediscovery Series in the U.S. in the Fall of next year. When I tried to get them to bring out <u>Stoner</u> as well they told me no one would be interested in an <u>academic</u>. How bad can it get? I had a very nice letter a few months ago from Nancy Williams who lives in a small town in Arkansas.[22]

---

20 Refers to W. H. Auden's 'Short Ode to the Cuckoo', dated June 1971 in the *Collected Poems*, 863. The poem opens:

> No one now imagines you answer idle questions
> — *How long shall I live? How long remain single?*
> *Will butter be cheaper?* — nor does your shout make
> husbands uneasy.

21 Oonagh, Niall's daughter, and her husband.

22 Nancy Williams, wife of John Williams (1922–94), who lived in Fayetteville, Arkansas, wrote to McGahern on 19 June 2003: 'I am grateful for everything you have done to see <u>Stoner</u> and <u>Augustus</u> into print in the UK. [. . .] I'm doubly lucky, to

We were in France in September for the publication of the last novel and learned that Michael Gresset isn't well.[23] We are in that age like in Auden's charming late Ode to the Cuckoo.

Mike Wreszin was here last year. We both liked his biography of Dwight McDonald.[24] He said he's in regular contact with Alberta Head and that she and her husband spend much time in casinos.

There's not much else.

I'm now a member of the Arts Council, and drink pints with the Minister, a nice man, John O'Donoghue, who isn't refined enough for some of the Elite.[25] I have caused trouble already. Of the 53 million the Government spends on the Arts only 7% gets to artists: singers, actors, writers, painters etc.

And we had a long beautiful summer.

Madeline sends her love,
with my love
John

Joe Kennedy

Foxfield

16 November 2003

Dear Joe,

Thank you for your letter and kind congratulations. The Lanaan award surprised me, surprised us both.[26] Galway approached me with a handsome offer, more than I expected, more than I wanted. There was no haggling, no agents, and I'm happy they're (mss) there, and they appear happy. You're

---

see the Vintage reprints, and to be introduced to your work. I haven't caught up with all of your books yet, but I'm a newly-minted and passionate fan of The Dark and Amongst Women.' Madeline McGahern Papers.

23 French academic who had spent a period at Colgate. See letter to Madeline of 20 September 1978.

24 Mike Wreszin, A Rebel in Defense of Tradition: The Life and Politics of Dwight Macdonald (New York: Basic Books, 1994).

25 John O'Donoghue b. 1956, who persuaded McGahern to take up a place on the Arts Council (2003–6), was a Fianna Fáil TD (member of parliament) for the Kerry South constituency from 1987 to 2011. He served as Minister for Arts, Sport and Tourism (2002–7) and subsequently as Ceann Comhairle (speaker) of Dáil Éireann.

26 McGahern was awarded the 2003 Lannan Literary Award for Fiction, valued at $125,000.

right about *X*, edited by David Wright and Patrick Swift. The Extracts? They were rewritten from a first novel, that was never published, but it has gone to Galway.[27] I'm glad I went on the Arts Council. The amount of money wasted on Administration & Officers & Specialists is shocking. Only 7% goes directly to painters, actors, writers etc., those who work. There's very little that can be done, unfortunately. Quinn has a little empire on the go.[28] I'm still in treatment, which isn't pleasant, but tolerable. The only invitations I take are those that would be churlish to refuse, like St Patrick's.[29] But they all seem to get in the newspapers. Other [*than*] that I'm just here and I try to write every day.

It would be very nice to meet John and Yourself, maybe after Christmas, for a drink or dinner. Please remember me to John. I like Maeve Brennan's work but I don't care for O Mordha.[30] We didn't get on when we worked together.

I hope you have a very happy Christmas and New Year

and with affection
John

27 *The End or the Beginning of Love*, now held in the McGahern Papers, NUIG.
28 Patricia Quinn was director of the Arts Council from 1996 until her resignation in March 2004.
29 McGahern was conferred with an honorary doctorate by St Patrick's College, Drumcondra in 2003.
30 McGahern had a long-standing interest in Maeve Brennan's work. See his letter to Michael McLaverty of 19 June 1961. Seán Ó Mordha had made a short documentary about McGahern in 1990.

2004

Dónal and Dolores Cleary
Foxfield

21 January 2004

Dear Donal and Dolores,
It was very nice to hear from you. I have very pleasant memories of evenings in Assams Park.[1]

Marie Reddan, the Librarian, U.C.G. might like to have the bell. I'm not sure. She is an easy person to deal with.[2]

Please remember me to Frank O'Dea with affection.
The Sergeant who used to come for P.E. stopped me recently in the school.[3]
He remembered Des. M. and was very funny about Miceál.[4]

Sean

With every good wish from Madeline and Sean. This was written before Christmas and wasn't posted – a mistake.

Sean

---

1 The Clearys lived in St Assams Park, Raheny where McGahern was a regular visitor during his time as a teacher at Belgrove.
2 Refers to the school bell that was rung at Belgrove and features at the opening of *The Leavetaking*. It passed into the possession of Dónal Cleary at his retirement. After McGahern's death, the bell was gifted to Madeline.
3 Sergeant Jim Ryan. Addressed as CS (Company Sergeant) Ryan by staff.
4 Des M. is Fr Desmond Millett, a one-time teaching colleague. See letter to Dónal Cleary of 6 January 1996. Miceál is Mícheál Kelleher, the principal of the school when McGahern worked there.

Colm Tóibín

Foxfield

7 March 2004

Dear Colm,

Thank you for <u>The Master</u> and the beautiful Chester Beatty selection.[5]

Madeline has started reading your novel and I'll read it as soon as I finish the first draft of what I'm writing, which is almost done.[6] I am hoping it will overcome my prejudice against books out of books.

Both of us wish it success in the world.

Please remember us to Caitríona

with affection

John

Neill Joy

[*Madeline McGahern*]

Foxfield

12 March 2004

Dear Neill,

Thank you for your letter. I'm glad you got the books, glad you liked Dick Walsh.[7] We used swim out at Dollymount when I was teaching there and he was at <u>The Irish Press</u>, 45 or so years ago.[8]

---

5 Tóibín's 2004 novel, published by Picador, in which the world is seen through the eyes of Henry James over a four-year period.

6 A reference to what was published as *Memoir* in 2005.

7 McGahern had sent three books to Joy: John Williams, *Stoner* and *Augustus*, and *Dick Walsh Remembered: Selected Columns from The Irish Times 1990–2002*.

8 McGahern wrote a foreword for the Dick Walsh book in which he remembers: 'I had the pleasure of his friendship for many years. This is irrelevant here other than to say that the man and his writing were of one piece. He always spoke in his own voice, even to strangers. [. . .] He was wonderful company and great fun, and he loved to talk. He spoke almost as well as he wrote, with a beautiful rhythmic phrasing.' See *LOTW*, 83–4.

Stoner, in particular, did very well both here and in Britain. All John Williams' are now going to be brought back into print in the U.S. Vintage Rediscoveries, The New York Review Imprint.[9]

These were wonderfully quiet months of work, but it starts to get busy soon. There are readings/lectures/tv. In April we go to San Francisco (4 days) Santa Fe (10 days). The Lancasters are in Santa Fe. They saw that I was appearing there and wrote. It'll be nice to see them again.[10]

We are travelling to Colgate with old friends, Seamus and Bernadette O'Grady. Seamus is head of External Studies in Galway. We'll probably fly to Kennedy, hire a car and drive to some hotel between New York and Colgate. We'll stay Friday and Saturday nights at the Inn. The lady at the University couldn't be more kind or helpful.[11] Seamus has to go back on Monday. I have one or two people I should see in New York and may wait till Wednesday. There is a slight chance my sister may come.

We remember all the kindnesses you both showed us over the years, and all the handballing fun you and I had, and one of the great pleasures will be to see you both again.

> Madeline sends her love
> and with my love
> John

9 Neill Joy wrote in thanks for the Williams books: 'It's nice to see you rescuing a US novelist by presenting him to an Irish reading public, and in that way, circuitously, to Mary and me.' Madeline McGahern Papers.

10 Bob Lancaster, a Minister of the Church, was married to Serena who worked in the Colgate library.

11 McGahern was conferred with an Honorary Doctorate of Letters at Colgate University's Commencement ceremony on Sunday 16 May 2004.

Frank Shovlin

Foxfield

2 May 2004

Dear Frank,[12]
Thank you for sending me your book and congratulations on the publication.[13]

I thought it good clear work, and the material was familiar. I grew up with those magazines.[14] It was interesting that there was no trace of Kate O'Brien or Michael McLaverty. I didn't realize how good K. O'B. was until much later. She was written out of that time as a serious writer while she was still alive.[15]

Are you moving back to Galway?[16]

I wish you and your work all good luck

Sincerely

John

---

12 For biographical details on Frank Shovlin, see letter of 15 March 2003.

13 Shovlin had gifted McGahern a copy of his book, *The Irish Literary Periodical 1923–1958* (Oxford: Clarendon Press, 2003).

14 Shovlin's book was a history of six mid-twentieth-century Irish literary periodicals: *The Irish Statesman* (1923–30); *The Dublin Magazine* (1923–58); *Ireland To-Day* (1936–8); *The Bell* (1940–54); *Envoy* (1949–51); and *Rann* (1948–53).

15 McGahern especially admired Kate O'Brien's 1934 novel *The Ante-Room*, published by Heinemann, which he taught at UCD in the late 1990s. O'Brien wrote one of the most enthusiastic reviews of *The Barracks* when it was published in 1963. See Kate O'Brien, *University Review* (now *Irish University Review*), vol. 3, no. 4 (1963), 59–60.

16 Shovlin and McGahern had first met through a seminar McGahern taught at UCG in spring 1993. On McGahern's teaching at Galway, see letter to Niall Walsh of 15 February 1993. At the time of the composition of this letter, Shovlin's wife Maura Kennedy was based in Galway where she was director of the Cúirt Literary Festival at which McGahern read alongside Michael Longley in 2001.

Ian Jack
[*Madeline McGahern*] (email)
Foxfield

24 June 2004

Dear Ian,[17]
I am delighted that the mss pleased you, and I'm happy for you to publish the extracts whenever you think best.[18]

I'm grateful for all the suggestions, and I'd be very grateful for anything else you might suggest. The Cavan–Leitrim is obviously right. Only at Arigna does it get close to Sligo. I'm sure Garradice Halt was the name of the station. I even have a vague, uncertain memory of seeing it written – but it was always called Aughawillian.[19] This is common. The lake below our house here is Lough Rowan, but nobody calls it anything other than Laura Lake (Lar Loch), which is what it is, a lake between two lakes.

I think the map is a great idea.[20] Would you have any suggestions for the title?[21] All the other comments I agree with.[22] I have already cut out

17 Ian Jack (1945–2022) was a British journalist, writer and editor. Having begun work as a journalist in Scotland, in 1970 he joined the *Sunday Times* in London, where he became a section editor and then a foreign correspondent-cum-feature writer with a special interest in South Asia and particularly India. From 1986 to 1989, he wrote for *The Observer* and *Vanity Fair*, and then joined the team that created the *Independent on Sunday*, which he edited from 1991 to 1995. His editorship of the quarterly *Granta* magazine, to which he had previously contributed as a writer, spanned forty-seven issues over twelve years to 2007.
18 This email forms part of a short and warm correspondence between McGahern and Jack in preparation for the appearance in *Granta* of an extract from the opening of *Memoir* titled 'The Lanes'.
19 Jack had pointed out to McGahern in an email of 21 June that he had misnamed the railway line in his memoir as the 'Sligo, Leitrim and Northern Counties' when it ought to be the 'Cavan and Leitrim'. Jack further pointed out that the station McGahern travelled from as a child was called Garradice Halt, not Aughawillan.
20 Jack had suggested that a map outlining the movements of McGahern and his family around various Leitrim and Roscommon locations such as Ballinamore, Aughawillan and Cootehall would strengthen the book. No map appears in the published *Memoir*.
21 As usual, McGahern was having trouble coming up with a name for his new book, eventually going with plain *Memoir*. See email to Neil Belton of 5 April 2005.
22 Jack suggested the following: a reconsideration of the working title – *Memoir* – to avoid giving the impression that the book was about McGahern from birth to

the scene of Guard Cannon taking The Barracks out of the library to read about himself. I was writing fast and then cutting towards a shape. I took it to Paris with me, and I feel that I'm getting my teeth into it at last. Over-writing around my father has been cut and sharpened, and new scenes have to be added.

Do you think it would be better to cut out the whole business about writing altogether, other than the concerns around The Leavetaking, and leave it to Moroney's library and the development of reading? Do the scenes in the sheep mart after my father's death, the building site in London, the maid in her later life thin out the narrative too much? Would it be better to concentrate it all back into the early life? As I said, I am very grateful and will be grateful for any further ideas. Nobody else has seen it. I told Bill Hamilton that I was sending you an unfinished copy because of a deadline. He knows he'll not get it until it's finished.

With every good wish

John

Neill Joy

[*Madeline McGahern*]

Foxfield

18 September 2004

Dear Neill,

Thank you for your letter. The enclosed re. John Williams may interest you. There's no need to return it. I think what J.W. meant was that the character <u>Stoner</u> had a good life in that he had <u>work</u>, a job he considered precious and valuable, which is more than can be said for most people.[23] I met a Californian book show host, connected with the book clubs, in Dublin recently, and he told me that young American writers are becoming interested in J.W. He wants me to go on his show when the new book comes out.

---

the present; some more signposting; an early, brief explanation as to how and why McGahern's father lived apart from his family; allowing the reader greater insight into how and when McGahern became a writer.

23 Neill Joy had written to McGahern about *Stoner* in a letter dated 18 August 2004: 'When you quote Williams' claim that it is a happy book, I gasped. [. . .] When Williams says it is a happy book he really means, I am sure, that he was happy in its composition and completion, and he deserved to see matters in that light.' Madeline McGahern Papers.

We had a fairly quiet time, and I finished the memoirs. They should be leaving the house next week. Granta will publish a long section in November. A tv crew will be here all next week. At the beginning of November we go to Japan for a week. This year is the centenary of Kavanagh's birth and I'm launching his Collected Poems in the Guinness store (K. loathed Guinness but drank whiskey by the pint). I'm looking forward to it as there's bound to be an unruly crowd.[24]

Madeline won her case against her tenant in Paris, who was fined heavily, and ordered to leave. She has now ignored the order and the eviction will take more time. It will happen eventually and could be slow.

It was a great pleasure to see you both again. I'd have liked to have stayed for a couple of weeks but that is what happens when you fall into the hands of the doctors. It must be lovely in Poolville now.

Madeline sends you both her love

and with my love

John

Sonny Mehta

[*Madeline McGahern*]

Foxfield

21 September 2004

Dear Sonny,[25]

I have just finished a memoir and I hope very much it will please you.

Ian Jack wrote looking for material and I showed him an earlier draft. He liked it and will publish a long section in the November Granta.

Bill Hamilton of A. M. Heath will be the agent, not Seldes. We spoke briefly about this and you were agreeable.

If you prefer, I can send the MSS directly to you if you contact me at the above.

---

24 Kavanagh's *Collected Poems*, edited by Antoinette Quinn, was published in 2004 by Allen Lane and the following year appeared as a Penguin Classic.
25 Sonny Mehta was for many years the editor-in-chief at Alfred A. Knopf and chairman of the Knopf Doubleday Publishing Group. For more, see letter to Tim Seldes of 14 February 1991.

I want to thank you again for all you did for both The Collected Stories and By the Lake,

And with much affection
John (McGahern)

Liam Kelly (email)
Foxfield

31 October 2004

Dear Liam,

Thank you for your note and the corrections. They were very useful, especially the spellings of the placenames.[26] I've changed the episode in which you are involved to a bad day in summer during the Maynooth holidays. Is there any exact story of how those people on the mountain were driven out of the North, or have the various stories merged into the usual vagueness?[27] I suppose it's better not to refer to McKiernan by name, in the sense of taking The Barracks from the library. It might be hurtful and it's not important.[28] He was certainly ambitious then, as well as being behind the times. All my sisters, in their different ways, are very happy with The Memoir. They have corroborated all the material and added certain things of their own that I had blanked out but are useful. Knopf have now bought The Memoir in the U.S., so it will have the same publishers as That They May Face the Rising Sun.[29] We go to Japan on Thursday and we'll be back on the 11th November. We hope we'll see you soon and that all goes well with your own work.

John

26 Kelly is a scrupulous local historian who was well placed to help McGahern with such issues as they arose in the composition of Memoir.
27 Kelly had told McGahern about the mass exodus of Catholics from Ulster counties to the hills and mountains of Leitrim, Sligo and Mayo, which took place in the winter of 1795 and the spring of 1796. Kelly has written in some detail about this movement of people in a book called A Flame Now Quenched: Rebels and Frenchmen in Leitrim 1793–1798 (Dublin: The Lilliput Press, 1998), 47–53. Kelly's father's family and McGahern's mother's family were both driven out of Ulster at that time.
28 Fr McKiernan (his actual name was MacKiernan) is, in fact, accused in Memoir of being responsible for having The Barracks removed from the shelves of Ballinamore library.
29 Here, at the end of his career, McGahern finally found a fully satisfactory and happy relationship with an American publisher thanks, largely, to a strong working relationship with Sonny Mehta at Knopf.

10 December 2004

Dear Neil,[30]

Thank you for your generous praise of the text and for going through it so painstakingly.[31] I've read through the notes carefully, and they all seem to make sense. They will be very useful as I go through the typescript for what should be a final, or near-final, revision. A very few were typos and some were already picked up. I'll send you the final version as soon as it is done, and if you spot anything I'll be grateful. I think I'd prefer to get a title for the book. Can you think of any titles? I've always had great difficulties with titles for longer works. There seems to be no such difficulties with short stories, which seem to name themselves. Was Maffey the British ambassador in the late 1940s in North Roscommon?[32] They had him down as Massey, since, for some reason, they connected him with the people who made the Massey-Ferguson tractors.

With every good wish

John

30 Neil Belton, Irish-born and educated at UCD, was then an editor at Faber. He also worked at Jonathan Cape and with *Granta* magazine, and is now editorial director at Head of Zeus. He is the author of *The Good Listener: Helen Bamber, a Life Against Cruelty* (London: Weidenfeld & Nicolson, 1998), which was awarded the 1999 *Irish Times* Literature Prize for Irish Non-fiction. His novel *A Game with Sharpened Knives*, based on the life of Erwin Schrodinger, was published to critical acclaim by Weidenfeld & Nicolson in 2005.

31 Refers to the text of what becomes published as *Memoir* in 2005.

32 Sir John Maffey (styled as Lord Rugby from 1947) served as British Representative in Ireland from 1939 to 1948. In 1948 the Oireachtas (the Irish legislature) passed the Republic of Ireland Act, under which Ireland withdrew from the Commonwealth the following year, and the name of the office was changed to 'Ambassador'. McGahern is checking this because *Memoir* refers to Maffey joining a 1940s shooting party at Rockingham House, near his childhood Cootehall home.

Belinda McKeon

Foxfield

12 December 2004

Dear Belinda,

Thank you for your very kind letter. All you have to do is telephone – we are here over the Christmas – and we can arrange a time or times.

Philip King said he admired your work and was interested in having you interview me at the time of the TV.[33] I told him there would be no difficulty on my side.

I'll be happy to support you in any way I can. Bring the forms with you when you come or post them to me if there's time pressure. If you can think of any other way I may be able to help just let me know.[34]

I'm looking forward to seeing you soon.

With affection

John

---

33 Philip King b. 1952 in Cork is a musician, film maker and broadcaster. He produced the television documentary *John McGahern – A Private World* in 2005.
34 McKeon was applying to study for an MFA at Columbia University.

2005

Seán Beattie

Foxfield

14 January 2005

Dear Sean Beattie,[1]
Thank you for your kind letter. I regret very much that I'll be unable to accept your invitation in October. I am cutting back on work and am unable to take on new engagements.

    I remember your mother's family. They lived beside P. J. O'Malley. My stepmother's family the McSherras also lived very close.[2]
I wish the Festival every success.
With good wishes
John McGahern

Niall Walsh Papers

Foxfield

20 January 2005

Dear Niall,
It was very nice that you liked the tv. I saw it in preview and got him to change a few small things, but other than that had no control. The director refused to take out the idiotic footage from Japan. I have not seen it since. It's unpleasant watching yourself, but Madeline says he pulled it together all right. It got a huge viewing 275,000+. The whole thing was rushed in the end and I'm just

---

1 Seán Beattie b. 1943 was chairman of a weekend literary festival, the Charles Macklin Autumn School, in Culdaff, Co. Donegal. In 2005 he wrote to McGahern inviting him to open the School, of which Brian Friel was Patron.
2 Beattie's grandparents were Mulligans and O'Malleys from Drumbrick, Boyle, Co. Roscommon where they were neighbours of McGahern's stepmother, Agnes McSherra.

sending out the final version of the memoir. Madeline tried to escape being filmed but the cameraman persuaded her to sit there. I'm glad he did.[3]

I'm halfway through the new course. It's every week so there's practically no recovery time. As usual Carney is aggressive, mixing chemo with the new stem cells. I got a bad enough bout of diarrhoea before Christmas but other than that have managed all right. One of his patients had to go into hospital for a number of days. I was supposed to speak in Washington this February but cancelled before Christmas. Other than that it's normal life and not as different as is supposed. There will be new scans when the course ends in February but the cancer seems to be held. The scans were good before this new course. When I began the memoir I didn't expect to have the time to finish. In some mysterious way these years have been more rich and full than any others. I hardly think about the disease at all other than as background. Maybe it is just the old body's plenitude.

Were you in Dublin and Scotland and Limerick over Christmas or did they join you in Ballinasloe? Please remember me to them all.

You might like to have the enclosed which appeared at Christmas.

Madeline joins me in wishing you a very Happy New Year.

John

Peter Guy

Foxfield

28 January 2005

Dear Mr Guy,[4]

I'm sorry I'll be unable to help you, as I have had to cut back on all commitments. I would not view any of the three writers you mention as 'realists'.[5]

With good wishes
John McGahern

3 Refers to the television documentary *John McGahern – A Private World*, directed by Pat Collins and first aired by RTÉ 1 on Tuesday 11 January 2005. Some footage of McGahern in Japan appears towards the end of the film.
4 Peter Guy b. 1980 was then a graduate student at NUIG and had written to McGahern asking him to comment on the idea that a school of literary realists had emerged in Ireland of the 1960s.
5 The three writers Guy gave as examples of this new school of realism were John Broderick, Edna O'Brien and John McGahern.

28 January 2005

Dear Neil,

L'Ecrivain at 7.30 will be fine, and we both look forward to seeing you then.[6] John Spain, the literary editor of the Indo, rang up about a week ago saying that negotiations were in progress with Will about the book.[7] He felt that Faber would not agree to either 'That They May Face the Rising Sun' or 'Amongst Women', and the book was most likely to be 'The Dark' or 'The Barracks'. 'Amongst Women' is on the Leaving, and continues to have high sales, roughly between 8,000 and 14,000 a year.[8] I'm just dishing this out from memory; it would earn the Indo money in two or three years. I imagine all those Indo copies would finish it off, and I don't trust marketing people when faced with a quick kill. I'd say to hold out for 'The Dark' or another book. But do we have any say?[9]

Spain said that if it was to be in the spring it would be decided shortly but that it was more likely that it would be published at the time of the memoir. What do you think? The Indo is plainly in competition with The Examiner, who have issued back copies of Roddy Doyle, Maeve Binchy, and one or two others in the same form. I suppose we'll have time to talk about it. Have you had a chance to look through the revisions? When you are satisfied would you send a copy to Bill Hamilton and Sonny Mehta? If you see anything that could be improved please tell me.

With every good wish

John

6 L'Ecrivain is a restaurant located on Dublin's Baggot Street.
7 John Spain, Dublin journalist then working with the *Irish Independent* group. Will Atkinson worked as a sales agent at Faber.
8 *Amongst Women* is still on the Leaving Certificate curriculum – Ireland's state examination for final year secondary students.
9 The *Independent* group issued an edition of *That They May Face the Rising Sun*.

Paul Armstrong

Foxfield

30 March 2005

Dear Dr Armstrong,[10]
Thank you for your kind letter. I vaguely remember The Magnet though I
do not think I was ever in the shop.[11] My years at the Brothers were 1948–
1953.[12] A charming man, a Mr Armstrong, who travelled for footwear and
was fond of whiskey, had a bar/shoe shop beside Flynns, across from the
clock.[13]

Once a writer's work is done I don't believe it lives again until it is brought
to life in a Reader's mind, and there will be as many versions of the book
as the Readers it finds. Then it belongs to its Readers, and what the writer
thinks is irrelevant: he has no more right than any other reader.

Naturally I hope it pleases and gives pleasure and that April 8 turns out a
happy evening.

With every good wish to you and to everybody attending the evening.

Sincerely

John McGahern

10 Dr Paul Armstrong, a medical doctor from Carrick-on-Shannon, Co. Leitrim,
wrote to McGahern inviting him to attend a book group in Lifford, Co. Donegal
of which Dr Armstrong was part. The group was reading *That They May Face the
Rising Sun*.

11 Armstrong's home was in the Carrick-on-Shannon shop, The Magnet.

12 The Presentation Brothers had a boys' secondary school in Carrick-on-Shannon
that was attended by McGahern and is remembered fondly by him in *Memoir* and
elsewhere.

13 This Mr Armstrong was no relation to Dr Armstrong's father. 'The Clock' is a
central landmark in Carrick-on-Shannon – much of what McGahern describes here is
still recognisable in the town today.

5 April 2005

Dear Neil,
I didn't get back till late last night from a meeting in Dublin. We'll be here all day today and most of tomorrow and back again Thursday evening. I had the very same fear about The Moons of Gloria. About a hundred titles have been thrown at the book, and none of them seem to stick. <u>Memoir</u> might be the right title. I'll try to think of something outside the text in the next few days, if there is that time. But I am happy with Memoir, if Faber thinks it's commercial enough.[14]

> With every good wish
> John

20 May 2005

Dear Neil,
I enjoyed A Game with Sharpened Knives. I liked especially the intelligence, the descriptions of the natural world as seen through science, the office scenes, the de Valera encounters, the whole shabbiness, moral and physical, of Dublin; and Clontarf, the marriage, the sea. I was less sure of the affair though the theatre set piece at the beginning was brilliant, and the recall of the war felt as too much material was being crammed in. I wonder if you know the novel Stoner by John Williams, which has as many similarities as differences with Sharpened Knives. I hope your novel has great good luck.

We are just back from Zurich. I gave a reading to the Joyce Institute, and we stayed with the ambassador and his wife, Joe and Irene Lynch, in Berne for a night. They are exceptionally pleasant. Joe had read and liked your

---

14 Belton had emailed on 4 April to say that Faber was 'all a bit frightened' by *The Moons of Gloria* as a possible title for McGahern's memoir. Other titles discussed include *The Lanes* and *Summer Lanes*, but Belton favoured *Memoir*.

novel. Declan was there a few weeks' ago.[15] As he probably told you, he was speaking on Ulysses at the Joyce Institute, and was greatly liked.

I'll probably see him in a couple of weeks at the launch of the University Review.[16] He has great energy and doesn't promote himself. When I taught at UCD some years back he made himself the least of men in order to encourage the younger lecturers and the students. It is how professors should behave but seldom do.

I am very happy with Memoirs, and leave the decision completely to you and Faber. Sonny was insistent on a title. I gave him a few titles, and Knopf went at once for All Will Be Well. He wanted to call the Rising Sun In the Village. By the Lake was a compromise, and it worked in America.[17]

With every good wish

John

Faber (email)

Foxfield

28 May 2005

Dear Neil,

I'm afraid I'm seldom kind when it comes to writing. I think it's too important. I hope Sharpened Knives has a long life and many readers.[18] I'll be happy to sign as many or all of the limited edition.[19] Kenny's of Galway have been tearing the Faber jackets off the more recent books and then doing them in their own limited editions.[20] I'm meeting Rachel and Will on Wednesday.[21]

---

15 Declan Kiberd was a mutual friend of Belton's and McGahern's.

16 *Irish University Review*, vol. 35, no. 1 (Spring–Summer 2005) was a John McGahern special.

17 McGahern was not keen on the titles chosen by Knopf but took a pragmatic approach.

18 Belton had emailed on 25 May to thank McGahern for the comments he made on *A Game with Sharpened Knives* in his email of 20 May.

19 Belton had asked McGahern if he could sign some of a limited run of 150 copies of *Memoir* for collectors.

20 Kenny's is a family-run book dealership in Galway founded by Des and Maureen Kenny, née Canning, in 1940. Mrs Kenny was a native of Mohill, the McGaherns' usual shopping town. When the bookshop and gallery were reopened on Galway's High Street after substantial refurbishment in 1996, McGahern performed the ceremony.

21 Faber employees.

I had a very nice evening with Declan – it was his 54th birthday – and I was reckoning I must have been 24 when I was teaching him in Clontarf. All the waves of Dollymount since then . . .

With every good wish
John

Niall Walsh Papers
Foxfield

4 August 2005

Dear Niall,

Thank you for your letter. It'd be pleasant to meet in Galway on the 22nd. Around the reading will probably be hopeless.[22] At 4 p.m. on the same day there's a small reception in the University for the opening of the Irish Studies Centre, at which I have to say a few words. Would you both like to come to that? There will not be many people and it'd be easier to talk and meet.

I have been on a new treatment since before Christmas, a new stem cell drug, which ½ the time they mix with the chemo. The results vary from patient to patient but in my case it appears to have been unusually successful. How long this will last nobody seems to know: it is still just maintenance treatment. The bad side is that the treatment is weekly with few breaks and it can be severe enough when the 2 drugs are mixed. I'm not looking forward to the next weeks when this will have to be juggled with the demands for publicity.

This must be a very busy time for you with family and visitors.
Please remember me to your friend. That was a pleasant meeting in Boyle. Madeline is in very good form and asks to be remembered to you. She is hoping that her tenant will finally be evicted from the Paris flat on September 15th.

With every good wish
John

22 McGahern read from *Memoir* to a packed house at Galway's Town Hall on the evening of 22 September 2005.

26 August 2005

Dear Neill,

It was a pleasure to get your letter, and to know that both of you are so well.

We wrote the Albrechts. Then after a long interval Madeline wrote Janette, merely restating her affection. She hasn't heard from her and I don't think she will. I think of Wil as being on the far right of hopelessness, and controlling everything, though it must be hard for him as well. We hear from Fred from time to time.[23] Iraq seems more and more a mess.[24] Robert Fisk writes regularly in the Ir. Independent.[25] I'm afraid Madeline gets angry every time George Bush's name comes up.[26] My theory is that they are there to control the oil and will stay. I met a photographer in Paris who did a tv documentary on oil. He told me the oil companies run Iraq, and if you utter a word of criticism they can have you out of the place in hours. He explained how he had to play along. Ruthless as they were, they didn't seem all that smart.

The word Mary's mother used was probably GRÁMHAR (Loving).[27] Next month the Ir. Independent will give away a free copy of the novel with the newspaper as the lead-off book in a series of Irish classics (some are far from classic).[28] As it was still selling 10,000 a year in Ireland they had to pay quite

23 Fred Busch.

24 The US, UK and allies invaded Iraq in March 2003 and thus began a long, drawn-out conflict. Fred Busch's son Ben, a US Marine, was, at the time of writing, on his third tour of duty in Iraq.

25 Robert Fisk (1946–2020) was a leading commentator on Middle Eastern politics for a number of news outlets.

26 George W. Bush b. 1946, 43rd President of the United States. Bush was a Republican who led his country into war in Afghanistan and Iraq.

27 In a letter of 19 August 2005, Neill Joy wrote of his Irish mother-in-law Bridie's reaction to the American edition of *That They May Face the Rising Sun*: 'she had very recently re-read By the Lake (US title), which we wanted her to have. She said what a kind, and caring book it is, and she used an Irish word for warm-and-tranquil, which I couldn't catch.' Madeline McGahern Papers.

28 The other nineteen titles in the series were Joseph O'Connor, *Star of the Sea*; Colm Tóibín, *The Blackwater Lightship*; John Banville, *The Book of Evidence*; Edna O'Brien, *The Country Girls*; J. P. Donleavy, *The Ginger Man*; Patrick McCabe, *The Butcher Boy*; Maeve Brennan, *The Springs of Affection*; Flann O'Brien, *At Swim-*

a bit. Next week the Memoir comes out. There'll be extracts tomorrow in both the Irish Times and The Guardian. They have given me a month off treatment. It is the first break since Christmas. Do you remember what the man in the doctor's surgery said all those years ago, 'When you're sick every day is a good day.'

There's not much else. We had a wonderful summer, and the meadows were easily gathered. The cows are sleek and fat. Three weeks ago a local woman (a suicide) drove into the lake in front of the house. A police helicopter found the car, with some kind of an imaging device. The whole lake was floodlit one night while they dragged the car and poor woman to shore. I miss Hamilton at this time of year. I loved the walk into the town along the old railway tracks when I was there 4 years ago.

They should have sent you the enclosed but probably did not.[29]

> Madeline sends you both her love
> and with my love
> John

Niall Walsh Papers

Foxfield

8 September 2005[30]

Dear Niall,

I asked Louis de Paor to send you an invitation for 3 to the opening of the Irish Studies Centre at 4 pm on the 22nd at U. C. G.[31] This will be done by

---

Two-Birds; William Trevor, *The Ballroom of Romance and Other Stories*; Molly Keane, *Good Behaviour*; Frank O'Connor, *Selected Stories*; Brian Moore, *The Lonely Passion of Judith Hearne*; Patrick Kavanagh, *Tarry Flynn*; Walter Macken, *Seek the Fair Land*; Mary Lavin, *In a Café and Other Stories*; Liam O'Flaherty, *The Informer*; Kate O'Brien, *The Ante-Room*; Seán O'Faoláin, *The Heat of the Sun and Other Stories*; Jennifer Johnston, *Captains and the Kings*.

29 Presumably a copy of *Memoir*.

30 This is McGahern's last extant letter to Niall Walsh.

31 McGahern had a long relationship with UCG, which had become the National University of Ireland Galway in 1997. In 1994 he was awarded an Honorary Doctorate in Literature by the university and, in January 2001, he was appointed Adjunct Professor of Irish Studies in recognition of a lifetime of creative achievement at the highest level. Louis de Paor was director of the Centre for Irish Studies, NUIG at the time this letter was written.

the President. I have just to be there for the ceremonial. If for any reason the invitations didn't arrive all you'd have to do is turn up.

Carney has given me a month off treatment but most of the time is taken up with demands for publicity. It usen't to be like this, but now it's like a small monster. There's a launch in Trinity next Monday 6–8 (again if you happen to be in Dublin and felt like attending all you'd have to do is turn up to the Long Hall) and I have to go to London the following morning and will be there till Sunday the 18th.

Madeline is in Paris. She's trying to recover her flat. The tenant is there illegally for over a year now. There's a police notice to evict her on September 15th. Sometimes it's not easy to get them to carry it out. I don't think it matters greatly but it'd be nice to be rid of the business.

We had a wonderful summer here and didn't have to go anywhere except for London (Hazlett's Hotel in Soho for a few days).

We are both looking forward to seeing you on the 22nd

and with affection

John

Colm Tóibín

Foxfield

28 November 2005

Dear Colm,

Thank you for your generous words about The Memoir.[32]

I'm sorry to be so slow in responding to The Master. Part of it was hesitation. I admired the writing and agreed with what Edmund White said but it did not take away my dislike of the literary as a theme for fiction. I had the same reaction to Michael Cunningham's The Hours. I could see the dyer's hand – but then my idea of fiction may be too narrow.[33]

Madeline was taken by surprise to see Caitríona step out of a big car in Paris, looking elegant and beautiful on her way to the prize ceremony. We

32 Tóibín had written to McGahern on 8 September of his admiration for Memoir: 'You write very beautifully in the book about reading, how at a certain age books can grip you. I think this book will make children of us all, engrossed and unselfconscious as we turn each page. I am very grateful to you for it.' Madeline McGahern Papers.
33 W. H. Auden's collected essays, The Dyer's Hand (New York: Random House, 1962), was a favourite book of McGahern's.

were both delighted and send our congratulations. It must have been a very happy day.[34]

With affection

John

Frances Byrnes (email)

Foxfield

5 December 2005

Dear Frances,
I thought the 'lyrical' Irish author was pretty bad – the description would be a big turn-off for me about another prose writer; and the harp music was another cliché, but I suppose neither was fully in your control. As for the rest, I don't think we could have done much better.[35] The book is going off to Mark Dwyer today. Would it be difficult to have copies of the readings? A few of my sisters, and some other people, are unable to get Radio Four.

Love

John

Colm Tóibín

Foxfield

16 December 2005

Dear Colm,
Thank you for your card and the LRB. I found the article fascinating and strangely sordid.[36] Why, do you think?

---

34 *The Master* had been awarded the Prix du Meilleur Livre Étranger for 2005 at an awards ceremony in Paris attended by Tóibín and his friend Catriona Crowe.
35 Extracts from *Memoir* were broadcast as 'Book of the Week' on BBC Radio 4 from Monday 5 December to Friday 9 December 2005 at 9.45 each morning and then repeated the following evening after midnight. The BBC continuity announcer had expanded the plain Presentation Details, adding the word 'lyrical' – as she saw it, to tempt listeners. This frustrated both McGahern and Byrnes.
36 An essay by Tóibín on *The Ferns Report*, an Irish government examination of clerical sexual abuse in Tóibín's native diocese, published in the *London Review of Books* for 1 December 2005.

In the late 1970s I was invited to speak in Maynooth.[37] I knew they thought they were being adventurous with a banned writer and was determined not to play the part. I gave a lecture on Ruskin's Sesame and Lilies, the idea of a public lending library, and how Proust via Marie Nordlingen both agreed and took issue with Ruskin's view.[38] Ledwith was the President and congratulated me afterwards, 'A thoroughly university evening, what Maynooth badly needs' which I took to mean that it was correct and dull, which was partly my aim.[39] My host was not Ledwith but McGinnity, the clerk of students.[40] Around him was the most outlandish gay court I have ever seen. They were all reading Tom Sharpe.[41] Exaggerated gestures. Refined voices. Witticisms that needed God's help. They had met Haughey and Fitzgerald (they despised Garret) and were fascinated by power without any experience of it, though they all felt Maynooth was at the very centre of power.[42] They also despised GAA types and their girl followers. I was fascinated. I suspect they were all celibates and had as little experience of sex as they had of power. At the still centre of the whole show was the bould McGinnity.

> Please remember me with affection to Caitríona
> I wish you both a very happy Christmas
> John

37 Ireland's largest and most prestigious seminary. Also home to Maynooth University.

38 John Ruskin's *Sesame and Lilies* (1865) was long a favourite essay of McGahern's.

39 Monsignor Micheál Ledwith is mentioned in Tóibín's *London Review of Books* essay as he served a term as dean of Tóibín's secondary school, St Peter's, Wexford and went on to be caught up in the sexual scandals that dogged the Irish Church through the 1990s and beyond. After leaving St Peter's, Ledwith went on to a stellar career in the Church, eventually becoming president of Maynooth in 1985.

40 Fr Gerard McGinnity, then senior dean at Maynooth, to whom a number of seminarians turned in 1984 with reports of improper sexual conduct by Mgr Ledwith. McGinnity was asked for his resignation from Maynooth the following year by Cardinal Ó Fiach, Ireland's top-ranked cleric, on the insistence of a number of bishops.

41 Tom Sharpe (1928–2013), English satirical novelist.

42 Charles J. Haughey and Garret FitzGerald were dominant Irish political figures of the 1980s, both serving as Taoiseach. Haughey, who had made a political comeback after being associated with arms smuggling to republicans in the early 1970s, was rarely far from controversy, while FitzGerald was perceived as a clever, if absentminded, liberal, frequently referred to colloquially as 'Garret the good'.

2006

Frances Byrnes (email)

Foxfield

17 January 2006

Dear Frances,
You and Mark will be very welcome here, but it looks as if the dates may not be right.[1] We have to go up to Dublin on the evening of the 24th, or very early on the morning of the 25th. We're crossing over to London on the 26th for the South Bank Show Awards, and we'll not be back until late on Sunday the 29th or Monday the 30th. The treatment seems to be going alright. I take very little interest in it. I'm told that the only difference between God and a consultant is that God doesn't know he is a consultant. All sorts of stuff about my father has come out of the woodwork since the publication of the Memoir. To carry the statue in the front of the procession would be in character.[2] He always knelt in the front seat of the church, and was the first to the Communion rail. Maybe that's why I belong to the crowd at the church door. If your dates change, let us know.
                    Much love
                    John

Faber (email)

Foxfield

19 January 2006

Dear Neil,
I knew you must have been busy. I go to Dublin today for treatment tomorrow, but will be back in the evening. I'm here until next Wednesday morning. We

---

1 Mark Lawlor, then Frances Byrnes's fiancé. They were married in August 2006.
2 Refers to the annual Corpus Christi procession described in *Memoir*.

cross to London on Thursday to the Savoy. That's very good news about the sales. I thought they were around 50 to 55,000. Also good news about the shortlist. I've come to the conclusion that all these awards are, more or less, a lottery. What is it that Auden says? Everybody had hats. Ours were of gold, paper all the rest, so we must have won.

The jacket looks fine to me. I have cleared everything out of the way but the story.[3] Bill Hamilton is well intentioned, sometimes too enthusiastic. I am working on it. After that it will be easy to pick and revise the rest of the stories. The trouble is that the present course of drugs is heavy, and it takes a long time to get through to the point where I can really work.

I'm looking forward to meeting you next week.

Every good wish
John

Stanley van der Ziel (email)[4]
[Foxfield]

14 February 2006

Dear Stanley,[5]
I assume you sent the review to elicit a response.[6]

3 Here McGahern is talking about his collected short stories, *Creatures of the Earth*, meant to both supersede *The Collected Stories* of 1992 and to stand as a final marker of what McGahern felt ought to represent his achievement as a short story writer. The 'story' he mentions is 'The White Boat', which he tried and failed (mainly due to his illness) to revise to his satisfaction and include in the collection.
4 This email is headed 'Not for Publication'.
5 Stanley van der Ziel, then a graduate student at UCD working towards a PhD on McGahern's writing under the supervision of Professor Declan Kiberd. He subsequently edited a selection of McGahern's non-fiction for Faber; see John McGahern, *Love of the World: Essays*, ed. Stanley van der Ziel, int. Declan Kiberd (London: Faber, 2009), and McGahern's plays as *The Rockingham Shoot and Other Dramatic Writings* (London: Faber, 2018). A much-revised and expanded version of his doctoral research was published as a monograph in 2016; see *John McGahern and the Imagination of Tradition* (Cork: Cork University Press, 2016).
6 Van der Ziel wrote a perceptive review of *Memoir* which he sent to McGahern. See *Irish University Review*, vol. 35, no. 2 (Autumn–Winter 2005), 463–9.

The aim of the book is stated clearly on page 260.[7] To have introduced the literary into such a narrative would have been as tactless as discussing Wordsworth to a world that had never heard of him. There was a long passage on the act of writing in an earlier draft, and it was cut for the same reason.

In Cleggan we had many friends. Only Patrick O'Malley is used.

Because of him, we nearly settled there. The narrative would have a different shape if we had. In the linking passage, the major omissions and the necessary inclusions are controlled similarly, and the style is that of reportage, the way it would filter back to the original world through newspapers or gossip.

The literary life around me is exaggerated. I could go through how tangential and flimsy it was, but it would take too long. Other than books, the main influence was Jimmy Swift. We met every Friday night for years. I remember being a little disappointed when I showed him McLaverty's work, and he dismissed it as too minor. I liked both McLaverty and his work, but we met only a few times. I remember he sent me a present of Edwin Muir's *Autobiography*.[8] As well as being a man of talent, McLaverty was an enthusiastic teacher. Everybody was a potential student, but I was too formed in my own views by then. I find him very true still when he writes about what he loves. As far as I remember, I never showed him any writing until it was published. When I met Kate O'Brien I hadn't read her work, nor did I know that she had written about my first book.[9] I admire her now, but at that time her work had been relegated to the status of women's magazine-writing by her rivals and the vagaries of literary fashion. I was introduced to Mary Lavin's salon by McLaverty.[10] He was suspicious of literary Dublin, and he thought it a safe house for a young man. I went there, mostly out of politeness, a few times. The trouble was that I wasn't on the lookout for safe houses.

7 Presumably McGahern is referring to the following passage: 'This is the story of my upbringing, the people who brought me up, my parents and those around them, in their time and landscape. My own separate life, in so far as any life is separate, I detailed only to show how the journey out of that landscape became the return to those lanes and small fields and hedges and lakes under the Iron Mountains.' See McGahern, *Memoir*, 260–1.

8 See letter to Michael McLaverty of 7 December 1962.

9 Kate O'Brien reviewed *The Barracks* for *University Review* (now *Irish University Review*), vol. 3, no. 4 (1963), 59–60. The review was almost wholly favourable and concludes thus: 'I commend it zestfully and with great satisfaction to all who care for the fictional form in art, and also to those who don't. Let them read here, and learn what an art the novel can be.'

10 It was in Mary Lavin's Lad Lane mews that McGahern, in the company of Nuala O'Faolain, first met Tom Kilroy. See letter to Mary Lavin of 26 January 1989.

The myth of Farmer John is not my doing. Over the years many TV crews have been here who wanted me to play the farmer. This I always refused. I was a writer who happened to live on a farm. I read lately in a couple of places that I hide my own sophistication or lack of it. That is for others to judge. Maybe I should buy a top hat and go to Dublin more often and talk about who's in and who's out and who met who in Paris in the 1920s. Jimmy Swift was one of the most deeply read men I ever knew, and you could never tell that he had read anything unless it came naturally into play. To do otherwise he would have viewed as bad manners, the bad manners of the mind.[11] To refer to Leitrim, which used to be a place to joke about, is sometimes a way of deflecting foolish questions without causing offence. Kavanagh and Beckett were definite influences, and I said so in my first TV interview when I was very young. Jimmy Swift got on distantly but well with Kavanagh. It was he who had Kavanagh's important later poems typed and copied, and he sent them away to his brother Paddy and David Wright, who published them in Nimbus and placed them with Longmans. Kavanagh then gave Jimmy the original manuscript. This is acknowledged in the recent edition of the Collected Poems, though such was Jimmy's nature that he would never want to claim any credit for himself.[12] I would have read nearly all these poems in manuscript, and read Beckett in the little magazines; and somehow that was more exciting than reading them in books. I'm not sure why. Maybe it was more immediate.

You are right to be wary of memoirs. I deliberately did not read Richard Murphy's The Kick.[13] I read the passage you refer to in Nuala O F's because her lawyers had her send it to me prior to publication.[14] Naturally, I told her to go ahead. I was attracted to Nuala when we were young, but it was not returned. She had a lover called Murray at the time, a writer/actor who was good looking and may have had some money. She took me to an attractive flat he had on Baggot Street. Looking back, the motive may have been some

---

11 A reference to one of McGahern's favourite quotes, taken from Proust: 'We can develop the power of our sensibility and our intelligence only within ourselves, in the depths of our spiritual life. But it is in this contact with other minds, which reading is, that the education of the "manners" of the mind is obtained.' See Marcel Proust, *On Reading Ruskin: Prefaces to La Bible d'Amiens and Sésame et les Lys with Selections from the Notes to the Translated Texts*, trans. and ed. Jean Autret, William Burford and Philip J. Wolfe, int. Richard Macksey (New Haven and London: Yale University Press, 1987), 125.

12 See Antoinette Quinn, 'Acknowledgements', in Patrick Kavanagh, *Collected Poems* (London: Penguin Books, 2005), x.

13 See Murphy, *The Kick*.

14 See Nuala O'Faolain, *Are You Somebody? The Life and Times of Nuala O'Faolain* (Dublin: New Island Books, 1996), 80–3.

form of revenge, but that's not certain. What is certain is that she made it clear the next day that it was an aberration, a one-night stand, and would not be repeated.[15] Nuala had many affairs and many admirers. I can only attribute my elevation in her memoir to the fact that I became better known with the years than the real suitors. What she wrote is fantasy, putting it at its kindest.[16]

I hope some of this is useful. Memory is uncertain. I had many letters that I was able to check. These showed me that I had often arranged things in different sequences in my mind. My sisters read the manuscript in draft, and naturally had different versions, or slightly different version, of the same event, and they recovered two important scenes that I had blanked out. My aim at all times was to get as close as possible to the facts.

Everybody reads a work differently. Thank you for all your attention to the text, which is probably more than it has earned.

With every good wish.

[*unsigned*]

Faber (email)

[*Foxfield*]

12 March 2006

Dear Neil,

A long e-mail came from you last Friday. For some reason these long e-mails block the system and eventually it was lost in cyberspace. Probably the

---

15 In *Are You Somebody?* O'Faolain recounts a relationship of 'a year or two' with McGahern in Dublin of the early 1960s, and concludes her memories of the affair thus: 'Maybe John toyed with certain possibilities as a way of settling himself. Certainly, we tried hard to know each other, if willing it could do it. I remember a miserable night – the last, I think – when we wandered the wintry streets for hours and still could not find any ease with each other. These things matter when you're young and have high standards. Nowadays, I bump into him once a year or so, and we just exchange friendly greetings. But I hardly know him less, in reality, than I did when we were meeting all the time.' 82–3.

16 In a letter dated 15 July 1996 from O'Faolain to McGahern she tells him of her intention to publish the memoir and asks him: 'So – is there anything you want to say to me about these quotations here?' She then adds a footnote, and at the bottom of the letter writes: 'I've been less than honest as it is, in my opinion'. Madeline McGahern Papers. It is clear that McGahern made no attempt to change what was sent or to interfere with the publication of *Are You Somebody?* as it stood.

simplest thing is to put it in the post. I'd be grateful if you would cast your eye over this prefatory note (sent separately). I've discarded stories I don't want to keep, but I'm open to your advice.[17] I'm now slowly going through the texts of the stories. I'd like to finish 'The White Boat'. Whether I'll have enough concentration to finish I won't know until I go back to it after going through the rest of the texts. I'll send you the completed text first without it. As always, I would be grateful for your editing and advice.

The good news from America is that All Will Be Well is reprinting. The first run was 16,000 copies.

With every good wish
John

Madeline McGahern (TS)

4 Mount Temple Road
Dublin 7

24 March 2006[18]

Dear Tom,[19]

I am sorry to be dictating this to you. Madeline brought yesterday the very kind letter you sent. I had to go back into the Mater again, where I am now. We had a run of very bad luck. We both got food poisoning while staying in The Savoy for the South Bank Show Awards.[20] As soon as that cleared, we got a bad flu bug. Madeline recovered easily enough, but since my own system has been shot up with chemotherapy for a number of years, I knew before I went into the Mater that I wouldn't make America, and I was right.[21] All the receptions and interviews, speeches, dinners, lunches, signings had to be cancelled. The book did alright without me; it might even have done better. It got an incredibly favourable reception. The one serious attack was by Denis

---

17 The discarded stories are 'Coming into his Kingdom', 'Bomb Box/The Key', 'Peaches', 'The Beginning of an Idea', 'The Stoat', 'Doorways' and 'Along the Edges'.
18 The McGaherns' Stoneybatter house.
19 Tom Callan, a solicitor in Boyle employed by the McGaherns.
20 Melvyn Bragg hosted the awards at the Southbank Centre, and the McGaherns stayed in the Savoy. The Evans, Braggs and McGaherns dined afterwards at the Garrick Club. Edna O'Brien presented the award.
21 John Bruton, who had been European Union ambassador to the United States since 2004, had invited the McGaherns to visit him and his wife Finola in Washington DC. The intention was for this trip to coincide with promotion of All Will Be Well.

Donoghue, my own Lord Oracle from U.C.D., but he is seen as so egocentric that it was thought to be as useful as a rave notice: it was all about himself, another sergeant's son.[22]

I think the record should be put straight, just in case. While you were away, we had a letter from Emmet McGarry's solicitor, polite and defeatist in tone. McGarry would take nothing less than a full apology, and he refused the offer of word changes. With the solicitor's letter was a large brown envelope marked 'Strictly Confidential' and <u>for my eyes only (Sean McGahern)</u>. The letter was long and extremely abusive; it may even have been defamatory. He accused me of fictionalizing his father's life, which I could not have known since I left their part of the country when I was nine or ten.[23] He also accuses me of giving an apology to Bishop McKiernan when I would not give one to his own family/blood relations, to whom I had caused much more serious injury. This is a lie.

McKiernan went to the Sunday Times and complained that *The Memoir* accused him of smoking, when he never smoked, and that he never took the book out of the library. All the evidence rested on Maggie's statement to me, which was to say that she told the future bishop to buy his cigarettes elsewhere until Sean's book was put back on the library shelves.[24]

22 Denis Donoghue's review of *Memoir* (published as *All Will Be Well: A Memoir* in the United States). Titled 'A Version of Pastoral', it appeared in the *New York Review of Books* for 23 March 2006. It is a strange, wrongheaded and at times meanspirited review in which, as McGahern comments above, Donoghue has too much to say about his own policeman father, is prudish about work like *The Pornographer* and 'Bank Holiday', condemns McGahern's stance on the Irish Troubles as narrow and simplistic, and – strangest of all – sees McGahern as having broken free from his canonical Irish predecessors: 'Some readers think of him in some relation to Beckett, but that seems extreme. Not being a poet, he is free of Yeats. He can circumvent Joyce by staying out of Dublin.' It is difficult to see how Donoghue could have got McGahern more wrong.

23 In *Memoir* McGahern paints an unflattering – if essentially harmless – picture of Francie McGarry, the local man who had married McGahern's aunt Katie McManus. See *Memoir*, 50–1.

24 The 'future Bishop' is Francis Joseph MacKiernan (1926–2005), a native of Aughawillan and a priest in Ballinamore at the time when *The Barracks* was published. He went on to a successful career in the Church, becoming Bishop of Kilmore in 1972. For a description of Aunt Maggie's reaction to the priest's attempted censorship of *The Barracks* in her hometown, see *Memoir*, 245. Liam Kelly negotiated a verbal settlement between McGahern and MacKiernan without the case going to law. In all future editions the deal was that MacKiernan's name would be left out of the text. See letter to Liam Kelly of 31 October 2004.

When the Sunday Times reporter rang me up, all I could say was that if Maggie's words weren't true the Bishop was owed an apology. A Sunday Times team of reporters investigated the incident and found that Maggie's story was substantially true. The young priest, the future bishop, did not physically take the book out of the library, but he controlled the library committee, and when Maggie learned that the book had been removed from the library shelves, she told the future bishop that he could take his custom elsewhere until Sean's book was returned to the shelves. In fairness to the Bishop, he never denied this and was polite, and he never asked for an apology – nor would he have been given one had he asked. If the case had been pursued further, the Bishop would have been seen to have been an even greater fool through trying to win on minor technicalities.

Out of this came another interesting feud. The county librarian, Vera McCarthy, and McKiernan had been having a long feud. While the librarian had no option but to obey the committee's orders, they could not stop her putting the removed book under the counter, which she did, recommending it happily. This gave me a richer text, and Bishop McKiernan was very satisfied with the agreed word changes. Again, he was very polite.

I only wrote about Francie McGarry in the light of how the McManus family viewed their sons-in-law, Frank McGahern and Francie McGarry. The central figure in the book is my own father, and McGarry is there only to give a consistency and a lightness to the McManus view. Of the two, my father was much more disliked; in fact, he was barred from their mountain dwelling, which was extremely unusual for the time. Francie McGarry could easily have been deleted from the text without damaging *The Memoir* in any way. I state clearly in the book that this narrow viewpoint was only my view. The one-and-a-half pages in which McGarry features in the book were all told to me by the McManus family, and I was able to check out the material when working on the book with my first cousin, Paddy McManus, whose own father was maligned in a number of the McGarry letters. My Uncle Jimmy McManus was one of the most attractive men I knew when I was growing up, the very opposite of the McGarry descriptions; but he was very independent minded and quick, and he did not suffer fools. We obviously see each other differently. By contrast, my father had 'great time' for Francie McGarry, much less time for Jimmy McManus.

I had no wish to extend the description of Francie McGarry beyond this narrow viewpoint, as I have no knowledge of his family life. I had already much material in reserve that I didn't use. For instance, one wet spring the McGarrys ran out of turf for the fire. The normal thing would have been to borrow a load of turf from one of his neighbours till he had his own turf saved, if his relationships were as good between him and his neighbours as the family asserts. Instead, he harnessed his horse and cart and drove the eight miles into the mountains to get turf from the McManuses. The ground was wet when he got there. He found Jimmy McManus putting out top-dressing with creels because he feared more rain. He had not enough dry turf around the house, but he had plenty of turf on the mountain. The house was closed and my grandmother was ill in bed. Jimmy asked Francie to put out a few creels for him while he went to the mountains for the turf. It was a long journey. These turf were usually taken home load by load at the end of each day's work when the new turf was being saved. When Jimmy returned with a load of turf in McGarry's cart, he found that not a creel of manure had been put out, and Francie McGarry had spent all the time Jimmy had been away rattling a stick in a little opening in my grandmother's window, presumably because she wouldn't get out of bed and was irked by her failure to open the house and dance attendance on him for the few hours. My grandmother already detested her two sons-in-law, but after this incident Francie was even more unpopular than my father. This story, as well as the others, can be corroborated independently of me. This description of his behaviour does not tally with the idealized, even noble, picture of the father that the family presents.

Families are often seen very differently when seen from inside their families, since they are seen from the outside. Through you I have tried to state this to Emmet McGarry, but nothing seems able to get past his anger and his desire for revenge.

Naturally, I would like to take your advice, but my own instinct at this time would be to leave things as they are. I don't believe McGarry can do anything, but I would like to leave these details of this sorry episode for the record without necessarily doing anything.

I hope I will be in better form when next we meet, and with warm regards from us both.

[*unsigned*]

26 March [2006]

Dear Paul,[25]
I was both disappointed and puzzled by your recent communications. At Christmas you enclosed a poem with your card that seemed to link Heaney and myself as a pair of literary hucksters.

You must know that I have found no sustenance in Heaney's verse for many years, and even the charm of the early work has worn badly. The effect of your piece was to create a certain sympathy for Heaney's own high position.

I have probably said more than enough about Denis Donoghue. He is entitled to his view. Neither of us did anything intentional to incur such a reaction from yourself. These are small things and are best forgotten about. The publishers do not seem to be bothered by it, and they have ordered another reprint.[26]

To my regret, I have never learned to use e-mail. Madeline has often agreed to send them on my behalf and the words were/are always mine. I would normally write by hand, but so much has been happening in the last months that it is easier to use e-mail.

I wish you well. What more can we say?
John

---

25 This note to Paul Durcan was dictated as an email in the final days of McGahern's life; it is the last known written communication from him – he died four days later, on 30 March 2006.
26 McGahern was angry about Donoghue's review of *All Will Be Well* in the *New York Review of Books*. See letter to Tom Callan of 24 March 2006.

ACKNOWLEDGEMENTS

Madeline McGahern first approached me in the summer of 2014 to discuss the possibility of editing her late husband's letters. Since that time we have come to know each other very well; nothing I say by way of an acknowledgement could adequately capture the debts I owe her. Through many long and enjoyable conversations with Madeline over the subsequent years in Leitrim, Liverpool, London and Paris, I have learned a great deal about John McGahern, his life and his works. I can only hope that the contents of this edition reflect the knowledge garnered. When I first began work on the many letters in Madeline's possession they had been catalogued by Luke Dodd via a series of invaluable tables that pointed to content, dates and recipients – these documents saved me months of work, as did the selfless help in preserving, xeroxing, filing and storing letters that had been given to Madeline by Bill Hamilton, Michael Keohane, Rosalyn Keohane and Jonathan Keohane. John's sister Monica Gilligan was exceptionally generous in answering a wide array of questions about her brother and the McGahern family; her help and kindness made my task both easier and more enjoyable.

A number of archivists and librarians have been unfailingly helpful. First among those to assist the project was Barry Houlihan at Special Collections, James Hardiman Library, National University of Ireland Galway, who went far beyond the call of duty to point me towards possible leads I would never otherwise have discovered. Robert Brown, the archivist at Faber & Faber, was a pleasure to work with and his help has played a vital part in bringing the work to fruition. Other archives to hold McGahern letters and which I wish to thank are: Harry Ransom Center, The University of Texas at Austin; Linen Hall Library, Belfast; University of Victoria, British Columbia; Stuart A. Rose Manuscript, Archives, and Rare Book Library, Emory University; Manuscripts and Archives Division, New York Public Library, Astor, Lenox, and Tilden Foundations; Special Collections and University Archives, University of Maryland Libraries; Lilly Library, Indiana University; Archive Department, Emerson College, Boston; BBC Written Archives Centre,

Reading; Special Collections, University College Dublin; Brotherton Library, University of Leeds; and the National Library of Ireland.

My old friend Patrick O'Sullivan commented on a section of this work in draft at an important moment and saved me from clumsiness of expression. The entire editorial team at Faber have been a delight to work with, and my copy-editor, Tamsin Shelton, saved me from numerous errors as well as making several suggestions that strengthen the book. As interns on the project, Lauren Price and Richard Snowden-Leak, undergraduate students of mine at the University of Liverpool, gave me extremely efficient and much-needed assistance in the summer of 2020. My colleagues at the Institute of Irish Studies have been an ever-present support. I was fortunate many years ago to have John Kelly as my moral tutor at St John's College, Oxford. His work on the letters of W. B. Yeats has been an inspiration and cannot be matched.

The following have all in various ways been generous with their time and resources, have shared their valuable thoughts with me about the project or were encouraging and kind at key stages of the work: Laura Albery, Kevin Bean, Neil Belton, Charlotte Buxton, Susanna Capon, Niall Carson, Michael Carter, Michael Chang, Mary Clayton, Jonathan Coleman, Iseult Coolahan, Marios Costambeys, Kathryn Court, Des Dockery, Maura Dooley, Martin Doyle, Keith and Siobhán Duggan, Martin Dyar, Leontia Flynn, John Foley, Tadhg Foley, Richard Ford, Roy Foster, Cliff Greenblatt, Michael Griffin, Donald S. 'Skip' Hays, Catherine Heaney, Sophia Hillan, Paddy Hoey, Neill Joy, Stephanie Judd, Margaret Kelleher, Bláithín and Miles Kennedy, Faye Kennedy, John and Karen Kenny, Liselotte Keogh, Declan Kiberd, Tom and Julia Kilroy, Rosie Lavan, Anne-Claire Leydier, Conor Linnie, Éamon Little, Kathleen MacMahon, Breandán MacSuibhne, John McAuliffe, Gregg McClymont, Maev McDaid, Brendan McGurk, Joanna Mackle, Catherine Manning, the late Kate Marsh, Vic Merriman, the late Richard Murphy, Deirdre Ní Chonghaile, Michael Nott, Eoin O'Connell, Bernard O'Donoghue, Eddie O'Kane, Liz O'Neill, Stephen O'Neill, Robert Palmer, Tom and Giti Paulin, Chris Perry, Valerie Parker-Chang, Anna Pilz, Pete Shirlow, my parents Collette and Frank Shovlin, and my brothers James, John and Peter Shovlin, Whitney Standlee, Tony Swift, Kersti Tarien, Anna Teekell, Dominic Turner and Richard Waterworth. Invitations to deliver public lectures about various aspects of the letters helped to focus and sometimes change my thinking. Thanks, in particular, are due to Nicholas Allen at the Willson Center for Humanities and Arts, University of Georgia; Dan Carey at the Moore Institute, National University of Ireland Galway; Patrick Griffin at the Keough-Naughton Institute for Irish Studies, University of Notre Dame; Paul Shovlin at the National Library of Ireland; and Enda Leaney at the Dublin City Libraries & Archives.

Several people very kindly gave me access to private correspondence from McGahern in their possession and thus make this book a truer reflection of the life: Paul Armstrong, Eamon Barrett, Seán Beattie, Rita Brehony, Frances Byrnes, Dónal and Dolores Cleary, Kathryn Court, Gerry Dawe, the late Alain Delahaye, Luke Dodd, Susanne Dumbleton, Luke Gibbons, Michael Gorman, Nicholas Grene, Peter Guy, Marius Harkin, DeWitt Henry, Mary Keelan, Liam Kelly, Joe Kennedy, Niall MacMonagle, Alen MacWeeney, Belinda McKeon, Joan O'Neill, Michael Prusse, Robin Robertson, James Ryan, Denis Sampson, Seán Sexton, Colm Tóibín, Stanley van der Ziel, Bob White and Pamela Woof.

The project would have taken considerably longer to complete had it not been for the generous funding supplied by a number of organisations. The award of a British Academy/Leverhulme Trust Senior Research Fellowship in 2018 was crucial and allowed me to concentrate wholly on the *Letters* for a full calendar year. A month spent with the McGahern Papers at the National University of Ireland Galway was made possible via the award of a Moore Institute Visiting Fellowship in April 2019. Further funding came from the University of Liverpool's School of Histories, Languages and Cultures and from the university's Institute of Irish Studies.

My wife Maura has been a great friend and supporter of the project from start to finish. My children, Frank and Beatrice, have witnessed their father's work on John McGahern their whole lives long and I appreciate their love and forbearance.

INDEX

Almeria, JMcG visits, 148, 149, 153, 154, 156, 163, 170
Altshuler, Miriam, 592, 619, 647, 649; **592n**, 635, 643, 648
Ambassador cinema, Dublin, 187
American Academy of Arts and Letters, 391n
American Centre, Paris, 228
American Embassy, Dublin, 572
American Embassy, Paris, 265
American Irish Foundation, 572
American Poetry Review, 527
Amherst College, 430n
Amis, Kingsley, 310n; *Ending Up*, 373n
Amongst Women (JMcG): influence of
  King Lear, 7n; and Three Blackbirds,
  Leytonstone, 151n; and de Montherlant:
  Chaos and Night, 160n; writing, 542n, 548,
  589, 591, 594–6, 598, 606–7, 610, 614,
  623, 630; title, 615, 619; UK edition (Faber
  & Faber), 597n, 612, 618, 620, 623, 632,
  634, 636, 640; US edition (Viking Penguin),
  529n, 619–20, 624, 627, 628–9, 631, 643,
  664, 682; French edition (*Entre toutes les
  femmes*; Presses de la Renaissance), 622,
  627, 631; paperback editions, 629n, 643,
  644, 647; and Chatto & Windus, 612; and
  Secker & Warburg, 561n; covers, 629n, 631,
  682; publicity, 625n, 629, 749n; reviews,
  619, 626, 637n, 733n; reception, 620–21,
  626, 628, 637, 639, 640, 678n, 771n; sales,
  625n, 629, 633, 634, 638, 640, 647, 648,
  785; reprints, 638, 682; serialised as *A Book
  at Bedtime*, 625, 630n; recorded for Irish
  radio, 644; television adaptation, 625, 661,
  683, 704, 709, 714, 728n; extract published
  in the *Sunday Independent*, 662; wins *Irish
  Times*-Aer Lingus prize, 632, 636n; and the
  Booker Prize, 632–4, 638; wins GPA Award,
  658, 661, 663, 716; included in Callil and
  Tóibín: *The Modern Library*, 721; on Irish
  Leaving Certificate curriculum, 785
An Garda Síochána, 556n
Anderson, Scott, 629
Andrew Edmonds' restaurant, London, 738n
Angers, University of: colloquy on JMcG and
  Alice McDermott, 725n
Anglo-Irish War (1919–21), 20n, 453n, 646n
Another Country (BBC Radio 3 series), 742n,
  753–4, 757–8, 760
Anvil (publisher), 571
Aosdána, 530, 538, 550, 573n, 580, 623,
  671, 706n

Aquinas, St Thomas, 49
Aquitaine Nord savings bank, 675n
Archers, The (BBC radio), 368n
Archery Tavern, Lancaster Gate, 186
Ardagh and Clonmacnois diocese, 584n
Ardara, Frank McGahern serves as garda
  sergeant, 168n
Ardcarne, burial of Frank McGahern, 441n
Arena Cinema (BBC), 307n
Arendt, Hannah, 255n
Argus (Drogheda), 84, 149n
Arigna mountains, 18
Arkansas, JMcG visits, 696
Arkansas Press, University of, 546n
Arkansas, University of, Fayetteville, 747n
Armstrong, Paul, 786, 786n
Arnold, Bruce: reviews *Getting Through*,
  460; *Jack Yeats*, 727n
Arnold, Matthew, 436
Arsenal FC, 237n, 454n
Arts Council (Great Britain): awards and
  bursaries to JMcG: 235, 236, 240n, 243,
  287, 289, 294, 299, 312, 354, 359, 447n,
  448; award to Richard Murphy, 219
Arts Council of Ireland: JMcG acknowledges,
  127; JMcG seeks support for publishing
  venture, 406; JMcG reports on Galway
  Writers' Workshop, 504; JMcG elected to
  Board, 767, 771, 772; personnel, 405n;
  establishment of Aosdána, 530n; Cnuas
  for Aosdána members, 573n; Macaulay
  Fellowship, 104n, 132; support for Lilliput
  Press, 676; support for TCD Writer
  Fellowship, 594n
Arts Theatre, Lamda, London, 293n
Arvon Foundation: Ted Hughes Arvon
  Centre, Lumb Bank, 544n, 545, 571, 655n;
  Totleigh Barton, 415, 505, 544
Aston Villa FC, 672n
Astoria hotel, St Petersburg, 142
Atascadero, California, 555n, 559, 688n
Atkinson, Will, 785, 788
Atlantic, The, 325n
Atlantic Monthly, 73, 265, 271, 275, 592;
  rejects 'The Country Funeral', 595n;
  publishes 'Korea', 249, 256n, 262, 264;
  publishes 'The Recruiting Officer', 243n,
  256n
Atlantic Monthly Press, 131n, 235n,
  242n, 245, 256n, 269, 277n, 325, 334,
  396, 434n, 440n, 449n; contracts and
  financial arrangements, 329, 331n, 347;

British Museum, London, 191
Brixton, London, 296n
Broadway, New York, 515
Brockway, James, 253, **253n**
Broderick, John, 784n
Brodkey, Harold: *This Wild Darkness*, 692
Brogan, Martin, 621
Broin, Joe, 141, 166
Bron, Eleanor, 646
Brooke-Rose, Christine: *Such*, 198n
Brooksbank, Miss (Faber & Faber), 280
Brown (literary editor of the *New York Times*), 113
Brown, Buchanan, 44, 44n
Brown University: alumni, 436n
Browne, Mrs James, 288, 301n
Browne, Josephine, 56n
Browne, Sir Thomas, 350, **350n**
Browning, Robert, 699, **699n**
Bruegel the Elder, Pieter, 749; *Landscape with the Fall of Icarus*, 21, 21n; *The Wedding*, 749
Brussels: Musées royaux des Beaux-Arts de Belgique, 21n
Bruton, Finola, 800n
Bruton, John, 538n, 701, 800n
Büchergilde Gutenberg: publishes German edition of *The Leavetaking* (*Abschiednehmen*), 393n
Buffalo, University of, 206
Buire-le-Sec, 516n, 532
Bulgakov, Mikhail: *The Master and Margarita*, 237
Buncrana, Co, Donegal, 168n
Bundoran, Co. Donegal, 168n
Bunting, John, 44, 44n
Buñuel, Luis, 175
Burford, William, 798n
Burgess, Anthony, 614
Burke, Donna, 721
Burke, Elizabeth, 742n
Burke, Tom, 721
Burroway, Janet, 296
Burtonport, Co. Donegal, 168n
Busby, Margaret, 533n
Busch, Ben, 790
Busch, Fred, 264, **264n**, 440, 441, 508, 543, 546, 557, 643, 705, 790; *Take This Man*, 543n
Bush, George W., 790, **790n**
Buswells Hotel, Dublin, 188
Butlin's, 166

By the Lake (JMcG), see *That They May Face the Rising Sun* (US edition)
Byatt, A. S., 632–3, 638; *Possession*, 632–3, 636
Byatt, A. S., and Peter Porter (eds.): *New Writing 6*, 572n, 684n
Byrne, Mr (Foxfield neighbour) 546
Byrne, Gay, 658n, 663
Byrnes, Frances, 678, 683, 684, 686, 690, 711, 712, 738, 742, 743, 753, 754, 756, 757, 758, 760, 761, 793, 795
Byrnes' pub, Davey, Dublin, 685n
Byron, George Gordon, Lord, 25, 262, 278, 532

Caen, JMcG visits, 675
Cafferty, Packie Joe, 584, 585
Cairns, Tom, 683n
Calder, Alexander, **496n**, 718
California, 559
California, University of, San Francisco, 704n
California Press, University of, 303
Callan, Tom, 800
Callan, Co. Kilkenny, 573n
Callil, Carmen, and Colm Tóibín (eds): *The Modern Library*, 721
Cambridge, University of, 184; alumni, 335n, 626n
Campbell, Roy, 406
Camus, Albert, 139n, 716n; *L'Homme Révolté*, 716n; *Le Mythe de Sisyphe*, 716n
Canadian Journal of Irish Studies, 480n, 715n; publishes 'The Creamery Manager', 593n
Canard, Le, 534, 535, 637n
Canny, Nicholas: *The Elizabethan Conquest of Ireland*, 687n; *Kingdom and Colony*, 687n; *Making Ireland British*, 687n
Capitol cinema, Dublin, 174
Capon, Edith, 476
Capon, Susanna, 285, 290, 298, 311, 319, 333, 335, 337, 359, 362, 363, 371, 586; 259, **285n**, 584, 585, 599, 723n
Captain (dog), 605n
Carey, Peter, 597n
Carleton, William, 177, **177n**, 500, 519; 'The Lough Derg Pilgrim', 177n; *Traits and Stories of the Irish Peasantry*, 177n, 246
Carney, Des, 754, 769, 784, 792
Carlson, Julia: *Banned in Ireland: Censorship and the Irish Writer*, 631n
Carlyle, Thomas, 735

Carmi, T., *see* Charney, Carmi
Carpentier y Valmont, Alejo, 224
Carr, Barbara, 379n
Carrefour des Littératures Européennes de
  Strasbourg, 616n, 624
Carrick-on-Shannon, Co. Leitrim, 306n,
  340n, 422n, 424, 611n, 622n, 676, 739n,
  744n, 786n
Carson, Ciaran, 401n
Cartano, Tony, 537n, 589, **589n**, 594n, 613,
  632, 643, 760n
Carter, Angela, 557n
Carter, Jimmy, 508n
Carty, Ciaran, 459n
Carysfort College of Education, 395n, 401, 407
Casavini, Pieralessandro (Austryn
  Wainhouse), 161, **161n**
Casement, Roger, 171
Casey, Dan, 665, 694
Casey, Eamonn, 655, **655n**
Casey, Kevin: *The Sinners' Bell*, 286n
Cassels, 45
Cassidy, Lar, 676
Castlebar, Co. Mayo, 660
Castlederg, Co. Tyrone, 86n, 381n, 481
Castlerea, Co. Roscommon, 18, 18n
Catherine the Great, 141n
Cavan, Co., 3n, 500, 696
Cayman Islands, 705n
Cayuga Lake, 465n
Cecil, Lord David, 198, **198n**
Censorship, 123n, 158n
Central Lancashire, University of, Preston:
  JMcG reading, 764n
Central Statistics Office, 273n
Centre Culturel Irlandais, Paris, 755
Centre National du Livre, Paris, 614n
Channel Four, 541n, 542, 646n, 692n
Chantilly, JMcG lecture, 624
Charabanc Theatre Company, 630n
Charlbury, Oxfordshire, 599
Charles Macklin Autumn School, Culdaff,
  Co. Donegal, 783n
Charley/Charlie (cat), 525, 555, 563, 584,
  585, 638
Charney, Carmi (T. Carmi), 64, 64n, 65
Chatto & Windus, 68n, 435n, 612n
Chatwin, Bruce, 557n
Chekhov, Anton, 83; *Platonov*, 172, 197;
  short stories, 47
Chelsea, London, 109
Chelsea FC, 237n

Cheltenham Literature Festival, 165, 170,
  172, 175, 758
Chester Beatty Museum, Dublin, 774
Chez Allard, Paris, 453, 586
Chicago, 93, 103, 112, 116, 478n, 696, 736n
Chicago, University of, 90n, 100n, 113n
Chicago Review, 101n, 102n, 103
Chinon, JMcG visits, 673
Christian Brothers, 305n
Christine de France, **336n**
'Christmas' (JMcG), 206, 390; sent to Knopf,
  211; early version submitted to the *New
  Yorker*, 212, 423n; and *Nightlines*, 266,
  267n, 270–71
Cigale Récamier, La, Paris, 586
Clandeboye Estate, Co. Down, 424n
Clapp, Susannah, 633n
Clark, Hap, 440
Clark, Orlo H., 704
Clarke, Austin, 119, **119n**
Cleary, Dónal, 411, 691, 773; **411n**
Cleary, Dolores, 773; 411, 691
Cleggan, Co. Galway, 87n, 90n, 103n, 135,
  152, 169n, 171n, 183, 184, 254, 287, 345,
  346, 356, 368, 797
Clifden, Co. Galway, 297, 299, 356, 630,
  632
Clifton, Harry, 736n
Clinton, Bill, 696
Clonmel, Co. Tipperary, 691
Clontarf, Dublin, 24, 608, 639, 769, 787, 789
Cloone, Co. Leitrim, 760
Cloudland ballroom, Rooskey, 78, 78n
Clough, Brian, 353n
Coetzee, J. M.: *Disgrace*, 722n
Cognac, 633, 634
Coifi, 218n
Cold War, 73n
Coleraine, 388, 409
Coleridge, Samuel Taylor: *Biographia
  Literaria*, 326n
Colgan, Michael, 645
Colgate, Hamilton, New York, 673n
Colgate University, 245; JMcG teaches at:
  87n, 301, 312n, 340n, 395, 403, 414n,
  417, 424–5, 451, 456, 458–9, 462, 492,
  514, 531, 534n, 546, 548, 550, 551, 554,
  582, 585, 634, 637, 638, 642, 643, 647,
  648, 665, 687–8, 693, 695–6, 735, 738,
  759, 764n, 765n, 775; Crawshaw Chair,
  557n; O'Connor Chair, 264, 267, 303;
  alumni, 466n; faculty, 336n, 341n, 423n,

de Bhaldraithe, Tomás, 30n
de la Mare, Giles, 280; and *The Dark*, 280;
    and Faber & Faber, 568n
De La Salle College, Waterford, 552, 569n
De Silva, Francesco, 119n
de Valera, Éamon, 397, 787
Dea (teacher), 657
'Dead Days, The' (BBC documentary film),
    176, 177, 182, 184–6, 188, 190, 192, 193
Deane, Seamus, 407n, 493n, 505, 557, 600n,
    630, 645n; *Reading in the Dark*, 733n
Defence of the Realm (film), 661
DeFiore and Company, 592n
Defoe, Daniel, 594n; *Moll Flanders*, 594n
Delacroix, Eugène: journals, 528
Delafield, Frances Katherine ('Kate'), **324n**
Delahaye, Alain, *509, 511, 512, 514, 516,*
    528, 531, 532, 537, 540, 547, 548, 549,
    551, 552, 553, 555, 558, 565, 571, 578,
    589, 613, 616, 617, 622, 624, 632, 649,
    651, 653, 654, 672, 674; 503n, **509n,**
    543, 550; *L'Être Perdu*, 511; *L'Éveil des*
    Traversées, 511n; poetry, 541n; and *The*
    Barracks, 578
Delahaye, Florence, 617
Delahaye, Pascale, 531, 537, 540, 566, 617
Delahaye, Sébastien, 540n, 549
Delehanty, James, 162, **162n**
Delvin, Co. Westmeath, 86
Denis Diderot, Université, 465n
Denmark, JMcG visits, 718
DePaul University, Chicago, 736n, 738n
Derrada Wood, Co. Leitrim, 556n
Derry, 164, 168n, 489, 515–16, 522;
    Guildhall, 580n
Des Pres, Terrence, 507, 508n, 557, **557n,**
    604, 671; *The Survivor*, 557n
Deux Magots, Les, Paris, 531n
Devlin, Alan, 678
Devlin, Anne, 581; *The Venus De Milo*
    Instead, 581n
Devlin, Denis, 109, **109n**
Dial Press, 434n, 503n
Diary of Anne Frank, The, 248n
Dick Walsh Remembered, 769, 774;
    introduction by JMcG, 774n
Dickens, Charles: *Our Mutual Friend*, 461
Dickey, James, 559, **559n**; *Deliverance*, 559n
Dickson, Christie, 542
Dictionary of Literary Biography, 714n
Dietzel, Gisela, 209, 232
Dillard, Annie, 442n

Dirty Dick pub, Bishopsgate, 223n
Dodd, Luke, 628, 674, *681, 684, 688;* **628n**
Dolan, Ted, 743
Dolan, Terry, 112
Dole, Bob, 696
Dollymount, Dublin, 774, 789
Dolmen Miscellany of Irish Writing, The,
    51n, 52n, 54, 58n, 59n, 68, 68n, 70, 70n,
    103n
Dolmen Press, 51n, 56n, 90n, 107n
Dolphin, Dublin, 114, 118, 188
Donegal, Co., 168, 381n, 448, 464, 699
Donleavy, J. P.: *The Ginger Man*, 790n
Donnelly, Anna Rose, 419n, 621
Donnelly, Jerome, 416, 419n, 420, 421n,
    555, 563, 584
Donnelly, Nancy, 419
Donnelly, Peter: reviews *The Pornographer*,
    483–4
Donoghue, Denis, 642, **642n**, 801, 804;
    Warrenpoint, 642n; reviews *Memoir*,
    800–801, 804
Doolan, Lelia, 335n
Dooley, Maura, 655, **655n**
'Doorways' (JMcG): originally 'Getting
    Through', 417; revisions, 429; discarded
    from *Creatures of the Earth*, 800n
Dostoyevsky, Fyodor, 17; *Notes from*
    Underground, 113
Double Life of Veronique, The (film), 282n
Doubleday, 164, 248n, 442n, 620n; *see also*
    Judith Jones
Dove Cottage, Grasmere, 421n
Down, Co., 737n
Doyle, Roddy, 785
Doyle, Tony, 625n, 683n, 728, **728n**
Drabble, Margaret, 379, 380n
Dreamland ballroom, Athy, 78, 78n
Dreyer, Carl Theodor, 137n
Drogheda, 84, 149n, 293, 728
Drogheda Independent, 149–50n
Dromod, Co. Leitrim, 484, 489, 514, 587,
    621, 629, 697
Druid Theatre Company, 630n, 641n
Drumboylan, Co. Roscommon, 306n
Drumcondra, Dublin, 140n
Drumderrig, Co. Leitrim, 604n
Drumlaheen, Lough, Co. Leitrim, 369n
Drumshanbo, Co. Leitrim, 359, 585
Dryden, John, 350
du Sautoy, Peter, 46n, 54n, 55n, 82, **82n,**
    234, 312; and *The Dark*, 126n, 128n,

Jack, Ian, 777, **777n**
Jacob Wirth's restaurant, 439
James, Henry, 774
James Tait Back prize, 198
Jammet's restaurant, Dublin, 129, 136
Japan, JMcG visits, 779, 780, 783
Jardin Le Bréa, Hôtel, Paris, 616
Jardine, Lisa, **756n**
Jarniewicz, Jerzy, 736n
Jebb, Julian, 198, **198n**, 457, 545; 'Heart of
  the Matter', 198n; reviews *The Dark*, 198n;
  reviews *The Leavetaking*, 384n; reviews
  Nightlines, 297
Jennings, Ollie, 595n
Jesenská, Milena, 303n
Jesus College, Oxford, 64n
Jimmy's Hall (film), 744n
Job, Book of, 192
John Lane (publisher), 223n
John Lehmann (publisher), 219n, 303
John McGahern – A Private World (TV
  documentary), 782n, 783–4
John Paul II, Pope, 488, **488n**; visit to
  Ireland, 488n
Johns Hopkins University, 247n; alumni,
  436n
Johnson, Lyndon B., 136n
Johnston, Adrienne, 213n
Johnston, Jennifer, 614n, 725; Captains and
  Kings, 791n
Johnston, Lucy, 213n
Johnston, Margaret, 149, **149–50n**, 213,
  300n
Johnston, Michael, 213n
Johnstons, The, 213n, 300n, 665
Jonathan Cape, 24n, 373n, 534n, 663n, 710,
  781n
Jones, Dick, 188, 199
Jones, Inigo, 262n
Jones, Judith, 187, 188, 199, 206, 248, **248n**
Jones, Julia, 606
Jones, Marie, 630n
Jones, Russell Celyn, 756, **756n**
Jones, Thom: 'Break on Through', 689n; *The
  Pugilist at Rest*, 689n
Jonson, Ben, 262
Jordan, Blainid, 305n, 362, 422, 437
Jordan, John, 52, **52n**, 154, 205, 580; 'Off
  the Barricade: A Note on Three Irish Poets',
  52n
Jordan, Michael, 608
Jordan, Neil, 458, 471, 505, 608; reviews

Getting Through ('A Rural Irony'), 458,
  459n
Jordan, Tom, 121n, 169n, 305, 315n, 362,
  375, 397, 411, 422, 437, 688, 691, 769
José Corti (publisher): and J. B. Yeats letters,
  700, 706, 707, 709
'Journée d'Adieu' (JMcG), 578
Joy, Edmund, 593–4, 605, 726
Joy, Mary, 423, 538, 591, 670, 685, 718, 725
Joy, Matthew ('Teo'), 336n, 594n, 726
Joy, Neill, 336, 423, 455, 513, 518, 522,
  538, 543, 563, 590, 591, 593, 595, 604,
  665, 670, 685, 686, 693, 699, 702, 704,
  718, 725, 727, 770, 774, 778, 790; 336n,
  438, 439, 465, 507
Joyce, James, 39, 52, 139, 152, 225, 284,
  293, 392n, 519, 526, 570, 607, 659n, 768,
  801; 'The Dead', 17, 77; *Dubliners*, 292,
  294, 333, 509n, 570; 'A Little Cloud',
  494n; *A Portrait of the Artist as a Young
  Man*, 253n, 383–4n, 486n; *Selected Letters
  of James Joyce*, 225, 246, 414n; *Stephen
  Hero*, 253n; *Ulysses*, 123, 130, 788
Joyce Institute, Zurich, 787–8
Joyce, Stanislaus, 61–2n, 225; *The Dublin
  Diary of Stanislaus Joyce*, 61, 61n, 64,
  64n, 246; *My Brother's Keeper*, 62n, 246;
  Portrait of the Artist as a Young Man, 185n

Kafka, Franz, 213, 255n, 303n; *Letters to
  Milena*, 303; *Metamorphosis*, 102, 104,
  109
Kalett, Jim, 462
Kallas, Aino, 222
Kallas, Oskar, 222n
Kanon, Joseph, 277, **277n**
Kansantheatre, Helsinki, 147
Kaplan, Fred: *Henry James: The Imagination
  of Genius*, 662, 669
Karikoski, Eeva, 124n, 126n
Katanga Province, Congo, 189n
Kavanagh, Patrick, 6, 6n, 45, 55n, 135–6,
  145n, 152, 154, 185, 191, 213, 230, 245,
  296, 519, 594, 619, 630, 639–40, 720,
  722, 779, 798; 'Prelude', 17, 17n; *Collected
  Poems*, 246, 779, 798; *Come Dance with
  Kitty Stobling*, 17n, 30n, 712n; 'The
  Hospital', 712n; 'The Paddiad', 30, 30n;
  Ploughman and Other Poems, 17n, 640;
  Tarry Flynn, 154, 244, 246, 791n; influence
  of, 14n, 17n; as critic, 17; rejected by Faber
  & Faber, 45n

Le Fanu, Sheridan, 281n
Leach, David, 683
Leavetaking, The (JMcG): first thoughts, 66n, 132n, 281, 298n; and Belgrove National Boys' School, 773n; and Patrick Gregory, 332n; Patrick Kavanagh, influence of, 17n; and JMcG's mother's final days, 208; Jimmy Swift as model for 'Lightfoot', 26n; and Niall Walsh, 308n, 344, 356; title, 351; UK publication (Faber & Faber), 346, 348, 351, 354, 365, 367–8, 373, 375, 379, 386–7, 403, 425; US publication (Atlantic-Little, Brown), 325, 353, 366–7, 368n, 390–91; Dutch edition (Contact), 389, 443; French edition, 537, 538n, 540, 543, 547–51, 556; German edition (*Abschiednehmen*; Büchergilde Gutenberg), 393n; paperback (Quartet), 350n, 443, 473n, 553; paperback (Penguin), 529n; and Random House, 328, 330–31, 443; blurb, 363–4; covers, 368, 377, 473; reviews and reception, 379, 382–4, 386, 388, 389, 392, 394, 403; sales, 385, 389–91, 407, 553, 556; foreign rights, 385, 389; reprints, 389–91, 407; revised edition (Faber & Faber), 550–52; extracts published in *New Review*, 354, 356; extract published in *Irish Press*, 373; TV dramatization (as *The Lost Hour*), 528; entered for Booker Prize, 373, 374; JMcG reads extracts at Newcastle University, 375; JMcG reads extracts at Harvard, 437; and 'A Matter of Death', 289n; and *Memoir*, 298n, 778n
Ledwidge, Francis, 453
Ledwith, Micheál, 794
Lee, Hermione, 619; reviews *Amongst Women*, 626; interviews JMcG re: *That They May Face the Rising Sun*, 752n
Lee, J. J.: *Ireland 1912–1985*, 687
Lee, Josephine ('Josie'), **304n**
Legge, David, 764–5, 769
Légion d'honneur, 51n
Lehane, Kevin, **121n**, 169, **169n**, 174, 203, 207, 211, 219–20, 271, 279, 305, 361–2, 422, 516; and *The Barracks* (stage adaptation), 259n; and 'Korea', 262; as poste restante for JMcG, 187; property hunting for JMcG, 150n
Leicester City FC, 672n
Leishman, J. B., 303n
Leitch, Maurice, 296, 401n
Leitrim, Co., 18, 151n, 287n, 356n, 358,

385, 388–9, 391, 394–5, 413, 415, 425n, 432, 435–7, 565, 766, 777, 780, 798; *see also* Foxfield
Leitrim County Council, 573n
Leitrim Gaelic football team, 418–20n, 420
Leitrim Observer, 419n, 420
Lemon & Durbridge, 620
Lemon Unna & Durbridge, 625
Leningrad, *see* St Petersburg
Lennon, Eeva, *see* Karikoski, Eeva
Lennon, Peter, 73, **73n**, 117, 124n, 126n, 155n, 162, 174, 184, 193, 359n, 401; *The Rocky Road to Dublin* (film), 73n
Lennon, Tony, 155, 169n
Leonard, Hugh (John Joseph Byrne), 253, **253n**, 261; *The Barracks* (stage adaptation), 253, 259, 261n; *Stephen D.*, 78, 79n, 253
Leonardo da Vinci, 24
Leopardi, Giacomo, 205, **205n**, 206; *Selected Prose and Poetry*, 206
Lessing, Doris, 93n
Letellier, Michelle, 606
Letter from America (BBC Radio 4), 501n
Levi, Primo, 119, **119n**, 160; *If This Is a Man*, 119, 160, 720n; *The Truce*, 160
Lewis, Gifford: *The Yeats Sisters and the Cuala*, 727n
Lewis, Norman: *Voices of the Old Sea*, 659
Lewis, Vivienne, 283
Leyris, Pierre, 267n, 318, **318n**, 322, 323n, 465
Liberal Party, 374
Libération, 565, 606, 631, 643, 768n; *Writers Speaking About Their Profession*, 631n
Licorne, La, Poitiers, 691n
Lifetimes (BBC Northern Ireland), 481–2n
Liffey, River, 4, 90n, 539
Lightfoot family, 4n
Lignes de Fond (JMcG), *see* Nightlines
'Like All Other Men' (JMcG); collected in *Firebird* (Penguin), 561n, 562n, 612n; and the *New Yorker*, 568; and *Yale Review*, 568
Lille, 675
Lille, University of, 512
Lilliput Press, 676–7, 680n, 748
Limerick, 118n
Limerick, University of, 566n
Linton, John, 303n, 703n
Lisbon, 734–6
Listener, The, 181n, 262, 264, 277, 307n; publishes 'The Bomb Box', 262, 264, 267;

and proposed Faber & Faber short story collection, 519; headmaster at St Thomas's Secondary School, Belfast, 15n, 48, 70n, 91, 147, 190 222; and Philip McDermott, 610; JMcG describes relationship with, 639–40, 797; 'After Forty Years', 77, 77n; *The Brightening Day* (*The Stranger*), 88, 147, 160, 170, 640; *The Choice*, 15; 'The Circus Pony', 15, 15n; *Collected Short Stories*, 77n; *School for Hope*, 15; *Truth in the Night*, 15; and 'Strandhill, the Sea', 91; on *The Dark*, 160; and 'Gold Watch', 509n

MacLeod, Alistair, 709, 710, 713, 724n, 726, 737; *As Birds Bring Forth the Sun and Other Stories*, 720n; 'The Closing Down of Summer', 720n; *Island*, 710n, 724n, 726, 729n; *The Lost Salt Gift of Blood*, 655n, 710, 724n; *No Great Mischief*, 726n, 731, 737; 'The Tuning of Perfection', 720n, 729n

McManus, Jimmy (JMcG's uncle), 563n, 802–3

McManus, Katie (JMcG's aunt), 801n

McManus, Maggie (JMcG's aunt), 36, 36n, 37, 86, 112, 563, 801–2

McManus, Paddy, 802

McManus, Pat (JMcG's uncle) 3n, 37, 37n, 159, 369n, 416–17, 419, 437, 563n, 601–5, 622, 636, 752; model for 'The Shah' in *That They May Face the Rising Sun*, 3n

McManus family, 802–3

Macmillan, New York, 46, 88, 108, 128, 170n, 189n, 456n; rejects *The Dark*, 128–30, 149; and *Winter Tales* anthology, 271–2; *see also The Barracks*

MacMonagle, Niall, 739, **739n**, 750

MacNamara, Brinsley (John Weldon), 86; *The Valley of the Squinting Windows*, 86n

McNamee, Eoin, 746n

MacNeice, Louis, 181, 334n, 362n; *The Dark Tower*, 362

McNiffe, Mary B., 697n

Macoby, Gina, 575, 577

McQuaid, John Charles, 177, **177n**

McShera, Agnes (JMcG's stepmother), 18n, 26n, 169n, 515, 546, 783n

McShera family, 783

MacWeeney, Alen, 627; 111, **111n**, 112, 121, **627n**

MacWeeney, Lesley, 108, **108n**, 111n

Madden, David, 139n

Madden, Deirdre, 706–7, 736n

'Madness/Creativity' (JMcG; pamphlet), 691n

Madrid, JMcG visit, 124n, 170, 283

Maffey, Sir John (later Lord Rugby), 781n

Magarshack, David, 172n

Magdalen College, Oxford, 41n, 659n

Magnet, The, Carrick-on-Shannon, 786

Maguire, Edward, 580, **580n**

Mahon, Derek, 363, 399n, 614n, 616

Mairie, Café de la, Paris, 337n

Malaga, 157n, 162

Man Alive, 370n, 375n, 376n, 390, 398; publishes 'A Slip-up', 390n, 394, 397; publishes 'The Stoat', 398n

Man Booker Prize, 756, 761

Manchester City FC, 237n

Manchester Guardian, *see Guardian*

Manchester United FC, 237n, 239n

Mandelstam, Nadezhda: *Hope Against Hope*, 399n

Mandelstam, Osip, 621n

The Manila Rope, The, see Veijo Meri: *The Manila Rope*

Mann, Thomas, 25, 35, 255n; *Confessions of Felix Krull, Confidence Man*, 25, 25n; 192; *The Magic Mountain*, 17

Manning, Bob, 256n, 262, 325, **325n**

Manning, Olivia, 158n; reviews *The Dark*, 158n

Mannion, Francie, 356

Mansfield, Katherine: *The Young Girl*, 15–16

Mantel, Hilary, 633n, 744n

Marcus, David, 373n, 473n, 540n

Márquez, Gabriel García: *A Hundred Years of Solitude*, 641

Marrakesh, JMcG visits, 700

Martel, Yann: *Life of Pi*, 756n, 761n

Martin, Mme, 537, 548, 549

Martin, Guy, 437

Martin, Marilyn, 437n

Martin Brian & O'Keefe, 145n, 189n

Marvell, Andrew, 48, 48n

Marx Brothers, 409n

Mason, James, 515n, 572

Mason, Ronald, 285n, 319, **319n**

Massachusetts Institute of Technology, 187n

Masters, Dexter, 276, **276n**

Mater Private Hospital, Dublin: JMcG's prostate operation, 654; JMcG treated for bowel cancer, 745–7, 754 JMcG treated for liver cancer, 765, 767, 800

Matson, Harold, 131, **131n**, 132, 172, 187, 189

Matson, Peter H., 129n

O'Faolain, Julia: *Godded and Codded*, 286n; *We Might See Sights!*, 286n
O'Faolain, Nuala, 493n, 505, 797n, 798; *Are You Somebody?*, 798–9
O'Faoláin, Seán, 24, **24n**, 304, 720; *Bird Alone*, 24, 24n; *The Heat of the Sun and Other Stories*, 791n
Offaly gaelic football team, 533n
Ó Fiach, Cardinal, 794
O'Flaherty, Liam, 281n; *The Informer*, 791
Ogilvie-Grant, Ian, 13th Earl of Seafield, 272n
O'Grady, Bernadette, 775
O'Grady, Desmond, 52n, 135, **135n**
O Grady/O'Grady, Seamus, 505, 740, 775
Ó hEithir, Breandán, 614n
O hEocha, Colm, 505n
O'Keefe, Timothy, 189, **189n**, 190–91
O'Kelly, Sean T., 117
'Old Man' The', *see* 'White Boat, The' (JMcG)
Old Wine Shades, London, 322, 344
'Oldfashioned' (JMcG): published by *Threshold*, 562n; and Penguin Books, 562; collected in *High Ground*, 562n; quoted in *Another Country*, 757
Olympia Press, 161
Olympia Theatre, Dublin, 253n, 259
Omagh, Co. Tyrone, 164n, 566n
O'Mahony, Michael, 569
O'Mahony, Pat, 569
O'Malley, Eileen, 289n, 291, 293n, 302
O'Malley, Ellen, 468
O'Malley, Ernie: *On Another Man's Wound*, 20n, 667n, 727, 745, 752; reviewed by JMcG ('Return of the Revolutionary'), in the *Irish Times*, 745n, 752
O'Malley, Mary, 22, 22n, 61, **61n**
O'Malley, Patrick, 797
O'Malley, Peter, 430, **430n**, 433n, 438, 446, 468, 495
O'Malley family, 783
O'Mara, Veronica (ed.): *PS . . . of course: Patrick Swift 1927–1983*, 658
O'Mordha, Sean, 607, 624, 761, 772
On the Buses (TV series), 646
O'Neill, Eugene: *The Iceman Cometh*, 657–8
O'Neill, Joan, 713; *Daisy Chain War*, 713
O'Neill's pub, Dublin, 495n
O'Nolan, Brian, 55n
O'Regan, Michael, 570–71, 584; *see also* Colleran, Gerard, and Michael O'Regan
O'Reilly, Carina, 755

Origo, Iris 206, **206n**; *Leopardi: A Study in Solitude*, 206n
Orion Press, 119n
Ormond, Conrad, 301n
Ormond, Dorothea, 301n
O'Reilly, Sean, 746n
O'Rourke, Fran, 293, 293n, 306
O'Rourke, Paddy, 634
O'Sullivan, Thaddeus, 678
Ó Tuairisc, Eoghan, 504n, 540; **540n**; *The Road to Brightcity* (trans.), 540n
Ó Tuairisc, Rita, 540
Ovid: *Metamorphoses*, 173n, 194
Oxford, 114, 121, 123, 146
Oxford, University of: alumni, 415; 532n faculty, 402n, 622
Oxford University Press (OUP), 206n, 232, 361; anthologies, 519, 522

P. J. Flaherty's pub, Galway, 183n
Pablo (dog), 466
Pakenham family, 188
Palermo, 693
Panther Books, 263, 350, 481; acquires paperback rights for *The Barracks* and *The Dark*, 156, 442; covers of *The Dark*, 282; and *Nightlines*, 298, 350; paperback rights for *Nightlines*, 309, 350, 442
Paor, Louis de, 744, 760; **744n**, 747, 791
'Parachutes' (JMcG), 482n: rejected by the *New Yorker*, 527n, 534n, 539n; published by *Encounter*, 534n, 562n; and Penguin Books, 562n; collected in *High Ground*, 534n
Paris, JMcG visits, 64, 116, 118, 124, 170–71, 228n, 233, 243n, 246, 253–5, 258–9, 267, 268, 270, 283, 318, 326, 332, 357–9, 397, 400, 491, 532, 534, 537, 538, 584n, 586, 588, 589, 598, 606, 614, 616, 624, 633, 634, 637, 653, 670, 693, 700, 755, 760, 767, 768n, 769, 778; *see also* Madeline Green, Niels Gron *and* Rue Christine flat
Paris Biennale, 108n
Paris Review, 527; rejects 'The Country Funeral', 595n
Pastoral Renewal, 696
Pater, Walter, 522
Patterson, Glenn, 716n
Paulin, Giti, 689n
Paulin, Michael, 689n
Paulin, Niall, 689n

334n, 443, 541, 620, 648, 699, 724n; *see also* Jacob Epstein

Random House Book of Twentieth-Century French Poetry, 541n

Rann, 776n

Ransom, John Crowe, 192n

Rea, Stephen, 645n, 757, 760

Reading, Douglas ('Doc'), 441, 466

Reading, Janey, 466

Reading, University of, 242, 245, 249, 272n, 273n, 290, 312, 315, 318, 319n; faculty, 435n, 708

Reagan, Ronald, 508n

'Recruiting Officer, The' (JMcG), 243, 257, 261; published by *Atlantic Monthly*, 256; and *Nightlines*, 266, 267n, 270–71

Reddan, Marie, 740; 773

Regan family, 31

Reid, Forrest, **405n**, 410, 519, 601; *Apostate*, 597, 601, 627; *Brian Westby*, 199, 200, 204, 205, 207–8, 210, 405–6, 408, 410, 597n; *Following Darkness*, 410n; *Peter Waring*, 410n

Reihill, Clare, 748; 561n, 612n, 663, 699

Reisz, Karel, 307n; *see also* Millar, Gavin, and Karel Reisz

Renoir, Jean, 179

Renvyle, Co. Galway, 606

Republic of Ireland Act (1948), 781n

Restorick, Stephen, 701n

Review (BBC), 307n

Review, The, 165, 268n, 354n; publishes JMcG short stories, 165n, 178n, 206n, 209n

Rexine, John E., 440, **440n**

Reynolds, Albert, **78n**

Reynolds, Jim, 78n

Reynolds, Lorna, 133, **133n**, 306, 504n; 'The Traveller', 306n; 'The Violet Plucked and Burnt', 306n

Rheims, JMcG visits, 675

Rhys, Jean, 93n, 318n

Richardson, Dorothy, 214n

Richler, Mordecai: *Solomon Gursky Was Here*, 633n

Rigney, James, 82

Rigney, Mary, 82n

Riley, Jonathan, 695, 748–9

Rilke, Clara, 111n

Rilke, Rainer Maria, 111, 303; *Duino Elegies*, 303n; *Fifty Selected Poems*, 303n; *The Notebooks of Malte Laurids Brigge*, 107, 303, 703n

Rinaldi, Angelo, 588, **588n**

Rio de Janeiro, 704n

Ritz, Paris, 273

Rivière, Jacques, 118, **118n**

Robertson, Robin, *561, 562, 611, 663, 699, 710, 724*; **561n**, 731, 748n, 749; *A Painted Field*, 699

Robinson, Marilynne, 546n; *Gilead*, 546n; *Housekeeping*, 546

Robinson, Mary, 634n, 705n

Rockefeller Foundation, 580n

Rockefeller Institute, New York, 177n, 183n, 187, 203

Rockefeller University Concerts, 187n

Rockingham estate, 32–3, 32n, 581, 781n

Rockingham Shoot, The (JMcG): and the BBC, 579, 581, 585n, 594–6

Rockingham Shoot and Other Dramatic Writings, The (JMcG; ed. Stanley van der Ziel), 249n, 796n

Rocky Horror Picture Show, The (film), 95n

Rodway, Norman, 285n

Rogers, John, 577, **577n**, 578

Rondeau, Daniel, 565–6n, 631n; *Les Fêtes partagées*, 566n

Ronsley, Joseph, 478n

Roosevelt, Franklin D., 696n

Rooskey, 518

Rosanov, Ivan, 221

Roscommon, Co., 3, 22, 152, 176–7, 291, 304n, 306n, 628, 777n

Rose Bowl, Pasadena, 499n

Roseanne (student; Chicago), 90, 92–3, 110

Roseland ballroom, Moate, 78, 78n

Rosenthal, Thomas Gabriel, 202, **202n**, 203, 266; at Secker & Warburg, 367n

Rosie (unidentified; Paris), 64, 64n

Ross, Alan John, *310, 312, 317, 389*; **310n**, 317

Rosslare, Co. Wexford, 656

Rothchild, Robert, 322, 339

Roussel, Frédérique, 768

Rowan, Lough, *see* Laura Lake

Rowe, Marsha, 614

Rowley, Alf, 766

Royal Belfast Academical Institution, 41n

Royal College of Surgeons, Dublin, 337n

Royal Court Theatre, London, 371n, 581n, 641n

Royal Dublin Socicty, 55n, 68, 632n

Royal Festival Hall, London, 655n

Royal Hotel, Boyle, 188

Southampton University, 667
Southern Illinois University, Carbondale, 173n
Spain, John, 785
Spanish Civil War, 124, 160n
Sparrow, John, 379n
Spectator, 132; reviews *The Dark*, 158
Spectrum, 78
Spender, Stephen, 303, 352
Spirit of Place (Radio 4 series), 678n
'Spoiled Poet Takes his Ordination Vows, The' (JMcG), 13–14
Spotlight, 376n
Stacco, Teresa, 46
Stafford-Clark, Maxwell Robert Guthrie Stewart ('Max'), 641, **641n**
Stand, 412n; publishes 'A Slip-up', 394, 409, 412n, 430
States of Mind (RTÉ), 485
Steevens' Hospital, Dr, Kilmainham, 4n
Steidl (publisher), 709
Stein, Jean, 592n, 647
Steinbeck, John, 28
Steiner, George, 365n
Steinman, Michael (ed.): *The Happiness of Getting it Down Right*, 719n
Stendhal, 48, 49, 61n
Stephenson, Francesca, 658
Stevens, Jocelyn, 147n
Stevens, Wallace, 722
'Stoat, The' (JMcG), 360, 653; recorded for BBC, 362–3, 364, 374, 376; published in *Vogue*, 363, 374, 376, 409; published in *Man Alive*, 370, 375n; revised, 652; discarded from *Creatures of the Earth*, 800n
Stockholm, JMcG visits, 142, 144
Stoneybatter, JMcG's house, 528n, 539n, 621n, 628n
Stoppard, Tom, 379, 380n
Strand, Paul, 749, **749n**; *Leaves, Orgeval, France, 1965*, 748n
'Strandhill, the Sea' (JMcG): original opening, 91; published in the *Irish Press*, 91n; published in the *New Yorker* (as 'Summer at Standhill'), 75n, 91n, 132, 423n; and *Nightlines*, 91n, 267n, 270–71; and Forrest Reid: *Brian Westby*, 199n, 208n; revisions, 263n
Strang, Barbara M. H., 379n
Strang, Colin, 379
Strangford, Co. Down, 170

Stranmillis teacher training college, 221
Strasbourg, 616
Straus, Roger, 634, 642
Strokestown, Co. Roscommon, 684n
Strokestown Park, 628n, 629, 674, 688n
Strongbow, 585
Stuart, Francis, 614n
Stuart, Ian, 211
Stubbs Gazette, 366
Studley-Herbert, Nina, 12th Countess of Seafield, 272n
Süddeutsche Zeitung, 242
Sudek, Josef, 749, **749n**
Sun, 149
Sunday Independent, 85n, 147n, 169n, 287n, 376n, 739n; publishes extract from *Amongst Women*, 662; reviews *Getting Through*, 458, 458–9n
Sunday Telegraph: reviews *Getting Through*, 457n; reviews *The Leavetaking*, 383n
Sunday Times, The, 103, 777n, 801–2; reviews *The Dark*, 198n
Sunday Tribune, 376n; reviews *High Ground*, 574n; reviews *The Power of Darkness*, 666n
Sunday World, 85n, 361, 376n, 448n, 470n
Sundell, John, 45
Suschitsky, Peter, 95, **95n**
'Swallows' (JMcG; short story), 298n, 301; published in *Evening Herald*, 299n, 300n, 317; published by the *London Magazine*, 312, 317, 409; revisions, 321
Swallows (JMcG; television film): screenplay, 307; broadcast, 371n
Swarthmore, JMcG visits, 673n, 736
Swedlin, Rosalie, 474
Sweeney, Father F. X., 502
Swift, Gary, 643n, 677
Swift, James (Jimmy), 26, 27, 29, 44, 61, 64, 65, 126, 129, 144, 145, 153, 156, 157, 181, 184, 193, 230, 370, 374, 469, 476, 484, 488, 491, 497, 517, 552, 554, 601, 657, 658, 677, 679; **26n**; on *The Barracks*, 65n; on Kierkegaard, 153n; prostate operation, 497; relationship with JMcG, 4n, 33, 35, 45n, 55, 105, 121n, 169n, 371n, 490, 589, 643n, 694, 797–8
Swift, Jonathan, 61n, 119, **119n**, 262
Swift, Julie, 32–3, 33n
Swift, Kathy, 32–3, 33n, 126, 554
Swift, Nora, 677
Swift, Oonagh, *see* Ryan, Oonagh

Western Ontario, University of, 502n
Western Washington State College, 232n
Westminster Abbey, London, 145n
Westport, Co, Mayo, 630n
Wharton, Edith, 729
'"What Are You, Sir?" Trinity College
   Dublin' (JMcG), 599n
'What Is My Language?' (JMcG), 624, 751n;
   published in the *Irish Review*, 624
'Whatever You Say, Say Nothing' (JMcG),
   687n; published in the *Irish Times*, 726n
Wheeler's restaurant, London, 345
'Wheels' (JMcG), 241, and *Nightlines*, 241n,
   267n, 270–71; previously 'My Future at
   my Back', 262; published in *Encounter*,
   264, 278; television film adaptation, 384n;
   JMcG reads at Harvard, 437n
Whelan, Tony, 8, 33, 45, 98, 109, 223; **8n**,
   9n; 'Working at the mill', 8n, 223n
Whelan family, 34, 98, 109
Whipps Cross Hospital, 29n, 216n
White, Edmund, 792
White, Patrick, 93n
White, Robert ('Bob'; 'R. S.'), 598, 638,
   598n; *Keats as a Reader of Shakespeare*,
   598
White, Sean J., **566n**
White, Tony, 145n, **184n**, 187, 216, 217,
   222, 240, 297; *see also* Green, Martin
'White Boat, The' (JMcG), 568, 572, 593,
   643n, 686, 716; published in *New Writing
   6*, 572n, 684, 714; revisions, 796n, 800
Whitehall Primary School, Chingford, 182n,
   186, 229, 235, 237, 239
'Why We're Here' (JMcG), 178; publications,
   178n, 206n, 209n; sent to Knopf, 211;
   adapted as *Sinclair* for radio, 249n, 285n,
   297; and *Nightlines*, 267n, 270–71
Wicklow, Co., 108, 193, 630n, 728
Wilbur, Richard, 438, **438n**
Wilde, Oscar, 509n, 520
Wilder, Thornton: *Our Town*, 449n
William Blake's bar, Enniskillen, 454, 494,
   614n, 654, 663n
Williams, John, 747, 751, 763, **770n**, 774n,
   775, 778; *Augustus*, 747, 763, 770, 774n;
   Stoner, 747, 763, 764n, 767, 770, 774n,
   775, 778, 787
Williams, Nancy, 770
Williams, Tennessee, 47
Wilson, David, 385
Wilson, Edmund, 688

Windsor, University of, Ontario 724n, 726
'Wine Breath, The' (JMcG), 416, 465;
   published in the *New Yorker*, 428, 432,
   433, 438n, 442n, 445; published in Hone
   (ed.), *Irish Ghost Stories*, 428n; collected in
   Getting Through, 426n
Winston, Clara, 255n
Winston, Justina ('Stina'), 251n, 255, 262,
   279
Winter Olympics (1980), 498
Winterson, Jeannette, 756, **756n**
Winton, Tim: *Dirt Music*, 756n
'Without Ceremony', *see* 'Parachutes' (JMcG)
Wodehouse, P. G., 44n
Wolfe, Philip J., 798n
Woman's Hour (BBC Radio 4), 678n
Woodbrook, 611, 636
Woodham-Smith, Cecil: *The Great Hunger*,
   246
Woods, Boolie, 621, 636
Woods, MacDara, 580, **580n**
Woods, Peter, 437, 439, 470, 485, 584,
   674–5
Woof, Pamela, 421
Woof, Robert, 421, **421n**
Wordsworth, Christopher: reviews *The
   Leavetaking*, 383–4n
Wordsworth, William, 77, 574n, 797
Wordsworth Trust, 421n
Wren, Sir Christopher, 344, 356
Wreszin, Mike, 436, 761, 771; *A Rebel in
   Defense of Tradition*, 436n, 771
Wright, David, 33, **31n**, 34, 40, 40n, 44, 45,
   45n, 55–6, 65, 66, 66n, 657, 679, 772, 798
Writers' Guild, 567n
Wrynn, Mrs, 541n
Wrynn family, 543
Wynn's restaurant, 642

X: A Quarterly Review, 31n, 34, 41–2, 41n,
   42, 42n, 45n, 46, 56, 56n, 132, 184n,
   313n, 314n, 444n, 679n, 772

Y (YMCA), 91st Street, New York, 666, 669,
   670, 673
Yaddo, Saratoga Springs, New York, 575
Yale Review, 568
Yates, Richard, 431n, **446n**, 468, 656;
   Revolutionary Road, 446, 471, 479, 656;
   reviewed by JMcG ('Terrible Tales from the
   Mart'), 656n
Yeats, Anne, 687, **687n**